# Deep Learning for Perception and Recognition: Method and Applications

# Deep Learning for Perception and Recognition: Method and Applications

Guest Editors

**Gaochang Wu**
**Zizhu Fan**
**Dong Pan**

MDPI

Basel • Beijing • Wuhan • Barcelona • Belgrade • Novi Sad • Cluj • Manchester

*Guest Editors*

Gaochang Wu
State Key Laboratory of Synthetical Automation for Process Industries
Northeastern University
Shenyang
China

Zizhu Fan
College of Computer Science and Technology
Shanghai Electric Power University
Shanghai
China

Dong Pan
School of Automation
Central South University
Changsha
China

*Editorial Office*
MDPI AG
Grosspeteranlage 5
4052 Basel, Switzerland

This is a reprint of the Special Issue, published open access by the journal *Sensors* (ISSN 1424-8220), freely accessible at: https://www.mdpi.com/journal/sensors/special_issues/51SL938P2D.

For citation purposes, cite each article independently as indicated on the article page online and as indicated below:

Lastname, A.A.; Lastname, B.B. Article Title. *Journal Name* **Year**, *Volume Number*, Page Range.

**ISBN 978-3-7258-6266-5 (Hbk)**
**ISBN 978-3-7258-6267-2 (PDF)**
**https://doi.org/10.3390/books978-3-7258-6267-2**

# Contents

# About the Editors

**Gaochang Wu**

Gaochang Wu works with the State Key Laboratory of Synthetical Automation for Process Industries at Northeastern University. His research interests include multimodal perception and recognition, light field imaging and processing, and computer vision for industrial applications. He has led four research projects, including a Young Scientists Fund project of the National Natural Science Foundation of China. He has authored or co-authored more than 40 technical papers, such as *IEEE TPAMI*, *CVPR*, and *ICML*. He was selected for the Youth Talent Support Program of the Chinese Association of Automation. His honors include the Excellent Doctoral Dissertation Award from the China Education Society of Electronics, the 2023 Liaoning Provincial Natural Science Award (Second Prize), and the First Prize in the ICME 2020 Grand Challenge on Densely Sampled Light Field Reconstruction.

**Zizhu Fan**

Zizhu Fan works with the College of Computer Science and Technology, Shanghai University of Electric Power. His research interests include pattern recognition, image processing, and explainable AI. He has led over 10 research projects, including a general project of the National Natural Science Foundation of China (NSFC), and a major project. He has authored more than 40 SCI-indexed papers, such as *IEEE TNNLS*, *TAI*, and *TIM*. He is the recipient of multiple science and technology awards, prominently including the Second Prize of the Jiangxi Provincial Natural Science Award (2017) and the Second Prize of the Heilongjiang Provincial Natural Science Award (2014). He serves as a member of the Big Data Professional Committee of the Chinese Society of Automation, an Editorial Board Member of the Journal of East China Jiaotong University, and also serves as a reviewer for over ten internationally renowned journals.

**Dong Pan**

Dong Pan works with Central South University, where his research centers on infrared thermography, temperature measurement, image processing, and the modeling and control of industrial processes. He has led five research projects, including a National Natural Science Foundation of China Young Scholars project, and has authored more than 40 SCI/EI-indexed papers. His contributions have resulted in 24 granted national invention patents. His recognitions include the Special Prize and First Prize for Scientific and Technological Progress from the Chinese Association of Automation, as well as the Jin Guofan Youth Scholar Award. He also serves as a member of the Early Career Advisory Board for journals such as *Measurement* and *Infrared and Laser Engineering*.

sensors MDPI

*Article*

# FFformer: A Lightweight Feature Filter Transformer for Multi-Degraded Image Enhancement with a Novel Dataset †

**Yongheng Zhang**

State Key Laboratory of Networking and Switching Technology, Beijing University of Posts and Telecommunications, No. 10 Xitucheng Road, Haidian District, Beijing 100876, China; zhangyongheng@bupt.edu.cn

† This article is a revised and expanded version of a conference paper entitled [Towards Robust Image Restoration: A Multi-Type Degradation Dataset for Outdoor Scenes], which was presented at [IEEE ICME2025, Nantes, France, 30 June–4 July 2025].

**Abstract:** Image enhancement in complex scenes is challenging due to the frequent co-existence of multiple degradations caused by adverse weather, imaging hardware, and transmission environments. Existing datasets remain limited to single or weather-specific degradation types, failing to capture real-world complexity. To address this gap, we introduce the Robust Multi-Type Degradation (RMTD) dataset, which synthesizes a wide range of degradations from meteorological, capture, and transmission sources to support model training and evaluation under realistic conditions. Furthermore, the superposition of multiple degradations often results in feature maps dominated by noise, obscuring underlying clean content. To tackle this, we propose the Feature Filter Transformer (FFformer), which includes: (1) a Gaussian-Filtered Self-Attention (GFSA) module that suppresses degradation-related activations by integrating Gaussian filtering into self-attention; and (2) a Feature-Shrinkage Feed-forward Network (FSFN) that applies soft-thresholding to aggressively reduce noise. Additionally, a Feature Enhancement Block (FEB) embedded in skip connections further reinforces clean background features to ensure high-fidelity restoration. Extensive experiments on RMTD and public benchmarks confirm that the proposed dataset and FFformer together bring substantial improvements to the task of complex-scene image enhancement.

**Keywords:** complex-scene image enhancement; multi-type degradation dataset; Feature Filter Transformer; Gaussian-filter self-attention

## 1. Introduction

In outdoor applications such as autonomous driving, security surveillance, and disaster response, high-quality visual imagery is essential for reliable decision-making and system performance. However, images captured in these scenarios are frequently corrupted by multiple coexisting factors, including adverse weather, environmental conditions, and hardware limitations. This reality underscores the need for robust image enhancement methods capable of handling diverse degradations to improve visual quality under real-world conditions.

Existing image enhancement datasets can be broadly divided into two categories. The first category targets a single degradation type, e.g., haze [1,2], rain [3,4], blur [5,6], or noise [7]. While these datasets enable effective restoration of the targeted distortion, they often fail when confronted with multiple co-occurring degradations, limiting their applicability in complex scenarios. The second category focuses on compound weather degradations; examples include BID2a and BID2b [8], which encompass rain, snow, and haze. While datasets like BID2 [8] represent a significant advance for restoring compound weather degradations (e.g., rain, haze, snow), their scope is primarily confined to these meteorological phenomena. They omit other critical degradation types prevalent in outdoor imaging, such as blur (from motion or defocus) and noise (from low-light or sensor limitations). Furthermore, the real-world images in these benchmarks typically exhibit only a single dominant degradation type, which does not fully capture the complex, multi-faceted degradation encountered in practice. These gaps underscore the urgent need for a dataset that covers the full spectrum of degradations encountered in outdoor scenes.

Early image enhancement methods have demonstrated effectiveness on individual tasks, e.g., dehazing [1,2], deraining [3,4], and deblurring [5,6], yet they generally fail when confronted with multiple, superimposed degradations typical of extreme outdoor conditions. More recent universal frameworks achieve promising results on diverse single degradations, but they still inadequately handle the complex mixtures of distortions found in challenging real scenes. Consequently, specialized solutions tailored to such harsh environments are essential for reliable visual information recovery.

To address these issues, this paper introduces the Robust Multi-Type Degradation dataset (RMTD)—a large-scale benchmark designed for outdoor image enhancement under multiple degradations—and proposes a dedicated solution, the FFformer. RMTD narrows the gap left by prior datasets by integrating a wide range of scene categories and degradation types, thereby enabling a comprehensive evaluation of enhancement robustness. Specifically, RMTD contains 10 outdoor scene classes—street, building, composite scene, natural landscape, scenic spot, transportation hub, person, residential area, highway, and others (Figure 1)—spanning urban to natural environments to ensure broad applicability. The dataset incorporates eight degradation types that reflect both meteorological and imaging-system challenges: light haze, dense haze, light rain, heavy rain, Gaussian blur, motion blur, Gaussian noise, and shot noise. These degradations are prevalent in outdoor imagery and particularly detrimental to visual quality, ensuring RMTD captures the most critical distortions observed in complex scenes. In total, RMTD provides 48,000 synthetic image pairs, each consisting of a multi-degradation image and its corresponding high-quality ground truth, making it the largest multi-degradation enhancement dataset to date. Additionally, 200 real-world multi-degradation images collected from the Internet form an extra test set for evaluating model robustness under authentic outdoor conditions.

To facilitate downstream evaluation, RMTD further furnishes over 3000 object-level annotations across 10 categories (car, truck, bus, person, motorcycle, backpack, handbag, bicycle, traffic light, and umbrella). These annotations enable assessment of enhancement algorithms from the perspective of object detection—a critical consideration for applications such as autonomous driving and surveillance. By integrating image-enhancement evaluation with detection performance, RMTD offers a comprehensive benchmark for validating the practical utility of enhancement techniques in real-world deployments.

The FFformer is an efficient and lightweight image enhancement model designed for complex scenes. It incorporates a Gaussian-Filtered Self-Attention (GFSA) mechanism and a Feature-Shrinkage Feed-forward Network (FSFN), which collectively address low-quality images with compounded degradations. Both GFSA and FSFN can not only effectively remove redundant noise introduced by different degradations but also reduce the computational cost of the model.

In the image encoder of FFformer, a Scale Conversion Module (SCM) is introduced, which enhances the features from different encoder layers and normalizes the scale of each layer. The features of these layers are aggregated through a Feature Aggregation Module (FAM) and then fed into the background decoder. Moreover, the Feature Enhancement

Block (FEB) in the residual structure further strengthens FFformer's ability to extract and enhance clear background features that are unaffected by degradations.

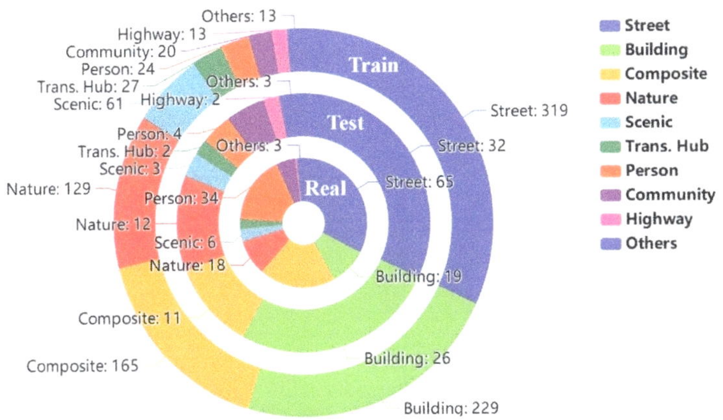


**Figure 1.** Nested doughnut charts illustrating the category distribution across the Train, Test, and Real-world subsets. From outer to inner, the rings represent the Train, Test, and Real subsets, respectively. The chart visualizes the proportion of the ten outdoor scene categories within each subset. The numerical values annotated on the charts indicate the exact number of images for each category.

The key contributions of this paper can be summarized as follows:

- We propose the RMTD dataset, the first large-scale comprehensive multi-degradation benchmark including both synthetic and real degraded images, providing valuable resources for complex-scene image enhancement research.
- We introduce the FFformer, an efficient image enhancement model based on Vision Transformers (ViT), which effectively removes redundant features from compounded degradations through its GFSA mechanism and FSFN.
- An SCM and an FAM are introduced in the image encoder to fully utilize the features of different-scale layers. Meanwhile, an FEB is integrated into the residual structure of the decoder to reinforce the clear background features.
- Extensive experiments on RMTD and other synthetic and real image datasets demonstrate that FFformer achieves leading performance in various complex scenes, proving the effectiveness of the proposed dataset and method in complex scene image enhancement.

## 2. Related Work

### 2.1. Image Restoration Datasets

Most existing image restoration datasets predominantly focus on specific types of degradation, such as rain [3,4], haze [1,2], snow [9], and blur [5,6]. Some desnowing datasets [10,11] include haze as a supplementary factor. However, real extreme weather conditions often involve multiple degradation factors occurring simultaneously, such as rain, haze, and blur.

Han et al. [8] proposed the Blind Image Decomposition task, which consists of two sub-tasks: Real Scenario Deraining in Driving and Real Scenario Deraining in General. This innovative task requires the simultaneous removal of rain, haze, and snow from a single image. To address this challenge, they collected clear background images and degradation masks for rain, haze, and snow from existing restoration datasets. The resulting datasets, named BID2a (driving scenario) and BID2b (general scenario), are significant for tackling multiple degraded image restoration tasks. However, the BID2 dataset has several limitations that our work aims to address. First, its degradation coverage is limited to weather effects (rain, haze, snow) and does not include other common types like blur or noise (see Table 1). Second, the real-world test set (BID2b) largely contains images with a single dominant weather degradation, failing to reflect the challenging scenario where multiple degradations co-exist. Additionally, BID2 lacks annotations for high-level computer vision tasks, which limits its utility for evaluating the impact of restoration on downstream applications. Moreover, the baseline Blind Image Decomposition Network (BIDeN), designed specifically for these datasets, features a simplistic structure that limits its versatility and generalizability.

**Table 1.** Comparison of dataset statistics and characteristics between RMTD and existing benchmarks.

| Dataset | Synthetic or Real | Number | Degradation Types | Real Test | Annotation |
|---|---|---|---|---|---|
| SIDD [7] | Real | 30,000 | Noise | Yes | No |
| RealBlur [6] | Real | 4556 | Blur | Yes | No |
| Rain1400 [3] | Synthetic | 14,000 | Rain | No | No |
| SPA [4] | Real | 29,500 | Rain | Yes | No |
| RESIDE [1] | Synthetic + Real | 86,645 + 4322 | Haze | Yes | RTTS |
| BID2a [8] | Synthetic | 3475 | 4 types | No | No |
| BID2b [8] | Synthetic + Real | 3661 + 1763 | 3 for train, 1 for test | Yes | No |
| RMTD | Synthetic + Real | 48,000 + 200 | 8 types | Yes | Test, Real |

To overcome these limitations, we introduce the RMTD dataset, which comprises both synthetic and real images affected by multiple degradations. Unlike existing datasets, RMTD captures the diverse degradation factors encountered in real multi-degraded scenarios. It serves as a comprehensive benchmark for evaluating image restoration methodologies within the challenging context of multi-degraded conditions.

### 2.2. *Image Restoration Methods*

#### 2.2.1. Specific Degraded Image Restoration

Early strategies for image restoration primarily focused on addressing individual degradations through corresponding a priori hypotheses [12–15]. For example, He et al. [12] introduced the dark channel prior (DCP) to estimate transmission maps and global atmospheric light for dehazing images, based on the observation that at least one channel in a patch has values close to zero. To mitigate potential loss of detailed information in the guidance image, Xu et al. [16] developed a refined guidance image for snow removal. Li et al. [14] utilized layer priors to effectively eliminate rain streaks, offering a robust solution for rain removal. Pan et al. [17] integrated the dark channel prior into image deblurring, while subsequent studies [18–20] further refined and enhanced the efficiency and performance of the DCP method.

The emergence of convolutional neural networks (CNNs) and visual transformers has ushered in a new wave of learning-based image restoration methods, yielding impressive results [4,9,11,21–26]. For instance, Li et al. [24] employed a depth refinement network to enhance edges and structural details in depth maps, leveraging a spatial feature transform layer to extract depth features for dynamic scene deblurring. Jiang et al. [27] tackled the image deraining problem by developing a Multi-Scale Progressive Fusion Network, demonstrating efficient and effective deraining capabilities. Additionally, Chen et al. [11] proposed the Hierarchical Decomposition paradigm within HDCWNet, offering an improved understanding of various snow particle sizes.

#### 2.2.2. General Degraded Image Restoration

Diverging from approaches focused on specific degraded images, several methods exhibit versatility in addressing multiple degradations, including challenges such as haze, rain, and noise [28–33]. For instance, Zamir et al. [28] introduced MPRNet, which employs a multi-stage architecture to progressively learn restoration functions for degraded inputs. Wang et al. [30] proposed U-Shaped Transformer (Uformer), leveraging a locally enhanced window (LeWin) Transformer block that performs non-overlapping window-based self-attention, thereby reducing computational complexity on high-resolution feature maps. Patil et al. [31] presented a domain translation-based unified method capable of simultaneously learning multiple weather degradations, enhancing resilience against real-world conditions. Additionally, Zhou et al. introduced an Adaptive Sparse Transformer (AST) designed to mitigate noisy interactions from irrelevant areas through an Adaptive Sparse Self-Attention block and a Feature Refinement Feed-forward Network. For handling unknown or mixed degradations, DAIR [34] proposes an implicit degradation prior learning framework. It adaptively routes and restores features based on degradation-aware representations inferred directly from the input, enhancing robustness in complex real-world scenarios.

While these methods effectively manage various degradation types within a unified framework, they often struggle when multiple degradation factors coexist simultaneously. To address this challenge, Han et al. [8] proposed the novel task of Blind Image Decomposition and introduced the BIDeN as a robust baseline. Building on this foundation, we propose the FFformer for multi-degraded image restoration, demonstrating effectiveness in removing degradations such as rain, haze, noise, and blur across diverse scenarios.

### 2.3. *ViT in Image Restoration*

The introduction of ViT into the field of image restoration has garnered considerable attention, owing to their ability to comprehend extensive dependencies within images. This capability is crucial for discerning the broader context and relationships among various image components. Recent research has highlighted the efficacy of ViT across a diverse range of image restoration applications [30,35–39].

Innovatively, Liang et al. [36] proposed SwinIR, a method for image restoration based on the Swin Transformer. SwinIR leverages multiple residual Swin Transformer blocks to effectively extract deep features for various restoration tasks. Similarly, Zamir et al. [35] introduced Restormer, a hierarchical encoder–decoder network constructed with Vision Transformer blocks. Restormer incorporates several key design elements in its multi-head attention and feed-forward network to capture long-range pixel interactions, making it applicable to large images. As a result, Restormer has demonstrated exceptional performance in restoring images affected by various degradation types. To enhance ViT efficiency for restoration, MG-SSAF [40] introduces a Spatially Separable MSA module that approximates global attention with linear complexity, coupled with a Multi-scale Global MSA module to maintain cross-window interactions, offering a lightweight yet effective design.

The integration of Vision Transformers into image restoration methodologies signifies a substantial advancement in utilizing transformer-based architectures to enhance the visual fidelity of degraded images. These developments underscore the adaptability and effectiveness of ViT in capturing intricate dependencies, ultimately facilitating superior image restoration outcomes.

### 2.4. *Feature Enhancement in Multi-Modal and Multi-Scale Learning*

The paradigm of feature enhancement extends beyond the domain of image restoration, serving as a fundamental technique to improve data quality and model representation power across various visual tasks. Recent research demonstrates its critical role in fusing information from different modalities or scales.

For instance, in the context of intelligent transportation systems, a trajectory quality enhancement method [41] leverages onboard images to calibrate and refine vehicle trajectory data. This work exemplifies how visual features can act as a high-fidelity prior to enhance the precision and reliability of another data modality (trajectory), showcasing a cross-modal feature enhancement strategy.

Similarly, in hyperspectral image (HSI) classification, an enhanced multiscale feature fusion network [42] highlights the importance of integrating features at different scales. By designing dedicated modules to aggregate contextual information from multiple receptive fields, it significantly boosts classification accuracy, underscoring the pivotal role of multi-scale feature fusion.

While the applications differ, these works share a common thread with our proposed FEB and FSFN modules: the core principle of actively guiding the model to reinforce more informative features. Our approach aligns with this philosophy but is specifically tailored for the challenge of image restoration under multiple degradations. The FEB enhances features across the encoder–decoder hierarchy to bridge the semantic gap, while the FSFN employs soft-thresholding to sparsify and purify features. Together, they form a cohesive feature enhancement framework within our FFFormer, dedicated to suppressing degradation artifacts and recovering clean image content.

## 3. The Robust Multi-Type Degradation Dataset

The RMTD dataset consists of 48,000 synthetic multi-degraded image pairs and 200 real-world images, designed to benchmark robust image restoration models across various degradation conditions. The synthetic dataset is divided into three subsets: Train (16,000 images), Test (1600 images), and Others (30,400 images). The Others subset is used as a flexible resource, which can be employed for validation or to supplement the training set, depending on the model's specific needs. The Real subset, containing 200 real-world images, offers an additional test set for evaluating model performance in uncontrolled, real-world scenarios. Table 1 compares RMTD with existing datasets.

### 3.1. Dataset Construction

This section describes the methodology used to construct the dataset, including the synthesis of multi-degraded images, the collection of real-world degraded images, and the object detection annotation process.

#### 3.1.1. Synthetic Multi-Degraded Image Generation

Synthetic multi-degraded images are generated from 3000 pristine clear outdoor images sourced from the Beijing-tour web [43]. These pristine images are categorized into 10 scenes (Figures 1 and 2), ensuring a diverse representation of outdoor environments. Each image is degraded by 8 degradation types, grouped into four categories: haze, rain, blur, and noise (Figure 3).

To simulate real-world conditions, each pristine image undergoes degradation by one of the four categories, with two settings per category, resulting in 16 unique degradation combinations per image. This approach captures both individual and compounded degradation effects, providing a comprehensive range of degradation scenarios for model evaluation. An example of a multi-degraded image, along with its ground truth and depth map, is shown in Figure 4.

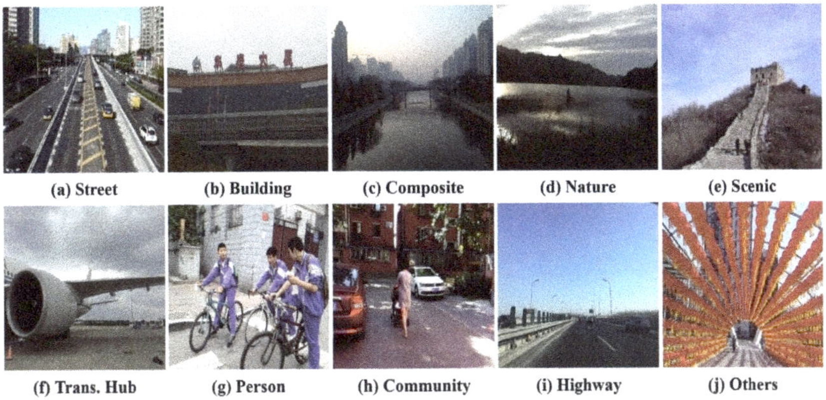


**Figure 2.** Ten scenes in the RMTD dataset.

**Figure 3.** Degradation configurations in the RMTD dataset. The multi-degraded images include four types of degradation (haze, rain, blur, noise) simultaneously.

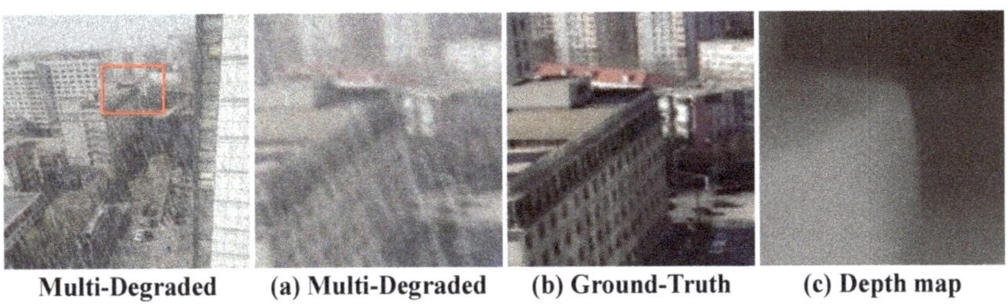


**Figure 4.** Illustration of a synthetic multi-degraded image with corresponding ground truth and depth map.

3.1.2. Haze Simulation

To realistically simulate hazy conditions, we adopt the physically grounded atmospheric scattering model [44]:

$$I(x) = J(x)t(x) + A(1 - t(x)), \quad (1)$$

where $I(x)$ and $J(x)$ represent the hazy image and the clean image, respectively, and $A$ denotes atmospheric light. The transmission map is given by $t(x) = e^{-\beta d(x)}$, where $\beta$ is the scattering coefficient of the atmosphere, and $d(x)$ is the distance between the object and the camera. We calculate the distance using MegaDepth [45]. The parameters for light and dense haze are carefully chosen to span common real-world conditions: for light haze, $A \in [0.5, 0.7]$, $\beta \in [0.6, 1.0]$; for dense haze, $A \in [0.7, 0.9]$, $\beta \in [1.0, 1.4]$. These ranges simulate phenomena from mild mist to heavy fog, effectively replicating the visibility degradation caused by atmospheric particles.

#### 3.1.3. Rain Simulation

Rain is synthesized to mimic its complex appearance in real captures. We generate realistic rain streaks using the method from [3]:

$$R = Trans(random(I), v, l), \tag{2}$$

where $I$ is the input image, $R$ is the rain mask, $random(I)$ is a random noise map with the same size of input image, $v$ is the minimal size of preserved rain, and $l$ is the average length of rain streaks. Rainy images are computed as:

$$O = I \cdot (1 - R) + (1 - \alpha)R, \tag{3}$$

where $O$ is the rainy image, $I$ is the pristine image, $R$ is the rain mask, and $\alpha$ controls streak transparency.

Parameters are set to cover varied precipitation intensities: light rain uses $v = 2, l = 10$, $\alpha = 0.8$, simulating sparse, fine streaks; heavy rain uses $v = 5, l = 15, \alpha = 0.6$, producing denser, more opaque rain layers that significantly obscure visibility.

#### 3.1.4. Blur Simulation

We simulate two prevalent types of blur encountered in practical imaging.

Gaussian blur approximates the effect of improper focus or atmospheric turbulence, implemented via convolution with a Gaussian point-spread function (PSF) [46]:

$$g(x, y) = (f \times h)(x, y), \tag{4}$$

where $f$ is the ideal scene, $h$ is the point-spread function (PSF), and $g$ is the observed image. The kernel severity $\sigma$ is sampled from $\{0.2, 0.4, 0.6, 0.8, 1.0\}$, covering a range from slight to noticeable softness.

Motion blur mimics camera shake or object movement. We employ a heterogeneous kernel model [47]:

$$Y(i,j) = \sum_{i',j'} K(i,j)(i',j')X(i+i',j+j'), \tag{5}$$

where $X$ denotes the sharp image and $K$ denotes a heterogeneous motion blur kernel map with different blur kernels for each pixel in $X$. Parameters (radius $\in [6, 9]$, $\sigma \in [1.0, 2.5]$) are randomized to generate diverse blur directions and intensities, closely resembling real motion artifacts.

#### 3.1.5. Noise Simulation

We model two dominant noise types in digital imaging.

Gaussian noise arises from sensor heat and electronic interference, following the distribution:

$$p(z) = \frac{1}{\sigma\sqrt{2\pi}} e^{-\frac{(z-\mu)^2}{2\sigma^2}}, \tag{6}$$

where $\mu$ is the mean, and $\sigma$ is the standard deviation. With $\mu = 0$ and $\sigma \in [0.04, 0.10]$, we simulate moderate to strong sensor noise prevalent in low-quality captures.

Shot noise (Poisson noise) stems from the photon-counting process in image sensors [48]:

$$P(X = k) = \frac{e^{-\lambda}\lambda^k}{k!}, \tag{7}$$

where $\lambda$ is the average rate of events per interval, and $k$ is the number of events. The severity parameter $\lambda$ is chosen from $\{50, 75, 100, 250, 500\}$, emulating various illumination conditions from low-light (high noise) to well-lit scenarios (low noise).

#### 3.1.6. Collection of Real-World Degraded Images

The Real subset consists of 200 real-world images collected from various online sources (e.g., Google, Baidu) to reflect diverse degradation conditions, including varying intensities of haze, rain, blur, and noise. These images cover all 10 outdoor scene categories (as shown in Figure 1), ensuring a broad representation of real-world environmental scenarios.

Unlike the synthetic images, these real-world images do not have ground truth data, making them an essential resource for evaluating model performance under uncontrolled and complex real-world conditions. As there are no direct reference points for comparison, these images challenge models to generalize well in the absence of perfect information, thus reflecting real-world use cases where ground truth may not be available.

For examples of real-world degraded images, refer to Figure 5, where representative samples from the Real subset are displayed.

**Figure 5.** Visualization of real multi-degraded images sampled from RMTD-Real subset. The Chinese text in the image consists of watermarks and traffic signs.

#### 3.1.7. Object Detection Annotations

To enhance the dataset's utility for downstream tasks, we incorporated object detection annotations into both the synthetic Test set and the real-world Real set. Annotations were created using the LabelImg tool [49] and saved in the PASCAL VOC format [50].

The dataset includes annotations for 10 object categories: car, truck, traffic light, person, motorbike, backpack, bus, handbag, bicycle, and umbrella. These categories are selected for their relevance to urban outdoor environments and applications like autonomous driving and urban surveillance.

The annotations serve two key purposes: (1) evaluating how well image restoration models preserve object features after degradation and (2) assessing the performance of object detection models under diverse degradation conditions. By testing detection on restored images, we can gauge the impact of restoration techniques on downstream tasks. Examples of annotated images are shown in Figure 6.

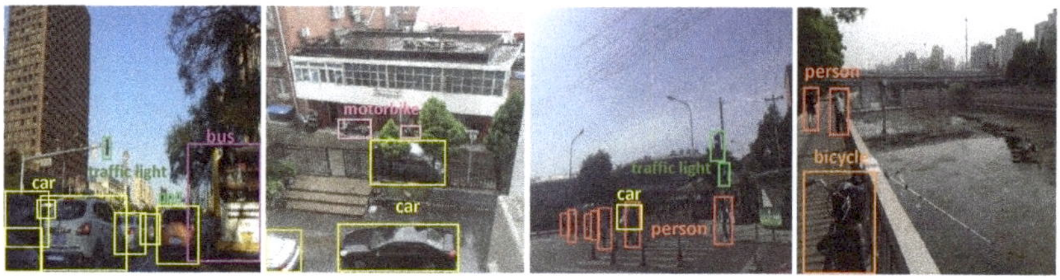


**Figure 6.** Visualization of object detection annotation boxes in outdoor scenes.

## *3.2. Dataset Statistics and Analysis*

### 3.2.1. Scene Distribution

RMTD spans 10 outdoor scene categories: Street, Building, Composite, Nature, Scenic, Transportation Hub, Person, Community, Highway, and Others. As shown in Figure 1, the dataset is designed to reflect a broad range of real-world environments, with "Street", "Building", and "Composite" scenes dominating, reflecting the dataset's urban focus. The inclusion of categories such as "Nature", "Scenic", and "Transportation Hub" ensures a diverse representation of outdoor environments. The "Others" category aggregates scenes that do not fit neatly into the other nine categories, ensuring further diversity and generalization across different environments.

### 3.2.2. Object Annotation Statistics

The distribution of object annotations is shown in Figures 7 and 8. In Figure 7, we observe that most images contain multiple annotated objects, with a significant number containing more than 15 object annotations. This highlights the dataset's complexity and relevance for real-world applications. Figure 8 presents the distribution of 3000 object boxes, where "car" and "person" dominate, reflecting the urban and transportation focus of RMTD. This distribution of annotations is consistent with common objects encountered in outdoor environments like urban streets.

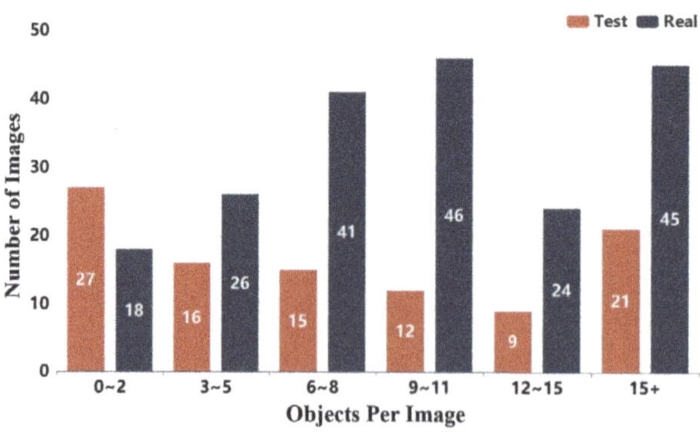


**Figure 7.** Distribution of object detection annotation boxes per image.

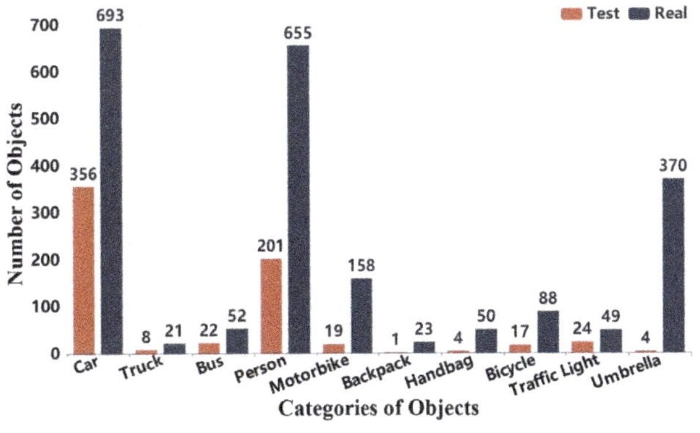


**Figure 8.** Category distribution of object detection annotation boxes.

3.2.3. Summary

RMTD addresses key limitations of prior datasets by combining synthetic and real-world images, supporting diverse degradation scenarios, and incorporating object detection annotations. These features make RMTD a comprehensive benchmark for evaluating robust image restoration techniques, particularly in urban environments, and for assessing the impact of restoration methods on downstream tasks like object detection.

## 4. Method

This section outlines the architecture of the proposed FFformer model, featuring novel components specifically designed for effective multi-degraded image restoration, including the GFSA, FSFN, SCM, FAM, and FEB.

### *4.1. Overall Pipeline*

As illustrated in Figure 9, the architecture of FFformer is built upon a hierarchical transformer encoder–decoder framework aimed at tackling the challenges associated with multi-degraded image restoration. Given a degraded input $I \in \mathcal{R}^{H \times W \times 3}$, FFformer initiates the process by extracting low-level features $X_0 \in \mathcal{R}^{H \times W \times C}$ using a $3 \times 3$ convolution, where $C$ represents the initial channel size. These initial features serve as a foundational representation capturing essential information from the input.

The extracted features then proceed through a 4-level encoder–decoder structure, which serves as the backbone of the FFformer architecture. Each encoder and decoder module contains multiple Feature Filter Transformer Blocks (FFTBs), specialized components crucial for managing multiple degradations in images. Within each FFTB, conventional mechanisms such as Multi-head Self-Attention (MSA) and Feed-forward Networks (FN) are replaced with our proposed GFSA and FSFN. These enhancements not only improve the model's ability to capture critical information and eliminate unnecessary degradations but also contribute to FFformer's lightweight design.

In the encoding stage, each encoder progressively reduces the spatial dimensions by half while doubling the channel size, facilitating a hierarchical abstraction of features. Multi-scale features are then processed through an SCM to adapt the scales for optimal utilization. Aggregated features from various encoder layers are fed into the image decoder via an additional FAM, ensuring comprehensive feature utilization.

Conversely, the decoding stage reconstructs the spatial dimensions by twofold while halving the channel size, enabling the network to generate a restored image that faithfully captures essential details. Departing from standard skip connections [30,51], which typically concatenate encoder and decoder features, FFformer incorporates the FEB. This block plays a critical role in further extracting and preserving features essential for multi-degradation restoration.

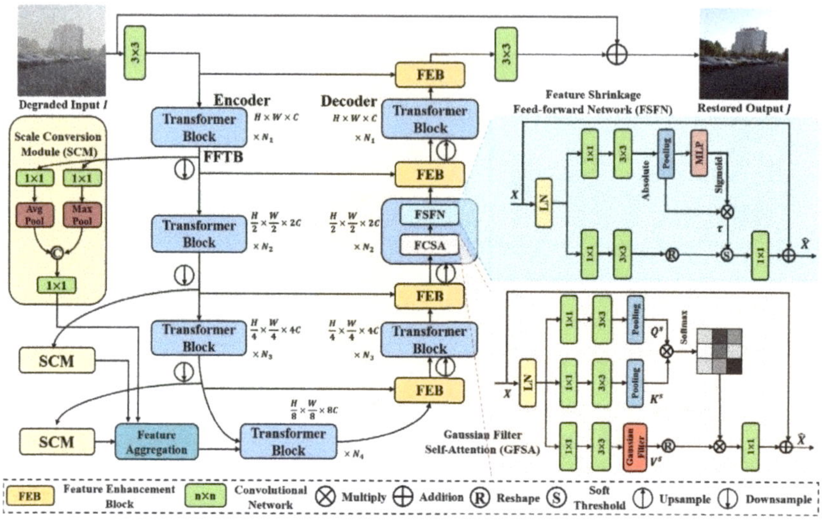


**Figure 9.** Overall architecture of the proposed FFformer for multi-degraded image restoration.

To maintain a balance between computational efficiency and information preservation, pixel-unshuffle and pixel-shuffle operations [52] are strategically employed for down-sampling and up-sampling of features.

After the decoding stage, a residual image $R \in \mathcal{R}^{H \times W \times 3}$ is generated through another $3 \times 3$ convolution, capturing the nuanced differences between the degraded input and the reconstructed features. Finally, the restored output is obtained as $O = R + I$. The entire network is trained by minimizing the $L_1$ norm loss:

$$\mathcal{L} = ||O - I_{gt}||_1, \tag{8}$$

where $I_{gt}$ denotes the ground truth and $|| \cdot ||$ denotes the $L_1$ norm. This loss function ensures the convergence of the network towards accurate restoration.

### 4.2. Gaussian Filter Self-Attention

In the task of complex scene multi-degraded image enhancement, the presence of multiple compounded degradation factors not only leads to a significant decline in image visual quality but also results in the features extracted by image enhancement networks being heavily contaminated with complex and high-proportion degradation factors. Relying solely on the inherent learning capabilities of deep neural networks to distinguish composite degradation features is not only challenging but also time-consuming, thereby increasing the risk of network overfitting. To address this issue, FFformer introduces a GFSA mechanism, incorporating the widely used Gaussian filter for signal denoising and smoothing in images into the self-attention mechanism of the visual Transformer structure. This approach aims to partially remove composite degradation factors at the feature level, thereby reducing the learning difficulty for the network. The two-dimensional Gaussian function is presented in Equation (6).

A significant contributor to the computational overhead in Transformers is the key-query dot product interaction within the self-attention layer [53,54]. To address this challenge, GFSA involves max-pooling the key-query features to a fixed size of $8 \times 8$ and computing cross-covariance across channels rather than across spatial dimensions. This strategic approach results in an attention matrix of size $\mathcal{R}^{C\times C}$, effectively alleviating the computational burden associated with traditional self-attention mechanisms.

The GFSA process begins with layer normalization, followed by $1 \times 1$ and $3 \times 3$ convolutions to prepare the input $X$ for subsequent operations. To leverage both pixel-wise cross-channel and channel-wise spatial context, two max-pooling layers are employed. These layers not only retain local information but also ensure a fixed feature size for both the key and query. The GFSA process can be expressed as:

$$Q^s = Pool(Conv(X)), K^s = Pool(Conv(X)), V^s = GF(Conv(X)), \tag{9}$$

$$\hat{X} = softmax(Q^s \cdot K^s/\lambda)V^s + X, \tag{10}$$

where $\lambda$ is an optional temperature factor defined by $\lambda = \sqrt{d}$.

The integration of Gaussian filtering within the self-attention mechanism is motivated by its frequency-domain properties. The Gaussian filter in the spatial domain is defined as:

$$G(x,y) = \frac{1}{2\pi\sigma^2} \exp^{-\frac{x^2+y^2}{2\sigma^2}}, \tag{11}$$

where $(x,y)$ are spatial coordinates and $\sigma$ is the standard deviation determining the filter's width. Through the Fourier transform, its representation in the frequency domain maintains a Gaussian shape:

$$G(u,v) = \exp^{-2\pi\sigma^2(u)}, \tag{12}$$

where $(u,v)$ are frequency-domain coordinates. The magnitude–frequency characteristic of the Gaussian filter is, therefore, a Gaussian function, which exhibits low-pass filtering properties.

In image processing, low-frequency components generally correspond to the primary structural information of an image, while high-frequency components often encompass noise and fine-texture details. By incorporating a Gaussian filter into the self-attention mechanism, we selectively attenuate high-frequency components in the feature maps. This operation directly affects the attention distribution by smoothing the calculated attention scores, making the model less sensitive to high-frequency noise and local perturbations. Consequently, it guides the model to focus on broader, more semantically consistent regions, thereby stabilizing the training process and enhancing feature quality by emphasizing robust, low-frequency information. This formulation captures the essence of the GFSA mechanism, demonstrating its ability to enhance the attention computation process while preserving the input features. The introduction of GFSA not only reduces computational overhead but also facilitates the efficient capture of essential information.

### 4.3. Feature Shrinkage Feed-Forward Network

While previous studies [30,55] have integrated depth-wise convolutions into feed-forward networks to enhance locality, they often overlook the inherent redundancy and noise in features critical for multi-degraded image restoration. To address this gap, we introduce the FSFN, a novel mechanism that employs a soft-threshold function to shrink feature values. This strategic approach aims to significantly reduce redundancy and eliminate unwanted degradations, thereby ensuring the robustness of the restoration process.

As depicted in Figure 9, the FSFN process begins with the input $X$, which undergoes normalization and convolution operations to prepare it for subsequent feature shrinkage.

The average score $M$ of size $\mathcal{R}^{1\times1\times C}$ is calculated as $M = GPool(|Conv(X)|)$, where $GPool$ represents global average pooling. The threshold $\tau$ is then defined as $\tau = M \cdot \text{sigmoid}(\text{MLP}(M))$. The overall FSFN process can be expressed as:

$$\hat{X} = SThold(Conv(LN(X))) + X, \tag{13}$$

where $SThold(x)$ is a soft-thresholding function defined as:

$$SThold(x) = \begin{cases} x - \tau & x > \tau \\ 0 & -\tau \leq x \leq \tau \\ x + \tau & x < -\tau \end{cases} \tag{14}$$

The theoretical motivation for this operation is twofold:

- Sparsity Promotion: The soft-thresholding function zeros out all feature elements whose absolute values are below the threshold $\tau$. This actively promotes sparsity in the feature representation, effectively filtering out a large number of weak or non-significant activations that are likely to be noise or less informative components.
- Noise Reduction: In signal processing theory, soft-thresholding is known to be the proximal operator for the L1-norm and is optimal for denoising signals corrupted by additive white Gaussian noise. By applying this principle to feature maps, the FSFN module acts as an adaptive feature denoiser. It shrinks the magnitudes of all features, aggressively pushing insignificant ones (presumed noise) to zero while preserving the significant ones (presumed signal).

Unlike the simple gating mechanisms in the Depthwise Feed-forward Network (DFN) [55], soft-thresholding provides a principled, data-driven approach to noise removal and feature selection. While DFN [55] primarily perform smoothing or weighting, soft-thresholding implements an explicit "shrink or kill" strategy, which is theoretically grounded in sparse coding and leads to a more robust and compact feature representation, particularly effective in the presence of complex, real-world degradations. The incorporation of FSFN within the FFformer framework significantly reduces redundancy, facilitating the effective elimination of degradations.

### 4.4. Scale Conversion Module and Feature Aggregation Module

To effectively harness the multi-scale features generated during the encoding process of FFformer, we introduce two key components: the SCM and the FAM. These modules are essential for enhancing feature representations and facilitating coherent integration across different scales.

The Scale Conversion Module is designed to resize feature representations while preserving critical information. It initiates the process by applying both max pooling and average pooling to the input feature $F_e^i$, reducing its spatial dimensions to $H/8 \times W/8$. This reduction captures important characteristics at a lower resolution, allowing for more efficient processing. The operations are defined as follows:

$$F_m^i = MaxPool(Conv(F_e^i)), \tag{15}$$

$$F_a^i = AvgPool(Conv(F_e^i)). \tag{16}$$

The outputs from both pooling operations are then concatenated and processed through another $1 \times 1$ convolution to expand the channel size to 8C:

$$F_k^i = Conv_1(Concat(F_m^i, F_a^i)). \tag{17}$$

This concatenation enriches the feature set by integrating both local and averaged information, ultimately enhancing feature representation.

Following the SCM, the FAM is employed to consolidate the processed features. The FAM consists of two $1 \times 1$ convolutional layers and incorporates a channel-wise self-attention mechanism to capture long-range dependencies within the feature maps. This integration is performed as follows:

$$F_u = Conv(Concat(F_k^i)), i = 1,2,3, \tag{18}$$

$$\hat{F_u} = Conv(CSA(F_u, F_u, F_u)) + F_u, \tag{19}$$

where $CSA(Q, K, V) = softmax(Q \cdot K^\top / \lambda)V$ denotes the channel-wise self-attention operation, with $\lambda$ as a learnable scaling factor. This attention mechanism selectively emphasizes significant features while downplaying irrelevant ones, enhancing the module's overall efficacy. Additionally, the integration of residual connections promotes stability and convergence during the learning process, further improving the performance of the module.

### 4.5. Feature Enhancement Block

The effectiveness of skip connections in U-Net-like architectures is often hampered by the semantic gap and spatial misalignment between encoder and decoder features. While prevalent feature enhancement modules, such as channel or spatial attention mechanisms, primarily focus on refining features within a single pathway, they are less effective in dynamically calibrating and fusing features from two distinct pathways (i.e., the decoder and the residual connection). To address this limitation, we propose the FEB. The key innovation of FEB lies in its dual-attention guided feature calibration and fusion mechanism, which explicitly and simultaneously models both cross-feature and intra-feature dependencies to achieve more effective skip connections.

Unlike traditional skip connections [30,51] that simply concatenate encoder and decoder outputs, the FEB introduces a more sophisticated approach to extracting and preserving critical features within a residual framework. As depicted in Figure 10, the FEB incorporates both cross-feature channel attention and intra-feature channel attention mechanisms, strategically designed to enhance the model's capability to utilize features effectively.

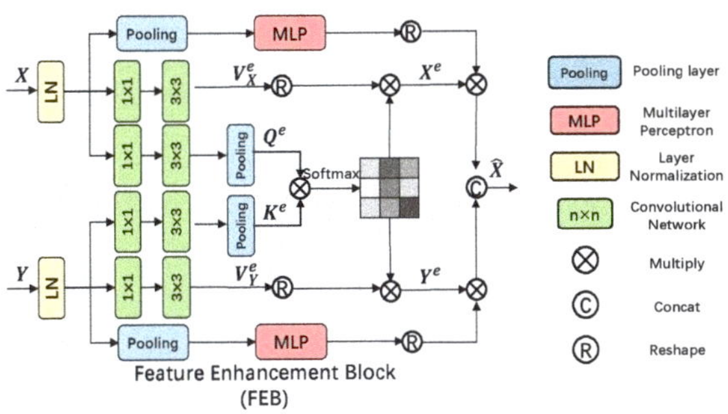


**Figure 10.** Implementation of the proposed FEB.

Given a decoder feature $X$ and a residual feature $Y$, the FEB initiates by computing the query, key, and value matrices for cross-feature attention. To distinguish these from the self-attention matrices in GFSA, we denote them with the superscript e (for "enhancement"): $Q^e = Pool(Conv(X))$, $K^e = Pool(Conv(Y))$, $V_X^e = Conv(X)$, and $V_Y^e = Conv(X)$. These computations facilitate the subsequent cross-feature channel attention mechanism. Similar to GFSA, the intermediate outputs are calculated as $X^e = \text{softmax}(Q^e \cdot K^e/\lambda)V_X^e$ and $Y^e = \text{softmax}(K^e \cdot Q^e/\lambda)V_Y^e$.

The FEB further incorporates intra-feature channel attention by applying global average pooling to each feature map, generating an attention matrix. The overall formulation of the FEB process is given by:

$$\hat{X} = Concat(X^e \cdot MLP(Gpool(LN(X))).Y^e \cdot MLP(Gpool(LN(Y)))). \quad (20)$$

This formulation captures the essence of the Feature Enhancement Block, highlighting its ability to synergistically combine cross-feature and intra-feature channel attention for improved extraction and preservation of vital features. By integrating the FEB within the residual structure, the model transcends basic concatenation, offering a refined and effective mechanism for enhancing crucial feature representation.

## 5. Experiments and Analysis

In this section, we provide a comprehensive comparison between our proposed FFformer and other state-of-the-art methods designed for task-specific and multi-degradation removal.

### 5.1. Datasets

Our experiments utilize the newly introduced RMTD dataset alongside subsets of the BID2a dataset, specifically the 5th (BID2a-5) and 6th (BID2a-6) subsets, as outlined by Han et al. [8]. The BID2a-5 dataset consists of synthetic images affected by rain and haze, while the BID2a-6 dataset presents the additional challenge of simultaneous disturbances from rain, haze, and snow. These datasets serve as valuable benchmarks for assessing the robustness and versatility of image restoration methods under various weather conditions.

### 5.2. Implementation Details

Our framework is implemented using PyTorch 1.10. For RMTD dataset, the models are trained on the Train subset, validated on 1600 images from the Others subset, and evaluated on the dedicated RMTD Test subset. This split ensures that the model is tuned and assessed on distinct data sources. We use the Adam optimizer with parameters ($\beta_1 = 0.9, \beta_2 = 0.999$) and a weight decay of $1 \times 10^{-4}$. The models are trained for 200 epochs with a batch size of 8. The training loss is the L1 loss between the predicted and ground-truth images. The initial learning rate is set to $1 \times 10^{-4}$ and is gradually reduced to $1 \times 10^{-6}$ using a cosine annealing scheduler [56] with a period of 200 epochs (T-max = 200) and no restarts. Input images are randomly cropped to a fixed patch size of 256 × 256 during training, while center cropping is applied for validation and testing. The architectural hyperparameters are set as follows: the number of FFformer blocks $N_1, N_2, N_3, N_4$ is $2, 4, 4, 6$, the number of attention heads in the GFSA modules is $1, 2, 4, 8$, and the base channel dimensions are $32, 64, 128, 256$.

### 5.3. Evaluation Metrics

To assess the performance of multi-degraded image restoration on labeled datasets RMTD-Syn, BID2a-5 [8], and BID2a-6 [8], we employ two widely used full-reference metrics: Peak Signal-to-Noise Ratio (PSNR in dB) [57] and Structural Similarity Index (SSIM) [58]. These metrics provide a quantitative assessment by comparing the restoration results with the corresponding ground truth images.

Additionally, we utilize two non-reference image quality evaluation indicators: BRISQUE [59], which measures potential losses of naturalness in images, and NIQE [60], which is based on a collection of statistical features constructed from a space-domain natural scene statistic (NSS) model.

### 5.4. Comparisons with State-of-the-Art Methods

We conduct a comprehensive comparison between FFformer and state-of-the-art restoration methods. The evaluated methods include four task-specific approaches (DerainNet [3], Principled-Synthetic-to-Real-Dehazing (PSD) [61], Complementary Cascaded Network (CCN) [62], Deblur-NeRF [63]) and seven generalized restoration methods (MPRNet [28], Uformer [30], Restormer [35], BIDeN [8], Weather-General and Weather-Specific (WGWS) [32], Patil et al. [31], Adaptive Sparse Transformer (AST) [33]). More details about the comparison methods are provided in Table 2.

**Table 2.** Details of the comparison methods.

| Category | Methods | Source |
|---|---|---|
| Task-specific Methods | DerainNet [64] | TIP' 2017 |
| | PSD [61] | CVPR' 2021 |
| | CCN [62] | CVPR' 2021 |
| | Deblur-NeRF [63] | CVPR' 2022 |
| Multiple Degradations Removal Methods | MPRNet [28] | CVPR' 2021 |
| | Uformer [30] | CVPR' 2022 |
| | Restormer [35] | CVPR' 2022 |
| | BIDeN [8] | ECCV' 2022 |
| | WGWS [32] | CVPR' 2023 |
| | Patil et al. [31] | ICCV' 2023 |
| | AST [33] | CVPR' 2024 |

Synthetic. Qualitative assessments on synthetic datasets are visually demonstrated in Figures 11–13. FFformer exhibits impressive capabilities in removing multiple degradations, producing high-quality images that closely resemble the ground truth. The quantitative results, as shown in Tables 3 and 4, highlight FFformer's consistent superiority over other methods, with PSNR and SSIM scores of 28.67 vs. 28.24 and 0.880 vs. 0.873, respectively, on the RMTD-Syn dataset. The satisfactory results obtained by FFformer on BID2a-5 and BID2a-6 further affirm its efficacy in restoring multi-degraded images across diverse synthetic datasets. This robust and versatile performance underscores FFformer's effectiveness in tackling the challenges posed by multi-degradations, solidifying its position as a reliable solution for various multi-degraded image restoration scenarios.

Real. To thoroughly evaluate the model's performance and generalization capability in authentic, uncontrolled outdoor scenarios, we conducted extensive experiments on the RMTD-Real. Furthermore, to directly address the model's ability to generalize across unseen degradation domains, we designed a cross-dataset validation experiment.

The quantitative results are summarized in Table 5. Crucially, the new Table 5 provides a cross-dataset analysis, where models were trained on different source datasets—BID2a, BID2b, and our RMTD-Syn—and evaluated on the target RMTD-Real set. The results confirm two key findings: First, training on our RMTD-Syn dataset yields the best performance on real-world images, even when compared to models trained on other real-world degradation datasets (BID2b). This demonstrates that the comprehensive multi-degradation simulation in RMTD effectively bridges the sim-to-real gap. Second, our FFformer consistently achieves the best no-reference quality metrics, attesting to its robustness and adaptability.

**Table 3.** PSNR ↑/SSIM↑ on three multiple degradation removal datasets. ↑ denotes that a higher value indicates better performance.

| Datasets | BID2a-5 [8] | BID2a-6 [8] | RMTD-Syn |
|---|---|---|---|
| **Degraded** | **14.05/0.616** | **12.38/0.461** | **15.09/0.410** |
| DerainNet [64] | 18.68/0.805 | 17.53/0.721 | 21.43/0.772 |
| PSD [61] | 22.17/0.855 | 20.57/0.809 | 26.97/0.839 |
| CCN [62] | 20.86/0.831 | 19.74/0.782 | 25.41/0.830 |
| Deblur-NeRF [63] | 21.10/0.840 | 20.12/0.797 | 26.87/0.843 |
| MPRNet [28] | 21.18/0.846 | 20.76/0.812 | 27.31/0.860 |
| Uformer [30] | 25.20/0.880 | 25.14/0.850 | 27.98/0.858 |
| Restormer [35] | 25.24/0.884 | 25.37/0.859 | 28.02/0.868 |
| BIDeN [8] | 27.11/0.898 | 26.44 /0.870 | 28.04/0.869 |
| WGWS [32] | 26.87/0.899 | 25.89/0.856 | 27.91/0.864 |
| Patil et al. [31] | 26.55/0.884 | 26.20/0.861 | 28.10/0.871 |
| AST [33] | 27.15/0.901 | 26.32/0.865 | 28.24/0.873 |
| FFformer (ours) | **27.41 /0.905** | **26.51/0.871** | **28.67/0.880** |

**Table 4.** No-reference BRISQUE↓/NIQE↓ on three multiple degradation removal datasets. ↓ denotes that a lower value indicates better performance.

| Datasets | BID2a-5 [8] | BID2a-6 [8] | RMTD-Syn |
|---|---|---|---|
| **Degraded** | **34.420/5.793** | **33.574/6.150** | **32.436/9.917** |
| DerainNet [64] | 33.877/5.742 | 32.015/6.062 | 30.617/4.967 |
| PSD [61] | 34.876/5.665 | 33.116/6.156 | 29.317/4.101 |
| CCN [62] | 33.624/5.736 | 34.394/6.134 | 30.261/4.575 |
| Deblur-NeRF [63] | 31.733/5.695 | 31.531/5.864 | 29.411/4.038 |
| MPRNet [28] | 31.348/5.567 | 32.377/5.969 | 28.518/3.950 |
| Uformer [30] | 30.627/5.324 | 31.001/5.599 | 29.690/4.183 |
| Restormer [35] | 29.137/5.346 | 30.482/5.504 | 30.234/3.870 |
| BIDeN [8] | 27.967/5.242 | 28.395/5.386 | 28.043/3.902 |
| WGWS [32] | 28.495/5.201 | 28.897/5.431 | 27.917/3.824 |
| Patil et al. [31] | 28.365/5.197 | 28.172/5.354 | 27.710/3.833 |
| AST [33] | 28.144/5.166 | 27.814/5.301 | 27.967/3.764 |
| FFformer (ours) | **27.134/5.084** | **26.313/5.146** | **26.451/3.685** |

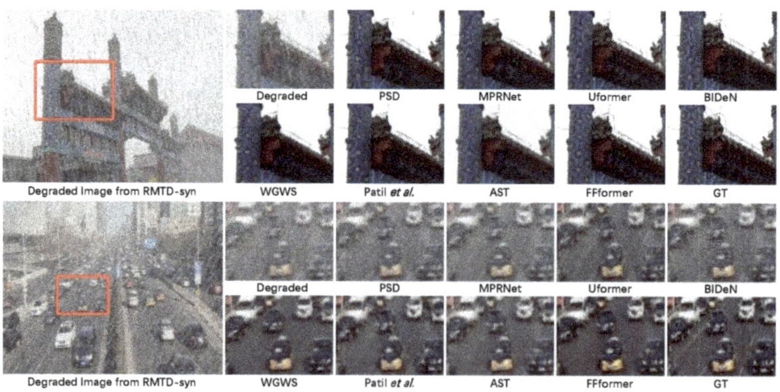


**Figure 11.** Qualitative restoration results on the RMTD-Syn dataset with PSD [61], MPRNet [28], Uformer [30], BIDeN [8], WGWS [32], Patil et al. [31], and AST [33].

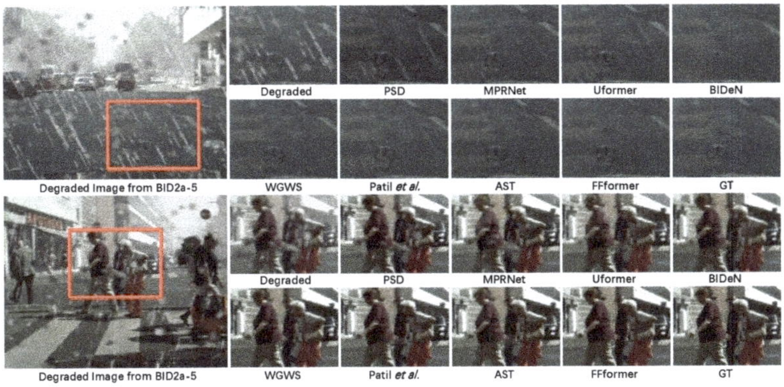


**Figure 12.** Qualitative restoration results on the BID2a-5 [8] with PSD [61], MPRNet [28], Uformer [30], BIDeN [8], WGWS [32], Patil et al. [31], and AST [33].

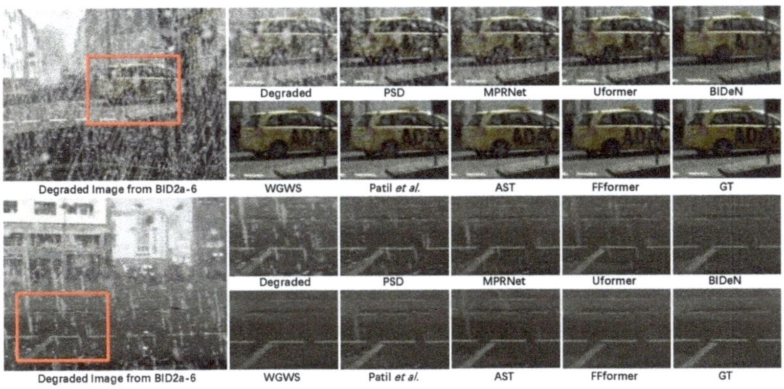


**Figure 13.** Qualitative restoration results on BID2a-6 [8] with PSD [61], MPRNet [28], Uformer [30], BIDeN [8], WGWS [32], Patil et al. [31], and AST [33].

**Table 5.** Cross-dataset generalization evaluation on the RMTD-Real test set. Models are trained on different source datasets (BID2a, BID2b, RMTD-Syn) and evaluated on the target RMTD-Real set using no-reference image quality metrics (BRISQUE↓/PIQE↓). Results demonstrate the superior effectiveness of the proposed RMTD-Syn dataset for generalizing to real-world multi-degradation scenarios and the robust performance of our FFformer.

| Training Set | BID2a [8] | BID2b [8] | RMTD-Syn |
|---|---|---|---|
| **Degraded** | **28.443/3.850** | **28.443/3.850** | **28.443/3.850** |
| DerainNet [64] | 29.431/3.871 | 29.991/3.955 | 29.624/3.844 |
| PSD [61] | 27.970/3.860 | 27.317/3.851 | 27.246/3.717 |
| CCN [62] | 28.412/3.812 | 27.961/3.974 | 28.791/3.901 |
| Deblur-NeRF [63] | 28.011/3.784 | 29.411/3.978 | 27.664/3.695 |
| MPRNet [28] | 27.318/3.759 | 27.118/3.801 | 26.417/3.672 |
| Uformer [30] | 28.682/3.647 | 29.013/3.661 | 27.011/3.590 |
| Restormer [35] | 27.302/3.756 | 27.034/3.720 | 26.181/3.604 |
| BIDeN [8] | 26.704/3.688 | 26.430/3.667 | 25.448/3.506 |
| WGWS [32] | 25.813/3.670 | 25.517/3.657 | 24.682/3.547 |
| Patil et al. [31] | 25.710/3.667 | 25.613/3.671 | 24.827/3.598 |
| AST [33] | 26.124/3.733 | 25.867/3.715 | 24.961/3.568 |
| FFformer (ours) | **25.012/3.562** | **25.334/3.541** | **23.437/3.427** |

Qualitatively, Figure 14 provides a compelling visual comparison. It shows that models trained on the weather-specific BID2b dataset struggles to fully restore a real-world image from RMTD-Real, which likely contains a complex mixture of degradations beyond just weather. In contrast, models trained on our diverse RMTD-Syn dataset successfully removes artifacts and recovers finer details.

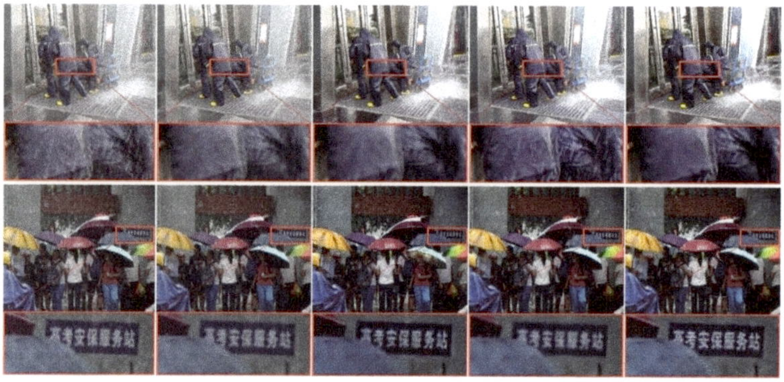

**(a) Degraded** **(b) Restormer-BID2b** **(c) Restormer-RMTD** **(d) WGWS-BID2b** **(e) WGWS-RMTD**

**Figure 14.** Visual comparison of models trained on different datasets and evaluated on RMTD-Real. The comparison between (**b**,**d**) models trained on BID2b and (**c**,**e**) models trained on RMTD-Syn demonstrates that training on our diverse synthetic dataset yields superior restoration of details and more effective degradation removal in complex real-world conditions. The image contains a Chinese sign, which translates to "Gaokao Security Service Station".

Finally, Figure 15 provides a critical analysis of the model's cross-dataset generalization capability. It showcases the restoration results of different models (all trained on our multi-degradation RMTD-Syn) when applied to real-world images from external sources (RTTS [1], SPA [4], BLUR-J [6]), each characterized by a single, dominant degradation type. The compelling performance across these diverse degradation domains demonstrates that the feature representations learned from our comprehensive RMTD-Syn dataset are highly robust and generalizable, effectively transferring to restoration tasks beyond the specific multi-degradation mixtures seen during training. Among them, our FFformer consistently produces the most visually pleasing results with the cleanest backgrounds and best-preserved details, solidifying its status as a robust and versatile solution for real-world image restoration.

Object Detection. The assessment of object detection performance, conducted using YOLOv8 [65] on restoration results, highlights FFformer's consistent superiority in accurately detecting objects within multi-degraded images. As shown in Table 6, FFformer outperforms alternative methods, demonstrating its exceptional ability to restore images while preserving crucial details necessary for reliable object detection. This comprehensive evaluation underscores FFformer's efficacy and robustness in restoring images affected by complex multi-degradations, positioning it as a state-of-the-art solution for multi-degraded image restoration tasks.

**Table 6.** Object detection results in mAP↑ using YOLOv8 [65].

| Datasets | RMTD-Syn | RMTD-Real |
|---|---|---|
| Degraded | 0.1580 | 0.5259 |
| Uformer [30] | 0.3710 | 0.5789 |
| BIDeN [8] | 0.3804 | 0.5893 |

**Table 6.** *Cont.*

| Datasets | RMTD-Syn | RMTD-Real |
|---|---|---|
| Patil et al. [31] | 0.3821 | 0.5876 |
| AST [33] | 0.3841 | 0.5955 |
| FFformer | **0.3965** | **0.6012** |
| Ground Truth | 0.4153 | - |

**Figure 15.** Cross-dataset generalization to real-world images with single degradations. All compared models were trained solely on the proposed RMTD-Syn dataset (multi-degradation) but are evaluated here on real images from external sources, each exhibiting a single dominant degradation (Hazy, Rainy, Blurry). The successful restoration across these different degradation domains demonstrates the strong generalization capability and robust feature learning fostered by our training dataset. Furthermore, our FFformer achieves the most visually pleasing results with the cleanest backgrounds and best-preserved details. The image contains a Korean advertisement poster implying low-cost rentals.

### *5.5. Ablation Studies*

The ablation study of the transformer architecture is summarized in Table 7 and Figure 16. The GFSA, which focuses on selecting local maximum features, outperforms the MSA, achieving a notable 0.26 dB gain in PSNR and a 0.007 gain in SSIM. Additionally, the feature value shrinkage introduced by the FSFN enhances its ability to filter redundant degradations, resulting in a 0.27 dB PSNR gain over the conventional FN [54] and a 0.08 dB PSNR gain over the DFN [55]. Overall, compared to the baseline, the architecture achieves a significant improvement with a 0.82 dB gain in PSNR and a 0.018 gain in SSIM.

The ablation study results presented in Table 8 and Figure 17 further illuminate the significant contribution of the FEB to the overall network improvement. FEB plays a crucial role, leading to a remarkable enhancement of 0.76 dB in PSNR and a substantial gain of 0.022 in SSIM. This underscores the effectiveness of FEB in refining and enriching feature representations, significantly contributing to FFformer's restoration performance.

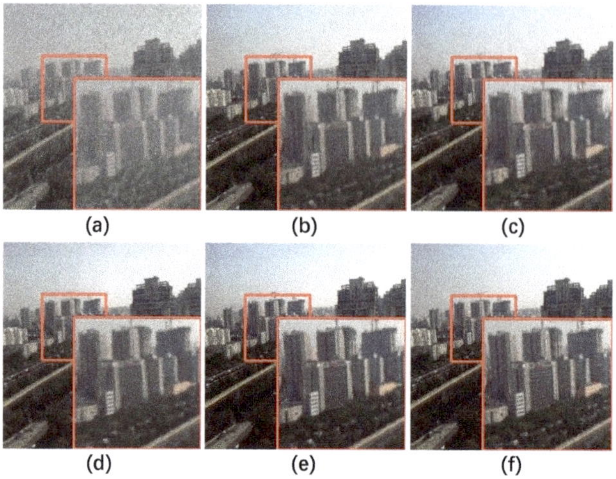


**Figure 16.** Qualitative ablation study results of the Feature Filter Transformer Block on RMTD-Syn dataset. (**a**) Degraded, (**b**) MSA + FN, (**c**) GFSA + FN, (**d**) MSA + FSFN, (**e**) GFSA + FSFN, (**f**) Ground Truth.

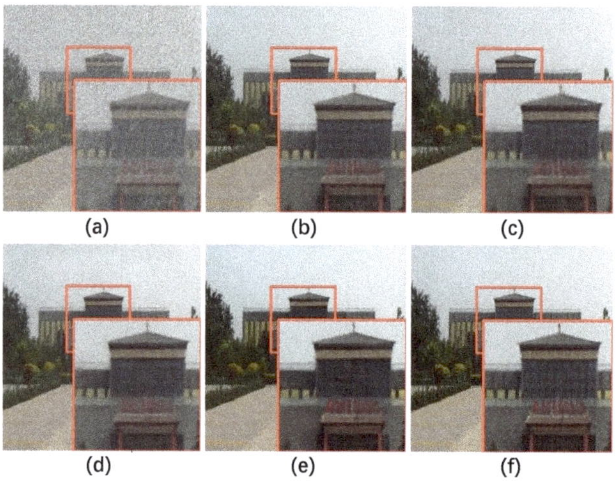


**Figure 17.** Qualitative ablation study results of the Feature Enhancement Block on RMTD-Syn dataset. (**a**) Degraded, (**b**) w/o FEB, (**c**) w/o intra-feature attention, (**d**) w/o cross-feature attention, (**e**) intra-feature + cross-feature attention, (**f**) Ground Truth.

**Table 7.** Quantitative ablation study results of the Feature Filter Transformer Block on RMTD-Syn dataset.

| Network | Component | PSNR ↑ | SSIM ↑ |
|---|---|---|---|
| baseline | MSA + FN [54] | 27.85 | 0.862 |
| Multi-head Attention | GFSA + FN [54] | 28.11 | 0.869 |
| Feed-forward Network | MSA + DFN [55] | 28.04 | 0.867 |
| | MSA + FSFN | 28.12 | 0.871 |
| Overall | GFSA + FSFN | **28.67** | **0.880** |

Table 8. Quantitative ablation study results of the Feature Enhancement Block on RMTD-Syn dataset.

| Setting | Cross-Feature Attention | Intra-Feature Attention | PSNR↑ | SSIM ↑ |
|---|---|---|---|---|
| (a) | | | 27.91 | 0.858 |
| (b) | ✓ | | 28.29 | 0.869 |
| (c) | | ✓ | 28.17 | 0.865 |
| (d) | ✓ | ✓ | **28.67** | **0.880** |

*5.6. Study of Hyper-Parameters and Model Complexity*

In this study, we investigate the impact of hyper-parameters and model complexity on the performance of FFformer. Four hyper-parameter configurations are tested, varying layer numbers, attention heads, and channel numbers. Specifically, we consider two settings for layer numbers: {4, 4, 4, 4} and {2, 4, 4, 6}, along with two settings for attention heads: {2, 2, 4, 4} and {1, 2, 4, 8}. The corresponding channel numbers are {64, 64, 128, 128} and {32, 64, 128, 256}, respectively. The comparison results are summarized in Table 9.

Table 9. Comparison of Hyper-parameters on RMTD-Syn dataset.

| Settings | Layer Nums | Attention Heads | PSNR↑/SSIM↑ |
|---|---|---|---|
| (a) | 4, 4, 4, 4 | 2, 2, 4, 4 | 26.97/0.862 |
| (b) | 4, 4, 4, 4 | 1, 2, 4, 8 | 28.10/0.868 |
| (c) | 2, 4, 4, 6 | 2, 2, 4, 4 | 28.17/0.867 |
| (d) | 2, 4, 4, 6 | 1, 2, 4, 8 | **28.67/0.880** |

Furthermore, the model complexity analysis in Table 10 reinforces FFformer's position as a lightweight model. It not only exhibits the lowest computational complexity but also achieves the fastest average inference time on 512 × 512 pixel images. This efficiency is attributed to the synergistic effects of feature size reduction and feature value shrinkage introduced by GFSA and FSFN. As shown in Figure 18, the FFformer is an efficient and lightweight image enhancement model for complex scene images. Consequently, FFformer excels in restoration performance and proves to be a practical and efficient solution for multi-degraded image restoration tasks, making it suitable for applications in systems such as autonomous driving and safety monitoring.

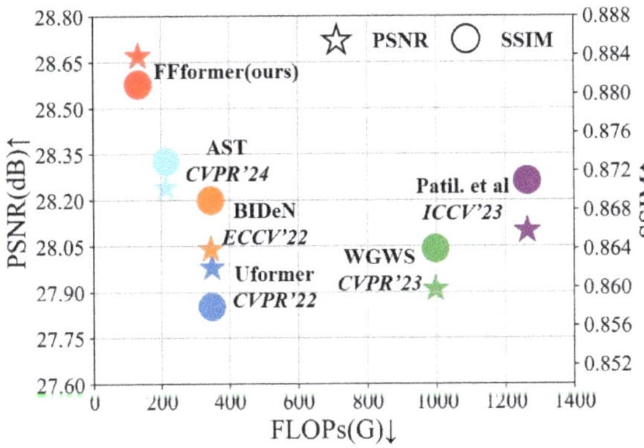


Figure 18. PSNR↑ and SSIM↑ vs. FLOPs↓ on the RMTD. FFformer outperforms state-of-the-art methods (AST [33] in cyan, BIDeN [8] in orange, Uformer [30] in blue, WGWS [32] in green, and Patil et al. [31] in purple) in both metrics while maintaining lower computational complexity.

**Table 10.** Comparison of Model Complexity.

| Model | FLOPs | Parameters | Inference Time |
|---|---|---|---|
| Uformer [30] | 347.6 G | 50.9 M | 0.1737 s |
| BIDeN [8] | 344.0 G | 38.6 M | 1.2140 s |
| WGWS [32] | 996.2 G | 12.6 M | 0.1919 s |
| Patil et al. [31] | 1262.9 G | 11.1 M | 0.1098 s |
| AST [33] | 213.6 G | 13.4 M | 0.1594 s |
| FFformer | 131.7 G | 17.2 M | 0.0847 s |

## 6. Conclusions

In conclusion, this paper introduces the Feature Filter Transformer (FFformer) as a specialized solution for multi-degraded image restoration. By leveraging the synergistic capabilities of the Gaussian Filter Self-Attention (GFSA) and Feature Shrinkage Feed-forward Network (FSFN), FFformer effectively compresses feature sizes and shrinks feature values simultaneously. Additionally, FFformer employs the innovative Scale Conversion Module (SCM) and Feature Aggregation Module (FAM) to adeptly handle multi-scale features within the image encoder. The integration of the Feature Enhancement Block (FEB) further refines the extraction of valuable multi-degradation features in the decoder.

Furthermore, we present the inaugural Robust Multi-Type Degradation (RMTD) dataset, a significant milestone in image restoration methodologies, as it encompasses multiple degradations simultaneously. The creation of RMTD represents a crucial advancement, providing a valuable resource for ongoing research and future developments in the field. Comparative experiments conducted on the RMTD dataset and other sources compellingly demonstrate FFformer's superior performance in multi-degraded image restoration. Ultimately, FFformer emerges as an innovative approach, promising robust solutions for applications reliant on accurate visual information under challenging weather conditions.

Looking ahead, our future work will focus on two key directions. First, we plan to extend our efficient restoration framework to enable comprehensive benchmarking against state-of-the-art large-scale generative and foundation models, which will require access to elevated computational resources. Second, we aim to continually expand the diversity and realism of the RMTD dataset by incorporating a wider spectrum of challenging real-world degradations.

**Funding:** This research received no external funding.

**Institutional Review Board Statement:** Not applicable.

**Data Availability Statement:** Dataset available on request from the author.

**Conflicts of Interest:** The author declares no conflicts of interest.

## References

1. Li, B.; Ren, W.; Fu, D.; Tao, D.; Feng, D.; Zeng, W.; Wang, Z. Benchmarking single-image dehazing and beyond. *IEEE Trans. Image Process.* **2018**, *28*, 492–505. [CrossRef]
2. Zhang, X.; Dong, H.; Pan, J.; Zhu, C.; Tai, Y.; Wang, C.; Li, J.; Huang, F.; Wang, F. Learning to restore hazy video: A new real-world dataset and a new method. In Proceedings of the CVPR, Nashville, TN, USA, 19–25 June 2021; pp. 9239–9248.
3. Fu, X.; Huang, J.; Zeng, D.; Huang, Y.; Ding, X.; Paisley, J. Removing rain from single images via a deep detail network. In Proceedings of the CVPR, Honolulu, HI, USA, 21–26 July 2017; pp. 3855–3863.
4. Wang, T.; Yang, X.; Xu, K.; Chen, S.; Zhang, Q.; Lau, R.W. Spatial attentive single-image deraining with a high quality real rain dataset. In Proceedings of the CVPR, Long Beach, CA, USA, 16–20 June 2019; pp. 12270–12279.
5. Nah, S.; Hyun Kim, T.; Mu Lee, K. Deep multi-scale convolutional neural network for dynamic scene deblurring. In Proceedings of the CVPR, Honolulu, HI, USA, 21–26 July 2017; pp. 3883–3891.

6. Rim, J.; Lee, H.; Won, J.; Cho, S. Real-world blur dataset for learning and benchmarking deblurring algorithms. In Proceedings of the ECCV, Glasgow, UK, 23–28 August 2020; pp. 184–201.
7. Abdelhamed, A.; Lin, S.; Brown, M.S. A high-quality denoising dataset for smartphone cameras. In Proceedings of the CVPR, Salt Lake City, UT, USA, 18–22 June 2018; pp. 1692–1700.
8. Han, J.; Li, W.; Fang, P.; Sun, C.; Hong, J.; Armin, M.A.; Petersson, L.; Li, H. Blind image decomposition. In Proceedings of the ECCV, Tel Aviv, Israel, 23–27 October 2022; pp. 218–237.
9. Liu, Y.F.; Jaw, D.W.; Huang, S.C.; Hwang, J.N. DesnowNet: Context-aware deep network for snow removal. *IEEE Trans. Image Process.* **2018**, *27*, 3064–3073. [CrossRef]
10. Chen, W.T.; Fang, H.Y.; Ding, J.J.; Tsai, C.C.; Kuo, S.Y. JSTASR: Joint size and transparency-aware snow removal algorithm based on modified partial convolution and veiling effect removal. In Proceedings of the Computer Vision–ECCV 2020: 16th European Conference, Glasgow, UK, 23–28 August 2020; pp. 754–770.
11. Chen, W.T.; Fang, H.Y.; Hsieh, C.L.; Tsai, C.C.; Chen, I.; Ding, J.J.; Kuo, S.Y. All snow removed: Single image desnowing algorithm using hierarchical dual-tree complex wavelet representation and contradict channel loss. In Proceedings of the IEEE/CVF International Conference on Computer Vision, Montreal, QC, Canada, 11–17 October 2021; pp. 4196–4205.
12. He, K.; Sun, J.; Tang, X. Single image haze removal using dark channel prior. *IEEE Trans. Pattern Anal. Mach. Intell.* **2010**, *33*, 2341–2353. [CrossRef] [PubMed]
13. Berman, D.; Treibitz, T.; Avidan, S. Non-local image dehazing. In Proceedings of the IEEE Conference on Computer Vision and Pattern Recognition, Las Vegas, NV, USA, 27–30 June 2016; pp. 1674–1682.
14. Li, Y.; Tan, R.T.; Guo, X.; Lu, J.; Brown, M.S. Rain streak removal using layer priors. In Proceedings of the IEEE Conference on Computer Vision and Pattern Recognition, Las Vegas, NV, USA, 27–30 June 2016; pp. 2736–2744.
15. Hu, Z.; Cho, S.; Wang, J.; Yang, M.H. Deblurring low-light images with light streaks. In Proceedings of the IEEE Conference on Computer Vision and Pattern Recognition, Columbus, OH, USA, 23–28 June 2014; pp. 3382–3389.
16. Xu, J.; Zhao, W.; Liu, P.; Tang, X. An improved guidance image based method to remove rain and snow in a single image. *Comput. Inf. Sci.* **2012**, *5*, 49. [CrossRef]
17. Pan, J.; Sun, D.; Pfister, H.; Yang, M.H. Blind image deblurring using dark channel prior. In Proceedings of the IEEE Conference on Computer Vision and Pattern Recognition, Las Vegas, NV, USA, 27–30 June 2016; pp. 1628–1636.
18. Meng, G.; Wang, Y.; Duan, J.; Xiang, S.; Pan, C. Efficient image dehazing with boundary constraint and contextual regularization. In Proceedings of the IEEE International Conference on Computer Vision, Sydney, Australia, 1–8 December 2013; pp. 617–624.
19. Li, Y.; Tan, R.T.; Brown, M.S. Nighttime haze removal with glow and multiple light colors. In Proceedings of the IEEE International Conference on Computer Vision, Santiago, Chile, 11–18 December 2015; pp. 226–234.
20. Chen, B.H.; Huang, S.C. An advanced visibility restoration algorithm for single hazy images. *Acm Trans. Multimed. Comput. Commun. Appl. (TOMM)* **2015**, *11*, 1–21. [CrossRef]
21. Qiu, C.; Yao, Y.; Du, Y. Nested Dense Attention Network for Single Image Super-Resolution. In Proceedings of the 2021 International Conference on Multimedia Retrieval, Taipei, Taiwan, 21–24 August 2021; pp. 250–258.
22. Du, X.; Yang, X.; Qin, Z.; Tang, J. Progressive Image Enhancement under Aesthetic Guidance. In Proceedings of the 2019 International Conference on Multimedia Retrieval, Ottawa, ON, Canada, 10–13 June 2019; pp. 349–353.
23. Dong, H.; Pan, J.; Xiang, L.; Hu, Z.; Zhang, X.; Wang, F.; Yang, M.H. Multi-scale boosted dehazing network with dense feature fusion. In Proceedings of the IEEE/CVF Conference on CVPR, Seattle, WA, USA, 14–19 June 2020; pp. 2157–2167.
24. Li, L.; Pan, J.; Lai, W.S.; Gao, C.; Sang, N.; Yang, M.H. Dynamic scene deblurring by depth guided model. *IEEE Trans. Image Process.* **2020**, *29*, 5273–5288. [CrossRef] [PubMed]
25. Wang, C.; Xing, X.; Yao, G.; Su, Z. Single image deraining via deep shared pyramid network. *Vis. Comput.* **2021**, *37*, 1851–1865. [CrossRef]
26. Cheng, B.; Li, J.; Chen, Y.; Zeng, T. Snow mask guided adaptive residual network for image snow removal. *Comput. Vis. Image Underst.* **2023**, *236*, 103819. [CrossRef]
27. Jiang, K.; Wang, Z.; Yi, P.; Chen, C.; Huang, B.; Luo, Y.; Ma, J.; Jiang, J. Multi-scale progressive fusion network for single image deraining. In Proceedings of the IEEE/CVF Conference on Computer Vision and Pattern Recognition, Seattle, WA, USA, 14–19 June 2020; pp. 8346–8355.
28. Zamir, S.W.; Arora, A.; Khan, S.; Hayat, M.; Khan, F.S.; Yang, M.H.; Shao, L. Multi-stage progressive image restoration. In Proceedings of the CVPR, Nashville, TN, USA, 19–25 June 2021; pp. 14821–14831.
29. Chen, W.T.; Huang, Z.K.; Tsai, C.C.; Yang, H.H.; Ding, J.J.; Kuo, S.Y. Learning multiple adverse weather removal via two-stage knowledge learning and multi-contrastive regularization: Toward a unified model. In Proceedings of the IEEE/CVF Conference on CVPR, New Orleans, LA, USA, 19–24 June 2022; pp. 17653–17662.
30. Wang, Z.; Cun, X.; Bao, J.; Zhou, W.; Liu, J.; Li, H. Uformer: A general u-shaped transformer for image restoration. In Proceedings of the IEEE/CVF Conference on CVPR, New Orleans, LA, USA, 19–24 June 2022; pp. 17683–17693.

31. Patil, P.W.; Gupta, S.; Rana, S.; Venkatesh, S.; Murala, S. Multi-weather Image Restoration via Domain Translation. In Proceedings of the ICCV, Paris, France, 2–6 October 2023; pp. 21696–21705.
32. Zhu, Y.; Wang, T.; Fu, X.; Yang, X.; Guo, X.; Dai, J.; Qiao, Y.; Hu, X. Learning Weather-General and Weather-Specific Features for Image Restoration Under Multiple Adverse Weather Conditions. In Proceedings of the CVPR, Vancouver, BC, Canada, 18–22 June 2023; pp. 21747–21758.
33. Zhou, S.; Chen, D.; Pan, J.; Shi, J.; Yang, J. Adapt or perish: Adaptive sparse transformer with attentive feature refinement for image restoration. In Proceedings of the CVPR, Seattle, WA, USA, 17–21 June 2024; pp. 2952–2963.
34. Monga, A.; Nehete, H.; Kumar Reddy Bollu, T.; Raman, B. Dairnet: Degradation-Aware All-in-One Image Restoration Network with Cross-Channel Feature Interaction. *SSRN* **2025**, SSRN:5365629.
35. Zamir, S.W.; Arora, A.; Khan, S.; Hayat, M.; Khan, F.S.; Yang, M.H. Restormer: Efficient transformer for high-resolution image restoration. In Proceedings of the CVPR, New Orleans, LA, USA, 19–24 June 2022; pp. 5728–5739.
36. Liang, J.; Cao, J.; Sun, G.; Zhang, K.; Van Gool, L.; Timofte, R. Swinir: Image restoration using swin transformer. In Proceedings of the IEEE/CVF International Conference on Computer Vision, Montreal, QC, Canada, 11–17 October 2021; pp. 1833–1844.
37. Lee, H.; Choi, H.; Sohn, K.; Min, D. Knn local attention for image restoration. In Proceedings of the IEEE/CVF Conference on Computer Vision and Pattern Recognition, New Orleans, LA, USA, 19–24 June 2022; pp. 2139–2149.
38. Song, Y.; He, Z.; Qian, H.; Du, X. Vision transformers for single image dehazing. *IEEE Trans. Image Process.* **2023**, *32*, 1927–1941. [CrossRef]
39. Chen, X.; Li, H.; Li, M.; Pan, J. Learning A Sparse Transformer Network for Effective Image Deraining. In Proceedings of the IEEE/CVF Conference on Computer Vision and Pattern Recognition, Vancouver, BC, Canada, 18–22 June 2023; pp. 5896–5905.
40. Yang, S.; Hu, C.; Xie, L.; Lee, F.; Chen, Q. MG-SSAF: An advanced vision Transformer. *J. Vis. Commun. Image Represent.* **2025**, *112*, 104578. [CrossRef]
41. Li, B.; Cai, Z.; Wei, H.; Su, S.; Cao, W.; Niu, Y.; Wang, H. A quality enhancement method for vehicle trajectory data using onboard images. *Geo-Spat. Inf. Sci.* **2025**, 1–26.
42. Yang, J.; Wu, C.; Du, B.; Zhang, L. Enhanced multiscale feature fusion network for HSI classification. *IEEE Trans. Geosci. Remote Sens.* **2021**, *59*, 10328–10347. [CrossRef]
43. Tour-Beijing. Available online: https://www.tour-beijing.com/real_time_weather_photo/ (accessed on 1 August 2023).
44. McCartney, E.J. *Optics of the Atmosphere: Scattering by Molecules and Particles*; American Institute of Physics: New York, NY, USA, 1976.
45. Li, Z.; Snavely, N. Megadepth: Learning single-view depth prediction from internet photos. In Proceedings of the CVPR, Salt Lake City, UT, USA, 18–22 June 2018; pp. 2041–2050.
46. Flusser, J.; Farokhi, S.; Höschl, C.; Suk, T.; Zitova, B.; Pedone, M. Recognition of images degraded by Gaussian blur. *IEEE Trans. Image Process.* **2015**, *25*, 790–806. [CrossRef]
47. Gong, D.; Yang, J.; Liu, L.; Zhang, Y.; Reid, I.; Shen, C.; Van Den Hengel, A.; Shi, Q. From motion blur to motion flow: A deep learning solution for removing heterogeneous motion blur. In Proceedings of the CVPR, Honolulu, HI, USA, 21–26 July 2017; pp. 2319–2328.
48. Consul, P.C.; Jain, G.C. A generalization of the Poisson distribution. *Technometrics* **1973**, *15*, 791–799. [CrossRef]
49. Tzutalin. Labelimg. Open Annotation Tool. Available online: https://github.com/HumanSignal/labelImg (accessed on 1 August 2024).
50. Everingham, M.; Van Gool, L.; Williams, C.K.; Winn, J.; Zisserman, A. The pascal visual object classes (voc) challenge. *Int. J. Comput. Vis.* **2010**, *88*, 303–338. [CrossRef]
51. Ronneberger, O.; Fischer, P.; Brox, T. U-net: Convolutional networks for biomedical image segmentation. In Proceedings of the Medical Image Computing and Computer-Assisted Intervention–MICCAI 2015: 18th International Conference, Munich, Germany, 5–9 October 2015; pp. 234–241.
52. Shi, W.; Caballero, J.; Huszár, F.; Totz, J.; Aitken, A.P.; Bishop, R.; Rueckert, D.; Wang, Z. Real-time single image and video super-resolution using an efficient sub-pixel convolutional neural network. In Proceedings of the IEEE Conference on CVPR, Las Vegas, NV, USA, 27–30 June 2016; pp. 1874–1883.
53. Vaswani, A.; Shazeer, N.; Parmar, N.; Uszkoreit, J.; Jones, L.; Gomez, A.N.; Kaiser, Ł.; Polosukhin, I. Attention is all you need. In Advances in neural information processing systems, Long Beach, CA, USA, 4–9 December 2017; pp. 30–40.
54. Dosovitskiy, A.; Beyer, L.; Kolesnikov, A.; Weissenborn, D.; Zhai, X.; Unterthiner, T.; Dehghani, M.; Minderer, M.; Heigold, G.; Gelly, S.; et al. An image is worth 16x16 words: Transformers for image recognition at scale. *arXiv* **2020**, arXiv:2010.11929.
55. Li, Y.; Zhang, K.; Cao, J.; Timofte, R.; Van Gool, L. Localvit: Bringing locality to vision transformers. *arXiv* **2021**, arXiv:2104.05707.
56. Loshchilov, I.; Hutter, F. Sgdr: Stochastic gradient descent with warm restarts. *arXiv* **2016**, arXiv:1608.03983.
57. Huynh-Thu, Q.; Ghanbari, M. Scope of validity of PSNR in image/video quality assessment. *Electron. Lett.* **2008**, *44*, 800–801. [CrossRef]

58. Wang, Z.; Bovik, A.C.; Sheikh, H.R.; Simoncelli, E.P. Image quality assessment: From error visibility to structural similarity. *IEEE Trans. Image Process.* **2004**, *13*, 600–612. [CrossRef]
59. Mittal, A.; Moorthy, A.K.; Bovik, A.C. No-reference image quality assessment in the spatial domain. *IEEE Trans. Image Process.* **2012**, *21*, 4695–4708. [CrossRef]
60. Mittal, A.; Soundararajan, R.; Bovik, A.C. Making a "completely blind" image quality analyzer. *IEEE Signal Process. Lett.* **2012**, *20*, 209–212. [CrossRef]
61. Chen, Z.; Wang, Y.; Yang, Y.; Liu, D. PSD: Principled synthetic-to-real dehazing guided by physical priors. In Proceedings of the CVPR, Nashville, TN, USA, 19–25 June 2021; pp. 7180–7189.
62. Quan, R.; Yu, X.; Liang, Y.; Yang, Y. Removing raindrops and rain streaks in one go. In Proceedings of the CVPR, Nashville, TN, USA, 19–25 June 2021; pp. 9147–9156.
63. Ma, L.; Li, X.; Liao, J.; Zhang, Q.; Wang, X.; Wang, J.; Sander, P.V. Deblur-nerf: Neural radiance fields from blurry images. In Proceedings of the CVPR, New Orleans, LA, USA, 19–24 June 2022; pp. 12861–12870.
64. Fu, X.; Huang, J.; Ding, X.; Liao, Y.; Paisley, J. Clearing the skies: A deep network architecture for single-image rain removal. *IEEE Trans. Image Process.* **2017**, *26*, 2944–2956. [CrossRef] [PubMed]
65. Jocher, G.; Chaurasia, A.; Qiu, J. YOLOv8. Available online: https://github.com/ultralytics/ultralytics (accessed on 20 October 2025).

sensors

MDPI

*Article*

# Modeling the Internal and Contextual Attention for Self-Supervised Skeleton-Based Action Recognition

**Wentian Xin [1], Yue Teng [2,*], Jikang Zhang [2], Yi Liu [2], Ruyi Liu [3], Yuzhi Hu [3] and Qiguang Miao [3]**

1 School of Information Science and Technology, Dalian Maritime University, Dalian 116026, China; wtxin@dlmu.edu.cn
2 Institute of Dataspace, Hefei Comprehensive National Science Center, Hefei 231283, China; zhangjikang@163.com (J.Z.); yiliu6@stu.xidian.edu.cn (Y.L.)
3 School of Computer Science and Technology, Xidian University, Xi'an 710071, China; ruyiliu@xidian.edu.cn (R.L.); yuzhihu@stu.xidian.edu.cn (Y.H.); qgmiao@xidian.edu.cn (Q.M.)
* Correspondence: yueteng@mail.ustc.edu.cn

**Abstract:** Multimodal contrastive learning has achieved significant performance advantages in self-supervised skeleton-based action recognition. Previous methods are limited by modality imbalance, which reduces alignment accuracy and makes it difficult to combine important spatial–temporal frequency patterns, leading to confusion between modalities and weaker feature representations. To overcome these problems, we explore intra-modality feature-wise self-similarity and inter-modality instance-wise cross-consistency, and discover two inherent correlations that benefit recognition: (i) Global Perspective expresses how action semantics carry a broad and high-level understanding, which supports the use of globally discriminative feature representations. (ii) Focus Adaptation refers to the role of the frequency spectrum in guiding attention toward key joints by emphasizing compact and salient signal patterns. Building upon these insights, we propose a novel language–skeleton contrastive learning framework comprising two key components: (a) Feature Modulation, which constructs a skeleton–language action conceptual domain to minimize the expected information gain between vision and language modalities. (b) Frequency Feature Learning, which introduces a Frequency-domain Spatial–Temporal block (FreST) that focuses on sparse key human joints in the frequency domain with compact signal energy. Extensive experiments demonstrate the effectiveness of our method achieves remarkable action recognition performance on widely used benchmark datasets, including NTU RGB+D 60 and NTU RGB+D 120. Especially on the challenging PKU-MMD dataset, MICA has achieved at least a 4.6% improvement over classical methods such as CrosSCLR and AimCLR, effectively demonstrating its ability to capture internal and contextual attention information.

**Keywords:** skeleton-based action recognition; multimodal learning; contrastive learning; frequency learning

## 1. Introduction

Human action recognition (HAR) has emerged as a critical area with wide-ranging applications across sensor-based domains, including consumer-level surveillance [1,2], autonomous driving [3,4], human-computer interaction [5,6], medical rehabilitation [7,8], sports analytics [9,10], and smart city systems [11,12]. Recent HAR methods utilize multimodal sensor data, such as RGB images, depth maps, and optical flow, to capture complementary information and improve recognition accuracy [13]. However, extracting accurate



https://doi.org/10.3390/s25216532

action representations from sensor-derived video is challenging due to background interference and inconsistent lighting, which could distort the relationships between human joints and reduce recognition accuracy [14,15].

Skeleton data provide 3D joint positions, motion details, and topological relationships, offering an efficient and compact representation of spatiotemporal features [16,17]. Although it highlights key attributes of human actions, extracting joint-level information often loses contextual semantics [18]. As a result, it becomes particularly challenging to accurately recognize actions with subtle semantic differences, such as distinguishing between 'reading' and 'writing', or 'pointing' and 'victory gesture' [19]. The absence of such semantic information makes it difficult even for experienced researchers to differentiate between similar skeletal patterns, let alone intelligent models [20,21]. As a result, multimodal fusion methods have become increasingly important, especially for fine-grained actions that rely heavily on semantic cues and interaction understanding [22]. Multimodal fusion approaches can generally be divided into two categories: RGB + Skeleton [14,23] and Semantics + Skeleton [24,25]. Although RGB + Skeleton methods achieve high accuracy [26], they require heavy computation and are unsuitable for lightweight applications. In contrast, semantics and skeleton are compact high-level representations, where semantics need some preprocessing, but inference remains more efficient than RGB methods [27]. Large-scale labeling is costly and error-prone, while self-supervised learning offers a way to reduce such challenges by removing supervision or generating pseudo-supervision [28,29].

Recently, several studies have advanced skeleton-based self-supervised and multimodal learning with novel mechanisms. For example, HiCLR [30] and HYSP [31] explored hierarchical consistency and hyperbolic learning to enhance representation robustness, yet they rely heavily on complex augmentation strategies, which may limit scalability. Skeleton-logoCLR [32] and CStrCRL [33] enhanced feature discrimination through global–local contrastive learning and gated graph modeling, yet they still rely mainly on structural cues without semantic understanding. In contrast, multimodal frameworks such as SAM-Net [34] and CFVL [35] integrated vision–language alignment, achieving better interpretability but incurring heavy computational costs. More recent cross-modal skeleton–language methods, such as ActionGCL [36] and CoCoDiff [37], introduced semantic-guided diffusion and contrastive consistency, but they struggle to maintain stable intra-modal self-similarity, leading to inconsistent representations. These limitations collectively highlight the need for a unified approach that can model both intra-modal self-similarity and inter-modal cross-consistency, motivating the design of our proposed framework.

Current self-supervised contrastive learning methods overlook several key aspects. First, relying on similarity measures in single-modal skeleton data suffers from contextual gaps, missing objects, and entangled spatiotemporal features, which weaken salient feature extraction and cause action misclassification. Second, most methods focus on spatiotemporal pairs while ignoring instance-wise consistency within a modality. Preserving internal structure is crucial for fine-grained details and accurate recognition. Third, point-wise temporal mappings fail to capture global dependencies, and noise, redundancy, and weak joint-movement representation further reduce discriminative power.

To systematically explore the relationship between inter-modal consistency and intra-modal self-similarity, and their combined effect on enhancing action recognition, we propose a novel framework called Modeling Internal and Contextual Attention (MICA). The framework enhances both feature-level and instance-level representations through two core components: the Feature Modulation and the Frequency-domain Spatial–Temporal Block (FreST).

Feature Modulation aligns skeletal motion data with corresponding semantic information by minimizing the representational distance between sample features and class-specific anchor points. Such alignment encourages precise decision boundaries and improves discrimination among similar actions. The effectiveness of this mechanism is visually demonstrated in the red sector area of Figure 1. FreST refines motion encoding by transforming skeleton sequences into the frequency domain, highlighting sparse yet informative joint movements. Adaptive filters suppress redundancy while preserving discriminative temporal-spatial features. By combining global and local frequency filtering, FreST captures structural variations and enhances action representations.

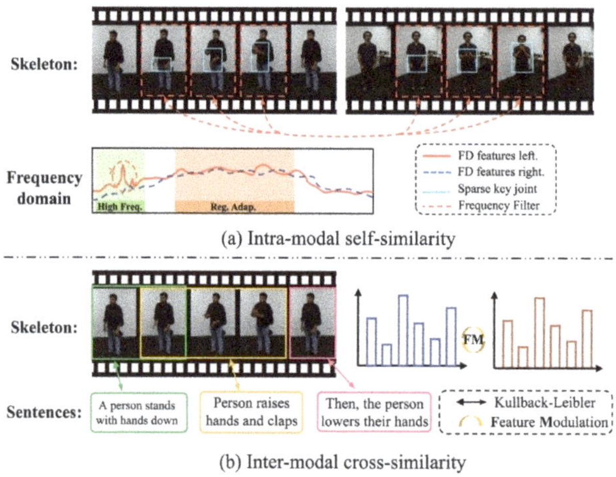


**Figure 1.** We illustrate two similarity mechanisms for feature association. (**a**) Intra-modal self-similarity: Analyzes skeleton sequences in the frequency domain (high-frequency, adaptive region, etc.) with features like left/right FD features, sparse key joints, and frequency filters to find single-modality associations. (**b**) Inter-modal cross-similarity: Achieves cross-modal association between skeleton sequences and text (e.g., 'A person stands with hands down') via KL divergence and Feature Modulation (FM).

Together, Feature Modulation and FreST provide a unified framework for cross-modal alignment and structural modeling, enabling context-aware attention with frequency-domain refinement. Extensive experiments across pre-training, linear evaluation, fine-tuning, and semi-supervised settings demonstrate significant performance gains without requiring extra labeled data. Visual validation further illustrates the skeleton–language action domain. To summarize, our main contributions are threefold:

- We propose a novel self-supervised framework named Modeling Internal and Contextual Attention (MICA), which enhances skeleton-based action recognition by jointly modeling intra-modal self-similarity and inter-modal cross-modal consistency.
- We introduce a Feature Modulation mechanism that constructs a skeleton–language conceptual domain by minimizing the expected information gain between modalities, enabling alignment of action representations in a shared semantic space.
- We design a Frequency-domain Spatial–Temporal Block (FreST) that adaptively filters sparse yet informative joint movements, leveraging global and local frequency filters to capture salient spatial–temporal patterns for fine-grained action recognition.

The remainder of this paper is organized as follows. Section 2 reviews related works on self-supervised learning, contrastive learning, and frequency-based skeleton action recognition. Section 3 introduces the preliminaries, including the skeleton encoder, semantic encoder, and semantic description learning. Section 4 presents the proposed Modeling Internal and Contextual Attention (MICA) framework in detail. Section 5 reports extensive experimental results and ablation studies on multiple benchmark datasets. Finally, Section 6 concludes the paper and discusses possible future research directions.

## 2. Related Works

In this section, we explore key techniques such as self-supervised learning, contrastive learning, multimodal contrastive learning, and frequency feature learning in skeleton-based action recognition.

**Self-supervised Learning with skeleton** aims to learn discriminative feature representations from unlabeled data to reduce the dependence on labeled data. Many efforts have been devoted to designing self-supervised learning frameworks to extract skeleton spatiotemporal motion features for benefiting recognition. Specifically, MS2L [38] performs motion prediction modeling by predicting future sequences, while integrating multi-task and jigsaw puzzle [39,40] recognition to solve the overfitting problem of single-task reconstruction. In addition, recent multimodal self-supervised frameworks such as SeBiReNet [41] and HiCo [42] have explored cross-modal consistency and hierarchical feature learning, providing valuable insights into the design of multi-stream skeleton representation models. However, it is difficult for these methods to compete with advanced supervised methods [43–45].

**Skeleton-based Contrastive learning** has demonstrated remarkable performance advantages in self-supervised model pre-training. It effectively enhances the discriminative ability of feature representations and improves model performance in downstream tasks. Contrastive learning has been popularized in skeleton-based action recognition recently, such as SkeletonCLR [28], AimCLR [46], ActCLR [47], and others [48,49]. In addition to contrastive paradigms, non-contrastive self-supervised methods have also shown great potential. For example, [17,50–52] learn spatiotemporal representations through masked auto-encoding without using contrastive objectives, effectively capturing fine-grained motion dynamics and frequency-aware structural dependencies in skeleton sequences. However, the information bottleneck (e.g., contextual gap and missing interaction objects) of single-modal skeleton data, and the complete entanglement of information caused by spatiotemporal modeling networks, contribute to the misclassification of similar actions.

**Semantic Augmentation Strategies on Multimodal Skeleton Action Recognition** have brought significant benefits to addressing the aforementioned information gap problem. Approaches such as CLIP [27] and ALIGN [53] achieve cross-modal understanding by learning to compare text and images. Integrating skeletal and linguistic semantics has become a powerful approach to enhance action recognition. Recent methods incorporate descriptive language into skeleton features using prompts, label embeddings, or generated text to enrich contextual understanding. For example, SMIE [54], SA-DVAE [55], and Text-CLS-Transformer [56] align skeleton and text spaces through mutual information maximization, variational modeling, or prompt-based joint embedding, while HSARL [57] introduces motion semantics from language models to improve generalization. Other approaches, such as LPSR [58], ActionGCL [36], and CoCoDiff [37], use contrastive objectives and latent diffusion to enforce consistency between skeleton representations and language embeddings, enhancing discrimination for ambiguous actions. At the structural level, CrossGLG [59], Neuron [60], and LGGT [61] construct skeleton–text association matrices guided by semantic priors to improve spatial–temporal modeling, and methods like GAP [24], MMFR [25], SAM-Net [34], CFVL [35], and SAT-GCN [62] further align inter-joint and inter-class structures using generative prompts and motion cues.

**Frequency Feature Learning** effectively addresses the inherent noise and redundancy present in skeleton data, thereby enhancing the ability to express salient information. DCT [63] introduced a frequency-domain learning approach, showcasing its effectiveness and advantages in a range of tasks (e.g., classification, detection, and segmentation). Frequency-domain compressed representation contains rich patterns for action recognition tasks. Frequency-domain MLPs [64] utilize MLPs in the frequency domain to address point-wise mappings and information bottlenecks in prediction tasks. Nonetheless, the frequency representation learning approach has seen limited application in skeleton-based action recognition.

**Summary and Distinction from Existing Works.** Despite remarkable progress, existing multimodal and skeleton contrastive learning methods still face two key limitations. First, most CLIP-based frameworks (e.g., ActionGCL [36], CoCoDiff [37]) rely on direct similarity maximization between modalities, which often leads to weak intra-modal consistency and insufficient control over semantic alignment. Second, recent frequency-domain methods (e.g., DCT [63], Frequency-MLPs [64]) improve signal compactness but treat frequency patterns as static representations, lacking adaptability to motion-dependent variations. In contrast, our proposed Modeling Internal and Contextual Attention (MICA) introduces two complementary modules: (1) Feature Modulation (FM), which models expected information gain to achieve fine-grained skeleton–language alignment while preserving intra-modal feature similarity; and (2) Frequency-domain Spatial–Temporal Block (FreST), which performs adaptive global–local frequency filtering on sparse joints to retain discriminative and context-aware spectral cues. Together, these designs provide a unified solution that simultaneously strengthens semantic alignment and spectral discrimination, two aspects that have rarely been optimized jointly in previous works.

## 3. Preliminaries

This section introduces foundational knowledge for semantic-guided skeleton-based action recognition, focusing on three key components: the skeleton encoder, the semantic encoder, and semantic description learning. These elements collectively form the basis of frameworks that align body motion and semantic meaning for improved action understanding.

### 3.1. Skeleton Encoder

Given a sequence of human body joints in 2D or 3D coordinates, the skeleton can be structured as a graph $\mathcal{G} = (\mathcal{V}, \mathcal{E})$, where $\mathcal{V} = (v_1, v_2, \ldots, v_N)$ denotes a set of $N$ joints (nodes), each $v_i$ representing the 3D coordinate of the $i$-th joint in the human body, and $\mathcal{E}$ defines the bones (edges) connecting them. For this undirected graph, an adjacency matrix $A \in \mathbb{R}^{N \times N}$ is used, where each entry $A_{i,j} = 1$ if joints $v_i$ and $v_j$ are directly connected, and 0 otherwise. The action sequence is represented by the joint feature set $\mathcal{X} = \{x_{t,n} \in \mathbb{R}^C \mid 1 \leq t \leq T, 1 \leq n \leq N\}$, where $x_{t,n}$ denotes the feature vector of joint $v_n$ at frame $t$, and $C$ represents the number of input channels (e.g., the 3D coordinates $(x, y, z)$ or other motion-related attributes such as velocity or confidence scores). The overall input can be written as a tensor $X \in \mathbb{R}^{T \times N \times C}$. With $X$ representing temporal features and $A$ capturing the spatial structure, a typical graph convolutional layer performs the update as follows:

$$X^{l+1} = \sigma(\tilde{\Lambda}^{-\frac{1}{2}} \tilde{A} \tilde{\Lambda}^{-\frac{1}{2}} X^l W^l), \tag{1}$$

where $\tilde{A} = A + I$ includes self-loops to preserve node features, and $\tilde{\Lambda}$ is the corresponding degree matrix, whose diagonal element $\tilde{\Lambda}_{ii} = \sum_j \tilde{A}_{ij}$ represents the number of connections (including self-loops) of node $v_i$. The function $\sigma(\cdot)$ applies a non-linear activation, and $W^l \in \mathbb{R}^{C_l \times C_{l+1}}$ is the trainable weight matrix at layer $l$. The skeleton encoding process can be simplified using the following formula:

$$S = E_s(\mathcal{S}_0), \tag{2}$$

where $\mathcal{S}_0 \in \mathbb{R}^{T \times N \times C}$ is the raw input tensor of joint features over time, $E_s(\cdot)$ is the learnable skeleton encoder that fuses spatial graph convolutions with temporal modeling to capture joint dependencies, and $S$ is the resulting compact spatiotemporal embedding for downstream tasks.

### 3.2. Semantic Encoder

Semantic action recognition transforms a textual description $\mathcal{T}_0$ (the raw input text) into an embedding vector $Z$ by applying a semantic encoder $E_t$, where $E_t$ refers to a pretrained transformer model such as CLIP or BERT. In this work, we adopt the CLIP text encoder because it provides a well-aligned multimodal embedding space that bridges visual and linguistic semantics. Unlike generic language models, CLIP has been trained on large-scale paired image–text data, enabling it to capture fine-grained action semantics and contextual cues that are crucial for skeleton–language alignment. This characteristic makes it particularly suitable for enhancing cross-modal consistency in self-supervised action recognition. The transformation is expressed as:

$$Z = E_t(\mathcal{T}_0), \quad Z \in \mathbb{R}^d, \tag{3}$$

where $d$ denotes the size of the semantic feature space used to match text with visual or skeletal information. Input descriptions can vary in form, including action names, synonymous expressions, structured part-based templates, or rich natural-language paragraphs.

### 3.3. Semantic Description Learning

To integrate semantic guidance into skeleton-based action representation, various strategies have been explored under different supervision paradigms. Despite differences in data and objectives, they aim to align skeleton and text features in a shared space, typically using contrastive learning that pulls positive pairs closer and pushes negatives apart. A typical bidirectional alignment is formulated as:

$$\begin{aligned} p_{S\to Z}(S_i) &= \frac{\exp(\mathrm{sim}(S_i, Z_i)/\tau)}{\sum_{j=1}^{B} \exp(\mathrm{sim}(S_i, Z_j)/\tau)}, \\ p_{Z\to S}(Z_i) &= \frac{\exp(\mathrm{sim}(Z_i, S_i)/\tau)}{\sum_{j=1}^{B} \exp(\mathrm{sim}(Z_i, S_j)/\tau)}, \end{aligned} \tag{4}$$

where $\mathrm{sim}(\cdot)$ is cosine similarity and $\tau$ is the temperature parameter. These probabilities are optimized using the Kullback–Leibler divergence:

$$\mathcal{L}_{\mathrm{KL}} = \tfrac{1}{2}\mathbb{E}_{(S,Z)}\Big[\mathrm{KL}(p_{S\to Z} \,\|\, y_{S\to Z}) + \mathrm{KL}(p_{Z\to S} \,\|\, y_{Z\to S})\Big], \tag{5}$$

where $y_{S\to Z}$ and $y_{Z\to S}$ are one-hot targets indicating positive pairs. In low-label or label-free settings, textual descriptions generated by large language models serve as weak supervision to guide representation learning. Finally, the overall training objective integrates the semantic contrastive loss with task-specific terms:

$$\mathcal{L}_{\mathrm{total}} = \mathcal{L}_{\mathrm{cls}} + \alpha \mathcal{L}_{\mathrm{KL}} \tag{6}$$

where $\mathcal{L}$cls is the cross-entropy loss for action classification. The hyperparameter $\alpha$ balances the contribution of the KL divergence. In summary, semantic description learning enriches skeleton-based action recognition by integrating structured or unstructured language as auxiliary supervision.

## 4. Methodology

In this section, we introduce MICA, which explores inter-modal consistency and intra-modal self-similarity and their correlations, benefiting recognition. MICA consists of Feature Modulation (FM) strategy (Section 4.1) combined with a Frequency-domain Spatial–temporal Block (FreST) method (Section 4.2). In addition, SkeletonCLR is introduced to encourage representations of different skeleton sequences to be pushed apart.

### 4.1. Feature Modulation

The overall framework of the proposed method includes two branches, as depicted in Figure 2. Within the skeleton branch, the input skeleton sequence undergoes data augmentation and topology mapping, passing through a stack of $N$ layers of GCN blocks, which incorporate the proposed frequency-domain spatiotemporal blocks, to encode and generate the skeleton feature representation. Similarly, in the lower branch, the text is processed through Byte-Pair Tokenization and then encoded into embeddings utilizing the CLIP text encoder.

Specifically, we employ the text encoder from the CLIP ViT-B/32 model to obtain sentence-level embeddings. Each action description or generated prompt sentence is first tokenized and then mapped into a 512-dimensional embedding space. These embeddings serve as semantic anchors for cross-modal alignment with skeleton features in the Feature Modulation module. During training, the CLIP encoder remains frozen to preserve its pretrained semantic structure while minimizing the expected information gain between modalities.

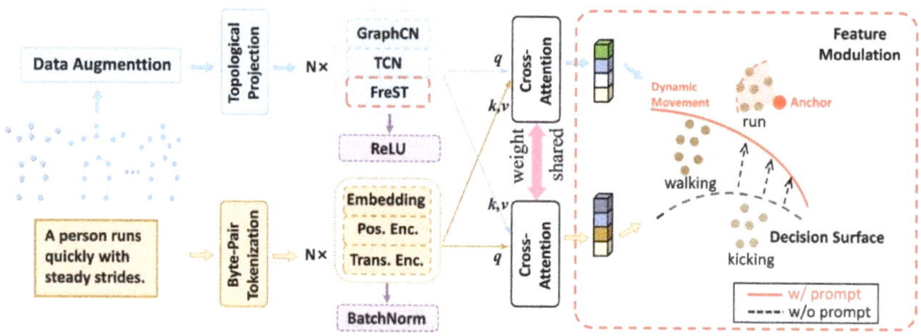


**Figure 2.** The overall structure of MICA, which is the cross-modal dual-encoder structure, consists of feature modulation and modality harmonizer. Feature modulation introduces text semantic information. The modality harmonizer solves the modal imbalance problem by cross-attention. Additionally, FreST is appended to the end of the skeleton encoder to capture frequency-domain features.

To elaborate further, we formulate the process of distillation as an optimization problem, where the text embedding $\mathcal{P}(\mathcal{X})$ is the true distribution, which is generated by a pretrained encoder. $\mathcal{Q}(\mathcal{X})$ is an approximate distribution used to fit $\mathcal{P}(\mathcal{X})$, which is encoded by a learnable graph convolutional neural network. The loss is defined as the expected information gain of $\mathcal{P}(\mathcal{X})$ with respect to $\mathcal{Q}(\mathcal{X})$, which measures the difference between two distributions.

The process of distillation can be formulated as an optimization problem where we aim to minimize the difference between two distributions. Specifically, the text embedding $\mathcal{P}(\mathcal{X})$ represents the true distribution, which is generated by a pretrained encoder. On the other hand, $\mathcal{Q}(\mathcal{X})$ is the approximate distribution, which we seek to learn and fit to $\mathcal{P}(\mathcal{X})$, using a graph convolutional neural network (GCN).

The goal is to bring $\mathcal{Q}(\mathcal{X})$ closer to $\mathcal{P}(\mathcal{X})$ by minimizing the discrepancy between these two distributions. This discrepancy is quantified by a loss function, often expressed in terms of the expected information gain (or Kullback–Leibler divergence) between $\mathcal{P}(\mathcal{X})$ and $\mathcal{Q}(\mathcal{X})$. The KL divergence, denoted as $D_{KL}(\mathcal{P}(\mathcal{X}) \parallel \mathcal{Q}(\mathcal{X}))$, measures how much information is lost when $\mathcal{Q}(\mathcal{X})$ is used to approximate $\mathcal{P}(\mathcal{X})$. The schematic code is shown as Algorithm 1. The loss function can be formally expressed as:

$$\begin{aligned} \mathcal{L}_{KL} &= \mathbb{E}_{\mathcal{P}(\mathcal{X})}[log\mathcal{P}(\mathcal{X}) - log\mathcal{Q}(\mathcal{X})] \\ &= D_{KL}(\mathcal{P}(\mathcal{X}) \| \mathcal{Q}(\mathcal{X})) \end{aligned} \tag{7}$$

**Algorithm 1** Pseudocode of FM in a PyTorch-like style

```
z_q, z_k, z_t: query/key embeddings and text embedding. (B × C)
queue_a: queue of N keys (C × N)
tau_s, tau_t: temperatures for student/teacher (scalars)

noise_for_q = torch.randn_like(q) × noise_std  # Gauss noise
noise_for_t = torch.randn_like(z_t) × noise_std

l_a = torch.mm(z_q + noise_for_q, queue_a)  # compute similarities
l_b = torch.mm(z_q + noise_for_q, z_t + noise_for_t)

loss_kl = loss_kld (l_b/tau_s, z_t/tau_t)

def
loss_kld ( inputs, targets):
    inputs, targets = F.log_softmax(inputs, dim = 1), F.softmax(
    targets, dim = 1)
    return F.kl_div(inputs, targets, reduction = 'batchmean')
```

The Feature Modulation (FM) module enhances action discrimination by adaptively emphasizing discriminative motion cues and suppressing redundant or highly correlated patterns across channels and temporal frequencies. By modulating feature responses conditioned on learned frequency–semantic representations, FM helps to separate subtle inter-class variations (e.g., 'drinking' vs. 'eating'), which often share similar motion trajectories but differ in temporal dynamics or joint coordination. This selective recalibration strengthens the representation's sensitivity to class-specific motion signatures, thereby improving the distinction between visually or kinematically similar actions.

### 4.2. FreST

Skeleton data usually consists of multiple temporal nodes, reflecting the motion trajectories of different human joints over time. The change frequency of these nodes can reveal key features of certain actions (e.g., speed, rhythm, and periodicity of actions). Specifically, the input skeleton sequence $x \in \mathbb{R}^{N \times C \times T \times V}$ passes through the Frequency Spatial Block (FreS) and Frequency Temporal Block (FreT), respectively, with feature optimization via their built-in adaptive frequency-domain filtering. FreS and FreT do not change the dimension of the input sequence. To avoid spatial–temporal feature coupling interference [14,17,21], which occurs when spatial topology and temporal motion cues are entangled within a single representation, a corresponding spatial or temporal decoupling module is added before each frequency-domain module. Such coupling can blur discriminative temporal dynamics with static spatial patterns, thereby reducing filtering precision. By decoupling, the module first separates the skeleton sequence's spatial topological features (e.g., relative joint positions) and temporal dynamic features (e.g., joint trajectories), then feeds the resulting single-dimensional representations into the subsequent frequency-domain module. This separation allows adaptive filters to focus more effectively on domain-specific variations, ultimately improving the accuracy of frequency-domain feature extraction.

As shown in Figure 3, the FreS module will be introduced below, and the working mechanism of the FreT module is the same. Specifically, after the input sequence is processed by the spatial decoupling module, its dimension is transformed from $\mathbb{R}^{N\times T\times V\times C} \rightarrow \mathbb{R}^{(NT)\times V\times C}$. In this context, the spatial domain refers to the coordinate space spanned by all skeletal joints, where each node $v_i \in \mathcal{V}$ corresponds to a specific physical joint location in the human body. The spatial relationships among these joints are defined by the adjacency matrix $\mathbf{A}$, which encodes the topological structure of the human skeleton. Subsequently, we convert the input $x[n]$, where $x[S] \in \mathbb{R}^{(NT)\times V\times C}$ for the spatial branch and $x[T] \in \mathbb{R}^{(NV)\times T\times C}$ for the temporal branch, into the frequency domain $\mathcal{F}$ by:

$$\begin{aligned}\mathcal{F}(\omega) &= \sum_{n=0}^{N-1} x[n] \cdot e^{-j\frac{2\pi}{N}\omega n} \\ &= \sum_{n=0}^{N-1} x[n]\left(\cos\left(\frac{2\pi}{N}\omega n\right) - j\sin\left(\frac{2\pi}{N}\omega n\right)\right)\end{aligned} \tag{8}$$

where $\mathcal{F}(\omega)$ is the signal (spectrum) in the frequency domain and represents the component of the signal at frequency $\omega$, $t$ is a temporal variable, and $j$ denotes the imaginary unit. Then, we define the 1D FFT operation in Equation (7) as: $F = \mathcal{F}[S] \in \mathbb{R}^{T\times C}$. $\hat{\mathcal{E}}_{i,j}$ is defined as the normalized energy, calculated as:

$$\hat{\mathcal{E}}_{i,j} = \frac{|X_{i,j}|^2}{media(\mathcal{E}) + \epsilon} \tag{9}$$

where $\mathcal{E}_{i,j}$ denotes the energy of the individual frequency component at $(i, j)$, median$(\mathcal{E})$ is the median value of all frequency component energies, and $\epsilon$ is a small constant (e.g., $\epsilon = 10^{-8}$) introduced to avoid numerical instability caused by zero denominators. This normalization ensures that the energy values are scaled relative to the central tendency of the energy distribution, facilitating consistent thresholding across different input signals.

$$\mathcal{F}_{\text{mask}} = \mathcal{F}(\omega) \odot \mathbb{I}(\hat{\mathcal{E}}_{i,j} > \tau) \tag{10}$$

where $\odot$ denotes element-wise multiplication, and $\mathbb{I}(\cdot)$ is the indicator function that generates a binary mask matrix: $\mathbb{I}(\hat{\mathcal{E}}_{i,j} > \tau) = 1$ if the normalized energy $\hat{\mathcal{E}}_{i,j}$ exceeds the threshold $\tau$, and 0 otherwise. Through this operation, frequency components with normalized energy above $\tau$ are retained in $\mathcal{F}_{\text{mask}}$, while those below the threshold are filtered out. Notably, the threshold $\tau$ is dynamically adjusted based on the temporal characteristics of the specific action being processed (e.g., motion intensity, frequency bandwidth of key action features), ensuring that critical frequency information (e.g., discriminative motion patterns) is preserved while suppressing high-frequency noise and redundant components that are irrelevant to the action semantics.

After applying adaptive filtering to the frequency-domain data, we introduce two types of learnable filters to further model frequency-domain characteristics. The global filter $\mathcal{W}_g$ operates directly on the original frequency-domain data $\mathcal{F}(\omega)$, enabling the model to capture global frequency correlations that may span the entire spectral range. In contrast, the local filter $\mathcal{W}_l$ is applied to the adaptively filtered result $\mathcal{F}_{\text{mask}}$, focusing on learning discriminative patterns within the frequency components deemed important by the adaptive thresholding step. Both filters are parameterized to handle complex-valued frequency-domain data, with their mathematical formulations given by:

$$\mathcal{W}_g = \mathcal{W}_g^r + j\mathcal{W}_g^i, \quad \mathcal{W}_l = \mathcal{W}_l^r + j\mathcal{W}_l^i \tag{11}$$

where $\mathcal{W}^r$ and $\mathcal{W}^i$ denote the real and imaginary parts of the complex-valued filters, respectively, and $j$ is the imaginary unit satisfying $j^2 = -1$. To initialize these filters in a stable manner, both $\mathcal{W}_g$ and $\mathcal{W}_l$ are sampled from a zero-mean Gaussian distribution with variance $\sigma^2$ (e.g., $\sigma^2 = 0.01$), ensuring that initial filter responses are moderate and avoid saturating subsequent computations.

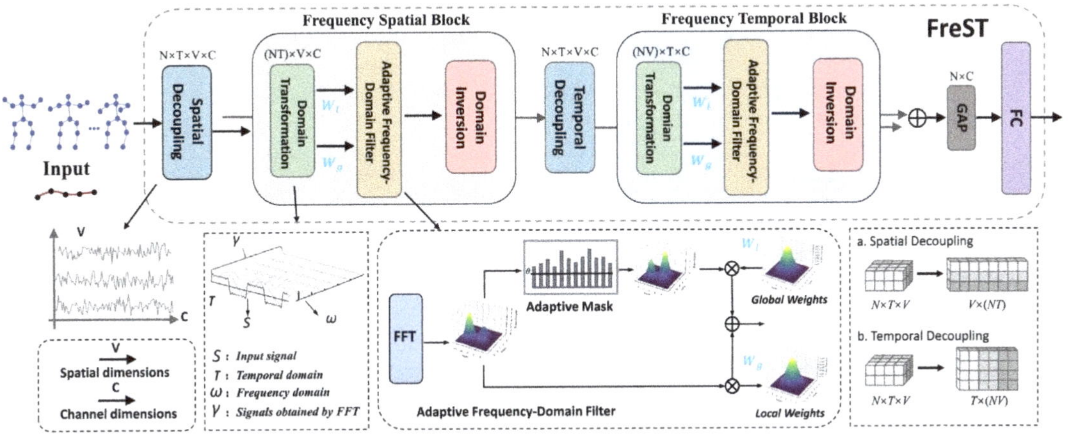


**Figure 3.** The overall overview of Frequency-domain Spatial-temporal block (FreST): the Frequency Spatial Block captures spatial dependencies by performing adaptive frequency-domain filtering in the spatial dimension; the Frequency Temporal Block captures temporal dependencies by performing adaptive frequency-domain filtering in the spatial dimension.

The application of these filters to the frequency-domain data is defined as:

$$\begin{aligned} \mathcal{F}_G &= \mathcal{W}_g \odot \mathcal{F}(\omega) \\ \mathcal{F}_L &= \mathcal{W}_l \odot \mathcal{F}_{\text{mask}} \end{aligned} \tag{12}$$

where $\mathcal{F}_G$ represents the globally filtered frequency features, capturing broad spectral patterns across the entire frequency domain, while $\mathcal{F}_L$ denotes the locally filtered features, which focus on the adaptively selected critical frequency components.

Finally, to integrate both global context and local discriminative details, the output frequency features are computed as the sum of the two filtered results: $\mathcal{F}_{\text{output}} = \mathcal{F}_G + \mathcal{F}_L$. This integration strategy ensures that the model preserves both coarse-grained global frequency characteristics and fine-grained local details, enhancing the representation capacity for complex spatiotemporal patterns in action recognition tasks.

**Modality Harmonizer.** After obtaining the enhanced frame-level feature $F_v^{\text{enh}}$ and the enhanced word-level feature $F_q^{\text{enh}}$, we apply cross-attention layers between $F_v^{\text{enh}}$ (as the query) and $F_q^{\text{enh}}$ (as the key and value) to facilitate interaction and alignment between modalities. The final aligned feature $F \in \mathbb{R}^{L_v \times D}$ is then derived using the standard cross-attention mechanism.

**Design Rationale of FreST.** The Frequency-domain Spatial–Temporal (FreST) block leverages the intrinsic spectral sparsity of skeletal motion to selectively retain action-relevant components while suppressing unstable oscillations. Concretely, an adaptive mask is formed using a threshold $\tau$ computed from the median spectral energy of each input sequence, so that filtering automatically tightens for noise-dominated spectra and relaxes for clean, low-frequency motions. FreST uses two learnable complex-valued filters: a global filter $\mathcal{W}_g$ that captures sequence-level rhythmic regularities and a local filter $\mathcal{W}_l$ that focuses on joint-wise short-range variations. This dual-filter parameterization aligns coarse temporal rhythm with fine spatial–temporal details in a single representation. Compared with time-domain smoothing, which operates on strongly correlated samples and often blurs subtle class-discriminative dynamics, frequency-domain selection compacts signal energy, stabilizes optimization, and preserves fine-grained motion signatures, thereby strengthening separability for visually or kinematically similar actions.

**Domain Inversion Module.** The Domain Inversion module functions as a core bridge between the frequency and spatial/temporal domains. It first converts the skeleton features back from the frequency domain to the original spatial or temporal space, ensuring that frequency-enhanced information can be seamlessly integrated into subsequent processing. Meanwhile, it refines the filtered frequency components by suppressing noise and preserving valid motion frequencies, thus improving the quality and stability of the reconstructed skeleton features.

### 4.3. Skeleton Instance Contrastive Loss

We employ identical skeleton encoders to enable contrastive learning at the feature-wise level between upward and downward skeleton modalities. Specifically, given an original skeleton sequence $S$, we apply two different augmentations, $\mathcal{T}$ and $\mathcal{T}'$, to generate the query and key samples, denoted as $x$ and $\hat{x} \in \mathbb{R}^{C \times T \times V}$, where $C$, $T$, and $V$ represent the number of channels, frames, and nodes, respectively. A query encoder $f_{\theta_q}$ and a momentum-based key encoder $f_{\theta_k}$ are employed. Following this, global average pooling (GAP) is applied to derive the query embeddings $z$ and key embeddings $\hat{z}$. To optimize the encoder representations and enforce similarity between positive pairs while distinguishing negatives, we adopt the InfoNCE loss as our training objective:

$$\mathcal{L}_{info} = -log\frac{exp(\hat{z}' \cdot z'/\tau)}{exp(\hat{z}' \cdot z'/\tau) + Z(\hat{z}') + exp(\tilde{z} \cdot z'/\tau)} \quad (13)$$

where $\cdot$ represents the dot product of calculating the similarity between the two normalized embeddings, and $\tau$ is the temperature hyperparameter (set to 0.2 by default). $Z(v) = \sum_{i=1}^{K} exp(v \cdot m_i/\tau)$ represents the similarity between embedding in view $v$ and memory queue $Q$, and $K$ represents the total number of samples stored in the queue $Q$. The parameters of the query encoder $f_{\theta_q}$ are updated by gradient backpropagation, while the parameters of the key encoder $f_{\theta_k}$ are updated to the moving average of the query encoder, which can be expressed as:

$$\theta_k = m\theta_k + (1-m)\theta_q \quad (14)$$

where $m \in [0, 1)$ is a momentum coefficient, usually close to 1, to maintain consistency in embedding in memory queues. Finally, the loss used to optimize the encoder can be formulated as:

$$\mathcal{L} = \mathcal{L}_{info} + \lambda\mathcal{L}_{KL} \quad (15)$$

where $\lambda$ is a hyperparameter to balance the different sample pairs. Additionally, we incorporate a Frequency-domain Signal Enhancement module (FreST) following the skeleton encoder. FreST enhances the model's ability to retain critical action information in the latent space by extracting sparse human joint information, which captures compressed signal energy. This feature extraction effectively boosts action recognition performance by emphasizing the most informative skeletal features.

# 5. Experiments

## 5.1. Datasets

**NTU RGB + D 60 (NTU 60):** [16] comprises 56,880 action samples from 40 subjects (ages 10 to 35) captured by Kinect v2. It provides four synchronized modalities: high-resolution RGB videos (1920 × 1080), depth maps, infrared frames (512 × 424), and 25-joint 3D skeleton data, covering 60 action classes including daily activities, health-related behaviors, and interpersonal interactions. Each action is recorded from three horizontal angles (−45°, 0°, +45°) and two subject-facing directions, resulting in six viewpoints. Additionally, 17 different camera setups introduce spatial diversity. Following the official evaluation protocols, two standard benchmarks are defined. In the cross-subject setting, samples from 20 subjects (a total of 40,320 sequences) are used for training, while the remaining 20 subjects (16,560 sequences) are held out for testing. In the cross-view setting, data captured by cameras 2 and 3 (37,920 samples) constitute the training set, and those recorded by camera 1 (18,960 samples) are used for testing.

**NTU RGB + D 120 (NTU 120):** [65] extends NTU 60 to 114,480 samples over 120 action classes, recorded via Kinect v2 from 106 subjects of varied ages and cultures. Samples span 96 environments and 155 camera views, offering RGB, depth, infrared, and 25-joint skeleton modalities. Two evaluation protocols are defined: Cross-Subject and Cross-Setup. Specifically, under the cross-subject protocol, samples from 53 subjects (approximately half of the participants) are used for training, while those from the remaining 53 subjects are reserved for testing. Under the Cross-Setup protocol, data captured in even-numbered setups constitute the training set, whereas samples recorded in odd-numbered setups are used for testing.

**PKU-MMD:** [66] is a medium-scale dataset designed for continuous action detection and multi-modality human activity analysis, captured with Kinect v2. It includes over 1000 untrimmed video sequences with synchronized RGB, depth, infrared, and 25-joint 3D skeleton data. The dataset is split into two parts with varying detection difficulty: Part I features clearly separated actions (1076 videos, 51 classes, 66 subjects), while Part II includes more challenging overlapping actions (1009 videos, 41 classes, 13 subjects). Under the protocol, Part I uses data from 57 subjects for training and 9 subjects for testing (944 and 132 videos, respectively). Part II serves as an independent test set consisting of 13 unseen subjects, used exclusively to evaluate cross-subject generalization—models are trained on Part I and tested on Part II.

## 5.2. Implementation Details

ST-GCN is adopted as the skeleton encoder. The number of input channels is set to the original 1/4, and the feature dimension is set to 512. For frequent learning, both global filters $\mathcal{W}_g$ and local filters $\mathcal{W}_l$ are normal distributions with a standard deviation of 0.02. For data augmentation, spatial *Shear* and temporal *Crop* are utilized to generate different skeleton views. For contrastive setting, we set $K$ = 32,768, $\tau = 0.2$, m = 0.999, and $\lambda = 0.01$. For optimization, we employ SGD with momentum (0.9) and weight decay (0.0001), training the model for 300 epochs with a learning rate of 0.1. Then, we evaluate our approach by comparing it to other methods across several protocols, including linear evaluation, fine-tuning, and semi-supervised evaluation. All experiments are conducted on PyTorch 1.4.0 using an RTX 3090ti (NVIDIA, Santa Clara, CA, USA). When training on the NTU60 dataset with a batch size of 128, the memory usage of a single RTX 3090 graphics card is 21 GB.

**Linear** Evaluation Protocol. We add a fully connected layer with a Softmax activation function on top of the frozen pretrained model, and train the classifier using supervised learning. The classifier is trained for 120 epochs with an initial learning rate of 5, which is reduced by a factor of 0.1 at the 80th epoch.

**Fine-tuning** Protocol. The fine-tuning protocol adds a linear classifier after the pre-trained model and trains the entire model for action recognition tasks. Unlike the linear evaluation approach, the pretrained model remains trainable in this protocol. We use supervised learning to train the entire model and compare its performance with other supervised methods.

**Semi-supervised Evaluation Protocol.** We first pre-train the encoder using all available unlabeled data. Then, we finetune the entire model with a small subset of labeled data, selecting either 1% or 10% of the labeled samples at random. Specifically, we employ this strategy to finetune the model using either 1% or 10% of the labeled data.

**Performance Evaluation Measures.** To ensure a fair and consistent comparison with prior work, we adopt widely used quantitative evaluation measures for skeleton-based action recognition. All reported results are based on Top-1 classification accuracy (%) under the standard cross-subject (xsub) and cross-view (xview) protocols of the NTU RGB + D 60 and 120 datasets. In addition, we assess the quality of the learned representations through multiple evaluation strategies, including linear evaluation, where the pretrained backbone is frozen and a linear classifier is trained on labeled data; k-nearest neighbor (k-NN) evaluation, which measures representation separability in feature space; and fine-tuning, where all model parameters are updated for the downstream task. For semi-supervised experiments, the model is trained on a small labeled subset combined with unlabeled samples to evaluate generalization under limited supervision. All metrics are computed per class and averaged (macro-average) over the dataset. These measures are consistent with recent self-supervised and multimodal skeleton learning benchmarks, ensuring the comparability and reproducibility of our experimental results.

**Fair Comparison Protocol.** To ensure a fair and transparent comparison with existing self-supervised and multimodal contrastive methods, we strictly adopted consistent backbone architectures, augmentation strategies, and training configurations across all experiments. Specifically, all methods use the ST-GCN backbone with identical input modalities and data preprocessing. During pre-training, the backbone parameters are unfrozen and updated jointly with the projection head, while during linear evaluation, the backbone is frozen and only the classifier layer is trained. Data augmentation (Spatial Shear and Temporal Crop), learning rate schedules, and optimizer settings (SGD with momentum 0.9 and weight decay 0.0001) are kept identical across all compared methods.

**Dataset Preprocessing.** Following the preprocessing strategy of SkeleMixCLR, we apply a unified and reproducible pipeline to ensure consistency across datasets. For each frame, 3D joint coordinates are centered at the hip joint and scaled by the average bone length to achieve translation and scale invariance. All skeleton sequences are temporally resampled to 64 frames using linear interpolation. Missing or noisy joints are linearly interpolated from adjacent frames along the temporal dimension, and samples with severely incomplete skeletons (typically more than 30% missing joints) are excluded to ensure data integrity. After preprocessing, the joint coordinates are normalized to the range of $[-1, 1]$ for stable model convergence. We also adopt skeleton-specific augmentations such as temporal cropping, joint jittering, and random rotation, consistent with SkeleMixCLR, to enhance generalization and robustness against sensor noise.

**Text Description Generation.** We follow the GAP [24] framework and employ a large-scale language model (GPT-3.5) as a knowledge engine to produce natural-language descriptions of actions. Given each action label, the model automatically generates both global descriptions and body-part-specific descriptions using structured prompts. For example, for the action 'put on a shoe,' the model outputs a global narrative ('The person bends down and puts their foot into the shoe') and detailed part-level semantics ('head tilts slightly forward; hand reaches down and grasps the shoe; leg bends at the knee, bringing the foot closer to the hand'). These descriptions are encoded using a pretrained CLIP text encoder, whose embeddings serve as semantic supervision for the skeleton encoder through a multi-part contrastive learning objective, allowing the model to align motion patterns with language-based semantics.

### *5.3. Comparison with State-of-the-Art Methods*

We first compare MICA with the advanced State-of-the-art methods. Table 1 shows comparison results of the three stream (e.g., joint, bone, and motion) on NTU RGB + D 60, NTU RGB + D 120, and PKU-MMD dataset using linear evaluation protocol. It is evident that our MICA method achieves state-of-the-art performance across each benchmark, indicating that our approach enables the model to effectively capture internal and contextual attention to learn discriminative feature representations. This achievement underscores the effectiveness of our approach in equipping the model to capture both internal and contextual attention, a capability crucial for learning highly discriminative feature representations. By focusing on modeling internal relationships within actions as well as contextual dependencies between them, our approach enhances the model's ability to accurately recognize complex action patterns. Importantly, this improvement is achieved without relying on additional labeled data, making our method efficient and adaptable for scenarios where labeled data are scarce. Furthermore, when compared to fully supervised methods like ST-GCN, our MICA method exhibits substantial gains, underscoring its potential to outperform traditional techniques in both accuracy and generalization across different datasets and action recognition tasks.

**Table 1.** Comparison to the state-of-the-art methods for action recognition accuracy on the NTU RGB + D 60, NTU RGB + D 120, and PKU-MMD I datasets under the linear evaluation protocol. G denotes GCN or ST-GCN, R denotes GRU, T denotes Transformer, and M denotes MAE. J, B, and M denote Joint, Bone, and Motion, respectively.

| Method | Publication | Architecture G ‖ R ‖ T ‖ M | Modality | NTU60 | | NTU120 | | PKU-MMD |
|---|---|---|---|---|---|---|---|---|
| | | | | X-Sub | X-View | X-Sub | X-Set | Part I |
| *Linear Evaluation Single-stream Results* (Arranged by Backbone Model and Publish Year) | | | | | | | | |
| SkeletonCLR [28] | CVPR'21 | • ‖ ○ ‖ ○ ‖ ○ | J | 68.3 | 76.4 | 56.8 | 55.9 | 80.9 |
| CrosSCLR [28] | CVPR'21 | • ‖ ○ ‖ ○ ‖ ○ | J | 78.7 | 84.9 | 68.7 | 69.6 | - |
| AimCLR [46] | AAAI'22 | • ‖ ○ ‖ ○ ‖ ○ | J | 74.3 | 79.7 | 63.4 | 63.4 | - |
| CMD [67] | ECCV'22 | ○ ‖ • ‖ ○ ‖ ○ | J | 79.8 | 86.9 | 70.3 | 71.5 | - |
| RVCTL [68] | CVPR'23 | ○ ‖ ○ ‖ • ‖ ○ | J | 74.7 | 79.1 | 68.0 | 68.9 | - |
| HYSP [31] | ICLR'23 | • ‖ ○ ‖ ○ ‖ ○ | J | 78.2 | 82.6 | 61.8 | 64.6 | 83.8 |
| HiCLR [30] | AAAI'23 | ○ ‖ ○ ‖ • ‖ ○ | J | 78.8 | 83.1 | 67.3 | 69.9 | 73.8 |
| ActCLR [47] | CVPR'23 | • ‖ ○ ‖ ○ ‖ ○ | J | 80.9 | 86.7 | 69.0 | 70.5 | - |
| SkeAttnCLR [69] | IJCAI'23 | • ‖ ○ ‖ ○ ‖ ○ | J | 80.3 | 86.1 | 66.3 | 74.5 | 87.3 |
| DMMG [70] | TIP'23 | • ‖ ○ ‖ ○ ‖ ○ | J | 82.1 | 87.1 | 69.6 | 70.1 | 90.7 |
| Skeleton-logoCLR [32] | TCSVT'24 | • ‖ ○ ‖ ○ ‖ ○ | J | 82.4 | 87.2 | 72.8 | 73.5 | 90.8 |
| CStrCRL [33] | TCSVT'24 | • ‖ ○ ‖ ○ ‖ ○ | J | 78.9 | 84.0 | 68.8 | 69.3 | - |
| STHMAE [17] | Sensors'25 | ○ ‖ ○ ‖ ○ ‖ • | J | 84.3 | 87.0 | 74.3 | 75.6 | - |
| **MICA (Ours)** | This work | • ‖ ○ ‖ ○ ‖ ○ | J | **84.4** | **87.8** | **71.7** | **75.4** | **91.8** |
| 3s-CrosSCLR [28] | CVPR'21 | • ‖ ○ ‖ ○ ‖ ○ | J + M + B | 77.8 | 83.4 | 67.9 | 66.7 | 84.9 |
| 3s-AimCLR [46] | AAAI'22 | • ‖ ○ ‖ ○ ‖ ○ | J + M + B | 78.9 | 83.3 | 68.7 | 69.6 | 87.8 |
| 3s-CMD [67] | ECCV'22 | ○ ‖ • ‖ ○ ‖ ○ | J + M + B | 84.1 | 90.0 | 74.0 | 75.2 | - |
| 3s-CPM [71] | ECCV'22 | • ‖ ○ ‖ ○ ‖ ○ | J + M + B | 84.8 | 90.9 | 74.6 | 76.1 | - |
| 3s-ActCLR [47] | CVPR'23 | • ‖ ○ ‖ ○ ‖ ○ | J + M + B | 85.1 | 91.4 | 75.4 | 76.0 | - |
| 3s-FDMAE [52] | SPL'25 | ○ ‖ ○ ‖ ○ ‖ • | J + M + B | 86.4 | 90.4 | 78.9 | 79.9 | 92.3 |
| **3s-MICA (Ours)** | This work | • ‖ ○ ‖ ○ ‖ ○ | J + M + B | **85.3** | **90.6** | **77.4** | **76.0** | **93.0** |

### 5.4. Ablation Studies

In this section, we conduct ablation experiments on NTU RGB + D 60, NTU RGB + D 120, and PKU-MMD joint modality to better verify the role of different submodules in our framework.

**Effectiveness of FM.** We analyze the impact of $\mathcal{L}_{FM}$. Specifically, we apply a forward ablation strategy to assess the FM module. Feature Modulation leverages textual semantics to guide the calculation of distribution differences. As shown in Table 2, experiments using only FM demonstrate excellent performance on popular human action benchmarks. Specifically, the joint modality on the NTU X-sub and X-view datasets achieves improvements of 1.8% and 1% over the baseline, respectively. These results validate the necessity of cross-modal, instance-wise similarity calculations, as well as the feasibility and efficiency of FM. The Frequency-domain Module (FM) effectively filters noise information through adaptive frequency-domain filtering technology; more critically, it can accurately distinguish actions with similar motion patterns from a high-level semantic perspective by means of prompts, as specifically illustrated in the comparative example of 'run' and 'walk' actions in Figure 2.

**Effectiveness of FreT.** As shown in Table 2, combining FreqT with $\mathcal{L}_{FM}$ resulted in a performance improvement of 2.3% under the NTU RGB + D 60 X-sub protocol, increasing from 82.5% to 84.8%. The FreqT strategy effectively enhanced the collaboration between the time domain and frequency domain within the encoder, enabling the model to better capture discriminative features related to actions. On other datasets and protocols, FreqT also demonstrated robust performance gains, indicating its broad applicability across different scenarios and a significant improvement in feature representation capability.

**Effectiveness of FreS.** As shown in Table 2, incorporating FreqS with the baseline $\mathcal{L}_{FM}$ consistently boosts performance, with a notable increase from 80.7% to 82.7% on the NTU RGB + D 60 X-sub protocol. This improvement highlights the effectiveness of FreqS in capturing spatial-frequency information crucial for recognizing complex actions. Across other datasets and protocols, we observe that FreqS contributes stable performance gains, demonstrating its generalizability and robustness.

**Table 2.** Exploration of different pre-training settings on the NTU-60, NTU-120, and PKU dataset. FM, FreqT, and FreqS denote Language-guided Feature Modulation, Frequency-domain Temporal block, and Frequency-domain Spatial block, respectively. w/ and w/o mean with and without the corresponding module.

| Pre-Training Settings | NTU RGB + D 60 | | NTU RGB + D 120 | | PKU-MMD | |
|---|---|---|---|---|---|---|
| | X-Sub | X-View | X-Sub | X-Set | Part I | Part II |
| w/o pre-training | 80.7 | 85.5 | 69.0 | 68.2 | 88.1 | 55.0 |
| w/ $\mathcal{L}_{FM}$ only | $82.5_{+1.8}$ | $86.5_{+1.0}$ | $70.6_{+1.6}$ | $69.7_{+1.5}$ | $89.2_{+1.1}$ | $55.7_{+0.7}$ |
| $\mathcal{L}_{FM} + FreqT$ | $83.0_{+2.3}$ | $86.6_{+1.1}$ | $70.9_{+1.9}$ | $72.5_{+4.3}$ | $90.3_{+2.2}$ | $56.2_{+1.2}$ |
| $\mathcal{L}_{FM} + FreqS$ | $82.7_{+2.0}$ | $86.8_{+1.3}$ | $71.1_{+2.1}$ | $71.8_{+3.5}$ | $91.2_{+3.1}$ | $55.9_{+0.9}$ |
| $FreqS + \mathcal{L}_{FM} + FreqT$ (ours) | $84.2_{+3.5}$ | $87.8_{+2.3}$ | $71.7_{+2.7}$ | $75.4_{+7.2}$ | $91.8_{+3.7}$ | $56.3_{+1.3}$ |

**Effectiveness of $\mathcal{W}_g$ and $\mathcal{W}_l$.** As shown in Table 3, we demonstrate the effectiveness of the global filter $\mathcal{W}_g$ and the local filter $\mathcal{W}_l$. Removing either $\mathcal{W}_g$ or $\mathcal{W}_l$ leads to a performance decrease of 0.7% and 0.5%, respectively, indicating the contribution of each filter to the overall model performance.

**Efficiency Analysis of FreST.** As summarized in Table 3, targeted ablation experiments validate the design of FreST. Removing the adaptive thresholding reduces recognition accuracy, while eliminating the global $\mathcal{W}_g$ or local $\mathcal{W}_l$ filter causes further performance drops of 0.7% and 0.5%, respectively, confirming their complementary roles. When the complete FreST module is applied, the overall accuracy improves by 3.5% compared with the baseline, with only 0.18 M additional parameters and 1.72 G FLOPs. These results indicate that the adaptive frequency selection and dual-filter structure achieve a favorable balance between model complexity and recognition performance, providing scalability for large-scale and real-time skeleton-based action recognition.

**Table 3.** Ablation study multiple analyses of model complexity on the proposed models. Acc denotes classification accuracy, #Params refers to the number of model parameters, and ~FLOPs represents approximate floating-point operations. w/ and w/o mean with and without the corresponding module. + and ✓indicate the inclusion of the corresponding component, while ✗ indicates its removal. $\mathcal{W}_g$ and $\mathcal{W}_l$ represent the global and local frequency filters, respectively.

| **Spatial–Temporal Aug. (NTU-60-Xsub-J)** | | | | **Semantic Compensation (NTU-60-Xsub-J)** | | | |
|---|---|---|---|---|---|---|---|
| Method | Acc (%) | #Params | ~FLOPs | Method | Acc (%) | #Params | ~FLOPs |
| SkeleMixCLR [29] | 80.7 | 1.90 M | ~1.70 G | SkeleMixCLR [29] | 80.7 | 1.70 M | ~1.72 G |
| $+\mathcal{L}_{FM}$ | 82.5 +1.8 | 1.90 M | ~1.70 G | $+\mathcal{L}_M$, *FreST* | **84.2** +3.5 | 2.08 M | ~1.72 G |
| ✓frequency spatial | 82.7 +2.0 | 1.90 M | ~1.70 G | ✗ $\mathcal{W}_l$ | 83.7 −0.5 | 2.08 M | ~1.72 G |
| ✓frequency temporal | **83.0** +2.3 | 1.90 M | ~1.70 G | ✗ $\mathcal{W}_g$ | 83.5 −0.7 | 2.08 M | ~1.72 G |
| CrosSCLR [28] | 77.8 | 2.45 M | ~2.10 G | ActCLR [47] | 80.9 | 2.01 M | ~1.72 G |

5.4.1. Performance Comparison

**Linear Evaluation.** As illustrated in Table 4, we compare MICA with state-of-the-art self-supervised methods on NTU-60 and NTU-120 under the linear evaluation protocol. MICA demonstrates superior performance over other methods in both single-stream and multi-stream settings. Specifically, MICA surpasses AimCLR by 7% and 7.5% on the X-sub and X-view protocols, respectively.

**Finetune Evaluation.** Table 4 provides comparisons on NTU RGB + D (60 & 120) under the finetune evaluation protocol, and our method leads 7% and 7.5% in X-sub and X-view protocols, respectively, compared to the more than 3s-AimCLR. The results suggest that our method captures more discriminative features and offers better robustness, further reinforcing its potential for real-world applications in action recognition.

**Table 4.** Linear evaluation and finetune results on NTU-60 and NTU-120. Numbers in blue and red reflect improvement and decline compared to SkeletonCLR [28], AimCLR [46], and ActCLR [47] with the same backbone, respectively.

| **Stream** | **Method** | **NTU-60** | | **NTU-120** | |
|---|---|---|---|---|---|
| | | **X-Sub** | **X-View** | **X-Sub** | **X-Set** |
| Linear Evaluation Protocol | | | | | |
| Single-stream | SkeletonCLR | 68.3 | 76.4 | 56.8 | 55.9 |
| | AimCLR | 74.3 | 79.7 | 63.4 | 63.4 |
| | ActCLR | 80.9 | 86.7 | 69.0 | 70.5 |
| | **MICA** | **84.2** +3.3 | **87.8** +1.1 | **71.7** +2.7 | **75.4** +4.9 |
| Multi-stream | 3s-CrosSCLR | 77.8 | 83.4 | 67.9 | 66.7 |
| | 3s-AimCLR | 78.9 | 83.8 | 68.2 | 68.8 |
| | 3s-ActCLR | 85.1 | 91.4 | 75.4 | 76.0 |
| | **3s-MICA** | **85.3** +0.2 | **90.6** −0.8 | **77.4** +2.0 | **76.0** +0.0 |
| Finetune Evaluation Protocol | | | | | |
| Single-stream | SkeletonCLR | 82.2 | 88.9 | 73.6 | 75.3 |
| | AimCLR | 83.0 | 89.2 | 76.4 | 76.7 |
| | ActCLR | 85.8 | 93.9 | 79.4 | 80.9 |
| | **MICA** | **86.0** +0.2 | **92.5** −1.4 | **78.2** −1.2 | **80.6** −0.3 |
| Multi-stream | 3s-CrosSCLR | 86.2 | 92.5 | 80.5 | 80.4 |
| | 3s-AimCLR | 86.9 | 92.8 | 80.1 | 80.9 |
| | 3s-ActCLR | 88.2 | 93.9 | 82.1 | 84.6 |
| | **3s-MICA** | **88.3** +0.1 | **94.1** +0.2 | **82.3** +0.2 | **84.9** +0.3 |

**Semi-supervised Evaluation.** Table 5 shows the comparisons on NTU RGB + D (60 & 120) under Semi-supervised evaluation protocol. In this setting, a portion of the labels is available for training, while the remaining labels are withheld, testing the capacity of the model to generalize from limited labeled data. Specifically, our method leads to 7% and 7.5% in X-sub and X-view protocols, respectively, compared to the 3s-AimCLR.

**Table 5.** Semi-supervised evaluation results on NTU-60 and NTU-120 dataset. The best scores are shown in bold.

| Method | NTU-60 | | PKU-MMD | |
|---|---|---|---|---|
| | X-Sub | X-View | Part I | Part II |
| 1% labeled data for semi-supervised evaluation: | | | | |
| $MS^2L$ [38] | 35.2 | - | 36.4 | 13.0 |
| 3s-CrosSCLR [28] | 51.1 | 50.0 | 49.7 | 10.2 |
| 3s-AimCLR [46] | 54.8 | 54.3 | 57.5 | 15.1 |
| 3s-CMD [67] | 55.6 | 55.5 | - | - |
| **3s-MICA (Ours)** | **56.0** +0.4 | **55.8** +0.2 | **62.9** +5.4 | **17.5** +2.4 |
| 10% labeled data for semi-supervised evaluation: | | | | |
| $MS^2L$ [38] | 65.2 | - | 70.3 | 26.1 |
| 3s-CrosSCLR [28] | 74.4 | 77.8 | 82.9 | 28.6 |
| 3s-AimCLR [46] | 78.2 | 81.6 | 86.1 | 33.4 |
| 3s-SDS-CL [72] | 77.2 | 83.0 | - | - |
| 3s-CMD [67] | 79.0 | 82.4 | - | - |
| 3s-SelMixCLR [29] | 79.9 | 83.6 | 87.7 | 41.0 |
| **3s-MICA (Ours)** | **80.2** +1.2 | **85.0** +2.0 | **88.6** +2.5 | **42.2** +1.2 |

**Quantitative Results.** To conduct multiple analyses of model complexity, we explore the #Params and FLOPs of our method as shown in Table 3. The addition of $\mathcal{L}_M$ does not change the number of parameters, but it results in a 1.8% improvement over the baseline, which is significant. The introduction of FreST increases the parameter count by 0.18 M, and considering the performance boost, this additional parameter burden is acceptable.

**Visualization.** Figure 4 shows the t-SNE visualization of MICA and SkeletonCLR on the NTU RGB + D 60 X-sub joint stream, based on 20 randomly selected action classes (different colors indicate different classes). At the abstract level, MICA demonstrates clearer class separation, indicating improved inter-class separability. At the concrete level, intra-class compactness is enhanced, suggesting better clustering within the same class. MICA outperforms SkeletonCLR in feature discrimination, effectively capturing the semantics of the selected action categories.

**Robustness and Sensitivity Analysis.** To further verify the robustness of MICA, we maintained the same random seed and key hyperparameter settings as SkeletonMixCLR (init_seed(2), $K = 32768$, $\tau = 0.2$, $m = 0.999$) and evaluated multiple CLIP-based semantic encoders under identical training conditions on an RTX 3090 GPU (NVIDIA, Santa Clara, CA, USA). The results summarized in Table 6 show that the framework achieves stable accuracy across different encoders, with ViT-B/32 performing best (84.40%) while maintaining a constant memory usage of 23.12 GB. These findings confirm that the proposed method is robust to encoder variation and insensitive to minor hyperparameter perturbations, ensuring both performance stability and practical efficiency.

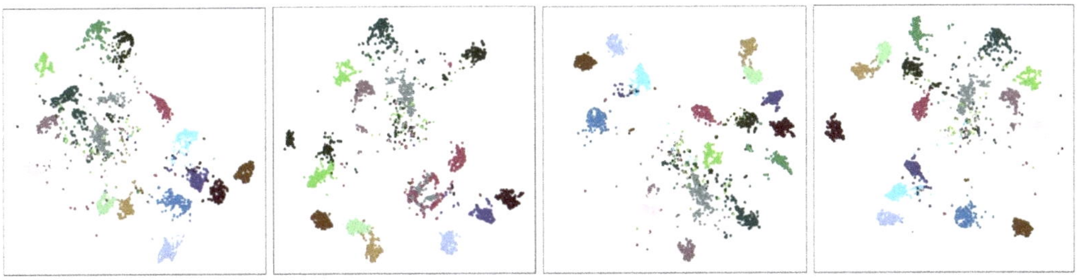


**Figure 4.** The t-SNE [73] visualization for ambiguous action groups on NTU RGB + D 60 dataset. Different colors indicate different classes.

**Table 6.** A ablation study of MICA different CLIP text encoders streaming a NVIDIA 3090 on an ntu-60 xsub joint stream connector with batch size set to 64.

| CLIP Text Encoder | Pre-Train | Acc@1 (%) | Memory (GB) |
|---|---|---|---|
| VIT/B-32 | text/img | 84.40 | 23.12 |
| VIT/B-16 | text/img | 84.33 | 23.12 |
| VIT/L-14 | text/img | 83.26 | 23.12 |
| ResNet-50 | text | 83.67 | 23.12 |

5.4.2. Limitations

While our framework achieves competitive results, several limitations remain. First, the performance may degrade when the input skeletons are severely corrupted or noisy, as the feature extraction relies on relatively stable joint trajectories. Incorporating denoising or uncertainty-aware modules could alleviate this issue in future work. Second, although Table 3 reports parameter counts and FLOPs, we note that both the Frequency Modulation (FM) and FreST modules introduce moderate computational and memory overhead, especially when processing long temporal sequences. Nonetheless, these components were designed with lightweight attention operations, maintaining a good balance between accuracy and efficiency. In addition, since all evaluations follow the official cross-subject and cross-view protocols of NTU RGB + D and PKU-MMD, k-fold cross-validation is not applicable in this context, but we acknowledge this as an inherent limitation of the standardized benchmark setting. Finally, our current implementation has been validated on medium-scale benchmarks; scaling to larger datasets or real-time deployment would require further optimization and possibly model compression techniques, which we plan to explore in future work.

## 6. Conclusions

In this paper, we propose an innovative self-supervised framework for skeleton-based action recognition, addressing key challenges in contrastive learning for cross-modal alignment and spatiotemporal feature extraction. Our approach, Modeling Internal and Contextual Attention (MICA), leverages a cross-modal dual-encoder structure with two key components: Feature Modulation and the Frequency-domain Spatial-Temporal block (FreST). Feature Modulation builds a robust skeleton–language feature space by enhancing intra-modality self-similarity and inter-modality instance-wise cross-consistency, thereby addressing the modality imbalance and enriching mutual information exchange. Meanwhile, FreST focuses on the frequency components of sparse key joints, enabling the model to prioritize action-relevant features through compact signal energy. Extensive experiments on the NTU-60, NTU-120, and PKU-MMD benchmarks validated the effectiveness of our approach, demonstrating significant improvements in performance across multiple evaluation protocols, including fine-tuning, linear evaluation, and semi-supervised learning.

**Author Contributions:** Conceptualization, W.X. and Y.L.; methodology, W.X.; software, Y.L.; validation, J.Z., R.L. and Y.H.; formal analysis, Y.H.; investigation, W.X.; resources, Y.L.; data curation, J.Z.; writing—original draft preparation, W.X.; writing—review and editing, Y.T.; visualization, Y.L.; supervision, Y.H.; project administration, Q.M.; funding acquisition, Y.T., R.L. and Q.M. All authors have read and agreed to the published version of the manuscript.

**Funding:** The work was jointly supported by the National Science and Technology Major Project under grant No. 2022ZD0117103, the National Natural Science Foundations of China under grant No. 62272364, the provincial Key Research and Development Program of Shaanxi under grant No. 2024GH-ZDXM-47, and Anhui Provincial Key Research and Development Program under grant No. 202423k09020005.

**Institutional Review Board Statement:** Not applicable.

**Informed Consent Statement:** Not applicable.

**Data Availability Statement:** Restrictions apply to the availability of these data. Data were obtained from Rose Lab and are available https://rose1.ntu.edu.sg/dataset/actionRecognition/ (accessed on 27 April 2022) with the permission of Rose Lab.

**Conflicts of Interest:** The authors declare no conflict of interest.

## References

1. Khan, M.A.; Javed, K.; Khan, S.A.; Saba, T.; Habib, U.; Khan, J.A.; Abbasi, A.A. Human action recognition using fusion of multiview and deep features: An application to video surveillance. *Multimed. Tools Appl.* **2024**, *83*, 14885–14911. [CrossRef]
2. Abbas, Y.; Jalal, A. Drone-based human action recognition for surveillance: A multi-feature approach. In Proceedings of the 2024 International Conference on Engineering & Computing Technologies (ICECT), Islamabad, Pakistan, 4 December 2024; pp. 1–6.
3. Xu, F.; Xu, F.; Xie, J.; Pun, C.-M.; Lu, H.; Gao, H. Action recognition framework in traffic scene for autonomous driving system. *IEEE Trans. Intell. Transp. Syst.* **2021**, *23*, 22301–22311. [CrossRef]
4. Kashevnik, A.; Ponomarev, A.; Shilov, N.; Chechulin, A. Threats detection during human-computer interaction in driver monitoring systems. *Sensors* **2022**, *22*, 2380. [CrossRef]
5. Dai, C.; Liu, X.; Xu, H.; Yang, L.T.; Deen, M.J. Hybrid deep model for human behavior understanding on industrial internet of video things. *IEEE Trans. Ind. Inform.* **2021**, *18*, 7000–7008. [CrossRef]
6. Vuletic, T.; Duffy, A.; Hay, L.; McTeague, C.; Campbell, G.; Grealy, M. Systematic literature review of hand gestures used in human computer interaction interfaces. *Int. J. Hum.-Comput. Stud.* **2019**, *129*, 74–94. [CrossRef]
7. Prati, A.; Shan, C.; Wang, K.I.-K. Sensors, vision and networks: From video surveillance to activity recognition and health monitoring. *J. Ambient. Intell. Smart Environ.* **2019**, *11*, 5–22. [CrossRef]
8. Tayyab, M.; Jalal, A. Disabled rehabilitation monitoring and patients healthcare recognition using machine learning. In Proceedings of the 2025 6th International Conference on Advancements in Computational Sciences (ICACS), Lahore, Pakistan, 18–19 February 2025; pp. 1–7.
9. Xu, J.; Yin, S.; Zhao, G.; Wang, Z.; Peng, Y. Fineparser: A fine-grained spatio-temporal action parser for human-centric action quality assessment. In Proceedings of the IEEE/CVF Conference on Computer Vision and Pattern Recognition, Seattle, WA, USA, 17–21 June 2024; pp. 14628–14637.
10. Xu, J.; Guo, Y.; Peng, Y. Finepose: Fine-grained prompt-driven 3d human pose estimation via diffusion models. In Proceedings of the IEEE/CVF Conference on Computer Vision and Pattern Recognition, Seattle, WA, USA, 17–21 June 2024; pp. 561–570.
11. Kashef, M.; Visvizi, A.; Troisi, O. Smart city as a smart service system: Human-computer interaction and smart city surveillance systems. *Comput. Hum. Behav.* **2021**, *124*, 106923. [CrossRef]
12. Mehmood, F.; Chen, E.; Akbar, M.A.; Zia, M.A.; Alsanad, A.; Alhogail, A.A.; Li, Y. Advancements in human action recognition through 5g/6g technology for smart cities: Fuzzy integral-based fusion. *IEEE Trans. Consum. Electron.* **2024**, *70*, 5783–5795. [CrossRef]
13. Sun, Z.; Ke, Q.; Rahmani, H.; Bennamoun, M.; Wang, G.; Liu, J. Human action recognition from various data modalities: A review. *IEEE Trans. Pattern Anal. Mach. Intell.* **2022**, *45*, 3200–3225. [CrossRef]

14. Duan, H.; Zhao, Y.; Chen, K.; Lin, D.; Dai, B. Revisiting skeleton-based action recognition. In Proceedings of the IEEE/CVF Conference on Computer Vision and Pattern Recognition, New Orleans, LA, USA, 18–24 June 2022; pp. 2969–2978.
15. Yue, R.; Tian, Z.; Du, S. Action recognition based on rgb and skeleton data sets: A survey. *Neurocomputing* **2022**, *512*, 287–306. [CrossRef]
16. Shahroudy, A.; Liu, J.; Ng, T.-T.; Wang, G. Ntu rgb+ d: A large scale dataset for 3d human activity analysis. In Proceedings of the IEEE Conference on Computer Vision and Pattern Recognition, Las Vegas, NV, USA, 26 June–1 July 2016; pp. 1010–1019.
17. Bian, C.; Yang, Y.; Wang, T.; Lu, W. Spatial–temporal heatmap masked autoencoder for skeleton-based action recognition. *Sensors* **2025**, *25*, 3146. [CrossRef] [PubMed]
18. Zhang, P.; Lan, C.; Zeng, W.; Xing, J.; Xue, J.; Zheng, N. Semantics-guided neural networks for efficient skeleton-based human action recognition. In Proceedings of the IEEE/CVF Conference on Computer Vision and Pattern Recognition, Seattle, WA, USA, 14–19 June 2020; pp. 1112–1121.
19. Cai, J.; Jiang, N.; Han, X.; Jia, K.; Lu, J. Jolo-gcn: Mining joint-centered light-weight information for skeleton-based action recognition. In Proceedings of the IEEE/CVF Winter Conference on Applications of Computer Vision, Virtual, 5–9 January 2021; pp. 2735–2744.
20. Yan, S.; Xiong, Y.; Lin, D. Spatial temporal graph convolutional networks for skeleton-based action recognition. In Proceedings of the Thirty-Second AAAI Conference on Artificial Intelligence, New Orleans, LA, USA, 2–7 February 2018.
21. Shi, L.; Zhang, Y.; Cheng, J.; Lu, H. Two-stream adaptive graph convolutional networks for skeleton-based action recognition. In Proceedings of the IEEE/CVF Conference on Computer Vision and Pattern Recognition, Long Beach, CA, USA, 15–20 June 2019; pp. 12026–12035.
22. Shafizadegan, F.; Naghsh-Nilchi, A.R.; Shabaninia, E. Multimodal vision-based human action recognition using deep learning: A review. *Artif. Intell. Rev.* **2024**, *57*, 178. [CrossRef]
23. Hu, Z.; Xiao, J.; Li, L.; Liu, C.; Ji, G. Human-centric multimodal fusion network for robust action recognition. *Expert Syst. Appl.* **2024**, *239*, 122314. [CrossRef]
24. Xiang, W.; Li, C.; Zhou, Y.; Wang, B.; Zhang, L. Generative action description prompts for skeleton-based action recognition. In Proceedings of the IEEE/CVF International Conference on Computer Vision, Paris, France, 2–3 October 2023; pp. 10276–10285.
25. Zhu, X.; Shu, X.; Tang, J. Motion-aware mask feature reconstruction for skeleton-based action recognition. *IEEE Trans. Circuits Syst. Video Technol.* **2024**, *34*, 10718–10731. [CrossRef]
26. He, T.; Chen, Y.; Gao, X.; Wang, L.; Hu, T.; Cheng, H. Enhancing skeleton-based action recognition with language descriptions from pre-trained large multimodal models. *IEEE Trans. Circuits Syst. Video Technol.* **2024**, *35*, 2118–2132. [CrossRef]
27. Radford, A.; Kim, J.W.; Hallacy, C.; Ramesh, A.; Goh, G.; Agarwal, S.; Sastry, G.; Askell, A.; Mishkin, P.; Clark, J.; et al. Learning transferable visual models from natural language supervision. In Proceedings of the International Conference on Machine Learning, PmLR, Virtual, 18–24 July 2021; pp. 8748–8763.
28. Li, L.; Wang, M.; Ni, B.; Wang, H.; Yang, J.; Zhang, W. 3d human action representation learning via cross-view consistency pursuit. In Proceedings of the IEEE/CVF Conference on Computer Vision and Pattern Recognition, Nashville, TN, USA, 20–25 June 2021; pp. 4741–4750.
29. Chen, Z.; Liu, H.; Guo, T.; Chen, Z.; Song, P.; Tang, H. Contrastive learning from spatio-temporal mixed skeleton sequences for self-supervised skeleton-based action recognition. *arXiv* **2022**, arXiv:2207.03065.
30. Zhang, J.; Lin, L.; Liu, J. Hierarchical consistent contrastive learning for skeleton-based action recognition with growing augmentations. In Proceedings of the AAAI Conference on Artificial Intelligence, Washington, DC, USA, 7–14 February 2023; Volume 37, pp. 3427–3435.
31. Franco, L.; Mandica, P.; Munjal, B.; Galasso, F. Hyperbolic self-paced learning for self-supervised skeleton-based action representations. *arXiv* **2023**, arXiv:2303.06242.
32. Hu, J.; Hou, Y.; Guo, Z.; Gao, J. Global and local contrastive learning for self-supervised skeleton-based action recognition. *IEEE Trans. Circuits Syst. Video Technol.* **2024**, *34*, 10578–10589. [CrossRef]
33. Hu, R.; Wang, X.; Chang, X.; Zhang, Y.; Hu, Y.; Liu, X.; Yu, S. Cstrcrl: Cross-view contrastive learning through gated gcn with strong augmentations for skeleton recognition. *IEEE Trans. Circuits Syst. Video Technol.* **2023**, *34*, 6674–6685. [CrossRef]
34. Liu, D.; Meng, F.; Mi, J.; Ye, M.; Li, Q.; Zhang, J. Sam-net: Semantic-assisted multimodal network for action recognition in rgb-d videos. *Pattern Recognit.* **2025**, *168*, 111725. [CrossRef]
35. Zeng, Q.; Dang, R.; Zhou, X.; Liu, C.; Chen, Q. Contrastive feedback vision-language for 3d skeleton-based action recognition. *IEEE Trans. Multimed.* **2025**, *27*, 4372–4385. [CrossRef]
36. Li, C.; Liang, W.; Yin, F.; Zhao, Y.; Zhang, Z. Semantic information guided multimodal skeleton based action recognition. *Inf. Fusion* **2025**, *123*, 103289. [CrossRef]
37. Zhao, Z.; Hua, H.; Li, J.; Wu, S.; Li, F.; Zhou, Y.; Li, Y. Cocodiff: Diversifying skeleton action features via coarse-fine text-co-guided latent diffusion. *arXiv* **2025**, arXiv:2504.21266.

38. Lin, L.; Song, S.; Yang, W.; Liu, J. Ms2l: Multi-task self-supervised learning for skeleton based action recognition. In Proceedings of the 28th ACM International Conference on Multimedia, Seattle, WA, USA, 16 October 2020; pp. 2490–2498.
39. Carlucci, F.M.; D'Innocente, A.; Bucci, S.; Caputo, B.; Tommasi, T. Domain generalization by solving jigsaw puzzles. In Proceedings of the IEEE/CVF Conference on Computer Vision and Pattern Recognition, Long Beach, CA, USA, 15–20 June 2019; pp. 2229–2238.
40. Liu, J.; Teshome, W.; Ghimire, S.; Sznaier, M.; Camps, O. Solving masked jigsaw puzzles with diffusion vision transformers. In Proceedings of the IEEE/CVF Conference on Computer Vision and Pattern Recognition, Seattle, WA, USA, 17–21 June 2024; pp. 23009–23018.
41. Nie, Q.; Liu, Z.; Liu, Y. Unsupervised 3d human pose representation with viewpoint and pose disentanglement. In Proceedings of the European Conference on Computer Vision, Glasgow, UK, 23–28 August 2020; pp. 102–118.
42. Dong, J.; Sun, S.; Liu, Z.; Chen, S.; Liu, B.; Wang, X. Hierarchical contrast for unsupervised skeleton-based action representation learning. In Proceedings of the AAAI Conference on Artificial Intelligence, Washington, DC, USA, 7–14 February 2023; Volume 37, pp. 525–533.
43. Xin, W.; Miao, Q.; Liu, Y.; Liu, R.; Pun, C.M.; Shi, C. Skeleton mixformer: Multivariate topology representation for skeleton-based action recognition. In Proceedings of the 31st ACM International Conference on Multimedia, Ottawa, ON, Canada, 29 October–3 November 2023; pp. 2211–2220.
44. Miao, Q.; Xin, W.; Liu, R.; Liu, Y.; Wu, M.; Shi, C.; Pun, C.M. Adaptive Pitfall: Exploring the Effectiveness of Adaptation in Skeleton-based Action Recognition. *IEEE Trans. Multimed.* **2024**, *27*, 56–71. [CrossRef]
45. Xin, W.; Lin, H.; Liu, R.; Liu, Y.; Miao, Q. Is really correlation information represented well in self-attention for skeleton-based action recognition? In Proceedings of the 2023 IEEE International Conference on Multimedia and Expo (ICME), Brisbane, Australia, 10–14 July 2023; pp. 780–785.
46. Guo, T.; Liu, H.; Chen, Z.; Liu, M.; Wang, T.; Ding, R. Contrastive learning from extremely augmented skeleton sequences for self-supervised action recognition. In Proceedings of the AAAI Conference on Artificial Intelligence, Virtual, 22 February–1 March 2022; Volume 36, pp. 762–770.
47. Lin, L.; Zhang, J.; Liu, J. Actionlet-dependent contrastive learning for unsupervised skeleton-based action recognition. In Proceedings of the IEEE/CVF Conference on Computer Vision and Pattern Recognition, Vancouver, BC, Canada, 17–24 June 2023; pp. 2363–2372.
48. Zhang, H. Contrastive mask learning for self-supervised 3d skeleton-based action recognition. *Sensors* **2025**, *25*, 1521. [CrossRef] [PubMed]
49. Liu, R.; Liu, Y.; Wu, M.; Xin, W.; Miao, Q.; Liu, X.; Li, L. SG-CLR: Semantic representation-guided contrastive learning for self-supervised skeleton-based action recognition. *Pattern Recognit.* **2025**, *162*, 111377. [CrossRef]
50. Wu, W.; Hua, Y.; Zheng, C.; Wu, S.; Chen, C.; Lu, A. Skeletonmae: Spatial-temporal masked autoencoders for self-supervised skeleton action recognition. In Proceedings of the 2023 IEEE International Conference on Multimedia and Expo Workshops (ICMEW), Brisbane, Australia, 10–14 July 2023; pp. 224–229.
51. Yang, S.; Liu, J.; Lu, S.; Hwa, E.M.; Hu, Y.; Kot, A.C. Self-supervised 3d action representation learning with skeleton cloud colorization. *IEEE Trans. Pattern Anal. Mach. Intell.* **2023**, *46*, 509–524. [CrossRef]
52. Liu, Y.; Shi, T.; Zhai, M.; Liu, J. Frequency decoupled masked auto-encoder for self-supervised skeleton-based action recognition. *IEEE Signal Process. Lett.* **2025**, *32*, 546–550. [CrossRef]
53. Jia, C.; Yang, Y.; Xia, Y.; Chen, Y.T.; Parekh, Z.; Pham, H.; Le, Q.; Sung, Y.; Li, Z.; Duerig, T. Scaling up visual and vision-language representation learning with noisy text supervision. In Proceedings of the International Conference on Machine Learning, PMLR, Virtual, 18–24 July 2021; pp. 4904–4916.
54. Zhou, Y.; Qiang, W.; Rao, A.; Lin, N.; Su, B.; Wang, J. Zero-shot skeleton-based action recognition via mutual information estimation and maximization. In Proceedings of the 31st ACM International Conference on Multimedia, Ottawa, ON, Canada, 29 October–3 November 2023; pp. 5302–5310.
55. Li, S.-W.; Wei, Z.-X.; Chen, W.-J.; Yu, Y.-H.; Yang, C.-Y.; Hsu, J.Y.-J. Sa-dvae: Improving zero-shot skeleton-based action recognition by disentangled variational autoencoders. In Proceedings of the European Conference on Computer Vision, Milan, Italy, 29 September–4 October 2024; pp. 447–462.
56. Zhou, M.; Li, X.; Zhang, D. Text-cls-transformer: Skeleton and label data-driven human action recognition method. In Proceedings of the 2024 Guangdong-Hong Kong-Macao Greater Bay Area International Conference on Digital Economy and Artificial Intelligence, Hongkong, China, 19–21 January 2024; pp. 332–336.
57. Wang, H.; Ma, X.; Kuang, J.; Gui, J. Heterogeneous skeleton-based action representation learning. In Proceedings of the Computer Vision and Pattern Recognition Conference, Nashville, TN, USA, 11–15 June 2025; pp. 19154–19164.
58. Chen, Q.; Liu, Y.; Huang, P.; Huang, J. Linguistic-driven partial semantic relevance learning for skeleton-based action recognition. *Sensors* **2024**, *24*, 4860. [CrossRef]

59. Gupta, P.; Sharma, D.; Sarvadevabhatla, R.K. Syntactically guided generative embeddings for zero-shot skeleton action recognition. In Proceedings of the 2021 IEEE International Conference on Image Processing (ICIP), Anchorage, AK, USA, 19–22 September 2021; pp. 439–443.
60. Chen, Y.; Guo, J.; Guo, S.; Tao, D. Neuron: Learning context-aware evolving representations for zero-shot skeleton action recognition. In Proceedings of the Computer Vision and Pattern Recognition Conference, Nashville, TN, USA, 11–15 June 2025; pp. 8721–8730.
61. Weng, L.; Lou, W.; Gao, F. Language guided graph transformer for skeleton action recognition. In Proceedings of the International Conference on Neural Information Processing, Changsha, China, 20–23 November 2023; pp. 283–299.
62. Hu, H.; Cao, Y.; Fang, Y.; Meng, Z. Semantics-assisted training graph convolution network for skeleton-based action recognition. *Sensors* **2025**, *25*, 1841. [CrossRef]
63. Xu, K.; Qin, M.; Sun, F.; Wang, Y.; Chen, Y.; Ren, F. Learning in the frequency domain. In Proceedings of the IEEE/CVF Conference on Computer Vision and Pattern Recognition, Seattle, WA, USA, 14–19 June 2020; pp. 1740–1749.
64. Yi, K.; Zhang, Q.; Fan, W.; Wang, S.; Wang, P.; He, H.; An, N.; Lian, D.; Cao, L.; Niu, Z. Frequency-domain mlps are more effective learners in time series forecasting. *Adv. Neural Inf. Process. Syst.* **2023**, *36*, 76656–76679.
65. Liu, J.; Shahroudy, A.; Perez, M.; Wang, G.; Duan, L.-Y.; Kot, A.C. Ntu rgb+ d 120: A large-scale benchmark for 3d human activity understanding. *IEEE Trans. Pattern Anal. Mach. Intell.* **2019**, *42*, 2684–2701. [CrossRef]
66. Liu, C.; Hu, Y.; Li, Y.; Song, S.; Liu, J. Pku-mmd: A large scale benchmark for continuous multi-modal human action understanding. *arXiv* **2017**, arXiv:1703.07475.
67. Mao, Y.; Zhou, W.; Lu, Z.; Deng, J.; Li, H. Cmd: Self-supervised 3d action representation learning with cross-modal mutual distillation. In Proceedings of the European Conference on Computer Vision, Tel Aviv, Israel, 23–27 October 2022; pp. 734–752.
68. Zhu, Y.; Han, H.; Yu, Z.; Liu, G. Modeling the relative visual tempo for self-supervised skeleton-based action recognition. In Proceedings of the IEEE/CVF International Conference on Computer Vision, Paris, France, 2–3 October 2023; pp. 13913–13922.
69. Hua, Y.; Wu, W.; Zheng, C.; Lu, A.; Liu, M.; Chen, C.; Wu, S. Part aware contrastive learning for self-supervised action recognition. *arXiv* **2023**, arXiv:2305.00666. [CrossRef]
70. Guan, S.; Yu, X.; Huang, W.; Fang, G.; Lu, H. DMMG: Dual min-max games for self-supervised skeleton-based action recognition. *IEEE Trans. Image Process.* **2023**, *33*, 395–407. [CrossRef]
71. Zhang, H.; Hou, Y.; Zhang, W.; Li, W. Contrastive positive mining for unsupervised 3d action representation learning. In Proceedings of the European Conference on Computer Vision, Tel Aviv, Israel, 23–27 October 2022; pp. 36–51.
72. Xu, B.; Shu, X.; Zhang, J.; Dai, G.; Song, Y. Spatiotemporal decouple-and-squeeze contrastive learning for semisupervised skeleton-based action recognition. *IEEE Trans. Neural Netw. Learn. Syst.* **2023**, *35*, 11035–11048. [CrossRef]
73. Van der Maaten, L.; Hinton, G. Visualizing data using t-SNE. *J. Mach. Learn. Res.* **2008**, *9*, 2579–2605.

*sensors*

*Article*

# Performance of Acoustic, Electro-Acoustic and Optical Sensors in Precise Waveform Analysis of a Plucked and Struck Guitar String

**Jan Jasiński *, Marek Pluta, Roman Trojanowski, Julia Grygiel and Jerzy Wiciak**

AGH University of Krakow, Department of Mechanics and Vibroacoustics, av. Mickiewicza 30, 30-059 Krakow, Poland; pluta@agh.edu.pl (M.P.); roman.cz.trojanowski@agh.edu.pl (R.T.); wiciak@agh.edu.pl (J.W.)
* Correspondence: jjasinsk@agh.edu.pl

**Abstract:** This study presents a comparative performance analysis of three sensor technologies—microphone, magnetic pickup, and laser Doppler vibrometer—for capturing string vibration under varied excitation conditions: striking, plectrum plucking, and wire plucking. Two different magnetic pickups are included in the comparison. Measurements were taken at multiple excitation levels on a simplified electric guitar mounted on a stable platform with repeatable excitation mechanisms. The analysis focuses on each sensor's capacity to resolve fine-scale waveform features during the initial attack while also taking into account its capability to measure general changes in instrument dynamics and timbre. We evaluate their ability to distinguish vibro-acoustic phenomena resulting from changes in excitation method and strength as well as measurement location. Our findings highlight the significant influence of sensor choice on observable string vibration. While the microphone captures the overall radiated sound, it lacks the required spatial selectivity and offers poor SNR performance 34 dB lower then other methods. Magnetic pickups enable precise string-specific measurements, offering a compelling balance of accuracy and cost-effectiveness. Results show that their low-pass frequency characteristic limits temporal fidelity and must be accounted for when analysing general sound timbre. Laser Doppler vibrometers provide superior micro-temporal fidelity, which can have critical implications for physical modeling, instrument design, and advanced audio signal processing, but have severe practical limitations. Critically, we demonstrate that the required optical target, even when weighing as little as 0.1% of the string's mass, alters the string's vibratory characteristics by influencing RMS energy and spectral content.

**Keywords:** non-contact sensing; sensor comparison; laser Doppler vibrometer (LDV); electro-acoustic transducer; musical acoustics; string vibration; electric guitar; waveform analysis

## 1. Introduction

The initial transient of a vibrating string contains critical information about the energy input, excitation mechanism, and interaction with the instrument body. In stringed instruments such as the guitar, this short-lived phase is perceptually important for timbre and identity recognition, and it plays a key role in both musical expression and sound synthesis applications. Despite its significance, the initial transient is difficult to capture with precision. It exhibits high-frequency content, non-linear behavior, and rapid temporal evolution, requiring measurement techniques with excellent time and spatial resolution.

Furthermore, the mechanical coupling between components complicates the isolation of the string's contribution using conventional acoustic recording methods.

Previous research has utilized various sensors to study instrument string vibrations, including microphones [1,2], electromagnetic pickups [2–4], contact pickups [5], and more recently, optical systems such as laser Doppler vibrometers (LDVs) [1,6], position sensitive detectors (PSD) [7], and high-speed cameras [1,8,9]. However, comparative studies evaluating the strengths and limitations of these methods—particularly under controlled excitation and measurement conditions—remain limited. Such studies have been conducted for instrument plate and body vibration measurements [10,11], but not for strings. Their results cannot be directly transferred, as strings differ substantially in mass, dimensions, and vibration amplitude. This gap hinders the ability to select suitable sensors for specific applications, such as instrument design [12], modeling of instruments [13], strings [14,15] and pickups [16], sound synthesis [17], and performance analysis [18].

This study provides a comparative evaluation of three sensor technologies—laser Doppler vibrometer, microphone, and magnetic pickup—for measuring guitar string vibration under varied excitation conditions. The laser Doppler vibrometer (LDV) provides high-resolution, non-contact measurement of the string velocity by detecting the Doppler shift of reflected laser light. This makes it particularly well suited for detailed analysis of vibrational modes and transient behaviour. The electromagnetic pickup, integral to the functioning of electric guitars, measures string motion through variations in magnetic flux induced by the vibration of ferromagnetic strings near a magnet and coil. While this signal reflects the transverse velocity of the string at the pickup location, it is inherently shaped by the pickup's position, design, and magnetic characteristics. The microphone detects acoustic pressure variations in air generated by the vibrating string. Although not commonly used with electric guitars, the focus on the very starting moments of the string's vibration means that we are not interested in the amplification that would come from the vibration of a guitar body in an acoustic guitar. Additionally, the microphone captures the radiated sound field, which is directly related to perceived timbre. Therefore, it is worth investigating whether precise string movement data can be extracted from such recordings. Together, these methods provide complementary perspectives on string vibration, ranging from precise physical characterization to musically functional signal capture. Measurements were conducted using a specially constructed stand, a simplified electric guitar platform, and three repeatable excitation methods. By analyzing the recordings, we assess each sensor's effectiveness in capturing selected vibro-acoustic phenomena related to excitation method and measurement position. The findings offer practical guidance for sensor selection in experimental design.

## 2. Experimental Method

### 2.1. Experimental Setup

The objective of the experimental setup was to eliminate as many external variables from the measured string vibrations as possible. To achieve this, a specialized stand was utilized to provide a stable mounting platform for the setup. A heavily simplified electric guitar served as the mounting for the pickups and string. It retains the proportions of a standard instrument, incorporating a guitar bridge, nut, key, and pickups, while featuring a simplified shape. This design ensures that the string vibrations are representative of a standard guitar while allowing for more repeatable mounting. The exact dimensions and design considerations that went into the creation of this simplified model are described in [4]. The corpus is clamped into the stand using dense foam, which provides stable placement while limiting vibration transfer between the instrument and the stand. This setup is shown in Figure 1. All measurements were conducted in a large anechoic chamber in the Department of Mechanics and Vibroacoustics of the AGH University of Krakow to minimize the impact of noise and interference on the experimental results.

**Figure 1.** Simplified electric guitar model mounted in the experimental stand.

The distance between the guitar bridge and the nut was 645 mm. The guitar pickups were mounted to the instrument and so the measuring point was chosen above them at 42 mm and 157 mm from the guitar bridge. To better observe certain vibro-acoustic phenomena caused by different excitation methods, the measuring point was selected on the shorter segment of the string, as divided by the excitation point. Consequently, the excitation point was chosen at 240 mm from the bridge to avoid proximity to any nodes of the first ten harmonic frequencies (excitation point to string length ratio equal to 0.372).

Experiments were conducted using two string diameters: a 1.17 mm (0.046 inch) steel core wound string and a 0.28 mm (0.011 inch) unwound steel string. D'Addario XL Nicklewound strings (D'Addario & Co., Farmingdale, NY, USA) were used. Strings were tuned to E2 (82.41 Hz) and B3 (246.94 Hz), respectively.

### 2.2. Measurement Methods

Three separate methods were utilized to measure the vibration of the string. To allow for the highest level of comparability between achieved results, the aim is for them to measure the vibration of the string at the same time, at the same point, and in the same direction.

Firstly, a Polytec VibraGo single-point laser Doppler vibrometer (LDV) was used (Polytec GmbH, Waldbronn, Germany). The vibrometer was positioned approx. 2 m away from the string and oriented perpendicularly to it. The vibrometers autofocus function was used to focus the laser onto the string. Due to the minimal size of the point at which vibrations are measured, it was not possible to conduct measurements without the use of a reflective sticker placed on the string. Without this sticker, the string would move outside the laser beam, resulting in sudden jumps in the recorded signal and incorrect measurements. A $3 \times 4$ mm rectangle of reflective tape, weighing 0.0056 g, proved sufficient to address this issue. This sticker and its influence on the vibration of the string will be analyzed and discussed in detail in Section 5.

The second measurement method involved a GRAS G46AE measurement microphone positioned near the string (GRAS Sound & Vibration, Holte, Denmark). The placement was as close as possible to the selected measurement point; however, due to the path of the laser vibrometer, the microphone had to be elevated. Consequently, the measurement direction is not identical.

The final measurement method utilized electromagnetic pickups mounted in the simplified electric guitar. Two pickups were used as follows: a single-coil Seymour Duncan SSL-5L and a humbucker Seymour Duncan SH-4 JB (Seymour Duncan, Santa Barbara, CA, USA). Both pickup configurations were employed to observe the differences in their measurement results. A humbucker consists of two coils wired in opposite polarity and positioned next to one another. This configuration cancels electromagnetic interference; however, its wider sensing aperture acts as a low-pass filter, averaging the string's motion over a larger area, which typically corresponds to a warmer perceived tone. In contrast, a brighter, more articulate sound is typically associated with single-coil pickups. It is not feasible to mount both pickups in the same position and orientation; therefore, they were left in their separate mounting locations, and measurements were conducted over both pickups.

All measurement instruments were recorded using a National Instruments NI 9234 input module (National Instruments Corporation, Austin, TX, USA) with a sampling rate of 51,200 Hz. The positioning of all measurement methods is shown in Figure 2.

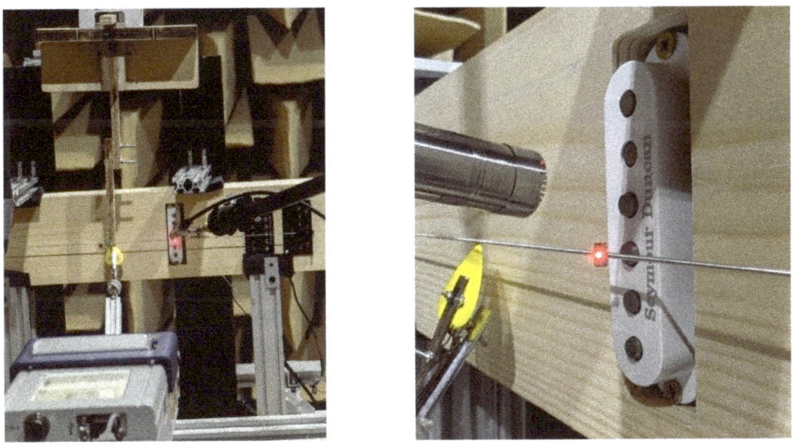


(a) (b)

**Figure 2.** Alignment of (**a**) excitation mechanisms and (**b**) measurement sensors.

### 2.3. Excitation Mechanisms

In order to eliminate string excitation as a variable, specialized mechanisms and solutions were designed and prepared for each excitation method. The first mechanism was designed to replicate a guitarist's use of a plectrum. This requires the plectrum to strike the string with an initial velocity and continue its movement along an arc trajectory until the string slips off the plectrum and rings out. The mechanism performs this through incorporating a leaf spring from a hair clip, connected to a hinge on one side and a latch on the other. When closed, the spring is under tension and bounces away upon release. By attaching a nylon guitar pick to the free end of the spring, this motion can be used for the repeatable plucking of a string. A hair tie is used to catch the spring and dampen its vibration. This method of string excitation has been demonstrated to be repeatable in previous research [4,19]. The constructed mechanism is illustrated in Figure 3a. More advanced automated plucking robots have been utilized to achieve higher levels of plucking repeatability [20,21]; however, such a solution was impractical due to spatial limitations, the required direction of plucking away from the guitar body, and the need for an unobstructed path from the vibrometer to the string.

(a) (b)

**Figure 3.** Constructed excitation mechanisms: (**a**) Plucker using a guitar plectrum mounted to a spring to mimic a guitar player. (**b**) Striker using a sideways-mounted guitar plectrum, mounted to a pendulum.

The second method of string excitation aims to provide a more defined, isolated pluck. A pluck requires the displacement of the string followed by its release. To achieve this, a copper wire is used. The wire is looped through the string at the excitation point and slowly pulled away from the instrument body. At a certain point, the wire breaks, releasing the string and allowing it to vibrate. Due to the repeatability of the copper wire, this method has previously been used for guitar string plucking [22,23] and has demonstrated a high level of repeatability [24]. In our experiment, the wire was pulled manually. Although automation of this process is possible for enhanced repeatability, the most common solution employs a solenoid [24]. However, this method is not viable when using electromagnetic guitar pickups, as the pulling coil generates significant electromagnetic interference, disrupting measurements.

The final method induces string vibration through a striking action. This is implemented using a pendulum mechanism with a nylon plectrum mounted perpendicular to the string. The pendulum is displaced to a predetermined angle and then released, allowing it to accelerate under gravity and strike the string with the edge of the plectrum. After impact, the pendulum rebounds and can be caught to prevent unwanted noise or interference with the string's vibration. The edge of the plectrum serves as the contact point to minimize the contact area with the string, thereby reducing damping effects on the induced vibrational modes. The constructed pendulum mechanism is illustrated in Figure 3b.

All excitation mechanisms were configured to induce initial vibrations at the same point and in the same direction, perpendicular to the guitar body, aligning with the measurement direction. Since the focus of this research is on sensor technologies rather than the differences between excitation methods, the methods were not normalized to one another. To ensure the comparability of recorded results between methods, a string excitation normalization methodology would be required [25]. The absence of such a method renders direct comparisons of amplitude and spectral content between excitation types impossible.

### 2.4. Experimental Procedure

The various components of the experimental method described in the preceding sections are brought together in the procedural flowchart shown in Figure 4. The diagram outlines the research process, from the initial preparation of the experimental setup to the iterative data acquisition loop, and the final stages of signal processing and analysis.

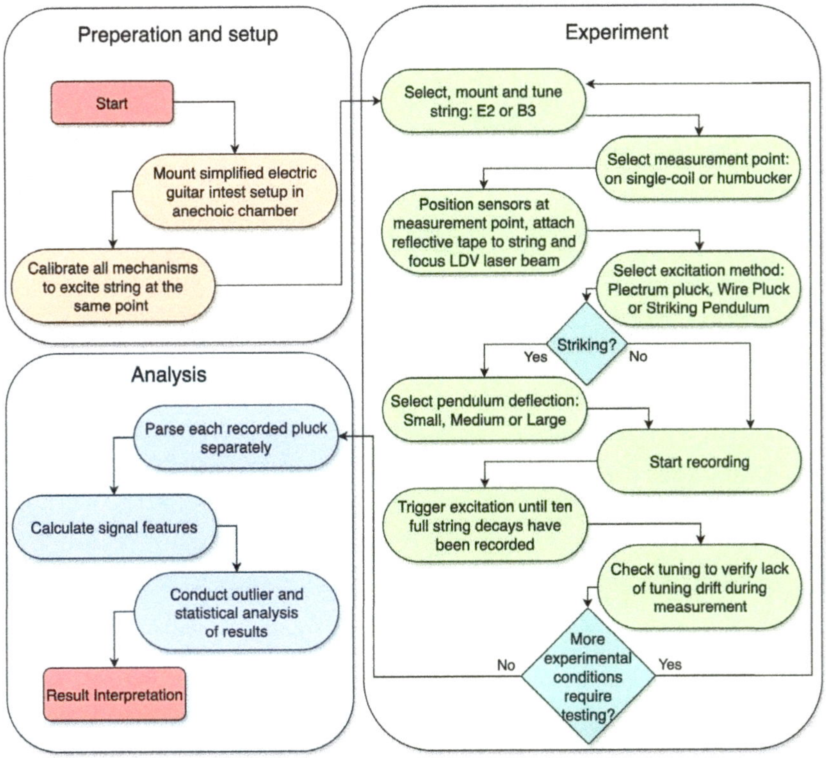


**Figure 4.** Diagram showing the experimental procedure including preparation, experimental recording, and data analysis.

## 3. Comparison of Sensor Performance

The focus of this paper is the capacity of each sensor to accurately record string vibrations, with particular emphasis on the initial phase of excitation. Thus, we will begin the comparison of each technology by investigating their ability to record specific phenomena. This will show their practical usability in the task of precise waveform analysis of a guitar string.

### 3.1. Sensor Differences Overview

The plucker mechanism equipped with a guitar plectrum (Figure 3a) provides a string excitation method that most closely resembles the actual playing conditions of a guitar. For this reason, it was selected as the starting point of the analysis. Figure 5 illustrates the moment of plucking as captured by all four sensors, whereas Figure 6 presents a segment of the same sound event two seconds after the initial pluck.

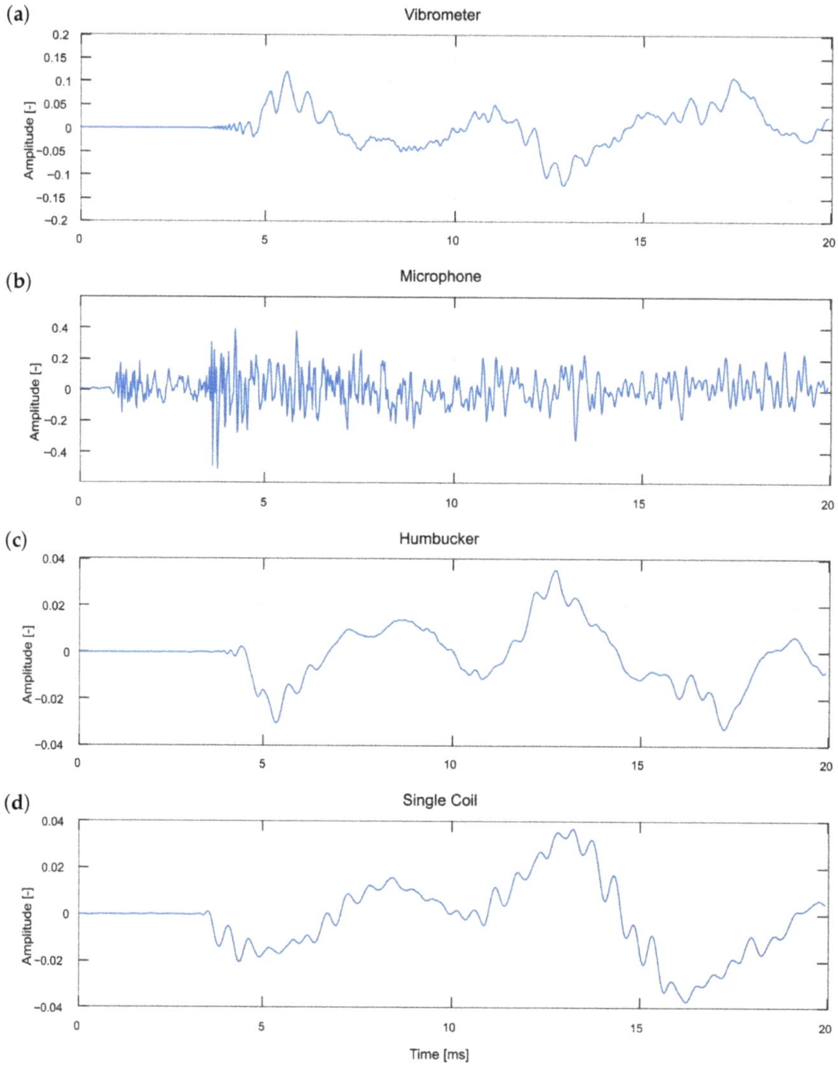


**Figure 5.** Close-up waveform comparison of an initial phase of the string plucking excitation, obtained using the plucker with a plectrum measured over the humbucker, for all four recording methods: (**a**) vibrometer, (**b**) microphone, (**c**) humbucker, and (**d**) single coil. The single coil measurements are not conducted in the same place along the string.

The first observation concerns the signal characteristics captured by each sensor. The microphone recording differs markedly from the other waveforms and also exhibits an earlier onset which is clearly visible in Figure 5, where the microphone signal precedes the responses of the other sensors by several milliseconds. This occurs because the microphone is the only sensor that detects air vibrations rather than the string itself. In the initial phase of the sound event (Figure 5), it registers the impulse-like noise generated by the excitation mechanism, which obscures the actual string vibrations. At this stage, no fundamental period is visible, and the waveform exhibits a noise-like character. In later stages, however, the signal becomes periodic, as illustrated in Figure 6. Combining microphone data with that obtained from any of the three remaining sensors may therefore provide a means of separating the excitation mechanism's sound from the string vibration. The gradual transition from a noise-like to a periodic signal is visible in the comparison between Figures 5 and 6, reflecting the decay of the excitation mechanism's transient.

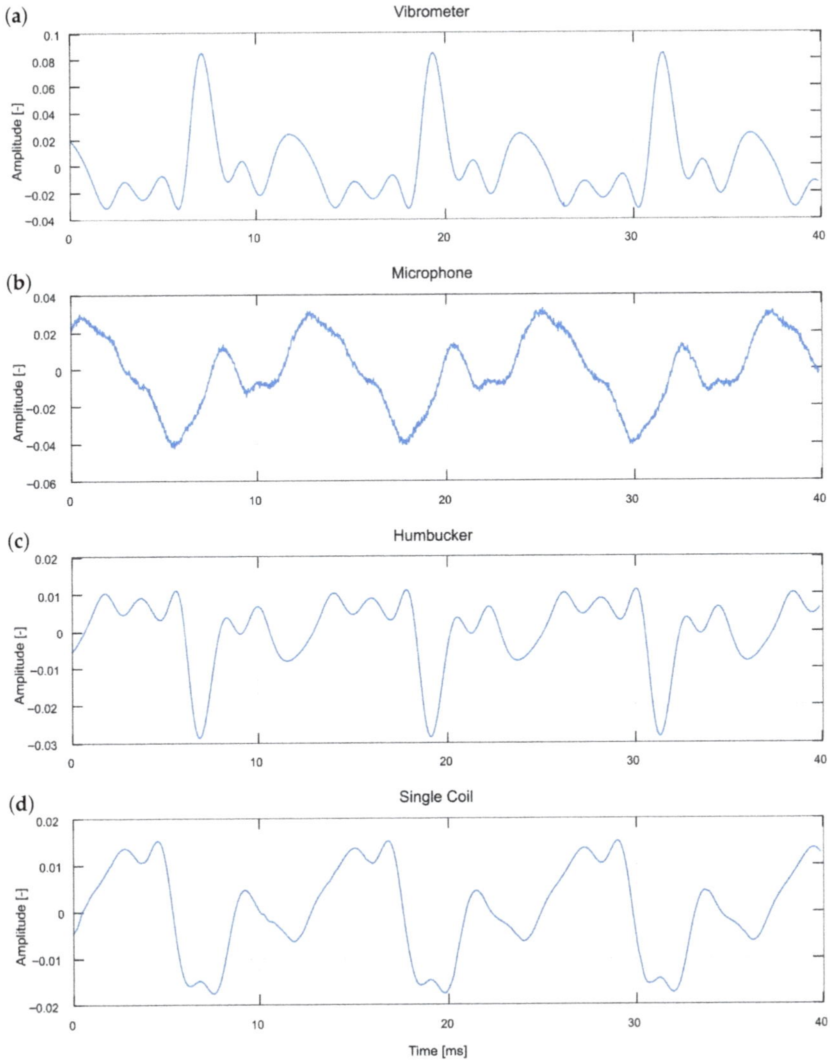


**Figure 6.** Close-up waveform comparison of the string plucking excitation, obtained using the plucker with a plectrum, two seconds after the pluck measured over the humbucker, for all four recording methods: (**a**) vibrometer, (**b**) microphone, (**c**) humbucker, and (**d**) single coil. The time scale is doubled compared to Figure 5. The single coil measurements are not conducted in the same place along the string.

The vibrometer signal is inverted relative to the two guitar pickups, since they measure string vibrations from opposite sides. Although their waveforms appear inverted, they remain consistent in timing, demonstrating that the sensors are phase-aligned apart from this polarity difference. A notable difference concerns the level of detail present in the waveforms. The microphone retains most of the high-frequency components, though many of these likely originate from the excitation mechanism rather than the string. During the initial phase of the sound event, the vibrometer and both pickups produce very similar waveforms, with the vibrometer exhibiting the greatest level of detail, followed by the single-coil pickup, and the least from the humbucker. This order is consistent with the humbucker's inherent low-pass filtering properties. After two seconds, this similarity significantly diminishes, with only the humbucker and vibrometer exhibiting comparable waveforms. The single-coil diverges from the vibrometer and humbucker signals, displaying mixed traits that partially resemble the microphone, suggesting a progressive loss of correlation between sensors over time. Although the microphone signal has become periodic, it superficially resembles the vibrometer signal, potentially due to measuring a different physical phenomenon or from the slightly different measurement perspective, as described in the experimental setup. The single-coil pickup waveform displays mixed characteristics of both the vibrometer and the microphone, which may in part also be attributed to the fact that the single coil measurements were not obtained at the same position along the string, as noted in the figure captions.

### 3.2. String Excitation When Striking

When a string is struck with a plectrum, the plectrum remains in contact with the string until the point of maximum displacement, after which the string rebounds and pushes the plectrum away. Consequently, the resulting vibration can be divided into two phases: (1) while the plectrum is in contact with the string and (2) after it has disengaged. In the first phase, the vibration is constrained not only at the string ends but also at the contact point. This effect has been theoretically described as the independent vibration of string segments, effectively creating shorter strings with correspondingly higher fundamental frequencies [26]. As a result, string vibrations during the onset are expected to exhibit a higher base frequency compared to the subsequent steady-state phase.

Figures 7 and 8 present waveforms recorded with different methods for two separate strikes, measured above the humbucker and the single coil, respectively. As noted earlier, the microphone signal is dominated by the excitation mechanism, which obscures the crucial initial phase of the event. By contrast, the vibrometer and humbucker clearly reveal the phenomenon of the string being divided by the plectrum: during the first 20 ms, four short vibration periods (indicated in red) can be observed before the signal transitions to the expected fundamental period of the entire string (indicated in green). In the single coil data, traces of the phenomenon are present, though the distinction between short and long periods is less pronounced than in the vibrometer and humbucker. It should be noted that although differences in measurement position (as in Figures 7 and 8) could influence the visibility of the phenomenon, the vibrometer consistently detected it at both positions. This indicates that the poorer performance of the single-coil pickup is attributable to the sensor characteristics rather than the measurement location.

Another marker of this effect is visible in the vibrometer and humbucker signals: during the initial short periods, the waveform exhibits a gradual increase in amplitude, reflecting the continued displacement of the string by the moving plectrum until disengagement occurs. This amplitude modulation is not evident in the single coil or microphone recordings, further highlighting the advantage of certain measurement methods.

The ratio of the short-period oscillations to the final fundamental period provides an estimate of the excitation point on the string, which, in this case, corresponds to 0.359 of the total string length. The vibrometer data, characterized by a sharper and more detailed waveform, facilitates precise identification of periodic markers. In contrast, the smoother humbucker waveform may be more effectively analyzed using autocorrelation rather than relying solely on visual inspection of waveform peaks.

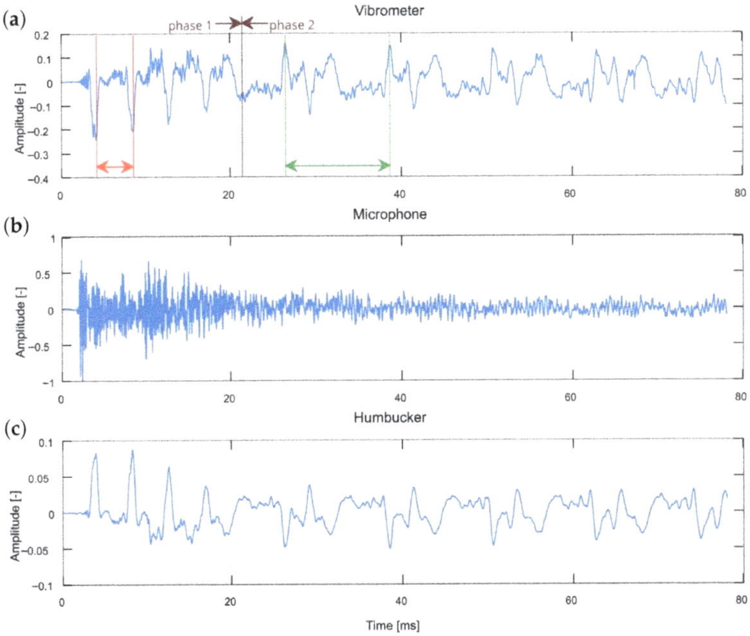


**Figure 7.** Comparison of striking excitation waveforms measured over the humbucker, for different recording methods: (**a**) vibrometer, (**b**) microphone, and (**c**) humbucker. Two phases can be observed as follows: 1—vibrations of a divided string segment, and 2—vibrations of the entire string. Red and green sections represent vibration periods in both phases.

### 3.3. Plucking Position and Measuring Point Estimation

Several methods have been proposed for estimating the plucking and measurement positions of a string based on recorded signals. These approaches include autocorrelation of spectral peaks [27], parametric pitch estimation [28], and, when precise recordings of string vibrations are available, analysis of wave reflection timing [26,29]. By capturing the temporal evolution of the string's transverse displacement with high precision, it is possible to examine the relative phase and amplitude content of its vibrational modes. The proportion and timing of reflected wave components provide sufficient information to infer the excitation position.

Wave reflections are most clearly observable in cases of clean excitation; thus, plucking with a copper wire will be analyzed. To enable proper identification of waveform features as successive reflections, a finite-difference simulation of an idealized string was performed and compared to the experimental recordings, as shown in Figure 9. The simulation was based on the one-dimensional wave equation:

$$\frac{\partial^2 u}{\partial t^2} = c^2 \frac{\partial^2 u}{\partial x^2}, \tag{1}$$

where $u(x,t)$ represents the displacement of a string and $c$ is the transverse wave velocity:

$$c = \sqrt{\frac{T_0}{\rho A}}, \tag{2}$$

where $T_0$ is the tension of a string, $\rho$ is the density of the string, and $A$ is the area of the cross-section of the string. The excitation and readout points in the simulation were adjusted to match those of the experiment.

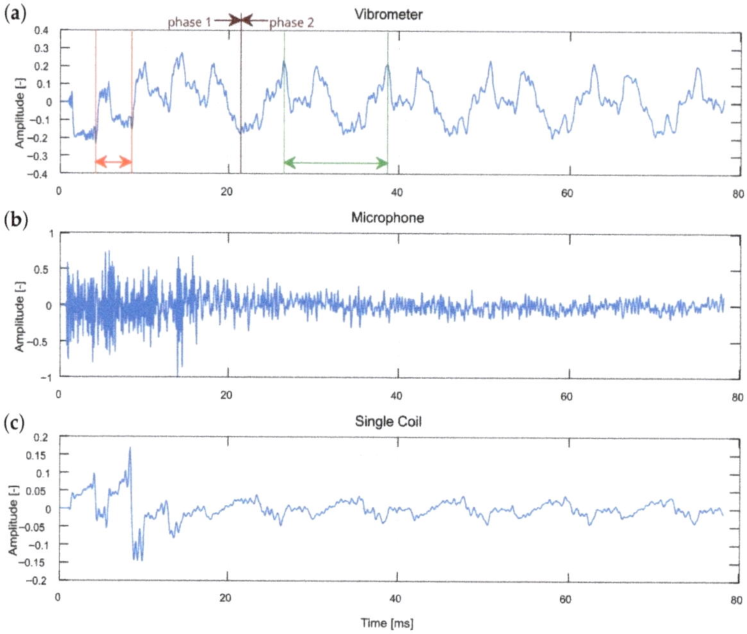


**Figure 8.** Comparison of striking excitation waveforms measured over the single coil, for different recording methods: (**a**) vibrometer, (**b**) microphone, and (**c**) single coil. Two phases can be observed as follows: 1—vibrations of a divided string segment, and 2—vibrations of an entire string. Red and green sections represent vibration periods in both phases.

The vibrometer recordings (Figure 9) correspond closely with the simulation results, allowing straightforward identification of all traveling impulses along the string. The fine temporal detail captured by the vibrometer enables accurate measurement of inter-impulse distances, yielding the results presented in Table 1. Among the tested sensors, only the vibrometer provides the level of precision required for such waveform analysis. The humbucker captures some, but not all, of the relevant impulses, while the single coil and microphone do not exhibit the necessary features.

**Table 1.** Comparison of physical measurement and estimation based on signal locations of measurement and excitation points.

| | **Physical Measurement** | **Signal-Based Estimation** |
|---|---|---|
| Excitation Location | $\frac{240\text{ mm}}{645\text{ mm}} \approx 0.372$ | $\frac{(414-184)\text{ samples}}{604\text{ samples}} \approx 0.381$ |
| Measurement Location | $\frac{157\text{ mm}}{645\text{ mm}} \approx 0.243$ | $\frac{(564-414)\text{ samples}}{604\text{ samples}} \approx 0.248$ |

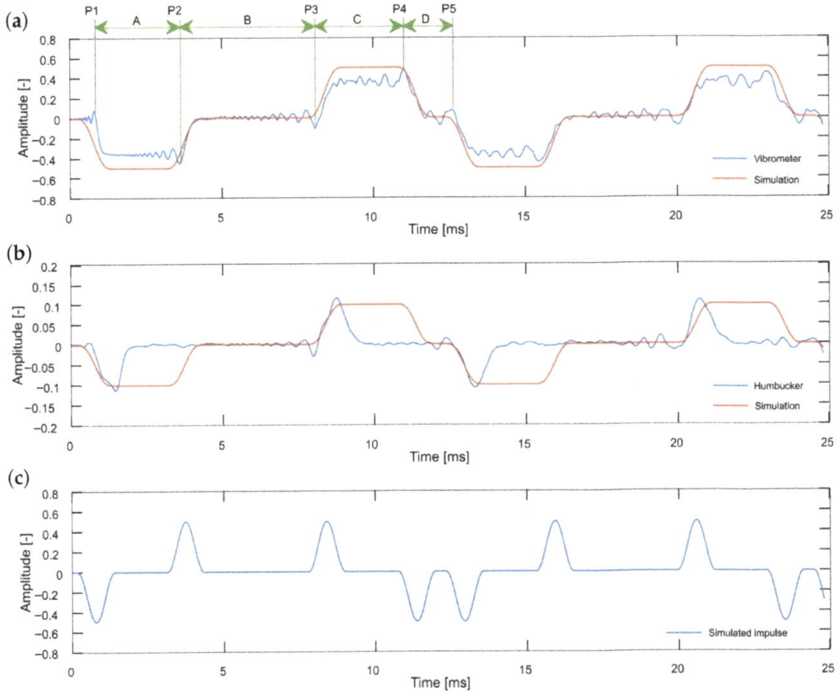


**Figure 9.** Analysis of plucking data obtained from vibrometer (**a**) and humbucker (**b**) observing string plucked by the copper wire, and from the finite-difference simulation (**c**). P1–P5 are subsequent impulses (straight or inverted, as shown on bottom, simulated plot) travelling over the measurement point. $T_0 = A + B + C + D$ is a single vibration period representing the fundamental frequency. $\frac{B}{T_0}$ allows us to estimate excitation position, and $\frac{C}{T_0}$ estimates measurement point, both as a fraction of a string length.

## 4. Measurement Method Characteristic Comparison

In this chapter, we will focus on a more general comparison of the sensors and their characteristics.

### 4.1. Signal-to-Noise Ratio

A way to evaluate the performance of each measurement technique is to calculate signal-to-noise ratio. This can be achieved through isolating segments of the recording in which there is no vibration of the string and comparing it to segments after plucking the string. The beginnings of plucks were located. Two second segments before and after these moments were cut to constitute the noise and signal signals. Plucks containing transient noise prior to string excitation were excluded from the analysis. To ensure comparability, all methods used the same signal segments for calculation. The signal-to-noise ratio (SNR) values were calculated using the formula:

$$\mathrm{SNR_{dB}} = 10\log_{10}\left(\frac{P_{\mathrm{signal}} + P_{\mathrm{noise}}}{P_{\mathrm{noise}}}\right) \tag{3}$$

In Equation (3), $P_{\mathrm{signal}}$ is the power of the signal segment and $P_{\mathrm{noise}}$ is the power of the noise segment. Given that the same level of background noise was present during the recording of the signal, the form of SNR that sums both powers in the numerator was selected as more appropriate. Figure 10 shows a comparison of SNR values calculated for each recording method.

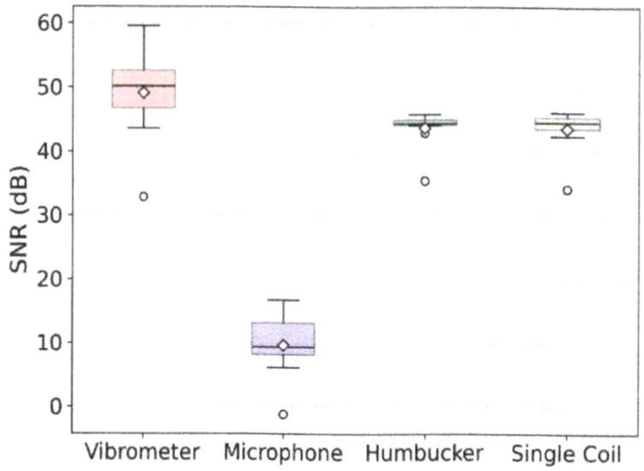


**Figure 10.** Comparison of SNR values calculated for different recording methods across N = 10 recorded strikes. Mean, median, IQR, typical values, and outliers are presented. Note: The humbucker measurements are not conducted in the same place along the string.

A few conclusions can be drawn from these results. The most important is the much lower values calculated for the microphone. This is due to two factors. Firstly, this reflects the inherently weak acoustic radiation of a single unamplified string in free air. Since the vibrating string is not amplified by any mechanical system, such as an acoustic guitar body, the signal level is low. Secondly, despite recording in an anechoic chamber, the microphone is still susceptible to noise generated by the operation of the plucking mechanisms. This shows the clear advantage of the optical and electro-acoustic methods in this experimental use case. The anechoic chamber provided both vibrational isolation and a low level of electric interference leading to high SNR values for these methods. The similar levels achieved by the single coil with 43.66 dB (SD = 2.9, N = 10) and humbucker with 43.74 dB (SD = 2.9, N = 10) suggest that the background electromagnetic interference was very low, rendering the interference cancellation provided by the humbucker unnecessary. Nonetheless, this factor should be considered when recording in less optimal environments. The highest SNR values were recorded for the vibrometer at 49.1 dB (SD = 6.9, N = 10); however, the advantage over the magnetic pickups was not substantial.

### *4.2. Response to Varying String Excitation Levels*

An aspect worthy of investigation is how each method captures the differences induced by variations in the initial striking speed. To this end, signals were recorded for three different initial pendulum deflection. To ensure the statistical reliability of the findings and to assess the reproducibility of each measurement, a total of N = 10 trials were recorded for each experimental condition. The strikes were recorded using a 240 frames-per-second video camera, and the velocity of the plectrum at the moment of striking was calculated through frame-by-frame analysis using the angular displacement and the length of the arm. The results are presented in Table 2.

To compare the sensors, each pluck was extracted with 0.5 s of time before the strike and 7 s of decay. The Root Mean Squared (RMS) values were calculated and averaged within each measurement series. The results obtained are presented in Figure 11. The focus is not on the absolute values but on the overall shape, which illustrates how each sensor records signals at varying dynamic levels. Consequently, the y-axis limits have been set so that the top and bottom positions for each sensor align at the same point.

**Table 2.** Measured velocity of the pendulum at the moment of striking for various initial pendulum deflections.

| Pendulum Deflection | Initial Deflection (°) | Measured Striking Velocity (m/s) |
|---|---|---|
| Small | 37 | 0.49 |
| Medium | 75 | 1.12 |
| Large | 112 | 1.74 |

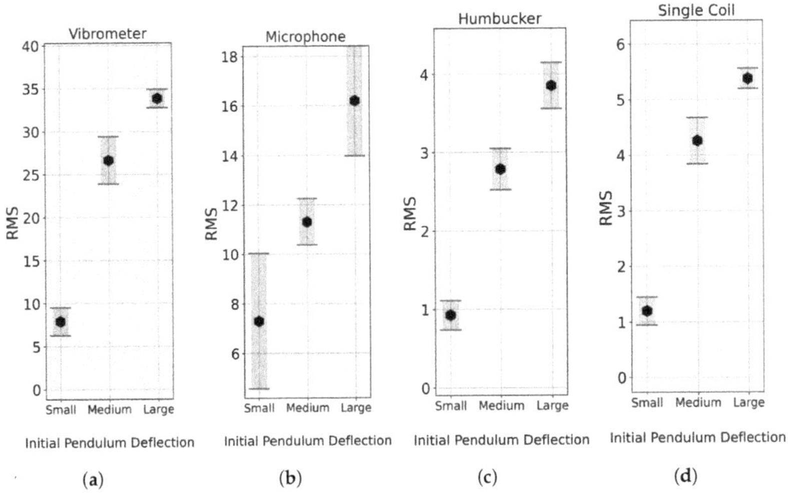


**Figure 11.** Comparison of average RMS of recorded signals for different initial pendulum displacements by different methods: (**a**) vibrometer (**b**) microphone (**c**) humbucker pickup, and (**d**) single coil pickup. All results are presented based on N = 10 trials, with the mean and standard deviation presented. Note: The humbucker measurements are not conducted in the same place along the string.

The obtained results demonstrate clear differences in the dynamic response and linearity of the sensors. It is important to note that a linear increase in striking velocity does not necessarily correspond to a linear increase in the generated string vibration energy. These results do not allow for the assertion of which shape is the most accurate and may only be used for comparative purposes. All methods successfully registered increased signal energy with higher striking velocity, as indicated by the non-overlapping standard deviation bars for each of the three dynamic levels across all sensors. The increases recorded by the vibrometer and the single coil exhibit very similar shapes. In contrast, the humbucker demonstrates a more linear shape, while the microphone is a clear outlier, as its results curve in the opposite direction. This indicates that the measurement methods possess different dynamic characteristics, with the vibrometer and single coil being the most similar. Lastly, since all methods effectively resolved the three dynamic levels, we can conclude that they all possess a sufficient dynamic range for typical guitar analysis.

### 4.3. Filter Transfer Functions

The next step was to visualize the spectral difference between the signal recorded between each method. To this end, the Filter Transfer Function was calculated for each method in relation to the vibrometer. It was chosen as the baseline due to the high quality of results it produced together with low noise. Recordings conducted for the same plucks were cut to the first two seconds, normalized to −23 LUFS [30], and their transfer functions were calculated and smoothed. This was performed for three strikes conducted using the medium setting of the pendulum. The achieved results are presented in Figure 12.

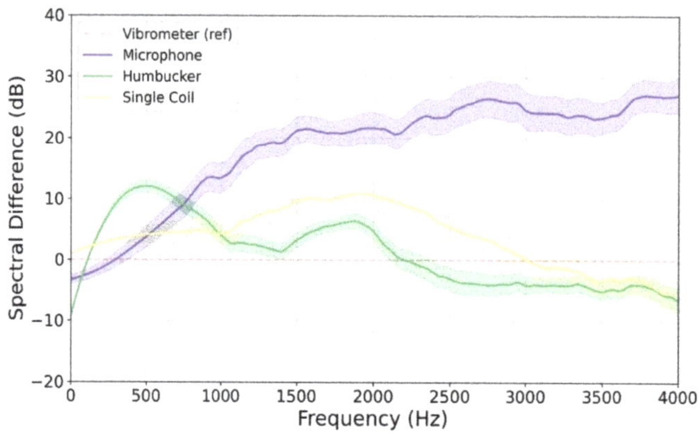


**Figure 12.** Comparison of smoothed average Filter Transfer Functions calculated for each method using the vibrometer as the reference. All values calculated across N = 10 strikes with the solid line representing the mean value and the shaded area showing standard deviation. Note: The humbucker measurements are not conducted in the same place along the string.

The functions obtained for both electromagnetic pickups are much closer to the results acquired with the vibrometer than those obtained from the microphone. This difference for the microphone increases with rising frequencies, likely due to a combination of captured noise captured and the influence of frequency-dependent acoustic radiation from the string. The characteristics of the pickups exhibit notable similarities, with the primary distinction being the poor performance of the humbucker at frequencies below 1 kHz and the single coil in the 1–3 kHz range, where values exceed 10 dB. Such a comparison between the magnetic pickups is not unexpected, as it aligns with previous theoretical and experimental research [31,32] which often frames a humbucker as having a low pass characteristic. The two coils wired in series in the humbucker increase the total inductance, capacitance, and resistance of the circuit. This, in turn, lowers the resonant frequency and reduces the Q-factor of the pickup's RLC circuit. The higher inductance impedes high-frequency current changes, while the increased resistance dampens the resonance. This results in an attenuation of high frequency content. Additionally, the wider magnetic aperture of the humbucker is sometimes mentioned as averaging string motion over a larger region, further filtering out higher spatial harmonics. It is worth noting that both magnetic pickup designs perform poorly at higher frequencies, with their frequency response functions deviating further from the reference vibrometer as frequencies increase.

## 5. Influence of the Reflective Tape on the String's Vibration

As described in Section 2.2, measurement of string vibration using the vibrometer required the use of a reflective tape affixed to the string. Without this tape, the string would move out of the laser's path, resulting in artifacts and inaccurate measurement results. This issue occurred despite attempts made while measuring the thicker string, with the excitation direction parallel to the laser's direction. The use of this tape does; however, raise the question of its influence on the measured string vibration. The smallest tape size that yielded accurate results was 3 × 4 mm. Despite using this tape, when plucking the string with a 0.14 mm diameter copper wire, the string's sticker moved out of the laser's path. This constitutes a strong pluck, exceeding the dynamics of regular guitar playing techniques. It illustrates issues that would arise at lower levels if a smaller reflective tape size were used. A spectrogram of the recording of this pluck using different methods is presented in Figure 13.

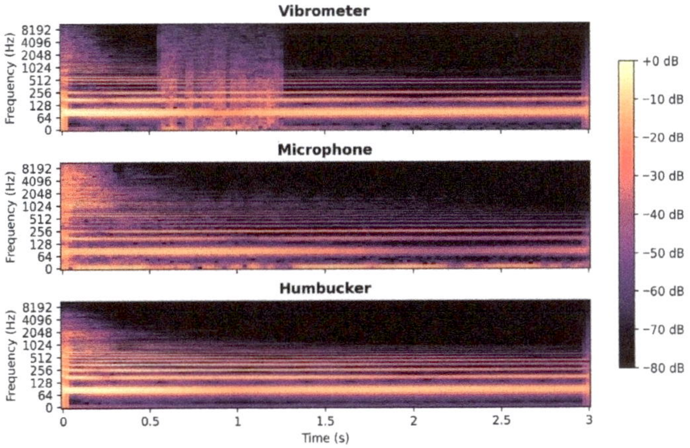


**Figure 13.** Spectrogram of pluck conducted with 0.014 mm diameter wire recorded with vibrometer, microphone, and humbucker.

When analysing the spectrogram of the vibrometer recording between 0.5 and 1.3 s, broad spectrum interference is present in the signal. This issue is not present in the recordings conducted using the microphone and humbucker, indicating that it is not a recording of a true phenomenon in the string's vibration. This noise is caused by the string vibrating at a magnitude which results in the sticker leaving the lasers path and thus making the resulting recording unusable. It is also worth noting that this happens despite the string being initially plucked in the direction of the laser. This is the reason why this noise is not present from the beginning of the pluck despite the string's vibration magnitude being highest at that moment. The string begins its vibration in the direction it was plucked, but as the vibration decay progresses, this plane of vibration dissolves into vibrations in both transversal polarizations [6]. These results show that the size of reflective tape cannot be further decreased to reduce weight.

Weighing the whole sheet, calculating the area density, and multiplying it by the area of the used 3 × 4 mm tape yields a weight of 0.0056 g. Comparing this weight to the effective segments of the thicker and thinner strings, 4.4 g and 0.3 g, respectively, demonstrates how this additional weight can pose issues when measuring thin strings. Lighter reflective tapes were also tested but their lack of rigidity caused them to bend and sway when affixed to the string resulting in incorrect measurements. It should also be noted that the sticker can influence the string's vibration not only through weight but through the increased resistance when moving against the air during vibration.

To show this measurement, recordings were conducted using the humbucker, with the thinner 0.28 mm string being plucked using a wire. Measurements were conducted without and with the reflected tape added to the string. A comparison of the achieved spectrums is shown on Figure 14.

The influence of the sticker is clearly evident, resulting in significant damping of certain harmonics and amplification of others. This is particularly visible in the 400–800 Hz and the 1400–1800 Hz ranges. The impact is also visible in the time envelope of the recorded sound. A comparison of RMS envelopes is shown on Figure 15.

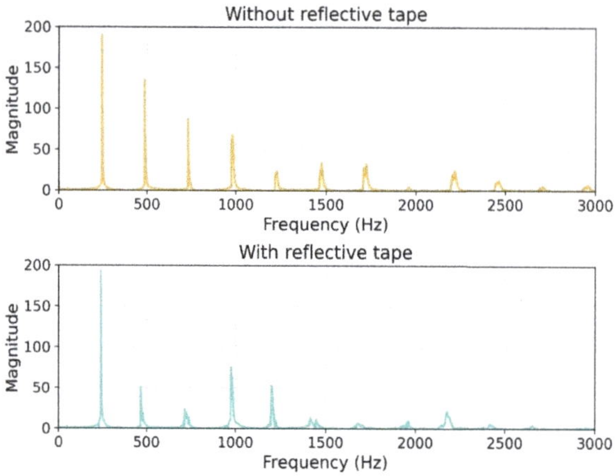


**Figure 14.** Magnitude spectrum comparison of wire plucks recorded using the humbucker for the 0.28 mm string without and with the vibrometer reflective tape adhered to the string.

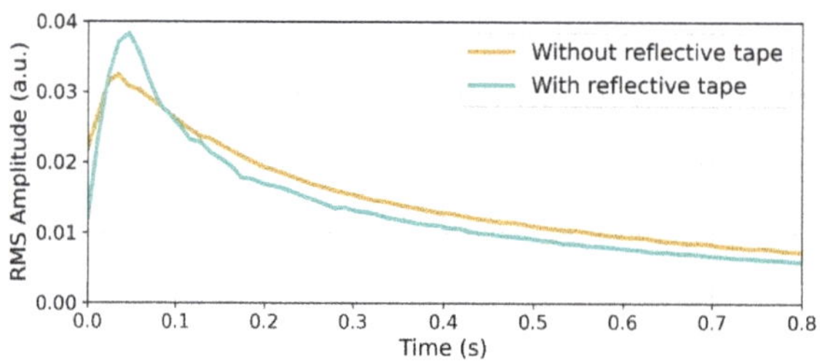


**Figure 15.** RMS envelope comparison of wire plucks recorded using the humbucker for the 0.28 mm string without and with the vibrometer reflective tape adhered to the string. "a.u." denotes "arbitrary units".

The additional mass clearly influences the temporal characteristics of the string's vibration. While the initial pluck is higher, the reflective tape introduces additional damping, evident in the faster decay of the blue curve.

These differences exceed the limits of imperceptibility, and such an influence on the measured phenomena is unacceptable for a measurement method. This indicates that, while laser vibrometry can achieve high precision, its potentially invasive nature, when requiring a target, presents a significant and sometimes prohibitive trade-off for lightweight structures such as guitar strings. It is important to note that a string gauge of 0.28 mm (0.011 inch) is realistic, as typical electric guitar sets have a high E string ranging from approximately 0.20 to 0.3 mm (0.008–0.012 inch).

*Measuring the Influence the LDV Optical Target Tape Has on a String's Vibration*

To better understand how the use of a vibrometer reflective sticker affects string dynamics, a series of experimental measurements were conducted. The experimental setup was identical to the previous recordings, with the exception of the string, which was a 1.12 mm (0.044 inch) with an active weight of 4.14 g, tuned to E2 (82.41 Hz). The vibration of the string was measured using all recording methods for an empty string (NoS) and with reflective stickers of various sizes attached to the string at the measurement point. Figure 16 shows the used fragments of reflective tape, and Table 3 presents a comparison of their parameters.

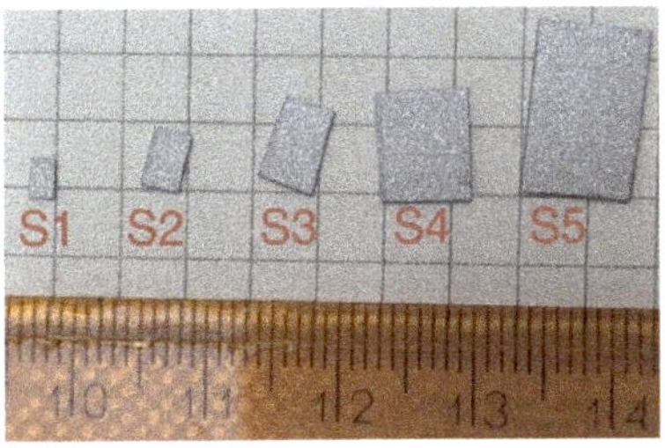


**Figure 16.** Reflective stickers used as optical targets for comparison. The labels S1–S5 indicate the configuration names assigned to each sticker.

**Table 3.** Dimensions and weights of the reflective stickers used.

| Configuration Name | Sticker Dimensions [mm] | Sticker Area [mm$^2$] | Sticker Mass [g] |
|---|---|---|---|
| NoS | 0 × 0 | 0 | 0 |
| S1 | 3 × 2 | 6 | 0.003 |
| S2 | 4 × 3 | 12 | 0.006 |
| S3 | 6 × 4 | 24 | 0.013 |
| S4 | 8 × 6 | 48 | 0.025 |
| S5 | 12 × 8 | 96 | 0.05 |

The first aspect worth investigating are the spectrums of the recorded signals. Figure 17 presents a comparison of spectra from a single excitation recorded for each tape configuration.

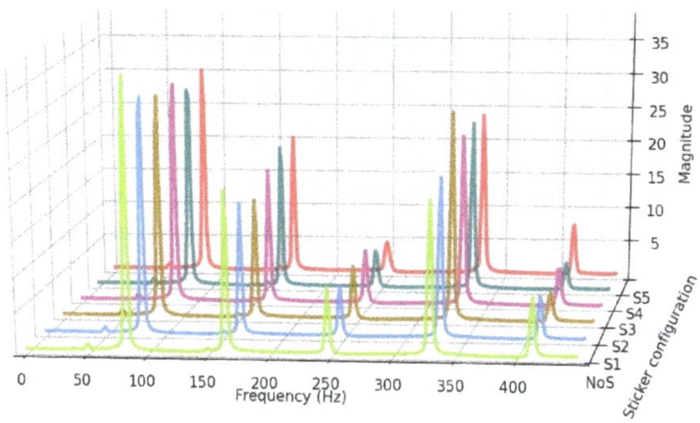


**Figure 17.** Average spectra of excitation series obtained from manual wire plucking, recorded with the humbucker for each sticker configuration. Results are averaged over N = 10 trials.

Analysis of the recorded, averaged spectra indicates that even the addition of the smallest sticker, S1, significantly alters the proportions of the harmonics. A sizeable decrease in the magnitudes of the first and second harmonics is observed, while the third and fourth harmonics are diminished to a lesser extent. As the tape size increases, this tendency remains but a clear characteristic of change does not manifest. This suggests that the sticker's effect is not purely mass-related but may depend on complex modal and aerodynamic interactions. Certain partials can be significantly affected, such as the fourth harmonic in S2 and the fifth harmonic in S5, which are notably stronger than for other stickers. A measurable shift in the string's base frequency was not observed for any sticker size. In the absence of a discernible trend, it is worthwhile to investigate signal parameters. The first parameter is the RMS of the signal, as presented in Figure 18.

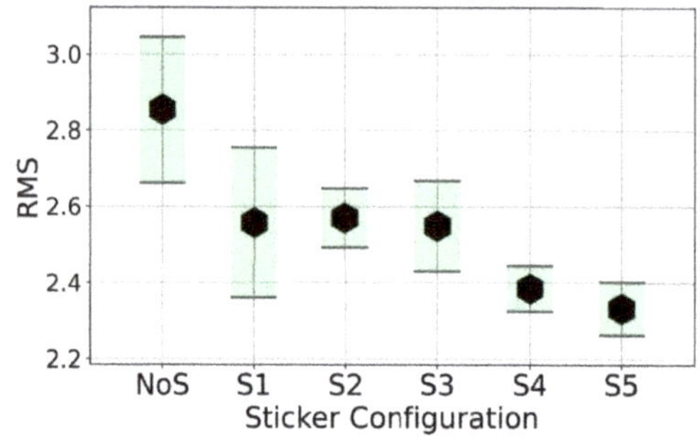


**Figure 18.** Average RMS values and standard deviations of humbucker recordings for wire plucking with various sticker configurations on the string. Results are averaged over N = 10 trials with the mean and standard deviation shown.

Analysis of the RMS clearly indicates that the addition of reflective tape consistently reduces the signal's energy. This observation holds true even for the smallest size, S1. Notably, the change is not consistent, with S1, S2, and S3 exhibiting similar values, although measurement uncertainty makes this relationship unclear. Another approach worth analyzing is investigating to what range the addition of a sticker influences the timbre of the played note. To this end, Figure 19 shows the change of spectral centroid over time for different stickers. Spectral centroid is an important parameter to investigate as it has been shown to highly correlate with listener perception of a sound's brightness [33].

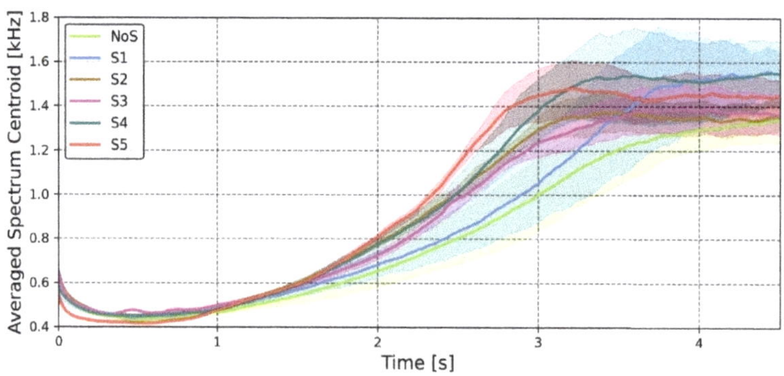


**Figure 19.** Average spectral centroid over time for wire plucking series, recorded with the humbucker for each sticker. Each configuration result represents N = 10 trials with the solid line representing the mean value and the shaded area showing standard deviation.

These results show, that although all configurations exhibit similar values initially, they begin to diverge after the first second and demonstrate significant differences during the third second of sound decay. These differences increase from the NoS values as the size of the sticker increases.

These results clearly illustrate the influence of the reflective sticker on string vibration. The differences are measurable and exceed the limits of perceptibility [34]. They are evident in both temporal and spectral analyses, as well as in the timbral features of the signal. This influence is observed even at a sticker size that is too small to provide a reliable optical target for the LDV, resulting in artifacts in the recorded signal. These results lead to the conclusion that when measuring instrument strings, LDVs cannot be used as a non-contact measurement method that does not influence the measured object.

This magnitude of change occurs despite the tape weighing only 0.1% of the string's mass. Several factors may contribute to this phenomenon. Firstly, the mass added by the sticker is concentrated in a small area. When converting the masses of the string and tape to linear density, the tape can constitute up to 10% of the string's density at that point. This means that it can disrupt the linear distribution of mass along the string, altering vibration modes and diminishing harmonicity. Secondly, the sticker adds not only mass but also surface area in the direction of initial excitation. This results in increased drag on the string, which enhances damping. Once again, this increase is localized, potentially disrupting the string's natural vibration. Thirdly, due to imperfect mounting, the sticker is not perfectly symmetrical on the string. Additionally, it is not perfectly stiff. These factors may cause evolving changes in vibration polarisation and type.

## 6. Discussion

The experimental results indicate that the choice of measurement technology is not neutral and involves significant trade-offs between precision and practicality. Each sensor captures a distinct aspect of the string's vibration, and no single method can be regarded as universally superior. Therefore, the selection is dependent on the specific research setup and question.

The laser vibrometer is considered the standard for non-contact, high-precision measurement. Its primary advantage is its ability to directly measure the mechanical motion of the string, providing exceptional immunity to confounding factors such as instrument body resonance and ambient acoustic noise. Inherent limitation to a single axis of measurement can be beneficial for analyzing the polarization modes of the string's vibration. Moreover, its designation as a measurement tool ensures a high level of reliability and repeatability. Nonetheless, this advantage is accompanied by a significant monetary cost. The method is sensitive to setup, requiring precise targeting of the laser on a reflective point. Critically, our results indicate that measuring a string's vibration requires a reflective sticker. This tape influences the string's vibration and renders the measurement of thin strings impossible. Even for thicker strings, the influence of the additional weight added to the string must be accounted for. This limitation needs to be recognized during experimental planning. The need for precise targeting also makes it highly impractical for studies involving human musicians, as any movement of the instrument renders the measurement unstable, confining its use to highly controlled laboratory settings.

In contrast to the vibrometer's isolated focus, the microphone offers a more general perspective on the vibration. It is also a specialized and calibrated measurement tool. It does not isolate the vibration of the string, being susceptible to the vibration of other elements, sound created by the test procedure and outside noise. The measurement of air vibration generated by the string instead of the string itself adds a level of delay and filtration. This means that the microphone is not adequate when conducting precise waveform analysis. It captures the holistic acoustic event as a human ear would perceive it, making it the most valid method for perceptual or psychoacoustic research.

Magnetic pickups offer a pragmatic compromise. They are low-cost, easy to position reliably, and share the vibrometer's immunity to ambient acoustic noise. However, they are susceptible to electromagnetic interference. They require ferromagnetic strings to function and, more importantly, act as inherent filters that influence the signal. No guitar pickups are designed for measurement purposes with a flat frequency response. Despite this, our measurement results show their ability to register precise waveform events at a level similar to the vibrometer.

*Sensing-Method Selection Based on Application Requirements*

When designing a measurement setup, the stated experimental goal will dictate which of the tested technologies can be used. The presented results can be employed to establish a practical set of systematic guidelines concerning use cases, strengths, and limitations that must be considered during experiment planning. Table 4 presents a comparison of measurement methods and what investigations they are appropriate for based on our results and analyses.

**Table 4.** Comparison of measurement methods regarding utilization use cases.

| Studied Problem | Precise Waveform Analysis | String Models Validation | Performance Analysis | Sound Synthesis Data | Instrument Timbre Analysis | Observing Vibration Polarities |
|---|---|---|---|---|---|---|
| **LDV** | Yes [1] | Yes | No | Yes | No | Yes |
| **Microphone** | No | No | Yes | Yes | Yes [1] | No |
| **Magnetic Pickups** | Yes | Yes | Yes | Yes | Yes | No |

[1] Most appropriate.

Additionally, sensor technology limitations mean that not all methods are possible to use depending on the requirements specific to every experimental situation. Table 5 presents which methods can be used depending on measurement scenarios.

**Table 5.** Comparison of measurement methods in regards to limitations resulting from experimental scenarios.

| Scenario | Nonferrous Strings | Light Strings | Instrument Mount Instability | Excitation Mechanism Noise | Noisy Environment | Electromagnetic Interference |
|---|---|---|---|---|---|---|
| **LDV** | Yes | No [1] | No | Yes | Yes | Yes |
| **Microphone** | Yes | Yes | Yes | No | Yes | No |
| **Magnetic Pickups** | No | Yes | Yes | No | Yes | No [2] |

[1] Due to requirement for optical target. [2] Single coil—no, Humbucker—conditionally yes.

To assist experimental design, the main takeaways regarding each measurement technology have been summarized in Table 6 for easy referencing.

**Table 6.** Comparison of measurement principles, strengths, limitations, and ideal use cases of different sensing methods for string vibration analysis.

| Feature | Laser Doppler Vibrometer (LDV) | Microphone | Magnetic Pickups |
|---|---|---|---|
| **Principle** | Measures transverse string velocity directly via Doppler shift of reflected laser light. | Measures acoustic pressure variations generated by the instrument. | Measures string velocity from variations in magnetic flux induced by vibrating ferromagnetic strings. |

**Table 6.** *Cont.*

| Feature | Laser Doppler Vibrometer (LDV) | Microphone | Magnetic Pickups |
|---|---|---|---|
| **Strengths** | **High Precision**: Exceptional micro-temporal fidelity; resolves fine waveform details; **High SNR**: Highest signal-to-noise ratio in a controlled environment; **Robustness**: Unaffected by acoustic and electromagnetic interference. | **Perceptual Relevance**: Captures the holistic acoustic event as a human would hear it; **Calibrated**: Standardized measurement tool for acoustic analysis. | **Pragmatic Compromise**: Good balance of high-fidelity waveform capture, practicality, and low cost; **Non-Invasive**: Does not require altering the string; **Acoustic immunity**: Unaffected by ambient acoustic noise. |
| **Limits** | **Invasive**: Requires reflective sticker that adds mass, unacceptably altering the vibration of thin strings; **High Cost**: Significantly more expensive than other methods; **Practicality**: Highly sensitive to setup and movement, limiting its use to controlled laboratory settings. | **Low Precision**: Inadequate for resolving fine-scale waveform phenomena on the string itself; **Low SNR**: Low signal level means it is susceptible to noise from the excitation mechanism and ambient sound; **Indirect Measurement**: Captures the radiated sound, not the direct string motion, introducing medium-related filtering and delays. | **Inherent Filtering**: Filters signal with non-flat frequency response, poor performance over 5 kHz; **Interference**: Vulnerable to electromagnetic interference; **Non-universal**: Only functions with ferromagnetic strings; **Consumer product**: No measurement equipment, uncertain repeatability, and performance limits. |
| **Use Case** | High-precision physical modeling and validation in controlled lab settings, but only for systems where the required optical target does not significantly alter the object's dynamics. | Psychoacoustic research, perceptual timbre analysis of the entire instrument, or studies where the radiated sound is the primary subject of interest. | Applied guitar research, performance analysis, and waveform-accurate modeling where target stability cannot be maintained or the invasiveness of an LDV target is unacceptable. |

## 7. Conclusions

In this study, three sensor technologies—microphone, magnetic pickups, and laser Doppler vibrometry (LDV)—were compared for their ability to capture the vibration of a guitar string under controlled excitation. The results showed that the choice of sensor strongly affects which aspects of string motion can be observed during the transient and decay of string motion.

The experiments confirmed that no single sensor can be considered universally superior. Instead, each method was found to be best suited to different research contexts. Laser Doppler vibrometry (LDV) offers unmatched precision in controlled laboratory studies; however, it necessitates an optical target, which, despite its low weight, influences the string's vibration. This influence is measurable in temporal, spectral, and timbral analyses. It must be taken into account when analysing results and renders the LDV ineffective for thin strings. Magnetic pickups provide a pragmatic balance of accuracy and usability for applied guitar research at a low cost. They allow precise waveform analysis but their inherent signal filtering must be taken into account when conducting more general timbre analysis. Microphones remain most relevant when perceptual or psychoacoustic questions regarding a full instrument are of interest rather then precise measurement of a single element vibration. In this configuration, the microphone did not provide sufficient precision for string vibration analysis.

Future work should address limitations of this study by exploring lighter or non-invasive optical markers, quantifying their impact on the measured physical system, implementing fully automated plucking mechanisms which minimise both acoustic and electromagnetic interference, and investigating how non-ideal measurement environments and scenarios influence the usability of specific measuring solutions. Further studies of sensor fidelity in the time domain would also clarify their relative suitability for waveform-accurate modeling and synthesis.

Overall, this study demonstrates that the choice of sensing technology represents a crucial methodological decision in guitar acoustics, with significant implications for experimental design and applied research in musical acoustics, particularly in physical modeling.

**Author Contributions:** J.J. and M.P. conceptualized and designed the study; J.W. and R.T. provided resources.; J.J., R.T. and J.G. conducted the investigation; J.J. and M.P. conducted formal analysis; J.J. created the visualizations; M.P. conducted simulations; J.J. wrote the first draft of the manuscript; M.P., J.J. and J.W. proofread and edited the final manuscript; M.P. was responsible for supervision. All authors have read and agreed to the published version of the manuscript.

**Funding:** This research was funded by the Department of Mechanics and Vibroacoustics of AGH University of Krakow, Poland, grant number 6.16.130.942.

**Institutional Review Board Statement:** Not applicable.

**Informed Consent Statement:** Not applicable.

**Data Availability Statement:** The data presented in this study are available upon request from the authors.

**Conflicts of Interest:** The authors declare no conflicts of interest.

## References

1. Chadefaux, D.; Le Carrou, J.L.; Le Conte, S.; Castellengo, M. Analysis of the harpsichord plectrum-string interaction. In Proceedings of the Stockholm Music Acoustics Conference (SMAC), Stockholm, Sweden, 30 July–3 August 2013.
2. Ray, T.; Kaljun, J.; Straže, A. Comparison of the Vibration Damping of the Wood Species Used for the Body of an Electric Guitar on the Vibration Response of Open-Strings. *Materials* **2021**, *14*, 5281. [CrossRef]
3. Perov, P.; Johnson, W.; Perova-Mello, N. The physics of guitar string vibrations. *Am. J. Phys.* **2016**, *84*, 38–43. [CrossRef]
4. Jasiński, J.; Oleś, S.; Tokarczyk, D.; Pluta, M. On the Audibility of Electric Guitar Tonewood. *Arch. Acoust.* **2021**, *46*, 138150. [CrossRef]
5. Lynch-Aird, N.; Woodhouse, J. Frequency Measurement of Musical Instrument Strings Using Piezoelectric Transducers. *Vibration* **2018**, *1*, 3–19. [CrossRef]
6. Brauchler, A.; Ziegler, P.; Eberhard, P. Examination of polarization coupling in a plucked musical instrument string via experiments and simulations. *Acta Acust.* **2020**, *4*, 9. [CrossRef]
7. Yang, C.H.; Wu, T.C. Vibration Measurement Method of a String in Transversal Motion by Using a PSD. *Sensors* **2017**, *17*, 1643. [CrossRef]
8. Whitfield, S.B.; Flesch, K.B. An experimental analysis of a vibrating guitar string using high-speed photography. *Am. J. Phys.* **2014**, *82*, 102–109. [CrossRef]
9. Birkett, S. Experimental investigation of the piano hammer-string interaction. *J. Acoust. Soc. Am.* **2013**, *133*, 2467–2478. [CrossRef] [PubMed]
10. Duerinck, T.; Segers, J.; Skrodzka, E.; Verberkmoes, G.; Leman, M.; Van Paepegem, W.; Kersemans, M. Experimental comparison of various excitation and acquisition techniques for modal analysis of violins. *Appl. Acoust.* **2021**, *177*, 107942. [CrossRef]
11. Rau, M.; Scavone, G. Measuring body vibrations of stringed instruments. *J. Acoust. Soc. Am.* **2024**, *156*, A92. [CrossRef]
12. Jasiński, J.; Wronka, W.; Chojnacka, K. Guitar timbre modification through active vibration control—Preliminary results. *Vib. Phys. Syst.* **2024**, *35*, 2024313-1–2024313-10. [CrossRef]
13. Kabała, A.; Barczewski, R. Shell-solid FEM model of a violin resonance body. *Vib. Phys. Syst.* **2020**, *31*, 2020308-1–2020308-8. [CrossRef]

14. Bilbao, S.; Ducceschi, M. Models of musical string vibration. *Acoust. Sci. Technol.* **2023**, *44*, 194–209. [CrossRef]
15. Ducceschi, M.; Bilbao, S. A Physical Model of the Prepared Piano. In Proceedings of the 26th International Congress on Sound and Vibration, Montreal, QC, Canada, 7–11 July 2019; Canadian Acoustical Association: Vaughan, ON, Canada, 2019.
16. Novak, A.; Guadagnin, L.; Lihoreau, B.; Lotton, P.; Brasseur, E.; Simon, L. Measurements and Modeling of the Nonlinear Behavior of a Guitar Pickup at Low Frequencies. *Appl. Sci.* **2017**, *7*, 50. [CrossRef]
17. Debut, V.; Antunes, J. Physical synthesis of six-string guitar plucks using the Udwadia-Kalaba modal formulation. *J. Acoust. Soc. Am.* **2020**, *148*, 575–587. [CrossRef]
18. Pàmies-Vilà, M.; Mayer, A.; Matusiak, E.; Chatziioannou, V. A method for the reproduction of cello bow kinematics using a robotic arm and motion capture. *Acta Acust.* **2024**, *8*, 45. [CrossRef]
19. Jasiński, J. Guitar sound hole modification and its effect on tone. *Vib. Phys. Syst.* **2023**, *34*, 2023202-1–2023202-10. [CrossRef]
20. Hanss, M.; Bestle, P.; Eberhard, P. A Reproducible Excitation Mechanism for Analyzing Electric Guitars. *PAMM* **2015**, *15*, 45–46. [CrossRef]
21. Mayer, A.; Lampis, A. *A Versatile Monochord Setup: An Industrial Robotic Arm as Bowing and Plucking Device*; Universität für Musik und darstellende Kunst Wien: Vienna, Austria, 2024. [CrossRef]
22. Woodhouse, J. Plucked guitar transients: Comparison of measurements and synthesis. *Acta Acust. United Acust.* **2004**, *90*, 945–965.
23. Türckheim, F.; Smit, T.; Hahne, C.; Mores, R. Novel Impulse Response Measurement Method for Stringed Instruments. In Proceedings of the 20th International Congress on Acoustics, ICA 2010, Sydney, Australia, 23–27 August 2010.
24. Smit, T.; Türckheim, F.; Mores, R. A highly accurate plucking mechanism for acoustical measurements of stringed instruments. *J. Acoust. Soc. Am.* **2010**, *127*, EL222–EL226. [CrossRef] [PubMed]
25. Tokarczyk, D.; Jasiński, J.; Pluta, M.; Wiciak, J. Coupling of Limit Switch Sensors and Stepper Motors with Acoustic Feedback for Positioning of a Cartesian Robot End Effector in the Study of Musical Instruments. *Sensors* **2025**, *25*, 1709. [CrossRef] [PubMed]
26. Fletcher, N.H.; Rossing, T.D. *The Physics of Musical Instruments*; Springer: New York, NY, USA, 1998. [CrossRef]
27. Mohamad, Z.; Dixon, S.; Harte, C. Pickup position and plucking point estimation on an electric guitar via autocorrelation. *J. Acoust. Soc. Am.* **2017**, *142*, 3530–3540. [CrossRef] [PubMed]
28. Hjerrild, J.M.; Græsbøll Christensen, M. Estimation of Guitar String, Fret and Plucking Position Using Parametric Pitch Estimation. In Proceedings of the ICASSP 2019—2019 IEEE International Conference on Acoustics, Speech and Signal Processing (ICASSP), Brighton, UK, 12–17 May 2019; pp. 151–155. [CrossRef]
29. Bilbao, S. *Numerical Sound Synthesis: Finite Difference Schemes and Simulation in Musical Acoustics*; John Wiley & Sons: Hoboken, NJ, USA, 2009.
30. *ITU-R BS.1770-5*; Algorithms to Measure Audioprogramme Loudness and True-Peak Audio Level. International Telecommunication Union: Geneva, Switzerland, 2023.
31. French, R.M. (Ed.) Guitar Electronics. In *Engineering the Guitar: Theory and Practice*; Springer: Boston, MA, USA, 2009; pp. 1–24. [CrossRef]
32. Kotiuga, P.R. Interwinding Distributed Capacitance and Guitar Pickup Transient Response. *IEEE Trans. Magn.* **2015**, *51*, 8000704. [CrossRef]
33. McAdams, S.; Giordano, B.L. The perception of musical timbre. In *Oxford Handbook of Music Psychology*; Hallam, S., Cross, I., Thaut, M.H., Eds.; Oxford University Press: Oxford, UK, 2008; pp. 72–80. [CrossRef]
34. Carral, S. Determining the Just Noticeable Difference in Timbre Through Spectral Morphing: A Trombone Example. *Acta Acust. United Acust.* **2011**, *97*, 466–476. [CrossRef]

sensors

MDPI

Article

# Progressive Multi-Scale Perception Network for Non-Uniformly Blurred Underwater Image Restoration

Dechuan Kong [1,2], Yandi Zhang [3], Xiaohu Zhao [2,*], Yanyan Wang [1] and Yanqiang Wang [1,*]

1 School of Artificial Intelligence, Henan Institute of Science and Technology, Xinxiang 453003, China; kdc@hist.edu.cn (D.K.); wang_yy@hist.edu.cn (Y.W.)

2 National and Local Joint Engineering Laboratory of Internet Application Technology on Mine, China University of Mining and Technology, Xuzhou 221116, China

3 School of Information Science and Engineering, Shenyang University of Technology, Shenyang 110870, China; zhangyd331@163.com

* Correspondence: zhaoxiaohu@cumt.edu.cn (X.Z.); wangyanqiang@hist.edu.cn (Y.W.)

**Abstract:** Underwater imaging is affected by spatially varying blur caused by water flow turbulence, light scattering, and camera motion, resulting in severe visual quality loss and diminished performance in downstream vision tasks. Although numerous underwater image enhancement methods have been proposed, the issue of addressing non-uniform blur under realistic underwater conditions remains largely underexplored. To bridge this gap, we propose PMSPNet, a Progressive Multi-Scale Perception Network, designed to handle underwater non-uniform blur. The network integrates a Hybrid Interaction Attention Module to enable precise modeling of feature ambiguity directions and regional disparities. In addition, a Progressive Motion-Aware Perception Branch is employed to capture spatial orientation variations in blurred regions, progressively refining the localization of blur-related features. A Progressive Feature Feedback Block is incorporated to enhance reconstruction quality by leveraging iterative feature feedback across scales. To facilitate robust evaluation, we construct the Non-uniform Underwater Blur Benchmark, which comprises diverse real-world blur patterns. Extensive experiments on multiple real-world underwater datasets demonstrate that PMSPNet consistently surpasses state-of-the-art methods, achieving on average 25.51 dB PSNR and an inference speed of 0.01 s, which provides high-quality visual perception and downstream application input from underwater sensors for underwater robots, marine ecological monitoring, and inspection tasks.

**Keywords:** underwater image enhancement; underwater non-uniform blur; multi-scale perception; hybrid interaction attention

## 1. Introduction

With the advancement of marine science and technology, high-definition underwater imaging has become increasingly vital for underwater applications such as underwater robotic navigation, seabed topographic mapping, and aquatic life monitoring [1,2]. However, underwater imaging is affected by a variety of factors, including light absorption, scattering effects, and relative motion between the camera and the dynamic scene, resulting in image degradation, especially the non-uniform spatial blur distribution. We perform Fourier analysis on underwater images, extract the direction and intensity of localized frequency domain energy, and map them into blur direction and intensity heatmaps to visualize underwater blur patterns. As illustrated in Figure 1, real-world underwater images

 https://doi.org/10.3390/s25175439

commonly exhibit non-uniform blur that varies in spatial extent and directional orientation, violating the common assumption of uniform blur kernels. Such degradation obscures critical visual cues, impairing the performance of downstream computer vision tasks. In autonomous underwater systems, the loss of structural information and motion cues due to non-uniform blur can lead to perceptual errors and decision-making biases, thereby posing challenges to the robustness and reliability of underwater operations.

(i)

(ii)

(iii)

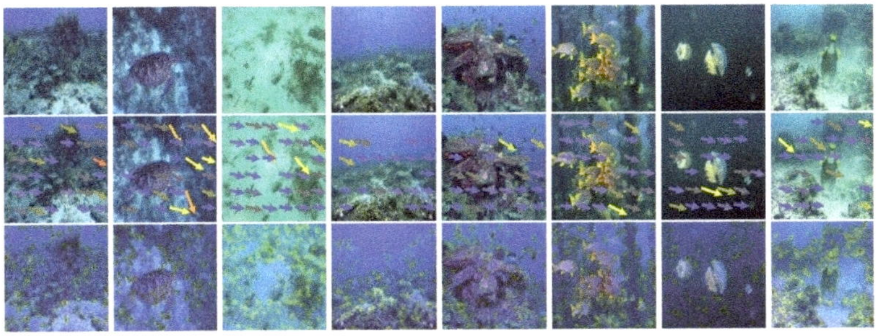

**Figure 1.** Illustration of non-uniform blur in underwater images. (**i**) The raw underwater images. (**ii**) The estimated blur trajectories, where the arrow directions and positions represent the motion blur vectors. (**iii**) The corresponding blur intensity heatmaps, where warmer colors indicate stronger blur magnitude.

To mitigate underwater image degradation, numerous hardware-based solutions have been developed, including specialized underwater cameras, structured lighting systems, and active imaging techniques such as laser illumination and time-gated imaging. These approaches aim to reduce visibility loss and scattering effects during image acquisition, thereby alleviating certain forms of blur. However, despite their potential to enhance raw image quality, such systems are commonly challenged for deployment in real-world environments due to their high cost, large physical footprint, and sensitivity to the environment. More critically, hardware-based methods do not explicitly address the underwater non-uniform blur arising from camera motion, moving objects, or dynamic water flow. This limitation has spurred increasing interest in algorithmic deblurring techniques, which can restore image sharpness directly from captured data without the need for auxiliary hardware.

Numerous studies have investigated traditional image enhancement techniques to address underwater image degradation. These methods typically leverage handcrafted priors and physical modeling to compensate for light attenuation and scattering. Common strategies include histogram equalization, white balance, gray-world assumptions, and Retinex-based methods for illumination decomposition. Some approaches further adapt atmospheric dehazing techniques, such as the Dark Channel Prior (DCP), to estimate the transmission map of underwater scenes. While these methods are relatively easy to deploy and interpretable, they generally assume static scenes and well-defined image structures, rendering them ineffective in the presence of the spatially non-uniform blur prevalent in real-world underwater environments. As a result, they commonly fail to recover fine image details and maintain structural consistency, limiting their utility in supporting high-level visual tasks.

With the growing application of deep learning (DL) in image restoration, learning-based methods for underwater image enhancement (UIE) have attracted increasing attention. Convolutional Neural Networks (CNNs) and Generative Adversarial Networks (GANs) are employed to correct color distortions, enhance contrast, and improve the visibility of underwater images, owing to their powerful feature extraction and representation learning capabilities. More recently, Transformer-based architectures have been introduced into underwater image enhancement and restoration tasks, demonstrating promising performance due to their global receptive field and long-range dependency modeling. However, most of these methods remain focused primarily on enhancing the visual quality of the image, lacking explicit mechanisms to model underwater image blur. Furthermore, the enhancement performance of the above networks often scales with their architectural complexity, which increases significantly in Transformer-based designs. This imposes substantial computational burdens, making real-time deployment in underwater applications impractical. Consequently, the performance of existing enhancement algorithms is frequently compromised under non-uniform blur conditions, underscoring the urgent need for dedicated deblurring frameworks tailored to the unique challenges of underwater environments.

Focusing on the challenge of non-uniform blur in underwater images, we propose PMSPNet, a Progressive Multi-Scale Perception Network. PMSPNet perceives and models blur features from multiple perspectives, encompassing both local and global receptive fields, contextual semantic information, as well as the direction and intensity of the blur. By integrating these diverse perceptual cues, the network effectively maximizes blur removal while enhancing overall image quality.

The main work of this article is summarized as follows:

- We propose a Progressive Multi-Scale Perception Network to effectively eliminate non-uniform blur in underwater images, enabling real-time underwater image enhancement.
- We introduce a Hybrid Interaction Attention Module that extracts and integrates local and global blur features to capture multi-view information and accurately perceive the direction and intensity of underwater blur.
- We design a Progressive Motion-Aware Perception Branch and a Progressive Feature Feedback Block to enable progressive fine-tuning of features, precise localization of blur, and efficient recovery of reconstruction details.
- We construct a Non-uniform Underwater Blur Dataset to provide a benchmark for evaluating underwater image deblurring algorithms. Extensive experiments demonstrate that the proposed method outperforms state-of-the-art approaches, validating its robustness and effectiveness.

The remainder of this article is organized as follows. Section 2 introduces related work. Section 3 describes the PMSPNet network. Section 4 presents the analysis and discussion of the experimental results, and Section 5 of this article concludes with a summary of the article and discusses potential future research areas.

## 2. Related Work

### 2.1. Hardware-Based Approach

To address the challenges of underwater image degradation, numerous hardware-based methods have been proposed. These approaches employ specialized imaging systems to capture higher-quality data at the point of acquisition, thereby reducing dependence on post-processing algorithms [3]. Some systems utilize auxiliary light sources or polarization filters to suppress scattering and backscatter effects [4,5]. In contrast, others adopt structured light or multi-camera setups to reconstruct clearer underwater scenes [6,7]. Notably, high-speed cameras and inertial measurement units (IMUs) have been leveraged to estimate and compensate for camera motion, thereby mitigating motion blur during image capture [8]. In parallel, the emergence of IoT-enabled sensor networks has driven research on adaptive routing, data reliability, and energy efficiency, which are critical for real-time underwater monitoring and communication systems [9–11]. These studies explore strategies such as cross-layer optimization, secure data aggregation, and energy-aware routing to improve the dependability and scalability of sensor-based infrastructures [12–14], providing complementary insights into the broader landscape of underwater sensing and communication. Integrating underwater image restoration techniques with efficient IoT-based sensing systems represents a promising direction, enabling both high-quality perception and reliable data delivery in challenging underwater environments. Although such hardware-enhanced systems can yield superior image quality under controlled conditions, they are commonly constrained by practical limitations, including high cost, limited deployment flexibility, and susceptibility to failure in dynamic or harsh underwater environments. Consequently, there is a pressing need for software-based solutions that can adaptively enhance underwater images without relying on specialized equipment, offering greater practicality, scalability, and robustness in real-world applications.

### 2.2. Traditional Approach

Traditional approaches to underwater image enhancement typically rely on physical priors or hand-crafted models to address degradation caused by absorption, scattering, and turbidity [15]. Zhou et al. employed a modified underwater image formation model incorporating depth estimation and color correction to effectively mitigate the effects of light absorption and scattering [16]. Ma et al. proposed an improved Retinex-based variational model that integrates information entropy smoothing and non-uniform illumination priors, enabling effective handling of uneven lighting in underwater images [17]. Liu et al. introduced an illumination-constrained, structure-preserving Retinex model with adaptive channel compensation and joint estimation of illumination and reflection, demonstrating competitive performance on turbid underwater images in both subjective and objective evaluations [18]. Zhou et al. combine pixel distribution remapping with a Retinex variational model and noise-texture priors, achieving notable improvements in color correction and contrast enhancement [19].

Beyond physics-based models, some methods focus on enhancing images by improving contrast, correcting color, or reducing haze based on prior knowledge or statistical assumptions without explicitly modeling the underwater imaging process. Zhang et al. proposed a principal component fusion method (PCFB) that enhances underwater images by fusing contrast-enhanced foregrounds and dehazed backgrounds using principal component analysis [20]. Zhang et al. introduced a multi-channel adaptive fusion approach that addresses color distortion and contrast loss through adaptive channel correction and dual-branch enhancement [21]. To accommodate images across different color gamuts, Zhang et al. proposed the RAG-IMF method, which integrates global–local color correction and multi-channel fusion in both RGB and LAB color spaces, thereby extending color gamut and improving quality metrics [22]. Similarly, Jha et al. developed the CBLA method, which performs RGB-based color correction and LAB-based contrast and naturalness restoration for effective underwater enhancement [23]. To preserve fine details, recent works have also explored multi-scale representations and frequency-domain techniques, leading to more robust enhancement across a variety of underwater scenes [24,25].

While the above approaches offer strong interpretability, their performance tends to degrade in highly dynamic underwater environments, where the underlying model assumptions are frequently violated. As a result, they are generally less effective in handling complex, non-uniform degradations such as motion blur and spatially varying illumination.

### 2.3. Data-Driven Approach

With the rapid advancement of deep learning, data-driven approaches have emerged as a powerful alternative for UIE [26]. Unlike traditional methods, data-driven techniques can implicitly model complex nonlinear degradations and adapt to diverse underwater conditions through training on large-scale datasets. Xue et al. addressed the limitations of conventional color spaces by introducing a learnable Underwater Scenes Orient (USO) color space and a Scene-Adapted Semantic-Aggregated Degradation-Decoupling (S2D2) framework [27]. Park et al. proposed a lightweight enhancement framework based on an adaptive standardization and normalization network, which effectively corrects distorted feature distributions and improves image contrast and brightness, all while maintaining low computational complexity [28].

In parallel, Generative Adversarial Networks (GANs) [29,30], particularly diffusion models [31,32], have further improved the capacity of neural networks to learn complex mappings between degraded underwater images and their high-quality counterparts. These models have demonstrated significant improvements in addressing color distortion, motion blur, and low contrast [33,34]. The recent success of Transformers in computer vision has further accelerated progress in underwater image enhancement [35,36]. Their powerful global modeling capabilities and context-aware mechanisms significantly improve detail restoration and color correction, resulting in more natural and visually appealing enhancement outcomes. Yang et al. introduced a progressive aggregation framework that utilizes a feature-prompted Transformer, combining global-local attention with multi-scale feature aggregation, to enhance detail preservation, color fidelity, and blur removal [37]. Huang et al. proposed an underwater enhancement network incorporating a cross-wise Transformer module and a feature supplementation strategy to capture inter-stage dependencies and compensate for feature loss [38]. Moreover, techniques involving multi-domain feature extraction, physics-guided priors, and unsupervised learning have been actively explored to improve the perceptual and generalization abilities of enhancement networks [39–42].

Despite their promising results, data-driven methods also face notable limitations. Convolutional Neural Networks (CNNs) struggle to capture long-range dependencies due to their localized and static receptive fields. Although Transformers effectively address this issue, their high computational cost limits their practicality, especially for deployment on resource-constrained edge devices. GAN-based models, while exhibiting strong feature generation capabilities, often suffer from limited generalization across diverse underwater scenes. Furthermore, the aforementioned methods require large volumes of training data, yet datasets specifically addressing underwater blur remain scarce. Therefore, the models are prone to domain bias, making them less effective in handling complex and variable non-uniform underwater blurred images.

## 3. Methods

To address the challenges, we propose PMSPNet, a Progressive Multi-Scale Perception Network, as illustrated in Figure 2. The network incorporates a Hybrid Interaction Attention Module (HIAM) to capture local details and global contextual dependencies, enabling an initial coarse perception of image blur features. Building upon this, we introduce the Progressive Motion-Aware Perception Branch (PMAB) and the Progressive Feature Feedback Block (PFFB), which can incrementally guide and refine the network's perceptual capability, thereby achieving accurate localization and representation of non-uniform blur regions. Furthermore, to facilitate more realistic and comprehensive training and evaluation, we construct a dedicated Non-uniform Underwater Blur Dataset (N2UD), which encompasses a wide range of blur patterns encountered in real-world underwater environments.

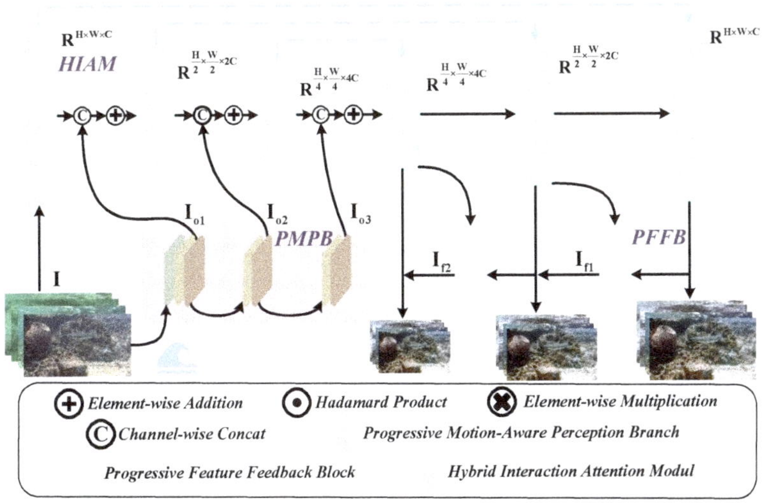


**Figure 2.** PMSPNet network architecture. Core components include the Hybrid Interaction Attention Module (HIAM), Progressive Motion-Aware Perception Branch (PMPB), and Progressive Feature Feedback Block (PFFB). The data come from the Non-uniform Underwater Blur Dataset (N2UD).

### 3.1. N2UD

To address the scarcity of underwater blur datasets, we constructed a specialized dataset by filtering an existing publicly available underwater image dataset. Specifically, we combined quantitative blur metrics with manual visual inspection to identify and select images exhibiting non-uniform blur. The resulting collection forms a new benchmark, termed the Non-uniform Underwater Blur Dataset (N2UD), which serves as a representative testbed for evaluating underwater deblurring algorithms under complex and realistic degradation conditions. As illustrated in Figure 3, N2UD includes underwater images affected by non-uniform blur across various resolutions and scenes, ensuring diversity and practical relevance.

**Figure 3.** The N2UD dataset, which contains various underwater environments and different degrees of non-uniform blur.

The quantitative blur metrics of which can be expressed as

$$\text{isBlurred} = \begin{cases} 1 & \delta_U + \delta_C + \delta_G + \delta_H > 1 \\ 0 & \text{otherwise} \end{cases}, \tag{1}$$

where $\delta_U$ denotes the underwater image sharpness measure, $\delta_C$ represents the global contrast level, $\delta_G$ is the mean image gradient, and $\delta_H$ corresponds to the high-frequency energy. When IsBlurred equals 1, it signifies that the image exhibits non-uniform blurring. The underwater image sharpness measure $\delta_U$ is defined as

$$\delta_U = \begin{cases} 1 & \frac{1}{k_1 k_2}\sum_{i=1}^{k_1}\sum_{j=1}^{k_2} 20 \cdot \log\left(\frac{I_{\max}^{(ij)}}{I_{\min}^{(ij)}+\epsilon}\right) < U_t \\ 0 & \text{otherwise} \end{cases}, \tag{2}$$

where the image is converted to the YUV color space and then partitioned into $k_1 \times k_2$ non-overlapping blocks; $I_{\max}^{(ij)}$ and $I_{\min}^{(ij)}$ represent the maximum and minimum luminance values, respectively, for the $(i,j)$th block; $\epsilon$ is a small constant ($10^{-6}$) to avoid division by zero; and $U_t$ is the corresponding threshold, set to 2.0. The $\delta_C$ is expressed as

$$\delta_C = \begin{cases} 1 & \frac{\sigma(\mathbf{I}_{\mathrm{LAB}}^{(l)})}{255} < C_t \\ 0 & \text{otherwise} \end{cases}, \tag{3}$$

where $\mathbf{I}_{\mathrm{LAB}}^{(l)}$ is the LAB color space of the input image $\mathbf{I}_{\mathrm{RGB}}$, $\sigma(\cdot)$ is the standard deviation, and $C_t$ is the corresponding threshold, set to 0.15. The $\delta_G$ is expressed as

$$\delta_G = \begin{cases} 1 & \frac{1}{N}\sum_{x=1}^{W}\sum_{y=1}^{H} \mathrm{M(x,y)} < G_t \\ 0 & \text{otherwise} \end{cases}, \tag{4}$$

where $N$ is the total number of pixels in the image; $W, H$ are the width and height of the image, respectively; and $G_t$ is the corresponding threshold, set to 15. The $\mathrm{M}(\cdot)$ is the gradient magnitude calculation for each pixel point, which is expressed as

$$\mathrm{M}(x,y) = \sqrt{\mathrm{G}_x(x,y)^2 + \mathrm{G}_y(x,y)^2}, \tag{5}$$

where $\mathrm{G}_x(\cdot,\cdot)$ and $\mathrm{G}_y(\cdot,\cdot)$ respectively perform Sobel filtering on the horizontal and vertical gradients of the grayscale image $\mathbf{I}_{\mathrm{gray}}$ of the original image $\mathbf{I}_{\mathrm{RGB}}$. The $\delta_H$ is expressed as

$$\delta_H = \begin{cases} 1 & \frac{\sum_{x=1}^{H}\sum_{y=1}^{W} |\mathrm{F_{HF}}(x,y)|}{\sum_{x=1}^{H}\sum_{y=1}^{W} |\mathrm{F}(x,y)|} < H_t \\ 0 & \text{otherwise} \end{cases}, \tag{6}$$

where $H_t$ is the corresponding threshold, set to 0.2. $\mathrm{F_{HF}}(\cdot)$ is expressed as

$$\mathrm{F_{HF}}(x,y) = \mathrm{F}(x,y) \cdot \mathrm{Mask(x,y)}, \tag{7}$$

where $\mathrm{F}(x,y)$ and $\mathrm{Mask(x,y)}$ are expressed as

$$\mathrm{F}(x,y) = \mathrm{FS}\left(\sum_{u=0}^{H-1}\sum_{v=0}^{W-1} \mathbf{I}_{\mathrm{gray}}(\mathrm{u,v}) \cdot \mathrm{e}^{-2\mathrm{ßi}\left(\frac{\mathrm{xu}}{\mathrm{H}}+\frac{\mathrm{yv}}{\mathrm{W}}\right)}\right), \tag{8}$$

$$\mathrm{Mask(x,y)} = \begin{cases} 0 & \sqrt{(x-c_u)^2 + (y-c_v)^2} \le r \\ 1 & \text{otherwise} \end{cases}, \tag{9}$$

where $\mathrm{FS}(\cdot)$ is a frequency shift that centers the zero-frequency (DC) component, and $\mathrm{Mask(x,y)} \in \{0,1\}^{H\times W}$ is a circular low-pass suppression mask centered at $(c_u, c_v) = (\frac{H}{2}, \frac{\mathrm{W}}{2})$, with radius $r = \frac{\min(\mathrm{H,W})}{4}$.

Considering that existing blur metrics may not fully capture the spatial variations of blur, we conducted manual visual inspections of each candidate image to refine the dataset. Based on evaluations by multiple experts specializing in visual perception, we retained only those images exhibiting noticeable non-uniform blur. This process ensures that the dataset accurately reflects the complex and spatially varying blur characteristics commonly observed in real-world underwater environments.

### *3.2. Hybrid Interaction Attention Module*

To enhance the network's capacity for deep feature extraction and precise localization of blurred regions in underwater scenes, we propose a Hybrid Interaction Attention Module (HIAM), as shown in Figure 4. Unlike traditional hybrid methods [43,44], HIAM, a cross-scale dual-channel design, utilizes an interactive cross-attention fusion dual-attention strategy for adaptive weighting control. This hybrid design enables collaborative modeling of localized blur features and global semantic structures, achieving coarse estimation of blurred feature extraction and localization.

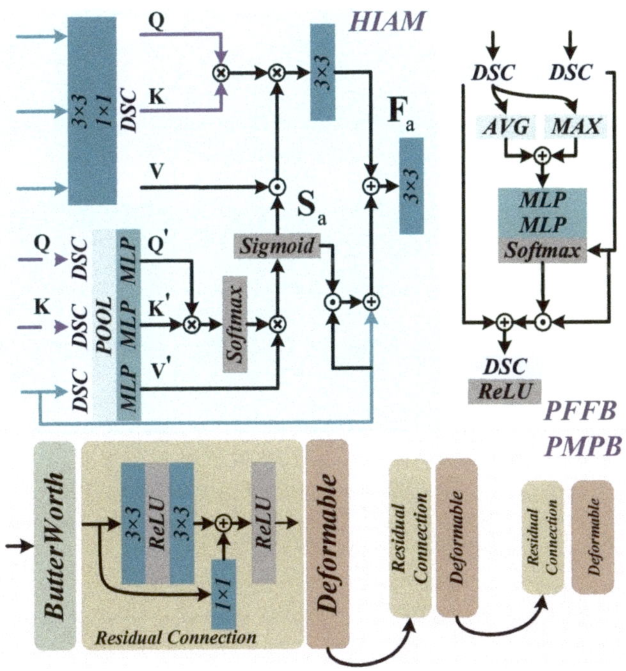


**Figure 4.** PMSPNet network components, including HIAM, PMPB, and PFFB.

Specifically, given an input feature $\mathbf{I} \in \mathbb{R}^{C\times H\times W}$, the process is represented as

$$\mathbf{F}_a = \mathrm{Conv}_{3\times 3}(\mathbf{L}_a(\mathbf{I}, \mathbf{S}_a) + \mathbf{G}_a(\mathbf{Q}^{'}, \mathbf{K}^{'}, \mathbf{I})), \tag{10}$$

where $\mathrm{Conv}_{3\times 3}(\cdot)$ indicates $3 \times 3$ convolution operation. The calculation process for other characters is as follows

Firstly, we obtain $\mathbf{Q}$, $\mathbf{K}$, and $\mathbf{V}$ as follows:

$$\mathbf{Q}, \mathbf{K}, \mathbf{V} = \mathrm{DSC}(\mathrm{Conv}_{1\times 1}(\mathrm{Conv}_{3\times 3}(\mathbf{I}, \mathbf{I}, \mathbf{I}))), \tag{11}$$

where $\mathrm{Conv}_{1\times 1}(\cdot)$ indicates $1 \times 1$ convolution operation, and $\mathrm{DSC}(\cdot)$ indicates depthwise separable convolution. Subsequently, $\mathbf{Q}^{'}$, $\mathbf{K}^{'}$, and $\mathbf{V}^{'}$ are obtained by

$$\mathbf{Q}^{'} = (\mathrm{P}_m(\mathrm{DSC}_q(\mathbf{Q})) + \mathrm{P}_a(\mathrm{DSC}_q(\mathbf{Q})))\mathbf{W}_Q, \tag{12}$$

$$\mathbf{K}^{'} = (\mathrm{P}_m(\mathrm{DSC}_k(\mathbf{K})) + \mathrm{P}_a(\mathrm{DSC}_k(\mathbf{K})))\mathbf{W}_K, \tag{13}$$

$$\mathbf{V}^{'} = (\mathrm{P}_m(\mathrm{DSC}_v(\mathbf{I})) + \mathrm{P}_a(\mathrm{DSC}_v(\mathbf{I})))\mathbf{W}_V, \tag{14}$$

where $\mathrm{P}_m(\cdot)$ and $\mathrm{P}_a(\cdot)$ are adaptive global max pooling and average pooling, and $\mathbf{W}_Q, \mathbf{W}_K, \mathbf{W}_V \in \mathbb{R}^{C\times d}$ are trainable matrices. $\mathbf{S}_a$ can be given by the following:

$$\mathbf{S}_a = \sigma_{\mathrm{sig}}(\sigma_{\mathrm{soft}}(\frac{\mathbf{Q}^{'}(\mathbf{K}^{'})^{\mathrm{T}}}{\sqrt{\mathbf{d}^{'}}})\mathbf{V}^{'}), \tag{15}$$

where $\sigma_{\mathrm{sig}}(\cdot)$ and $\sigma_{\mathrm{soft}}(\cdot)$ are Sigmoid and Softmax activation functions, and $\mathbf{d}^{'}$ is the dimension of the key vector. Thus, $\mathbf{L}_a(\mathbf{I}, \mathbf{S}_a)$ can be expressed as

$$\mathbf{L}_a(\mathbf{I}, \mathbf{S}_a) = \mathrm{Conv}_{3\times 3}(\frac{\mathbf{Q}(\mathbf{K})^{\mathrm{T}}}{\sqrt{\mathbf{d}}}(\mathbf{V} \odot \mathbf{S}_a)), \tag{16}$$

where $\odot$ is a pointwise multiplication operation. $\mathbf{G}_a(\mathbf{Q}^{'}, \mathbf{K}^{'}, \mathbf{I})$ can be expressed as

$$\mathbf{G}_a(\mathbf{Q}^{'}, \mathbf{K}^{'}, \mathbf{I}) = \mathbf{S}_a \odot \mathbf{I} + \mathbf{I}. \tag{17}$$

### 3.3. *Progressive Motion-Aware Perception Branch*

To further enhance the modeling of aware features in underwater non-uniform blur scenarios, we introduce a Progressive Motion-Aware Perception Branch (PMPB), as depicted in the lower part of Figure 4. This module progressively refines the localization of non-uniform blur features in a coarse-to-fine manner, thereby strengthening the network's multi-level perception of structural details.

Specifically, a two-dimensional Butterworth filter is applied to the input image to perform frequency adjustment. This operation amplifies the response of blurred regions across varying frequency components, improving the network's sensitivity to related features [45,46]. The filtering process is defined as

$$\mathbf{I}_{\mathrm{b}} = \mathrm{L2R}(\mathrm{Concat}(\mathcal{H}_{\mathrm{hf}}(\mathbf{L}), \mathbf{A}, \mathbf{B})), \tag{18}$$

where $\mathrm{L2R}(\cdot)$ converts the image from LAB to RGB color space; $\mathrm{Concat}(\cdot)$ is a channel splicing operation; and $\mathbf{L} = \mathbf{I}_{\mathrm{LAB}}^{(l)}$, $\mathbf{A} = \mathbf{I}_{\mathrm{LAB}}^{(a)}$, and $\mathbf{B} = \mathbf{I}_{\mathrm{LAB}}^{(b)}$ are the luminance and color channels in the LAB space, respectively. $\mathcal{H}_{\mathrm{hf}}(\cdot)$ represents high-frequency extraction operations, expressed as

$$\mathcal{H}_{\mathrm{hf}}(\mathbf{L}) = \Re(\tilde{\mathbf{L}}_{\mathrm{spatial}}), \tag{19}$$

where $\Re(\cdot)$ denotes the real part of a complex number. $\tilde{\mathbf{L}}_{\mathrm{spatial}}$ can be expressed as

$$\tilde{\mathbf{L}}_{\text{spatial}} = \mathcal{F}^{-1}(\tilde{\mathbf{L}}_s), \tag{20}$$

where $\mathcal{F}^{-1}\cdot$ is the inverse fast Fourier transform (IFFT). $\tilde{\mathbf{L}}_s$ can be expressed as

$$\tilde{\mathbf{L}}_s = \text{IS}(\tilde{\mathbf{L}}), \tag{21}$$

$$\tilde{\mathbf{L}} = \hat{\mathbf{L}} \cdot (1 - \mathbf{H}_{\text{bw}}), \tag{22}$$

where $\text{IS}(\cdot)$ indicates that the centralized spectrum diagram will be restored to its original layout. $\hat{\mathbf{L}} \in \mathbb{C}^{B\times 1\times H\times W}$ can be expressed as

$$\hat{\mathbf{L}} = \text{FS}(\mathcal{F}(\mathbf{L})), \tag{23}$$

where $\mathcal{F}(\cdot)$ is the fast Fourier transform (FFT).

The Butterworth filter $\mathbf{H}_{\text{bw}}$ is constructed as

$$\mathbf{H}_{\text{bw}}(u,v) = \frac{1}{1 + (\frac{D_0}{\sqrt{(u-\frac{H}{w})^2+(v-\frac{W}{2})^2+\epsilon}})^{2n}}, \tag{24}$$

where $D_0$ is the cutoff frequency, $n$ is the filter order, and $\epsilon$ is the anti-decimation constant, set to $10^{-6}$.

Subsequently, the frequency domain enhanced image $\mathbf{I_b}$ is subjected to initial feature extraction, which is denoted as

$$\mathbf{I_i} = \sigma_{\text{re}}(\text{Conv}_{1\times1}(\mathbf{I_b}) + \text{Conv}_{3\times3}(\sigma_{\text{re}}(\text{Conv}_{3\times3}(\mathbf{I_b})))), \tag{25}$$

where $\sigma_{\text{re}}(\cdot)$ is the ReLU activation function.

Finally, we introduce Deformable Convolution [47] to adaptively adjust the sampling position for more accurate perception and feature extraction of the non-uniform blur region, which is expressed as

$$\mathbf{I_o^{p_0}} = \sum_{k=1}^{K} \mathbf{w}_k \cdot (\sum_{q\in\mathcal{N}(p_0+\mathbf{p}_k+\triangle\mathbf{p}_k)} \text{G}(q, p_0 + \mathbf{p}_k + \triangle\mathbf{p}_k) \cdot \mathbf{I_i^q}), \tag{26}$$

where $\mathbf{I_o^{p_0}}$ is the value of the output feature map at position $p_0$; $\mathbf{w}_k$ is the weight of the $k$th position of the convolution kernel; $\mathcal{N}$ is a bilinear interpolating neighborhood; $\text{G}(q,\cdot)$ is the interpolated weight, satisfying $\sum_q \text{G}(q,\cdot) = 1$; $\mathbf{p}_k$ is the $k$th standard sampling offset in the convolution kernel; $\triangle\mathbf{p}_k$ is the learnable offset of the $k$th position; and $\mathbf{I_i^q}$ is the value of the input feature $\mathbf{I_i}$ at position $q$.

The fine features are fed into the backbone to provide it with feature guidance, which is expressed as

$$\mathbf{F_a} = \mathbf{I_o} + \text{Conv}_{3\times3}(\text{Concat}(\mathbf{F_a}, \mathbf{I_o})). \tag{27}$$

### 3.4. Progressive Feature Feedback Block

To achieve lossless extraction of hierarchical semantic features during reconstruction, we propose a Progressive Feature Feedback Block (PFFB), as illustrated in Figure 4. This module facilitates inter-layer information interaction by constructing a hierarchical feedback pathway, allowing recovered features from subsequent stages to guide and refine the representation learning in previous stages. The structure of the PFFB is represented as

$$\mathbf{F}_{\mathrm{f}} = \sigma_{\mathrm{re}}(\mathrm{DSC}_1(\mathbf{F}_{\mathrm{att}} + \mathbf{F}_m)), \tag{28}$$

where $\mathbf{F}_{\mathrm{att}}$ can be expressed as

$$\mathbf{F}_{\mathrm{att}} = \sigma_{\mathrm{soft}}(\mathrm{MLP}_{1,2}(\mathrm{P}_m(\mathbf{F}_m) + \mathrm{P}_m(\mathbf{F}_{\mathrm{m}}))) \odot \mathrm{DSC}_2(\mathbf{F}_{\mathrm{up}} + \mathbf{F}_{\mathrm{cu}}), \tag{29}$$

where $\mathbf{F}_m = \mathrm{DSC}_3(\mathbf{F}_{\mathrm{up}} + \mathbf{F}_{\mathrm{cu}})$, $\mathrm{MLP}_{1,2}(\cdot)$ is a multilayer perceptron, and $\mathbf{F}_{\mathrm{up}}$ and $\mathbf{F}_{\mathrm{cu}}$ are the previous and current level recovery features in the decoder, respectively.

*3.5. Loss Function*

To increase visual quality and perceptual fidelity of the restored image, we design a composite loss function that jointly enforces constraints on color accuracy, structural consistency, frequency response, and perceptual realism. This multi-objective formulation ensures that the restored images align closely with ground truth data and exhibit enhanced perceptual quality. The overall loss is defined as

$$\mathcal{L}_t = \mathcal{L}_{\mathrm{charb}} + \lambda_{\mathrm{fft}} \cdot \mathcal{L}_{\mathrm{fft}} + \lambda_{\mathrm{lab}} \cdot \mathcal{L}_{\mathrm{lab}} + \lambda_{\mathrm{lch}} \cdot \mathcal{L}_{\mathrm{lch}} + \mathcal{L}_{\mathrm{vgg}} + \mathcal{L}_{\mathrm{color}}, \tag{30}$$

where $\mathcal{L}_{\mathrm{charb}}$, $\mathcal{L}_{\mathrm{fft}}$, $\mathcal{L}_{\mathrm{lab}}$, $\mathcal{L}_{\mathrm{lch}}$, $\mathcal{L}_{\mathrm{vgg}}$, and $\mathcal{L}_{\mathrm{color}}$ are charbonnier loss, fast fourier transform loss, LAB color loss, LCH color loss, perceptual loss, and color constancy loss, respectively. $\lambda_{\mathrm{fft}}$, $\lambda_{\mathrm{lab}}$, and $\lambda_{\mathrm{lch}}$ are the corresponding weighting coefficients, set to $1 \times 10^{-1}$, $1 \times 10^{-6}$, and $1 \times 10^{-2}$, respectively. $\mathcal{L}_{\mathrm{charb}}$ is defined as

$$\mathcal{L}_{\mathrm{charb}}(x, y) = \frac{1}{N}\sum_{i=1}^{N}\sqrt{(x_i - y_i)^2 + \epsilon^2}, \tag{31}$$

where $x$ and $y$ are the predicted image and ground truth, and $N$ is the total number of pixels in the image. $\mathcal{L}_{\mathrm{fft}}$ is defined as

$$\mathcal{L}_{\mathrm{fft}}(x, y) = \|\mathcal{F}(x) - \mathcal{F}(y)\|_1, \tag{32}$$

where $||\cdot||_1$ is L1 loss. $\mathcal{L}_{\mathrm{lab}}$ is defined as

$$\mathcal{L}_{\mathrm{lab}}(x, y) = \mathcal{L}_{\mathrm{l}}(x, y) + \alpha \cdot \mathcal{L}_{\mathrm{ab}}(x, y), \tag{33}$$

where $\alpha$ is the weighting coefficient, set to 1. $\mathcal{L}_{\mathrm{l}}(\cdot)$ and $\mathcal{L}_{\mathrm{ab}}(\cdot)$ are the brightness and color channel loss in the LAB channel, defined as

$$\mathcal{L}_{\mathrm{l}}(x, y) = \frac{1}{N}\sum_{i=1}^{N}|L_x^{(i)} - L_y^{(i)}|, \tag{34}$$

$$\mathcal{L}_{\mathrm{ab}}(x, y) = \frac{1}{N}\sum_{i=1}^{N}\sum_{k=1}^{N} P_y^{(i,k)} \cdot \log(\frac{P_y^{(i,k)}}{P_x^{(i,k)} + \epsilon}) \approx -\frac{1}{N}\sum_{i=1}^{N}\sum_{k=1}^{N} P_y^{(i,k)} \cdot \log(P_x^{(i,k)} + \epsilon), \tag{35}$$

where $P_x^{(i,k)}$ and $P_y^{(i,k)}$ are the softmax weights for the $k$th bin at the $i$th pixel position of images $x$ and $y$. $\mathcal{L}_{\mathrm{lch}}$ is defined as

$$\mathcal{L}_{\mathrm{lch}} = \mathcal{L}_{\mathrm{ll}} + \mathcal{L}_{\mathrm{lc}} + \mathcal{L}_{\mathrm{lh}}, \tag{36}$$

where $\mathcal{L}_{\mathrm{ll}}$ and $\mathcal{L}_{\mathrm{lc}}$ represent brightness and chromaticity L1 loss (reference Equation (34)), and $\mathcal{L}_{\mathrm{lh}}$ represents hue distribution loss (reference Equation (35)) in LCH color space.

In addition, $\mathcal{L}_{\text{vgg}}$ utilizes the multi-scale features of the VGG19 network to measure the differences between the enhanced image and the reference image in the high-level semantic space. $\mathcal{L}_{\text{color}}$ achieves color balance consistency by minimizing the pairwise Euclidean distances between the $R$, $G$, and $B$ channels.

## 4. Experiments

### 4.1. Datasets

We train and evaluate the proposed network using the constructed N2UD dataset and compare its performance against state-of-the-art methods on N2UD and three publicly available underwater image enhancement benchmarks: EUVP [48], LSUI [49], and UIEB [50]. Additionally, to assess the practical benefits of the enhanced images in real-world scenarios, we conduct downstream task evaluations on the DUO dataset [51], demonstrating the model's effectiveness in supporting higher-level underwater vision tasks.

#### 4.1.1. N2UD

The N2UD dataset comprises 3201 real underwater image pairs, each consisting of a non-uniformly blurred image and its corresponding reference. Among these, 2246 pairs were used for training, 624 for testing, and 322 for validation. The dataset consists of several publicly available underwater image enhancement datasets. Using a combination of quantitative blur metrics with manual visual inspection, we screened high-quality non-uniform blur image pairs. Specifically, the dataset includes 555 images from the EUVP dataset, 2190 from the LSUI dataset, and 465 from the UIEB dataset. The selected images span a range of resolutions, from $256 \times 256$ to $1280 \times 720$, and diverse underwater environments and imaging conditions. The dataset is available at https://github.com/UI2025/N2UD, accessed on 28 August 2025.

#### 4.1.2. EUVP

The EUVP dataset is designed to support the enhancement of color and structural details in real-world underwater images. It employs multiple underwater sensors (GoPros, Aqua AUV's uEye cameras, low-light USB cameras, and Trident ROV's HD camera) to capture underwater images and conduct marine exploration and human-robot cooperative experiments in different locations under various visibility conditions. It contains both paired and unpaired collections of approximately 20,000 images, covering a broad spectrum of underwater environments, lighting conditions, and viewpoints. The dataset includes both real and synthetically degraded underwater images at various resolutions, making it suitable for training and evaluating deep learning-based underwater image enhancement models. The dataset is available at https://irvlab.cs.umn.edu/resources/euvp-dataset, accessed on 17 May 2025.

#### 4.1.3. LSUI

The LSUI dataset, filtered and screened based on various real underwater image data, is a large-scale collection of 4279 real-world underwater images captured across multiple scenes, including shallow waters, deep sea, coral reefs, and shipwrecks. It encompasses a wide variety of conditions in terms of lighting, water quality, and color degradation. LSUI emphasizes real data distributions and high scene complexity, making it well-suited for studying naturally occurring underwater degradations. The dataset is available at https://lintaopeng.github.io/_pages/UIE%20Project%20Page.html, accessed on 17 May 2025.

#### 4.1.4. UIEB

The UIEB dataset collects and processes underwater images on different platforms and includes private underwater shooting videos. It is one of the most widely used benchmarks in underwater image enhancement. It includes 890 real-world underwater images of varying resolutions, most of which have been enhanced by domain experts to form a high-quality paired dataset. It is commonly used for both subjective and objective evaluation of enhancement algorithms. In addition, UIEB includes a challenging subset, Challenging-60, comprising 60 challenging unpaired samples used to test algorithmic robustness under extreme conditions. The dataset is available at https://li-chongyi.github.io/proj_benchmark.html, accessed on 17 May 2025.

#### 4.1.5. DUO

The DUO dataset is a high-quality benchmark designed for underwater object detection (UOD) tasks. These data were obtained by collecting underwater images through underwater photography and labeling them, and they were used to study the perception decisions and sensor sensitivity issues of underwater robots. It contains 7782 images captured from diverse underwater environments, including shallow and deep water, turbid regions, and varied lighting conditions. The dataset features a wide array of target types, including starfish, sea urchins, and fish, along with substantial variation in scene structure, imaging quality, and target scale. All images are provided at a uniform resolution of $1920 \times 1080$, with 6671 images allocated for training and 1111 for testing. In this work, we utilize the trained enhancement model to augment the DUO dataset and perform downstream detection tasks, thereby validating the positive influence of our method on higher-level vision applications. The dataset is available at https://github.com/chongweiliu/DUO, accessed on 18 May 2025.

### 4.2. *Experimental Configuration*

#### 4.2.1. Implementation Details

The proposed network was implemented using the PyTorch 2.0.1 framework and trained on a Linux-based system equipped with a GeForce RTX 3090 GPU (24 GB), 250 GB of memory, and 80 Intel(R) Xeon(R) Gold 5218R processors (2.10 GHz). The training was performed using the Adam optimizer with an initial learning rate of $1 \times 10^{-4}$. A cosine learning rate scheduling strategy with a warm-up phase was employed, in which the learning rate was gradually increased during the first 10 epochs, after which it followed a cosine decay schedule. The network was trained for 200 epochs with a batch size of 8. To improve the model's robustness and generalization capability, standard data augmentation techniques such as random horizontal and vertical flipping were applied during training. To prevent overfitting and ensure stable convergence, an early stopping mechanism was employed, in which training was terminated if the validation loss failed to improve for 10 consecutive epochs. Furthermore, random seeds were fixed across all experiments to guarantee reproducibility of the reported results.

#### 4.2.2. Evaluation Metrics

To comprehensively assess the performance of the proposed method in restoring underwater images affected by non-uniform blur, we employed a diverse set of evaluation metrics covering full-reference, no-reference, perceptual, and sharpness-based aspects. For full-reference evaluation, we used the Peak Signal-to-Noise Ratio (PSNR), the Structural Similarity Index (SSIM), and the Feature Similarity Index (FSIM) to quantify pixel-level fidelity and structural consistency between the restored images and their ground-truth counterparts. To evaluate perceptual quality, we adopted LPIPS [52], which measures perceptual similarity using deep feature representations and aligns better with human visual perception.

For no-reference evaluation, we employed underwater-specific quality metrics, including UIQM [53] and UCIQE [54], to evaluate key visual attributes such as color fidelity, contrast, and clarity. Additionally, we introduced NIQE [55], a natural image quality evaluator, and URanker [56], a human preference-based perceptual scoring model, to further assess image naturalness and subjective quality. To evaluate the preservation of fine details and edge sharpness, we incorporated high-frequency sharpness metrics, including Laplacian variance, Tenengrad, and Brenner gradient, each capturing edge clarity and detail recovery from different computational perspectives.

The integration of these complementary metrics enables a comprehensive and objective evaluation of image enhancement performance, ensuring the model's robustness and practical applicability in real-world underwater scenarios and downstream tasks.

### 4.3. Performance Comparison

#### 4.3.1. N2UD

To comprehensively evaluate the effectiveness of the proposed method, we conducted extensive experiments on the constructed N2UD dataset using both full-reference and no-reference image quality assessment metrics. The results are presented in Tables 1 and 2.

**Table 1.** Comparison of performance on the N2UD dataset, where evaluation includes full-reference image quality metrics and resource consumption metrics. All results are reported in the format of mean ± standard deviation. ↑ indicates that a higher value is better, while ↓ indicates that a lower value is better.

| Methods | PSNR ↑ | SSIM ↑ | FSIM ↑ | LPIPS ↓ | Params (M) ↓ | FLOPs (G) ↓ | Time (s) ↓ |
|---|---|---|---|---|---|---|---|
| WFAC [25] | 15.73 ± 3.21 | 0.66 ± 0.14 | 0.77 ± 0.09 | 0.35 ± 0.10 | - | - | 0.38 |
| WWPF [57] | 17.48 ± 3.59 | ±0.73 ± 0.13 | 0.82 ± 0.07 | 0.28 ± 0.11 | - | - | 0.26 |
| HFM [58] | 17.31 ± 3.18 | 0.76 ± 0.11 | 0.88 ± 0.06 | 0.31 ± 0.14 | - | - | 0.53 |
| HLRP [59] | 12.80 ± 1.97 | 0.22 ± 0.07 | 0.64 ± 0.05 | 0.51 ± 0.08 | - | - | 0.01 |
| ACDC [60] | 16.63 ± 2.90 | 0.70 ± 0.12 | 0.82 ± 0.07 | 0.34 ± 0.11 | - | - | 0.22 |
| MMLE [61] | 17.80 ± 3.73 | 0.73 ± 0.12 | 0.82 ± 0.07 | 0.29 ± 0.11 | - | - | 0.08 |
| PCDE [62] | 15.40 ± 2.96 | 0.62 ± 0.14 | 0.75 ± 0.08 | 0.39 ± 0.11 | - | - | 0.29 |
| TEBCF [63] | 17.90 ± 2.30 | 0.69 ± 0.12 | 0.80 ± 0.08 | 0.30 ± 0.09 | - | - | 1.24 |
| CycleGAN [29] | 23.91 ± 4.72 | 0.83 ± 0.11 | 0.91 ± 0.05 | 0.24 ± 0.01 | 22.76 | 99.364 | 0.03 |
| U-Shape [49] | 24.32 ± 3.87 | 0.83 ± 0.11 | 0.92 ± 0.04 | 0.22 ± 0.06 | 31.59 | 26.10 | 0.05 |
| FUnIE-GAN [48] | 21.42 ± 3.49 | 0.79 ± 0.09 | 0.90 ± 0.04 | 0.28 ± 0.06 | 3.59 | 26.72 | 0.06 |
| Histoformer [64] | 13.96 ± 2.25 | 0.30 ± 0.14 | 0.64 ± 0.07 | 0.72 ± 0.07 | 25.71 | 44.42 | 0.03 |
| Phaseformer [65] | 24.13 ± 3.17 | 0.64 ± 0.11 | 0.93 ± 0.04 | 0.21 ± 0.09 | 1.78 | 14.12 | 0.03 |
| UIR-PolyKernel [66] | 22.19 ± 4.62 | 0.84 ± 0.09 | 0.92 ± 0.04 | 0.25 ± 0.09 | 1.89 | 13.68 | 0.01 |
| CCL-Net [67] | 23.81 ± 5.39 | 0.83 ± 0.20 | 0.91 ± 0.10 | 0.23 ± 0.16 | 0.55 | 37.36 | 0.06 |
| PUIE-Net [68] | 24.40 ± 3.78 | 0.91 ± 0.08 | 0.96 ± 0.04 | 0.17 ± 0.08 | 0.83 | 150.69 | 0.13 |
| USUIR [69] | 18.79 ± 2.86 | 0.79 ± 0.10 | 0.89 ± 0.04 | 0.32 ± 0.08 | 0.23 | 14.88 | 0.01 |
| SGUIE [70] | 24.13 ± 4.50 | 0.87 ± 0.09 | 0.93 ± 0.04 | 0.20 ± 0.08 | 18.63 | 20.16 | 0.02 |
| PMSPNet | 25.51 ± 3.98 | 0.92 ± 0.09 | 0.95 ± 0.04 | 0.19 ± 0.08 | 4.44 | 26.77 | 0.01 |

As shown in Table 1, traditional image processing methods exhibit generally poor performance across full-reference metrics. Specifically, their PSNR values typically fall below 18 dB, and LPIPS scores often exceed 0.3, indicating significant limitations in perceptual quality and visual fidelity. These methods struggle to adaptively model complex blur degradation, which severely limits their scalability in real-world applications. Furthermore, traditional methods are often computationally intensive and inefficient. Some require up to 1.24 s to process a single image, rendering them unsuitable for time-sensitive tasks. In contrast, deep learning-based UIE methods demonstrate more robust performance. GAN-based approaches offer modest improvements in some metrics. CycleGAN achieves relatively high SSIM (0.83 ± 0.11) and LPIPS (0.24 ± 0.01) compared to traditional methods. However, it exhibits considerable PSNR variance (±4.72), highlighting a lack of consistency and reliability in generative adversarial models. U-Shape, leveraging a multi-scale architecture, performs well across all full-reference metrics but still falls short of the performance achieved by PMSPNet. Among recently proposed Transformer-based methods, HistFormer suffers from mode collapse issues, leading to degraded performance across multiple metrics. Additionally, it incurs a high computational cost (44.42 GFLOPs) and slower inference speeds. PhaseFormer, in contrast, shows a more balanced performance. However, its relatively low SSIM indicates limitations in preserving structural integrity. PUIE-Net achieves favorable results across most metrics, yet its complexity is a concern, with computational overhead reaching 150.69 GFLOPs and inference time extending to 0.13 s per image. SGUIE performs well in FSIM and LPIPS, reflecting strengths in perceptual quality. Nonetheless, its overall effectiveness remains inferior when compared to PMSPNet. PMSPNet achieves superior performance in both objective metrics and computational efficiency, confirming its robustness and practical applicability for real-world underwater deblurring tasks.

**Table 2.** Comparison of performance on the N2UD dataset, where evaluation is based on no-reference image quality metrics. All results are reported in the format of mean ± standard deviation. ↑ indicates that a higher value is better, while ↓ indicates that a lower value is better.

| Methods | UIQM ↑ | UCIQE ↑ | NIQE ↓ | URANKER ↑ | Laplacian ↑ | Tenengrad ↑ | Brenner ↑ |
|---|---|---|---|---|---|---|---|
| WFAC [25] | 3.16 ± 0.33 | 0.42 ± 0.02 | 6.02 ± 3.46 | 2.49 ± 0.89 | 0.11 ± 0.18 | 0.53 ± 0.23 | 2044.20 ± 1559.13 |
| WWPF [57] | 2.85 ± 0.40 | 0.44 ± 0.04 | 5.43 ± 2.20 | 2.50 ± 0.741 | 0.05 ± 0.08 | 0.44 ± 0.17 | 1291.93 ± 911.55 |
| HFM [58] | 2.91 ± 0.37 | 0.47 ± 0.03 | 5.49 ± 2.02 | 2.35 ± 0.81 | 0.02 ± 0.06 | 0.31 ± 0.14 | 662.62 ± 639.15 |
| HLRP [59] | 2.62 ± 0.67 | 0.49 ± 0.07 | 5.78 ± 2.25 | 1.69 ± 0.96 | 0.03 ± 0.03 | 0.39 ± 0.09 | 1016.97 ± 489.98 |
| ACDC [60] | 3.34 ± 0.20 | 0.38 ± 0.03 | 5.24 ± 1.78 | 2.68 ± 0.76 | 0.04 ± 0.08 | 0.42 ± 0.15 | 990.85 ± 790.32 |
| MMLE [61] | 2.77 ± 0.41 | 0.44 ± 0.04 | 5.56 ± 2.42 | 2.53 ± 0.86 | 0.07 ± 0.10 | 0.46 ± 0.19 | 1504.57 ± 1072.266 |
| PCDE [62] | 2.66 ± 0.68 | 0.46 ± 0.03 | 5.50 ± 1.98 | 2.59 ± 0.74 | 0.06 ± 0.08 | 0.50 ± 0.17 | 1671.21 ± 995.43 |
| TEBCF [63] | 3.00 ± 0.35 | 0.45 ± 0.02 | 5.60 ± 1.75 | 2.42 ± 0.69 | 0.049 ± 0.07 | 0.46 ± 0.14 | 1274.67 ± 699.73 |
| CycleGAN [29] | 3.19 ± 0.42 | 0.41 ± 0.06 | 4.62 ± 1.30 | 1.50 ± 0.81 | 0.01 ± 0.01 | 0.26 ± 0.10 | 448.48 ± 291.55 |
| U-Shape [49] | 3.10 ± 0.46 | 0.38 ± 0.05 | 5.05 ± 1.37 | 1.35 ± 0.74 | 0.01 ± 0.01 | 0.22 ± 0.09 | 313.03 ± 202.13 |
| FUnIE-GAN [48] | 3.10 ± 0.43 | 0.43 ± 0.05 | 4.17 ± 0.90 | 1.80 ± 0.78 | 0.02 ± 0.02 | 0.30 ± 0.14 | 607.95 ± 504.67 |
| Histoformer [64] | 3.09 ± 0.27 | 0.31 ± 0.04 | 12.00 ± 3.09 | 0.74 ± 0.54 | 0.01 ± 0.01 | 0.12 ± 0.04 | 99.17 ± 76.09 |
| Phaseformer [65] | 2.77 ± 0.39 | 0.43 ± 0.06 | 7.75 ± 6.61 | 1.26 ± 0.79 | 0.02 ± 0.03 | 0.24 ± 0.10 | 399.73 ± 353.68 |
| UIR-PolyKernel [66] | 2.91 ± 0.62 | 0.38 ± 0.07 | 5.09 ± 1.38 | 1.18 ± 0.99 | 0.01 ± 0.02 | 0.24 ± 0.13 | 435.62 ± 447.07 |
| CCL-Net [67] | 3.03 ± 0.48 | 0.41 ± 0.06 | 5.56 ± 2.05 | 1.46 ± 0.76 | 0.02 ± 0.03 | 0.26 ± 0.11 | 488.43 ± 408.52 |
| PUIE-Net [68] | 3.00 ± 0.51 | 0.40 ± 0.06 | 5.55 ± 1.85 | 1.42 ± 0.85 | 0.02 ± 0.02 | 0.25 ± 0.11 | 430.14 ± 375.36 |
| USUIR [69] | 2.96 ± 0.30 | 0.46 ± 0.03 | 4.80 ± 1.15 | 1.51 ± 0.82 | 0.01 ± 0.01 | 0.29 ± 0.11 | 528.35 ± 372.24 |
| SGUIE [70] | 2.96 ± 0.56 | 0.38 ± 0.07 | 5.46 ± 1.52 | 1.31 ± 0.90 | 0.01 ± 0.02 | 0.22 ± 0.11 | 350.12 ± 326.33 |
| PMSPNet | 3.46 ± 0.41 | 0.46 ± 0.06 | 5.30 ± 1.61 | 1.73 ± 0.79 | 0.01 ± 0.01 | 0.22 ± 0.09 | 319.80 ± 254.67 |

As shown in the no-reference image quality evaluation results in Table 2, although some methods perform reasonably well on individual metrics, a noticeable gap remains in overall quality. Notably, PMSPNet consistently leads across multiple perceptual quality metrics, such as UIQM and UCIQE, indicating that its enhanced images exhibit more natural color, clarity, and contrast, aligning well with human visual preferences. Interestingly, some traditional methods achieve higher scores on sharpness-based metrics, such as Tenengrad and Brenner. This contrasts with their overall inferior performance on full-reference and other no-reference metrics. The root cause of this "contradiction" is that many current reference-free metrics capture only specific local attributes, failing to reflect comprehensive image quality or perceptual realism.

The vision comparisons in Figure 5 further support this conclusion. While traditional methods can enhance local edge sharpness, they often suffer from over-sharpening, resulting in structural distortions, unnatural textures, or even pattern collapse, leading to a visually unrealistic "pseudo-enhancement" effect. In contrast, deep learning-based methods leverage strong feature representation and adaptive learning to restore degraded details more comprehensively. By capturing complex, non-uniform blur patterns across multiple scales and dimensions, PMSPNet achieves accurate regional restoration while preserving structural clarity and avoiding artifacts. This results in improved naturalness, semantic consistency, and stronger generalization in real-world conditions.

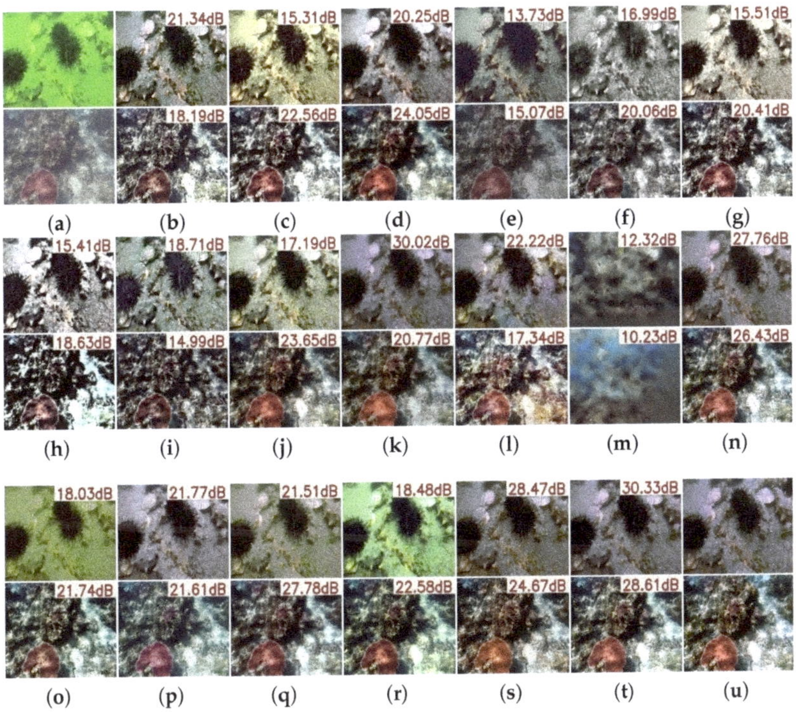


**Figure 5.** Visual comparison on the N2UD dataset, with the PSNR value of the image shown in the upper-right corner of the image. (**a**) Raw images. (**b**) WFAC [25]. (**c**) WWPF [57]. (**d**) HFM [58]. (**e**) HLRP [59]. (**f**) ACDC [60]. (**g**) MMLE [61]. (**h**) PCDE [62]. (**i**) TEBCF [63]. (**j**) CycleGAN [29]. (**k**) U-Shape [49]. (**l**) FUnIE-GAN [48]. (**m**) Histoformer [64]. (**n**) Phaseformer [65]. (**o**) UIR-PolyKernel [66]. (**p**) CCL-Net [67]. (**q**) PUIE-Net [68]. (**r**) USUIR [69]. (**s**) SGUIE [70]. (**t**) PMSPNet. (**u**) Ground Truth.

To further validate model robustness, Figure 6 presents the statistical distribution of three representative full-reference metrics. Traditional methods exhibit low and tightly clustered scores, indicating limited and inconsistent enhancement. Deep learning-based methods perform better overall. PMSPNet shows the highest median and maximum values, especially exceeding 35 dB in PSNR, and maintains stable, high distributions in SSIM and FSIM. The low dispersion of PMSPNet scores reflects its adaptability across various scenes, attributed to its hybrid interaction attention and progressive motion-aware modules, which jointly enhance spatially non-uniform blur modeling and semantic detail recovery.

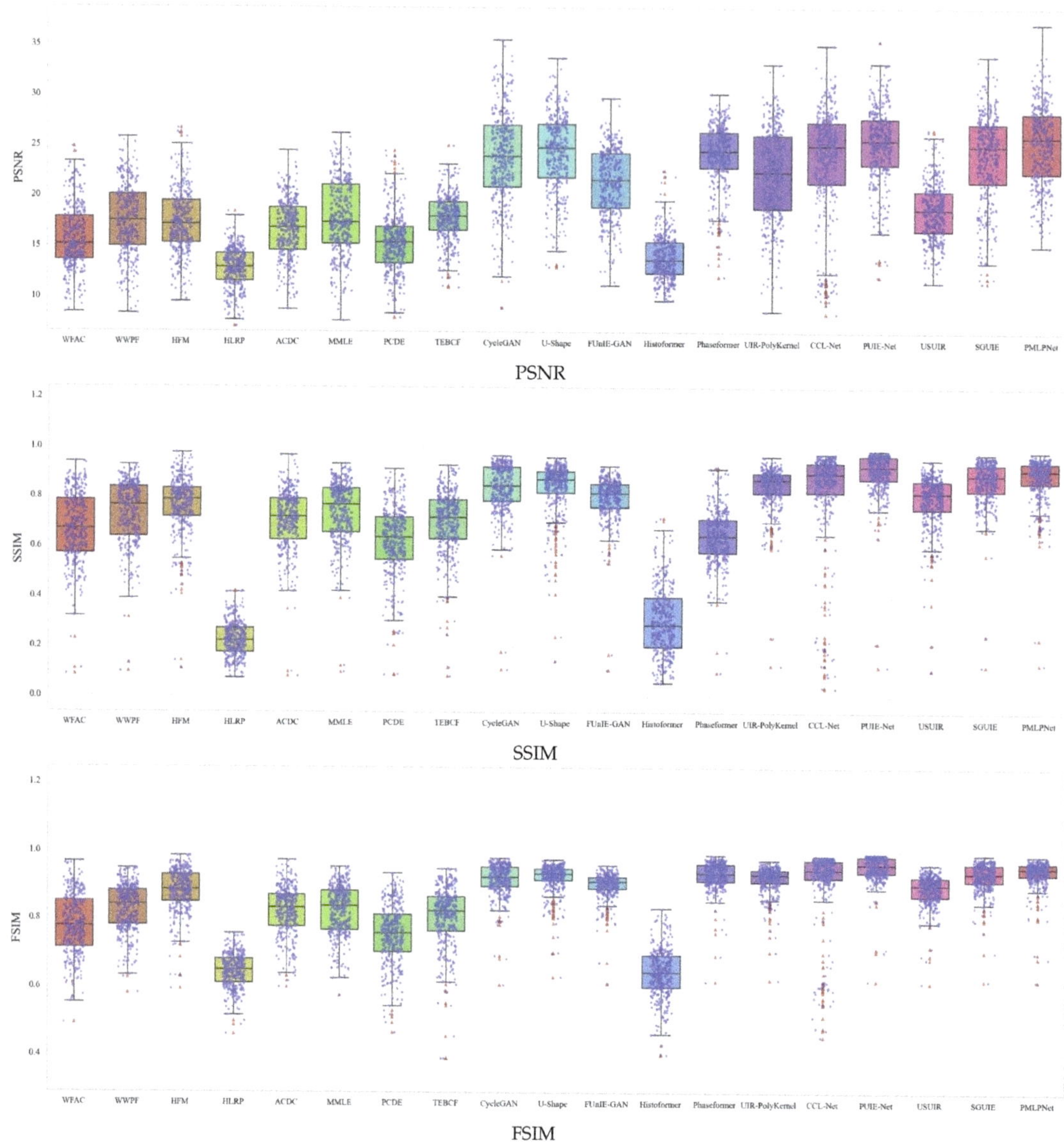


**Figure 6.** Box plot comparison of PSNR, SSIM, and FSIM on the N2UD dataset.

### 4.3.2. EUVP

To further assess the generalization capability of the proposed network, we evaluated pre-trained models on the EUVP dataset. As shown in Table 3, PMSPNet achieves the best performance across nearly all full-reference metrics, including PSNR (25.81), SSIM (0.85), and FSIM (0.94), and the lowest LPIPS (0.21), demonstrating superior fidelity and perceptual quality. In no-reference perceptual assessments, PMSPNet remains competitive, achieving a UIQM of 3.09, a UCIQE of 0.36, and a URanker of 1.16, consistently outperforming some existing methods.

**Table 3.** Comparison of performance on the EUVP dataset, where evaluation includes full-reference and no-reference image quality metrics. All results are reported in the format of mean ± standard deviation. ↑ indicates that a higher value is better, while ↓ indicates that a lower value is better.

| Methods | PSNR ↑ | SSIM ↑ | FSIM ↑ | LPIPS ↓ | UIQM ↑ | UCIQE ↑ | URANKER ↑ |
|---|---|---|---|---|---|---|---|
| WFAC [25] | 13.24 ± 2.43 | 0.54 ± 0.10 | 0.68 ± 0.07 | 0.45 ± 0.10 | 2.81 ± 0.26 | 0.43 ± 0.02 | 2.97 ± 0.90 |
| WWPF [57] | 14.62 ± 2.83 | 0.60 ± 0.10 | 0.75 ± 0.05 | 0.39 ± 0.09 | 2.68 ± 0.33 | 0.45 ± 0.04 | 2.16 ± 0.81 |
| HFM [58] | 15.13 ± 2.74 | 0.66 ± 0.10 | 0.82 ± 0.04 | 0.44 ± 0.11 | 2.93 ± 0.25 | 0.49 ± 0.03 | 2.44 ± 0.99 |
| HLRP [59] | 11.41 ± 1.86 | 0.17 ± 0.06 | 0.61 ± 0.04 | 0.60 ± 0.06 | 2.65 ± 0.59 | 0.50 ± 0.06 | 2.09 ± 0.99 |
| ACDC [60] | 14.42 ± 2.61 | 0.60 ± 0.10 | 0.75 ± 0.07 | 0.46 ± 0.09 | 3.34 ± 0.15 | 0.38 ± 0.03 | 2.98 ± 0.81 |
| MMLE [61] | 14.12 ± 2.69 | 0.59 ± 0.09 | 0.72 ± 0.06 | 0.41 ± 0.10 | 2.56 ± 0.31 | 0.45 ± 0.04 | 2.78 ± 0.98 |
| PCDE [62] | 13.55 ± 2.48 | 0.52 ± 0.13 | 0.68 ± 0.08 | 0.47 ± 0.11 | 2.37 ± 0.56 | 0.47 ± 0.02 | 2.97 ± 0.80 |
| TEBCF [63] | 17.07 ± 2.55 | 0.68 ± 0.09 | 0.79 ± 0.07 | 0.35 ± 0.07 | 2.82 ± 0.36 | 0.45 ± 0.03 | 2.59 ± 0.81 |
| CycleGAN [29] | 22.68 ± 3.52 | 0.79 ± 0.07 | 0.89 ± 0.04 | 0.29 ± 0.06 | 3.11 ± 0.50 | 0.40 ± 0.06 | 1.30 ± 0.85 |
| U-Shape [49] | 24.92 ± 3.78 | 0.83 ± 0.07 | 0.93 ± 0.02 | 0.23 ± 0.05 | 2.97 ± 0.62 | 0.38 ± 0.05 | 1.18 ± 0.84 |
| FUnIE-GAN [48] | 24.06 ± 2.60 | 0.79 ± 0.05 | 0.90 ± 0.02 | 0.27 ± 0.04 | 2.88 ± 0.57 | 0.41 ± 0.05 | 1.36 ± 0.82 |
| Histoformer [64] | 14.82 ± 2.88 | 0.33 ± 0.14 | 0.65 ± 0.07 | 0.71 ± 0.08 | 3.12 ± 0.23 | 0.30 ± 0.04 | 0.80 ± 0.50 |
| Phaseformer [65] | 23.58 ± 2.64 | 0.61 ± 0.07 | 0.91 ± 0.02 | 0.27 ± 0.06 | 2.63 ± 0.51 | 0.40 ± 0.05 | 0.98 ± 0.81 |
| UIR-PolyKernel [66] | 24.92 ± 3.86 | 0.87 ± 0.05 | 0.93 ± 0.02 | 0.22 ± 0.04 | 2.85 ± 0.74 | 0.40 ± 0.06 | 1.37 ± 0.90 |
| CCL-Net [67] | 24.55 ± 3.17 | 0.84 ± 0.07 | 0.93 ± 0.02 | 0.23 ± 0.04 | 2.97 ± 0.60 | 0.38 ± 0.06 | 1.34 ± 0.80 |
| PUIE-Net [68] | 24.71 ± 2.70 | 0.85 ± 0.06 | 0.93 ± 0.02 | 0.20 ± 0.04 | 2.97 ± 0.61 | 0.37 ± 0.06 | 1.12 ± 0.76 |
| USUIR [69] | 17.53 ± 2.47 | 0.73 ± 0.08 | 0.86 ± 0.03 | 0.35 ± 0.08 | 2.82 ± 0.22 | 0.47 ± 0.04 | 1.78 ± 0.89 |
| SGUIE [70] | 25.48 ± 3.23 | 0.84 ± 0.06 | 0.92 ± 0.03 | 0.24 ± 0.05 | 2.83 ± 0.71 | 0.38 ± 0.06 | 1.12 ± 0.87 |
| PMSPNet | 25.81 ± 3.22 | 0.85 ± 0.07 | 0.94 ± 0.02 | 0.21 ± 0.04 | 3.09 ± 0.46 | 0.36 ± 0.05 | 1.16 ± 0.78 |

As illustrated in Figure 7, visual comparisons further substantiate PMSPNet's advantages. Compared to prior methods, PMSPNet produces images with sharper edges, more natural color reproduction, and enhanced contrast. Traditional methods such as HLRP, ACDC, and MMLE suffer from color shifts, amplified noise, or loss of structural detail. Although deep learning methods like CycleGAN and U-Shape show improved enhancement, they still exhibit color deviations or insufficient deblurring in complex scenes. In contrast, PMSPNet effectively restores clarity and color fidelity even under severe degradation, delivering results that are perceptually closest to the ground truth.

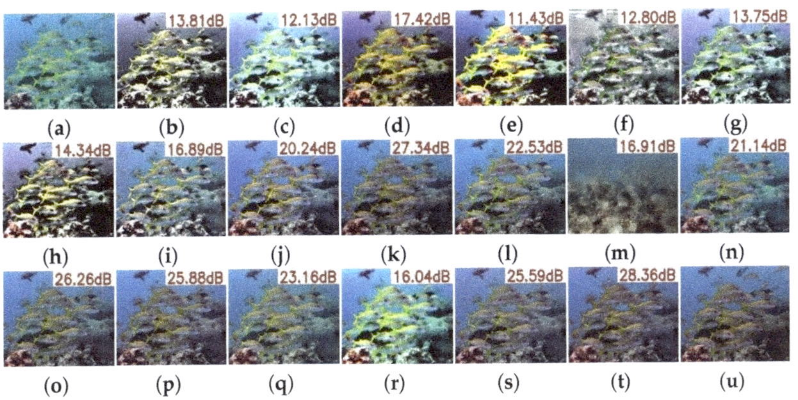

**Figure 7.** Visual comparison on the EUVP dataset, with the PSNR value of the image shown in the upper-right corner of the image. (**a**) Raw image. (**b**) WFAC [25]. (**c**) WWPF [57]. (**d**) HFM [58]. (**e**) HLRP [59]. (**f**) ACDC [60]. (**g**) MMLE [61]. (**h**) PCDE [62]. (**i**) TEBCF [63]. (**j**) CycleGAN [29]. (**k**) U Shape [49]. (**l**) FUnIE-GAN [48]. (**m**) Histoformer [64]. (**n**) Phaseformer [65]. (**o**) UIR-PolyKernel [66]. (**p**) CCL-Net [67]. (**q**) PUIE-Net [68]. (**r**) USUIR [69]. (**s**) SGUIE[70]. (**t**) PMSPNet. (**u**) Ground Truth.

#### 4.3.3. LSUI

Table 4 presents the evaluation results on the LSUI dataset. PMSPNet achieves the highest scores across key full-reference metrics, along with the lowest LPIPS, indicating superior fidelity and perceptual quality in the restored images. In the no-reference evaluation, PMSPNet also ranks first in UIQM and second in UCIQE, further demonstrating its effectiveness in enhancing visual quality. In contrast, traditional methods and other deep learning-based approaches show reduced performance across most metrics due to their limited capacity to manage complex color degradation and structural blurring prevalent in underwater environments.

**Table 4.** Comparison of performance on the LSUI dataset, where evaluation includes full-reference and no-reference image quality metrics. All results are reported in the format of mean ± standard deviation. ↑ indicates that a higher value is better, while ↓ indicates that a lower value is better.

| Methods | PSNR ↑ | SSIM ↑ | FSIM ↑ | LPIPS ↓ | UIQM ↑ | UCIQE ↑ | URANKER ↑ |
|---|---|---|---|---|---|---|---|
| WFAC [25] | 15.35 ± 3.09 | 0.61 ± 0.14 | 0.73 ± 0.09 | 0.37 ± 0.08 | 2.76 ± 0.45 | 0.43 ± 0.02 | 2.55 ± 0.84 |
| WWPF [57] | 17.51 ± 3.44 | 0.70 ± 0.12 | 0.81 ± 0.06 | 0.30 ± 0.08 | 2.76 ± 0.41 | 0.45 ± 0.05 | 2.59 ± 0.65 |
| HFM [58] | 17.63 ± 2.93 | 0.74 ± 0.11 | 0.87 ± 0.06 | 0.33 ± 0.11 | 2.80 ± 0.31 | 0.47 ± 0.03 | 2.41 ± 0.73 |
| HLRP [59] | 13.04 ± 1.87 | 0.22 ± 0.08 | 0.64 ± 0.04 | 0.55 ± 0.05 | 2.80 ± 0.58 | 0.47 ± 0.09 | 1.65 ± 0.88 |
| ACDC [60] | 16.96 ± 2.63 | 0.71 ± 0.12 | 0.82 ± 0.06 | 0.33 ± 0.10 | 3.34 ± 0.18 | 0.38 ± 0.03 | 2.63 ± 0.72 |
| MMLE [61] | 17.59 ± 3.15 | 0.69 ± 0.11 | 0.79 ± 0.06 | 0.31 ± 0.08 | 2.55 ± 0.44 | 0.45 ± 0.04 | 2.59 ± 0.80 |
| PCDE [62] | 15.25 ± 2.30 | 0.59 ± 0.11 | 0.73 ± 0.07 | 0.40 ± 0.09 | 2.32 ± 0.57 | 0.47 ± 0.03 | 2.75 ± 0.69 |
| TEBCF [63] | 17.95 ± 2.05 | 0.68 ± 0.12 | 0.80 ± 0.08 | 0.31 ± 0.08 | 2.93 ± 0.33 | 0.45 ± 0.03 | 2.58 ± 0.64 |
| CycleGAN [29] | 24.93 ± 4.32 | 0.85 ± 0.11 | 0.92 ± 0.05 | 0.23 ± 0.09 | 3.21 ± 0.37 | 0.42 ± 0.06 | 1.63 ± 0.71 |
| U-Shape [49] | 24.94 ± 3.54 | 0.84 ± 0.11 | 0.92 ± 0.04 | 0.22 ± 0.07 | 3.10 ± 0.41 | 0.39 ± 0.05 | 1.38 ± 0.61 |
| FUnIE-GAN [48] | 21.47 ± 3.32 | 0.80 ± 0.10 | 0.90 ± 0.04 | 0.28 ± 0.06 | 3.09 ± 0.38 | 0.43 ± 0.05 | 1.84 ± 0.64 |
| Histoformer [64] | 14.05 ± 2.04 | 0.31 ± 0.14 | 0.65 ± 0.07 | 0.72 ± 0.07 | 3.07 ± 0.28 | 0.31 ± 0.04 | 0.70 ± 0.56 |
| Phaseformer [65] | 24.64 ± 3.14 | 0.64 ± 0.11 | 0.93 ± 0.04 | 0.20 ± 0.09 | 2.79 ± 0.33 | 0.44 ± 0.06 | 1.29 ± 0.70 |
| UIR-PolyKernel [66] | 22.22 ± 4.20 | 0.84 ± 0.09 | 0.92 ± 0.04 | 0.26 ± 0.09 | 2.91 ± 0.54 | 0.38 ± 0.07 | 1.16 ± 0.90 |
| CCL-Net [67] | 25.15 ± 4.45 | 0.87 ± 0.15 | 0.94 ± 0.08 | 0.19 ± 0.12 | 3.02 ± 0.43 | 0.41 ± 0.06 | 1.52 ± 0.67 |
| PUIE-Net [68] | 26.21 ± 3.63 | 0.90 ± 0.09 | 0.95 ± 0.04 | 0.18 ± 0.08 | 3.06 ± 0.44 | 0.39 ± 0.06 | 1.39 ± 0.65 |
| USUIR [69] | 18.86 ± 2.74 | 0.80 ± 0.11 | 0.89 ± 0.04 | 0.33 ± 0.08 | 2.96 ± 0.29 | 0.45 ± 0.04 | 1.44 ± 0.75 |
| SGUIE [70] | 24.59 ± 4.40 | 0.87 ± 0.10 | 0.93 ± 0.04 | 0.19 ± 0.08 | 2.96 ± 0.49 | 0.39 ± 0.07 | 1.37 ± 0.78 |
| PMSPNet | 26.46 ± 3.91 | 0.92 ± 0.09 | 0.96 ± 0.03 | 0.13 ± 0.07 | 3.31 ± 0.38 | 0.45 ± 0.06 | 1.51 ± 0.70 |

The visual results in Figure 8 further highlight the advantages of PMSPNet. Traditional algorithms often leave residual blur or introduce significant color distortions. While learning-based models such as U-Shape and CCL-Net show improved results, they still suffer from over-smoothing and color shifts, particularly in fine details. In comparison, PMSPNet effectively recovers key textures, preserves natural color tones, and enhances contrast, producing visually more realistic and aesthetically pleasing results.

#### 4.3.4. UIEB

The UIEB dataset presents a broad spectrum of underwater imaging challenges, including severe color distortion, low contrast, and complex lighting conditions. As shown in Table 5, PMSPNet outperforms most compared methods across full-reference and no-reference metrics. Specifically, it achieves a PSNR of 22.43 dB, SSIM of 0.86, and a low LPIPS of 0.21, reflecting strong reconstruction accuracy and perceptual similarity. While methods like CCL-Net and SGUIE yield competitive results, their higher variance in metrics such as URanker and UIQM suggests inconsistent performance. In contrast, PMSPNet delivers high-quality results, demonstrating robustness across varying underwater degradation types.

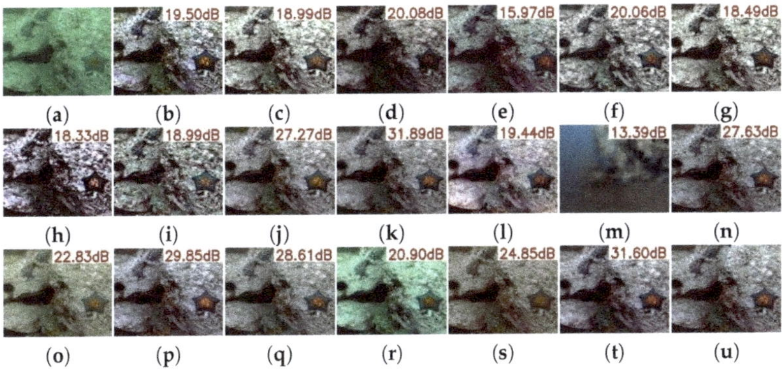


**Figure 8.** Visual comparison on the LSUI dataset, with the PSNR value of the image shown in the upper-right corner of the image. (**a**) Raw image. (**b**) WFAC [25]. (**c**) WWPF [57]. (**d**) HFM [58]. (**e**) HLRP [59]. (**f**) ACDC [60]. (**g**) MMLE [61]. (**h**) PCDE [62]. (**i**) TEBCF [63]. (**j**) CycleGAN [29]. (**k**) U-Shape [49]. (**l**) FUnIE-GAN [48]. (**m**) Histoformer [64]. (**n**) Phaseformer [65]. (**o**) UIR-PolyKernel [66]. (**p**) CCL-Net [67]. (**q**) PUIE-Net [68]. (**r**) USUIR [69]. (**s**) SGUIE [70]. (**t**) PMSPNet. (**u**) Ground Truth.

**Table 5.** Comparison of performance on the UIEB dataset, where evaluation includes full-reference and no-reference image quality metrics. All results are reported in the format of mean ± standard deviation. ↑ indicates that a higher value is better, while ↓ indicates that a lower value is better.

| Methods | PSNR ↑ | SSIM ↑ | FSIM ↑ | LPIPS ↓ | UIQM ↑ | UCIQE ↑ | URANKER ↑ |
|---|---|---|---|---|---|---|---|
| WFAC [25] | 15.39 ± 2.25 | 0.66 ± 0.13 | 0.74 ± 0.10 | 0.35 ± 0.11 | 2.79 ± 0.52 | 0.43 ± 0.02 | 2.39 ± 0.79 |
| WWPF [57] | 17.52 ± 2.71 | 0.76 ± 0.10 | 0.84 ± 0.08 | 0.25 ± 0.11 | 2.75 ± 0.54 | 0.44 ± 0.04 | 2.54 ± 0.89 |
| HFM [58] | 17.76 ± 3.44 | 0.79 ± 0.11 | 0.89 ± 0.07 | 0.26 ± 0.14 | 2.93 ± 0.52 | 0.47 ± 0.03 | 2.33 ± 0.98 |
| HLRP [59] | 13.33 ± 1.58 | 0.19 ± 0.07 | 0.64 ± 0.04 | 0.55 ± 0.07 | 3.10 ± 0.67 | 0.43 ± 0.09 | 1.46 ± 0.88 |
| ACDC [60] | 17.70 ± 3.20 | 0.78 ± 0.10 | 0.86 ± 0.08 | 0.27 ± 0.12 | 3.39 ± 0.35 | 0.38 ± 0.02 | 2.57 ± 0.85 |
| MMLE [61] | 17.35 ± 2.91 | 0.73 ± 0.11 | 0.80 ± 0.08 | 0.29 ± 0.11 | 2.46 ± 0.57 | 0.45 ± 0.04 | 2.56 ± 0.96 |
| PCDE [62] | 15.20 ± 3.67 | 0.61 ± 0.19 | 0.75 ± 0.12 | 0.38 ± 0.13 | 2.27 ± 0.94 | 0.44 ± 0.02 | 2.69 ± 0.81 |
| TEBCF [63] | 17.68 ± 2.51 | 0.76 ± 0.13 | 0.84 ± 0.11 | 0.25 ± 0.10 | 2.84 ± 0.38 | 0.46 ± 0.03 | 2.60 ± 0.87 |
| CycleGAN [29] | 19.44 ± 4.28 | 0.77 ± 0.10 | 0.88 ± 0.06 | 0.27 ± 0.09 | 3.19 ± 0.50 | 0.40 ± 0.06 | 1.15 ± 1.02 |
| U-Shape [49] | 20.72 ± 3.59 | 0.81 ± 0.10 | 0.89 ± 0.06 | 0.21 ± 0.07 | 3.25 ± 0.43 | 0.37 ± 0.05 | 1.39 ± 1.09 |
| FUnIE-GAN [48] | 18.02 ± 2.10 | 0.76 ± 0.07 | 0.88 ± 0.04 | 0.29 ± 0.08 | 3.42 ± 0.21 | 0.43 ± 0.05 | 2.09 ± 1.06 |
| Histoformer [64] | 12.50 ± 1.62 | 0.23 ± 0.13 | 0.59 ± 0.09 | 0.73 ± 0.05 | 3.15 ± 0.22 | 0.32 ± 0.04 | 0.80 ± 0.47 |
| Phaseformer [65] | 22.41 ± 3.28 | 0.68 ± 0.15 | 0.93 ± 0.04 | 0.16 ± 0.09 | 2.82 ± 0.47 | 0.43 ± 0.05 | 1.48 ± 1.03 |
| UIR-PolyKernel [66] | 17.72 ± 4.06 | 0.80 ± 0.10 | 0.90 ± 0.05 | 0.24 ± 0.11 | 2.96 ± 0.78 | 0.38 ± 0.07 | 1.07 ± 1.44 |
| CCL-Net [67] | 16.93 ± 5.99 | 0.64 ± 0.31 | 0.79 ± 0.17 | 0.38 ± 0.27 | 3.16 ± 0.52 | 0.41 ± 0.06 | 1.32 ± 0.97 |
| PUIE-Net [68] | 22.43 ± 3.95 | 0.90 ± 0.07 | 0.94 ± 0.05 | 0.13 ± 0.07 | 3.09 ± 0.49 | 0.39 ± 0.07 | 1.45 ± 1.27 |
| USUIR [69] | 19.95 ± 3.41 | 0.82 ± 0.09 | 0.91 ± 0.06 | 0.24 ± 0.10 | 3.18 ± 0.35 | 0.46 ± 0.03 | 1.56 ± 0.98 |
| SGUIE [70] | 20.42 ± 4.47 | 0.86 ± 0.09 | 0.92 ± 0.05 | 0.19 ± 0.11 | 3.10 ± 0.63 | 0.37 ± 0.07 | 1.25 ± 1.35 |
| PMSPNet | 22.43 ± 3.37 | 0.86 ± 0.08 | 0.92 ± 0.05 | 0.21 ± 0.10 | 3.27 ± 0.39 | 0.39 ± 0.05 | 1.53 ± 1.08 |

As illustrated in Figure 9, PMSPNet excels at restoring fine structures and maintaining natural color tones, even in severely degraded scenarios. Compared to methods like UIR-PolyKernel and HistFormer, which often produce over-smoothed textures or color shifts, PMSPNet effectively reconstructs edges and preserves the texture of marine organisms. It also avoids common artifacts, such as excessive blue saturation or overly enhanced contrast, frequently observed in other approaches. This balance across metrics highlights the visual fidelity and realism of PMSPNet, making it both quantitatively superior and perceptually compelling.

In summary, the above experiments demonstrate that PMSPNet can effectively remove underwater non-uniform blur, generating clearer structures, more natural colors, and fewer artifacts and exhibiting strong generalization across diverse underwater scenes. Compared to both traditional and deep learning-based baselines, PMSPNet achieves an optimal trade-off between detail preservation and deblurring, especially under challenging conditions, validating the effectiveness and robustness of the proposed approach.

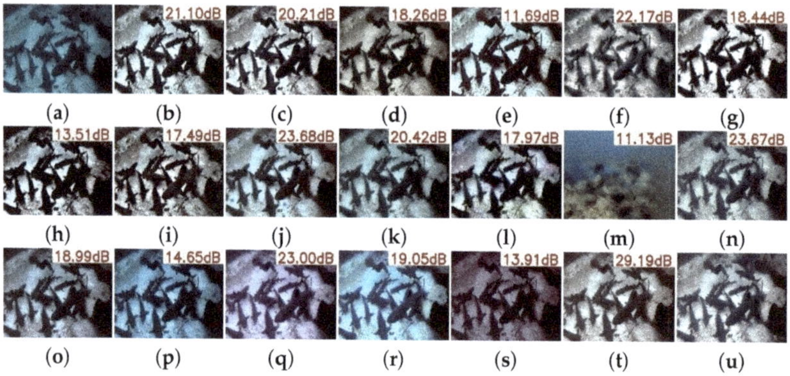


**Figure 9.** Visual comparison on the UIEB dataset, with the PSNR value of the image shown in the upper-right corner of the image. (**a**) Raw image. (**b**) WFAC [25]. (**c**) WWPF [57]. (**d**) HFM [58]. (**e**) HLRP [59]. (**f**) ACDC [60]. (**g**) MMLE [61]. (**h**) PCDE [62]. (**i**) TEBCF [63]. (**j**) CycleGAN [29]. (**k**) U-Shape [49]. (**l**) FUnIE-GAN [48]. (**m**) Histoformer [64]. (**n**) Phaseformer [65]. (**o**) UIR-PolyKernel [66]. (**p**) CCL-Net [67]. (**q**) PUIE-Net [68]. (**r**) USUIR [69]. (**s**) SGUIE[70]. (**t**) PMSPNet. (**u**) Ground Truth.

### 4.4. Ablation Study

To validate the effectiveness of the proposed components in PMSPNet, we conduct comprehensive ablation experiments by removing key modules and evaluating the impact of different loss function combinations. Furthermore, we assess the scalability of the proposed algorithm in downstream tasks.

#### 4.4.1. Butterworth Filter

We introduce a Butterworth filter in the input stage of the PMPB to improve the frequency correspondence and mitigate the aliasing phenomenon. As shown in Table 6, although removing the module results in a slight increase in PSNR by 0.47, all other evaluation metrics exhibit a decline. In particular, SSIM drops to 0.88, UIQM decreases to 3.08, and UCIQE falls to 0.39. These results underscore the module's effectiveness in enhancing structural clarity and perceptual quality as perceived by the human visual system. As illustrated in Figure 10b, the absence of this module leads to noticeable blurring and color artifacts, particularly around object edges and in background regions. This further confirms the module's critical role in improving the overall structural integrity of the image and enhancing the network's sensitivity to spatially non-uniform blur.

**Table 6.** Comparison of performance using different components, where evaluation includes full-reference and no-reference image quality metrics. All results are reported in the format of mean ± standard deviation. ↑ indicates that a higher value is better. ✓ indicates the model is evaluated w/ the corresponding module, while ✗ denotes the model is evaluated w/o the corresponding module.

| ButterWorth | Deformable | PMPB | PFFB | PSNR ↑ | SSIM ↑ | FSIM ↑ | UIQM ↑ | UCIQE ↑ |
|---|---|---|---|---|---|---|---|---|
| ✗ | ✓ | ✓ | ✓ | 25.98 ± 4.20 | 0.88 ± 0.09 | 0.94 ± 0.04 | 3.08 ± 0.40 | 0.39 ± 0.06 |
| ✓ | ✗ | ✓ | ✓ | 17.18 ± 5.14 | 0.73 ± 0.13 | 0.87 ± 0.06 | 2.31 ± 0.84 | 0.41 ± 0.08 |
| ✗ | ✗ | ✗ | ✓ | 25.99 ± 4.29 | 0.89 ± 0.09 | 0.94 ± 0.04 | 3.09 ± 0.39 | 0.40 ± 0.06 |
| ✓ | ✓ | ✓ | ✗ | 24.78 ± 4.07 | 0.87 ± 0.09 | 0.94 ± 0.04 | 3.08 ± 0.41 | 0.39 ± 0.06 |
| ✓ | ✓ | ✓ | ✓ | 25.51 ± 3.98 | 0.92 ± 0.09 | 0.95 ± 0.04 | 3.46 ± 0.41 | 0.46 ± 0.06 |

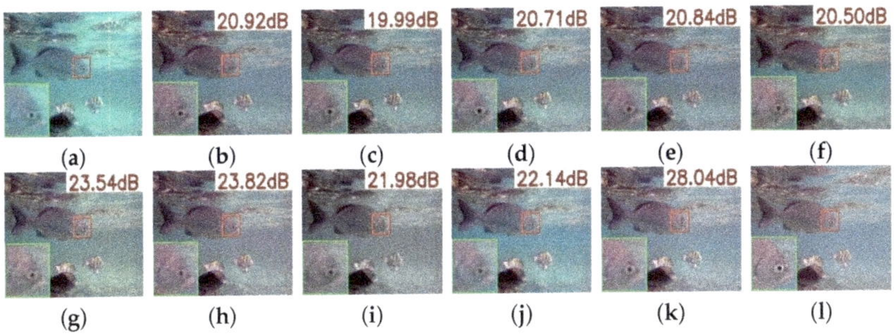


**Figure 10.** Visual comparison of networks using different components and loss functions. PSNR is shown in the top-right, and the bottom-left presents a zoomed-in view of the red-boxed region. (**a**) Raw image. (**b**) w/o Butterworth. (**c**) w/o Deformable Convolution. (**d**) w/o PFFB. (**e**) w/o PMPB. (**f**) w/o FFT loss. (**g**) w/o FFT and LAB loss. (**h**) w/o FFT, LAB and LCH loss. (**i**) w/o FFT, LAB, LCH, and VGG loss. (**j**) w/o FFT, LAB, LCH, VGG, and Color loss. (**k**) PMSPNet. (**l**) Ground Truth.

#### 4.4.2. Deformable Convolution

The high dynamics of deformable convolution enable precise localization and directional modeling of non-uniform blur, allowing the network to effectively capture regionally continuous blur patterns and apply accurate weighting to key features. As shown in Table 6, the removal of deformable convolution results in a substantial decline across all evaluation metrics, with PSNR dropping sharply to 17.18, indicating a significant reduction in reconstruction quality. Furthermore, the network's overall stability is noticeably compromised. As illustrated in Figure 10c, the network without this module struggles to preserve object boundaries and spatial consistency, and the residual blur remains largely unaddressed. These results demonstrate that deformable convolution significantly enhances the network's capacity to identify critical image features and improves the modeling of local structures, which is essential for effective UIE under non-uniform degradation conditions.

#### 4.4.3. Progressive Motion-Aware Perception Branch

The PMPB integrates a Butterworth filter and deformable convolution to progressively capture the spatial distribution of blur and guide feature extraction in the backbone, enabling a coarse-to-fine refinement of blur localization. As shown in Table 6, while the removal of PMPB results in a slight increase in PSNR, it reduces the overall stability of the network. This observation also validates the complementary roles of HIAM and PMPB: HIAM facilitates multi-directional feature perception and coarse localization of blur, whereas PMPB further refines this localization, enhancing the network's generalization and robustness. Additionally, the observed decline in metrics such as SSIM confirms PMPB's contribution to structural clarity and perceptual quality. As illustrated in Figure 10d, the absence of PMPB increases color distortion and reduces image sharpness, particularly in fine structures. These results underscore the importance of PMPB in preserving texture details and scale-aware representations, achieving a critical balance between global semantic understanding and local detail restoration.

#### 4.4.4. Progressive Feature Feedback Block

The PFFB hierarchically integrates multi-level features by facilitating cross-layer feedback, enabling the fusion of spatial details with deep semantic representations. As shown in Table 6, the removal of this module leads to increased information loss during image reconstruction, which diminishes the network's adaptive reconstruction capability, resulting in a consistent, albeit modest, degradation across all evaluation metrics. Figure 10e reveals noticeable artifacts and diminished smoothness, particularly along background contours, indicating the loss of critical structural details. These results demonstrate that PFFB plays a vital role in regulating cross-layer information flow, guiding adaptive feature reweighting, and reducing reconstruction-induced information loss. Consequently, it contributes significantly to improving structural fidelity and perceptual consistency in enhanced underwater images.

#### 4.4.5. Loss Function

We investigated the impact of different loss components on the overall performance of the proposed network. As illustrated in Table 7, removing most auxiliary losses leads to a notable decline across multiple evaluation metrics. Among these, the FFT, LAB, and LCH loss functions contribute most significantly to performance improvement, enhancing objective image quality and perceptual fidelity. In particular, the inclusion of the LAB loss enhances network stability, underscoring the importance of multi-domain color perception. While the VGG and Color losses did not yield substantial improvements in numerical metrics, they contributed positively to visual quality by enhancing hue perception and overall appearance. Figure 10f–k demonstrates that models trained without specific loss terms suffer from excessive smoothing or unnatural color shifts. In contrast, the complete loss configuration consistently generates underwater images with sharper edges, more balanced color tones, and enhanced visual appeal, validating the effectiveness of each component.

**Table 7.** Comparison of performance using different loss functions, where evaluation includes full-reference and no-reference image quality metrics. All results are reported in the format of mean ± standard deviation. ↑ indicates that a higher value is better. ✓ indicates the model is evaluated w/ the corresponding module, while ✗ denotes the model is evaluated w/o the corresponding module.

| Charbonnier | FFT | LAB | LCH | VGG | Color | PSNR ↑ | SSIM ↑ | FSIM ↑ | UIQM ↑ | UCIQE ↑ |
|---|---|---|---|---|---|---|---|---|---|---|
| ✓ | ✗ | ✗ | ✗ | ✗ | ✗ | 24.00 ± 3.98 | 0.86 ± 0.09 | 0.91 ± 0.04 | 2.90 ± 0.45 | 0.41 ± 0.07 |
| ✓ | ✗ | ✗ | ✗ | ✗ | ✓ | 21.27 ± 4.31 | 0.83 ± 0.09 | 0.91 ± 0.04 | 2.95 ± 0.41 | 0.35 ± 0.06 |
| ✓ | ✗ | ✗ | ✗ | ✓ | ✓ | 21.43 ± 4.21 | 0.83 ± 0.09 | 0.91 ± 0.04 | 3.08 ± 0.37 | 0.35 ± 0.06 |
| ✓ | ✗ | ✗ | ✓ | ✓ | ✓ | 22.53 ± 4.36 | 0.84 ± 0.09 | 0.92 ± 0.04 | 3.08 ± 0.37 | 0.37 ± 0.06 |
| ✓ | ✗ | ✓ | ✓ | ✓ | ✓ | 24.06 ± 3.84 | 0.85 ± 0.09 | 0.92 ± 0.04 | 3.08 ± 0.38 | 0.39 ± 0.06 |
| ✓ | ✓ | ✓ | ✓ | ✓ | ✓ | 25.51 ± 3.80 | 0.92 ± 0.09 | 0.95 ± 0.04 | 3.46 ± 0.41 | 0.46 ± 0.06 |

#### 4.4.6. Blur Perceptual Localization

To further investigate the contribution of components to blur perception, we visualize the heatmaps generated under various ablation settings in Figure 11, using the second column of Figure 1 as a representative example. When the Butterworth filter is removed, the heatmap exhibits higher noise levels, indicating a weakened ability to extract key features and accurately capture blur-related information. The removal of deformable convolution and the PFFB markedly impairs the network's capacity for accurately identifying and localizing blurred regions. These components are essential for enabling coarse-to-fine blur localization and iterative attention modulation. Eliminating the PMPB module causes the network's attention to drift while demonstrating the capability of HIAM in achieving coarse localization of blur features.

From the perspective of loss functions, removing the FFT loss impairs the network's ability to capture frequency-domain information, thereby diminishing its capacity to identify and localize blur across multiple spatial domains. VGG, LAB, and LCH losses contribute to guiding the network's attention toward perceptually and semantically important regions, facilitating more accurate blur localization. While Color loss has a relatively smaller effect on network performance, it plays a crucial role in suppressing over-sharpening, thereby enhancing visual naturalness.

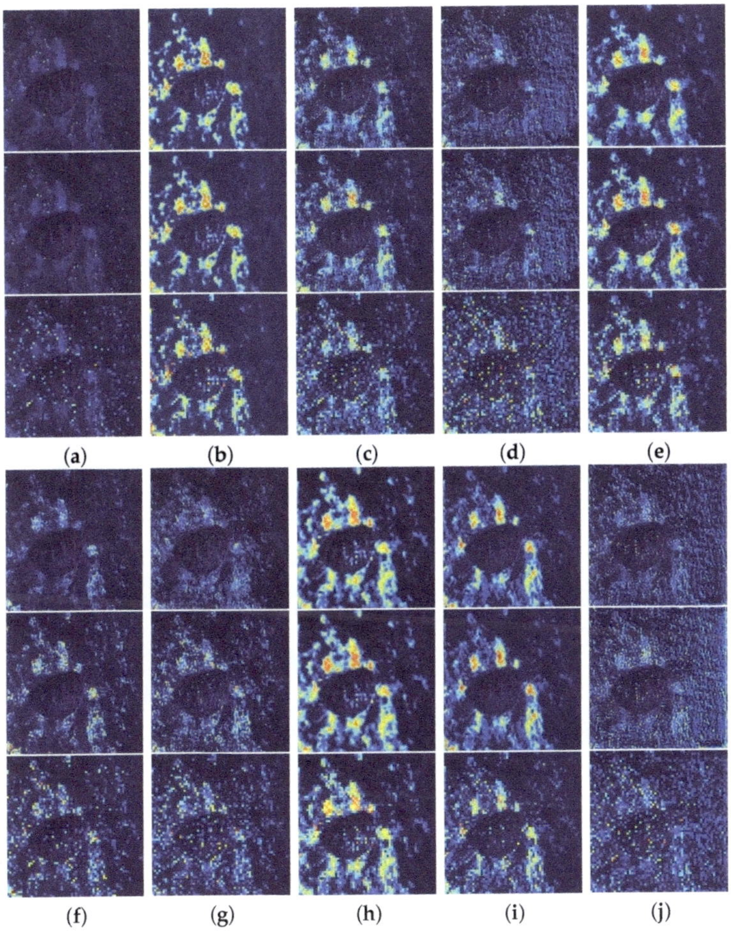

**Figure 11.** Visualization of blur localization under different components and loss functions. Each group of three images corresponds to the enhanced outputs at three different scales. (**a**) w/o Butterworth. (**b**) w/o Deformable Convolution. (**c**) w/o PFFB. (**d**) w/o PMPB. (**e**) w/o FFT loss. (**f**) w/o FFT and LAB loss. (**g**) w/o FFT, LAB, and LCH loss. (**h**) w/o FFT, LAB, LCH, and VGG loss. (**i**) w/o FFT, LAB, LCH, VGG, and Color loss. (**j**) PMSPNet.

In contrast, the proposed model exhibits the most concentrated and semantically accurate activation responses, highlighting blurred regions. These results validate the effectiveness of our architectural design and multi-component loss in improving the network's capability for blur perception and structural fidelity restoration in underwater environments.

4.4.7. Downstream Task Evaluation

To further validate the practical benefits of the proposed method, we conducted evaluations on downstream tasks, including classic feature extraction and underwater object detection (UOD).

As illustrated in Figure 12, we applied SIFT keypoint detection and Canny edge detection to assess the influence of enhancement on low-level visual features. The first row shows the SIFT results, while the second row displays the Canny edges. Traditional methods often fail to preserve sufficient structural detail, introducing noise and blurring in non-salient regions, which results in some key edges being obscured or missing. In contrast, images enhanced by PMSPNet exhibit clear contours and rich edge information, closely matching the ground truth, demonstrating that PMSPNet effectively enhances geometric clarity, facilitating better feature localization.

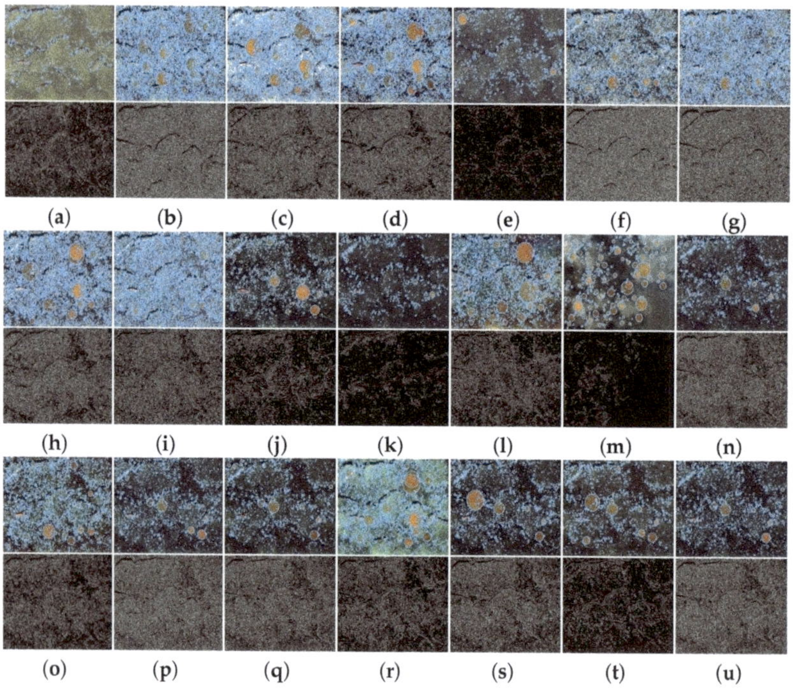


**Figure 12.** Visual comparison of SIFT keypoint and Canny edge detection results. The first row presents the visualization of SIFT keypoints, while the second row displays the corresponding Canny edge detection results. (**a**) Raw image. (**b**) WFAC [25]. (**c**) WWPF [57]. (**d**) HFM [58]. (**e**) HLRP [59]. (**f**) ACDC [60]. (**g**) MMLE [61]. (**h**) PCDE [62]. (**i**) TEBCF [63]. (**j**) CycleGAN [29]. (**k**) U-Shape [49]. (**l**) FUnIE-GAN [48]. (**m**) Histoformer [64]. (**n**) Phaseformer [65]. (**o**) UIR-PolyKernel [66]. (**p**) CCL-Net [67]. (**q**) PUIE-Net [68]. (**r**) USUIR [69]. (**s**) SGUIE [70]. (**t**) PMSPNet. (**u**) Ground Truth.

To assess high-level perception, we applied YOLOv12 [71] for underwater object detection. A YOLOv12 model pre-trained on the original DUO dataset was used to detect objects in images enhanced by different methods. As shown in Figure 13, traditional enhancement approaches often introduce significant color distortions, which impair detection performance. Deep learning-based baselines exhibit limited performance in small object detection, primarily due to underperformance in detail preservation. In contrast, PMSPNet-enhanced images have more accurate and stable detection outcomes, achieving higher confidence scores and better alignment with the original detection results. Notably, because YOLOv12 was trained on the original images, detection performance is best in raw images.

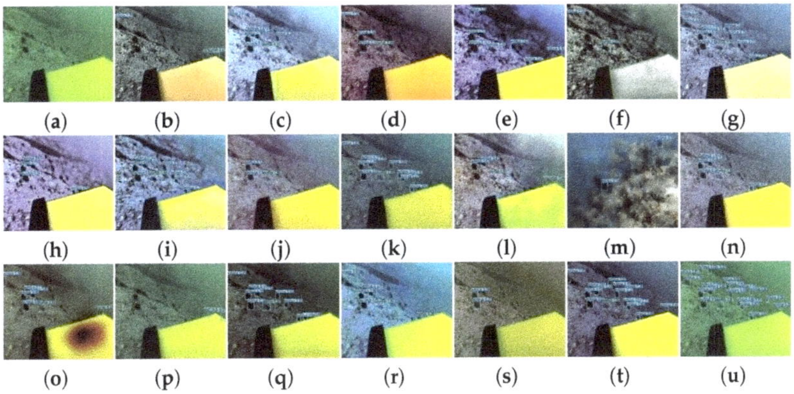

**Figure 13.** Comparison of YOLOv12 detection effects on enhanced underwater images from the DUO dataset. (**a**) Raw image. (**b**) WFAC [25]. (**c**) WWPF [57]. (**d**) HFM [58]. (**e**) HLRP [59]. (**f**) ACDC [60]. (**g**) MMLE [61]. (**h**) PCDE [62]. (**i**) TEBCF [63]. (**j**) CycleGAN [29]. (**k**) U-Shape [49]. (**l**) FUnIE-GAN [48]. (**m**) Histoformer [64]. (**n**) Phaseformer [65]. (**o**) UIR-PolyKernel [66]. (**p**) CCL-Net [67]. (**q**) PUIE-Net [68]. (**r**) USUIR [69]. (**s**) SGUIE [70]. (**t**) PMSPNet. (**u**) Detection effect of raw image.

The above results demonstrate that PMSPNet not only improves perceptual image quality but also preserves semantic fidelity, making it well-suited for integration into real-world underwater robotic systems and visual monitoring pipelines.

4.4.8. Limitation Analysis

Although PMSPNet demonstrates superior performance in non-uniform underwater image deblurring, several limitations remain. Due to the incorporation of multi-scale perception and progressive feedback mechanisms, the model introduces additional computational overhead, which may restrict its real-time deployment on extremely resource-constrained underwater robotic platforms. While the proposed N2UD dataset covers diverse non-uniform blur patterns, it still cannot fully represent the wide spectrum of degradations in real-world underwater environments, such as extreme turbidity, lighting fluctuations, or dynamic background interference. While we validated the universality of PMSPNet on downstream tasks such as detection, edge detection, and keypoint localization, comprehensive evaluations on segmentation tasks remain limited. In addition, this study primarily focuses on algorithm-level comparisons. Integrating advanced hardware-oriented solutions, such as novel imaging sensors or optical acquisition systems, represents another promising research direction.

Future work will focus on addressing these issues by optimizing the network components to improve their flexibility, enabling lightweight and real-time deployment. Moreover, we will expand the dataset with more challenging real-world scenarios and extend the validation to segmentation tasks.

## 5. Conclusions

This article proposes PMSPNet, a Progressive Multi-Scale Perception Network designed for the challenging task of non-uniform underwater image deblurring. PMSPNet incorporates a Hybrid Interaction Attention Module (HIAM) to effectively capture fine-grained visual textures and long-range contextual dependencies, enabling robust modeling of feature ambiguity and spatial disparity. Furthermore, the Progressive Motion-Aware Perception Branch (PMPB) is introduced to explicitly represent spatial orientation variations and progressively refine the localization of blur-affected regions. In addition, the Progressive Feature Feedback Block (PFFB) enhances feature reconstruction by leveraging multi-level information in a feedback manner, improving feature restoration quality. To enable reliable evaluation, we construct the N2UD dataset, which contains diverse non-uniform blur patterns representative of real-world underwater environments. Extensive experiments on real-world datasets validate the superiority of our method in terms of both quantitative metrics and visual quality. While achieving an inference speed of 0.01 s, it reached the highest PSNR of 25.51 dB and SSIM of 0.92 on the N2UD dataset. PMSPNet also demonstrates clear advantages in downstream tasks such as edge detection and object recognition, which enhances the visual reliability of underwater perception systems, facilitating downstream tasks such as object detection, recognition, and navigation in robotic platforms. Future efforts will focus on extending PMSPNet for real-time deployment in underwater robotic systems. Moreover, extending PMSPNet to handle real-time underwater video restoration and multimodal fusion with sonar or depth data remains a promising direction. In addition, diffusion-based generative models, despite their current limitations in computational efficiency, offer great potential for modeling complex blur patterns and realistic underwater degradations. Integrating the strengths of diffusion models into underwater deblurring frameworks will be an important avenue for our future research.

**Author Contributions:** Conceptualization, D.K.; methodology, D.K. and Y.Z.; software, D.K. and Y.Z.; validation, X.Z. and Y.W. (Yanyan Wang); formal analysis, D.K. and Y.Z.; investigation, D.K. and Y.W. (Yanyan Wang); resources, D.K. and X.Z.; data curation, Y.Z. and Y.W. (Yanqiang Wang); writing—original draft preparation, D.K. and Y.Z.; writing—review and editing, D.K. and Y.Z.; visualization, X.Z. and Y.W. (Yanqiang Wang); supervision, X.Z.; project administration, D.K. and Y.Z.; funding acquisition, D.K. All authors have read and agreed to the published version of the manuscript.

**Funding:** This research was funded by the Science and Technology Project of Henan Province, grant numbers 242102211025, 252102211059, and 252102210114.

**Data Availability Statement:** Publicly available datasets were analyzed in this study. These data can be found at https://github.com/UI2025/N2UD (N2UD), accessed on 28 August 2025; https://irvlab.cs.umn.edu/resources/euvp-dataset (EUVP), accessed on 17 May 2025; https://lintaopeng.github.io/_pages/UIE%20Project%20Page.html (LSUI), accessed on 17 May 2025; https://li-chongyi.github.io/proj_benchmark.html (UIEB), accessed on 17 May 2025; and https://github.com/chongweiliu/DUO (DUO), accessed on 18 May 2025.

**Conflicts of Interest:** The authors declare no conflicts of interest.

## References

1. Zhou, J.; Liu, C.; Long, B.; Zhang, D.; Jiang, Q.; Muhammad, G. Degradation-Decoupling Vision Enhancement for Intelligent Underwater Robot Vision Perception System. *IEEE Internet Things J.* **2025**, *12*, 17880–17895. [CrossRef]
2. Sun, L.; Wang, Y.; Hui, X.; Ma, X.; Bai, X.; Tan, M. Underwater Robots and Key Technologies for Operation Control. *Cyborg Bionic Syst.* **2024**, *5*, 0089. [CrossRef]
3. González-Sabbagh, S.P.; Robles-Kelly, A. A Survey on Underwater Computer Vision. *ACM Comput. Surv.* **2023**, *55*, 1–39. [CrossRef]
4. Shen, L.; Reda, M.; Zhang, X.; Zhao, Y.; Kong, S.G. Polarization-Driven Solution for Mitigating Scattering and Uneven Illumination in Underwater Imagery. *IEEE Trans. Geosci. Remote Sens.* **2024**, *62*, 1–15. [CrossRef]
5. Li, Y.; Chen, Y.; Zhang, J.; Li, Y.; Fu, X. An Underwater Image Restoration Method With Polarization Imaging Optimization Model for Poor Visible Conditions. *IEEE Trans. Circuits Syst. Video Technol.* **2025**, *35*, 3924–3939. [CrossRef]
6. Cai, W.; Zhu, J.; Zhang, M. Multi-modality object detection with sonar and underwater camera via object-shadow feature generation and saliency information. *Expert Syst. Appl.* **2025**, *287*, 128021. [CrossRef]
7. Wu, H.; Liu, Z.; Li, C.; Wang, H.; Zhai, Y.; Dong, L. A laser field synchronous scanning imaging system for underwater long-range detection. *Opt. Laser Technol.* **2024**, *175*, 110849. [CrossRef]
8. Xu, S.; Zhang, K.; Wang, S. AQUA-SLAM: Tightly Coupled Underwater Acoustic-Visual-Inertial SLAM With Sensor Calibration. *IEEE Trans. Robot.* **2025**, *41*, 2785–2803. [CrossRef]

9. He, Y.; Han, G.; Hou, Y.; Lin, C. Environment-Tolerant Trust Opportunity Routing Based on Reinforcement Learning for Internet of Underwater Things. *IEEE Trans. Mob. Comput.* **2025**, *24*, 6348–6360. [CrossRef]
10. Xu, C.; Song, S.; Liu, J.; Pan, M.; Xu, G.; Cui, J.H. Joint Power Control and Multipath Routing for Internet of Underwater Things in Varying Environments. *IEEE Internet Things J.* **2025**, *12*, 15197–15210. [CrossRef]
11. Jiang, B.; Feng, J.; Cui, X.; Wang, J.; Liu, Y.; Song, H. Security and Reliability of InternSecurity and Reliability of Internet of Underwater Things: Architecture, Challenges, and Opportunities. *ACM Comput. Surv.* **2024**, *57*, 1–37. [CrossRef]
12. Draz, U.; Ali, T.; Yasin, S.; Chaudary, M.H.; Yasin, I.; Ayaz, M.; Aggoune, E.H.M. Hybrid Underwater Localization Communication Framework for Blockchain-Enabled IoT Underwater Acoustic Sensor Network. *IEEE Internet Things J.* **2025**, *12*, 16858–16885. [CrossRef]
13. Rupa, C.; Varshitha, G.S.; Divya, D.; Gadekallu, T.R.; Srivastava, G. A Novel and Robust Authentication Protocol for Secure Underwater Communication Systems. *IEEE Internet Things J.* **2025**. [CrossRef]
14. Zhu, R.; Boukerche, A.; Yang, Q. An Efficient Secure and Adaptive Routing Protocol Based on GMM-HMM-LSTM for Internet of Underwater Things. *IEEE Internet Things J.* **2024**, *11*, 16491–16504. [CrossRef]
15. Chandrasekar, A.; Sreenivas, M.; Biswas, S. PhISH-Net: Physics Inspired System for High Resolution Underwater Image Enhancement. In Proceedings of the IEEE/CVF Winter Conference on Applications of Computer Vision (WACV), Waikoloa, HI, USA, 3–8 January 2024; pp. 1506–1516.
16. Zhou, J.; Yang, T.; Ren, W.; Zhang, D.; Zhang, W. Underwater image restoration via depth map and illumination estimation based on a single image. *Opt. Express* **2021**, *29*, 29864–29886. [CrossRef]
17. Ma, H.; Huang, J.; Shen, C.; Jiang, Z. Retinex-inspired underwater image enhancement with information entropy smoothing and non-uniform illumination priors. *Pattern Recognit.* **2025**, *162*, 111411. [CrossRef]
18. Liu, S.; Zheng, Y.; Li, J.; Lu, H.; An, D.; Shen, Z.; Wang, Z. Turbid Underwater Image Enhancement with Illumination-Constrained and Structure-Preserved Retinex Model. *IEEE Trans. Circuits Syst. Video Technol.* **2025**. [CrossRef]
19. Zhou, J.; Wang, S.; Lin, Z.; Jiang, Q.; Sohel, F. A Pixel Distribution Remapping and Multi-Prior Retinex Variational Model for Underwater Image Enhancement. *IEEE Trans. Multimed.* **2024**, *26*, 7838–7849. [CrossRef]
20. Zhang, W.; Liu, Q.; Feng, Y.; Cai, L.; Zhuang, P. Underwater Image Enhancement via Principal Component Fusion of Foreground and Background. *IEEE Trans. Circuits Syst. Video Technol.* **2024**, *34*, 10930–10943. [CrossRef]
21. Qiang, H.; Zhong, Y.; Zhu, Y.; Zhong, X.; Xiao, Q.; Dian, S. Underwater Image Enhancement Based on Multichannel Adaptive Compensation. *IEEE Trans. Instrum. Meas.* **2024**, *73*, 1–10. [CrossRef]
22. Zhang, T.; Su, H.; Fan, B.; Yang, N.; Zhong, S.; Yin, J. Underwater Image Enhancement Based on Red Channel Correction and Improved Multiscale Fusion. *IEEE Trans. Geosci. Remote Sens.* **2024**, *62*, 1–20. [CrossRef]
23. Jha, M.; Bhandari, A.K. CBLA: Color-Balanced Locally Adjustable Underwater Image Enhancement. *IEEE Trans. Instrum. Meas.* **2024**, *73*, 1–11. [CrossRef]
24. Wang, Y.; Hu, S.; Yin, S.; Deng, Z.; Yang, Y.H. A multi-level wavelet-based underwater image enhancement network with color compensation prior. *Expert Syst. Appl.* **2024**, *242*, 122710. [CrossRef]
25. Zhang, W.; Liu, Q.; Lu, H.; Wang, J.; Liang, J. Underwater Image Enhancement via Wavelet Decomposition Fusion of Advantage Contrast. *IEEE Trans. Circuits Syst. Video Technol.* **2025**, *35*, 7807–7820. [CrossRef]
26. Kong, D.; Zhang, Y.; Zhao, X.; Wang, Y.; Cai, L. MUFFNet: Lightweight dynamic underwater image enhancement network based on multi-scale frequency. *Front. Mar. Sci.* **2025**, *12*, 1541265. [CrossRef]
27. Xue, X.; Yuan, J.; Ma, T.; Ma, L.; Jia, Q.; Zhou, J.; Wang, Y. Degradation-Decoupled and semantic-aggregated cross-space fusion for underwater image enhancement. *Inf. Fusion* **2025**, *118*, 102927. [CrossRef]
28. Park, C.W.; Eom, I.K. Underwater image enhancement using adaptive standardization and normalization networks. *Eng. Appl. Artif. Intell.* **2024**, *127*, 107445. [CrossRef]
29. Zhu, J.Y.; Park, T.; Isola, P.; Efros, A.A. Unpaired Image-To-Image Translation Using Cycle-Consistent Adversarial Networks. In Proceedings of the IEEE International Conference on Computer Vision (ICCV), Venice, Italy, 22–29 October 2017.
30. Kong, D.; Mao, J.; Zhang, Y.; Zhao, X.; Wang, Y.; Wang, S. Dual-Domain Adaptive Synergy GAN for Enhancing Low-Light Underwater Images. *J. Mar. Sci. Eng.* **2025**, *13*, 1092. [CrossRef]
31. Ho, J.; Jain, A.; Abbeel, P. Denoising Diffusion Probabilistic Models. In *Proceedings of the Advances in Neural Information Processing Systems*; Larochelle, H., Ranzato, M., Hadsell, R., Balcan, M., Lin, H., Eds.; Curran Associates, Inc.: Red Hook, NY, USA, 2020; Volume 33, pp. 6840–6851.
32. Rombach, R.; Blattmann, A.; Lorenz, D.; Esser, P.; Ommer, B. High-Resolution Image Synthesis with Latent Diffusion Models. In Proceedings of the IEEE/CVF Conference on Computer Vision and Pattern Recognition (CVPR), New Orleans, LA, USA, 18–24 June 2022; pp. 10684–10695.
33. Li, W.; Wu, X.; Fan, S.; Wei, S.; Gowing, G. INGC-GAN: An Implicit Neural-Guided Cycle Generative Approach for Perceptual-Friendly Underwater Image Enhancement. *IEEE Trans. Neural Netw. Learn. Syst.* **2025**, *36*, 10084–10098. [CrossRef] [PubMed]

34. Qing, Y.; Liu, S.; Wang, H.; Wang, Y. DiffUIE: Learning Latent Global Priors in Diffusion Models for Underwater Image Enhancement. *IEEE Trans. Multimed.* **2025**, *27*, 2516–2529. [CrossRef]
35. Liu, Z.; Lin, Y.; Cao, Y.; Hu, H.; Wei, Y.; Zhang, Z.; Lin, S.; Guo, B. Swin Transformer: Hierarchical Vision Transformer Using Shifted Windows. In Proceedings of the IEEE/CVF International Conference on Computer Vision (ICCV), Montreal, BC, Canada, 11–17 October 2021; pp. 10012–10022.
36. Dosovitskiy, A.; Beyer, L.; Kolesnikov, A.; Weissenborn, D.; Zhai, X.; Unterthiner, T.; Dehghani, M.; Minderer, M.; Heigold, G.; Gelly, S.; et al. An Image is Worth 16x16 Words: Transformers for Image Recognition at Scale. *arXiv* **2021**, arXiv:2010.11929. [CrossRef]
37. Yang, J.; Zhu, S.; Liang, H.; Bai, S.; Jiang, F.; Hussain, A. PAFPT: Progressive aggregator with feature prompted transformer for underwater image enhancement. *Expert Syst. Appl.* **2025**, *262*, 125539. [CrossRef]
38. Huang, Z.; Wang, X.; Xu, C.; Li, J.; Feng, L. Underwater variable zoom: Depth-guided perception network for underwater image enhancement. *Expert Syst. Appl.* **2025**, *259*, 125350. [CrossRef]
39. Song, J.; Xu, H.; Jiang, G.; Yu, M.; Chen, Y.; Luo, T.; Song, Y. Frequency domain-based latent diffusion model for underwater image enhancement. *Pattern Recognit.* **2025**, *160*, 111198. [CrossRef]
40. Yin, J.; Wang, Y.; Guan, B.; Zeng, X.; Guo, L. Unsupervised Underwater Image Enhancement Based on Disentangled Representations via Double-Order Contrastive Loss. *IEEE Trans. Geosci. Remote Sens.* **2024**, *62*, 1–15. [CrossRef]
41. Liu, X.; Jiang, Y.; Wang, Y.; Liu, T.; Wang, J. MDA-Net: A Multidistribution Aware Network for Underwater Image Enhancement. *IEEE Trans. Geosci. Remote Sens.* **2025**, *63*, 1–13. [CrossRef]
42. Liang, D.; Chu, J.; Cui, Y.; Zhai, Z.; Wang, D. NPT-UL: An Underwater Image Enhancement Framework Based on Nonphysical Transformation and Unsupervised Learning. *IEEE Trans. Geosci. Remote Sens.* **2024**, *62*, 1–19. [CrossRef]
43. Guo, X.; Chen, X.; Wang, S.; Pun, C.M. Underwater Image Restoration Through a Prior Guided Hybrid Sense Approach and Extensive Benchmark Analysis. *IEEE Trans. Circuits Syst. Video Technol.* **2025**, *35*, 4784–4800. [CrossRef]
44. Ji, X.; Chen, S.; Hao, L.Y.; Zhou, J.; Chen, L. FBDPN: CNN-Transformer hybrid feature boosting and differential pyramid network for underwater object detection. *Expert Syst. Appl.* **2024**, *256*, 124978. [CrossRef]
45. J., S.; L., A.K. An explainable artificial intelligence driven fall system for sensor data analysis enhanced by butterworth filtering. *Eng. Appl. Artif. Intell.* **2025**, *158*, 111364. [CrossRef]
46. Kurinjimalar, R.; Pradeep, J.; Harikrishnan, M. Underwater Image Enhancement Using Gaussian Pyramid, Laplacian Pyramid and Contrast Limited Adaptive Histogram Equalization. In Proceedings of the 2024 IEEE 3rd World Conference on Applied Intelligence and Computing (AIC), Gwalior, India, 27–28 July 2024; pp. 729–734. [CrossRef]
47. Dai, J.; Qi, H.; Xiong, Y.; Li, Y.; Zhang, G.; Hu, H.; Wei, Y. Deformable Convolutional Networks. In Proceedings of the IEEE International Conference on Computer Vision (ICCV), Venice, Italy, 22–29 October 2017.
48. Islam, M.J.; Xia, Y.; Sattar, J. Fast Underwater Image Enhancement for Improved Visual Perception. *IEEE Robot. Autom. Lett.* **2020**, *5*, 3227–3234. [CrossRef]
49. Peng, L.; Zhu, C.; Bian, L. U-Shape Transformer for Underwater Image Enhancement. *IEEE Trans. Image Process.* **2023**, *32*, 3066–3079. [CrossRef]
50. Li, C.; Guo, C.; Ren, W.; Cong, R.; Hou, J.; Kwong, S.; Tao, D. An Underwater Image Enhancement Benchmark Dataset and Beyond. *IEEE Trans. Image Process.* **2020**, *29*, 4376–4389. [CrossRef] [PubMed]
51. Liu, C.; Li, H.; Wang, S.; Zhu, M.; Wang, D.; Fan, X.; Wang, Z. A Dataset and Benchmark of Underwater Object Detection for Robot Picking. In Proceedings of the 2021 IEEE International Conference on Multimedia & Expo Workshops (ICMEW), Shenzhen, China, 5–9 July 2021; pp. 1–6. [CrossRef]
52. Zhang, R.; Isola, P.; Efros, A.A.; Shechtman, E.; Wang, O. The Unreasonable Effectiveness of Deep Features as a Perceptual Metric. In Proceedings of the IEEE Conference on Computer Vision and Pattern Recognition (CVPR), Salt Lake City, UT, USA, 18–22 June 2018.
53. Panetta, K.; Gao, C.; Agaian, S. Human-Visual-System-Inspired Underwater Image Quality Measures. *IEEE J. Ocean. Eng.* **2016**, *41*, 541–551. [CrossRef]
54. Yang, M.; Sowmya, A. An Underwater Color Image Quality Evaluation Metric. *IEEE Trans. Image Process.* **2015**, *24*, 6062–6071. [CrossRef] [PubMed]
55. Mittal, A.; Soundararajan, R.; Bovik, A.C. Making a "Completely Blind" Image Quality Analyzer. *IEEE Signal Process. Lett.* **2013**, *20*, 209–212. [CrossRef]
56. Guo, C.; Wu, R.; Jin, X.; Han, L.; Zhang, W.; Chai, Z.; Li, C. Underwater Ranker: Learn Which Is Better and How to Be Better. *Proc. AAAI Conf. Artif. Intell.* **2023**, *37*, 702–709. [CrossRef]
57. Zhang, W.; Zhou, L.; Zhuang, P.; Li, G.; Pan, X.; Zhao, W.; Li, C. Underwater Image Enhancement via Weighted Wavelet Visual Perception Fusion. *IEEE Trans. Circuits Syst. Video Technol.* **2024**, *34*, 2469–2483. [CrossRef]
58. An, S.; Xu, L.; Deng, Z.; Zhang, H. HFM: A hybrid fusion method for underwater image enhancement. *Eng. Appl. Artif. Intell.* **2024**, *127*, 107219. [CrossRef]

59. Zhuang, P.; Wu, J.; Porikli, F.; Li, C. Underwater Image Enhancement with Hyper-Laplacian Reflectance Priors. *IEEE Trans. Image Process.* **2022**, *31*, 5442–5455. [CrossRef]
60. Zhang, W.; Wang, Y.; Li, C. Underwater Image Enhancement by Attenuated Color Channel Correction and Detail Preserved Contrast Enhancement. *IEEE J. Ocean. Eng.* **2022**, *47*, 718–735. [CrossRef]
61. Zhang, W.; Zhuang, P.; Sun, H.H.; Li, G.; Kwong, S.; Li, C. Underwater Image Enhancement via Minimal Color Loss and Locally Adaptive Contrast Enhancement. *IEEE Trans. Image Process.* **2022**, *31*, 3997–4010. [CrossRef]
62. Zhang, W.; Jin, S.; Zhuang, P.; Liang, Z.; Li, C. Underwater Image Enhancement via Piecewise Color Correction and Dual Prior Optimized Contrast Enhancement. *IEEE Signal Process. Lett.* **2023**, *30*, 229–233. [CrossRef]
63. Yuan, J.; Cai, Z.; Cao, W. TEBCF: Real-World Underwater Image Texture Enhancement Model Based on Blurriness and Color Fusion. *IEEE Trans. Geosci. Remote Sens.* **2022**, *60*, 1–15. [CrossRef]
64. Peng, Y.T.; Chen, Y.R.; Chen, G.R.; Liao, C.J. Histoformer: Histogram-Based Transformer for Efficient Underwater Image Enhancement. *IEEE J. Ocean. Eng.* **2025**, *50*, 164–177. [CrossRef]
65. Khan, M.R.; Negi, A.; Kulkarni, A.; Phutke, S.S.; Vipparthi, S.K.; Murala, S. Phaseformer: Phase-Based Attention Mechanism for Underwater Image Restoration and Beyond. In Proceedings of the 2025 IEEE/CVF Winter Conference on Applications of Computer Vision (WACV), Tucson, AZ, USA, 28 February–4 March 2025; pp. 9618–9629. [CrossRef]
66. Guo, X.; Dong, Y.; Chen, X.; Chen, W.; Li, Z.; Zheng, F.; Pun, C.M. Underwater Image Restoration via Polymorphic Large Kernel CNNs. In Proceedings of the ICASSP 2025-2025 IEEE International Conference on Acoustics, Speech and Signal Processing (ICASSP), Hyderabad, India, 6–11 April 2025; pp. 1–5. [CrossRef]
67. Liu, Y.; Jiang, Q.; Wang, X.; Luo, T.; Zhou, J. Underwater Image Enhancement with Cascaded Contrastive Learning. *IEEE Trans. Multimed.* **2025**, *27*, 1512–1525. [CrossRef]
68. Fu, Z.; Wang, W.; Huang, Y.; Ding, X.; Ma, K.K. Uncertainty Inspired Underwater Image Enhancement. In *Proceedings of the Computer Vision–ECCV 2022: 17th European Conference, Tel Aviv, Israel, 23–27 October 2022*; Proceedings, Part XVIII; Springer: Berlin/Heidelberg, Germany, 2022; pp. 465–482. [CrossRef]
69. Fu, Z.; Lin, H.; Yang, Y.; Chai, S.; Sun, L.; Huang, Y.; Ding, X. Unsupervised Underwater Image Restoration: From a Homology Perspective. *Proc. AAAI Conf. Artif. Intell.* **2022**, *36*, 643–651. [CrossRef]
70. Qi, Q.; Li, K.; Zheng, H.; Gao, X.; Hou, G.; Sun, K. SGUIE-Net: Semantic Attention Guided Underwater Image Enhancement with Multi-Scale Perception. *IEEE Trans. Image Process.* **2022**, *31*, 6816–6830. [CrossRef] [PubMed]
71. Tian, Y.; Ye, Q.; Doermann, D. YOLOv12: Attention-Centric Real-Time Object Detectors. *arXiv* **2025**, arXiv:2502.12524.

*sensors*

MDPI

*Article*

# Wind Turbine Blade Defect Recognition Method Based on Large-Vision-Model Transfer Learning

**Xin Li [1], Jinghe Tian [1,*], Xinfu Pang [1], Li Shen [1], Haibo Li [1] and Zedong Zheng [2]**

[1] Key Laboratory of Energy Saving and Controlling in Power System of Liaoning Province, Shenyang Institute of Engineering, Shenyang 110136, China; 12023201117@stu.sie.edu.cn (X.L.); pangxf@sie.edu.cn (X.P.); shenli@sie.edu.cn (L.S.); lihb@sie.edu.cn (H.L.)

[2] School of Computing and Mathematical Sciences, University of Leicester, Leicester LE1 7RH, UK; zz288@leicester.ac.uk

* Correspondence: tianjh@sie.edu.cn

**Abstract:** Timely and accurate detection of wind turbine blade surface defects is crucial for ensuring operational safety and improving maintenance efficiency with respect to large-scale wind farms. However, existing methods often suffer from poor generalization, background interference, and inadequate real-time performance. To overcome these limitations, we developed an end-to-end defect recognition framework, structured as a three-stage process: blade localization using YOLOv5, robust feature extraction via the large vision model DINOv2, and defect classification using a Stochastic Configuration Network (SCN). Unlike conventional CNN-based approaches, the use of DINOv2 significantly improves the capability for representation under complex textures. The experimental results reveal that the proposed method achieved a classification accuracy of 97.8% and an average inference time of 19.65 ms per image, satisfying real-time requirements. Compared to traditional methods, this framework provides a more scalable, accurate, and efficient solution for the intelligent inspection and maintenance of wind turbine blades.

**Keywords:** defect detection; DINOv2; Stochastic Configuration Network; wind blades; YOLOv5 network

## 1. Introduction

### 1.1. Literature Review

As wind is a renewable energy source, wind power generation does not emit greenhouse gases or other pollutants (unlike traditional thermal power generation), thereby supporting the achievement of carbon peaking and neutralization. Severe weather and gravity-related factors will affect the long-term stable operation of wind turbine blades outdoors. Blade defects, such as paint chipping, cracking damage, and oil stains, usually develop over time. Regular inspection of wind turbine blades is currently carried out manually or with the assistance of drones. Manual detection usually requires workers to climb up tall wind turbine towers to conduct visual inspections, posing high safety risks, and this method is prone to misjudgment and missed detection. In addition, the efficiency of manual inspection is low, and it is difficult to quickly cover many wind turbines on large wind farms. Therefore, it is vital to judge blade defects safely and effectively to allow the continuous and reliable operation of a wind turbine.

In Ref. [1], the Bayesian classification method was used to classify the vibration signals generated by cracks, corrosion, loose connections, and other faults. In Ref. [2], RPCA was employed to reduce the data dimensions of vibration signals. The wind turbine blade inspection blade data set was deemed significant, and traditional machine learning was found to have low processing efficiency for large-scale data and high data quality requirements. Traditional machine learning methods must manually design and extract features, and over-reliance on prior knowledge is subject to influence by subjective factors.

In recent years, owing to advancements in deep learning advancements, neural-network-based methods have become the standard approach to wind turbine blade recognition. In Ref. [3], a characteristic map of vibration signals was input into an MCNN to extract the features of different defect types, and the ART network was used as a classifier. In Ref. [4], the Haar-AdaBoost cascade classifier was used to determine the damaged area, and then the variant VGG16 was used to classify the types of damage. However, the Haar features of this method need to be artificially designed in order to improve the model's generalization ability. In Ref. [5], the Otsu algorithm was used to remove the complex background in blade images, and then AlexNet combined with transfer learning was used for feature extraction. Finally, a random forest was used to classify defect types. In Ref. [6], a two-stage object detection network, Faster-RCNN, with a backbone of Inception-ResNet-v2 was used to identify and classify blade defects, and the images were enhanced via flipping, brightness transformation, Gaussian blur, and other methods. In Ref. [7], the ADMM algorithm was used to reduce the weight of VGG11 for blade defect detection. In Ref. [8], the improved ResNet50 was used to replace the backbone VGG part of the SSD network to realize blade defect detection. In Ref. [9], a UAV was used to circle a wind turbine blade in order to obtain blade images, and AlexNet was used for damage classification. In Ref. [10], a multi-feature fusion residual structure named ResNet34 was proposed, with a smaller network depth than the original ResNet34. In Ref. [11], a DCNN pre-trained on ImageNet was used as a feature extractor, and an SVM was used as a classifier to classify blade defects. In Ref. [12], combined with transfer learning, ResNet101 was fine-tuned as the backbone network of an R-CNN to realize the identification of three defects: damage, cracks, and oil pollution. The improved k-means algorithm was used to reduce the influence of complex backgrounds. Although this method successfully classified these three types of defects, its accuracy still needs to be improved. In Ref. [13], VGG16 with an attention mechanism and an adaptive learning rate was used as a feature extractor. In Ref. [14], MASK-RCNN and MRNet were combined to reduce background influence. In Ref. [15], the authors compared the performance of ResNet50 and AlexNet in blade defect recognition tasks, and the results showed that ResNet50 was better. The authors of [16–20] all used the original or improved YOLO-series algorithms to realize defect recognition, added attention mechanisms to reduce the influence of blade image background on defect features, or used lightweight models to increase reasoning speed and lower computational power consumption. In recent years, foundation models have received extensive attention in both the language and vision domains. Large-scale language models, such as GPT and BERT, are pre-trained on vast textual corpora for language comprehension and generation. In contrast, visual foundation models such as DINOv2 and CLIP are pre-trained on large-scale image datasets to extract general-purpose visual representations. DINOv2 offers strong generalization and feature representation capabilities, particularly in complex visual environments and small-sample scenarios, making it well-suited for tasks such as wind turbine blade defect classification. In Ref. [21], a fuzzy-system-based genetic algorithm was designed to perform adaptive segmentation of trajectory sequences, enabling global optimization through dynamic mutation and crossover strategies. The core ideas of adaptive structure adjustment and optimization are relevant to visual detection in complex environments. In Ref. [22], a dual-scale complementary spatial–spectral joint model was introduced for hyperspectral image classification, improving the robustness of feature representation by integrating multi-scale spatial and spectral information. There are also recent studies offering important references for building efficient, generalizable models in the field of defect detection. In Ref. [23], an energy-efficient mechanical fault diagnosis method named SpikingFormer was proposed, inspired by neural dynamics and metric learning. This method addresses the challenge of limited sample availability in industrial scenarios by combining low-energy computing with prototype-based classification. In Ref. [24], a multi-source domain adversarial transfer network that adheres to a dual-fusion strategy was developed to enhance fault diagnosis performance in cross-domain and noisy environments. This approach integrates both feature-level and decision-level information to improve generalization. These studies reflect recent advancements in deep learning-based fault diagnosis, highlighting the importance of robustness, domain adaptation, and efficient representation learning. In Ref. [25], a meta-learning framework named MDGCML was proposed to address imbalanced open-set domain generalization in fault diagnosis. By coordinating gradients across domains and classes, it enabled balanced decision boundaries and fast adaptation to unknown conditions. This method demonstrates strong generalization in few-shot and cross-domain scenarios, offering valuable insights for robust industrial diagnosis. A summary of related work is shown in Table 1.

**Table 1.** Summary of related work.

| References | Wind Turbine Blade Positioning | Blade Defect Feature Extraction | Blade Defect Classification |
|---|---|---|---|
| [1] | - | Descriptive statistical parameters + J48 decision tree algorithm | Bayesian classification |
| [2] | - | RPCA | RPCA |
| [3] | - | MCNN | ART |
| [4] | Haar-AdaBoost | Improved VGG16 | Fully connected layer of VGG16 |
| [5] | Otsu algorithm | AlexNet | Random forest |
| [6] | - | Inception-ResNet-v2 | Fully connected layer of Faster-RCNN |
| [7] | - | Improved VGG11 | Fully connected layer of VGG11 |
| [8] | - | ResNet50 | Fully connected layer of SSD |
| [9] | - | AlexNet | AlexNet |
| [10] | - | Improved ResNet34 | Fully connected layer of |
| [11] | - | DCNN | SVM |
| [12] | Improved k-means algorithm | Fine-tuned ResNet101 | Fully connected layer of R-CNN |
| [13] | - | Improved VGG16 | Fully connected layer of VGG16 |
| [14] | MR algorithm | ResNet50 | DenseNet-121 |
| [15] | - | ResNet50 | Fully connected layer |
| [16] | - | CSPDarknet+RepVGG | Fully connected layer of YOLOvX |
| [17] | - | CSPDarknet | Fully connected layer of YOLOv5 |
| [18] | - | CSPDarknet | Fully connected layer of YOLOv5 |
| [19] | - | MobileNetv3 | Fully connected layer of YOLOv5 |
| [20] | - | CSPDarknet | Fully connected layer |
| This study | YOLOv5 | Feature extraction of DINOv2 large vision model | Stochastic Configuration Network |

### 1.2. Motivation and Contributions

The analysis of vibration signals during the detection of defects in wind turbine blades is a standard method that has been applied in previous studies. However, it is hindered by environmental interference, poor real-time performance, and high equipment costs, and it is not suitable for large-scale wind turbine blade defect detection tasks. Therefore, defect detection methods based on visual images have become the mainstream. (1) Traditional machine learning requires the manual design of features, relying on domain experts' knowledge and experience. The process of feature extraction for high-dimensional data and unstructured data is time-consuming and complex. (2) The performance of existing deep learning methods depends on image quality. Noise in the complex background of an image of a wind turbine blade may be confused with defective features of the blade. For example, background elements such as sky, clouds, and earth may look similar to blade defects, resulting in false or missed detection. (3) To ensure continuous and stable operation of a wind turbine and avoid excessively long downtimes (causing more severe damage to the blades), wind turbine blade defects should be detected in real time.

The following contributions were made to solve the above problems and improve the accuracy of wind turbine blade defect detection:

(1) An end-to-end defect detection framework for wind turbine blades was constructed, comprising three key stages—blade region localization, defect feature extraction, and defect classification—thus forming a complete visual detection process.

(2) Over-fitting suppression and robustness enhancement in blade positioning were achieved using YOLOv5. The images of wind turbine blades taken by drones show different perspectives at different angles. Changes in light will also affect the brightness or darkness (via shadows) of the blade surface, thus affecting the model's generalizability. Therefore, we suppressed over-fitting using Mixup, brightness transformation, flipping, random scaling, and Mosaic methods for image enhancement. These augmentations improve the model's ability to generalize across unseen scenarios, contributing to the robustness of the system. After positioning, the augmented and cropped blade regions were used as inputs for the subsequent classification process, ensuring that the DINOv2-based feature extraction and SCN-based classification operated on inputs that had already been optimized for variability and complexity, allowing the system to maintain high performance across diverse real-world conditions. This augmentation strategy effectively enhances the end-to-end robustness of the proposed defect recognition framework.

(3) We performed feature extraction of wind turbine blades based on a transfer-learning DINOv2 large vision model. In traditional feature extraction methods, features must be manually selected based on previous experience. After dimensionality reduction, some data information may be lost, resulting in limited feature expression ability. For wind turbine blade defect recognition, we propose using the DINOv2 large vision model to extract the features of the blade. This model autonomously extracts image features and possesses strong generalization capabilities, significantly enhancing the accuracy of detecting defects in turbine blades.

(4) We achieved wind turbine blade defect classification based on an SCN. The existing wind turbine blade defect detection methods have low accuracy, but using the SCN classifier can effectively improve accuracy.

The remaining parts of this study are structured as follows. The second section describes the problems inherent in wind turbine blade defect recognition and introduces the specific steps of wind turbine blade defect detection and recognition, including YOLOv5-based blade area positioning, the feature extraction of wind turbine blades via the DINOv2 large vision model, and stochastic-configuration-network-based wind turbine blade defect classification. The third section provides the details of the simulation experiment. The fourth section is a summary of our work.

## 2. Wind Turbine Blade Positioning and Defect Recognition

### *2.1. Framework for Wind Turbine Blade Defect Recognition*

Wind turbines are generally installed in windy areas such as hills, mountains, coastal regions, and vast plains. Regular maintenance of wind turbine blades is essential to ensuring the safe operation of wind turbines and prolonging their service lives. Wind turbines are generally tens of meters high. Manual blade inspection is highly risky, inefficient, and prone to subjective limitations if a turbine has been erected in a harsh natural environment. Therefore, we propose using a UAV to capture images of wind turbine blades for automatic defect detection. The process includes three parts: First, locate the blade area in the image and remove the background that does not contain the blade. Second, input the image of the blade area obtained via positioning into the defect recognition algorithm. Finally, note the position of the blade area and the corresponding defect type in the original image. This process is depicted in Figure 1.

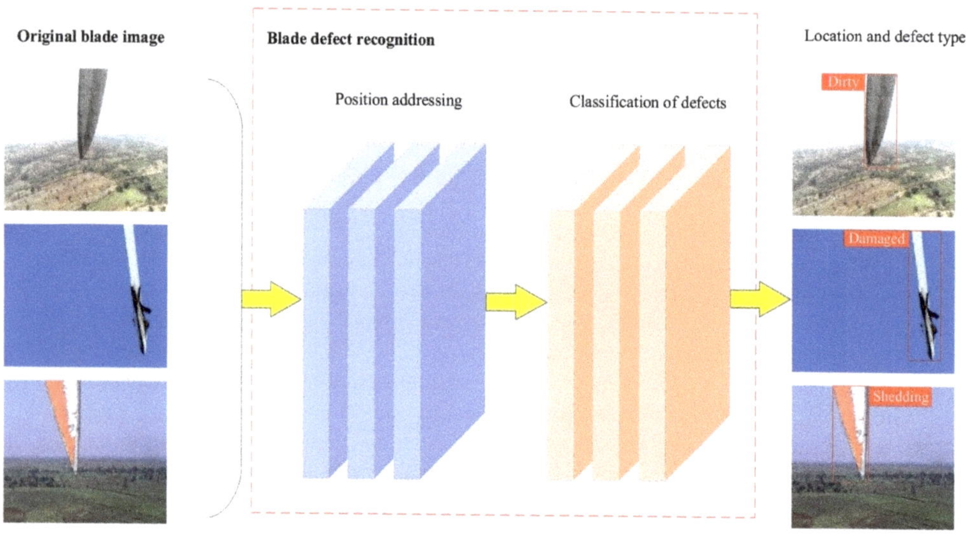


**Figure 1.** Wind turbine blade-positioning and defect classification.

Wind turbine blade defect recognition has three parts: blade area positioning, blade feature extraction, and blade defect classification. A framework of this strategy is shown in Figure 2. (1) Wind turbine blade area positioning is determined. Original UAV-captured images containing complex backgrounds are input into the YOLOv5 object detection model. YOLOv5 accurately locates the blade regions, which are then cropped for further processing. This process effectively isolates the blade from noisy backgrounds, improving downstream feature extraction. (2) The localized blade images are resized and fed into the large vision model DINOv2, which generates a 384-dimensional feature vector representing the visual characteristics of the image. These features are robust and discriminative, and they generalize well under conditions involving complex textures. (3) The 384-dimensional feature vector extracted from the DINOv2 model is fed into a Stochastic Configuration Network for defect classification. An SCN is an incremental learning model capable of dynamically constructing its network structure while ensuring universal approximation.

It selects hidden nodes based on predefined error tolerance and activation constraints, allowing for fast convergence and high classification accuracy. This process outputs the final predictions for each defect type, including damage, paint shedding, and dirt buildup.

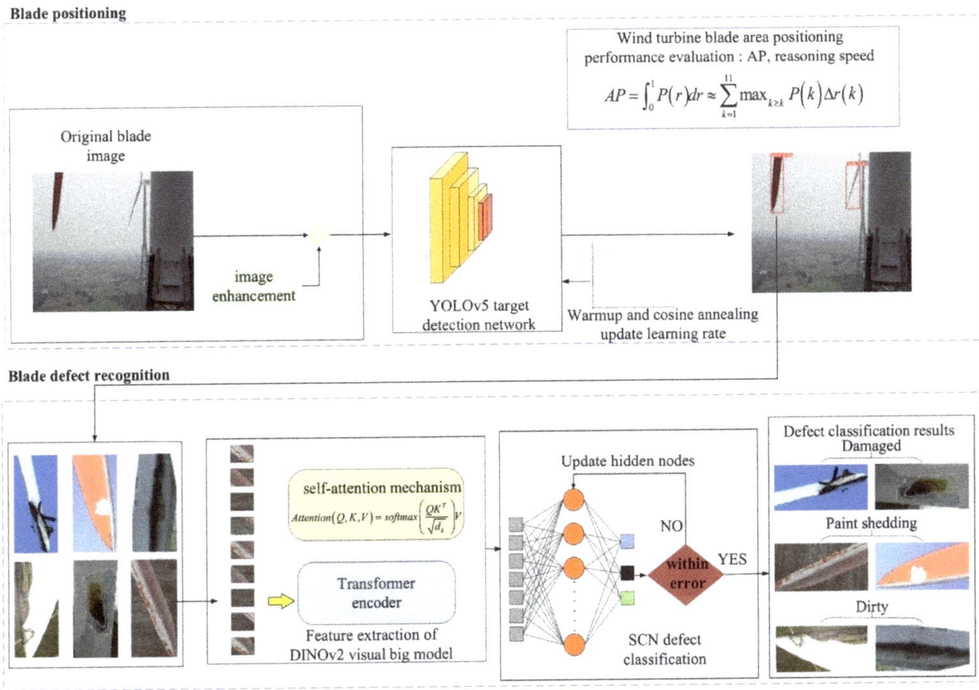


**Figure 2.** Framework of the wind turbine blade defect recognition process.

### 2.2. Wind Turbine Blade Area Positioning Method

The next step entails locating the blade in an image and removing the complex background. The YOLOv5 detection network, known for its speed, accuracy, and simple design, is utilized to identify and localize wind turbine blade areas, aiding in efficient monitoring and analysis. The blades in the original wind turbine blade dataset image are extracted to avoid confusion between the blades' surface defects and the background information precipitated by the feature extraction process, thereby helping the classifier improve recognition accuracy.

YOLOv5 is a single-stage detector [26–28]. Owing to its high efficiency, accuracy, and ease of use, it is widely used in industrial automation, automatic driving, medical imaging, and other fields. The YOLOv5 target detection model adds a CSP structure to the backbone network based on YOLOv3 [29,30]. Its structure includes backbone feature extraction, neck feature fusion, and head target prediction. The wind turbine blade area positioning process based on YOLOv5 is shown in Figure 3.

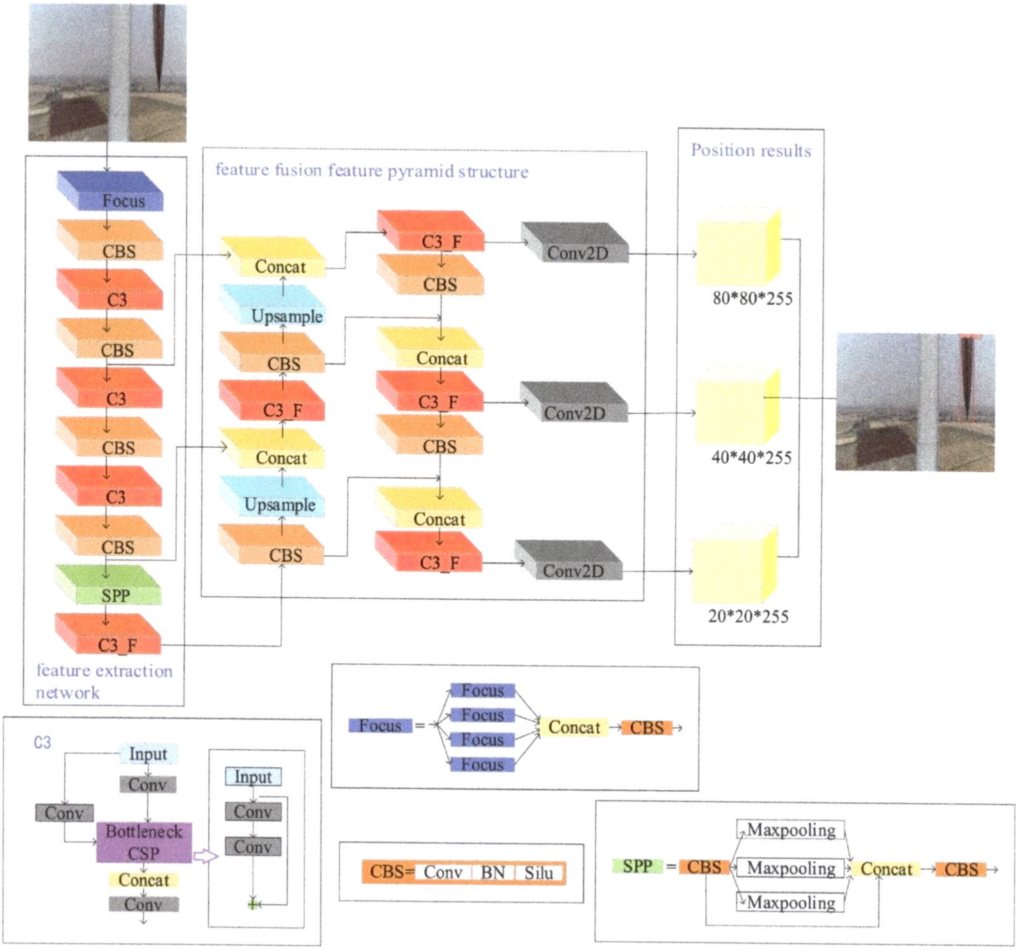


**Figure 3.** A flow chart of wind turbine blade area positioning based on YOLOv5.

The steps of the wind turbine blade area positioning algorithm based on YOLOv5 are as follows:

**Step 1: Wind turbine blade feature extraction.**

The original wind turbine blade image dataset—with a significant background area—captured by the UAV is input into the YOLOv5 backbone feature extraction network. Focus, CBS, C3, and SPP modules are applied to successfully extract and enhance the images.

The CBS module includes Conv (convolution), BN (batch normalization), and Silu activation functions for feature extraction. The activation function expressions are given in Equations (1) and (2), and the batch normalization process is shown in Algorithm 1. The C3 module can perform feature extraction by stacking the convolutional layers (Conv) and the BottleneckCSP module.

$$Silu(x) = x \times Sigmoid(x) \tag{1}$$

$$Sigmoid(x) = \frac{1}{1 + e^{-x}} \tag{2}$$

**Algorithm 1:** Batch normalization

**Input:** $A = \{x_1, x_2, x_3, \ldots x_n\}$, $n$ is the input batch size
**Output:** $B = \{y_1, y_2, y_3 \cdots y_i\}$
1 **For** $i$ = 1 to $n$ **do**
2 Calculate the input mean: $\mu_A = \frac{1}{n}\sum_{i=1}^{n} x_i$
3 Calculate variance: $\sigma_A^2 = \frac{1}{n}\sum_{i=1}^{n}(x_i - \mu_A)^2$
4 Normalize each input using variance and mean: $\widetilde{x}_i = \frac{x_i - \mu_A}{\sqrt{\sigma_A^2 + \varepsilon}}$, $\varepsilon$ is a nonzero decimal number
5 Introducing learnable parameters $\gamma, \beta$ perform linear transformation: $y_i = \gamma\hat{x}_i + \beta$
6 **End For**

**Step 2: Wind turbine blade feature fusion.**

The SPP module performs maximum pooling on the feature map by pooling kernels of different sizes. Then, it performs splicing operations to obtain a new feature map, which improves the model's adaptability to various sizes of wind turbine blades and helps express blade features. After the convolution operation, the resolution of the feature map is improved via nearest-neighbor upsampling so that this map can be fused with other feature maps to form a multi-scale feature pyramid, which can improve the detection ability of the network for different sizes of blades. The nearest neighbor upsampling is shown in Equation (3).

$$x_{src} = \frac{x_{dst} Width_{scc}}{Width_{dst}},\ y_{src} = \frac{y_{dst} Height_{src}}{Height_{dst}} \tag{3}$$

Here, $x_{src}$ is the abscissa of a pixel in the original image, $y_{src}$ is the ordinate of a pixel in the original image, $Width_{src}$ is the width of the original image, $Height_{src}$ is the height of the original image, $x_{dst}$ is the abscissa of the corresponding pixel of the target image, $y_{dst}$ is the ordinate of the corresponding pixel of the target image, $Width_{dst}$ is the width of the target image, and $Height_{dst}$ is the height of the target image.

**Step 3: Obtain the wind turbine blade area results.**

Feature decoding is performed on the feature pyramid of the wind turbine blade neck. The head network predicts the position and size of the wind turbine blade bounding box in each image through the convolution and activation layers. It distinguishes the wind turbine blade from the background area. After upsampling, the original image size is restored, and the position of the wind turbine blade is framed.

### 2.3. Classification of Wind Turbine Blade Defects

Wind turbine blade defect classification includes feature extraction and dimension reduction with data classification. Firstly, the DINOv2 large vision model is used to extract the features of the YOLOv5-located blade images. To meet the requirements of a limited-resource environment and fast reasoning, the DINOv2 ViT-S/14 model was selected as the feature extractor. The embedding dimension of the model is 384 [31], and the obtained wind turbine blade feature vector has 384 elements. Then, the Stochastic Configuration Network is used to classify the feature vectors after data dimensionality reduction. Finally, the probability values of various defect types of wind turbine blades can be obtained.

#### 2.3.1. Method for Extracting Features Utilizing DINOv2

The wind turbine blade area extracted by YOLOv5 still contains a bit of background imagery. To reduce the redundant features generated by the background and the feature dimensions of the defective blade, the number of calculations carried out by the classifier is diminished, and classification efficiency is improved. Accordingly, the DINOv2ViT-S/14 model is used as the feature extractor for blade area in combination with transfer learning [31]. A flow chart of feature extraction via the DINOv2 large vision model is shown in Figure 4, and the corresponding algorithm is shown in Algorithm 2. DINOv2ViT-s/14 extracts features from unlabeled wind turbine blade image data through self-supervised learning. The student model learns the output of the teacher model and improves feature expression ability through knowledge distillation [32]. The ViT neural network has an attention mechanism that can capture the global information of an image, and parallel computing improves the running speed of the model. The attention mechanism is shown in Equation (4).

$$Attention(Q,K,V) = softmax\left(\frac{QK^T}{\sqrt{d_k}}\right)V \tag{4}$$

In this equation, $Q$ is the query matrix, $K$ is the key matrix, $V$ is the value matrix, and $d_k$ is the key dimension.

**Algorithm 2:** DINOv2 wind turbine blade feature extraction algorithm

**Input:** blade image $X_i \in \mathbb{R}^{224\times224\times3}$, $\varepsilon = 10^{-6}$
**Output:** blade feature vector $y \in \mathbb{R}^{384}$

1 The blade image is divided into 16×16 image blocks with 14 × 14 pixels, and the wind turbine image is obtained: $X_c \in \mathbb{R}^{256\times14\times14\times3}$
2 Flatten the three-channel $X_c$ to get $X_f \in \mathbb{R}^{256\times588}$
3 $X_f$ is linearly projected onto a 384-dimensional vector space to obtain $X_{fc\_1} = X_f A^T + b$, $A \in \mathbb{R}^{384\times588}$, $X_{fc\_1} \in \mathbb{R}^{256\times384}$
4 To distinguish the relative position of sequence elements, embedded position encoding, $X_{fc\_1} \in \mathbb{R}^{257\times384}$
5 **For** $i$ = 1 to 12 **do**
6 Layer normalization: $X_{LN\_1} = \frac{X_{fc\_1}-E[X_{fc\_1}]}{\sqrt{Var[X_{fc\_1}]+\varepsilon}} \cdot \gamma + \beta$
7 Attention mechanism: $X_{att} = Attention(X_{LN\_1}, X_{LN\_1}, X_{LN\_1})$
8 Layer normalization: $X_{LN\_2} = \frac{X_{att}-E[X_{att}]}{\sqrt{Var[X_{att}]+\varepsilon}} \cdot \gamma + \beta$
9 The first fully connected layer of multi-layer perceptron: $X_{fc\_2} = X_{att}{A_1}^T + b$, $A_1 \in \mathbb{R}^{1536\times384}$, $X_{fc\_2} \in \mathbb{R}^{257\times1536}$
10 The second fully connected layer of multi-layer perceptron: $X_{fc\_3} = X_{fc\_2}{A_2}^T + b$, $A_2 \in \mathbb{R}^{384\times1536}$, $X_{fc\_3} \in \mathbb{R}^{257\times384}$
11 **End For**
12 Layer normalization: $X_{LN\_3} = \frac{X_{fc\_3}-E[X_{fc\_3}]}{\sqrt{Var[X_{fc\_3}]+\varepsilon}} \cdot \gamma + \beta$
13 The blade feature vector $y$ is the first row element of $X_{LN\_3}$

2.3.2. Feature Vector Classification Based on a Stochastic Configuration Network

The wind turbine blade feature vector extracted by DINOv2 has many dimensions and a large quantity of data, and it is difficult to manually distinguish the characteristics of different types of defects. Therefore, the Stochastic Configuration Network [33], which can automatically learn the classification rules from the input feature vector, is used as the classifier. It is robust and can quickly fit the data. The Stochastic Configuration Network is a random-learning algorithm with a supervision mechanism. The algorithm contains a small number of initial hidden layer nodes. According to the residual error in the input wind turbine blade feature vector fitting process and the preset tolerance error, a judgement is made regarding whether to increase the number of hidden layer nodes. Equation (7) is the current node residual calculation process. The self-monitoring mechanism randomly assigns the weights and deviations of the hidden layer, and the network structure is shown in Figure 5. In Equations (5) and (6), all the feature vectors of wind turbine blades extracted by DINOv2 are superimposed into a matrix and input into the Stochastic Configuration Network to reduce the error by automatically updating the number of hidden layer nodes until the tolerance error is satisfied. Finally, the probability values of different types of wind turbine blade defects are output.

$$Y_{L-1}(x) = \sum_{j=1}^{L-1} \beta_j sigmoid\left(\omega_j^T x + b_j\right), L = 1,2,3,\ldots,n;\ f_0 = 0 \tag{5}$$

$$sigmoid(x) = \frac{1}{1 - e^{-x}} \tag{6}$$

$$e_{L-1} = f - f_{L-1} = \left[e_{L-1,1}, e_{L-1,2}, \ldots, e_{L-1,n}\right] \tag{7}$$

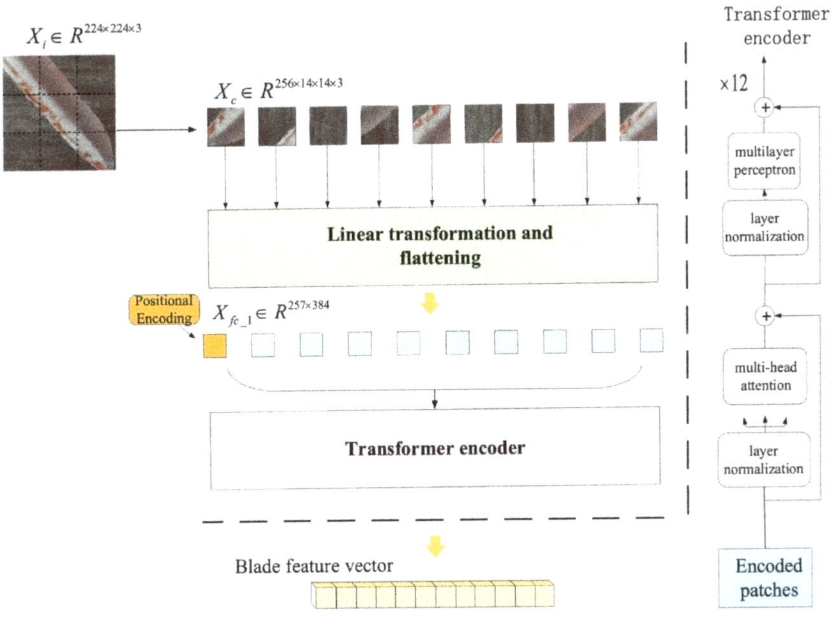


**Figure 4.** A structural diagram of the characteristics of the wind turbine blades obtained via DINOv2.

Suppose the output residual error cannot meet the preset tolerance error. In that case, the number of hidden layer nodes is automatically increased. The output of the $L$ hidden nodes can be expressed as Equation (8).

$$h_L = sigmoid\left(\omega_L^T x + b_L\right) \tag{8}$$

**Theorem 1 [31]:** *Suppose span* $(\Gamma)$ *is dense in* $L_2$ *space, and* $\forall h \in \Gamma, 0 \leq \|h\| \leq b_h$. *Given that* $0 < r < 1$ *and a non-negative sequence* $\{\mu_L\}, \mu_L \leq 1 - r$ *and* $lim_{L\to+\infty}\mu_L = 0$, *for* $L = 1,2\ldots$, *denoted by Equation (9),*

$$\delta_L = \sum_{q=1}^{m} \delta_{L,q}, \delta_{L,q} = (1 - r - \mu_L)\|e_{L-1}\|^2, q = 1,2,\ldots,m \tag{9}$$

*If $h_L$ satisfies the following inequality*

$$\langle e_{L-1}, h_L \rangle^2 \geq {b_h}^2 \delta_{L,q}, q = 1, 2, \ldots, m \tag{10}$$

*the output weights can be evaluated as follows:*

$$[\beta_1^*, \beta_2^*, \ldots, \beta_L^*] = \underset{\beta}{argmin} \left\| f - \sum_{j=1}^{L} \beta_j h_j(X) \right\| \tag{11}$$

*Then, we obtain* $\lim_{L \to +\infty} \| f - f_L^* \| = 0$, *where* $f_L^* = \sum_{j=1}^{L} \beta_j^* h_j(X), \beta_j^* = \left[ \beta_{j,1}^*, \beta_{j,2}^*, \ldots, \beta_{j,m}^* \right]^{\mathrm{T}}$.

Theorem 1 demonstrates that the universal approximation capability of SCNs is theoretically guaranteed through the constraint of Inequality (10). Therefore, the continual addition of new hidden nodes based on (10) and (11) ensures that the model's error will converge within the tolerance error.

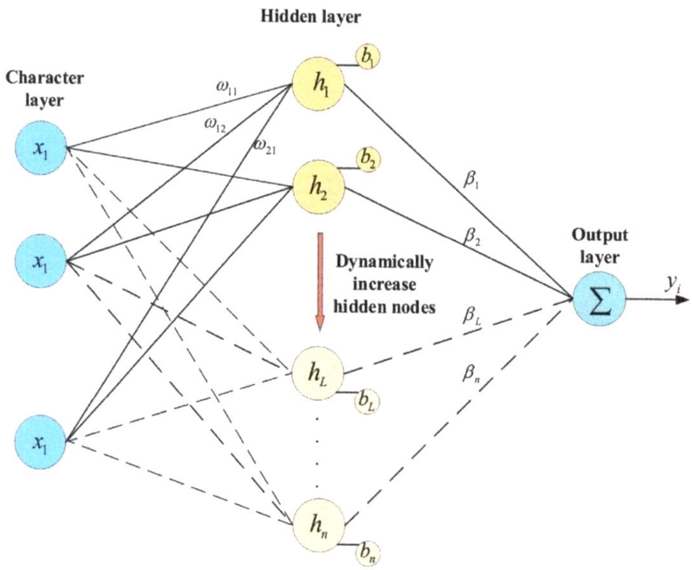


**Figure 5.** A structural diagram of the Stochastic Configuration Network.

## 3. Experimental Validation and Evaluation

### 3.1. Experimental Environment

The software and hardware equipment required for the experiment in this study are shown in Table 2.

**Table 2.** Experimental equipment.

| Computer Software and Hardware | Version/Model |
|---|---|
| GPU | Nvidia RTX 4090 (24 GB) |
| Python | 3.8 |
| CPU | Intel Xeon Platinum 8352 V |
| CUDA | 11.3 |
| Operating System | Ubuntu 22.04 |
| Pytorch | 1.10 |

### 3.2. Model Architecture and Parameter Setting

(1) The entire model architecture consists of three sequential modules: YOLOv5 for blade area localization, DINOv2 for visual feature extraction, and the Random Configuration Network (SCN) for defect classification. In the first stage, YOLOv5 was used for object detection. Before being input into YOLOv5, the original images captured by the unmanned aerial vehicle were adjusted to dimensions of 640 × 640, and the YOLOv5 output was used to crop the bounding box of the wind turbine blade area. In the second stage, the image of the wind turbine blade, following positioning and pruning, was resized to 224 × 224 and passed into the DINOv2 ViT-S/14 large vision model. This model output a 384-dimensional feature vector, representing the semantic and spatial information of the blade surface. In the third stage, the SCN received the DINOv2 feature vector and classified it. The SCN constructed a single-hidden layer feedforward neural network, randomly generated hidden nodes, and calculated the weights of the analytical output. The final prediction indicated whether the type of defect was damage, peeling paint, or dirt buildup. The integration of transformer-based feature extractors and adaptive SCN classifiers contributes to the overall accuracy and robustness of the proposed framework.

(2) In the blade-positioning experiment, the batch size of YOLOv5 was set to $n$ = 16, the number of training instances was set to 100, the learning rate was set to $\eta$ = 0.01, and the momentum was set to $\gamma$ = 0.937. Choosing a lower learning rate and momentum can accelerate convergence and reduce oscillation. To accelerate the convergence of the model, improve its generalizability, and avoid premature over-fitting, Warmup and cosine annealing learning rates are used. When model training began, the Warmup preheating learning rate was selected, as shown in Equation (12). The cosine annealing strategy is shown in Equation (13).

$$Warmup\_lr = lr_{in} + (lr_{\max} - lr_{in}) \cdot \frac{epoch_{now}}{epoch_{tt}} \tag{12}$$

$$lr = \frac{1}{2} lr_{\max} \left(1 + cos\left(\frac{\pi \times epoch_{now}}{epoch_{tt}}\right)\right) \tag{13}$$

where $lr_{in}$ is the initial learning rate of training, $lr_{\max}$ is the preset learning rate, $epoch_{now}$ is the current training round, and $epoch_{tt}$ denotes the total training rounds.

(3) In the defect type recognition experiment, the maximum number of hidden nodes ($L_{\max}$ = 500), the tolerance error ($\varepsilon$ = 0.0001), and the maximum number of candidate nodes ($T_{\max}$ = 100) were randomly configured. Selecting 500 hidden nodes can effectively guarantee the complete convergence of the SCN, and selecting 100 maximum candidate nodes can ensure that the error is minimized every time the SCN updates hidden nodes.

### 3.3. Analysis of Wind Turbine Blade Area Positioning

The dataset used for blade area positioning was obtained from a public online resource. It consists of 4590 high-resolution images of wind turbine blades captured by drones under different conditions. These images cover different perspectives, lighting changes, and backgrounds, such as hills, skies, and grasslands. The dataset was randomly divided into three subsets in an 8:1:1 ratio using a Python script, with 3672 images for training, 459 images for validation, and 459 images for testing. This random division ensured the data distribution was balanced and facilitated repeatable experimental evaluation. Some examples of the blade area positioning dataset are shown in Figure 6.

To effectively avoid over-fitting of the YOLOv5 target detection network in the early training stage, various image data enhancement techniques were adopted to enrich the diversity and complexity of the dataset. These techniques include Mosaic enhancement, which dramatically increases the diversity of datasets by combining multiple images into one image, and the flipping are rotation of the images. These two geometric transformation techniques can simulate the wind turbine blade images taken by the UAV from different perspectives so that the model can adapt to the positioning tasks at various angles. By changing the chromaticity, the wind turbine blade images under different illumination and weather conditions were simulated by adjusting the brightness, contrast, and saturation of the images to improve the model's robustness. By adding noise, the enhancement method simulates image noise in the natural environment, helping the model learn how to accurately detect the target in images containing noise. The image enhancement methods are shown in Figure 7.

**Figure 6.** Example images from the wind turbine blade area positioning dataset.

The prediction results from the wind turbine blade area positioning experiment can be classified into four cases: instances where a positive sample was correctly classified as a positive sample, i.e., a True Positive (TP); instances where positive samples were mistakenly identified as negative samples, i.e., False Negatives (FNs); instances where negative samples were mistakenly identified as positive samples, i.e., False Positives (FPs); and instances where negative samples have been correctly identified as such, i.e., True Negatives (TNs). These four situations correspond to two evaluation indicators for evaluating the performance of wind turbine blades, namely, Precision and Recall, and the corresponding calculation equations are shown in Equations (14) and (15), respectively. Given the difficulty of direct integral calculation, we used the interpolation method to simplify the process. Specifically, it was used to calculate the average value of the accuracy rate at different recall rate levels to obtain the AP value. This index can comprehensively reflect the performance of the blade position detection network; it can be calculated as shown in Equation (16).

$$precision = \frac{TP}{TP + FP} \tag{14}$$

$$recall = \frac{TP}{TP + FN} \tag{15}$$

$$AP = \int_0^1 P(r)dr \approx \sum_{n=1}^{11} \max_{\tilde{n} \geq n} P(\tilde{n}) \Delta r(n) \tag{16}$$

The YOLO series single-stage target detection model and Faster-RCNN two-stage model were used to locate the wind turbine blades in this experiment. The accuracy of each model in locating wind turbine blades is shown in Table 3. AP: 50 represents the average accuracy calculated when the IOU threshold is 0.5, and the formula for calculating the IOU is shown in Equation (17). The IOUs of the predicted and actual bounding boxes were calculated. If the IOU $\geq 0.5$, the prediction result was considered correct.

$$IOU = \frac{area\left(B_p \cap B_{ab}\right)}{area\left(B_p \cup B_{ab}\right)} \tag{17}$$

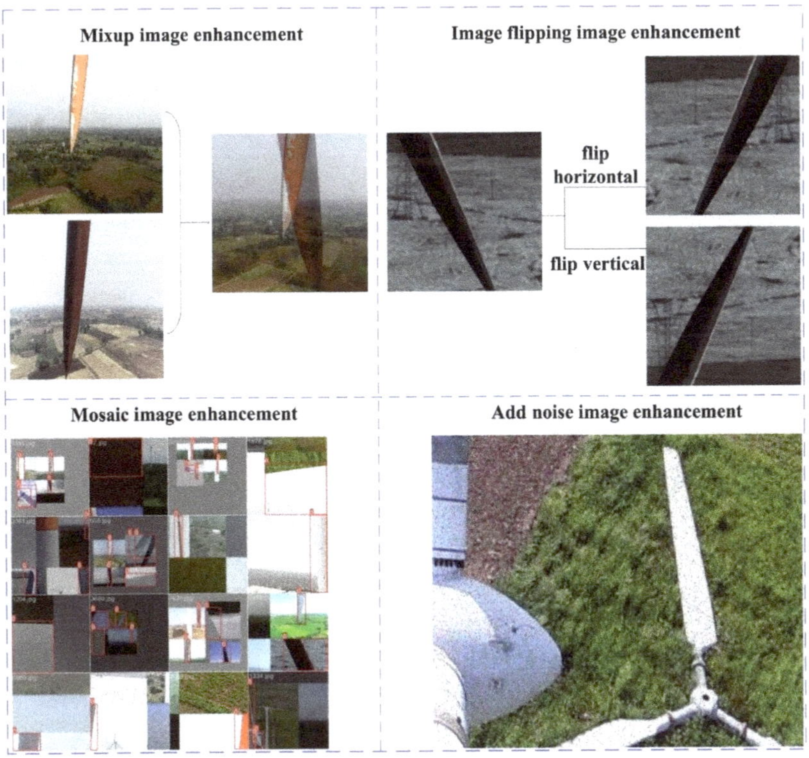


**Figure 7.** Wind turbine blade area positioning data enhancement methods.

**Table 3.** Localization accuracy of wind turbine blade area for each model.

| Blade-Positioning Model | AP:50 | Reasoning Speed |
|---|---|---|
| YOLOv3 | 0.993 | 10.3 ms |
| YOLOv5 | 0.994 | 9.0 ms |
| YOLOv7 | 0.941 | 8.1 ms |
| YOLOv8 | 0.990 | 21.9 ms |
| YOLOv9 | 0.994 | 31.3 ms |
| FasterRCNN | 0.909 | 9.6 ms |

In this equation, $B_p$ is the model's prediction boundary, and $B_{ab}$ is the actual boundary of the wind turbine blade.

As shown in Table 3, YOLOv5 had the best accuracy and speed and is the preferred model for wind turbine blade area positioning tasks. The accuracy of the FasterRCNN two-stage target detection network was much lower than that of the YOLO series, and its inference speed was also lower than that of YOLOv5 and YOLOv7. Under our experimental conditions, involving the use of an RTX4090 graphics card, YOLOv5's speed in locating the original image of a single wind turbine blade reached 9.0 ms, meeting the real-time requirements of wind turbine inspection tasks. The experimental results regarding YOLOv5's ability to locate wind turbine blades are shown in Figure 8.

**Figure 8.** YOLOv5 wind turbine blade positioning.

Figure 9a–d show the trend of the learning rate during the training process. Warmup and cosine decay strategies were adopted. After three rounds of preheating, the learning rate reached the preset value and then decayed with the cosine curve. In the Warmup rounds, a lower learning rate was used for training to avoid over-fitting and reduce the oscillation of the training process. After the model became stable, the preset learning rate was used for training. The cosine annealing strategy allows the learning rate to change according to the cosine function during the training process, allowing a smooth attenuation of the learning rate.

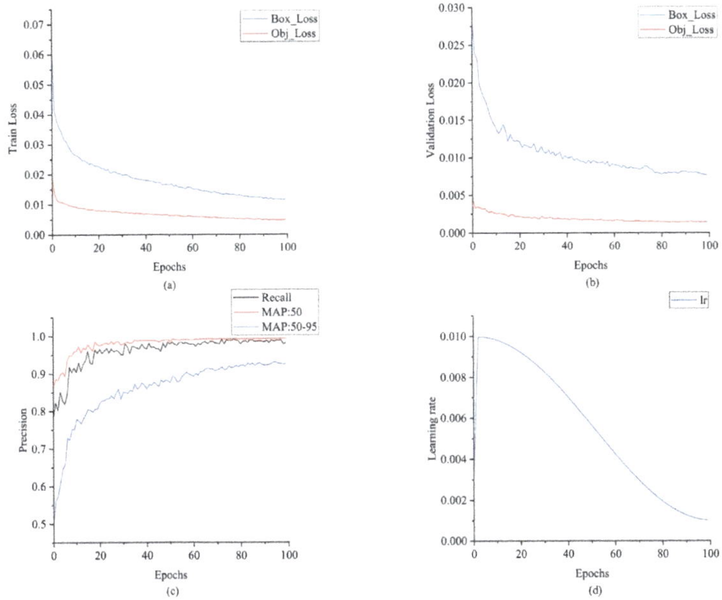


**Figure 9.** YOLOv5 training curve: (**a**) training set loss curve; (**b**) verification set loss curve; (**c**) recall, MAP:50, and MAP50-95; and (**d**) learning rate.

### 3.4. Analysis of Wind Turbine Blade Defect Classification

The dataset used to classify wind turbine blade defects consisted of the blade area images located by YOLOv5, comprising a total of 2989 images. The specific categories and division of wind turbine blade images are shown in Table 4.

**Table 4.** Division and statistics of wind turbine blade defect dataset.

| Sample | Damage | Paint Shedding | Dirt Buildup |
|---|---|---|---|
| Training set | 647 | 687 | 758 |
| Validation set | 138 | 148 | 163 |
| Testing set | 139 | 147 | 162 |
| Total images | 924 | 982 | 1083 |

The feature vectors extracted by DINOv2ViT-s/14, ResNet50, and ResNet18 were reduced to three-dimensional space using the t-SNE algorithm to realize feature visualization [34]. t-SNE can reduce the dimensions of a feature vector and adapt to human observation. However, it also leads to a loss of some feature information. The feature vectors extracted by DINOv2ViT-s/14 allowed for the classification of the wind turbine defects into three categories. The vectors extracted by ResNet18 and ResNet50 are very chaotic, making the defect classification accuracy of the Stochastic Configuration Network low. Feature visualization is shown in Figure 10.

As shown in Figure 11, using the pre-trained DINOv2ViT-s/14 model as the feature extractor and an SCN as the classifier yielded the highest wind turbine blade defect classification accuracy. The feature vector extracted by PCA had the lowest classification accuracy, mainly because PCA does not rely on prior experience and can only capture the linear features of the data, making it difficult to deal with high-dimensional data such as images. When combined with DINOv2ViT-s/14 and transfer learning, ResNet's feature extraction effect with respect to ImageNet pre-training was better than that of PCA. Therefore, the feature extraction method consisting of applying DINOv2 and ResNet combined with transfer learning effectively improved the accuracy of the classifier.

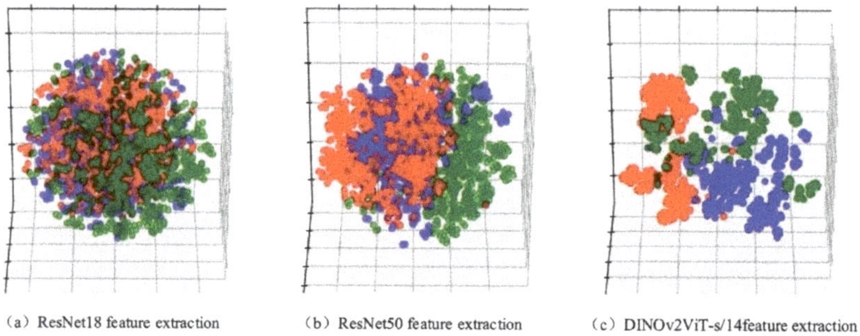


**Figure 10.** Wind turbine blade feature visualization: (**a**) ResNet18, (**b**) ResNet50, and (**c**) DINOv2ViT-s/14 feature extraction.

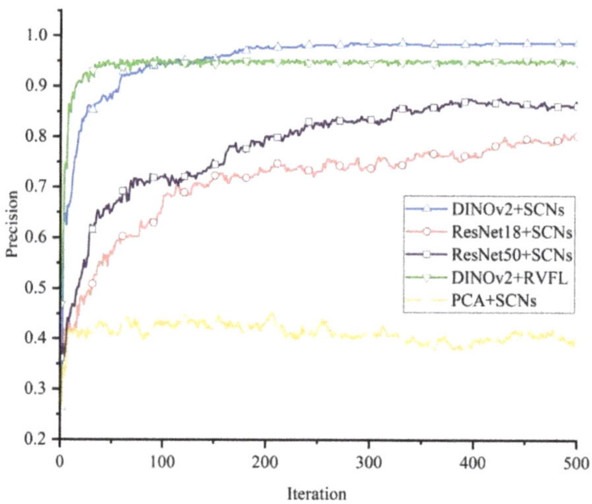


**Figure 11.** Experimental curve of defect classification.

As shown in Table 5, which compares the SCN and other classification algorithms, K-means clustering yielded a value of $k = 3$, and the KNN yielded an initial $k = 5$; SVM adopts a linear kernel function, and the evaluation standard for random forest is the Gini coefficient. The experimental results show that the SCN with automatically updated nodes and randomly assigned weights and offsets can reduce the error, effectively fit wind turbine blade data exhibiting different defect types, and improve the accuracy of defect classification. The results show that the performance of DINOv2 is significantly better than that of ResNet18 for the same classifier, reflecting the enhancement of its visual representation learning ability. When using the features extracted by DINOv2, SCN exhibited the best classification performance among all the evaluated classifiers, verifying that the SCN has stronger discriminative learning and recognition ability. The DINOv2 + SCN method exhibited good feature extraction ability and could effectively classify defective wind turbine blades.

**Table 5.** Experimental results of wind turbine blade defect classification.

| Wind Turbine Blade Defect Classification Algorithm | Accuracy |
|---|---|
| DINOv2 + SCN | 0.987 |
| DINOv2 + Kmeans | 0.515 |
| DINOv2 + KNN | 0.982 |
| DINOv2 + SVM | 0.906 |
| DINOv2 + random forest | 0.983 |
| DINOv2 + RVFL | 0.958 |
| ResNet50 + SCN | 0.873 |
| ResNet18 + SCN | 0.795 |
| PCA + SCN | 0.453 |
| RESNet18 + KNN | 0.759 |
| RESNet18 + Kmeans | 0.360 |
| DINOv2 + SCN (No YOLOv5 positioning) | 0.944 |

To evaluate the feasibility of real-time deployment, the inference speed of each component in the proposed defect recognition framework was measured. The YOLOv5-based blade-positioning module achieved an average inference time of 9.0 ms per image, while the DINOv2 model required 10.60 ms for feature extraction. The SCN classifier completed defect-type classification with a time of only 0.05 ms per image. The total end-to-end inference time was approximately 19.65 ms, which corresponds to over 50 frames per second (FPS). This result demonstrates that the proposed method satisfies the requirements for real-time blade defect detection.

To evaluate the contribution of the blade region localization stage, an ablation experiment was conducted by removing the YOLOv5-based positioning module. Under these conditions, the original UAV images containing background elements such as sky, hills, and vegetation were directly input into the DINOv2 feature extractor without being cropped. As shown in Table 5, the classification accuracy dropped from 0.987 (with YOLOv5) to 0.944 (without YOLOv5). This result confirms that YOLOv5 can effectively suppress background interference and enable more focused and accurate feature extraction by DINOv2, thereby improving overall classification performance.

## 4. Conclusions

To address the low positioning efficiency for wind turbine blades, we used the YOLOv5 target detection network to remove complex background areas and retain the areas containing the blades. Aiming to address the poor robustness of feature extraction, poor adaptability to different defect types, and the low accuracy of defect classification for defective wind turbine blades, we propose a method for detecting and classifying defects in wind turbine blades based on using DINOv2ViT-s/14 as a feature extractor and a random configuration network, combined with transfer learning, as a classifier. Our conclusions are as follows.

(1) The original image data contain many complex background images, interfering with detecting blade defects. YOLOv5 was used to crop the blade areas. To avoid premature over-fitting of YOLOv5, several image enhancement techniques were applied to enhance dataset diversity. This strategy broadened data variation, improving model generalization and robustness.

(2) To address the problem wherein the traditional feature extraction method relies on prior experience, manual design, and the extraction of features, resulting in poor expression ability and low classification accuracy, we used DINOv2ViT-s/14 combined with transfer learning as a feature extractor and a random configuration network as a classifier., The accuracy of classifying defective wind turbine blades reached 98.7% using this method.

In this study, when using an Nvidia RTX4090 GPU, the AP: 50 of the wind turbine blade area was 99.4%, the inference speed for a single picture was 9.0 ms, and the wind turbine blade defect classification accuracy was 98.7%. The proposed method outperforms existing techniques in both accuracy and speed for wind turbine blade image positioning and defect classification.

While the proposed method effectively classifies the surface defects of wind turbine blades, it does not provide information about the shape or extent of the defects, limiting its ability to support finer-grained maintenance strategies that rely on a quantitative analysis of defect areas. Future work will explore the integration of segmentation networks to extract the exact locations and sizes of defects, enabling severity-level estimation and enhancing the practical value of the system in condition-based maintenance scenarios.

**Author Contributions:** Conceptualization, J.T.; methodology, X.L. and J.T.; software, X.L.; validation, X.L.; formal analysis, X.L.; investigation, X.L. and J.T.; resources, H.L.; data curation, X.L.; writing—original draft, X.L. and J.T.; writing—review and editing, Z.Z.; visualization, X.L.; supervision, L.S.; project administration, L.S.; funding acquisition, X.P. and J.T. All authors have read and agreed to the published version of the manuscript.

**Funding:** This work was supported by the Natural Science Foundation of Liaoning Province, China (2023JH2/101700261, 2024-MS-217); the Department of Education of Liaoning Province, China (LJ222411632035, LJ212411632075); and the Shenyang Science and Technology Plan Project (24-213-3-29).

**Institutional Review Board Statement:** Not applicable.

**Informed Consent Statement:** Not applicable.

**Data Availability Statement:** The data that support the findings of this study are available from the corresponding author upon reasonable request.

**Conflicts of Interest:** The authors declare that they have no conflicts of interest.

## Abbreviations

| | |
|---|---|
| YOLO | You Only Look Once |
| SCN | Stochastic Configuration Network |
| DINO | DETR with Improved Denoising Anchor Boxes |
| CNN(Conv) | Convolutional Neural Network |
| Faster-RCNN | Faster Region Convolutional Neural Network |
| VGG | Visual Geometry Group Network |
| ResNet | Residual Network |
| SSD | Single-Shot Multi-Box Detector |
| SVM | Support Vector Machine |
| RPCA | Recursive Principal Component Analysis |
| MCNN | Multi-Channel Convolutional Neural Network |
| ART | Adaptive Resonance Theory |
| CSP | Cross-Stage Partial Network |
| CBS | Conv + Batch Normalization + Silu |
| SPP | Spatial Pyramid Pooling |
| BN | Batch Normalization |
| Silu | Sigmoid Linear Unit |
| AP | Average Precision |
| IOU | Intersection over Union |
| PCA | Principal Component Analysis |
| t-SNE | t-Distributed Stochastic Neighbor Embedding |

| KNN | K Nearest Neighbor |
|---|---|
| K-means | k-Means Clustering |

## References


1. Joshuva, A.; Sugumaran, V. A Comparative Study of Bayes Classifiers for Blade Fault Diagnosis in Wind Turbines through Vibration Signals. *Struct. Durab. Health Monit.* **2017**, *12*, 69–90.
2. Rezamand, M.; Kordestani, M.; Carriveau, R.; Ting, D.S.-K.; Saif, M. A New Hybrid Fault Detection Method for Wind Turbine Blades Using Recursive PCA and Wavelet-Based PDF. *IEEE Sens. J.* **2020**, *20*, 2023–2033. [CrossRef]
3. Wang, M.H.; Lu, S.D.; Hsieh, C.C.; Hung, C.C. Fault Detection of Wind Turbine Blades Using Multi-Channel CNN. *Sustainability* **2022**, *14*, 1781. [CrossRef]
4. Guo, J.; Liu, C.; Cao, J.; Jiang, D. Damage Identification of Wind Turbine Blades with Deep Convolutional Neural Networks. *Renew. Energy* **2021**, *174*, 122–133. [CrossRef]
5. Yang, X.; Zhang, Y.; Lv, W.; Wang, D. Image Recognition of Wind Turbine Blade Damage Based on a Deep Learning Model with Transfer Learning and an Ensemble Learning Classifier. *Renew. Energy* **2021**, *163*, 386–397. [CrossRef]
6. Shihavuddin, A.S.; Chen, X.; Fedorov, V.; Nymark Christensen, A.; Andre Brogaard Riis, N.; Branner, K.; Bjorholm Dahl, A.; Reinhold Paulsen, R. Wind Turbine Surface Damage Detection by Deep Learning Aided Drone Inspection Analysis. *Energies* **2019**, *12*, 676. [CrossRef]
7. Xu, D.; Wen, C.; Liu, J. Wind Turbine Blade Surface Inspection Based on Deep Learning and UAV-Taken Images. *J. Renew. Sustain. Energy* **2019**, *11*, 053305. [CrossRef]
8. Lv, L.; Yao, Z.; Wang, E.; Ren, X.; Pang, R.; Wang, H.; Zhang, Y.; Wu, H. Efficient and Accurate Damage Detector for Wind Turbine Blade Images. *IEEE Access* **2022**, *10*, 2169–3536. [CrossRef]
9. Zhao, X.Y.; Dong, C.Y.; Zhou, P.; Zhu, M.J.; Ren, J.W.; Chen, X.Y. Detecting Surface Defects of Wind Turbine Blades Using an AlexNet Deep Learning Algorithm. *IEICE Trans. Fundam. Electron. Commun. Comput. Sci.* **2019**, *E102-A*, 1817–1824. [CrossRef]
10. Zhu, J.; Wen, C.; Liu, J. Defect Identification of Wind Turbine Blade Based on Multi-Feature Fusion Residual Network and Transfer Learning. *Energy Sci. Eng.* **2022**, *10*, 219–229. [CrossRef]
11. Yu, Y.; Cao, H.; Yan, X.; Wang, T.; Ge, S.S. Defect Identification of Wind Turbine Blades Based on Defect Semantic Features with Transfer Feature Extractor. *Neurocomputing* **2020**, *376*, 1–9. [CrossRef]
12. Mao, Y.; Wang, S.; Yu, D.; Zhao, J. Automatic Image Detection of Multi-Type Surface Defects on Wind Turbine Blades Based on Cascade Deep Learning Network. *Intell. Data Anal.* **2021**, *25*, 463–482. [CrossRef]
13. Liu, Z.H.; Chen, Q.; Wei, H.L.; Lv, M.Y.; Chen, L. Channel-Spatial Attention Convolutional Neural Networks Trained with Adaptive Learning Rates for Surface Damage Detection of Wind Turbine Blades. *Measurement* **2023**, *217*, 113097. [CrossRef]
14. Zhang, C.; Wen, C.; Liu, J. Mask-MRNet: A Deep Neural Network for Wind Turbine Blade Fault Detection. *J. Renew. Sustain. Energy* **2020**, *12*, 053302. [CrossRef]
15. Yang, P.; Dong, C.; Zhao, X.; Chen, X. The Surface Damage Identifications of Wind Turbine Blades Based on ResNet50 Algorithm. In Proceedings of the 2020 39th Chinese Control Conference (CCC), Shenyang, China, 27–29 July 2020.
16. Yao, Y.; Wang, G.; Fan, J. WT-YOLOX: An Efficient Detection Algorithm for Wind Turbine Blade Damage Based on YOLOX. *Energies* **2023**, *16*, 3776. [CrossRef]
17. Ran, X.; Zhang, S.; Wang, H.; Zhang, Z. An Improved Algorithm for Wind Turbine Blade Defect Detection. *IEEE Access* **2022**, *10*, 122171–122181. [CrossRef]
18. Foster, A.; Best, O.; Gianni, M.; Khan, A.; Collins, K.; Sharma, S. Drone Footage Wind Turbine Surface Damage Detection. In Proceedings of the 2022 IEEE 14th Image, Video, and Multidimensional Signal Processing Workshop (IVMSP), Nafplio, Greece, 26–29 June 2022.
19. Zhang, Y.; Yang, Y.; Sun, J.; Ji, R.; Zhang, P.; Shan, H. Surface Defect Detection of Wind Turbine Based on Lightweight YOLOv5s Model. *Measurement* **2023**, *220*, 113222. [CrossRef]
20. Zhang, R.; Wen, C. SOD-YOLO: A Small Target Defect Detection Algorithm for Wind Turbine Blades Based on Improved YOLOv5. *Adv. Theory Simul.* **2022**, *5*, 2100631. [CrossRef]
21. Ran, X.; Suyaroj, N.; Tepsan, W.; Lei, M.; Ma, H.; Zhou, X.; Deng, W. A Novel Fuzzy System-Based Genetic Algorithm for Trajectory Segment Generation in Urban Global Positioning System. *J. Adv. Res.* 2025, in press. [CrossRef] [PubMed]
22. Chen, H.; Sun, Y.; Li, X.; Zheng, B.; Chen, T. Dual-Scale Complementary Spatial-Spectral Joint Model for Hyperspectral Image Classification. *IEEE J. Sel. Top. Appl. Earth Obs. Remote Sens.* **2025**, *18*, 6772–6789. [CrossRef]
23. Wang, C.; Yang, J.; Jie, H.; Zhao, Z.; Wang, W. An Energy-Efficient Mechanical Fault Diagnosis Method Based on Neural-Dynamics-Inspired Metric SpikingFormer for Insufficient Samples in Industrial Internet of Things. *IEEE Internet Things J.* **2025**, *12*, 1081–1097. [CrossRef]

24. Wang, C.; Jie, H.; Yang, J.; Gao, T.; Zhao, Z.; Chang, Y.; See, K.Y. A Multi-Source Domain Feature-Decision Dual Fusion Adversarial Transfer Network for Cross-Domain Anti-Noise Mechanical Fault Diagnosis in Sustainable City. *Inf. Fusion* **2025**, *115*, 102739. [CrossRef]
25. Wang, C.; Shu, Z.; Yang, J.; Zhao, Z.; Jie, H.; Chang, Y.; Jiang, S.; See, K.Y. Learning to Imbalanced Open Set Generalize: A Meta-Learning Framework for Enhanced Mechanical Diagnosis. *IEEE Trans. Cybern.* **2025**, *55*, 1464–1475. [CrossRef] [PubMed]
26. Zheng, Y.; Liu, Y.; Wei, T.; Jiang, D.; Wang, M. Wind Turbine Blades Surface Crack-Detection Algorithm Based on Improved YOLO-v5 Model. *J. Electron. Imaging* **2023**, *32*, 033012. [CrossRef]
27. Redmon, J.; Divvala, S.; Girshick, R.; Farhadi, A. You Only Look Once: Unified, Real-Time Object Detection. In Proceedings of the IEEE Conference on Computer Vision and Pattern Recognition, Las Vegas, NV, USA, 27–30 June 2016; pp. 779–788.
28. Redmon, J.; Farhadi, A. YOLO9000: Better, Faster, Stronger. In Proceedings of the IEEE Conference on Computer Vision and Pattern Recognition, Honolulu, HI, USA, 21–26 July 2017; pp. 6517–6525.
29. Redmon, J.; Farhadi, A. YOLOv3: An Incremental Improvement. *arXiv* **2018**, arXiv:1804.02767. [CrossRef]
30. Liu, X.; Liu, C.; Jiang, D. Wind Turbine Blade Surface Defect Detection Based on YOLO Algorithm. In Proceedings of the International Congress and Workshop on Industrial AI and eMaintenance 2023, Luleå, Sweden, 13–15 June 2023; pp. 367–380.
31. Oquab, M.; Darcet, T.; Moutakanni, T.; Vo, H.; Szafraniec, M.; Khalidov, V.; Fernandez, P.; Haziza, D.; Massa, F.; El-Nouby, A.; et al. DINOv2: Learning Robust Visual Features without Supervision. *arXiv* **2023**, arXiv:2304.07193.
32. Caron, M.; Touvron, H.; Misra, I.; Jegou, H.; Mairal, J.; Bojanowski, P.; Joulin, A. Emerging Properties in Self-Supervised Vision Transformers. In Proceedings of the IEEE/CVF International Conference on Computer Vision (ICCV), Montreal, BC, Canada, 11–17 October 2021; pp. 9650–9660.
33. Wang, D.; Li, M. Stochastic Configuration Networks: Fundamentals and Algorithms. *IEEE Trans. Cybern.* **2017**, *47*, 3466–3479. [CrossRef] [PubMed]
34. van der Maaten, L.; Hinton, G. Visualizing Data Using t-SNE. *J. Mach. Learn. Res.* **2008**, *9*, 2579–2605.

sensors

MDPI

Article

# Automated Anomaly Detection in Blast Furnace Shaft Static Pressure Using Adversarial Autoencoders and Mode Decomposition

Xiaodong Sun [1], Jie Zhu [2], Bing Tang [2] and Zhaohui Jiang [1,*]

[1] School of Automation, Central South University, Changsha 410083, China; xiaodong.sun@cisdi.com.cn
[2] CISDI Information Technology (Chongqing) Co., Ltd., Chongqing 401122, China; jie.zhu@cisdi.com.cn (J.Z.); bing.tang@cisdi.com.cn (B.T.)
* Correspondence: jzh0903@csu.edu.cn; Tel.: +86-158-7429-1486

**Abstract:** Monitoring the blast furnace shaft static pressure is crucial for maintaining a stable ironmaking process. Traditional rule-based methods and manual inspections suffer from high labor costs and inconsistent standards. This article proposes a new unsupervised anomaly detection framework that combines adversarial autoencoder with variational mode decomposition (VMD). Firstly, using VMD combined with sample entropy calculation and clustering algorithm, the trend, period, and other components of multidimensional signals are extracted, and then these components are integrated into an improved adversarial training autoencoder to detect global and local anomalies. The proposed method has an accuracy of 0.95, a recall rate of 0.91, and an F1 score of 0.93. Which demonstrates the method effectively captures multi-scale anomalies including value bias, morphological changes, and sudden fluctuations, while providing analysts with interpretable anomaly detail diagnosis.

**Keywords:** blast furnace monitoring; time-series anomaly detection; adversarial autoencoder; variational mode decomposition; unsupervised learning

## 1. Introduction

Blast furnace operators need to determine the blast furnace production status and make appropriate operational adjustments based on time-series signals (such as temperature, pressure, etc.) collected by sensors installed at different positions of the furnace. The distribution of gas flow inside the blast furnace is a critical factor affecting stable and smooth operation. To more comprehensively understand the gas flow distribution state within the blast furnace, many steel plants have introduced shaft static pressure measurement signals. Shaft static pressure is measured by evenly installing pressure sensors around the cooling walls at specific layers of the blast furnace. Different abnormal patterns of shaft static pressure often indicate abnormal gas flow distribution inside the furnace. Currently, the primary method for monitoring abnormal states of shaft static pressure requires operators to observe signal curves in real time, which consumes significant human effort and is difficult to standardize due to differences in analytical logic among operators. Therefore, constructing an automated algorithm for blast furnace shaft static pressure anomaly detection has become necessary. This method can significantly reduce the workload of blast furnace operators, standardize evaluation logic, and improve the stability of production control.

In traditional industrial fields, such as blast furnace process control systems (PCS), the anomaly detection logic for key indicators mainly relies on explicit expression rules and corresponding thresholds [1,2]. The drawback of this method is its high requirement for threshold setting, typically requiring process experts to adjust numerous parameters. Additionally, changes in raw materials, operational systems, and other influencing factors cause corresponding changes in the data distribution of blast furnace conditions and their monitoring indicators. This necessitates continuous threshold adjustments to adapt to complex changes in furnace conditions, making traditional rule-based anomaly detection methods difficult to apply in actual production processes. To optimize this situation, subsequent academic research proposed a series supervised machine learning (SML) based parameter optimization methods to achieve automatic adaptive parameter adjustment or fuzzy logic control (FLC) [3,4], but these still require manual design of rule-based process feature extraction as a foundation.

Since the key monitoring indicators in the blast furnace production process are time-series signal data collected through multiple sensors, the anomaly detection of these key indicators can be abstracted as a multidimensional time-series anomaly detection algorithm task. In recent years, researchers have developed various methods to address this problem. The most commonly used techniques can be divided into two major categories: traditional statistical models and deep learning-based approaches. Among them, statistical model-based methods include: distance-based models using Dynamic Time Warping (DTW) [5]; time-series prediction models represented by ARIMA [6]; and clustering algorithms represented by DBSCAN [7]. These traditional statistical models primarily focus on single-variable time-series anomaly detection. However, for multidimensional time-series anomaly detection as encountered in this study, these methods often perform unsatisfactorily due to the curse of dimensionality.

Deep learning algorithms for time-series anomaly detection [8–18] can be broadly categorized into two types. One type involves establishing prediction models to calculate prediction errors, such as recurrent neural networks (RNN) and Long Short-Term Memory (LSTM) networks [19,20], which extend traditional statistical model-based time-series prediction methods into the domain of deep learning. Since anomaly detection in industrial applications often lacks large amounts of labeled negative samples to support prediction model training, most prediction error-based models compare predicted values with observed values. This requires predicting time-series over extended periods, where high accuracy in long-term prediction is a prerequisite for effective anomaly detection models—a problem that has long challenged the industrial sector. The other type uses encoder-decoder architectures to reconstruct observed values and calculate reconstruction errors, with common models including autoencoder neural network (AE) and Variational Autoencoders (VAE) [21–24]. However, VAE models often struggle to learn true posterior distributions, which affects the quality of reconstruction [25,26].

In response to the aforementioned technical challenges, the academic community has attempted to enhance the generative performance of Variational Autoencoders (VAEs) by incorporating the adversarial mechanism of Generative Adversarial Networks (GANs), leading to the development of the Adversarial Autoencoder (AAE) algorithmic framework [25,26]. Within the domain of anomaly detection, the existing literature primarily explores AAE algorithms through two distinct research trajectories: the first category focuses on adaptive designs of generators and discriminators [27], aiming to improve anomaly recognition accuracy by optimizing feature extraction efficacy during adversarial training; the second category endeavors to integrate AAE with conventional anomaly detection models such as Isolation Forest and Support Vector Data Description (SVDD) [28,29], thereby reinforcing detection robustness in specific scenarios through ensemble learning strategies. Existing research demonstrates that the performance optimization of anomaly detection models critically depends on domain-specific customized modeling. Throughout this process, the effectiveness of data feature representation emerges as a pivotal constraining factor. For industrial time-series signals, time-frequency analysis techniques including Fourier Transform and Wavelet Transform have been extensively employed as data preprocessing methods. Among these, Variational Mode Decomposition (VMD) has garnered significant attention due to its prominent advantages in processing non-stationary signals with strong interference. In the field of anomaly monitoring, current studies on VMD methodology predominantly manifest in two aspects: The first involves adaptive selection mechanism design for critical parameters such as modal quantities [30]; The second combines VMD with deep learning models like Convolutional Autoencoders (CAE) to achieve anomaly identification in multidimensional industrial signals (e.g., hydro-turbine unit monitoring data [31]. Notably, the majority of the existing literature integrating VMD with neural networks concentrates on time-series prediction tasks, such as the construction of crude oil price prediction models based on VMD and Bidirectional Long Short-Term Memory (BiLSTM) networks [32]. However, the data characteristics in the aforementioned research contexts exhibit substantial differences from the blast furnace shaft static pressure data investigated in this study. Specifically, existing methods typically employ post-processing strategies such as Intrinsic Mode Functions (IMFs) component screening or convolutional feature extraction. When applied to blast furnace static pressure signal analysis, these approaches confront two primary limitations: firstly, inadequate adaptability to multi-scale signal characteristics under complex blast furnace operating conditions; secondly, insufficient interpretability of the feature processing procedures. In light of this, the present study proposes an innovative analytical framework tailored to the data characteristics of blast furnace shaft static pressure, aiming to achieve automated detection and interpretation of anomalous signals within this specific context.

The shaft static pressure sensors are evenly installed on multiple layers of blast furnace stave coolers, collectively characterizing the three-dimensional pressure field inside the furnace [33]. Therefore, unlike traditional anomaly detection that only considers temporal anomalies in time-series signals, this study also needs to consider spatial anomalies such as changes in relative magnitudes between different signals. Process experts refer to this analysis as furnace profile analysis, which was previously conducted by manually observing changes in relative values between different sensor signals to determine whether the furnace profile had changed.

During temporal anomaly detection, operations such as burden charging and blast injection cause shaft static pressure data to exhibit superimposed multiple periodicities with variable cycle lengths. Traditional manual observation methods can filter out these interference patterns using prior knowledge or experience to focus on abnormal fluctuations outside normal periodic variations. However, a key challenge in this study is how models that minimize overall reconstruction error can overcome these interferences to detect truly meaningful anomalies.

Due to the difficulty in obtaining labeled samples for blast furnace shaft static pressure and the challenge of precisely defining anomalies through rules, traditional supervised models cannot be used in model selection. To address these issues, this paper proposes an empirical mode decomposition method combined with reconstruction error for shaft static pressure anomaly detection. The contribution of our method are as follows:

1. Proposed an anomaly monitoring method specifically for blast furnace shaft static pressure data. This method enables label-free anomaly detection while maintaining interpretable results that support further analysis incorporating process knowledge, transforming the current manual visual monitoring practice for anomaly detection.

2. Developed an innovative algorithmic framework combining improved Variational Mode Decomposition (VMD) with H-AAE network for anomaly detection. This framework

specifically addresses the data characteristics of non-fixed-length periodicity in our dataset by optimizing VMD decomposition results through sample entropy and k-means clustering, achieving adaptive separation and reconstruction of trend, periodic, and detail variation components. These physically meaningful components are then integrated with the H-AAE network to enable simultaneous detection of different types of global and local anomalies.

3. Proposed a modified autoencoder H-AAE that incorporates concepts from Generative Adversarial Networks (GAN) and Huber loss function. This model ensures stability and computational efficiency by integrating GAN concepts into the autoencoder framework, while enhancing robustness in detecting both anomaly segments and points through the modified Huber loss function.

The rest of this document is organized as follows. Section 2 describes the details of the main process background and issues of the proposed method in this paper. Section 3 describes the main methodology proposed in this paper. Section 4 provides an industrial validation based on real data. Section 5 summarizes the work of this paper and its contributions.

## 2. Process Introduction and Problem Description

### 2.1. Blast Furnace Ironmaking Process

The production process of ironmaking focuses on the reduction in iron from ores and other natural forms of iron-containing compounds. The main methods of ironmaking include blast furnace, direct reduction and smelting. The basic principle is the reduction in ores to hot metal by physical and chemical reactions in a special atmosphere (reductants CO, $H_2$, C, appropriate temperature, etc.). Most of the ore is used as raw material for ironmaking, except for a small portion of the ore. Blast furnace ironmaking is the main method of modern ironmaking and an important part of steel production. This method of ironmaking was developed and perfected on the basis of ancient open-hearth ironmaking. Although many new ironmaking methods have been researched and developed in different countries around the world, this method still accounts for more than 95% of the world's iron production due to its high pressure furnace ironmaking technology, good economy, simple process, large output, high productivity and low energy consumption. In the ironmaking process, iron is made by loading raw materials (sintered ore, pelletized ore, iron ore), fuels (e.g., coke, pulverized coal), and other auxiliary materials (e.g., limestone, dolomite, manganese ore, etc.) into the furnace in a certain proportion to be smelted). Hot air is injected in certain proportions from the top of the blast furnace through the perimeter of the blast furnace to the bottom of the hot blast furnace, where they contribute to the combustion of the coke (depending on the blast furnace, pulverized coal, heavy oil, natural gas, and other auxiliary fuels may also be injected). At high temperatures, the coking coal is burned in the presence of oxygen in the air inside the drum. At high temperatures, the coking coal is burned by the oxygen in the blast furnace air, producing carbon monoxide and hydrogen. Raw materials, fuels plus smelting under the furnace and other processes, gas under the furnace and on the furnace discharge, heat transfer, reduction, smelting, decarburization effect and ore production in turn, adding slag iron ore raw materials to join and the combination of the flow in the furnace, the bottom of the furnace intermittent melting iron pots, sent to the steelmaking plant. At the same time, the production of blast furnace gas, blast furnace slag two kinds of by-products, the main non-ferrous metal impurities in the iron water, combined with limestone and other fluxes, from the output of the slag, all of which is used as a raw material for the production of cement, after water quenching; the production of the blast furnace gas produced by the outlet, after dust removal, into the hot blast furnace, blast furnace and coke oven, boiler, and other fuels. The main structure of the blast furnace is shown in the Figure 1.

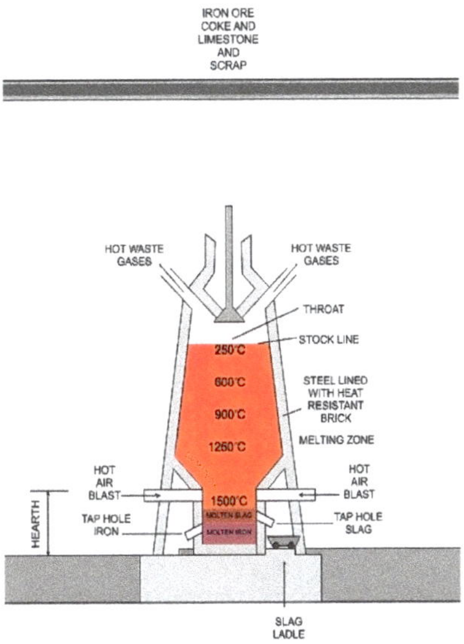


**Figure 1.** Main structure of blast furnace.

### *2.2. Problem Description*

During the production of the blast furnace, hot blast is injected through tuyeres, which includes fuels such as pulverized coal or natural gas. The hot air reacts with iron ore (mainly iron oxides), and the C in the blast material seizes the O in the iron ore, generating CO and $CO_2$ that are discharged from the top of the blast furnace, and at the same time, the iron ore is reduced to hot metal. The hot air above forms a gas flow with reducing atmosphere in the blast furnace. Whether the blast furnace gas flow distribution is reasonably distributed, directly affects the reaction state of the blast furnace. Ensuring the reasonable distribution of airflow is the key to ensure the stable operation of the blast furnace.

Traditionally, the monitoring of blast furnace airflow status is mainly carried out through blast pressure, top pressure and other indicators for rough monitoring, and it is difficult to determine the overall airflow distribution in different locations of the blast furnace. In order to have a more detailed and comprehensive understanding of the blast furnace airflow distribution status, some steel mills in the blast furnace part of the stave coolers in multiple directions, circumferentially embedded embedded pressure sensors, to realize the different positions of the blast furnace radial gas flow profile status of real-time monitoring.

The operational stability of a blast furnace is closely tied to whether its shaft static pressure remains within normal ranges. For instance, certain anomalies in shaft static pressure may signal critical abnormalities like gas channeling within the furnace. Consequently, process experts must closely monitor changes in blast furnace shaft static pressure during operations (see Figure 2).

Due to the blast furnace there are burden charging, blast injection and other cyclical operations, such operations on the static pressure of the furnace at various points will have a cyclical impact, and due to changes in the production rhythm, errors, and other reasons, the length of such cycles is approximate but not the same. At the same time, for the judgment of airflow distribution anomalies in addition to each pressure measurement point itself is abnormal, multi-sensor between the relative value of the disorder is also one of the key anomalies that needs to be monitored.

Traditional anomaly detection methods commonly used in manufacturing, such as rule-based systems or simple degradation trend analysis, fail to meet the monitoring demands of the static pressure of the blast furnace shaft. Currently, no automated algorithms for identifying such anomalies are industrially deployed. Steel enterprises primarily rely on experienced operators to manually detect abnormalities through manual pattern recognition. However, as blast furnaces operate continuously 24/7, the intense workload of monitoring static pressure leads to frequent missed detections. This underscores the necessity to develop an automated monitoring algorithm tailored to the unique data characteristics of blast furnace static pressure.

Therefore, the rule-based anomaly recognition commonly used in the manufacturing industry is difficult to adapt to the monitoring scenario of the static pressure of the furnace, and the current iron and steel enterprises mainly recognize anomalies through the manual observation of experienced operators. Due to the 24 h uninterrupted production of the blast furnace, the intensity of the operator's observation of the static pressure of the furnace is very high, and it is prone to omission of judgment and other problems. It is necessary to design a set of algorithms to adapt to the data characteristics of the static pressure of the furnace and realize automatic monitoring.

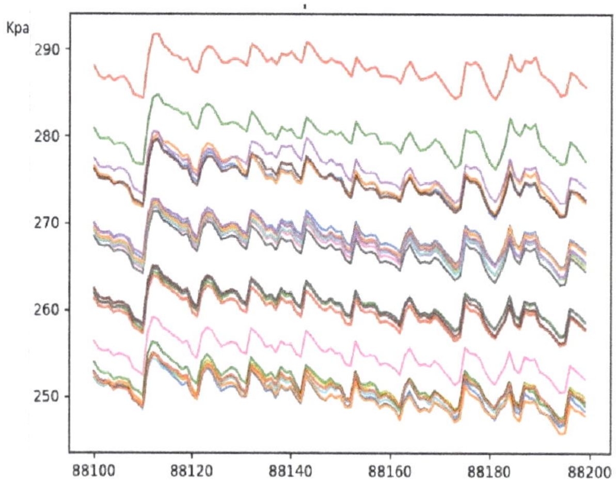


**Figure 2.** Furnace Static Pressure Data Fragment.

### 2.3. Problem Formulation

In this study, the shaft static pressure anomaly detection problem can be abstracted as a multidimensional time-series anomaly detection task. In time-series analysis, a single-variable time-series can typically be represented as a sequence of data points with temporal ordering:

$$x = \{x_1, x_2, x_3, \ldots, x_n\} \tag{1}$$

where $x_i$ represents the data value at the $i$-th time point, and $n$ is the total length of the time series.

The shaft static pressure data constitutes a multidimensional time-series variable. Assuming a blast furnace has $m$ static pressure detection sensors labeled in positional order, the $j$-th time-series signal can be denoted as $x^j$, where $j \in \{1, 2, \ldots, m\}$.

Anomaly detection typically involves analyzing and making judgments on specific segments or windows of the time series. This study employs sliding window segmentation for detection segments. Assuming a window width of $t$ and a step size of $k$, the $i$-th time segment can be represented as:

$$W_i = \begin{bmatrix} x^1_{i\cdot k+1} & x^1_{i\cdot k+2} & \cdots & x^1_{i\cdot k+t} \\ x^2_{i\cdot k+1} & x^2_{i\cdot k+2} & \cdots & x^2_{i\cdot k+t} \\ \vdots & \vdots & \ddots & \vdots \\ x^m_{i\cdot k+1} & x^m_{i\cdot k+2} & \cdots & x^m_{i\cdot k+t} \end{bmatrix} \quad (2)$$

where $i$ is the window index and $k$ is the step size ($k \in \{0, 1, 2, \ldots\}$). The detection of anomalies in shaft static pressure essentially involves identifying anomalies in matrix $W_i$.

Since there are no labeled anomaly samples in the studied scenario, it is hard to evaluate the model using metrics like accuracy and recall from classification tasks.This paper adopts the idea of unsupervised algorithms, defining that the anomaly degree of a segment $W_i$ increases with the distance $(W_i, W_c)$ from the normal state $W_c$ (represented by most segments). Note that $W_c$ is not necessarily a matrix but represents the concept of the normal state.A method will be designed to calculate the distance $(W_i, W_c)$ for the static pressure scenario.

## 3. Method

This section is divided into three parts: Anomaly Detection Method, Time-Series Data Processing, and implementation details.

### 3.1. Anomaly Detection Method

For the normal state representation $W_c$, this study adopts a reconstruction error-based approach. The encoder of the Autoencoder (AE) maps input $W_i$ to latent variables $Z$, while the decoder reconstructs the input space through $R$. Since the primary task in this scenario involves detecting temporal segment anomalies, segment-level anomalies may manifest as various patterns such as trend shifts, fluctuations, or occasional extreme values. The L2 loss is highly sensitive to extreme values, which could lead the model to become less sensitive to other types of anomalies.To enhance robustness against outliers, the original L2 loss is replaced with the Huber loss, whose sensitivity to anomalies can be controlled via parameter $\delta$. The AE is trained by minimizing the Huber loss between inputs and reconstructions:

$$\min\{\mathcal{H}_\delta(W_i, \mathrm{AE}(W_i))\} \quad (3)$$

where the Huber loss is defined as:

$$\mathcal{H}_\delta(a,b) = \begin{cases} \frac{1}{2}(a-b)^2 & \text{if } |a-b| \le \delta \\ \delta|a-b| - \frac{1}{2}\delta^2 & \text{otherwise} \end{cases} \quad (4)$$

To balance computational efficiency and industrial applicability, the adversarial training architecture from [26] is integrated with the AE. This hybrid framework consists of an encoder $E$ and two decoders $D_1$, $D_2$. The core adversarial objectives are reformulated using Huber loss:

$$\begin{cases} \min\limits_{\mathrm{AE}_1}\{\mathcal{H}_{\delta_1}(W_i, \mathrm{AE}_2(\mathrm{AE}_1(W_i)))\} \\ \max\limits_{\mathrm{AE}_2}\{\mathcal{H}_{\delta_2}(W_i, \mathrm{AE}_2(\mathrm{AE}_1(W_i)))\} \end{cases} \quad (5)$$

The anomaly scoring function is accordingly modified to:

$$\mathcal{A}(\widehat{W_i}) = \alpha\mathcal{H}_{\delta_3}\left(\widehat{W_i}, \mathrm{AE}_1(\widehat{W_i})\right) + \beta\mathcal{H}_{\delta_4}\left(\widehat{W_i}, \mathrm{AE}_2(\mathrm{AE}_1(\widehat{W_i}))\right) \tag{6}$$

with $\alpha + \beta = 1$, where $\delta_1$–$\delta_4$ are tunable hyperparameters optimized through cross-validation for specific industrial environments. This design mitigates the oversensitivity of L2 loss to outliers while preserving its stability in smooth regions.

Since this study uses a reconstruction error-based anomaly detection approach and assumes the training set is approximately normal or contains minimal anomalies, the anomaly threshold is set as the 99th percentile of the training set scores:

$$T = Q_{0.99}\left(\mathcal{A}(\widehat{W})\right) = \inf\left\{x \in \mathbb{R} : P\left(\mathcal{A}(\widehat{W}) \le x\right) \ge 0.99\right\} \tag{7}$$

### 3.2. Time Series Data Processing

While the adversarial training architecture described above can construct $W_c$, its optimization objective focuses on minimizing the overall Huber difference in the data. However, the shaft static pressure data contains multiple superimposed periodicities with variable lengths. Solely considering overall error tends to overlook detailed anomalies, which affects model performance. To address this data characteristic, the time-series segments used for anomaly detection are decomposed.

Variational Mode Decomposition (VMD) is a non-recursive signal processing method that decomposes time-series data into a series of Intrinsic Mode Functions (IMFs) with finite bandwidth. Compared to traditional Empirical Mode Decomposition (EMD), VMD obtains IMF components through iterative optimization, effectively avoiding mode mixing and producing more accurate and stable decomposition results. The VMD objective function can be expressed as:

$$\begin{cases} \min\left\{\sum_{k=1}^{K}\left\|\partial_t\left[\left(\delta(t) + \frac{j}{\pi t}\right) * u_k(t)\right]e^{-j\omega_k t}\right\|_2^2\right\} \\ \text{s.t.} \sum_{k=1}^{K} u_k = f(t) \end{cases} \tag{8}$$

where $\partial_t$ denotes the partial derivative, $\delta(t)$ is the Dirac delta function, "$*$" represents the convolution operation, $K$ is the total number of components, and $f(t)$ is the original signal.

For the decomposed signal components, process experts focus on overall trend changes and short-term detailed variations. From the perspective of visual inspection aligned with process analysis logic, some components represent overall trends while others represent detailed changes. In terms of information content, these two types of components exhibit significant differences, which can be distinguished by calculating sample entropy that characterizes time-series complexity. Therefore, this study designs a method combining sample entropy with k-means clustering to extract components representing overall trends and detailed variations from the VMD decomposition results and classify them accordingly.

The calculation logic is as follows:

1. Given a time series: $\{x(i),\ i = 1, 2, \ldots, n\}$.
2. Sequence segmentation: Divide the time series into $k = n - m + 1$ vectors using a window length $m$. Each vector sequence is represented as: $X_i(t) = \{x_i(t),\ x_{i+1}(t),\ \ldots,\ x_{i+m-1}(t)\}$.
3. Distance calculation: Compute the distance between each $m$-dimensional vector sequence and all other $k$ $m$-dimensional vector sequences. The distance is defined as the maximum absolute difference between corresponding elements of two vectors:

$$d_{ij} = \max\{|x_{i+k}(t) - x_{j+k}(t)|\},\ k = 0, 1, \ldots, m-1 \tag{9}$$

4. Threshold definition: $F = r \cdot SD$, where $r$ is a coefficient (typically 0.1–0.25) and $SD$ is the standard deviation of the sequence.
5. Ratio statistics: Count the ratio of $m$-dimensional vector sequences with distances exceeding $F$ to the total number (excluding self-comparisons), denoted as $C_m(i)$. Calculate the average of all $C_m(i)$, denoted as $\varnothing_m(t)$.
6. Sample entropy calculation: Repeat steps 2–5 with window length $m+1$ to obtain $\varnothing_{m+1}(t)$. Compute sample entropy using:

$$\text{SampEn}(t) = \ln \varnothing_m(t) - \ln \varnothing_{m+1}(t) \tag{10}$$

7. Sample entropy clustering: Cluster the VMD-decomposed sequences using k-means into three categories representing trend, cycle, and residual fluctuations. Combine components within each cluster to form three final components: $W_i^1$ (trend), $W_i^2$ (cycle), and $W_i^3$ (residual).

Using these three components as input, the adversarial training-based reconstruction error minimization method is applied for anomaly detection. Three anomaly scores are obtained: $\mathcal{A}(\widehat{W_i^1})$, $\mathcal{A}(\widehat{W_i^2})$, and $\mathcal{A}(\widehat{W_i^3})$. The final anomaly detection results are the union of anomalies detected from all three components.

### 3.3. Implementation Framework

The complete implementation workflow of the proposed unsupervised anomaly detection algorithm for blast furnace multidimensional shaft static pressure data is shown in Figure 3.

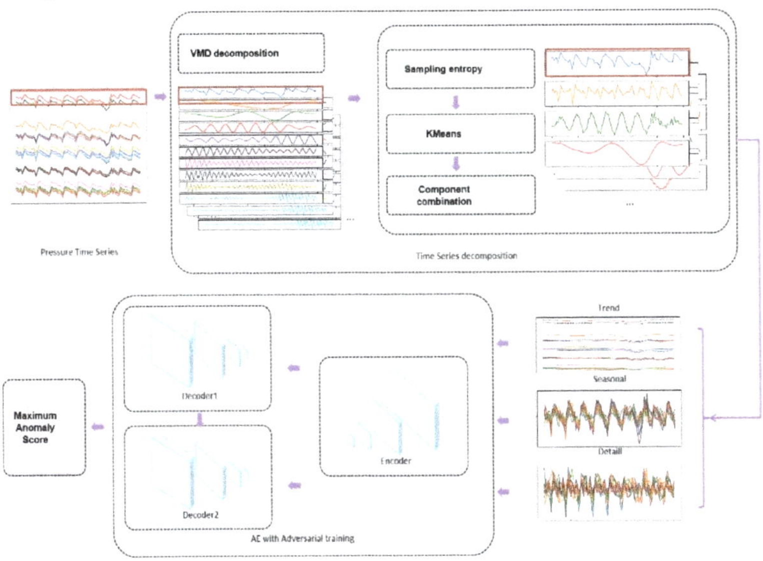


**Figure 3.** Workflow of the anomaly detection algorithm.

The algorithm steps are described as follows:

1. **Step 1**: Perform VMD decomposition on the raw data to obtain multiple components. Since subsequent steps involve post-processing the VMD decomposition results, this paper does not focus on adaptive parameter adjustment for VMD. The raw data are preliminarily split into 10 components, retaining dynamic baseline drift, with the convergence criterion set to "$10^{-7}$".

2. **Step 2**: Due to the variable-length periodic characteristics of the data and the need for model interpretability, post-processing of the IMF components decomposed in Step 1 is required. Key steps include calculating the sample entropy of different components, standardizing the data to eliminate dimensional effects, and setting the tolerance to 0.1 to balance robustness and noise impact. Further, k-means clustering is applied to the entropy values, categorizing the components into three classes—trend, periodic, and residual (remaining details)—based on data morphology. Thus, the number of clusters is set to 3. The clustered components are recombined to decompose the original time series data into trend, periodic, and residual components. This separation mitigates the influence of periodic fluctuations and impact-type anomalies on model performance.
3. **Step 3**: Since the shaft static pressure data is multi-dimensional time series, after decomposing each time series via VMD and regrouping them into three components, identical component types across multiple dimensions are grouped to form three 2D arrays. These arrays are individually input into the improved H-AAE network for training and anomaly detection. Given the presence of multiple anomaly types in this scenario, each with distinct physical meanings and operational implications, the detected anomaly results from each component in the H-AAE model are combined via a union operation. All anomalies are presented to process experts, who evaluate the necessity and approach for handling them by integrating other production parameters.

## 4. Experiments

### 4.1. Dataset Description

Due to frequent changes in operating conditions during steel production that lead to data distribution shifts, high-frequency model retraining using recent data is typically required in actual production. To validate the model's effectiveness, this study selects time segments containing shaft static pressure anomalies and their preceding periods for training and testing, effectively simulating real production conditions.

The experimental dataset consists of real minute-level shaft static pressure data collected from multiple sensors at a steel plant, totaling 7500 min. The first 3500 min are designated as the training set (assumed to contain almost no anomalies), and the remaining 4000 min as the test set.

### 4.2. Evaluation Methodology

Time-series segments are obtained through sliding window partitioning with specified window widths. In this dataset, anomalies are manually labeled by process experts at the window level. Windows containing anomalies are labeled as 1, and normal windows as 0.

The primary evaluation metrics are precision, recall, and F1-score:

$$\text{Precision} = \frac{TP}{TP + FP} \tag{11}$$

$$\text{Recall} = \frac{TP}{TP + FN} \tag{12}$$

$$F_1\text{-score} = \frac{2 \cdot \text{Precision} \cdot \text{Recall}}{\text{Precision} + \text{Recall}} \tag{13}$$

where $TP$ represents true positives, $FP$ false positives, and $FN$ false negatives.

### 4.3. Experimental Results

The shaft static pressure data exhibits periodicity and certain trend characteristics. Whether providing richer data information for anomaly state detection or supplying fundamental analysis data (such as long-term furnace profile trends and short-term local gas flow analysis) for process experts through decomposition, developing an algorithm that correctly decomposes trend, cycle, and residual components is crucial.

### 4.3.1. Comparison Experimental Results

Since the periodic fluctuations in shaft static pressure are related to the burden distribution cycle, traditional approaches typically perform decomposition using STL method [34,35] with a fixed 10-min cycle. However, due to variable gas flow patterns inside the blast furnace, the actual period length and morphology of shaft static pressure are inconsistent. Therefore, this paper proposes a VMD decomposition method combined with sample entropy and clustering algorithms. The decomposition effects are compared in Figure 4.

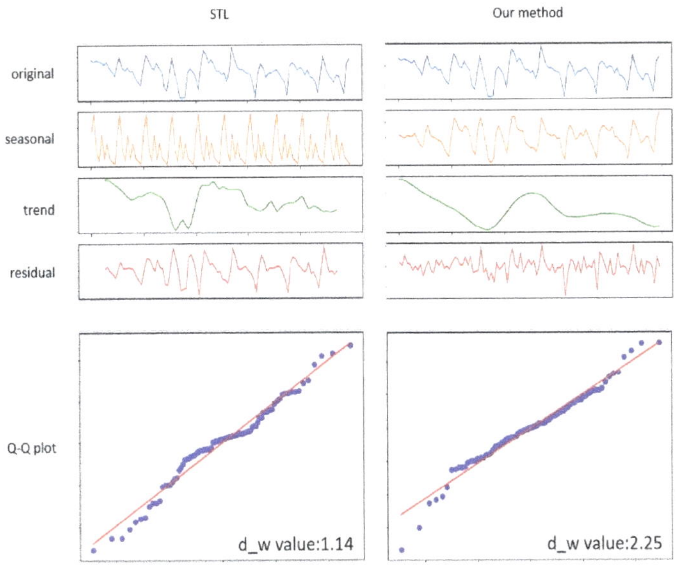


**Figure 4.** Comparison of decomposition effects (**Left**: STL, **Right**: Proposed Method).

Key observations from Figure 4 include:

- The upper part of Figure 4 illustrates the contrasting extraction effects of STL and the proposed method on trend, periodic, and residual components. By observing the morphology of each component in the time-series plots, it is evident that the original data exhibits oscillatory periodic fluctuations with variations in cycle length and morphological details, alongside a gradual declining trend. The proposed method achieves accurate extraction of the actual periodic patterns while successfully isolating significant trend components, ensuring the extracted features maintain physically interpretable characteristics. In contrast, STL decomposition requires predefined cycle lengths, leading to extracted periodic components that deviate markedly from observed patterns. This suboptimal periodic extraction further causes incomplete separation of trend and residual components from cyclic influences. Notably, residual components fail to reliably identify impact type anomalies due to uncorrected periodic interference.
- The lower part of Figure 4 further analyzes the decomposed residual components using Q–Q plots. Results indicate that residuals from our method show no significant autocorrelation (Durbin–Watson statistic between 1.5 and 2.5), with most scatter

points clustered near and parallel to the red reference line. In contrast, STL residuals demonstrate moderate positive autocorrelation (DW = 1.14), exhibiting oscillatory scatter patterns around the red line. The Q–Q plot also reveals that extreme residual values correspond to localized anomalies.

This paper conducts a comparison between its proposed model and various classical unsupervised anomaly detection models. In this paper, four unsupervised classical models supporting multi-dimensional anomaly recognition, namely IsoForest, LOF, PCA, and HBOS, are selected for comparison. Since the method of this paper mainly recognizes segment anomalies, for full comparison, the above classical models are used to capture the anomalies firstly, and then the sliding window is cut according to 60 window widths and 1 as the step size, and the proportion of anomalies in the sliding window is higher than 20%, then the segment is considered to be anomalous. The results of the comparison experiments are shown in the following Table 1.

**Table 1.** Performance comparison of different models.

| Model | Precision | Recall | F1-Score |
|---|---|---|---|
| IsoForest | 1.00 | 0.46 | 0.63 |
| LOF | 1.00 | 0.19 | 0.31 |
| PCA | 0.82 | 0.50 | 0.62 |
| HBOS | 1.00 | 0.49 | 0.66 |
| Proposed | 0.95 | 0.91 | 0.93 |

The test fragment specific labeled anomalies are plotted against the anomalies recognized by the different algorithms as follows:

The pink semi-transparent box in the above figure indicates the abnormality segments identified by manual marking or algorithm. As this paper intercepts the time series data fragments for anomaly identification by means of sliding window, the window width is temporarily set at 60, so the starting point of the anomaly fragments labeled in the figure is earlier than the actual anomaly moment, but it does not affect the effect of real-time on-line alarms in actual production, and it does not affect the effect of real-time on-line alarms in actual production. The Figure 5 reveals that process experts have flagged anomalies worth attention, including abnormally high/low values, sudden drops/increases, significant trend shifts, and abnormal fluctuations. Among the classic anomaly detection algorithms selected for comparison, only PCA identifies some notable trend variations, while others primarily detect extreme value outliers. Quantitative analysis shows recall rates of 0.46, 0.19, 0.50, and 0.49 for Isolation Forest, LDF, PCA, and HBOS, respectively, with the highest recall being merely 0.5, indicating severe under-detection issues in traditional methods. The proposed algorithm demonstrates superior accuracy and recall, effectively capturing diverse anomalies like numerical deviations, fluctuation patterns, and abrupt changes. Subsequent ablation experiments will clarify which modules significantly contribute to recall improvement.

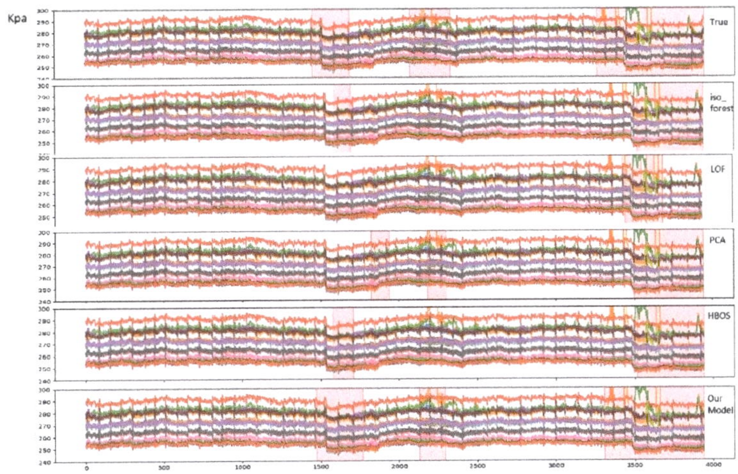


**Figure 5.** Anomaly detection comparison (Ground Truth vs. Algorithm Results).

#### 4.3.2. Ablation Experimental Results

Further ablation experiments comparing different models are presented in Table 2. The proposed method achieves 0.93 F1-score, outperforming baseline models.

**Table 2.** Performance comparison of different models.

| Model | Precision | Recall | F1-Score |
|---|---|---|---|
| AE | 0.88 | 0.82 | 0.85 |
| H-AAE | 0.92 | 0.82 | 0.86 |
| Proposed | 0.95 | 0.91 | 0.93 |

Figure 6 compares manual annotations with algorithmic detection results. The pink translucent boxes represent human expert annotations, while blue boxes show algorithm detections.

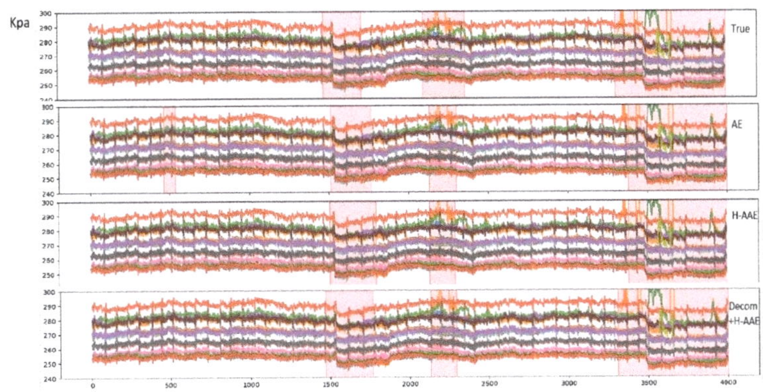


**Figure 6.** Anomaly detection comparison (Ground Truth vs. Algorithm Results).

Notably, while most models can detect significant trend anomalies (e.g., sustained high/low values), our method better captures morphological changes and sudden transitions that align with manual expert judgments. Further analysis of detection results from different components is shown in Figure 7.

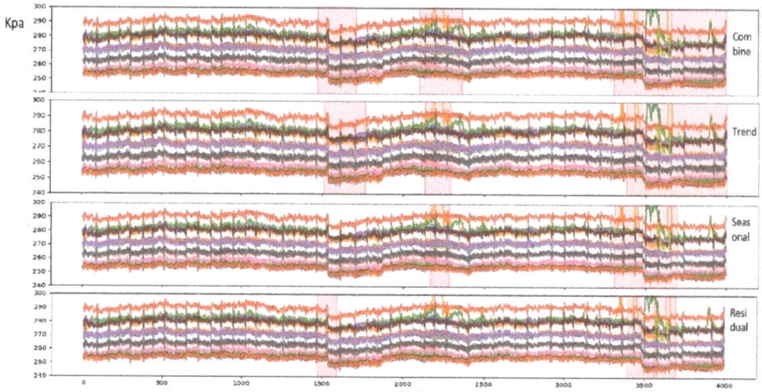


**Figure 7.** Anomaly detection by component (Trend/Cycle/Residual).

- **Anomaly Segment Annotation**: The pink semi-transparent boxes in the figure indicate anomaly segments manually labeled or algorithmically identified. Due to the sliding window approach (window width = 60) used in this study for extracting time-series data fragments, the annotated anomaly start points precede actual anomaly timestamps. This design does not compromise the real-time online alarm performance in practical production.
- **Model Comparison**: Observations from Figure 6 reveal that while both AE and H-AAE models can identify anomaly segments overlapping with manual annotations, the AE model only detects anomalies characterized by "significant sustained elevation or reduction" in specific segments. For example:The second anomaly segment identified by AE corresponds to a sharp global decline followed by gradual recovery; The third AE-detected anomaly segment reflects a distinct "bulge" morphology in the data; The fourth AE-detected segment combines both "bulge" and sharp decline anomalies; Additionally, AE erroneously flags the first anomaly segment due to poor robustness. To address AE's robustness limitations, this study integrates GAN mechanisms and modifies the loss function, enabling H-AAE to recognize broader anomaly types. The modified H-AAE avoids AE's false identifications (e.g., Segment 1) but remains reliant on detecting "significant sustained variations", showing only marginal metric improvements.

  After introducing VMD postprocessing to decompose trend, periodic, and residual components, the model demonstrates enhanced performance: our model identifies anomalies during early trend declines (e.g., Anomaly segment 1 corresponding to AE's Segment 1 and H-AAE's Segment 2), demonstrating short-term trend detection capability; e.g., Anomaly segment 3 (mapped to AE's Segment 4 and H-AAE's Segment 3) successfully captures short-term fluctuations; quantitative metrics show substantial improvements in accuracy and recall, confirming the critical role of signal decomposition.
- **Component-Wise Anomaly Analysis**: Trend Component: Detects significant long-term increases/decreases. Undecomposed data risks masking other anomaly types under dominant trends; Periodic Component: Improved via Huber-modified loss functions, effectively identifying transient or sustained "fluctuation" patterns; Residual Component: Captures spike anomalies and short-term deviations, enabling early micro-anomaly warnings. Final anomaly results combine outputs from all three components. Component-specific anomaly types aid fault diagnosis and severity assessment, enhancing interpretability; Fusion logic adapts dynamically to operational requirements, enabling refined detection and alert strategies.

While most models detect extreme-value anomalies, our method excels in identifying subtle anomalies (e.g., morphological shifts, abrupt changes) akin to expert judgment. The trend, periodic, and residual components, respectively, specialize in global trends, cyclical fluctuations, and transient peaks, with flexible fusion strategies supporting customized industrial needs.

## 5. Conclusions

This paper conducts an in-depth investigation into the anomaly detection problem in static pressure data. Given the scarcity of anomaly samples and the lack of labeled datasets, we propose an unsupervised anomaly detection approach based on reconstruction errors. First, to address the issues of traditional autoencoder (AE) models being sensitive to outliers and having poor stability, we introduce the Huber loss function into the AE framework to mitigate the sensitivity of L2 loss to outliers, and integrate a dual-decoder generative adversarial network (GAN) to enhance model stability through adversarial training. Second, to tackle the challenges posed by the variable-length periodic patterns in shaft static pressure data, where anomaly detection based on raw data often fails to capture multi-category anomalies such as trend deviations and periodic disruptions, we employ Variational Mode Decomposition (VMD) to decompose the original signals. This decomposition is further optimized through sample entropy analysis and clustering, adaptively separating the signals into trend, periodic, and residual components while ensuring residual normality and eliminating autocorrelation. By feeding these decomposed components into the adversarially enhanced AE model, our method achieves multi-dimensional detection of long-term trend shifts, periodic pattern disruptions, and transient fluctuations. Comparative and ablation experiments validate the superiority of the hybrid framework. Furthermore, the interpretable component-level results derived from this decomposition enable operators to perform detailed analysis of different anomaly types and implement targeted adjustment measures.

**Author Contributions:** X.S.: Proposed the research scenario and dataset; Designed the overall research framework and core algorithm architecture. J.Z.: Implemented the algorithmic concepts into functional code. B.T.: Reviewed the algorithm design; Identified optimization opportunities and provided critical feedback. Z.J.: Supervised the paper's academic rigor and structural coherence; Revised the manuscript for clarity, logic, and compliance with publishing standards. All authors have read and agreed to the published version of the manuscript.

**Funding:** This research was funded by Chongqing Natural Science Foundation OF FUNDER grant number CSTB2024NSCQ-BSX0011.

**Informed Consent Statement:** Informed consent was obtained from all subjects involved in the study.

**Data Availability Statement:** Where data is unavailable due to privacy restrictions.

**Conflicts of Interest:** Author Jie Zhu and Bing Tang were employed by the company CISDI Information Technology (Chongqing) Co., Ltd. The remaining authors declare that the research was conducted in the absence of any commercial or financial relationships that could be construed as a potential conflict of interest.

## References

1. Amano, S.; Takarabe, T.; Nakamori, T.; Oda, H.; Taira, M.; Seki, T. Expert System for Blast Furnace Operation at Kimitsu Works. *ISIJ Int.* **1990**, *30*, 105–110. [CrossRef]
2. Yang, T.; Yang, S.; Zuo, G.; Wei, H.; Xu, J.; Zhou, Y. An expert system for abnormal status diagnosis and operation guide of a blast furnace. *IFAC Proc. Vol.* **1992**, *25*, 59–63. [CrossRef]

3. Gao C.; Ge, Q.; Jian L. Rule extraction from fuzzy-based blast furnace SVM multiclassifier for decision-making. *IEEE Trans. Fuzzy Syst.* **2013**, *22*, 586–596. [CrossRef]
4. Wang, H.; Sheng, C.; Lu, X. Knowledge-Based Control and Optimization of Blast Furnace Gas System in Steel Industry. *IEEE Access* **2017**, *5*, 25034–25045. [CrossRef]
5. Cui, L.; Zhang, Q.; Shi, Y.; Yang, L.; Wang, Y.; Wang, J.; Bai, C. A method for satellite time series anomaly detection based on fast-DTW and improved-KNN. *Chin. J. Aeronaut.* **2023**, *36*, 149–159. [CrossRef]
6. Kozitsin, V.; Katser, I.; Lakontsev, D. Online forecasting and anomaly detection based on the ARIMA model. *Appl. Sci.* **2021**, *11*, 3194.
7. Çelik, M.; Dadaşer-Çelik, F.; Dokuz, A.Ş. Anomaly detection in temperature data using DBSCAN algorithm. In Proceedings of the 2011 International Symposium on Innovations in Intelligent Systems and Applications, Istanbul, Turkey, 15–18 June 2011; pp. 91–95.
8. Zamanzadeh Darban, Z.; Webb, G.I.; Pan, S.; Aggarwal, C.C.; Salehi, M. Deep learning for time series anomaly detection: A survey. *ACM Comput. Surv.* **2024**, *57*, 1–42. [CrossRef]
9. Kim, J.; Kang, H.; Kang, P. Time-series anomaly detection with stacked Transformer representations and 1D convolutional network. *Eng. Appl. Artif. Intell.* **2023**, *10*, 105964.
10. Belay, M.A.; Blakseth, S.S.; Rasheed, A.; Rossi, P.S. Unsupervised anomaly detection for IoT-based multivariate time series: Existing solutions, performance analysis and future directions. *Sensors* **2023**, *23*, 2844.
11. Ding, C.; Sun, S.; Zhao, J. MST-GAT: A multimodal spatial-temporal graph attention network for time series anomaly detection. *Inf. Fusion* **2023**, *89*, 527–536. [CrossRef]
12. Chen, Y.; Zhang, C.; Ma, M.; Liu, Y.; Ding, R.; Li, B.; He, S.; Rajmohan, S.; Lin, Q.; Zhang, D. Imdiffusion: Imputed diffusion models for multivariate time series anomaly detection. *arXiv* **2023**, arXiv:2307.00754. [CrossRef]
13. Zeng, F.; Chen, M.; Qian, C.; Wang, Y.; Zhou, Y.; Tang, W. Multivariate time series anomaly detection with adversarial transformer architecture in the Internet of Things. *Future Gener. Comput. Syst.* **2023**, *144*, 244–255. [CrossRef]
14. Xu, H.; Wang, Y.; Jian, S.; Liao, Q.; Wang, Y.; Pang, G. Calibrated one-class classification for unsupervised time series anomaly detection. *IEEE Trans. Knowl. Data Eng.* **2024**, *36*, 5723–5736. [CrossRef]
15. Li, H.; Zheng, W.; Tang, F.; Zhu, Y.; Huang, J. Few-shot time-series anomaly detection with unsupervised domain adaptation. *Inf. Sci.* **2023**, *649*, 119610. [CrossRef]
16. Zheng, M.; Man, J.; Wang, D.; Chen, Y.; Li, Q.; Liu, Y. Semi-supervised multivariate time series anomaly detection for wind turbines using generator SCADA data. *Reliab. Eng. Syst. Saf.* **2023**, *235*, 109235. [CrossRef]
17. Wang, R.; Liu, C.; Mou, X.; Gao, K.; Guo, X.; Liu, P.; Wo, T.; Liu, X. Deep contrastive one-class time series anomaly detection. In Proceedings of the 2023 SIAM International Conference on Data Mining (SDM), Minneapolis, MN, USA, 27–29 April 2023; pp. 694—702.
18. He, X.; Li, Y.; Tan, J.; Wu, B.; Li, F. OneShotSTL: One-shot seasonal-trend decomposition for online time series anomaly detection and forecasting. *arXiv* **2023**, arXiv:2304.01506. [CrossRef]
19. Ergen, T.; Kozat, S.S. Unsupervised anomaly detection with LSTM neural networks. *IEEE Trans. Neural Netw. Learn. Syst.* **2019**, *31*, 3127–3141. [CrossRef]
20. Malhotra, P.; Ramakrishnan, A.; An, G.; Vig, L.; Agarwal, P.; Shroff, G. LSTM-based encoder-decoder for multi-sensor anomaly detection. *arXiv* **2016**, arXiv:1607.00148.
21. Gong, D.; Liu, L.; Le, V.; Saha, B.; Mansour, M.R.; Venkatesh, S.; Hengel, A.V.D. Memorizing normality to detect anomaly: Memory-augmented deep autoencoder for unsupervised anomaly detection. In Proceedings of the IEEE/CVF International Conference on Computer Vision, Seoul, Korea, 27 October–2 November 2019; pp. 1705–1714.
22. Chen, H.; Liu, H.; Chu, X.; Liu, Q.; Xue, D. Anomaly detection and critical SCADA parameters identification for wind turbines based on LSTM-AE neural network. *Renew. Energy* **2021**, *172*, 829–840. [CrossRef]
23. Wang, Z.; Pei, C.; Ma, M.; Wang, X.; Li, Z.; Pei, D.; Rajmohan, S.; Zhang, D.; Lin, Q.; Zhang, H.; et al. Revisiting VAE for Unsupervised Time Series Anomaly Detection: A Frequency Perspective. In Proceedings of the ACM on Web Conference 2024, Singapore, 13–17 May 2024; pp. 3096–3105.
24. Huang, T.; Chen, P.; Li, R. A semi-supervised VAE based active anomaly detection framework in multivariate time series for online systems. In Proceedings of the ACM Web Conference 2022, Lyon, France, 25–29 April 2022; pp. 1797–1806.
25. Niu, Z.; Yu, K.; Wu, X. LSTM-based VAE-GAN for time-series anomaly detection. *Sensors* **2020**, *20*, 3738. [CrossRef]
26. Audibert, J.; Michiardi, P.; Guyard, F.; Marti, S.; Zuluaga, M.A. USAD: Unsupervised anomaly detection on multivariate time series. In Proceedings of the 26th ACM SIGKDD International Conference on Knowledge Discovery & Data Mining, Virtual, 6–10 July 2020; pp. 3395–3404.
27. Zhang, H.; Song, Z.; Yang, J.; Gao, Y. Adversarial Autoencoder Empowered Joint Anomaly Detection and Signal Reconstruction From Sub-Nyquist Samples. *IEEE Trans. Cogn. Commun. Netw.* **2023**, *9*, 618–628. [CrossRef]

28. Liu, H.; Zhao, B.; Guo, J.; Zhang, K.; Liu, P. A lightweight unsupervised adversarial detector based on autoencoder and isolation forest. *Pattern Recognit.* **2024**, *147*, 110127. [CrossRef]
29. Zhou, Y.; Liang, X.; Zhang, W.; Zhang, L.; Song, X. VAE-based Deep SVDD for anomaly detection. *Neurocomputing* **2021**, *453*, 131–140.
30. Liu, S.; Lang, X.; Wu, J.; Zhang, Y.; Lei, C.; Su, H. Corrective variational mode decomposition to detect multiple oscillations in process control systems. *Control Eng. Pract.* **2025**, *154*, 106123.
31. Wang, H.; Liu, X.; Ma, L.; Zhang, Y. Anomaly detection for hydropower turbine unit based on variational modal decomposition and deep autoencoder. *Energy Rep.* **2021**, *7*, 938–946. [CrossRef]
32. Guan, K.; Gong, X. A new hybrid deep learning model for monthly oil prices forecasting. *Energy Econ.* **2023**, *128*, 107136. [CrossRef]
33. Ergun, S. Pressure drop in blast furnace and in cupola. *Ind. Eng. Chem.* **1953**, *45*, 477–485. [CrossRef]
34. Clevel, R.B.; Clevel, W.S.; McRae, J.E. STL: A seasonal-trend decomposition. *J. Off. Stat.* **1990**, *6*, 3–73.
35. Yang, S.; Deng, Z.; Li, X.; Zheng, C.; Xi, L.; Zhuang, J.; Zhang, Z.; Zhang, Z. A novel hybrid model based on STL decomposition and one-dimensional convolutional neural networks with positional encoding for significant wave height forecast. *Renew. Energy* **2021**, *173*, 531–543. [CrossRef]

*sensors*

MDPI

*Article*

# Invisible CMOS Camera Dazzling for Conducting Adversarial Attacks on Deep Neural Networks

**Zvi Stein, Adir Hazan * and Adrian Stern**

School of Electrical and Computer Engineering, Ben-Gurion University of the Negev, Beer-Sheva 8410501, Israel; tzviste@post.bgu.ac.il (Z.S.); stern@bgu.ac.il (A.S.)
* Correspondence: hazanad@post.bgu.ac.il

**Abstract:** Despite the outstanding performance of deep neural networks, they remain vulnerable to adversarial attacks. While digital domain adversarial attacks are well-documented, most physical-world attacks are typically visible to the human eye. Here, we present a novel invisible optical-based physical adversarial attack via dazzling a CMOS camera. This attack involves using a designed light pulse sequence spatially transformed within the acquired image due to the camera's shutter mechanism. We provide a detailed analysis of the photopic conditions required to keep the attacking light source invisible to human observers while effectively disrupting the image, thereby deceiving the DNN. The results indicate that the light source duty cycle controls the tradeoff between the attack's success rate and the degree of concealment needed.

**Keywords:** adversarial attack; PSF; rolling shutter; CMOS

## 1. Introduction

Deep Neural Networks (DNNs) have revolutionized the field of image analysis and processing, delivering state-of-the-art performance across a range of applications. However, these systems are inherently vulnerable to adversarial attacks [1], which introduce subtle perturbations to the input signal that cause the DNNs to make incorrect predictions. The concept of adversarial examples, commonly known as *attacked images*, was first introduced a decade ago by Szegedy et al. [2], demonstrating that DNNs could be easily misled by seemingly minor modifications to input images. Since then, numerous approaches for generating adversarial examples have been explored [3], highlighting the significant security concerns surrounding DNN-based systems.

The underlying mechanism for adversarial susceptibility lies in the way DNNs process images. Rather than learning the actual semantic content of the image, these networks often rely on superficial or spurious features for classification, as described by Goodfellow et al. as a "Potemkin village" of features [4]. This explains why two images that are visually indistinguishable from human vision can be classified differently by a DNN, revealing a vulnerability that adversarial attacks exploit. These attacks often aim to minimize the perturbations applied to an image so that the changes are not noticeable to the human eye while still causing a misclassification.

Adversarial attacks on DNNs can be divided into digital and physical attacks. While digital attacks manipulate image pixels, they often struggle to transfer to the physical world due to dynamic conditions and deployment challenges. Physical attacks alter real-world objects' visual characteristics and pose a threat but are typically invasive, requiring visible changes that can be easily dismissed and detected by human vision. However, optical-based physical adversarial attacks are non-invasive and generate perturbations that mimic natural effects, making them harder to detect and better suited for real-world applications [5]. Despite advancements in imperceptibility, many of these attacks still have an obvious trace in the physical domain, limiting their effectiveness and feasibility, with achieving complete invisibility to the human eye remaining an unresolved challenge.

This paper introduces and demonstrates a novel optical-based physical adversarial attack that leverages the rolling shutter mechanism of CMOS sensors. The proposed attack is designed to be invisible in the physical domain, ensuring that the attacking light source remains undetectable to the scene observer. This involves a designed light pulse sequence spatially transformed during the image acquisition, effectively disrupting the camera's image processing to deceive DNNs with a high attack success rate. Furthermore, our approach does not require precise alignment of the adversarial spatial pattern with the target object location, offering greater flexibility in real-world scenarios. A successful invisible attack is achieved when the beam of Attacking MOdulated Light Source (AMOLS) covers the camera aperture, such that the following are achieved:

1. The peak irradiance is sufficient to dazzle the sensor temporarily;
2. The average irradiance remains below the sensitivity threshold of the human eye.

The following summarizes the primary contributions of this work:

- We propose a physical domain adversarial attack on DNNs that receive images from a CMOS camera. The attack involves directing a light source toward the camera; however, the presence of the projected light is completely unnoticed by observers in the scene.
- We introduce an optical attack that is based on dazzling a camera sensor by sending short pulses. We investigate the effect of the projected pulses on the image captured by the CMOS camera. We evaluate the irradiance required to attack the image.
- We explore the relationship between the human eye's ability to distinguish the attacking light source directed at the camera and the disruption of DNN performance caused by the influence of the pulsed laser beam. We analyze the photopic conditions required to ensure that the attacking light source remains invisible to human observers while still effectively disrupting the acquired image to mislead the classifier model.
- We evaluate the trade-off between the success of DNN attacks caused by dazzling pulses and their invisibility to the human eye. Our findings indicate that the duty cycle of the light source can be adjusted to manage the balance between the attack's success rate and the level of concealment required.
- We present simulated and real experimental results to demonstrate the effectiveness of our attack.

## 2. Related Works

While most studies on adversarial attacks have focused on the digital domain, where perturbations are added to pixel values, growing efforts have expanded into the physical domain [6]. Examples of physical-world attacks typically include using adversarial objects or imaging system manipulations to fool DNN models. These modifications may include simple changes, such as adding elements like stickers, eyeglasses, earrings, and others to a real-world object [7], to more complex approaches. The more complex methods typically involve optical-based techniques [5], including temporarily projecting specifically crafted adversarial perturbations onto target objects [8], among others, or strategically illuminating target objects using infrared light sources [9]. Furthermore, synthesizing Three-Dimensional (3D) adversarial objects has been proposed to confuse classifier models [10], and imaging projection transformation in a 3D physical environment was demonstrated to deceive object detection systems effectively [11]. These examples highlight the growing applicability of adversarial attacks in real-world settings.

Recent studies on physical adversarial examples have increasingly focused on manipulating imaging systems themselves. For instance, Liu et al. [12] induced perturbations in the captured image through an electromagnetic injection attack. They focused on CCD sensors but noted that CMOS sensors, which have an independent measurement unit for each pixel, provide greater resilience to electromagnetic interference, making them more robust against such threats. Additionally, Duan et al. [13] employed a laser beam attack to create spatially tailored perturbations; however, they noted that this approach has a limited success rate in dynamic conditions. Many physical adversarial attacks require precise alignment of the adversarial spatial pattern with the target object placement. Moreover, Liu et al. [14] inject their attack after image acquisition, targeting the data lane between the camera sensor and the endpoint device. This requires physical access to the sensor-enabled system, which is practically infeasible in certain situations.

In this work, we develop an invisible camera dazzling attack that leverages the rolling shutter mechanism inherent in CMOS sensors. Unlike the continuous-wave operation of light sources, where the degree of dazzle on CMOS sensors can be depicted by the dazzling area or the number of saturated pixels [15], temporally modulated light can produce adjustable stripes in a captured image—introducing a unique approach to injecting adversarial spatial patterns. The rolling shutter effect is primarily studied in the context of mitigating distortions caused by fast-moving objects that approach the camera's scanning frequency [16]. Accordingly, models have been developed to correct these distortions. Moreover, it was proposed that a smartphone camera can be used for visible light communications to detect and convert a temporal signal into spatial patterns by exploiting the rolling shutter effect of CMOS sensors [17].

Adversarial attacks leveraging the rolling shutter mechanism have been introduced in references [18–22], where temporally modulated LEDs are used to illuminate a target object, as shown in Figure 1a. This results in distortions in the acquired image due to the camera's row-wise scanning process. The first configuration [18] was introduced as a black-box backdoor attack on face recognition systems, where illuminating the entire scene induces perturbations employing the rolling shutter effect. While the first two studies [18,19] utilize programmable RGB LEDs, resulting in an adversarial signal with three adjustable components of Red, Green, and Blue, later work [20] demonstrated the use of a common commercial LED with a modulator to control the frequency of the emitted white light. In addition, further schemes [21,22] expanded the application of the white light attack method, showcasing the generalization and transferability of adversarial samples across different models and tasks, including traffic sign recognition systems and lane detection models. However, these approaches require comprehensive illumination of the whole scene and usually fail to remain invisible to the human eye. Despite the light pulse sequence being designed with a modulation frequency that prevents flickering perceived by the human eye, the illumination source still appears steady and is not stealthy to the human observer in the scene.

Here, we propose to employ an AMOLS beam that directly illuminates the camera's aperture as shown in Figure 1b, taking advantage of the rolling shutter's scanning process to induce real-world adversarial perturbations on the acquired image. Since the pulsed light beam is directed toward the camera rather than reflecting off a target object (see Figure 1), the average power requirements are significantly reduced compared to previous methods. While Kohler et al. [23] and Yan et al. [24] introduced such *a camera* attack utilizing a laser and exploiting the rolling shutter mechanism, their approaches still leave an obvious trace of the attack in the physical domain and remain visible to the human eye.

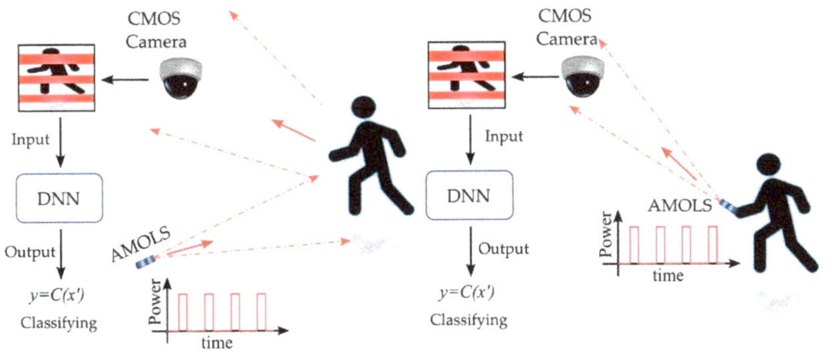


**Figure 1.** Practical physical-world adversarial attack. The attack can be carried out either (**a**) by temporally modulating a light source to illuminate the entire scene, which reflects light pulses onto the CMOS sensor, or (**b**) by directing a pulsed laser beam specifically at a CMOS sensor. The red arrows indicate the propagation direction of the light.

Since the integration time of the human eye is significantly longer than the acquisition time of each row in a rolling shutter scanning process, a high-frequency modulated signal is seen as continuous by the human eye. If denoting the duty cycle of the AMOLS as $D$, the intensity perceived by the human eye can be expressed as follows:

$$I_{eye} = D \cdot I_{source}. \tag{1}$$

That is, the human eye only perceives the signal's average power. Consequently, it is possible to control this intensity by appropriately reducing the duty cycle of the AMOLS. In this paper, we explore the relationship between the effectiveness of a duty cycle during a direct camera attack and the ability to distinguish the AMOLS implementation. First, we review the effect of AMOLS on the camera and determine the irradiance needed to produce the desired disruptive effect on the camera. Next, we evaluate the dazzling irradiance on the human eye and determine the conditions that influence the eye's ability to perceive and recognize the light source. Finally, after establishing the irradiance requirements, we examine the efficiency of image distortion caused by the designed pulse sequence on a well-known classifier, the Residual Neural Network (ResNet50) architecture, through simulations and experiments.

## 3. Materials and Methods

### 3.1. Dazzle Effect with Rolling Shutter Camera

The spatial spread of a point source in the image plane is conventionally described by the diffraction of the Point Spared Function (PSF), generally given by the Fourier transformation of the entrance pupil. However, particularly for bright power sources (e.g., a laser source), other effects such as stray light scattering and halo [25] may occur in addition to the PSF diffraction, which may be considerably more significant than the PSF. The dazzling effect is demonstrated in Figure 2, where the measurement is acquired from a laptop camera (installed on a DELL-INSPIRON laptop with 0.92 Megapixel, 88° diagonal viewing angle). The AMOLS average power was 5 mW with ∼ 3.5 mm spot diameter. As shown in Figure 2, a notable dazzling effect is observed when utilizing such a power level.

**Figure 2.** Experimental PSF measurement. The camera's response to placed point source within the field of view. The radiant flux measured in the object plane is ~50 mW/cm$^2$.

Previous studies on infrared imagers [26,27] have empirically shown that the diameter of the saturated area in the image plane, denoted as $x_{sat}$, can be approximated as follows:

$$x_{sat} \propto \left( \frac{I_0}{I_{sat}} \right)^{\frac{1}{3}} \tag{2}$$

where $I_0$ and $I_{sat}$ are the laser irradiance and the saturation level, respectively. Based on results for visible light using a CMOS camera [28,29] a minimum average irradiance of 50 mW/cm$^2$ during each row exposure is required, and at least 0.1 mW/cm$^2$ pick irradiance to achieve dazzling with shorter pulses. We experimentally found that similar conditions hold for the camera used in this work, as observed in Figure 2.

Next, the dazzling effect formed in the attacked image is examined. With a rolling shutter camera, every row in the frame collects ambient light during different periods. As shown in Figure 3, the $i$-th row of the sensor records the light integrated during the period from $t_i - t_{exp}$ till $t_i$, while for the following row $i+1$, the integration time will be until $t_i + t_{read}$, where $t_{read}$ denotes the reading time of a single row and $t_{exp}$ denotes the exposure time of a single row. The duration of scanning each frame, denoted by $t_{frame}$, can be expressed as follows [16]:

$$t_{frame} = t_{read}(N_r + N_{rH}) + t_{exp}. \tag{3}$$

where $N_r$ and $N_{rH}$ are the number of pixel rows and the number of hidden pixel rows in each frame, respectively.

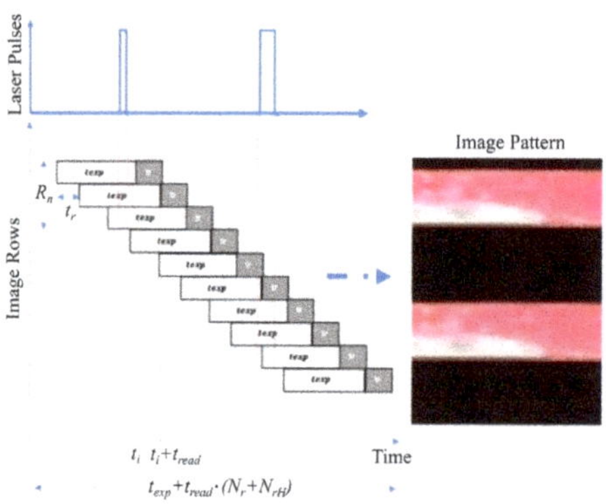


**Figure 3.** A schematic illustration of the rolling shutter effect caused by dazzling AMOLS. The rolling shutter mechanism transforms the temporal signal with a designed sequence of laser pulses (marked in blue at the top) into spatial distortion. This distortion occurs during different periods of reading and exposure for the pixel rows in the frame (indicated by white and gray blocks). As a result, a stripe-like pattern emerges in the acquired image (right).

The ratio $R_n = t_{exp}/t_{read}$ determines the number of exposed rows at any given time (see Figure 4). Thus, $R_n$ is referred to as the row's exposure constant. It is worth highlighting that if the pulse duration generated by the AMOLS is shorter than $t_{read}$, exactly $R_n$ rows will be dazzled, regardless of the pulse width. For instance, both pulses with a duration $1\,\mu s$ and $2\,\mu s$ will produce the same pattern when using a typical camera with a reading time of $t_{read} \approx 30\ \mu s$. The experimentally obtained dazzle pattern for the rolling shutter sensor when the AMOLS is applied is shown in Figure 4, along with the simulated stripe-line pattern utilizing $R_n = 37$ obtained with a calibration process. The simulation result corresponds well with the experimental measurement, with a structural similarity of 93%.

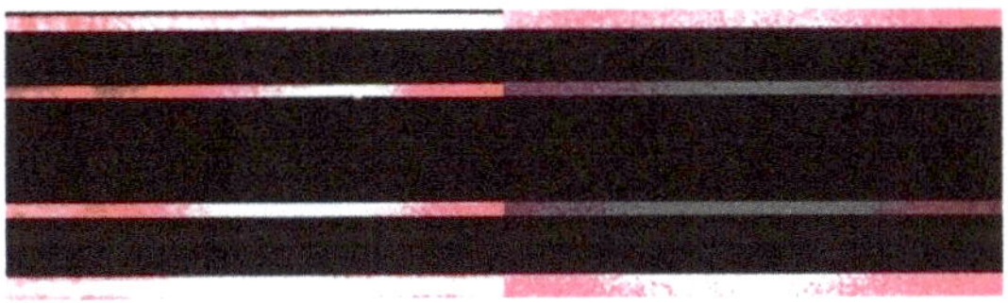

(a) (b)

**Figure 4.** Dazzle effect of rolling shutter sensor by a modulated light source. (**a**,**b**) The resulting dazzle pattern for AMOLS via (**a**) experiment and (**b**) simulation with $R_n = 37$.

### 3.2. Photopic Conditions for Invisibility

This section focuses on determining the photometric conditions required to keep the AMOLS effectively invisible. The attack scenario is depicted in Figure 5, where a target object (car) and the AMOLS are placed in front of a camera while an observer is near the camera at an angle $\theta$ relative to the optical axis. The acquired image is then fed to DNN to classify the target. Consider that the AMOLS power is set to produce an irradiance of $e = 50\ \text{mW}/\text{cm}^2$ at the sensor plane when active. The average power $E$ received by the observer's eyes from the AMOLS is influenced by the duty cycle of the AMOLS during the frame exposure period. The light source duty cycle denoted by $D$ determines the average power of the light source, which can be expressed as $E = e \cdot D$. In addition, assuming the AMOLS is smaller than the human eye's angular resolution, the strictest condition would be the concentration of the seen power from any given source. Thus, a larger angular extent covered by the AMOLS would yield a lower peak power.

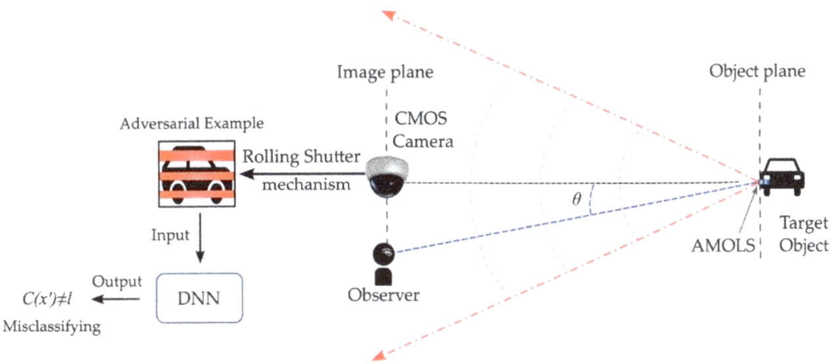


**Figure 5.** Invisible AMOLS implementation for direct camera attack. A target object (e.g., a car) is placed in the camera's field of view, and a light source directly illuminates the camera (by sending a beam between the red arrows). The task of the DNN is to classify the acquired image. When applying the AMOLS, it must remain invisible to an observer at an angle $\theta$ relative to the optical axis.

By denoting the background brightness by $L_b$ and the AMOLS brightness by $L_{AS}$, the contrast can be given by the following:

$$C = \frac{L_{AS} - L_b}{L_b}, \tag{4}$$

Previous studies by H.R. Blackwell [30] and W. Adrian [31] investigated the threshold contrast $C_{thr}$ required to detect an object. According to W. Adrian, a target contrast of 1 at a small angle is sufficient to recognize the target. Since radiance is a physical quantity conserved throughout an optical system, it dictates the brightness. When the solid angle covered by the target is smaller than the system's resolving power, the AMOLS brightness has the following form [32]:

$$L_{AS} = E \cdot 683 \cdot V_\lambda \cdot \Omega_{eye}^{-2} \ \left[\mathrm{cd} \cdot \mathrm{m}^{-2}\right], \tag{5}$$

where $V_\lambda$ denotes the photopic efficacy and $\Omega_{eye}$ is the resolving power of the human eye (representing the strictest condition regarding the received power). Employing a camera model to represent the eye model, C.A. Williamson and L.N. McLin [33,34] proposed a scattering function based on empirical findings by J. Vos et al. [35], with an effective solid angle collected by the eye:

$$f_{eye}(\theta, A, p, L_b) = S \cdot L_b^T \cdot g_{eye}(\theta, A, p) \ \left[\mathrm{sr}^{-1}\right], \tag{6}$$

where $g_{eye}$ can be determined by the off-axis angle $\theta$ (see Figure 5), the age $A$ (in years), and the eye pigment $p$, which is given by the following:

$$g_{eye}(\theta, A, p) = \frac{10}{\theta^3} + \left[\frac{5}{\theta^2} + \frac{0.1p}{\theta}\right]\left[1 + \left(\frac{A}{62.5}\right)^2\right] + 0.0025p \ [\mathrm{sr}^{-1}], \tag{7}$$

Substituting the term of the average power $E$, and the angular resolution by $f_{eye}$, the AMOLS brightness expressed in Equation (5) takes the following form:

$$L_{AS} = e \cdot D \cdot 683 \cdot V_\lambda \cdot f_{eye} \ \left[\mathrm{cd} \cdot \mathrm{m}^{-2}\right], \tag{8}$$

Finally, by substituting Equation (8) into Equation (4), the light source duty cycle can be expressed by the following:

$$D = L_b^{1-T} \frac{C_{thr}(L_b) + 1}{e \cdot 683 \cdot V_\lambda \cdot S \cdot g_{eye}(\theta, A, p)}. \tag{9}$$

Figure 6 shows the light source duty cycle $D$ required for dazzling as a function of the background illumination for various viewing aspect angles. As the aspect angle increases, the effective radiance on the retina decreases. Consequently, the contrast decreases with the increasing background brightness, requiring more power to exceed the threshold. It is observed from the results shown in Figure 6 that for observers placed at an angle greater than 10 degrees, a duty cycle of 0.5% is sufficient to keep the source invisible, regardless of the background illumination level. The following sections will present a technique that can be operated even at lower duty cycle percentages.

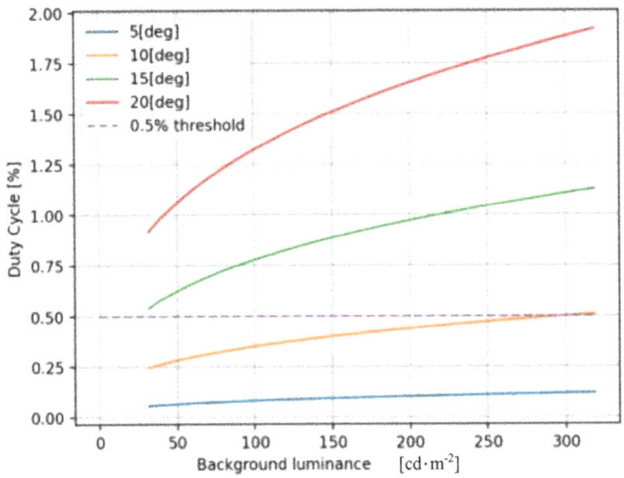


**Figure 6.** The duty cycle $D$ of the AMOLS at the threshold of human discrimination as a function of the background luminance for various viewing angles $\theta$.

### 3.3. Generating the Physical Adversarial Attack

Following the formalism in [2], the problem of finding an adversarial example can be formally defined as follows:

$$\begin{aligned} &\text{minimize } ||x' - x||_2^{\,2} \\ &\text{s.t. } C(x') \neq l \\ &x' \in [0,1]^n, \end{aligned} \tag{10}$$

where $x$ is the undistributed image, $x'$ is the perturbated image, $l$ represents the ground truth label of the image $x$, and $C(x)$ denotes the DNN used as a classifier. Periodically, solving such a problem can be incredibly complex, which leads to solving a more straightforward problem instead, as suggested in [36]. In brief, the goal is to find a small perturbation $\delta = x' - x$, which can be applied to an image $x$ to alter its classification while ensuring that the resulting image remains valid. Considering that the Softmax $V_n$ is applied on top of the DNN logits, the loss function mapping an image $x$ to a positive real number can be described as follows

$$f(x) = Loss_{C,\,l}(V_n(x)), \tag{11}$$

Accordingly, instead of formulating the constraint minimization problem as in Equation (10), one can use an alternative formulation and solve the following problem:

$$\begin{aligned} &\text{minimize } ||\delta||_0 - \alpha \cdot f(x+\delta) \\ &\text{s.t. } x+\delta \in [0,\, 1]^n. \end{aligned} \tag{12}$$

where $\alpha$ represents the ratio between the magnitude of the disturbance and its effect's intensity on the output, and $||\cdot||_0$ denotes the zero norm.

In our case, we aim to establish a relation between the pulsed laser activity and the resulting adversarial perturbation caused by the rolling shutter mechanism of the CMOS camera. This mechanism converts the temporal signal of the designed laser pulse sequence into a spatial distortion within the acquired image. $\mathbf{E}_{eff}$ is an $N$-dimensional binary row vector representing the pulsed laser activity, which can be expressed by $N = (N_r + N_{rH})/R_n$, where $R_n$ denotes the number of dazzled pixel rows by each pulse and $(N_r + N_{rH})$ indicates the sensor's total number of pixel rows (see Section 3.1). Specifically, a unit value at the $i$-th component of this vector $\mathbf{E}_{eff}[i] = 1$, indicates a pulse occurring at the time $t = i \cdot t_{frame}/N$, and dazzles the sensor's pixel rows from $i \cdot R_n$ to $(i+1) \cdot R_n$. Thus, the indices of the dazzled pixel rows in the acquired image can be obtained by substituting each unit entry of the pulsed laser activity vector $\mathbf{E}_{eff}^T$ with a size $R_n$ vector of ones, which is given by the following:

$$\mathbf{E}_r^T = \mathbf{E}_{eff}^T \bigotimes \mathbf{1}_{R_n}^T \tag{13}$$

where $\otimes$ is the Kronecker product and $\mathbf{1}_{R_n}^T$ is an $R_n$-dimensional column vector of ones. Consequently, $\mathbf{E}_r^T$ is an $N \cdot R_n$-dimensional binary column vector in which unit entries indicate the dazzled sensor's pixel rows. Next, the resulting dazzle pattern in the acquired $N \times M$ image (e.g., Figure 4) can be obtained by the following:

$$\delta = \mathbf{E}_r^T \bigotimes \mathbf{1}_M = \left(\mathbf{E}_{eff}^T \bigotimes \mathbf{1}_{R_n}^T\right) \bigotimes \mathbf{1}_M, \tag{14}$$

where $\mathbf{1}_M$ is a size $M$ vector of ones corresponding to the number of pixel columns in the acquired image. Instead of formulating the minimization problem following Equation (12), we now use an alternative formulation expressed in terms of the pulsed laser activity vector $\mathbf{E}_{eff}$—the problem then becomes as follows: given $x$, find $\delta$ that satisfies the following:

$$\begin{gathered} \text{minimize} \left|\left|\mathbf{E}_{eff}^T\right|\right|_0 - \alpha \cdot f(x+\delta) \\ \text{s.t. } \delta \in [0,\ 1]^n, \end{gathered} \tag{15}$$

In practice, to implement a typical gradient-based optimization algorithm (such as SGD or ADAM) for solving Equation (15), we replace the binary vector derived from Equation (14). Rather than optimizing over the variable $\delta$ defined above, we change the variables and optimize over $\boldsymbol{\omega}^T$, which has the following form:

$$\delta = \left[\left(\frac{1}{2}\tanh\left(\boldsymbol{\omega}^T\right) + 1\right) \bigotimes \mathbf{1}_{R_n}^T\right] \bigotimes \mathbf{1}_M, \tag{16}$$

where $\delta \in [0,\ 1]^n$, and $\boldsymbol{\omega}^T$ has the same dimensions as $\mathbf{E}_{eff}^T$.

Since the exact moment of camera exposure is unknown to the attacker in a real-world setting, applying the AMOLS, consisting of a designed sequence of laser pulses, yields a dazzling pattern with a random horizontal shift. Considering the asynchrony between the attacking light pulse sequence and the camera's exposure moment, we utilize the Expectation over Transformation (EoT) method [10] as follows:

$$\text{minimize } \mathbb{E}_{t_0 \sim T}\left\{\left|\left|\mathbf{E}_{eff}^T\right|\right|_0 - \alpha \cdot f(x+\delta)\right\}. \tag{17}$$

where $T$ is the space of all possible instances of frame exposure, denoted as $t_0$.

## 4. Results and Discussion

This section presents the feasibility of conducting invisible adversarial attacks on DNNs in the physical domain by dazzling the camera. In addition, we evaluate the AMOLS performance using optimal dazzle patterns following the method described in Section 3.3, considering the pulsed laser activity depicted in Section 3.1. In the following sections, we employ both simulations and real experiments. First, we conduct simulations to investigate the effect of the AMOLS duty cycle while maintaining a constant pulse width. Next, we optically demonstrate the attack and examine its sensitivity to the pulse width.

### 4.1. Effectiveness of the AMOLS

We evaluate the effectiveness of the AMOLS based on the duty cycle of a pulsed laser (as discussed in Section 3.2) while keeping a constant pulse width. The ResNet50 classifier [37] and the standard cross-entropy loss function are utilized to simulate the adversarial attacks on the image classification model. Figure 7 shows simulation results of the loss function depending on the AMOLS duty cycle for two cases: where an object covers (1) approximately 40% of the field of view (FOV), and (2) approximately 85% of the FOV. These results focus on the "Coffee mug" as the target object, with the highest obtained values for each examined duty cycle as a result of optimizing the attack (as discussed in Section 3.3). It can be empirically determined that loss function values exceeding 2 exhibit poor classifier performances, resulting in misclassification across a significant number of input images—specifically, this enhances the effectiveness of the AMOLS. The results presented in Figure 7 indicate that when the duty cycle is set lower than 0.2%, the attack remains feasible—yet the classification model tends to yield better results when the target object covers $\sim$ 40% of the FOV. Conversely, increasing the AMOLS duty cycle substantially raises the loss, thereby enhancing the effectiveness of the attack in the case of an object occupying $\sim$ 40% of the FOV. Additionally, for a target object that covers $\sim$ 85% of the FOV, the attack proves effective across the entire duty cycle range examined, with a milder dependence on changes in the AMOLS duty cycle.

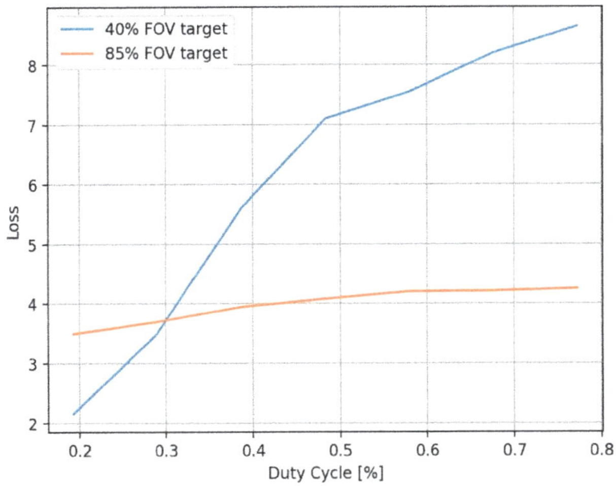


**Figure 7.** The effectiveness of the proposed attack on the loss function and its dependency on the duty cycle $D$ of the pulsed laser beam.

In addition, we examined a range of target objects during the attack, imaged from various angles of view corresponding to different classes—several samples are shown in Figure 8a. An analysis of the effect of the AMOLS duty cycle, while maintaining constant pulse width, on the classifier's loss function across diverse input images is shown in Figure 8b. We empirically found the critical values of the cross-entropy loss function at which the DNN begins to misclassify objects across different classes, considering an offset in the obtained loss curves above these critical values. It is observed from the results shown in Figure 8b that an AMOLS duty cycle of 0.4%, which corresponds to a designed sequence of 4 laser pulses, successfully fools the classifier in all cases.

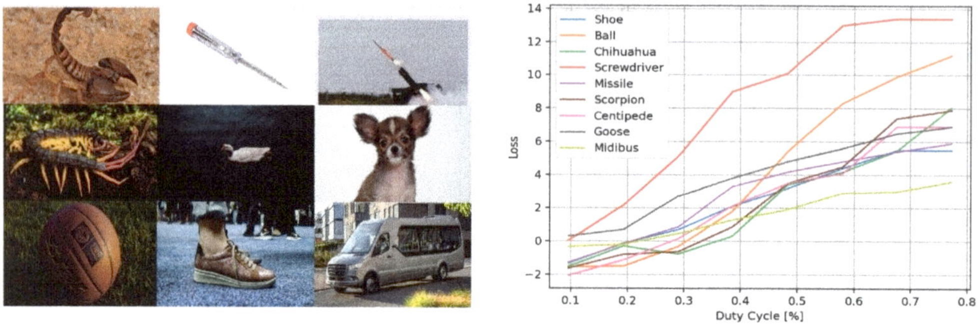


(a) (b)

**Figure 8.** The AMOLS is applied to different objects. (**a**) Examples of attacked images. (**b**) The dependence of the loss function on the attacking light source duty cycle for various objects.

### 4.2. *Real Experiments on Physical-World Adversarial Attack*

We carried out real experiments to evaluate the feasibility of the proposed optical-based physical adversarial attacks in real-world scenarios formed by converting the light temporal signal to a spatial distortion within the acquired image. A coffee mug is used as the target object and placed inside the FOV of a laptop camera (installed on a DELL-INSPIRON laptop with 0.92 Megapixel, 88° diagonal viewing angle). For the attack, a pulsed laser beam is directed at the camera from a position adjacent to the object, produced from a 650 nm dot diode laser, with an average power of 5 mW and a spot size of 3.5 mm. A sequence of pulses is designed to generate the adversarial dazzle pattern following the optimization method described in Section 3.2, where the temporal modulating signal is produced utilizing the Arduino-Uno microcontroller board. The camera captures both the light reflected from the object and the light emitted by the AMOLS. The acquired images are then fed to the DNN for classification. We conducted our experiments with no ambient light, as this represents the most challenging condition for our problem setting, which requires the light source to remain invisible to a human observer. As illustrated in Figure 6, as the background illumination decreases, the allowable AMOLS illumination budget that can remain invisible also decreases. Conversely, a lower AMOLS illumination budget challenges the success of attacks, as indicated by the reduced classification loss shown in Figure 8b.

Figure 9a,b shows two optical-based physical adversarial examples and their corresponding predictions from the image classification model. These examples were generated from two separate exposure shots, where the AMOLS used different pulse widths. It is worth mentioning that the attacking light pulse sequence is not synchronized with the camera's exposure moment (see Section 3.3), leading to variations in the dazzle pattern across each frame, specifically introducing a horizontal shift. Videos showing the footage from the attacked camera sequence are provided in the Supplementary Materials. Additional examples can be found on the GitHub repository associated with this paper at https://github.com/ZviSteinOpt/RollingShutterAttack/tree/main (accessed on 1 April 2025). The invisible CMOS camera dazzling attack induces misclassification across the input images, significantly reducing the classifier's confidence in the correct 500th class, as shown in Figure 9c.

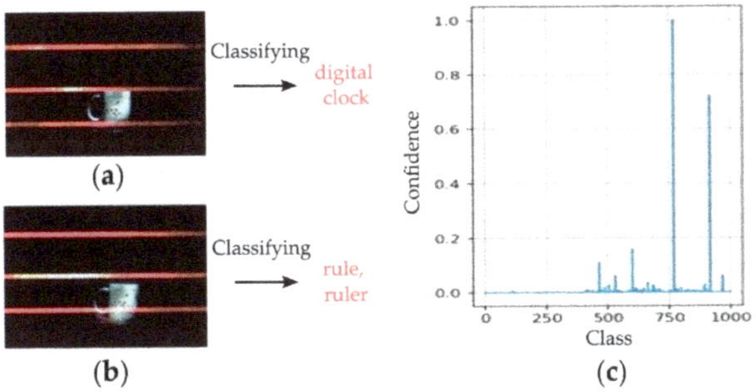


**Figure 9.** Results of AMOLS realization on an image classification model. Physical-world adversarial examples generated via two shots recording when setting different AMOLS activities: (**a**) pulse width of 1 μs with $D = 0.01\%$, and (**b**) pulse width of 70 μs with $D = 0.85\%$. (**c**) The DNN's confidence in the predicted results across the 1000 classes it was trained on, with the index for the correct "coffee mug" label being #500.

The distribution of predictions made by a targeted DNN model across various classes during the optical-based physical adversarial attacks is depicted in Figure 10. It is based on 254 repeated trials, where the AMOLS operates four pulses, having a pulse duration of 1 μs. The results indicate that the designed attack achieved an 85% success rate under these conditions. The results shown in Figure 11 indicate that a higher attack success rate can be achieved by increasing the pulse width. When the AMOLS pulse width exceeds approximately 70 μs, the physical-world attack success rate approaches 98%. However, following Section 3.2, increasing the pulse width reduces the range of concealed viewing angles (see Figure 6). These exhibit a tradeoff between the angular realm achieving invisibility and the success rate of the physical-world attack as the AMOLS duty cycle varies. Considering that the camera captures 30 frames per second, a pulse of 1 μs corresponds to a low duty cycle of 0.012% ($D = 100 \cdot 4 \cdot 1\ \mu s \cdot 30 s^{-1} = 0.012\%$), whereas a pulse duration of 70 μs results in a higher duty cycle of 0.84%. It can be observed from the results shown in Figure 6 that setting a duty cycle of 0.01% ensures the AMOLS activity remains invisible to the observer located at angles greater than approximately 5° from the optical axis. In comparison, a duty cycle of 0.85% could be sufficient to maintain the invisibility of optical-based physical adversarial attacks at a viewing angle of 15°.

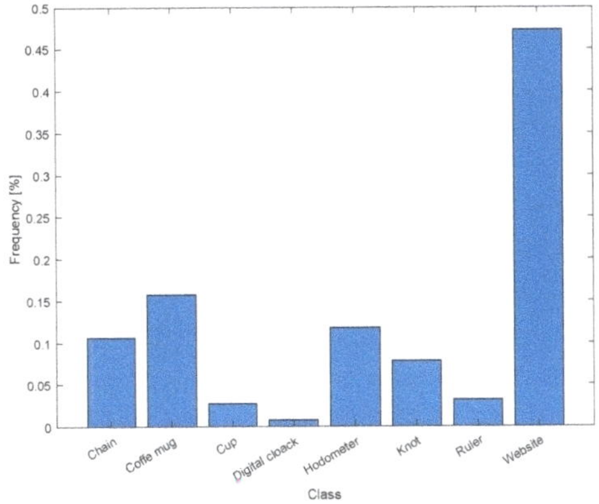


**Figure 10.** The frequency distribution of the DNN predictions during the attack. While the object's correct label is a "coffee mug", the attack exhibits an attack success rate of 85%.

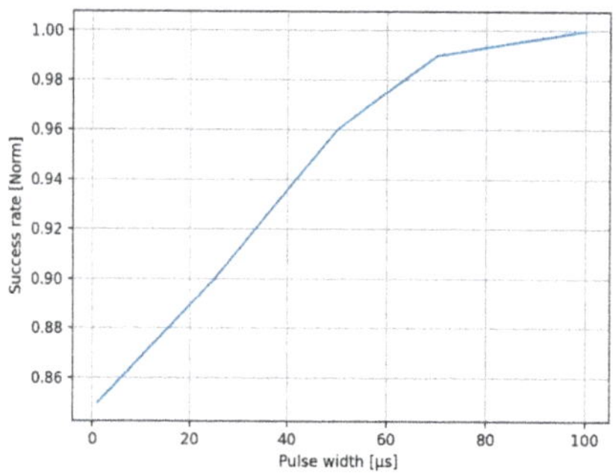


**Figure 11.** The average attack success rate as a function of the AMOLS pulse width.

The performance and properties of our attack are summarized in Table A1 in Appendix A, together with a comparison to that of other physical adversarial attacks involving image sensors.

## 5. Conclusions

In summary, we introduced a novel method for conducting optical-based physical adversarial attacks on DNN. The attack is demonstrated by directing a pulsed light at a CMOS camera. The rolling shutter mechanism of the camera converts the temporal signal, which consists of the designed sequence of light pulses, into a spatial distortion within the physical-world adversarial image. The photometric conditions and light pulse characteristics are analyzed to dazzle the CMOS camera sufficiently, thereby fooling the DNN model while keeping the AMOLS activity invisible to observers in the environment.

We demonstrated that the light source duty cycle enables the control of the tradeoff between the attack's success rate and the required angular degree of concealment. For instance, with the proposed method, an 85% success rate for the physical-world attack can be achieved while ensuring the invisibility of light source activity to the observer except for a narrow angular range of 5° from the optical axis. However, the attack success rate could be increased to 98% by allowing a slight reduction of 10° in the angular concealment range.

**Supplementary Materials:** The following supporting information can be downloaded at: https://www.mdpi.com/article/10.3390/s25072301/s1. The following supporting videos show the footage from the attacked camera sequence when setting different AMOLS activities. Video S1: pulse width of 1 μs with $D = 0.01\%$, and Video S2: pulse width of 70 μs with $D = 0.85\%$.

**Author Contributions:** Conceptualization, A.S. and A.H.; methodology, Z.S.; software, Z.S.; validation, Z.S., A.H. and A.S.; investigation, Z.S.; data curation, Z.S.; writing—original draft, Z.S.; writing—review and editing, A.H. and A.S.; supervision, A.H. and A.S.; project administration, A.S. All authors have read and agreed to the published version of the manuscript.

**Funding:** This research received no external funding.

**Institutional Review Board Statement:** Not applicable.

**Informed Consent Statement:** Not applicable.

**Data Availability Statement:** The original data presented in the study are openly available in the GitHub repository at https://github.com/ZviSteinOpt/RollingShutterAttack/tree/main (accessed on 1 April 2025).

**Conflicts of Interest:** The authors declare no conflicts of interest.

## Appendix A

**Table A1.** Comparison of physical adversarial attacks involving the image sensors.

| Physical World Attack | Attack Mechanism | Targeting Camera Sensors | Adversary Physical Access | Achievable Attack Success Rate | Invisibility Criterion |
|---|---|---|---|---|---|
| EM Injection [12] | CCD interface | ✓ | X Near distances | 50% ∼ 94% [a] | ✓ |
| *AdvLB* [13] | Spatial laser beam | X | X | 77.43% ∼ 100% [b] | X |
| CamData Lane [14] | Camera data lane | X | ✓Camera interface | 89.2% ∼ 96% [c] | – |
| RS Backdoor Attack [18] | CMOS dazzling | ✓ | X | 40% ∼ 88% [d] | X [f] |
| Adversarial RS [19] | CMOS dazzling | ✓ | X | ∼ 84% | X [f] |
| Our Attack | Invisible AMOLS | ✓ | X | 85% ∼ 98% [e] | ✓ |

[a] Average performance from various viewpoints depending on the threat model. [b] Depending on indoor or outdoor attacks. [c] Depending on the DNN model. [d] Based on simulation study or physical-domain study. [e] Depending on the observer zone location restriction (Figure 5). [f] Designed to prevent visible flickering, although the illumination source may be seen shining. RS—Rolling Shutter. X and ✓ represent whether the attacks target the camera sensors to inject their perturbations, require physical access by the adversary, or satisfy the invisibility criterion in the physical domain. — represents a designed attack assuming adversary physical access.

## References


1. Heaven, D. Why deep-learning AIs are so easy to fool. *Nature* **2019**, *574*, 163–166. [CrossRef] [PubMed]
2. Szegedy, C.; Zaremba, W.; Sutskever, I.; Bruna, J.; Erhan, D.; Goodfellow, I.; Fergus, R. Intriguing properties of neural networks. In Proceedings of the International Conference on Learning Representations (ICLR), Banff, AB, Canada, 14–16 April 2014.
3. Yuan, X.; He, P.; Zhu, Q.; Li, X. Adversarial Examples: Attacks and Defenses for Deep Learning. *IEEE Trans. Neural Netw. Learn. Syst.* **2019**, *30*, 2805–2824. [CrossRef] [PubMed]
4. Goodfellow, I.J.; Shlens, J.; Szegedy, C. Explaining and harnessing adversarial examples. In Proceedings of the International Conference on Learning Representations (ICLR), San Diego, CA, USA, 7–9 May 2015.
5. Fang, J.; Jiang, Y.; Jiang, C.; Jiang, Z.L.; Liu, C.; Yiu, S.M. State-of-the-art optical-based physical adversarial attacks for deep learning computer vision systems. *Expert Syst. Appl.* **2024**, *250*, 123761. [CrossRef]
6. Wang, J.; Wang, C.; Lin, Q.; Luo, C.; Wu, C.; Li, J. Adversarial attacks and defenses in deep learning for image recognition: A survey. *Neurocomputing* **2022**, *514*, 162–181.
7. Wei, H.; Tang, H.; Jia, X.; Wang, Z.; Yu, H.; Li, Z.; Satoh, S.I.; Van Gool, L.; Wang, Z. Physical adversarial attack meets computer vision: A decade survey. *IEEE Trans. Pattern Anal. Mach. Intell.* **2024**, *46*, 9797–9817. [CrossRef] [PubMed]
8. Lovisotto, G.; Turner, H.; Sluganovic, I.; Strohmeier, M.; Martinovic, I. SLAP: Improving Physical Adversarial Examples with Short-Lived Adversarial Perturbations. *arXiv* **2020**, arXiv:2007.04137.
9. Zhou, Z.; Tang, D.; Wang, X.; Han, W.; Lu, X.; Zhang, K. Invisible Mask: Practical attacks on face recognition with infrared. *arXiv* **2018**, arXiv:1803.04683v1.
10. Athalye, A.; Engstrom, L.; Ilyas, A.; Kwok, K. Synthesizing Robust Adversarial Examples. In Proceedings of the 35th International Conference on Machine Learning, Stockholm, Sweden, 10–15 July 2018.
11. Cui, J.; Guo, W.; Huang, H.; Lv, X.; Cao, H.; Li, H. Adversarial examples for vehicle detection with projection transformation. *IEEE Trans. Geosci. Remote Sens.* **2024**, *62*, 5632418. [CrossRef]
12. Liu, Z.; Lin, F.; Ba, Z.; Lu, L.; Ren, K. MagShadow: Physical Adversarial Example Attacks via Electromagnetic Injection. *IEEE Trans. Dependable Secur. Comput.* **2025**, 1–17. [CrossRef]
13. Duan, R.; Mao, X.; Qin, A.K.; Chen, Y.; Ye, S.; He, Y.; Yang, Y. Adversarial laser beam: Effective physical-world attack to dnns in a blink. In Proceedings of the IEEE/CVF Conference on Computer Vision and Pattern Recognition, Nashville, TN, USA, 20–25 June 2021; pp. 16062–16071.
14. Liu, W.; He, W.; Hu, B.; Chang, C.H. A practical man-in-the-middle attack on deep learning edge device by sparse light strip injection into camera data lane. In Proceedings of the 2022 IEEE 35th International System-on-Chip Conference (SOCC), Belfast, UK, 5–8 September 2022; IEEE: Piscataway, NJ, USA, 2022; pp. 1–6.
15. Wang, X.; Xu, Z.; Zhong, H.; Cheng, X.A.; Xing, Z.; Zhang, J. Fresnel Diffraction Model for Laser Dazzling Spots of Complementary Metal Oxide Semiconductor Cameras. *Sensors* **2024**, *24*, 5781. [CrossRef] [PubMed]
16. Chia-Kai, L. Analysis and Compensation of Rolling Shutter Effect. *IEEE Trans. Image Process.* **2008**, *17*, 1323–1330. [CrossRef] [PubMed]
17. Danakis, C.; Afgani, M.; Povey, G.; Underwood, I.; Haas, H. Using a CMOS Camera Sensor for Visible Light Communication. In Proceedings of the IEEE Globecom Workshops, Anaheim, CA, USA, 3–7 December 2012.
18. Li, H.; Wang, Y.; Xie, X.; Liu, Y.; Wang, S.; Wan, R.; Chau, L.P.; Kot, A.C. Light Can Hack Your Face! Black-box Backdoor Attack on Face Recognition Systems. *arXiv* **2020**, arXiv:2009.06996.

19. Sayles, A.; Hooda, A.; Gupta, M.; Chatterjee, R.; Fernandes, E. Invisible Perturbations: Physical Adversarial Examples Exploiting the Rolling Shutter Effect. In Proceedings of the IEEE/CVF Conference on Computer Vision and Pattern Recognition, Nashville, TN, USA, 20–25 June 2021; pp. 14666–14675.
20. Chen, Z.; Lin, P.; Jiang, Z.L.; Wei, Z.; Yuan, S.; Fang, J. An illumination modulation-based adversarial attack against automated face recognition system. In Proceedings of the Information Security and Cryptology: 16th International Conference, Inscrypt 2020, Guangzhou, China, 11–14 December 2020; Revised Selected Papers. Springer International Publishing: Cham, Switzerland, 2021; pp. 53–69.
21. Shen, Y.; Cheng, Y.; Lin, Y.; Long, S.; Jiang, C.; Li, D.; Dai, S.; Jiang, Y.; Fang, J.; Jiang, Z.L.; et al. MLIA: Modulated LED illumination-based adversarial attack on traffic sign recognition system for autonomous vehicle. In Proceedings of the 2022 IEEE International Conference on Trust, Security and Privacy in Computing and Communications (TrustCom), Wuhan, China, 9–11 December 2022; IEEE: Piscataway, NJ, USA, 2022; pp. 1020–1027.
22. Fang, J.; Yang, Z.; Dai, S.; Jiang, Y.; Jiang, C.; Jiang, Z.L.; Liu, C.; Yiu, S.M. Cross-task physical adversarial attack against lane detection system based on LED illumination modulation. In Proceedings of the Chinese Conference on Pattern Recognition and Computer Vision (PRCV), Xiamen, China, 13–15 October 2023; Springer Nature: Singapore, 2023; pp. 478–491.
23. Köhler, S.; Lovisotto, G.; Birnbach, S.; Baker, R.; Martinovic, I. They See Me Rollin': Inherent Vulnerability of the Rolling Shutter in CMOS Image Sensors. In Proceedings of the 37th Annual Computer Security Applications Conference, Virtual, 6–10 December 2021; pp. 399–413.
24. Yan, C.; Xu, Z.; Yin, Z.; Mangard, S.; Ji, X.; Xu, W.; Zhao, K.; Zhou, Y.; Wang, T.; Gu, G.; et al. Rolling colors: Adversarial laser exploits against traffic light recognition. In Proceedings of the 31st USENIX Security Symposium (USENIX Security 22), Boston, MA, USA, 10–12 August 2022; pp. 1957–1974.
25. Nilson, D.G.; Hill, D.N.; Evans, J.C. *Thomson Scattering Stray Light Reduction Techniques Using a CCD Camera*; Lawrence Livermore National Laboratory: Livermore, CA, USA, 1997.
26. Schleijpen, R.H.M.A.; Dimmeler, A.; Eberle, B.; van den Heuvel, J.C.; Mieremet, A.L.; Beckman, H.; Mellier, B. Laser Dazzling of Focal Plane Array Cameras. In Proceedings of the Defense and Security Symposium, Orlando, FL, USA, 10 October 2007.
27. Schleijpen, H.M.A.; Carpenter, S.R.; Mellier, B.; Dimmeler, A. Imaging Seeker Surrogate for IRCM evaluation. In Proceedings of the Optics/Photonics in Security and Defence, Stockholm, Sweden, 5 October 2006.
28. Santos, C.N.; Chrétien, S.; Merella, L.; Vandewal, M. Visible and near-infrared laser dazzling of CCD and CMOS cameras. In Proceedings of the Technologies for Optical Countermeasures XV, Berlin, Germany, 9 October 2018.
29. Eberle, B.; Kinerk, W.T.; Koerber, M.; Öhgren, J.; Ritt, G.; Santos, C.N.; Schwarz, B.; Steinvall, O.; Tipper, S.M.; Vandewal, M.; et al. NATO SET-249 joint measurement campaign on laser dazzle effects in airborne scenarios. In *Proceedings Volume 11161, Technologies for Optical Countermeasures XVI*; SPIE: Bellingham, WA, USA, 2019; pp. 119–138.
30. Blackwell, H.R. Contrast Thresholds of the Human Eye. *J. Opt. Soc. Am.* **1946**, *36*, 624–643. [CrossRef] [PubMed]
31. Adrian, W. Visibility of targets: Model for calculation. *Light Res. Technol.* **1989**, *21*, 181–188.
32. Paschotta, R. RP Photonics Encyclopedia. Available online: https://www.rp-photonics.com/radiance.html (accessed on 1 April 2025).
33. Williamson, C.A.; McLin, L.N. Nominal ocular dazzle distance (NODD). *Appl. Opt.* **2015**, *54*, 1564–1572. [CrossRef]
34. McLin, L.N.; Smith, P.A.; Barnes, L.E.; Dykes, J.R. Scaling laser disability glare functions with "K" factors to predict dazzle. In *International Laser Safety*; AIP Publishing: Albuquerque, NM, USA, 2015.
35. Vos, J.; Cole, B.; Bodmann, H.-W.; Colombo, E.; Takeuchi, T.; van den Berg, T.J.T.P. *CIE Equations for Disability Glare*; CIE TC: Vienna, Austria, 2002.
36. Carlini, N.; Wagner, D. Towards Evaluating the Robustness of Neural Networks. In Proceedings of the 2017 IEEE Symposium on Security and Privacy (SP), San Jose, CA, USA, 22–26 May 2017.
37. He, K.; Zhang, X.; Ren, S.; Sun, J. Deep Residual Learning for Image Recognition. In Proceedings of the 2016 IEEE Conference on Computer Vision and Pattern Recognition (CVPR), Las Vegas, NV, USA, 27–30 June 2016.

sensors

MDPI

Article

# HGF-MiLaG: Hierarchical Graph Fusion for Emotion Recognition in Conversation with Mid-Late Gender-Aware Strategy

Yihan Wang [1,†], Rongrong Hao [1,†], Ziheng Li [1], Xinhe Kuang [1], Jiacheng Dong [1], Qi Zhang [1], Fengkui Qian [1] and Changzeng Fu [1,2,3,*]

[1] Sydney smart technology college, Northeastern University, Qinhuangdao Campus, Qinhuangdao 066004, China; 202219206@stu.neuq.edu.cn (Y.W.); 202219259@stu.neuq.edu.cn (R.H.); 202219039@stu.neuq.edu.cn (Z.L.); 202319257@stu.neuq.edu.cn (X.K.); 202219071@stu.neuq.edu.cn (J.D.); 202212078@stu.neu.edu.cn (Q.Z.); 2372410@stu.neu.edu.cn (F.Q.)

[2] Osaka University, Toyonaka Campus, Osaka 560-0043, Japan

[3] Hebei Key Laboratory of Marine Perception Network and Data Processing, Northeastern University, Qinhuangdao Campus, Qinhuangdao 066004, China

* Correspondence: changzeng.fu@irl.sys.es.osaka-u.ac.jp

† These authors contributed equally to this work.

**Abstract:** Emotion recognition in conversation (ERC) is an important research direction in the field of human-computer interaction (HCI), which recognizes emotions by analyzing utterance signals to enhance user experience and plays an important role in several domains. However, existing research on ERC mainly focuses on constructing graph networks by directly modeling interactions on multimodal fused features, which cannot adequately capture the complex dialog dependency based on time, speaker, modalities, etc. In addition, existing multi-task learning frameworks for ERC do not systematically investigate how and where gender information is injected into the model to optimize ERC performance. To address the above problems, this paper proposes a Hierarchical Graph Fusion for ERC with Mid-Late Gender-aware Strategy (HGF-MiLaG). HGF-MiLaG uses hierarchical fusion graph to adequately capture intra-modal and inter-modal speaker dependency and temporal dependency. In addition, HGF-MiLaG explores the effect of the location of gender information injections on ERC performance, and ultimately employs a Mid-Late multilevel gender-aware strategy in order to allow the hierarchical graph network to determine the proportion of emotion and gender information in the classifier. Empirical results on two public multimodal datasets(i.e.,IEMOCAP and MELD), demonstrate that HGF-MiLaG outperforms existing methods.

**Keywords:** emotion recognition; hierarchical graph fusion; mid-late multilevel gender-aware strategy; multi-task learning

## 1. Introduction

With the rapid development of AI technology, the application of emotion recognition in conversation (ERC) in human-computer interaction (HCI) has gained widespread attention. ERC technology is capable of recognizing the emotion of speakers by analyzing signals (i.e., audio, video, text, etc.) in utterance. By recognizing and responding to emotional state of users, machines can provide a more personalized and empathetic interaction experience, deepening the human emotional connection between humans and machines, thus enhancing user experience [1,2]. Additionally, ERC has played a significant role in the fields of opinion mining in social media [3], doctor-patient interaction in clinical practice [4], depression diagnosis [5], and electronic learning environments [6].

In ERC, understanding and utilizing contextual information is particularly important [7]. Capture of speaker dependency and temporal dependency can provide rich contextual understanding. Speaker dependency refers to emotional interactions between individuals in a conversation [8]. This dependency includes changes in not only the individual's own emotional state, but also emotional interactions between different speakers. For example, as shown in Figure 1, an example of intra-speaker dependency is that in u7, the son expresses frustration, an emotional state that may have been influenced by his own previous utterances (u3, u5). An example of inter-speaker dependency is that in u10, the son expresses concern about his mother's angry feelings, which may have been influenced by his mother's angry utterance in u8 and u9. Temporal dependency involves changes in emotional states over time in a conversation. Past utterance influences the trajectory of future utterance, and future utterance may fill in missing information in the past utterance [9]. For example, as shown in Figure 1, 'frustrated' in u5 is influenced by 'sad' in u4, and it is also supplemented by the information of the emotion state of 'sad' of u6 at the next time step. Therefore, the ability to adequately capture speaker dependency and temporal dependency in a conversation is crucial to improve the performance of ERC. HiGRU [10] combined attention and recurrent neural networks to capture neighboring utterance through three main components, but it failed to take speaker dependency into account. To this end, DialogueGCN [11] captured inter-speaker dependence and intra-speaker dependence through a graph network, but it used only textual information and failed to take full advantage of complementarities between different modalities of information, which led to poor performance in complex emotion recognition tasks. Therefore, researchers started to focus on how to integrate information from different modalities using graph networks, proposing cross-modal multi-head attention mechanisms [12,13] and cross-modal feature complementation [14]. However, existing approaches mainly focus on fusing multimodal features and directly modeling the relationships, which cannot adequately capture speaker dependency and temporal dependency within and across modalities. This may lead to a degradation of the overall performance of the model when there are differences in the quality of information across unimodality.

Additionally, adding auxiliary tasks to ERC can improve the performance of the model significantly. Existing multi-task learning, such as the auxiliary tasks in speaker recognition [15], emotion shift detection (ESD-ERC model) [16], facial expression perception (Facial MMT framework) [17], provided additional supervised signals to the ERC model, which helped to improve the model's understanding and prediction of emotional states. However, most multitask learning fails to utilize gender information effectively, or does not systematically examine how and where gender information is injected into the model to optimize ERC performance. Studies have shown that males and females differ in emotion expression, and these differences are not only reflected in the audio characteristics of speech, such as pitch, intensity, and sound quality, but may also affect the accuracy of emotion recognition [18]. Ignoring gender information can lead to models that fail to model individual differences effectively, thus affecting the personalization and accuracy of emotion recognition.

To address these limitations, this paper introduces Hierarchical Graph Fusion and Mid-Late Gender-aware Strategy (HGF-MiLaG). HGF-MiLaG **captures the emotional dynamics of a conversation by constructing Hierarchical Fusion Graph in order to enhance the model's understanding of semantics and emotions.** Specifically, the hierarchical fusion graph is constructed by first constructing unimodal graphs for each modality to capture intra-modal dependency, and then building multimodal graph that enables inter-modal information integration and capture inter-modal speaker dependency, the combination of which is the basis of the hierarchical graph fusion strategy. For the construction of each graph, we model conversations with the help of directed graphs in order to model speaker dependency and temporal dependency. Each node in the graph represents a utterance and the edges represent dependency between utterances. We input the built graph into a graph convolutional network [9] to propagate contextual information. Meanwhile, to address the problem of ignored gender information, we **introduce the Mid-Late multilevel gender-aware strategy, and the gender prediction subtask was designed as an auxiliary task to enhance contextual understanding and individual difference recognition for emotion recognition.** Considering that mid-stage fusion with feature interaction and fusion at the middle layer of the model can more utilize complementary information between tasks effectively, while late-stage fusion can fuse data from different tasks flexibly. Therefore, in the process of optimizing the multitasking mechanism, we propose an innovative approach of **injecting gender-auxiliary information into both the unimodal graph structure with speaker dependency and temporal dependency (mid-stage), and the multimodal graph structure (late-stage), in order to allow the hierarchical graph network to decide how much gender and emotion information to use.**

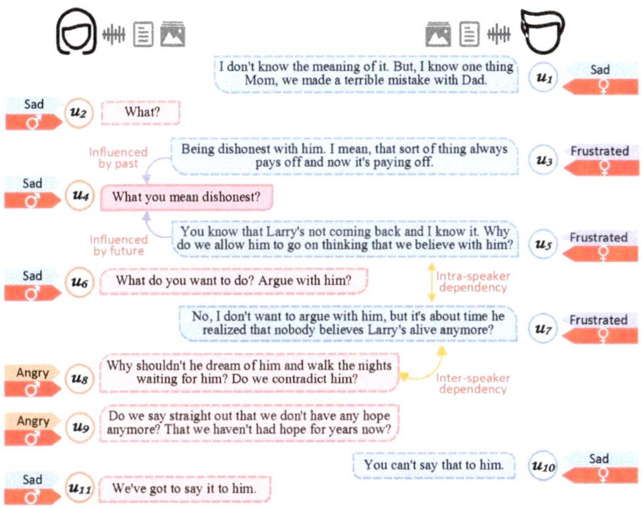


**Figure 1.** Example of a multimodal dialog scene: The dialog is drawn from textual, audio, and visual modalities. The dialog demonstrates the complexity of communication and emotional relationships faced by the mother and the son when dealing with the loss of a loved one as an intra-familial issue, reflecting speaker-dependent and temporal-dependent relationships.

In particular, it should be noted that due to the involvement of gender labels, we need to face up to the potential bias brought about by the use of gender information for modelling. In the data processing process, if there is gender imbalance in the training data or under-representation of emotion data of certain genders, it may lead to bias in the learning process of the model, which in turn may lead to unfair results in practical applications. For example, if the amount of female emotion data is much larger than that of male, the model may identify female emotions more accurately, while the judgement of male emotions is biased. Therefore, in subsequent studies, we will always be highly cautious to circumvent potential biases and ensure the fairness and social value of the model.

General speaking, our main contributions and innovations of this work are as follows:

**1. Hierarchical graph fusion:** In order to capture and integrate complex dependency in multimodal data, we propose a hierarchical graph fusion strategy. This strategy first constructs three unimodal graphs to capture speaker dependency and temporal dependency within modalities, and then constructs a multimodal graph to represent inter-modal dependency, which ultimately enhances the model's ability to recognize emotionally relevant features, and provides a richer and more dynamic perspective for the ERC task.

2. **Mid-Late multi-Level gender-aware strategy:** In order to improve the accuracy of the model in emotion node classification and prediction tasks, we adopt a Mid-Late multi-level gender-aware strategy approach to inject gender information. Taking into account the advantages of the Mid-Late fusion strategy that feature interaction and fusion at the middle layer of the model can utilize the complementary information between tasks more effectively, and the late-stage fusion that can flexibly fuse the data from different tasks, we finally adopt the simultaneous injection of gender-auxiliary information in both the unimodal graph structure with speaker-dependent and temporal-dependent features (mid-stage) and the multimodal graph structure (late-stage) to improve the model's performance on a emotion classification task. We further explore the effect of the location of gender information injection on ERC performance in Section 5, and the results corroborate our ideas.

We evaluated the proposed model on the IEMOCAP and MELD dialog datasets and compared it with existing methods. The experimental results show that the model has competitive performance over the chosen competitors on both datasets. The rest of the paper is organized as follows: we present related work in Section 2. The details of our proposed methodology are given in Section 3. The experiments are detailed in Section 4. Results and discussions are presented in Section 5, and Section 6 briefly summarizes our work.

## 2. Related Works

### 2.1. Graph Neural Network

In the field of conversational emotion recognition, graph neural networks (GNNs) provide a powerful framework for modeling speaker dependency in conversations due to their excellent relational modeling capabilities. Ghosal et al. [11] applied graph neural networks to ERC for the first time by proposing the DialogueGCN model, which solved the context propagation problem that existed in recurrent neural network (RNN)-based models. However, the method mainly focused on textual information and does not integrate multimodal data. To solve this problem, Hu et al. [12] proposed a multimodal graph convolutional network (MMGCN) based on DialogueGCN, which improves the accuracy of emotion recognition by exploiting the dependency between modalities. However, MMGCN crudely connected the utterance to all other utterances within the modality, which brought additional noise. For this reason, Li et al. [19] proposed a novel multimodal fusion method (GraphMFT) based on graph neural networks, which reduced the noise by constructing multiple heterogeneous graphs and introducing an improved graph attention network. However, the above GNN-based method establishes utterance dependency under a fixed window and thus tends to over-consider contextual information that is weakly or irrelevantly related to the current utterance. Therefore, Gan et al. [20] proposed a model for recognizing emotions in conversations using graph neural networks, supplemented with novel context filters and feature correction mechanisms, which yielded superior performance in the task of conversational emotion recognition. The graph neural network model of HAM-GNN proposed by Fu et al. [21] efficiently models conversational behavior labels by capturing interactions between speakers and contextual semantics, enabling efficient conversational behavior classification. It can be concluded that graph neural networks (GNNs) have made significant progress in the field of ERC. In this paper, we propose the hierarchical graph fusion strategy to adequately capture intra-modal and inter-modal dependency.

### 2.2. Multi-Task Learning

Multi-task learning is an efficient machine learning strategy [22] that enhances the generalization ability of a model by training multiple related tasks simultaneously. The core advantage of this approach is the ability to share knowledge points and utilize the correlation between tasks to enhance the learning efficiency of each task. Ruder [23] pointed out that the use of a multi-task learning approach can simultaneously optimize multiple emotion-related subtasks during the training process, which not only helps to reduce the overfitting problem of the model, but also improves the recognition effect. In addition, collaboration between the tasks also promotes complementary information between modalities and effectively avoids affecting the performance of the whole model due to insufficient data or noise in one modality [24]. A typical example is the multimodal emotion recognition model based on multi-task learning proposed by Wang et al. [25], which improved modal fusion by setting auxiliary tasks to learn more emotionally inclined visual and audio representations. Xue et al. [26] investigated and proposed a self-supervised dynamic fusion model for multi-task multimodal interactive learning, centered on text modality and supplemented by audio modality and video modality, using distribution similarity loss function and heterogeneity loss function to learn commonality characterization and characteristic characterization of modalities. Based on this, multi-task learning is used to obtain the consistency and difference characterization of the modalities. These studies have fully demonstrated the potential of multitask learning in multimodal emotion recognition. In this paper, we further introduce a multitask learning module for Mid-Late multilevel gender-aware strategy to enhance contextual understanding and individual difference recognition for emotion recognition, thus further improving the performance of the model.

### 2.3. Auxiliary Information Fusion

Individual difference modeling is one of the key directions for optimization of ERC, which belongs to the subtask of auxiliary information fusion [27]. In the process of individual difference modeling, the location factor of fusion is crucial, and different fusion locations can significantly affect the model performance. Depending on the location of the fusion, the research methods are primarily divided into early-stage fusion, mid-stage fusion, and late-stage fusion.

Early-stage fusion strategies mainly inject auxiliary information at the input layer [28]. For example, in the field of multimodal emotion analysis, research in Tian et al. [29] improved model performance by incorporating weakly labeled emotion information based on emoji filtering into word vector representations and introducing external feature extraction algorithms. This approach simplifies the subsequent processing by merging data from different modalities right at the data preprocessing stage. However, the disadvantage of early-stage fusion is that it may lead to under-modeling of high-dimensional feature space and complex relationships between modalities [30]. Late-stage fusion strategies merge information from different tasks in the final stage of the model. For example, Zadeh et al. [31] proposed the Multi-Attention Recurrent Network (MARN). MARN recognizes emotions by merging information from different modalities in the final stage of the model. The disadvantage of late fusion is that it may not adequately capture information about interactions between different modalities because each modality is processed independently, which may lead to information loss [32]. The mid-stage fusion strategy, on the other hand, performs feature interaction and fusion at the middle layer of the model [31]. Wu et al. [33] proposed a multimodal emotion recognition method based on the assistance of affective information, which simultaneously improves the performance of emotion classification and emotion recognition tasks by means of joint learning. Specifically, the method encoded modality internal information through a private network layer and achieved mid-stage fusion by jointly learning the main and auxiliary tasks through a shared network layer. The mid-stage fusion strategy provides a way to balance the disadvantages of early-stage and late-stage fusion due to its ability to perform feature interaction and fusion at the middle layer of the model, which can utilize the complementary information between the tasks more effectively, improving the accuracy and robustness of emotion recognition.

Therefore, in the process of optimizing the multitasking mechanism, we propose an innovative approach of injecting both gender-auxiliary information into the unimodal graph structure with speaker dependency and temporal dependency (mid-stage) and the multimodal graph structure (late-stage), which is done in order to allow the hierarchical graph network to decide on the proportion of gender information and emotion information utilized.

## 3. Method

This section describes the proposed method in this paper in detail. The overall architecture of our method is shown in Figure 2, including context encoding, construction of hierarchical graph based on graph networks, injection of gender information and emotion prediction.

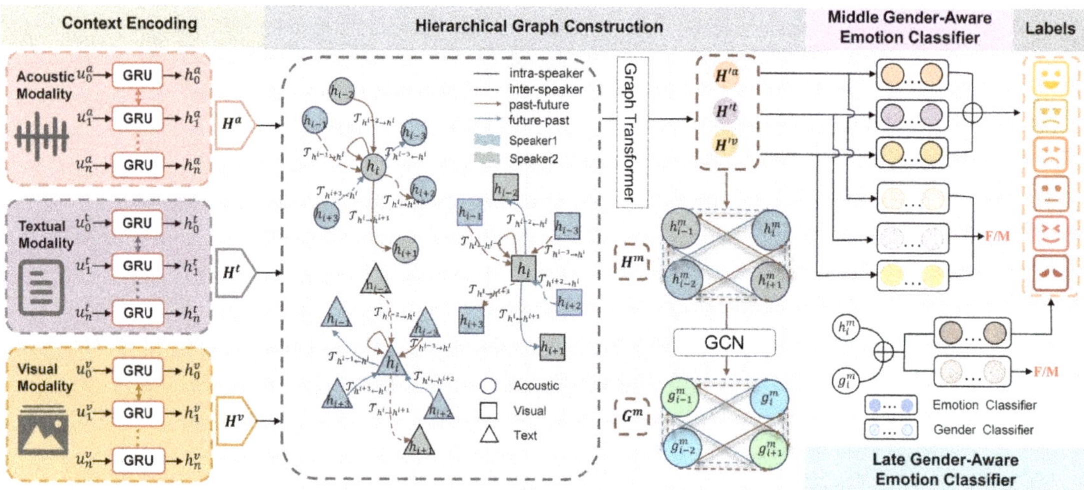


**Figure 2.** The overall architecture of the proposed HGF-MiLaG, including context encoding, creation of hierarchical graph based on graph networks, auxiliary tasks gender information injection and emotion prediction.

### 3.1. Task Definition

In the ERC scenario, each dialog contains M utterances $\{u_1, u_2, \ldots, u_M\}$, and each utterance incorporates information from three modalities: audio ($u_i^a$), text ($u_i^t$), and video ($u_i^v$). The core task of ERC is to assign each utterance in the dialog a emotion label $\{y_1, y_2, \ldots, y_M\}$. Our model exploits the speaker dependency and temporal dependency within and across modalities, and proposes a hierarchical graph fusion strategy. In addition, in order to improve the accuracy of emotion recognition, a Mid-Late multilevel gender-aware strategy is adopted to incorporate gender information as an auxiliary task in the model training.

### 3.2. Unimodal Feature Extraction

AUDIO: We used the OpenSmile toolkit and its IS10 configuration [34] for audio feature extraction. During feature extraction, the window length was set to 25 ms, the step size to 10 ms, and the frames were windowed using a Hamming window. Finally, the acoustic features of each speech are represented as a 1582-dimensional feature vector.

TEXT: We use RoBERTa model [10] to extract the context independent utterance level feature vector. Specifically, we fine-tune the RoBERTa Large model so that each utterance can be generated by the model as a 1024-dimensional feature vector representation.

VISUAL: In line with previous methods [35], we extract visual features using the DenseNet model [36] to generate a feature vector of dimension 342 for each utterance.

### 3.3. Hierarchical Graph Fusion

#### 3.3.1. Context Encoding

To obtain the contextual information of each modality, we refer to DialogueGCN [11] and use bidirectional gated recurrent unit ($\overleftrightarrow{GRU}$).

$$h_i^{(a,t,v)} = \overleftrightarrow{GRU}\left(u_i^{(a,t,v)}, h_{i(\pm 1)}^{(a,t,v)}\right) \tag{1}$$

where $u_i^{(a,t,v)}$ is the context-independent feature representation of utterance i from the audio, textual, and visual modalities, respectively. $h_i^{(a,t,v)}$ denotes the sequential contextual utterance of the output of each modal encoder.

#### 3.3.2. Hierarchical Fusion Graph Construction

We construct directed graphs for each modality to dynamically capture speaker dependency and temporal dependency between utterances. A conversation with M utterances is represented as three unimodal graphs $\mathcal{G}^{(a,t,v)} = (\mathcal{V}^{(a,t,v)}, \mathcal{E}^{(a,t,v)}, \mathcal{T}^{(a,t,v)})$, where $\mathcal{V}^{(a,t,v)}$ stands for vertices, $\mathcal{E}^{(a,t,v)}$ stands for edges, and $\mathcal{T}^{(a,t,v)}$ stands for edge types.

**Vertex:** Each utterance in a conversation contains three modalities, so each utterance is represented as a vertex $v_i^{(a,t,v)} \in V^{(a,t,v)}$ in the directed graph of audio, textual and visual modalities, respectively. Where each vertex is initialized with the feature vector $h_i^{(a,t,v)}$ encoded in the corresponding context.

**Edge:** In a graph, an edge represents a connection between vertices. In our model, it is assumed that each utterance in a set of conversations has a direct dependency on all other utterances in the conversation, i.e., a conversation is constructed as a fully connected graph.

**Edge Types:** In dialog analysis, the connectivity relations between edges need to be considered in terms of speaker dependency and temporal dependency. Specifically, speaker dependency includes intra-speaker ($S_{intra}$) dependency and inter-speaker ($S_{inter}$) dependency. In this paper, only two speakers ($s1$ and $s2$) are considered for conversational emotion recognition, so there are four relationship types for speaker dependency, i.e., speaker 1 self-dependency, speaker 2 self-dependency, speaker 1's dependency on speaker 2, and speaker 2's dependency on speaker 1. Temporal dependency considers the order in which utterance appears in a conversation, i.e., there are two types of relations: dependency of present utterance on future utterance and dependency of future utterance on present utterance. We use $\alpha_{i,j}^{(a,t,v)} \in (0,1)$ to encode speaker dependency in three unimodal graphs: when there is some speaker dependency between two vertices, $\alpha_{i,j}^{(a,t,v)}$ is 1; otherwise, $\alpha_{i,j}^{(a,t,v)}$ is 0. Similarly, we encode the temporal dependence by $\beta_{i,j}^{(a,t,v)} \in (0,1)$. Thus for each modality there are at most 8 different relation types $\mathcal{T}^{(a,t,v)} = (\alpha_{i,j}^{(a,t,v)}, \beta_{i,j}^{(a,t,v)})$.

**Graph Transformer:** We introduce the Graph Transformer model [37] to update the feature vectors of vertices and the weights of edges in unimodal graphs to obtain speaker-dependent and temporal-dependent vertex features. The model incorporates the classical multi-head attention mechanism, making it applicable to graph-structured data.

$$h_i^{(a,t,v)\prime} = W_1^{(a,t,v)} h_i^{(a,t,v)} + \frac{1}{N_{\mathcal{T}}} \sum_{\tau \in \mathcal{T}} \sum_{j \in N_i} \theta_{i,j}^{\tau(a,t,v)} W_2^{(a,t,v)} h_j^{(a,t,v)} \tag{2}$$

where $W_n^{(a,t,v)}$ is the trainable matrix, $N_{\mathcal{T}}$ denotes the total number of relation types of edges, $N_i$ denotes the total number of utterances, and $\theta_{i,j}^{\tau(a,t,v)}$ is the attention coefficients computed by the multi-head dot product attention mechanism.

$$\theta_{i,j}^{\tau(a,t,v)} = \mathrm{Softmax}\left( \frac{(W_3^{(a,t,v)} h_i^{(a,t,v)})^\top (W_4^{(a,t,v)} h_j^{(a,t,v)})}{\sqrt{D}} \right) \tag{3}$$

where D is the dimension of the model.

Inspired by the studies of Chudasama et al. [37] and Deng et al. [38], we introduce a multi-modal cross-modal attention mechanism to fuse three unimodal features. The multimodal feature is finally represented by $H_m$.

Similar to the construction of per-modal graphs, we utilize the output multimodal feature representation $H_m$ to construct the multimodal graph structure $\mathcal{G}^m = (\mathcal{V}^m, \mathcal{E}^m, \mathcal{T}^m)$ via speaker dependency and temporal dependency, where $\mathcal{V}^m$ are the nodes, $\mathcal{E}^m$ are the edges, and $\mathcal{T}^m$) are the type of relationship of the edges. Our goal is to utilize the graph structure to more fully integrate the multimodal features of different information dynamics.

Based on the multimodal graph construction, we utilize the graph convolutional network RGCN to deal with different types of relationships between different types of interactions such as intra-speaker and inter-speaker interactions. The capability of RGCN lies in its ability to learn unique representations of different types of relationships, which provides richer contextual information for our model.

First, the multimodal feature representation $H_m$ is input to the RGCN, which combines information from neighboring nodes as well as specific relationship types to update the feature representation of a node.

$$h_i^{m\prime} = \sigma(\vartheta_{\text{root}} \cdot h_i^m + \sum_{\tau \in \mathcal{T}} \sum_{j \in N(i)} \frac{1}{|\mathcal{N}(i)|} \vartheta_\tau \cdot h_j^m) \tag{4}$$

where $\vartheta_{\text{root}}$ is a learnable parameter of the RGCN for combining the features of the node itself and its neighboring nodes. $N(i)$ is the set of neighboring nodes of node $i$ under relation type $\tau$. $\vartheta_\tau$ is the learnable weight matrix associated with relation type $\tau$. $\sigma(.)$ is the ReLU activation function.

After RGCN processing, we use the Weisfeiler-Lehman algorithm [39] to further refine and summarize graph-related features. The WL algorithm encodes the topology of the graph by iteratively updating the feature representations of the nodes, thus generating a feature vector for each node containing information about the global graph structure. The WL processing can increase the model's ability to perceive the overall structure of the graph.

$$m_i = W_{\text{Mult}}^{(1)} \cdot h_i^{m\prime} + W_{\text{Mult}}^{(2)} \sum_{j \in N(i)} \omega_{i,j} \cdot h_j^{m\prime} \tag{5}$$

where $\omega_{i,j}$ is the edge weight from source node $j$ to target node $i$.

### 3.4. Mid-Late Gender-Aware Emotion Feature Classifier

In this section, we introduce a gender prediction task that aims to integrate gender information as an auxiliary feature into our model. The goal of the auxiliary task is to predict the gender attributes of the dialog participants, thus enriching the model's understanding of user characteristics. In this way, our model is able to more accurately capture and reflect gender-related emotional features in conversations, which ultimately improves the accuracy of the model's main task of emotion recognition. To achieve this goal, we design a multi-task learning framework [23] inspired by existing hard parameter sharing strategies [40] and customized for our research goals. In particular, we adopt a Mid-Late multilevel gender-aware approach to inject gender information, which is a way to improve the performance of the model's emotion classification task by simultaneously injecting gender-auxiliary information in both the speaker-dependent and temporal-dependent unimodal graph structure (mid-stage), and in the fused multimodal graph structure (late-stage). Based on this, we constructed a lightweight multi-task GNN model, HGF-MiLaG, which shares all the convolutional layers between gender prediction and emotion prediction tasks to improve the accuracy of emotion recognition.

#### 3.4.1. Middle Gender-Aware Emotion Classifier

In a unimodal gender-aware emotion classification task, feature vectors $h_i^{(a,t,v)'}$ of each modal utterance are fed into respective mid-stage gender-aware emotion classifiers to predict emotion labels and gender labels. Specifically, the classifiers first compute the unnormalized emotion or gender category labels $C_{i,emo}^{(a,t,v)}$ and $C_{i,gen}^{(a,t,v)}$ via a ReLU activation function, and then apply a Softmax function to obtain the probability distributions $P_{i,emo}^{(a,t,v)}$ and $P_{i,gen}^{(a,t,v)}$. Ultimately, the model selects the category with the highest probability as the emotion or gender labels $\hat{y}_{i,emo}^{(a,t,v)}$ and $\hat{y}_{i,gen}^{(a,t,v)}$ for each modal prediction. The features of the two tasks are represented as:

$$C_{i,emo}^{(a,t,v)} = \mathrm{ReLU}\left(W_e h_i^{(a,t,v)'} + b_e\right) \tag{6}$$

$$P_{i,emo}^{(a,t,v)} = \mathrm{Softmax}\left(W_{pe} C_{i,emo}^{(a,t,v)} + b_{pe}\right) \tag{7}$$

$$\hat{y}_{i,emo}^{(a,t,v)} = \mathrm{argmax}(P_{i,emo}^{(a,t,v)}) \tag{8}$$

$$C_{i,gen}^{(a,t,v)} = \mathrm{ReLU}\left(W_g h_i^{(a,t,v)'} + b_g\right) \tag{9}$$

$$P_{i,gen}^{(a,t,v)} = \mathrm{Softmax}\left(W_{pg} C_{i,gen}^{(a,t,v)} + b_{pg}\right) \tag{10}$$

$$\hat{y}_{i,gen}^{(a,t,v)} = \mathrm{argmax}(P_{i,gen}^{(a,t,v)}) \tag{11}$$

where $C_{i,emo}^{(a,t,v)}$ and $C_{i,gen}^{(a,t,v)}$ denote the score vectors for emotion or gender categorization after processing by ReLU activation function, $P_{i,emo}^{(a,t,v)}$ and $P_{i,gen}^{(a,t,v)}$ are the obtained emotion and gender probability distributions, $\hat{y}_{i,emo}^{(a,t,v)}$ and $\hat{y}_{i,gen}^{(a,t,v)}$ are the emotion and gender labels predicted by the model, which is the most probable category in the probability distribution.

#### 3.4.2. Late Gender-Aware Emotion Classifier

To avoid omitting the initial multimodal representation information from the final emotion output, the processed multimodal representation $m_i$ and the unprocessed multimodal representation $h_i^m$ were concatenated together as a joint multimodal representation input into a late gender-aware emotion classifier, going through the following steps:

$$m_i' = \mathrm{Concat}(m_i, h_i^m) \tag{12}$$

$$M' = [m'_0, m'_1, \ldots, m'_t] \tag{13}$$

In order to capture the temporal dynamics of emotions in the dialog, i.e., to take into account the influence of the emotional dynamics of previous speeches on the emotions of current speeches in the model, we constructed the module of temporal attention, and input the feature sequences $M'$ into the formula of temporal attention to get the attention weights $\xi^m$. After processing, the model can reflect the evolution and dynamics of the emotional state in the dialog.

$$\xi^m = \text{softmax}(m_i'^T W_M) M' \cdot M'^T \tag{14}$$

where $W_M$ is a trainable weight matrix used to map features to a new space to capture temporal relationships.

$\xi^m$ is fed into the multimodal classifier to obtain the multimodal part of the output $P^m_{i,emo}$ and $P^m_{i,gen}$.

$$C^m_{i,emo} = \text{ReLU}(\xi^m m'_i + b_e) \tag{15}$$

$$P^m_{i,emo} = \text{Softmax}(W_{pe} C^m_{i,emo} + b_{pe}) \tag{16}$$

$$C^m_{i,gen} = \text{ReLU}(\xi^m m'_i + b_g) \tag{17}$$

$$P^m_{i,gen} = \text{Softmax}(W_{pg} C^m_{i,gen} + b_{pg}) \tag{18}$$

Ultimately, the probability distribution $P^{(a,t,v)}_{i,emo}$ for emotion category and $P^{(a,t,v)}_{i,gen}$ for gender category obtained by the mid-state gender-aware emotion classifier as well as the probability distribution $P^m_{i,emo}$ for each emotion category and $P^m_{i,gen}$ for each gender category obtained by the late-state gender-aware emotion classifier are combined as the final prediction of each utterance's emotion label or gender labeling tool.

$$P_{i,emo} = P^m_{i,emo} + \sum_{k \in \{a,t,v\}} \delta_k P^k_{i,emo} \tag{19}$$

$$\hat{y}_{i,emo} = \arg\max(P_{i,emo}) \tag{20}$$

$$P_{i,gen} = P^m_{i,gen} + \sum_{k \in \{a,t,v\}} \delta_k P^k_{i,gen} \tag{21}$$

$$\hat{y}_{i,gen} = \arg\max(P_{i,gen}) \tag{22}$$

where $\hat{y}_{i,emo}$ and $\hat{y}_{i,gen}$ are the emotion and gender labels predicted by the utterance $u_i$ respectively. $\delta_{a,t,v}$ is a pre-determined hyperparameter.

In the Mid-Late multilevel gender-aware strategy, the model learns both emotion and gender features simultaneously by jointly optimizing the loss function, and the parameter update of the model is guided by the jointly optimized loss function, which enables the model to capture the complex interactions between the gender features and the emotion expression, and thus largely improves the overall performance of HGF-MiLaG.

### 3.4.3. Loss Function

Throughout the process, we use a single loss function to train all classifiers simultaneously. Given that categorical cross-entropy is well-suited for classification tasks and L2 regularization helps mitigate overfitting [41], we employ categorical cross-entropy as the loss function and incorporate L2 regularization to train our model in an end-to-end manner via backpropagation. Since there is a gender task involved, the total loss function is the sum of the loss functions of the gender classification task and the emotion classification task. It is composed as:

$$\text{Loss} = \alpha \cdot \text{Loss}_{\text{emo}} + \beta \cdot \text{Loss}_{\text{gen}} \tag{23}$$

where $\alpha$ is the weight of emotion information and $\beta$ is the weight of gender information, the sum of the weights is 1. The weights of the two pieces of information are determined through a hierarchical graph network.

$$\text{Loss}_{\text{emo}}^{(a,t,v,m)} = -\frac{1}{N}\sum_{i=1}^{N} \log \text{P}_{i,\text{emo}}^{(a,t,v,m)} \cdot \left[\text{y}_{i,\text{emo}}^{(a,t,v,m)}\right] + \lambda\|\Theta\|_2 \tag{24}$$

$$\text{Loss}_{\text{emo}} = \sum_{k\in\{a,t,v,m\}} \theta_k \cdot \text{Loss}_{\text{emo}}^{k} \tag{25}$$

$$\text{Loss}_{\text{gen}}^{(a,t,v,m)} = -\frac{1}{N}\sum_{i=1}^{N} \log \text{P}_{i,\text{gen}}^{(a,t,v,m)} \cdot \left[\text{y}_{i,\text{gen}}^{(a,t,v,m)}\right] + \lambda\|\Theta\|_2 \tag{26}$$

$$\text{Loss}_{\text{gen}} = \sum_{k\in\{a,t,v,m\}} \delta_k \cdot \text{Loss}_{\text{gen}}^{k} \tag{27}$$

where N is the number of utterances in the conversation, $\text{y}_{i,\text{emo}}^{(a,t,v,m)}$ and $\text{y}_{i,\text{gen}}^{(a,t,v,m)}$ are the base truth labels for a single emotion prediction or gender prediction task respectively. Specifically, $y_i = 1$ if the emotion or gender type of a sample utterance $i$ belongs to the $i$th class, and $y_i = 0$ otherwise. $\lambda$ is the L2-regularity weight, $\Theta$ is the set of trainable parameters, and $\theta$ and $\delta$ are the weights of the respective modality (including multimodality) associated with emotion and gender, respectively.

## 4. Experiment

### 4.1. Dataset

We evaluated our proposed HGF-MiLaG in two public datasets: **IEMOCAP** [42] and **MELD** [43].

**IEMOCAP:** This dataset records the performances of 10 actors in 5 binary sessions covering 12 h of audio-visual data as well as textual transcriptions. Each session involved 2 actors and was segmented into individual utterances. Each utterance was labeled with one of the following six emotion labels: happy, sad, neutral, excited, frustrated, and angry.

**MELD:** This dataset is a large multimodal multi-party affective dialogue dataset that contains more than 13,000 utterance fragments extracted from the classic American TV show "Friends", which are organized into approximately 1400 dialogues. Each utterance in the dialog is labeled with one of the following seven emotions: neutral, anger, disgust, fear, joy, sadness, surprise.

### 4.2. Baseline

To validate the effectiveness of our proposed hierarchical graph fusion with Mid-Late gender-aware strategy, we compared it with several previous baselines. The baselines include DiagueGCN [11], DiagueCRN [44], MMGCN [12], COGMEN [8], GraphCFC [14], GA2MIF [13], GraphMFT [19], GCCL [45], and HiMul-LGG [46]. The details of these models are shown below.

**DiagueGCN** improves the accuracy of emotion recognition by constructing a directed graph to capture the dependency between individual speeches in a conversation, including inter-dependency and intra-dependency between speakers, and utilizing graph convolutional networks to propagate the contextual information in these dependency.

**DiagueCRN** mimics unique human cognitive thinking by designing a multi-round reasoning module in the cognitive stage to iteratively perform intuitive retrieval processes and conscious reasoning processes, thus providing a deeper understanding of the conversational context and identifying the key cues that trigger the current emotion.

**MMGCN** is a graph convolutional network model that fuses audio, visual, and textual modalities to enable information interaction by constructing graphs and establishing intermodal edge connections, and injecting speaker embeddings to capture speaker dependency. The model employs a spectral domain graph convolutional network and extends to deep layers to enhance emotion recognition performance.

**COGMEN** is a cognitive graph-based emotion recognition model focused on modeling the process of human emotion understanding. The model captures the emotional dynamics in a conversation by combining local information (internal and external dependency between speakers) and global information (conversation context) using Graph Convolutional Networks (GCN) and Graph Transformers.

**GraphCFC** effectively mitigates the heterogeneity gap problem in multimodal fusion by using multiple subspace extractors and the pairwise cross-modal complementation (PairCC) strategy. By extracting multiple edges from the graph, the GNN can capture key contextual and interaction information in the message delivery more accurately. In addition, the model designs the GAT-MLP structure, which provides a new unified framework for multimodal learning.

**GA2MIF** focuses on contextual modeling and cross-modal modeling by utilizing multi-head directed graph attention networks (MDGATs) and multi-head paired cross-modal attention networks (MPCATs), respectively, and is able to capture the long-term contextual information within modalities and the complementary information between modalities efficiently.

**GraphMFT** integrates data objects from different modalities by constructing a graph that utilizes multiple improved graph attention networks to capture intra-modal contextual information and inter-modal complementary information.

**GCCL** is a multimodal emotion recognition framework that captures speaker, temporal, and inter-modal dependency and integrates multimodal information through a graph-based module. The framework includes a emotion consensus learning unit and a consensus-aware unit with an attention mechanism that ensures individual diversity and inter-modal semantic consistency as well as maintains category-level semantic associations across samples.

**COLD Fusion** quantifies modality-specific probability or data uncertainty to predict emotion through calibration and ordinal latent distribution fusion. It learns unimodal temporal contextual latent distributions by limiting variance and designs softmax distribution matching loss for uncertainty-weighted fusion. The method significantly improves the generalisation performance and robustness of emotion recognition on multiple datasets.

**HiMul-LGG** employs a hierarchical decision fusion strategy to ensure cross-modal feature consistency and a local-global graph neural network architecture to enhance intermodality and intra-modality speaker dependency. In addition, HiMul-LGG utilizes a cross-modal multi-head attention mechanism to facilitate inter-modal interactions.

### *4.3. Experiment Setup*

In this study, all experiments were run on NVIDIA GeForce RTX 4060 laptop Gpus (NVIDIA Corporation, Santa Clara, CA, USA). The training framework uses PyTorch 2.5.1 (developed by Facebook AI Research Team), Python version 3.9.0, CUDA Toolkit version 12.4 (NVIDIA Corporation, Santa Clara, CA, USA). During training, the Adam optimizer is used to train our network with the dropout rate of 0.1 and the learning rate set to 0.0003. And the batch size is set to 32 for all datasets. For context encoding, the number of units of the GRUs used is set to 160. The hidden dimension of the hidden layer of the hierarchical fusion graph and the hidden dimension of the temporal attention are also set to 160. The weights of the emotion information and the gender information are set to 0.7 and 0.3, respectively. The pre-determined hyper-parameters $\delta_{a,t,v}$ are 0.1, 0.7, and 0.2, respectively. Our evaluation method is the same as that of the chosen baseline article method, where the weighted average F1 scores and the average accuracies are used to evaluate the performance of HGF-MiLaG.

## 5. Results and Discussion

In this section, experimental results will be reported to evaluate the proposed HGF-MiLaG. Firstly, an overall comparison of HGF-MiLaG with all baseline methods will be made. Then, the effects of different components in the ablation experiments on HGF-MiLaG are discussed. Further, we specifically discuss the effect of injecting gender information at different locations on the effectiveness of model implementation. Next, we explore the effects of different time window settings on HGF-MiLaG. Finally, we also performed an error analysis of our method.

### *5.1. Comparison with Baseline Models*

Our model obtained optimal weighted average F1 scores on both the IEMOCAP and MELD datasets. Table 1 compares the experimental results of HGF-MiLaG with other baseline models (mentioned in Section 4.2). As can be seen from Table 1, for the IEMOCAP dataset, the accuracy and F1 score of HGF-MiLaG are 70.98% and 71.92%, respectively, which are 0.86% and 1.11% more accurate than the current state-of-the-art models HiMul-LGG and GCCL, respectively, and the F1 scores are 0.80% and 1.73% more accurate, respectively. In addition, we show the corresponding F1 scores for each emotion label in detail in the table, and HGF-MiLaG shows significant improvement on the emotion label of Happy. Notably, the F1 scores of HGF-MiLaG are significantly higher than the current state-of-the-art models GCCL and AVL COLD Fusion for all six emotion categories.For the MELD dataset, the accuracy and F1 scores of HGF-MiLaG are 66.22% and 65.26%, respectively, and similarly, compared to the accuracies of HiMul-LGG and GCCL models by 0.01% and 3.40%, respectively, and F1 scores by 0.08% and 4.98% over the HiMul-LGG and GCCL models, respectively.

Based on these results, the HGF-MiLaG model exhibits superior performance on both datasets, which is mainly attributed to the synergistic effect of hierarchical graph fusion and Mid-Late multilevel gender-aware strategy. The hierarchical graph fusion strategy effectively captures speaker dependency and temporal dependency within and across modalities by constructing unimodal and cross-modal graph structures. This enables the model to better understand the complex modal relationships and temporal dynamics in emotional expressions. The Mid-Late multilevel gender-aware strategy further enhances the model's contextual understanding of emotion recognition and its ability to recognise individual differences by simultaneously injecting gender-auxiliary information in both the middle and late stages of the model. Gender plays a key role in emotion expression, and there are often differences in the way males and females express their emotions. By introducing gender information, the model is able to better distinguish these differences, thus improving the overall recognition accuracy. The combination of these two approaches enables the model to not only capture rich modal and temporal information, but also deeply understand gender differences in emotion expressions, thus achieving better performance in complex emotion recognition tasks.

**Table 1.** Comparison with the baseline model: assessment metrics include Acc., F1 and Wa-F1, representing accuracy (%), F1 score (%) and weighted average F1 score (%), respectively. The best performance is indicated in bold.

| Model | IEMOCAP | | | | | | | | MELD | |
|---|---|---|---|---|---|---|---|---|---|---|
| | Happy F1 | Sad F1 | Neutral F1 | Angry F1 | Excited F1 | Frustrated F1 | Acc. | Wa-F1 | Acc. | Wa-F1 |
| DiagueGCN | 41.28 | 82.52 | 64.33 | 65.18 | 73.18 | 64.46 | 66.85 | 66.78 | 59.58 | 58.17 |
| DiagueCRN | 53.23 | 83.37 | 62.96 | 66.09 | 75.40 | 66.07 | 67.16 | 67.21 | 61.11 | 58.67 |
| MMGCN | 37.61 | 79.84 | 62.26 | **74.29** | 75.00 | 63.68 | 67.28 | 66.67 | 61.07 | 57.33 |
| COGMEN | 51.90 | 81.70 | 68.60 | 66.00 | 75.30 | 58.20 | 68.20 | 67.60 | - | - |
| GraphCFC | 43.08 | **84.99** | 64.70 | 71.35 | **78.86** | 63.70 | 69.13 | 68.91 | 61.42 | 58.86 |
| GA2MIF | 46.15 | 84.50 | 68.38 | 70.29 | 75.99 | 66.49 | 69.75 | 70.00 | 61.65 | 58.94 |
| GraphMFT | 45.99 | 83.12 | 63.08 | 70.30 | 76.92 | 63.84 | 67.90 | 68.07 | 61.30 | 58.37 |
| GCCL | 54.05 | 81.10 | 70.28 | 68.21 | 72.17 | 64.00 | 69.87 | 69.29 | 62.82 | 60.28 |
| AVL COLD Fusion | 43.70 | 60.20 | 48.90 | 58.40 | 61.60 | 57.90 | **82.70** | 55.10 | - | - |
| HiMul-LGG | 53.95 | 79.92 | **71.66** | 67.56 | 72.00 | **68.46** | 70.12 | 70.22 | 66.21 | 65.18 |
| HGF-MiLaG | **59.16** | 83.94 | 70.60 | 68.60 | 74.20 | 66.21 | **70.98** | **71.02** | **66.22** | **65.26** |

### 5.2. Ablation Study

To better understand the role of our model components, we performed ablation experiments on key components of HGF-MiLaG. The results are shown in Table 2.

Effect of MiLaG. We first explored the impact of the Mid-Late multilevel gender-aware strategy on the model's emotion categorization task. For this purpose, we removed the gender-auxiliary information injection module, and what can be seen is that the accuracy decreased by 1.11% and the F1-weighted average score by 1.01% in the IEMOCAP dataset, and the accuracy decreased by 0.31% and the F1-weighted average score by 0.35% in the MELD dataset. Introducing gender-auxiliary information can provide the model with additional a priori knowledge to help it better capture individual differences in emotion expression. This strategy can enhance the model's contextual understanding of emotion recognition and make it more accurate in handling emotion classification tasks. This fully demonstrates the effectiveness of introducing gender-auxiliary information in ERC. It can enhance the model's contextual understanding of emotion recognition and individual difference recognition.

Impact of the MG. We then explored the impact of multimodal graphs on the model emotion classification task. For this purpose, we removed the multimodal fusion graph and relied solely on the three unimodal graph classifiers for emotion classification, in which case we can see a decrease of 5.55% in accuracy and 5.57% in F1-weighted average score for the IEMOCAP dataset, and a decrease of 0.58% in accuracy and 0.37% in F1-weighted average score for the MELD dataset. The reason for this is that there is complementarity and correlation between different modes, for example, intonation and rhythm of speech can enhance the intensity of emotion in text, while visual information (such as facial expressions) can further assist the recognition of emotion. As an effective intermodal information integration tool, multimodal graph can fuse information of different modes and capture intermodal speaker dependency and temporal dependency. This cross-modal fusion can make up for the deficiency of unimodal information and improve the accuracy and robustness of emotion classification. The fact that the classification performance decreases drastically proves the effectiveness of the multimodal map and the introduction of the multimodal map, which enables cross-modal information integration and thus captures inter-modal speaker dependency and temporal dependency.

Impact of UG. another core of HGF-MiLaG is the unimodal graph. It is responsible for modeling intra-modal speaker dependency and temporal dependency. For this reason, we removed the three unimodal graphs, and the final emotion classification results were determined by the multimodal classifier only, as can be seen by the fact that in the IEMOCAP dataset, the accuracy was reduced by 1.97% and the F1-weighted average score by 1.93%, and in the MELD dataset, the accuracy was reduced by 0.19% and the F1-weighted average score was reduced by 0.51%. According to the dynamic theory of emotion, the expression and transmission of emotion are sequential and dependent. Unimodal graphs can capture this dynamic change of emotion by modeling the temporal dependencies within the modes. In addition, modeling speaker dependence can further enhance the accuracy of emotion recognition, since the emotional expression styles and habits of different speakers may differ. The effectiveness of the unimodal graph lies in its ability to dig deep into the complex relationships within the modes and provide richer semantic and structural information for emotion classification. This demonstrates the validity of the unimodal graphs.

**Table 2.** Ablation experiments of HGF-MiLaG: assessment metrics include Acc. and Wa-F1. The best performance is indicated in bold.

| Method | IEMOCAP | | MELD | |
|---|---|---|---|---|
| | Acc. | Wa-F1 | Acc. | Wa-F1 |
| HGF-MiLaG | **70.98** | **71.02** | **66.22** | **65.26** |
| w/o MiLaG | 69.87 | 70.01 | 65.91 | 64.91 |
| w/o MG | 65.43 | 65.45 | 65.64 | 64.89 |
| w/o UG | 69.01 | 69.09 | 66.03 | 64.75 |

### 5.3. Comparison with Different Position of Gender Injection

In this section, we explore the effect of the location of gender injection on the IEMOCAP dataset, i.e., early, middle, late, and mid-late injection, on the model performance. The results in Table 3 clearly show that injecting gender information in the Mid-Late stage significantly improves the accuracy and weighted F1 scores of the model. Specifically, the F1 scores of injecting gender information in the Mid-Late stage are improved by 1.33%, 1.38%, and 1.81% compared to the F1 scores of injecting gender information in the early, middle, and late stages, respectively. This is due to the unique advantages of Mid-Late multilevel gender aware strategies: Middle stage fusion excels in capturing information about mid-level associations between different modalities, effectively balancing the advantages and disadvantages of early and late fusion. While early fusion facilitates the integration of information at the initial stage, it may lead to information loss or excessive smoothing due to premature merging of features from different modalities. On the other hand, late fusion allows for more flexible processing of data from different tasks in later stages of the model, but may not effectively capture inter-modal associations. The Mid-Late multilevel gender-aware strategy exploits mid-level correlation information by combining the advantages of middle stage fusion and late stage fusion, while maintaining the flexibility and robustness of late-stage fusion. This multilevel gender-aware strategy ensures that the model can better adapt to the complexity of multimodal data, thereby improving its overall performance.

To better understand the effect of gender injection location on the model, we used t-SNE to visualize the potential representations learned by different gender information injection locations on the IEMOCAP test set. Figures 3a–c show the visualization results for gender information injected alone in the early, middle, and late stages, respectively, and Figure 3d shows the visualization results for gender information injected simultaneously in the middle and late stages. Compared with injecting gender information at early, middle, and late stages, our Mid-Late multilevel gender-aware strategy has significantly optimized the clustering of the same emotional category and increased the distance and clarity of boundaries between different emotional categories. Specifically, the representations of sad and happy are clearly distinguishable. Moreover, the overlapping areas of excited, frustrated, and neutral with other emotional categories have been significantly reduced. These results show that MiLaG is able to learn structured representations with clustered levels, improving the model's ability to recognize emotion categories.

**Table 3.** Comparison of effects across different gender injection locations on the IEMOCAP dataset. The best performance is indicated in bold.

| Position | IEMOCAP | |
|---|---|---|
| | **Acc.** | **Wa-F1** |
| Early | 69.50 | 69.69 |
| Middle | 69.38 | 69.64 |
| Late | 69.25 | 69.21 |
| Mid-Late | **70.98** | **71.02** |

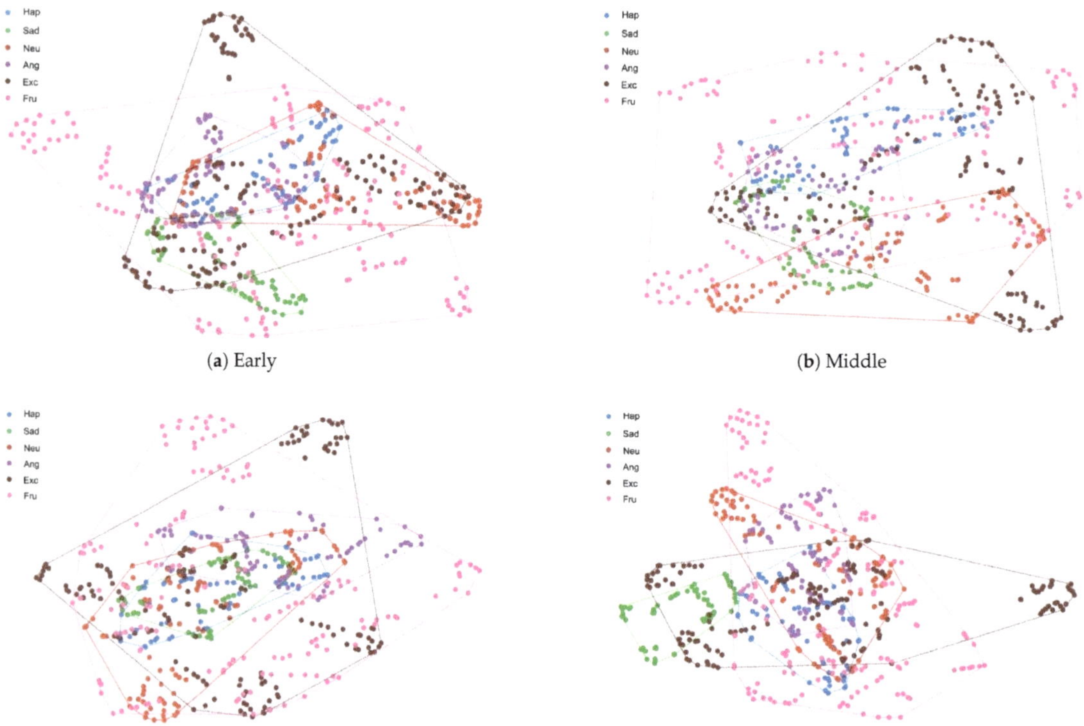


(**a**) Early (**b**) Middle

(c) Late (**d**) Mid-Late

**Figure 3.** T-SNE visualization of the learned features using different methods on the IEMOCAP test set. In these figures, we use blue, green, red, purple, brown and pink to represent happy, sad, neutral, anger, excited and frustrated, respectively.

## 5.4. Effect of Window Size

In this section, we discuss the effect of different window sizes on the performance of HGF-MiLaG. Figure 4a,b show the changes in accuracy and weighted F1 values of HGF-MiLaG corresponding to different window sizes on the IEMOCAP and MELD datasets, respectively.

IEMOCAP dataset sees a trend that both F1-w scores and accuracy rates show an increasing and then decreasing trend. The highest values of both F1-w score and accuracy are reached at a window size of 10, both of which are 0.712. while the lowest values of these two metrics are found at window sizes of 0 and 1, which are about 0.679 and 0.677, respectively. the model performance is best at a window size of 10. The model's performance first improves as the size of the contextual window increases, but beyond a certain size, the effect of the model's enhancement gradually diminishes, the even to the point of showing a downward trend. The possible reason for this is that shorter context windows cannot capture these long-term dependency, while longer windows help the model to capture these dependency, but beyond a certain length, the increased context information may contain too much noise or irrelevant data, which in turn reduces the model's recognition ability. Specifically, the optimal window on the IEMOCAP dataset is 10.

The same phenomenon also occurs in the MELD dataset, but with a lower degree of variability and more volatility, where the optimal window is 12. The F1-w scores and accuracy of HGF-MiLaG fluctuate over a small range with window size, and the overall scores are low.The F1-w scores do not vary much between a window size of 0 and 20, with the highest value being about 0.651 and the lowest about 0.645.The accuracy similarly does not vary much between a window size of 0 and 20, with the highest value being about 0.664 and the lowest about 0.657.This indicates that in the second graph, the window size has less effect on the model performance and the performance is more stable. The possible reason for this variability is that the MELD dataset is constructed based on dialogues from the Old Friends TV series, where some of the neighboring utterances are not contiguous in the actual scenarios, making the results somewhat uncertain and requiring longer distances for contextual modeling. In this section, we conclude that the number of windows (i.e., the number of nodes) in graph construction has a significant impact on the model, and that choosing appropriate forward and backward time steps can maximize the model performance and improve the model's ability for emotion classification tasks.

(**a**) Accuracy and F1 scores on the IEMOCAP dataset (**b**) Accuracy and F1 scores on the MELD dataset

**Figure 4.** T-SNE visualization of the learned features using different methods on the IEMOCAP test set. In these figures, we use blue, green, red, purple, brown and pink to represent happy, sad, neutral, anger, excited and frustrated, respectively.

### 5.5. *Insight from Output*

To further evaluate the performance of the model, we show in Figure 5 the confusion matrix of HGF-MiLaG on the IEMOCAP and MELD test sets, which is used to assess the quality of the model's prediction output. With the confusion matrix on the IEMOCAP test set (Figure 5a), we observe that the HGF-MiLaG model has some limitations in distinguishing emotional nuances. For example, the model exhibits low discrimination in recognizing anger vs. frustrated and happy vs. excited. This suggests that the model has room for improvement in capturing subtle differences in emotion.

We have further analysed the MELD test set to compare the model output distribution with the true distribution of the dataset. The results show that the model output distribution is highly consistent with the true distribution of the MELD dataset, and there is no data imbalance that causes the model to over-concentrate on outputting dominant labels.

Specifically, although the emotion labels Anger, Disgust and Fear have a small number of samples and can be easily misclassified as the Neutral label with the largest number of samples, the overall prediction results show that the model's predicted probability distributions of the emotion labels match with the actual distribution of the dataset. For example, the model's higher prediction probability for the Neutral label matches the actual situation in the MELD dataset where neutral emotion expressions are more common. This is not a flaw in the model, but rather a reflection of its ability to accurately reflect real-world emotion distributions. In real-world emotion analysis scenarios, the distribution of emotions is inherently uneven, and neutral emotion expressions are usually more common, with strong emotions (e.g., anger, disgust, etc.) being relatively less common, which is related to the natural distribution of people's daily language expressions and emotional states.

For visual presentation, we draw a histogram of the distribution of the model's output labels (see Figure 6) and compare it with the true distribution of the MELD dataset. As can be seen from the figure, the model predictions are highly consistent with the real distribution, further confirming the model's adaptability to real-world emotion distribution.

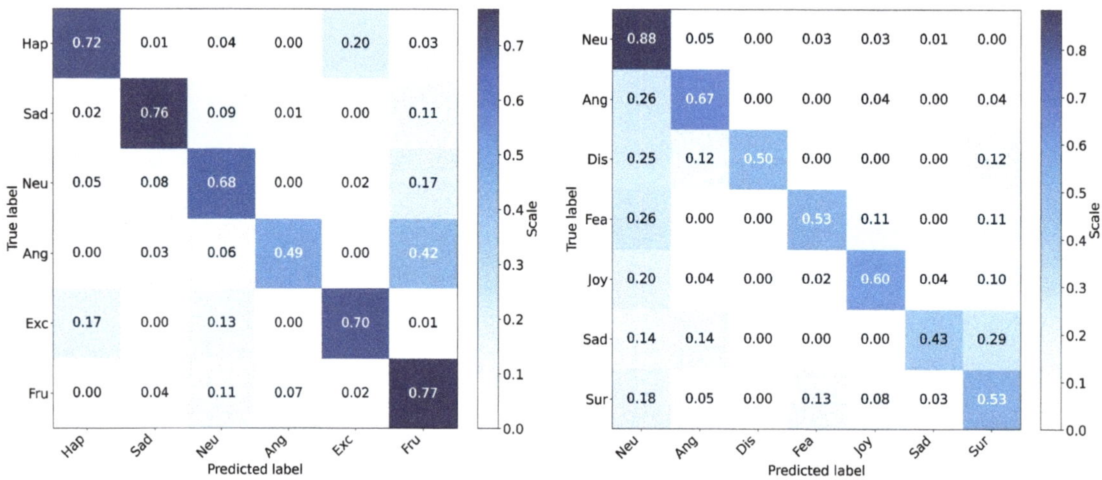


(**a**) IEMOCAP (**b**) MELD

**Figure 5.** Normalized confusion matrix of HGF-MiLaG on IEMOCAP and MELD test sets. Rows indicate predicted labels and columns indicate true labels.

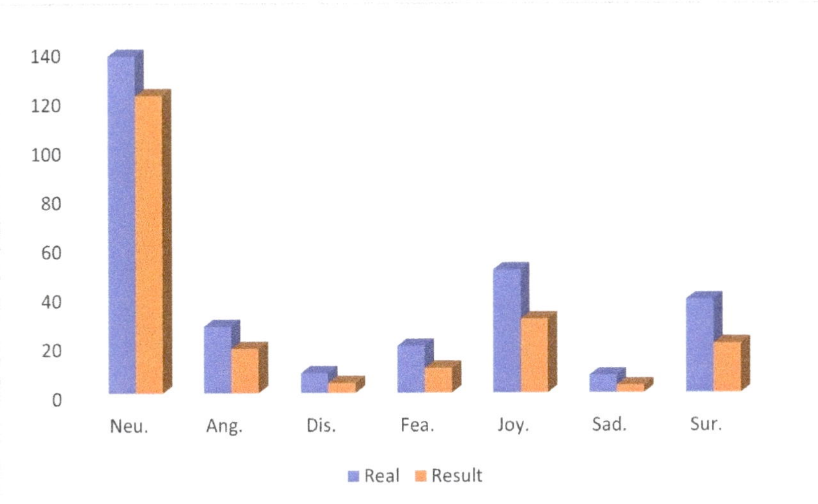


**Figure 6.** Comparison of model predictions and true emotion label distributions on the MELD test set

## 6. Conclusions

In this study, we present the innovative HGF-MiLaG model for analyzing conversational emotional states, and the model adequately combines the hierarchical graph fusion and the Mid-Late multilevel gender-aware strategy to improve the performance of the model's affective classification task. We provide insights into the performance of our model by comparing it to other baselines and related works in the IEMOCAP and MELD datasets suitable for our experiments. The results reported on both datasets establish the superiority of the HGF-MiLaG model performance. The results of the ablation experiments validate the contribution of the key components of HGF-MiLaG to the model, and show that the hierarchical fusion graph is able to capture speaker-dependency and temporal dependency within and across modalities, and that the introduction of gender-auxiliary information in the ERC strengthens the model's contextual understanding of emotion recognition and the identification of individual differences. Further, we explored the effect of the location of gender information injection on the performance of ERC, and finally adopted the Mid-Late multilevel gender-aware strategy to realize the ability to let the hierarchical graph network have the ability to decide the proportion of emotion and gender information in the classifier by itself. We believe that this study fully reveals the importance of graph-based modeling techniques and the incorporation of gender-auxiliary tasks at optimal locations for emotion recognition tasks, and that our work has taken an important step forward in the field of modeling the dynamics of complex information for multimodal emotion recognition in conversations. In future work, we will continue to push multimodal learning with a focus on solving the previously mentioned problem of similar emotion discrimination, as well as improving HGF-MiLaG to enhance the model's ability to deal with sample label imbalance. In addition, we would like to apply our model to more practical settings, similar to the multimodal dialog generation domain, etc., to understand the utility of our model.

**Author Contributions:** Conceptualization, Y.W. and R.H.; Methodology, Y.W. and R.H.; Software, Z.L.; Validation, X.K.; Formal analysis, F.Q.; Investigation, Z.L.; Data curation, J.D. and Q.Z.; Writing—review & editing, C.F.; Visualization, X.K.; Supervision, F.Q. and C.F.; Project administration, J.D. and Q.Z. All authors have read and agreed to the published version of the manuscript.

**Funding:** This research was funded by the National Natural Science Foundation of China (Grant No. 62306068) Project and the Natural Science Foundation of Hebei Province, China (Grant No. F2024501002).

**Institutional Review Board Statement:** Not applicable.

**Informed Consent Statement:** Not applicable.

**Data Availability Statement:** The data presented in this study are openly available.

**Acknowledgments:** The authors extend their thanks for the creators of the IEMOCAP and MELD datasets for making their data publicly available, which greatly supported their research.

**Conflicts of Interest:** The authors declare no conflicts of interest.

## References

1. Pereira, R.; Mendes, C.; Costa, N.; Frazão, L.; Fernández-Caballero, A.; Pereira, A. Human-Computer Interaction Approach with Empathic Conversational Agent and Computer Vision. In *Artificial Intelligence for Neuroscience and Emotional Systems*; International Work-Conference on the Interplay Between Natural and Artificial Computation; Springer Nature: Cham, Switzerland, 2024; pp. 431–440.
2. Votintseva, A.; Johnson, R.; Villa, I. Emotionally Intelligent Conversational User Interfaces: Bridging Empathy and Technology in Human-Computer Interaction. In *Human-Computer Interaction*; International Conference on Human-Computer Interaction; Springer Nature: Cham, Switzerland, 2024; pp. 404–422.
3. Messaoudi, C.; Guessoum, Z.; Ben Romdhane, L. Opinion mining in online social media: A survey. *Soc. Netw. Anal. Min.* **2022**, *12*, 25. [CrossRef]
4. Huang, C.W.; Wu, B.C.; Nguyen, P.A.; Wang, H.H.; Kao, C.C.; Lee, P.C.; Rahmanti, A.R.; Hsu, J.C.; Yang, H.C.; Li, Y.C.J. Emotion recognition in doctor-patient interactions from real-world clinical video database: Initial development of artificial empathy. *Comput. Methods Programs Biomed.* **2023**, *233*, 107480. [CrossRef] [PubMed]
5. Li, J.; Zhao, Y.; Zhang, H.; LiMember, W. J.; Fu, C.; Lian, C.; Shan, P. Image Encoding and Fusion of Multi-modal Data Enhance Depression Diagnosis in Parkinson's Disease Patients. *IEEE Trans. Affect. Comput.* **2024**, *early access*. [CrossRef]
6. Imani, M.; Montazer, G. A. A survey of emotion recognition methods with emphasis on E-Learning environments. *J. Netw. Comput. Appl.* **2019**, *147*, 102423. [CrossRef]
7. Poria, S.; Majumder, N.; Mihalcea, R.; Hovy, E. Emotion recognition in conversation: Research challenges, datasets, and recent advances. *IEEE Access* **2019**, *7*, 100943–100953. [CrossRef]
8. Joshi, A.; Bhat, A.; Jain, A.; Singh, A. V.; Modi, A. COGMEN: COntextualized GNN based multimodal emotion recognition. *arXiv* **2022**, arXiv:2205.02455.
9. Defferrard, M.; Bresson, X.; Vandergheynst, P. Convolutional Neural Networks on Graphs with Fast Localized Spectral Filtering. In Proceedings of the 30th Annual Conference on Neural Information Processing Systems (NIPS), Barcelona, Spain, 5–10 December 2016.
10. Jiao, W.; Yang, H.; King, I.; Lyu, M. R. HiGRU: Hierarchical Gated Recurrent Units for Utterance-level Emotion Recognition. *arXiv* **2019**, arXiv:1904.04446.
11. Ghosal, D.; Majumder, N.; Poria, S.; Chhaya, N.; Gelbukh, A. DialogueGCN: A graph convolutional neural network for emotion recognition in conversation. In Proceedings of the 2019 Conference on Empirical Methods in Natural Language Processing (EMNLP-IJCNLP), Hong Kong, China, 3–7 November 2019; pp. 154–164.
12. Hu, J.; Liu, Y.; Zhao, J.; Jin, Q. MMGCN: Multimodal fusion via deep graph convolution network for emotion recognition in conversation. In Proceedings of the 59th Annual Meeting of the Association for Computational Linguistics & 11th International Joint Conference on Natural Language Processing (Volume 1: Long Papers), Virtual Event, 1–6 August 2021; pp. 5666–5675.
13. Li, J.; Wang, X.; Lv, G.; Zeng, Z. GA2MIF: Graph and attention based two-stage multi-source information fusion for conversational emotion detection. *IEEE Trans. Affect. Comput.* **2024**, *15*, 130–143. [CrossRef]
14. Li, J.; Wang, X.; Lv, G.; Zeng, Z. GraphCFC: A Directed Graph Based Cross-Modal Feature Complementation Approach for Multimodal Conversational Emotion Recognition. *IEEE Trans. Multimed.* **2024**, *26*, 77–89. [CrossRef]
15. Li, J.; Zhang, M.; Ji, D.; Liu, Y. Multi-task learning with auxiliary speaker identification for conversational emotion recognition. *arXiv* **2020**, arXiv:2003.01478.
16. Gao, Q.; Cao, B.; Guan, X.; Gu, T.; Bao, X.; Wu, J.; Liu, B.; Cao, J. Emotion recognition in conversations with emotion shift detection based on multi-task learning. *Knowl.-Based Syst.* **2022**, *248*, 108861. [CrossRef]
17. Zheng, W.; Yu, J.; Xia, R.; Wang, S. A Facial Expression-Aware Multimodal Multi-task Learning Framework for Emotion Recognition in Multi-party Conversations. In Proceedings of the 61st Annual Meeting of the Association for Computational Linguistics (Volume 1: Long Papers), Toronto, ON, Canada, 9–14 July 2023; 2023; pp. 15445–15459.

18. Cao, X.; Li, H.; Wang, W. A study on gender differences in speech emotion recognition based on corpus. *J. Nanjing Univ. (Nat. Sci.)* **2019**, *55*, 758–764.
19. Li, J.; Wang, X.; Lv, G.; Zeng, Z. GraphMFT: A graph network based multimodal fusion technique for emotion recognition in conversation. *Neurocomputing* **2023**, *550*, 126427. [CrossRef]
20. Gan, C.; Zheng, J.; Zhu, Q.; Jain, D. K.; Štruc, V. A graph neural network with context filtering and feature correction for conversational emotion recognition. *Inf. Sci.* **2024**, *658*, 120017. [CrossRef]
21. Fu, C.; Su, Y.; Su, K.; Liu, Y.; Shi, J.; Wu, B.; Liu, C.; Ishi, C.T.; Ishiguro, H. HAM-GNN: A hierarchical attention-based multi-dimensional edge graph neural network for dialogue act classification. *Expert Syst. Appl.* **2025**, *261*, 125459. [CrossRef]
22. Caruana, R. Multitask Learning. *Mach. Learn.* **1997**, *28*, 41–75. [CrossRef]
23. Ruder, S. An Overview of Multi-Task Learning in Deep Neural Networks. *arXiv* **2017**, arXiv:1706.05098.
24. Xie, Y.; Yang, K.; Sun, C. J.; Liu, B.; Ji, Z. Knowledge-interactive network with sentiment polarity intensity-aware multi-task learning for emotion recognition in conversations. In Proceedings of the Findings of the Association for Computational Linguistics: EMNLP 2021, Punta Cana, Dominican Republic, 16–20 November 2021; pp. 2879–2889.
25. Wang, X.; Zhang, M.; Chen, B.; Wei, D.; Shao, Y. Dynamic weighted multitask learning and contrastive learning for multimodal sentiment analysis. *Electronics* **2023**, *12*, 2986. [CrossRef]
26. Xue, P.; Li, Y.; Wang, S.; Liao, J.; Zheng, J.; Fu, Y.; Li, D. Sentiment classification method based on multitasking and multimodal interactive learning. In Proceedings of the 22nd China National Conference on Computational Linguistics, Harbin, China, 3–5 August 2023; pp. 315–327.
27. Ma, Z.; Jia, W.; Zhou, Y.; Xu, B.; Liu, Z.; Wu, Z. Personality Enhanced Emotion Generation Modeling for Dialogue Systems. *Cogn. Comput.* **2024**, *16*, 293–304. [CrossRef]
28. Cai, C.; He, Y.; Sun, L.; Lian, Z.; Liu, B.; Tao, J.; Xu, M.; Wang, K. Multimodal sentiment analysis based on recurrent neural network and multimodal attention. In Proceedings of the 2nd on Multimodal Sentiment Analysis Challenge, Virtual Event, 24 October 2021; pp. 61–67.
29. Tian, H.; Gao, C.; Xiao, X.; Liu, H.; He, B.; Wu, H.; Wang, H.; Wu, F. SKEP: Sentiment knowledge enhanced pre-training for sentiment analysis. *arXiv* **2020**, arXiv:2005.05635.
30. Zhao, F.; Zhang, C.; Geng, B. Deep Multimodal Data Fusion. *ACM Comput. Surv.* **2024**, *56*, 216. [CrossRef]
31. Zadeh, A.; Liang, P. P.; Poria, S.; Vij, P.; Cambria, E.; Morency, L. P. Multi-attention recurrent network for human communication comprehension. In Proceedings of the AAAI Conference on Artificial Intelligence, New Orleans, LA, USA, 2–7 February 2018; Volume 32, No. 1.
32. Nagrani, A.; Yang, S.; Arnab, A.; Jansen, A.; Schmid, C.; Sun, C. Attention bottlenecks for multimodal fusion. *Adv. Neural Inf. Process. Syst.* **2021**, 34, 14200–14213.
33. Wu, L.; Liu, Q.; Zhang, D.; Wang, J.; Li, S.; Zhou, G. Multimodal emotion recognition with auxiliary sentiment information. *Beijing Da Xue Xue Bao* **2020**, *56*, 75–81.
34. Schuller, B.; Batliner, A.; Steidl, S.; Seppi, D. Recognising realistic emotions and affect in speech: State of the art and lessons learnt from the first challenge. *Speech Commun.* **2011**, *53*, 1062–1087. [CrossRef]
35. Fu, C.; Liu, C.; Ishi, C. T.; Yoshikawa, Y.; Iio, T.; Ishiguro, H. Using an android robot to improve social connectedness by sharing recent experiences of group members in human-robot conversations. *IEEE Robot. Autom. Lett.* **2021**, *6*, 6670–6677. [CrossRef]
36. Huang, G.; Liu, Z.; Van Der Maaten, L.; Weinberger, K. Q. Densely connected convolutional networks. In Proceedings of the IEEE Conference on Computer Vision and Pattern Recognition, Honolulu, HI, USA, 21–26 July 2017; pp. 4700–4708.
37. Chudasama, V.; Kar, P.; Gudmalwar, A.; Shah, N.; Wasnik, P.; Onoe, N. M2fnet: Multi-modal fusion network for emotion recognition in conversation. In Proceedings of the IEEE/CVF Conference on Computer Vision and Pattern Recognition, New Orleans, LA, USA, 18–24 June 2022; pp. 4652–4661.
38. Deng, L.; Liu, B.; Li, Z. Multimodal Sentiment Analysis Based on a Cross-Modal Multihead Attention Mechanism. *Comput. Mater. Contin.* **2024**, *78*, 1. [CrossRef]
39. Morris, C.; Ritzert, M.; Fey, M.; Hamilton, W.L.; Lenssen, J.E.; Rattan, G.; Grohe, M. Weisfeiler and Leman go neural: Higher-order graph neural networks. In Proceedings of the AAAI Conference on Artificial Intelligence, Honolulu, HI, USA, 29–31 January 2019; Volume 33, No. 01, pp. 4602–4609.
40. Foggia, P.; Greco, A.; Saggese, A.; Vento, M. Multi-task learning on the edge for effective gender, age, ethnicity and emotion recognition. *Eng. Appl. Artif. Intell.* **2023**, *118*, 105651. [CrossRef]
41. Ciampiconi, L.; Elwood, A.; Leonardi, M.; Mohamed, A.; Rozza, A. A survey and taxonomy of loss functions in machine learning. *arXiv* **2023**, arXiv:2301.05579.
42. Busso, C.; Bulut, M.; Lee, C.C.; Kazemzadeh, A.; Mower, E.; Kim, S.; Chang, J.N.; Lee, S.; Narayanan, S.S. IEMOCAP: Interactive emotional dyadic motion capture database. *Lang. Resour. Eval.* **2008**, *42*, 335–359. [CrossRef]

43. Poria, S.; Hazarika, D.; Majumder, N.; Naik, G.; Cambria, E.; Mihalcea, R. MELD: A Multimodal Multi-Party Dataset for Emotion Recognition in Conversations. In Proceedings of the 57th Annual Meeting of the Association for Computational Linguistics, Florence, Italy 28 July–2 August 2019; Association for Computational Linguistics: Florence, Italy, 2019; pp. 527–536.
44. Hu, D.; Wei, L.; Huai, X. DialogueCRN: Contextual Reasoning Networks for Emotion Recognition in Conversations. *arXiv* **2021**, arXiv:2106.01978.
45. Dai, Y.; Li, J.; Li, Y.; Lu, G. Multi-modal graph context extraction and consensus-aware learning for emotion recognition in conversation. *Knowl. Based Syst.* **2024**, *298*, 111954. [CrossRef]
46. Fu, C.; Qian, F.; Su, K.; Su, Y.; Wang, Z.; Shi, J.; Liu, Z.; Liu, C.; Ishi, C.T. HiMul-LGG: A hierarchical decision fusion-based local–global graph neural network for multimodal emotion recognition in conversation. *Neural Netw.* **2025**, *181*, 106764. [CrossRef] [PubMed]

*sensors*

MDPI

*Article*

# A Projective-Geometry-Aware Network for 3D Vertebra Localization in Calibrated Biplanar X-Ray Images

**Kangqing Ye, Wenyuan Sun, Rong Tao and Guoyan Zheng ***

Institute of Medical Robotics, School of Biomedical Engineering, Shanghai Jiao Tong University, Shanghai 200240, China; yekangq@sjtu.edu.cn (K.Y.); wenyuansun1998@sjtu.edu.cn (W.S.); rongt@nvidia.com (R.T.)
* Correspondence: guoyan.zheng@sjtu.edu.cn

**Abstract:** Current Deep Learning (DL)-based methods for vertebra localization in biplanar X-ray images mainly focus on two-dimensional (2D) information and neglect the projective geometry, limiting the accuracy of 3D navigation in X-ray-guided spine surgery. A 3D vertebra localization method from calibrated biplanar X-ray images is highly desired to address the problem. In this study, a projective-geometry-aware network for localizing 3D vertebrae in calibrated biplanar X-ray images, referred to as ProVLNet, is proposed. The network design of ProVLNet features three components: a Siamese 2D feature extractor to extract local appearance features from the biplanar X-ray images, a spatial alignment fusion module to incorporate the projective geometry in fusing the extracted 2D features in 3D space, and a 3D landmark regression module to regress the 3D coordinates of the vertebrae from the 3D fused features. Evaluated on two typical and challenging datasets acquired from the lumbar and the thoracic spine, ProVLNet achieved an identification rate of 99.53% and 98.98% and a point-to-point error of 0.64 mm and 1.38 mm, demonstrating superior performance of our proposed approach over the state-of-the-art (SOTA) methods.

**Keywords:** landmark localization; biplanar X-ray imaging; projective geometry

## 1. Introduction

Biplanar X-ray imaging is widely used in image-guided spine surgery due to its low radiation dose and acquisition cost [1]. However, the lack of 3D information negatively affects navigation accuracy [2], which can be addressed by localizing 3D anatomical landmarks like vertebral body centers. The localization of landmarks in 3D space facilitates 2D/3D registration [3], 3D reconstruction [4–9], surgical navigation [2], and spinal geometry estimation [10].

Various Deep Learning (DL)-based methods have been developed for vertebra localization in both single [11–16] and biplanar [4,17–22] X-ray images. Payer et al. [13] proposed the SpatialConfiguration-Net (SCN) for medical landmark localization in a single image, which achieved superior performance and inspired various vertebra localization methods [14,15]. Unlike single-view localization methods, an effective biplanar fusion module is required in dual-view localization methods. The approaches to localizing landmarks in 3D space from calibrated biplanar images is generally divided into two categories: coordinate-level fusion methods and feature-level fusion methods. The coordinate-level fusion methods [5,6,17,18] triangulate coordinates of landmarks detected by a 2D single-view localization method, while the feature-level fusion methods [4,19–22] integrate features from both images, facilitating aggregation of biplanar information in the feature space. Given their advantages, this paper primarily focuses on the feature-level fusion methods.

Feature-level fusion is commonly achieved by either concatenating 2D features from each view [4,19–24] or constraining the landmark prediction using a consistency condition based on the assumption of orthogonality [25]. By concatenating images of both views, Aubert et al. [4,19] and Galbusera et al. [24] utilized biplanar information in vertebra localization. Furthermore, Wu et al. [20] proposed the X-module, which combined biplanar feature integration through summation and concatenation, thereby enhancing adolescent scoliosis assessments. The X-module has been adopted in other studies as well [21,22]. Huang et al. [25] achieved biplanar fusion in intraoperative long-film X-ray images by ensuring identical z-coordinates for the vertebrae in a Faster R-CNN framework. Despite these efforts, current methods neglect the projective geometry between views, failing to align the features from both views. Recently, a few multi-view fusion methods [26, 27] have been developed in multi-view 3D human pose estimation. However, directly applying them to the biplanar X-ray localization task may lead to suboptimal results due to the non-informative features [26] and the lack of 3D information [27]. Table 1 provides a comparative overview of the state-of-the-art (SOTA) dual-view localization methods, in terms of their backbone networks, fusion level, and fusion strategies.

**Table 1.** Overview of the state-of-the-art (SOTA) dual-view localization methods.

| Methods | Backbone | Fusion Level | Fusion Strategy |
|---|---|---|---|
| 2D ResNet [28] | ResNet | Coordinate-level | Triangulation of 2D coordinates |
| 2D SCN [13] | SCN | Coordinate-level | Triangulation of 2D coordinates |
| Alg [26] | ResNet | Feature-level | Gradient-based triangulation |
| Vol [26] | ResNet | Feature-level | Unprojecting 2D features into 3D space |
| Adafuse [27] | ResNet | Feature-level | Fusion of predicted heatmaps in 3D space |
| Ours | SCN | Feature-level | Unprojecting 2D features into 3D space |

In this paper, an end-to-end projective-geometry-aware network, referred to as ProVLNet, is proposed for 3D vertebra localization in calibrated biplanar X-ray images. The design of ProVLNet features three components: a Siamese 2D feature extractor, a spatial alignment fusion module, and a 3D landmark regression module. The workflow of the proposed method begins with extracting features from both anterior–posterior (AP) and lateral (LAT) images through two weight-sharing 2D feature extractors. The output features are then unprojected and fused into 3D aggregated features by the spatial alignment fusion module. Finally, the 3D landmark regression module computes 3D coordinates from these aggregated features.

Our contribution can be summarized as follows:

- A novel end-to-end network called ProVLNet is proposed, which incorporates projective geometry to localize vertebrae in 3D space from calibrated biplanar X-ray images.
- A spatial alignment fusion module and a 3D landmark regression module are carefully designed, aiming to capture underlying 3D information by aligning 2D features from biplanar views in 3D space and to resolve semantic ambiguity in 3D landmark detections.
- Comprehensive experiments were conducted on two typical yet challenging datasets acquired from the lumber and the thoracic spine, demonstrating superior performance of our proposed approach over the state-of-the-art (SOTA) methods.

## 2. Method

### 2.1. Architecture Overview

Figure 1 presents the overall pipeline of ProVLNet. Although the network can be easily extended to multi-view scenarios, this paper mainly focuses on the widely used biplanar setup. The inputs to ProVLNet are anterior–posterior (AP) and lateral (LAT) X-ray images $x_i \in \mathbb{R}^{H\times W}, i \in \{AP, LAT\}$ ($H$ and $W$ represent the spatial dimension) and the associated projection matrix $P_i \in \mathbb{R}^{3\times 4}$ which can be used to project 3D coordinates to 2D image space. The overall pipeline of our method is as follows. First, two weight-sharing 2D feature extractors generate 2D features $M_i = f_\theta(x_i) \in \mathbb{R}^{H\times W\times K}$ and the associated fusion weights $\mathbf{w}_i \in \mathbb{R}^K$, where K is the number of feature channels. Then, a spatial alignment fusion module unprojects these 2D features into 3D space to generate the corresponding 3D features $V_i \in \mathbb{R}^{64\times 64\times 64\times K}$ based on projective geometry. From the unprojected 3D features $V_i$ and the associated fusion weights $\mathbf{w}_i$, a weighted summation is calculated to obtain the fused 3D features $V_{agg} \in \mathbb{R}^{64\times 64\times 64\times K}$. Finally, a 3D landmark regression module, which includes a 3D SCN $u_\phi$ [13] with parameters $\phi$ and a soft-argmax function $\sigma$, is used to regress the 3D coordinates of all L landmarks. In particular, the 3D SCN regresses distinct heatmaps $V_{processed} \in \mathbb{R}^{64\times 64\times 64\times L}$ from the 3D fused features $V_{agg}$, which are taken as the input to the soft-argmax function to calculate the landmark coordinates $y \in \mathbb{R}^{3\times L}$. Our network is fully differentiable and supports end-to-end training, which can be formulated as:

$$y = \sigma(u_\phi(\mathcal{F}_\mathbf{w}(f_\theta(x_{AP}), P_{AP}, f_\theta(x_{LAT}), P_{LAT}))), \tag{1}$$

where $\mathcal{F}(\cdot)$ represents the spatial alignment fusion module.

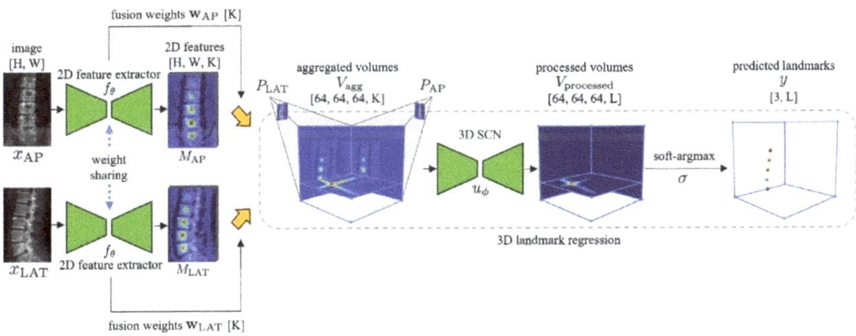


**Figure 1.** A schematic illustration of the overall pipeline of the proposed ProVLNet. The yellow arrows represent the spatial alignment fusion module. SCN represents the SpatialConfiguration-Net. Dimensions of data are indicated within square brackets.

### 2.2. 2D Feature Extractor

A Siamese-architecture-based 2D feature extractor is designed to extract features from the AP and the LAT images. Features extracted by the two weight-sharing 2D feature extractors are fed into the spatial alignment fusion module as described in the next section.

Figure 2 illustrates the network architecture of our 2D feature extractor, which takes a 2D SCN as the backbone to produce local appearance features. In the 2D SCN, the heatmap produced by the local appearance component $\mathbb{H}_i^{LA} \in \mathbb{R}^{H\times W\times L}$ is multiplied with the heatmap produced by the spatial configuration component $\mathbb{H}_i^{SC} \in \mathbb{R}^{H\times W\times L}$ to generate the predicted heatmap $h_i \in \mathbb{R}^{H\times W\times L}$. Moreover, the 2D features of the last layer before $\mathbb{H}_i^{LA}$ are denoted as $M_i \in \mathbb{R}^{H\times W\times K}$, which are unprojected into 3D space to obtain the 3D features $V_i$ as described below. Additionally, a fusion weight branch is designed to generate $\mathbf{w}_i \in \mathbb{R}^K$ from the bottom-level features of the local appearance component. Both $V_i$ and $\mathbf{w}_i$ are taken as the input to the spatial alignment fusion module to calculate a weighted 3D feature aggregation.

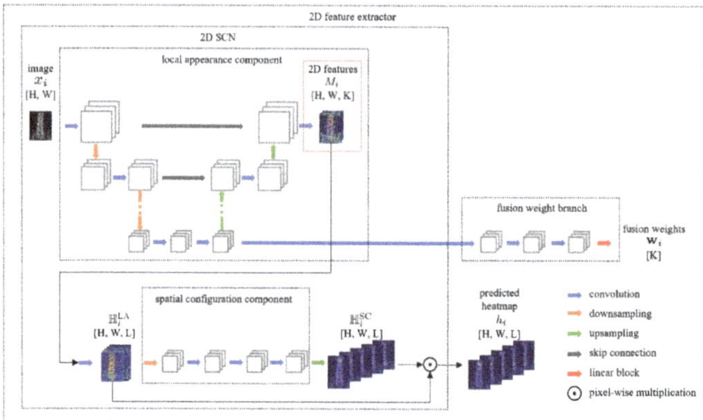


**Figure 2.** A schematic illustration of the network architecture of the 2D feature extractor, which takes a 2D SCN as the backbone. $\mathbb{H}_i^{\mathrm{LA}}$ represents the output heatmap of the local appearance component, and $\mathbb{H}_i^{\mathrm{SC}}$ represents the output heatmap of the spatial configuration component. The architecture of the local appearance component of the 2D SCN is a 5-layer U-Net [29]. The spatial configuration component includes an average pooling layer that downsamples the features, three convolutional layers, and an upsampling layer that rescales the features to their original size. Empty boxes represent intermediate features. Dimensions of data are indicated within square brackets.

## 2.3. Spatial Alignment Fusion Module

In this module, 2D features $M_i \in \mathbb{R}^{\mathrm{H}\times\mathrm{W}\times\mathrm{K}}, i \in \{\mathrm{AP}, \mathrm{LAT}\}$ extracted from the AP and the LAT images are unprojected into 3D features $V_i \in \mathbb{R}^{64\times64\times64\times\mathrm{K}}$ to incorporate projective geometry. These 3D features are then fused to produce $V^{\mathrm{agg}} \in \mathbb{R}^{64\times64\times64\times\mathrm{K}}$. An example of the $k$-th ($k \in [1, \mathrm{K}]$) channel of $V^{\mathrm{agg}}$ is shown in Figure 3. Initially, a cubical volume is defined in 3D space as the target for feature unprojection. The center of the cube is determined using a linear algebraic triangulation approach [26] based on the centers of the AP and the LAT images. The $64 \times 64 \times 64$ voxel cube represents a physical space of $250 \times 250 \times 250$ mm$^3$, capable of containing all vertebrae imaged by biplanar X-ray images in our experimental setup.

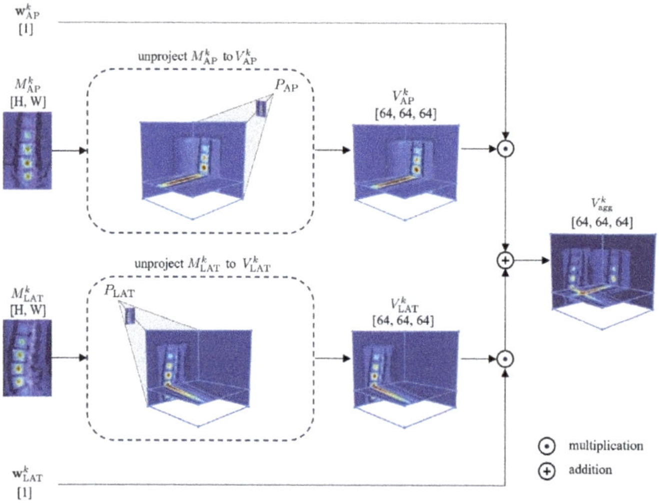


**Figure 3.** The aggregation of the 2D features $M_i^k$ in the spatial alignment fusion module. Dimensions of data are indicated within square brackets.

To unproject the $k$-th channel of 2D features $M_i$, denoted as $M_i^k$, into the $k$-th channel of the 3D features $V_i$, denoted as $V_i^k$, correspondences between voxels in $V_i^k$ and pixels in $M_i^k$ are established as follows. Specifically, by applying the defined center, physical dimensions, and size of the cube, the 3D coordinate $\mathbf{r}_v^{3D} \in \mathbb{R}^3$ of voxel $v$ in $V_i^k$ is obtained. Then, the projection matrix $P_i$ is utilized to project the 3D coordinate $\mathbf{r}_v^{3D}$ into the 2D coordinate $\mathbf{r}_v^{2D} \in \mathbb{R}^2$. The value of voxel $v$ is set to the value of the pixel at $\mathbf{r}_v^{2D}$ in $M_i^k$, which is obtained through bilinear sampling.

To account for the influence of different features across two distinct views, a weighted summation of $V_i^k$ is computed to obtain the 3D aggregated feature $V_{\text{agg}}^k \in \mathbb{R}^{64\times64\times64}$, with weights $\mathbf{w}_i^k$ learned from the 2D feature extraction process (Figure 3):

$$V_{\text{agg}}^k = \sum_i (\mathbf{w}_i^k \cdot V_i^k) / \sum_i \mathbf{w}_i^k. \quad (2)$$

## 2.4. 3D Landmark Regression

In order to accurately localize landmarks from the 3D aggregated feature $V_{\text{agg}}^k$, one has to reduce the ambiguity by suppressing false positive responses in the areas with similar structures. This is achieved by employing a 3D SCN, which has a two-branch structure that is well suited for this task, to process $V_{\text{agg}}$ with the ultimate goal to produce 3D heatmaps $V_{\text{processed}} \in \mathbb{R}^{64\times64\times64\times L}$ for L landmarks.

The structure of the 3D SCN is similar to the 2D SCN used in the 2D feature extractor, where the convolutional layers in the 2D SCN are replaced by their 3D counterparts. With a large receptive field, the spatial configuration component of the 3D SCN robustly predicts the coordinate of a single landmark out of all landmarks in $\mathbb{H}^{\text{LA}}$. Such a design naturally incorporates the underlying 3D information.

In order to maintain the differentiability of the entire network, a soft-argmax function is employed instead of argmax to extract landmark coordinates from $V_{\text{processed}}$. The first step is to compute the softmax across the spatial axes:

$$V_{\text{processed}}'^{l} = \exp\left(V_{\text{processed}}^{l}\right) / \left(\sum_{64}\sum_{64}\sum_{64} \exp\left(V_{\text{processed}}^{l}\right)\right), \quad (3)$$

where $l$ represents the $l$-th ($l \in [1, \text{L}]$) channel.

Then, the centroid of $V_{\text{processed}}'^{l}$ is calculated to obtain the predicted landmark $y^l \in \mathbb{R}^3$, which is approximately the argmax point:

$$y^l = \sum_{64}\sum_{64}\sum_{64} \mathbf{r} \cdot V_{\text{processed}}'^{l}(\mathbf{r}), \quad (4)$$

where $\mathbf{r} = (r_x, r_y, r_z)^T$ represents the world coordinate of the voxel in volumes.

## 2.5. Loss

The total loss is the aggregation of the losses from the Siamese 2D feature extractor and the 3D landmark regression:

$$\mathcal{L}_{\text{total}} = \mathcal{L}_{\text{2D}} + \mathcal{L}_{\text{3D}}. \quad (5)$$

The 2D loss $\mathcal{L}_{\text{2D}}$ measures the similarity between the SCN's predicted heatmaps $h_i \in \mathbb{R}^{\text{H}\times\text{W}\times\text{L}}$ and the ground truth Gaussian heatmaps $g_i \in \mathbb{R}^{\text{H}\times\text{W}\times\text{L}}$. To resolve the foreground–background class imbalance, a combination of Dice loss and Mean Squared Error (MSE) loss is used:

$$\mathcal{L}_{2D} = \sum_i \mathcal{L}_{\text{Dice}}(h_i, g_i) + \sum_i \mathcal{L}_{\text{MSE}}(h_i, g_i). \tag{6}$$

As for the 3D loss $\mathcal{L}_{3D}$, a typical L1 loss with a heatmap regularization term is used to maximize the value at the 3D ground truth landmarks, ensuring the existence of a peak for each anatomical landmark:

$$\mathcal{L}_{3D} = \sum_l \left| y^l - y^l_{\text{gt}} \right| - \alpha \cdot \log\left( V^l_{\text{output}}\left( y^l_{\text{gt}} \right) \right), \tag{7}$$

where $\alpha$ is a parameter weighting the influence of the second term.

## 3. Experiments and Results

### 3.1. Datasets

Comprehensive experiments were conducted on two typical yet challenging datasets of digitally reconstructed radiograph (DRR) images which were simulated from Computed Tomography (CT) scans. In our simulation system, the source-detector distance was set to 2000 mm, with an isocenter distance of 1000 mm. The projection was parameterized by the left/right anterior oblique (LAO/RAO) angle, which was randomly varied between $-15^\circ$ and $+15^\circ$, around the perfect AP and the LAT views. The 3D landmark ground truth was established by localizing vertebral body centers in the CT scans and then transforming the coordinates of the centers into the world coordinates system. The 2D landmark ground truth was obtained by projecting the 3D landmark ground truth to 2D image space.

**Lumbar Spine dataset**: The Lumbar Spine dataset contains DRR images generated from an in-house dataset of 130 CT scans, each containing the L1–L5 vertebrae. These CT scans were divided into three subsets: 100 for training, 10 for validation, and 20 for testing. For each of these CT scans, we generated 10 AP and 10 LAT views with a size of $1536 \times 1024$ pixels on a 450 mm $\times$ 300 mm detector plane, resulting in a total of $130 \times 10 \times 10$ pairs of biplanar DRR images.

**Thoracic Spine dataset**: The Thoracic Spine dataset was generated from CT data collected from MICCAI (Medical Image Computing and Computer Assisted Interventions) VerSe19 and VerSe20 challenges [30]. A total of 235 CT scans containing thoracic vertebrae were selected and cropped into 1465 smaller volumes, each containing four consecutive thoracic vertebrae. These volumes were divided into three subsets: 993 for training, 153 for validation, and 319 for testing, ensuring that all volumes from the same scan were grouped in the same subset. For each CT scan, an AP and a LAT view were generated with a size of $1024 \times 1024$ pixels on a 300 mm $\times$ 300 mm detector plane.

### 3.2. Metrics

Three commonly used metrics are adopted to evaluate localization results.

**Point-to-point error (PE)**: The PE for each anatomical landmark is calculated as the Euclidean distance between the predicted and the ground truth landmark position. The mean and standard deviation of PE across all test images are reported, denoted as $\text{PE}_{\text{all}}$.

**Image-specific point-to-point error (IPE)**: The IPE for a specific image is the average of the PE values for that image. To provide a comprehensive overview, cumulative IPE distribution graphs, which can illustrate the proportion of images that reach various IPE values in our test dataset, are presented.

**Landmark identification rate ($\mathbf{ID_{rate}}$)**: The $\text{ID}_{\text{rate}}$ is the ratio between the accurately identified landmarks and the total number of vertebrae. A landmark is considered accurately identified if the distance between the predicted and the ground truth locations is below 5.0 mm.

### 3.3. Implementation Details

The proposed method was implemented with the PyTorch framework. The input images were rescaled to a size of 768 × 512 pixels for the Lumbar Spine dataset and a size of 512 × 512 pixels for the Thoracic Spine dataset. Empirically, the number of channels K for the 2D features $M$ was set to 16, and the parameter $\alpha$ in Equation (7) was set to 0.01. The number of landmarks, $L$, that ProVLNet could detect was set to 5 for the Lumbar Spine dataset and 4 for the Thoracic Spine dataset. ProVLNet was trained for 1500 epochs on the Lumbar Spine dataset and 500 epochs on the Thoracic Spine dataset, considering the larger size of the Thoracic Spine dataset compared to the Lumbar Spine dataset. The Adam optimizer was adopted with a learning rate of 0.001 and a batch size of 4. All experiments were conducted on a single NVIDIA GeForce RTX 3090 GPU. To compare ProVLNet with other state-of-the-art (SOTA) methods, a Wilcoxon signed-rank test was performed with a significance level of 0.01.

### 3.4. Comparison Methods

In this study, our proposed ProVLNet was compared with two coordinate-level fusion methods [13,28] and three feature-level fusion methods [26,27]:

- 2D ResNet [28]: this method predicts 2D coordinates by a network based on ResNet-152 and determines the 3D coordinates by triangulation [26].
- 2D SCN [13]: this method predicts 2D coordinates by 2D SCN architecture [13] and determines the 3D coordinates by triangulation [26].
- Alg [26]: this is a baseline method introduced in [26], which enables gradient propagation for triangulating coordinates.
- Vol [26]: this is another method introduced in [26], which incorporates 3D information by unprojecting 2D features into 3D space.
- Adafuse [27]: this method fuses predicted 2D heatmaps based on epipolar geometry.

### 3.5. Results

#### 3.5.1. Results on the Lumbar Spine Dataset

Table 2 compares the vertebra localization performance of ProVLNet with others on the Lumbar Spine dataset. ProVLNet outperforms other methods with an $ID_{rate}$ of 99.53% and a $PE_{all}$ of 0.64 mm. The $PE_{all}$ is reduced by about 50% over the second-best method (Vol [26]). Such improvement is statistically significant, as evidenced by the results of the Wilcoxon signed-rank test ($p = 2.6 \times 10^{-10}$). Figure 4a illustrates the cumulative IPE distributions for the Lumbar Spine dataset. The IPE of over 99% images provided by ProVLNet is under 3 mm, while the proportion of all other methods is below 95%. Figure 5 visualizes the localization results. ProVLNet identifies all vertebrae successfully, outperforming others.

**Table 2.** Overview of vertebra localization performance comparison on the Lumbar Spine dataset (mean ± SD). The best results are highlighted in bold.

| Method | $ID_{rate}$ (%) | $PE_{all}$ (mm) |
|---|---|---|
| 2D ResNet [28] | 95.68 | 1.53 ± 3.95 |
| 2D SCN [13] | 97.30 | 1.62 ± 3.08 |
| Alg [26] | 96.18 | 1.72 ± 3.88 |
| Vol [26] | 97.76 | 1.27 ± 5.42 |
| Adafuse [27] | 96.97 | 3.98 ± 19.02 |
| Ours | **99.53** | **0.64 ± 0.57** |

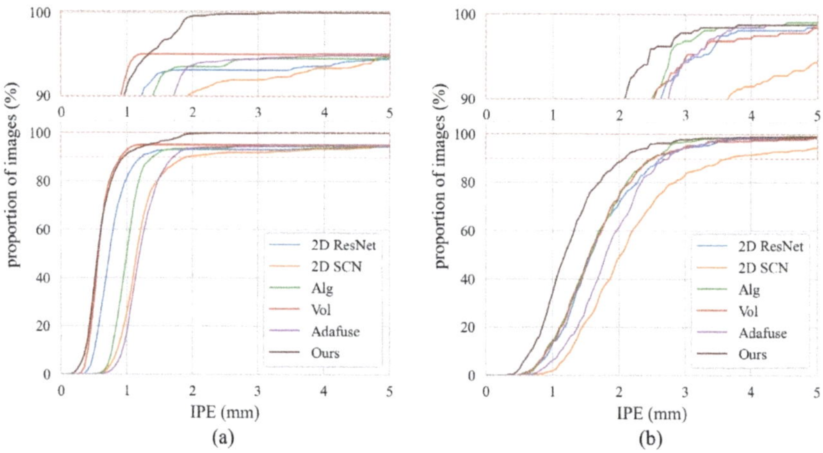


**Figure 4.** Cumulative distributions of IPE on the Lumbar Spine dataset (**a**) and the Thoracic Spine dataset (**b**). The top part shows a zoomed-in view of the dashed red box.

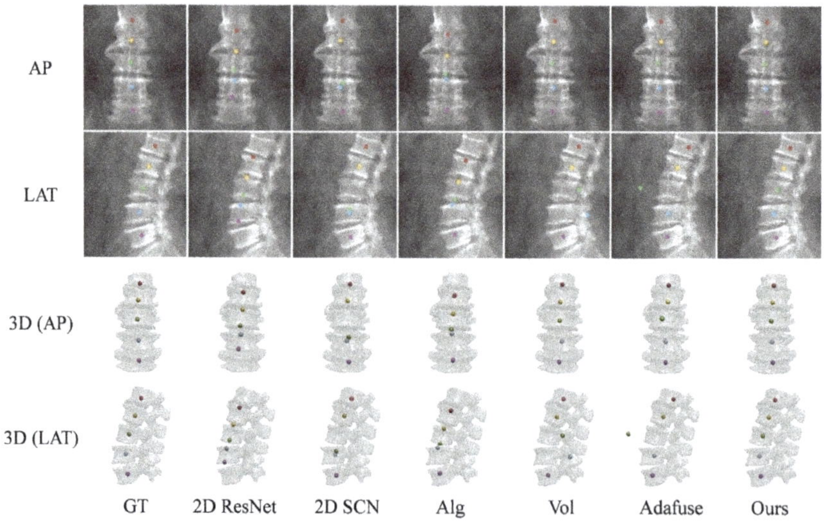


**Figure 5.** Landmark detection on the Lumbar Spine dataset using different methods: 2D ResNet [28], 2D SCN [13], Alg [26], Vol [26], and Adafuse [27]. The first two rows show the AP and the LAT views of projected landmarks, while the last two rows visualize landmarks in 3D space. The colored dots are the detected body centers of different lumbar vertebrae: red (L1), yellow (L2), green (L3), blue (L4), and purple (L5). GT: ground truth.

### 3.5.2. Results on the Thoracic Spine Dataset

Table 3 compares the vertebra localization performance of ProVLNet with others on the Thoracic Spine dataset. As one can see from this table, in comparison with other SOTA methods, ProVLNet achieves the best results with an $ID_{rate}$ of 98.98% and a $PE_{all}$ of 1.38 mm. The $PE_{all}$ is reduced by about 20% over the second-best method (Alg [26]) ($p = 1.1 \times 10^{-9}$). Figure 4b illustrates the cumulative IPE distributions for the Thoracic Spine dataset. As one can see from this figure, ProVLNet prevails over other SOTA methods with the highest proportion of images in the range of 0.5–4 mm. The localization results are visualized in Figure 6. Again, ProVLNet performs localization with the best precision, particularly for the last two vertebrae in the lateral view.

**Table 3.** Overview of vertebra localization performance comparison on the Thoracic Spine dataset (mean ± SD). The best results are highlighted in bold.

| Method | $ID_{rate}$ (%) | $PE_{all}$ (mm) |
|---|---|---|
| 2D ResNet [28] | 98.59 | 1.76 ± 1.23 |
| 2D SCN [13] | 94.67 | 2.40 ± 2.17 |
| Alg [26] | 98.74 | 1.68 ± 1.08 |
| Vol [26] | 98.43 | 1.73 ± 1.25 |
| Adafuse [27] | 98.74 | 1.92 ± 1.08 |
| Ours | **98.98** | **1.38 ± 1.72** |

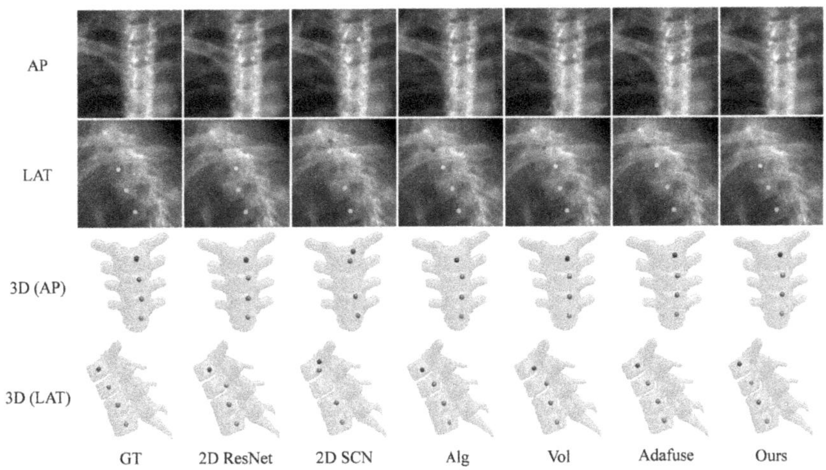


**Figure 6.** Landmark detection on the Thoracic Spine dataset using different methods: 2D ResNet [28], 2D SCN [13], Alg [26], Vol [26], and Adafuse [27]. The first two rows show the AP and the LAT views of projected landmarks, while the last two rows visualize landmarks in 3D space. The colored dots are the detected body centers of different thoracic vertebrae. GT: ground truth.

### 3.5.3. Ablation Study

An ablation study on the Lumbar Spine dataset was conducted to evaluate the effectiveness of the spatial alignment fusion module and the 3D landmark regression module. The results are presented in Table 4. The baseline, represented in the first row, is the backbone network of the Siamese 2D feature extractor, consistent with the 2D SCN [13] in Table 2. The approach in the second row integrates the 2D SCN and the spatial alignment fusion module with the 3D Convolutional Neural Network (CNN) from the Vol method [26] to determine landmark coordinates. According to Table 4, incorporating the spatial alignment fusion module leads to a 0.73% increase in $ID_{rate}$, and the addition of the 3D landmark regression module contributes to a further 1.5% improvement. Correspondingly, the $PE_{all}$

metric shows improvements of 0.62 mm and 0.36 mm, respectively. Figure 7 shows the cumulative distributions of IPE for the methods in Table 4. It shows that for all IPE values, our method achieves the highest proportion.

**Table 4.** Quantitative results of the ablation study on the Lumbar Spine dataset. The best results are highlighted in bold. Fusion: spatial alignment fusion.

| | Components | | | Results | |
|---|---|---|---|---|---|
| **Method** | **2D SCN** | **Fusion** | **3D Landmark Regression** | **$ID_{rate}$ (%)** | **$PE_{all}$ (mm)** |
| 2D SCN | ✓ | | | 97.30 | 1.62 ± 3.08 |
| 2D SCN + Fusion | ✓ | ✓ | | 98.03 | 1.00 ± 2.56 |
| Ours | ✓ | ✓ | ✓ | **99.53** | **0.64 ± 0.57** |

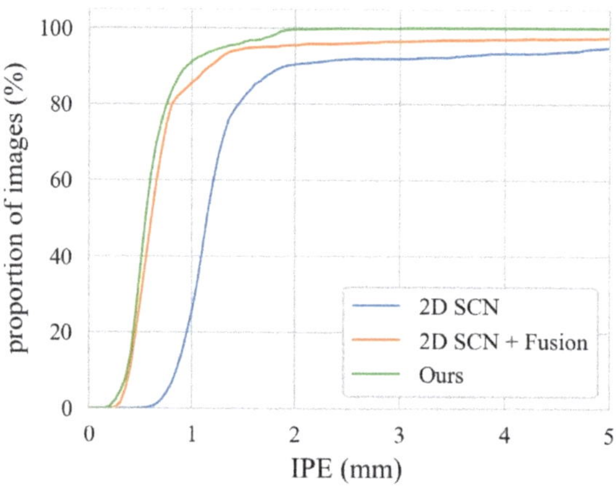


**Figure 7.** Cumulative distributions of IPE on the Lumbar Spine dataset of ablation study.

3.5.4. Analysis of Intermediate Features

Qualitatively, Figure 8 shows the intermediate features when detecting the body center of the L4 vertebra from a given pair of AP and LAT images, which can be used to illustrate the efficacy of ProVLNet. Specifically, using the images from Figure 8a as inputs, the Siamese 2D feature extractor generates aligned local appearance features, with one representative channel shown in Figure 8b. These features effectively highlight the detected vertebral body centers, but the ambiguity between adjacent vertebrae remains. The spatial alignment fusion module then fuses these features based on projective geometry and outputs the aggregated 3D features displayed in Figure 8c. The aggregated 3D features from the spatial alignment fusion module highlight areas at the 3D vertebral body centers, capturing the underlying 3D information. Following this, the 3D SCN, which is a component of the 3D landmark regression module, outputs the predicted heatmaps as shown in Figure 8d. Each channel in these heatmaps represents a specific landmark. As one can see from Figure 8d, the ambiguity is resolved by the 3D SCN, where false positive responses in adjacent vertebrae shown in Figure 8c are suppressed.

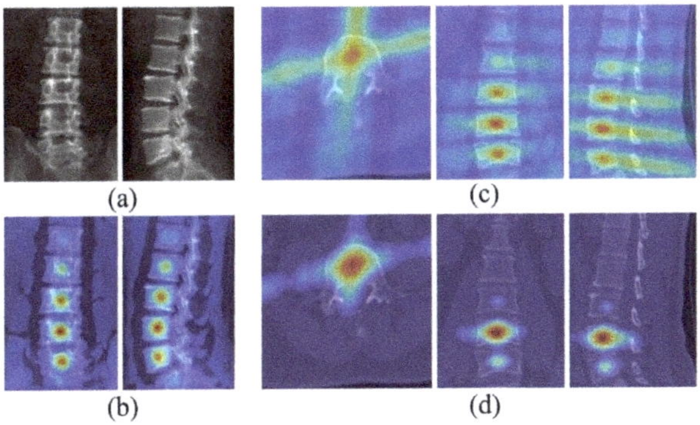


**Figure 8.** Visualization of the intermediate features when detecting the body center of the L4 vertebra from a given pair of AP and LAT images. (**a**) Original input image; (**b**) output from the Siamese 2D feature extractor; (**c**) 3D unprojection of features before 3D SCN (transverse, coronal, sagittal views); (**d**) output after 3D SCN (transverse, coronal, sagittal views).

## 4. Discussion and Conclusions

In this paper, an end-to-end network referred to as ProVLNet was proposed. ProVLNet was designed to incorporate projective geometry for accurate localization of vertebrae in 3D space from calibrated biplanar X-ray images. In particular, 2D local appearance features were first extracted by a Siamese 2D feature extractor. The extracted 2D appearance features were then fused in 3D space by a carefully designed spatial alignment fusion module. Finally, 3D coordinates of all landmarks were predicted by a 3D landmark regression module. Comprehensive experiments were conducted on two typical yet challenging datasets to validate the efficacy of the proposed ProVLNet. Quantitatively and qualitatively, the experimental results demonstrated the superior performance of the proposed ProVLNet over other SOTA methods.

It is apparent that the coordinate-level fusion methods such as 2D ResNet [28] and the 2D SCN [13] generate suboptimal results, as demonstrated by the quantitative results presented in Tables 2 and 3. This is largely due to the fact that these methods learn to detect 2D landmarks from the AP and the LAT image independently, followed by a 3D coordinate triangulation to generate the final results. Thus, rather than incorporating the projection geometry into the learning process, these methods only use it in the coordinate triangulation step, leading to suboptimal results. Although methods such as Alg [26] and Adafuse [27] exploit epipolar geometry to integrate biplanar information, they do not incorporate underlying 3D information, resulting in lower performance. In contrast, by incorporating the projection geometry into the learning process and by including a 3D landmark regression module, our proposed ProVLNet can not only implicitly model the 3D anatomical landmark prior but also reasonably handle ambiguity in landmark detections, leading to superior results on both datasets.

It is worth comparing the proposed ProVLNet with the Vol method [26] as both methods are designed to incorporate 3D information. Compared with the Vol method [26], our method benefited from a decomposition strategy that divided the main task into two sub-problems: the extractions of 2D features with ambiguous candidate predictions and the reduction in ambiguity in 3D space. Such a strategy was proved to be effective for anatomical landmark detection tasks [13], as demonstrated quantitatively and qualitatively by the results presented in Tables 2 and 3 and Figures 4–6.

The effectiveness of the carefully designed spatial alignment fusion module and the 3D landmark regression module was demonstrated by the ablation results shown in Table 4 and Figure 8. By unprojecting 2D features into 3D space based on projective geometry, the spatial alignment fusion module captured the underlying 3D information, as demonstrated by an example shown in Figure 8c. The 3D landmark regression module further resolved the ambiguity in landmark detections by suppressing false positive responses in adjacent vertebrae, as demonstrated by an example shown in Figure 8d.

There exist limitations in the present study. First, the number of vertebrae in the calibrated biplanar images that ProVLNet can detect was fixed, i.e., 5 for the Lumbar Spine dataset and 4 for the Thoracic Spine dataset. Extending our method to handle the arbitrary number of vertebrae will be our future work. Second, due to the difficulty in organizing calibrated biplanar X-ray images in clinical scenarios, we only validated our method on synthetic datasets. One way to generalize the trained models to calibrated biplanar X-ray images in clinical scenarios in the future is to explore unsupervised domain adaptation technique [31]. Nevertheless, since all the methods were compared on the same datasets, the results that we obtained in this study demonstrated the superior performance of ProVLNet over other SOTA methods.

In summary, we proposed a projective-geometry-aware network called ProVLNet to localize 3D vertebrae in calibrated biplanar X-ray images. It incorporates 3D information into the landmark detection process via a carefully designed spatial alignment fusion module. The remaining ambiguity in landmark detections are further resolved by the 3D landmark regression module. ProVLNet outperformed other SOTA methods when evaluated on two typical and challenging datasets acquired for the lumbar and the thoracic spine. It holds the potential to be applied to clinical scenarios of X-ray-guided spine surgery.

**Author Contributions:** Conceptualization, G.Z.; methodology, K.Y., W.S., R.T., and G.Z.; software, K.Y. and W.S.; validation, K.Y. and W.S.; formal analysis, K.Y.; investigation, K.Y.; writing—original draft preparation, K.Y.; writing—review and editing, K.Y., W.S., R.T., and G.Z.; visualization, K.Y.; supervision, G.Z.; project administration, G.Z.; funding acquisition, G.Z. All authors have read and agreed to the published version of the manuscript.

**Funding:** This study was partially supported by the National Natural Science Foundation of China via project U20A20199.

**Institutional Review Board Statement:** Not applicable.

**Informed Consent Statement:** Not applicable.

**Data Availability Statement:** The data presented in this study are available on reasonable request from the corresponding author.

**Conflicts of Interest:** The authors declare no conflicts of interest.

## Abbreviations

The following abbreviations are used in this manuscript:

| | |
|---|---|
| AP | Anterior–posterior |
| CT | Computed Tomography |
| DRR | Digitally reconstructed radiograph |
| LAO | Left anterior oblique |
| LAT | Lateral |
| MICCAI | Medical Image Computing and Computer Assisted Interventions |
| RAO | Right anterior oblique |
| SCN | SpatialConfiguration-Net |
| SOTA | State-of-the-art |
| 2D | Two-dimensional |
| 3D | Three-dimensional |

## References


1. Sommer, F.; Goldberg, J.L.; McGrath, L.; Kirnaz, S.; Medary, B.; Härtl, R. Image Guidance in Spinal Surgery: A Critical Appraisal and Future Directions. *Int. J. Spine Surg.* **2021**, *15*, S74–S86. [CrossRef]
2. Thakkar, S.C.; Thakkar, R.S.; Sirisreetreerux, N.; Carrino, J.A.; Shafiq, B.; Hasenboehler, E.A. 2D versus 3D Fluoroscopy-Based Navigation in Posterior Pelvic Fixation: Review of the Literature on Current Technology. *Int. J. Comput. Assist. Radiol. Surg.* **2017**, *12*, 69–76. [CrossRef] [PubMed]
3. Kim, H.; Lee, K.; Lee, D.; Baek, N. 3D Reconstruction of Leg Bones from X-Ray Images Using CNN-Based Feature Analysis. In Proceedings of the 2019 International Conference on Information and Communication Technology Convergence (ICTC), Jeju Island, Republic of Korea, 16–18 October 2019; pp. 669–672.
4. Aubert, B.; Vazquez, C.; Cresson, T.; Parent, S.; De Guise, J.A. Toward Automated 3D Spine Reconstruction from Biplanar Radiographs Using CNN for Statistical Spine Model Fitting. *IEEE Trans. Med Imaging* **2019**, *38*, 2796–2806. [CrossRef] [PubMed]
5. Zhou, L.; Wu, G.; Zuo, Y.; Chen, X.; Hu, H. A Comprehensive Review of Vision-Based 3D Reconstruction Methods. *Sensors* **2024**, *24*, 2314. [CrossRef]
6. Bayareh Mancilla, R.; Tan, B.P.; Daul, C.; Gutiérrez Martínez, J.; Leija Salas, L.; Wolf, D.; Vera Hernández, A. Anatomical 3D modeling using IR sensors and radiometric processing based on structure from motion: Towards a tool for the diabetic foot diagnosis. *Sensors* **2021**, *21*, 3918. [CrossRef] [PubMed]
7. Yan, H.; Dai, J. Reconstructing a 3D Medical Image from a Few 2D Projections Using a B-Spline-Based Deformable Transformation. *Mathematics* **2022**, *11*, 69. [CrossRef]
8. Lechelek, L.; Horna, S.; Zrour, R.; Naudin, M.; Guillevin, C. A hybrid method for 3d reconstruction of mr images. *J. Imaging* **2022**, *8*, 103. [CrossRef]
9. Göbel, B.; Reiterer, A.; Möller, K. Image-Based 3D Reconstruction in Laparoscopy: A Review Focusing on the Quantitative Evaluation by Applying the Reconstruction Error. *J. Imaging* **2024**, *10*, 180. [CrossRef]
10. Hu, Z.; Vergari, C.; Gajny, L.; Liu, Z.; Lam, T.P.; Zhu, Z.; Qiu, Y.; Man, G.C.W.; Yeung, K.H.; Chu, W.C.W.; et al. Comparison of 3D and 2D Characterization of Spinal Geometry from Biplanar X-Rays: A Large Cohort Study. *Quant. Imaging Med. Surg.* **2021**, *11*, 3306–3313. [CrossRef]
11. Liang, Y.; Lv, J.; Li, D.; Yang, X.; Wang, Z.; Li, Q. Accurate Cobb Angle Estimation on Scoliosis X-Ray Images via Deeply-Coupled Two-Stage Network With Differentiable Cropping and Random Perturbation. *IEEE J. Biomed. Health Inform.* **2022**, *27*, 1488–1499. [CrossRef]
12. Cheng, L.W.; Chou, H.H.; Cai, Y.X.; Huang, K.Y.; Hsieh, C.C.; Chu, P.L.; Cheng, I.S.; Hsieh, S.Y. Automated Detection of Vertebral Fractures from X-Ray Images: A Novel Machine Learning Model and Survey of the Field. *Neurocomputing* **2024**, *566*, 126946. [CrossRef]
13. Payer, C.; Štern, D.; Bischof, H.; Urschler, M. Integrating Spatial Configuration into Heatmap Regression Based CNNs for Landmark Localization. *Med. Image Anal.* **2019**, *54*, 207–219. [CrossRef] [PubMed]
14. Reddy, P.K.; Kanakatte, A.; Gubbi, J.; Poduval, M.; Ghose, A.; Purushothaman, B. Anatomical Landmark Detection Using Deep Appearance-Context Network. In Proceedings of the 2021 43rd Annual International Conference of the IEEE Engineering in Medicine & Biology Society (EMBC), Virtual, 30 October–5 November 2021; pp. 3569–3572.
15. Kim, K.C.; Cho, H.C.; Jang, T.J.; Choi, J.M.; Seo, J.K. Automatic Detection and Segmentation of Lumbar Vertebrae from X-Ray Images for Compression Fracture Evaluation. *Comput. Methods Programs Biomed.* **2021**, *200*, 105833. [CrossRef] [PubMed]
16. Rahmaniar, W.; Suzuki, K.; Lin, T.L. Auto-CA: Automated Cobb Angle Measurement Based on Vertebrae Detection for Assessment of Spinal Curvature Deformity. *IEEE Trans. Biomed. Eng.* **2023**, *71*, 640–649. [CrossRef] [PubMed]
17. Liao, H.; Lin, W.A.; Zhang, J.; Zhang, J.; Luo, J.; Zhou, S.K. Multiview 2D/3D Rigid Registration via a Point-Of-Interest Network for Tracking and Triangulation. In Proceedings of the 2019 IEEE/CVF Conference on Computer Vision and Pattern Recognition (CVPR), Long Beach, CA, USA, 16–20 June 2019; pp. 12630–12639.
18. Bousigues, S.; Gajny, L.; Abihssira, S.; Heidsieck, C.; Ohl, X.; Hagemeister, N.; Skalli, W. 3D reconstruction of the scapula from biplanar X-rays for pose estimation and morphological analysis. *Med Eng. Phys.* **2023**, *120*, 104043. [CrossRef]
19. Aubert, B.; Vidal, P.A.; Parent, S.; Cresson, T.; Vazquez, C.; De Guise, J. Convolutional Neural Network and In-Painting Techniques for the Automatic Assessment of Scoliotic Spine Surgery from Biplanar Radiographs. In Proceedings of the Medical Image Computing and Computer-Assisted Intervention—MICCAI 2017, Quebec City, QC, Canada, 10–14 September 2017; Descoteaux, M., Maier-Hein, L., Franz, A., Jannin, P., Collins, D.L., Duchesne, S., Eds.; Lecture Notes in Computer Science; Springer: Cham, Switerland, 2017; pp. 691–699.
20. Wu, H.; Bailey, C.; Rasoulinejad, P.; Li, S. Automated Comprehensive Adolescent Idiopathic Scoliosis Assessment Using MVC-Net. *Med. Image Anal.* **2018**, *48*, 1–11. [CrossRef] [PubMed]
21. Wang, L.; Xu, Q.; Leung, S.; Chung, J.; Chen, B.; Li, S. Accurate Automated Cobb Angles Estimation Using Multi-View Extrapolation Net. *Med. Image Anal.* **2019**, *58*, 101542. [CrossRef] [PubMed]

22. Zhang, K.; Xu, N.; Guo, C.; Wu, J. MPF-Net: An Effective Framework for Automated Cobb Angle Estimation. *Med. Image Anal.* **2022**, *75*, 102277. [CrossRef] [PubMed]
23. Li, Y.; Liang, W.; Zhang, Y.; An, H.; Tan, J. Automatic Lumbar Vertebrae Detection Based on Feature Fusion Deep Learning for Partial Occluded C-Arm X-Ray Images. In Proceedings of the 2016 38th Annual International Conference of the IEEE Engineering in Medicine and Biology Society (EMBC), Orlando, FL, USA, 16–20 August 2016; pp. 647–650.
24. Galbusera, F.; Niemeyer, F.; Wilke, H.J.; Bassani, T.; Casaroli, G.; Anania, C.; Costa, F.; Brayda-Bruno, M.; Sconfienza, L.M. Fully Automated Radiological Analysis of Spinal Disorders and Deformities: A Deep Learning Approach. *Eur. Spine J.* **2019**, *28*, 951–960. [CrossRef] [PubMed]
25. Huang, Y.; Jones, C.K.; Zhang, X.; Johnston, A.; Waktola, S.; Aygun, N.; Witham, T.F.; Bydon, A.; Theodore, N.; Helm, P.A.; et al. Multi-Perspective Region-Based CNNs for Vertebrae Labeling in Intraoperative Long-Length Images. *Comput. Methods Programs Biomed.* **2022**, *227*, 107222. [CrossRef] [PubMed]
26. Iskakov, K.; Burkov, E.; Lempitsky, V.; Malkov, Y. Learnable Triangulation of Human Pose. In Proceedings of the 2019 IEEE/CVF International Conference on Computer Vision (ICCV), Seoul, Republic of Korea, 27 October–2 November 2019; pp. 7717–7726.
27. Zhang, Z.; Wang, C.; Qiu, W.; Qin, W.; Zeng, W. AdaFuse: Adaptive Multiview Fusion for Accurate Human Pose Estimation in the Wild. *Int. J. Comput. Vis.* **2021**, *129*, 703–718. [CrossRef]
28. Xiao, B.; Wu, H.; Wei, Y. Simple baselines for human pose estimation and tracking. In Proceedings of the European Conference on Computer Vision (ECCV), Munich, Germany, 8–14 September 2018; pp. 466–481.
29. Ronneberger, O.; Fischer, P.; Brox, T. U-net: Convolutional networks for biomedical image segmentation. In Proceedings of the Medical Image Computing and Computer-Assisted Intervention–MICCAI 2015: 18th International Conference, Munich, Germany, 5–9 October 2015; Proceedings, Part III 18; Springer: Berlin/Heidelberg, Germany, 2015; pp. 234–241.
30. Sekuboyina, A.; Husseini, M.E.; Bayat, A.; Löffler, M.; Liebl, H.; Li, H.; Tetteh, G.; Kukačka, J.; Payer, C.; Štern, D.; et al. VerSe: A Vertebrae Labelling and Segmentation Benchmark for Multi-Detector CT Images. *Med. Image Anal.* **2021**, *73*, 102166. [CrossRef] [PubMed]
31. Jin, H.; Che, H.; Chen, H. Unsupervised domain adaptation for anatomical landmark detection. In Proceedings of the International Conference on Medical Image Computing and Computer-Assisted Intervention, Vancouver, BC, Canada, 8–12 October 2023; Springer: Berlin/Heidelberg, Germany, 2023; pp. 695–705.

sensors

MDPI

Article

# DeiT and Image Deep Learning-Driven Correction of Particle Size Effect: A Novel Approach to Improving NIRS-XRF Coal Quality Analysis Accuracy

**Jiaxin Yin [1,2], Ruonan Liu [1,2], Wangbao Yin [1,2,*], Suotang Jia [1,2] and Lei Zhang [1,2,*]**

1 State Key Laboratory of Quantum Optics and Quantum Optics Devices, Institute of Laser Spectroscopy, Shanxi University, Taiyuan 030006, China; 202222618045@email.sxu.edu.cn (J.Y.); 202322618022@email.sxu.edu.cn (R.L.); tjia@sxu.edu.cn (S.J.)

2 Collaborative Innovation Center of Extreme Optics, Shanxi University, Taiyuan 030006, China

* Correspondence: ywb65@sxu.edu.cn (W.Y.); k1226@sxu.edu.cn (L.Z.)

**Abstract:** Coal, as a vital global energy resource, directly impacts the efficiency of power generation and environmental protection. Thus, rapid and accurate coal quality analysis is essential to promote its clean and efficient utilization. However, combined near-infrared spectroscopy and X-ray fluorescence (NIRS-XRF) spectroscopy often suffer from the particle size effect of coal samples, resulting in unstable and inaccurate analytical outcomes. This study introduces a novel correction method combining the Segment Anything Model (SAM) for precise particle segmentation and Data-Efficient Image Transformers (DeiTs) to analyze the relationship between particle size and ash measurement errors. Microscopic images of coal samples are processed with SAM to generate binary mask images reflecting particle size characteristics. These masks are analyzed using the DeiT model with transfer learning, building an effective correction model. Experiments show a 22% reduction in standard deviation (SD) and root mean square error (RMSE), significantly enhancing ash prediction accuracy and consistency. This approach integrates cutting-edge image processing and deep learning, effectively reducing submillimeter particle size effects, improving model adaptability, and enhancing measurement reliability. It also holds potential for broader applications in analyzing complex samples, advancing automation and efficiency in online analytical systems, and driving innovation across industries.

**Keywords:** coal quality analysis; near-infrared spectroscopy (NIRS); X-ray fluorescence (XRF); particle size effect; image segment; data-efficient image transformer (DeiT)

## 1. Introduction

Coal, as a critical global energy resource, directly impacts the efficiency of power generation, coal preparation, and coal chemical industries, as well as their environmental effects [1,2]. Therefore, rapid and accurate coal quality analysis plays a crucial role in promoting the clean and efficient utilization of coal [3]. Key indicators of coal quality include ash, volatile matter, calorific value, and sulfur content, which determine the combustion performance and environmental characteristics of coal [4].

Traditional coal quality analysis methods include LIBS [5,6], XRF [7], NIRS [8] and Dual-Energy X-ray Analysis (DEXA) [9,10]. These methods, with their high sensitivity, rapid response, and non-destructive characteristics, offer certain advantages in terms of accuracy. However, they often face challenges such as complex sample preparation, lengthy analysis times, and susceptibility to human interference. To address these issues, NIRS-XRF combined spectroscopy [11] has emerged as an analytical technique that integrates the strengths of near-infrared spectroscopy (NIRS) and X-ray fluorescence spectroscopy (XRF). It provides higher accuracy and reliability, particularly in overcoming the limitations of single techniques [12].

NIRS excites molecular vibrations in the sample using specific wavelengths of light, generating unique absorption spectra that precisely reflect the organic components of the sample [13]. Meanwhile, XRF employs high-energy X-rays to excite atoms in the sample, producing characteristic fluorescence spectra that efficiently and reliably measure inorganic elements [14]. The combination of these two techniques enables highly stable and comprehensive detection of coal components, facilitating the rapid and accurate analysis of key coal quality indicators. For example, Gao et al. [15] developed a fast calorific value analyzer for coal using NIRS-XRF technology, employing a partial least squares regression (PLSR) algorithm with an overall-segmented model. They achieved a standard deviation of 0.09 MJ/kg when measuring the calorific value of four coal products with a particle size of 0.2 mm. Additionally, they proposed a method for identifying coal types using random forests and applying corresponding PLSR sub-models to predict calorific value, effectively addressing the measurement challenges posed by varying coal types in complex applications like coking and coal washing industries. Similarly, Li et al. [16] proposed an automatic classification method for coking coal by combining NIRS-XRF fusion spectroscopy, principal component analysis (PCA), and t-distributed stochastic neighbor embedding (t-SNE) for dimensionality reduction. They classified the samples using support vector machines (SVM) and built regression models with PLSR. This approach significantly improved the prediction accuracy of ash, volatile matter, and sulfur content in coal samples with a particle size of 0.2 mm. The determination coefficient ($R^2$) for ash reached 0.9987, with a root mean square error of prediction (RMSEP) of 0.31%.

In practical applications, grinding samples to a 0.2 mm particle size often causes blockages in grinders, leading to equipment downtime and increased maintenance costs, which in turn affect the overall operational efficiency of the system. In contrast, coal samples with a particle size of 1mm can be obtained directly through simple crushing processes, which are more convenient and significantly improve the efficiency of online coal detection. However, the NIRS-XRF analysis of 1mm coal samples is subject to interference from uneven surface particle distribution and particle size variations [17,18]. This is because a 1 mm particle size represents the D50 median diameter, meaning 50% of particles are smaller than or equal to this size. Larger particles may cause uneven light scattering and absorption [19]. To improve the accuracy and consistency of NIRS-XRF analysis for coal samples with a particle size of 1 mm or larger, effective correction of particle size effects has become a key issue that needs urgent resolution.

Conventional particle size correction methods, such as Multiplicative Scatter Correction (MSC) [20], Polynomial Multiplicative Scatter Correction (PMSC) [21], Standard Normal Variate Correction) [22], and Extended Multiplicative Scatter Correction (EMSC) [23], can partially reduce the impact of physical factors on spectral data and are widely used in industries such as agriculture [24] and pharmaceuticals [25]. However, these methods primarily rely on spectral data for correction and fail to account for the influence of spatial distribution and morphological characteristics of particles. In contrast, image segmentation technology can directly capture the spatial distribution and morphological information of sample particles, allowing for more precise correction of spectral changes caused by uneven particle size, thus providing more accurate correction results.

This study focuses on developing a particle size effect correction method based on machine vision and image deep learning, aiming to make NIRS-XRF prediction models insensitive to variations in particle size distribution. Specifically, the Segment Anything

Model (SAM) [26] is used to achieve precise particle segmentation of microscopic images of coal samples, generating binary mask images that reflect particle size distribution characteristics. Then, Data-Efficient Image Transformers (DeiTs) [27] are employed to train these mask images and the associated ash measurement errors, establishing a particle size effect correction model for NIRS-XRF coal quality measurements. By validating the effectiveness of this method through experiments, we aim to provide an innovative solution to the particle size effect issue in spectral analysis.

## 2. Materials and Methods

### *2.1. Experiment*

#### 2.1.1. Experiment Setup

The NIRS-XRF combined coal quality analysis experimental setup used for particle size effect correction comprises the following five modules as shown in Figure 1:

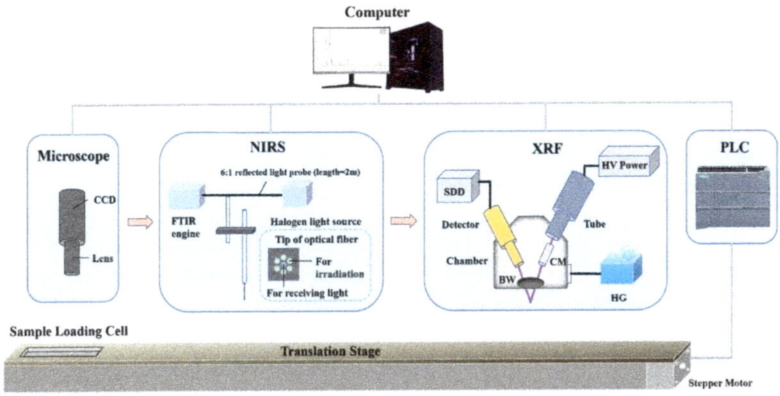


**Figure 1.** NIRS-XRF combined coal quality analysis setup for particle size effect correction (CCD: charge-coupled device, FTIR: Fourier-transform infrared spectroscopy, HV Power: high voltage power, HG: hydrogen generator, BW: beryllium window, CM: collimator, SDD: silicon drift detector, PLC: programmable logic controller).

1. NIRS Module: A Fourier-transform infrared spectrometer (C15511-01, Hamamatsu Photonics, Hamamatsu, Japan) is employed, with a working wavelength range of 1100–2500 nm, a spectral resolution of 5.7 nm, a signal-to-noise ratio of 10,000:1, and a spectral repeatability of $\pm$0.5 nm. The exposure time is set to 15 s. The light source is a halogen lamp (AvaLight-HAL-S Mini, Avantes, Apeldoorn, The Netherlands) with a working wavelength range of 360–2500 nm, a color temperature of 2700 K, and a service life exceeding 13,000 h.
2. XRF Module: This energy-dispersive structure is equipped with an X-ray tube (VF-50J, Varex Imaging, Salt Lake City, UT, USA) with a maximum power of 50 W and a rhodium target cathode. The tube voltage and current are set to 14 kV and 0.4 mA, respectively. A silicon drift detector (VIAMP, KETEK, Munich, Germany) with a graphene window is included, featuring a peak integration time of 0.1 μs and an integration time of 30 s. To prevent low energy X-ray fluorescence signals from being absorbed by air, a hydrogen generator (SFH-300, Shen Fen Analytical Instruments, Shanghai, China) supplies hydrogen with 99.99% purity at a flow rate of 150 mL/min to the measurement chamber.
3. Microscopic Imaging Module: Located between the sample pool's initial position and the NIRS analysis module, this module includes a CCD microscope (RY-602, Renyue Electronics, Shanghai, China) and a ring-shaped auxiliary light. The microscope

features 1× optical magnification, ~30× electronic magnification, and a working distance of 120 mm, with a field of view of 18 mm × 10 mm. The light provides an illumination of 55,000 Lux with an optimized angle to ensure uniform illumination on the coal sample surface.

4. Sample Transport Module: The core component is a one-dimensional motorized linear stage located beneath the NIRS and XRF modules, with an effective travel distance of 600 mm, a repeatability of 0.03 mm, and a moving speed of 20 mm/s. The sample loading cell mounted on this module measures 130 mm × 30 mm × 10 mm.
5. Analysis and Control Module: This module consists of a computer (equipped with an NVIDIA GeForce RTX 4090 GPU) and a programmable logic controller (PLC, SIEMENS S7-1200), responsible for timing control and data processing during the measurement process. The experimental operation software, developed on the LabVIEW platform, provides a user-friendly interface, allowing users to input sample information, select measurement methods, and monitor and display the progress and results in real time.

During the experiments, microscope images, NIRS spectra, and XRF energy spectra were collected from a central square area on the sample loading cell of the sample transport module, as shown in Figure 2. The left side shows the sample loading cell captured by a standard camera, while the right side provides a detailed view of the central square area (9 mm × 9 mm, green square) in the measurement region, captured by a microscope and highlighted by the green square. This area was used for collecting microscope images, NIRS spectra, and XRF energy spectra. We carefully calibrated the movement distances between these modules to ensure alignment of the same area for data collection, using adhesive labels and X-ray film for precise alignment.

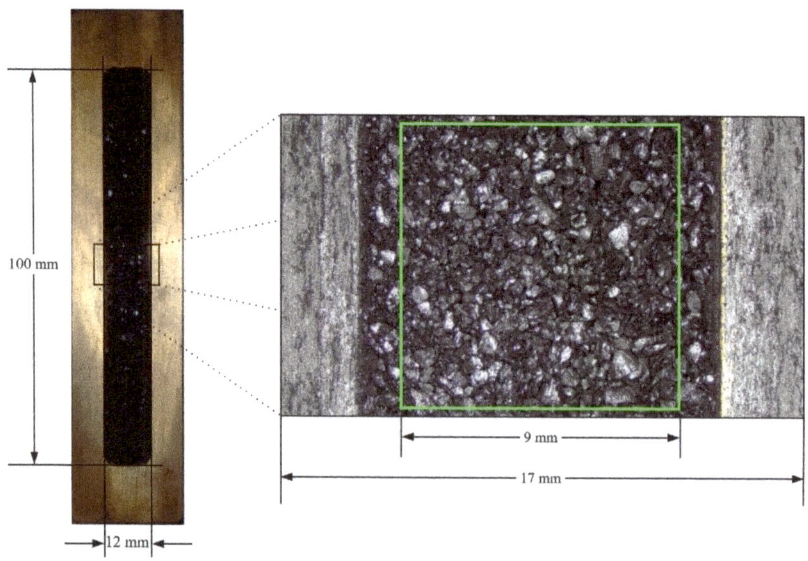


**Figure 2.** Schematic diagram of the sample cell and the corresponding magnified image showing the measurement area.

The experimental setup operates as follows: first, microscopic imaging (~5 s) is performed, followed sequentially by NIRS (~15 s) and XRF detection (~30 s). The entire process takes approximately 1 min. After completion, the sample pool returns to its initial position, and all data are saved and recorded. Special attention is required to align the near-infrared and X-ray beam spots to the same size and ensure consistent sample irradiation areas. This ensures that the microscopic images can be accurately cropped and correspond to the respective spectra. The experimental environment is maintained at 22–25 °C with a humidity of 40–50%.

2.1.2. Samples

In this study, eight coal samples were collected from the coal preparation plant of Shanxi Sunshine Coking Group, all with a median particle size of 1 mm. These samples were classified as coking coal according to the Chinese National Standard GB/T5751-2009 Classification of Coals in China. The ash content standard values were determined following the Chinese National Standard GB/T212-2008 Methods for Chemical Analysis of Coal to ensure accuracy and authority.

The previously established ash prediction model based on 0.2 mm coal samples was used as the standard model. The eight 1 mm samples were used for particle size effect correction to ensure the standard ash prediction model maintained accurate prediction capabilities across samples with varying particle size distributions.

Each coal sample was placed in the sample pool, leveled, and tested 100 times, resulting in 100 microscopic images and 100 initial ash measurement values for each sample. For model training, 90 images were randomly selected from each sample, with the remaining 10 images used for testing. Thus, the dataset consisted of 720 training images and 80 testing images.

*2.2. Construction of the Particle Size Effect Correction Model*

The overall construction process of the particle size effect correction model is shown in Figure 3. For the microscopic images of the coal samples, systematic preprocessing, image segmentation, and post-processing are performed to generate binary mask images. The difference between the predicted ash values from the standard model and the actual ash values is then calculated. This forms a dataset comprising 224 × 224 pixels mask images and ash difference values, used for training and testing the correction model.

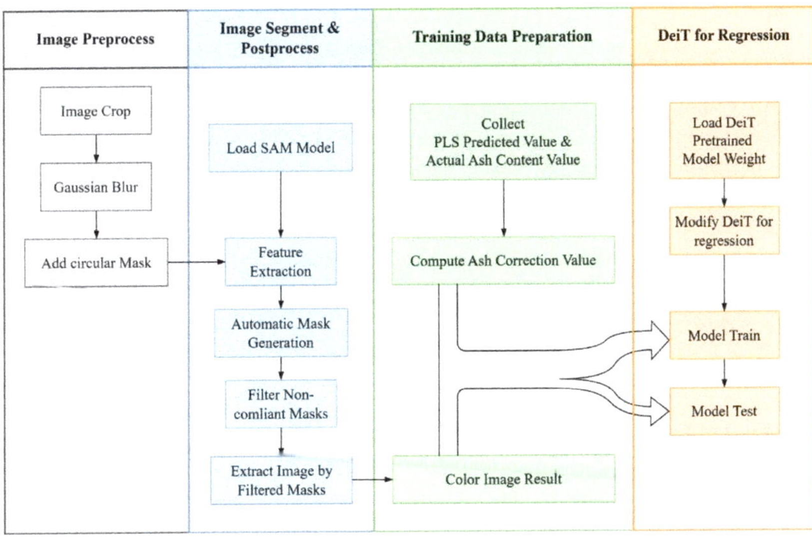


**Figure 3.** Overall construction process of the particle size effect correction model.

2.2.1. Image Preprocessing and Post-Processing

The original images cover a large area, so they are first center-cropped to reduce the pixel size to 1000 × 1000. To minimize noise, Gaussian filtering is applied for image smoothing. Since the spectral acquisition region is circular, a circular mask is used to process the images, ensuring the size matches the mask's outer boundary while maintaining a pixel size of 1000 × 1000.

For accurate coal particle segmentation, the SAM model is utilized to produce high-precision panoptic segmentation maps and extract the mask for each coal particle. The segmentation masks are sorted and filtered to remove abnormal sizes and discard smaller masks in overlapping regions.

The filtered segmentation masks are combined into a single mask image. Using this mask, valid segmented coal particle regions are extracted from the original image and resized to 224 × 224 pixels for subsequent model training and testing.

2.2.2. Segment Anything Model

Image segmentation is a core task in computer vision [28], aiming to divide an image into multiple meaningful regions or objects for further analysis or processing. Traditional image segmentation methods, such as thresholding, edge detection [29], region growing [29], watershed algorithms [30] and normalized cuts [31], rely on handcrafted features and low-level image information. While effective for simple scenarios, these methods often fail when handling complex or irregularly shaped objects. With advancements in deep learning, methods such as U-Net [32] and Mask R-CNN [33] have significantly improved segmentation capabilities through large-scale data training and end-to-end learning. However, these methods typically require extensive labeled data and task-specific architecture design, limiting their generalizability and applicability across tasks.

Against this backdrop, the Segment Anything Model (SAM) emerges as an innovative image segmentation method. Trained on vast amounts of data, SAM captures diverse visual concepts and supports cross-domain transfer learning, greatly enhancing its generality for segmentation tasks in various applications [26]. Its key advantage lies in its ability to perform efficient and precise segmentation even in the absence of abundant labeled data, automatically adapting to different scenarios. This capability is particularly valuable in complex, dynamic environments. SAM has been widely applied in areas such as medical image analysis [34], remote sensing image processing [35], object detection in autonomous driving [36], industrial inspection [37] and agricultural pest identification [38,39]. Its exceptional flexibility and efficiency make it particularly suitable for tasks involving complex structures or diverse environments.

The SAM model combines the strengths of CNNs and transformers to form an efficient image segmentation method. CNNs excel at extracting local features and recognizing spatial structural information within images, making them particularly suitable for tasks with prominent local patterns. At the same time, transformers, through their self-attention mechanism, capture global information and exploit long-range dependencies in images. This combination allows SAM to extract fine details while also understanding the global context of an image, achieving more precise and robust segmentation. In particular, when processing the panoptic segmentation of coal particle images, SAM effectively addresses differences in particle morphology and the complexity of image backgrounds, providing more accurate segmentation results.

Figure 4 illustrates the basic structure of the SAM model [26], which consists of three main components: an Image Encoder, a Prompt Encoder, and a Mask Decoder. First, the Image Encoder (based on the Vision Transformer) extracts features from the input image, generating an embedded representation of the image (Image Embedding). Next, the

Prompt Encoder converts user-provided prompts (such as points, bounding boxes, or text) into embeddings. These embeddings are combined with the image embeddings and input into the Mask Decoder. Finally, the Mask Decoder integrates the image features and prompt information to generate the final segmentation mask. This overall structure effectively combines global image features with the guidance of prompt information, enabling the SAM model to flexibly adapt to various segmentation tasks.

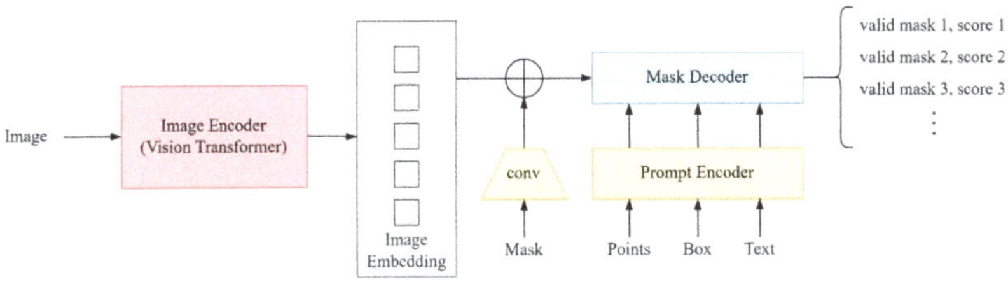


**Figure 4.** Basic structure of the SAM model.

In this study, SAM is applied to the task of panoptic segmentation of coal particle images. Coal samples exhibit complex particle morphology with significant variation between samples, making traditional segmentation methods challenging. SAM excels in adapting to diverse image characteristics and effectively completing segmentation tasks without requiring extensive labeled data [24]. For coal particle images, SAM accurately identifies and separates particles of different sizes, generating binary mask images that reflect coal particle morphology. Figure 5 demonstrates SAM's strong capability in coal particle image processing. Compared to traditional methods, SAM not only improves segmentation accuracy but also significantly enhances the model's adaptability to complex and dynamically changing scenarios. Using SAM for coal particle image segmentation provides high-quality data support for subsequent analyses such as coal quality detection and particle size effect correction, advancing coal analysis technology.

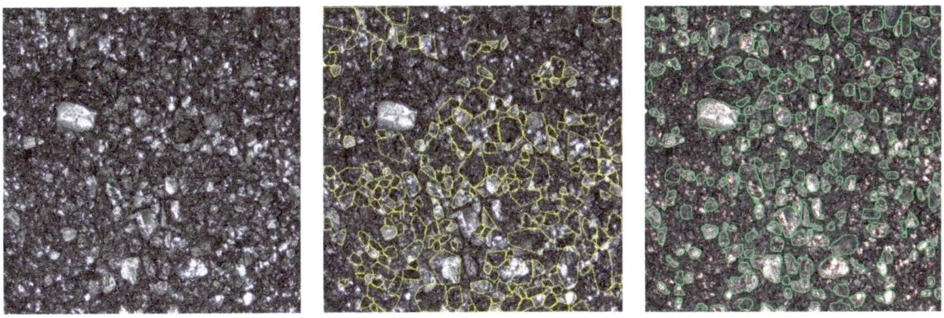


**Figure 5.** Comparison of different segmentation methods. (**a**) Coal sample original microscopic image; (**b**) Watershed segmentation using convex hull analysis; (**c**) SAM segmentation.

### 2.2.3. PLSR Model

We previously developed an ash content prediction model for coal with a median particle size of 0.2 mm, implemented on our experimental platform using Partial Least Squares Regression (PLSR). We collected near-infrared and X-ray fluorescence spectral data. These data are preprocessed to reduce noise and enhance quality. Principal Component Analysis (PCA) is then applied to extract relevant features from the processed spectra, focusing on the principal components associated with ash content, such as specific wavelengths in the NIRS spectrum or element concentrations measured by XRF. A PLSR model is constructed to establish the relationship between the extracted features and ash content. The model's output is the predicted ash content, which has not been corrected for particle size effects. The model was validated on 0.2 mm coal powder samples, demonstrating excellent performance with a repeatability standard deviation (SD) of less than 0.2%, indicating high accuracy in ash content prediction. The next step will involve addressing particle size effects through a correction model, targeting coal with a median particle size of 1 mm.

### 2.3. Correction Model

#### 2.3.1. DeiT Model

The core of the particle size effect correction model lies in using particle size distribution data to adjust the ash content of coal samples, effectively reducing measurement errors caused by particle size differences and improving the accuracy of ash measurement. The process begins by calculating the ash error as the difference between the actual ash content and the measured value of the sample. This error is then normalized and regularized, serving as the target value for ash error correction. For model design, 224 × 224 pixel three-channel color images are used as training inputs. These mask images incorporate comprehensive physical information about larger particles on the coal sample surface, including shape, color, position, and size.

In recent years, deep learning has achieved significant breakthroughs in image analysis [40], leading to the development of numerous efficient models. Among these, transformer models have demonstrated exceptional performance in tasks such as image classification, owing to their powerful feature extraction and global information modeling capabilities, exemplified by ViT [41]. The core mechanism of transformer models is self-attention, which captures long-range dependencies within images and provides a global receptive field. In contrast, CNN models [42] have local receptive fields that require multiple layers of convolution and pooling to gradually expand their receptive field. However, traditional transformer models require large datasets for training, which poses a challenge in coal composition analysis due to the high cost of acquiring large-scale coal image datasets.

To address this limitation, this study adopts the concept of transfer learning and employs the Data-efficient Image Transformers (DeiTs) Model. DeiT is an improved transformer model that uses a training method called "distillation" to enhance performance on small datasets. Distillation involves a knowledgeable teacher model (usually a high-performing traditional model, such as a CNN) guiding a student model (DeiT) to learn more effectively, as illustrated in Figure 6 [43]. This approach enables DeiT to learn meaningful image features from smaller datasets, which is crucial for analyzing coal images with limited data.

Specifically, the task involves mapping coal images to a floating-point number representing the ash error (actual ash value minus the measured value), essentially performing image regression. The DeiT model's core mechanism, self-attention, efficiently captures relationships between different regions of an image, which is critical for understanding the microstructure and compositional distribution of coal. By pretraining on large general-purpose image datasets, DeiT learns generic image features. Subsequently, the pretrained DeiT model is fine-tuned on the coal image dataset to better adapt to coal-specific characteristics and accurately predict relevant physical and chemical properties. The structural design and workflow based on the DeiT deep learning model are as follows:

- Backbone Model: This study uses DeiT Base as the backbone model. Its architecture is based on Vision Transformer (ViT) and consists of multiple transformer encoders capable of extracting global features from input images. The model accepts 224 × 224 × 3 images as input, performs linear projection and positional encoding, divides the image into 16 × 16 patches, and maps these patches into fixed-length embedding vectors. Each embedding vector is processed through a multi-head self-attention mechanism and a feed-forward network to capture global feature relationships.

- Adaptation for Regression Tasks: To adapt to the regression task for ash correction, the DeiT classification head is replaced with a regression head. The original classification head is modified to a linear layer with a single output node for predicting continuous values. The input dimension of the new linear layer matches the final embedding features of DeiT (768 dimensions), while the output dimension is set to 1 to generate ash correction predictions.
- Feature Extraction and Regression Output: Preprocessed images are fed into the backbone DeiT model, where multi-layer transformer encoders extract global image features. The regression head then produces the ash correction prediction. The transformer structure effectively models complex spatial distributions and ash variation patterns within coal particle images through its global modeling capability.

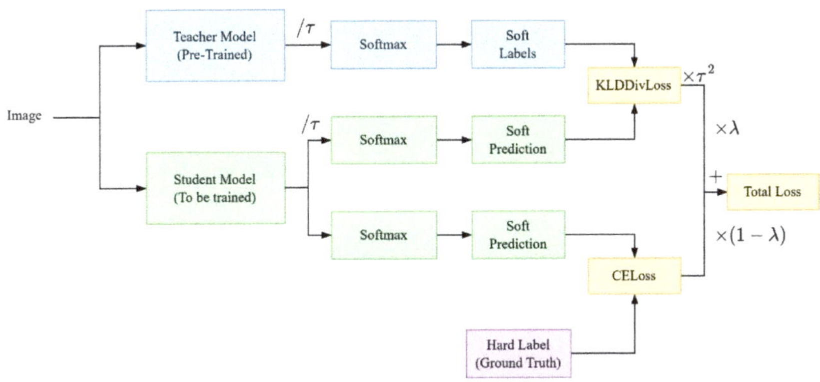


**Figure 6.** Teacher–student distillation training in DeiT model.

Compared to traditional CNNs, DeiT directly models global feature interactions through its multi-head self-attention mechanism, eliminating the dependency of convolution operations on local regions. Furthermore, DeiT's data efficiency allows it to perform well on smaller labeled datasets by leveraging pretrained models. By adapting the regression head to task-specific needs, this method achieves a direct mapping from coal particle images to ash predictions, providing robust support for multimodal feature integration and analysis of complex feature relationships.

Unlike traditional image analysis methods that rely on handcrafted features, DeiT automatically learns intricate image characteristics, avoiding the complexity and subjectivity of manual feature design. Its global receptive field further enhances its ability to capture the overall structure of coal images, which is crucial for composition analysis tasks requiring consideration of global structures. As a complementary tool to CNNs, DeiT provides a powerful modeling approach for ash correction tasks, improving both prediction accuracy and generalization capability. Therefore, using DeiT for regression tasks to correct ash measurement errors is highly appropriate.

### 2.3.2. Model Evaluation

To evaluate the established particle size effect correction model, this study uses Standard Deviation (SD) and Root Mean Square Error (RMSE) as assessment metrics to measure the model's accuracy and repeatability in prediction results.

SD measures the model's repeatability, reflecting the consistency of ash prediction results obtained from multiple measurements of the same coal sample under identical conditions. A smaller SD value indicates better repeatability of the model's ash predictions. The calculation formula is as follows:

$$SD = \sqrt{\frac{\sum_{i=1}^{n}\left(X_i - \overline{X}\right)^2}{n-1}} \quad (1)$$

where $X_i$ represents the corrected ash value from the i-th measurement of the same coal sample, $\overline{X}$ represents the average of all predicted values for the coal sample during repeated measurements, and $n$ denotes the total number of repeated measurements.

RMSE is a widely used error evaluation metric primarily designed to quantify the deviation between the model's predicted ash values and the actual ash values of coal samples. Compared to Mean Absolute Error (MAE), RMSE is more sensitive to larger errors due to its inclusion of a squared term, which amplifies the impact of significant errors. Therefore, RMSE is better suited for scenarios requiring a focus on penalizing large errors and more effectively reflects the model's stability and precision in predictions. The calculation formula is as follows:

$$RMSE = \sqrt{\frac{\sum_{i=1}^{n}\left(Y_i - \overline{Y}\right)^2}{n}} \quad (2)$$

where $Y_i$ represents the actual ash value of the coal sample, $\overline{Y}$ represents the predicted value, and $n$ denotes the total number of samples.

## 3. Results

### 3.1. Impact of Particle Size on NIRS and XRF Spectra

In the experimental analysis, the reproducibility of NIRS spectra (Figure 7) and XRF energy spectra (Figure 8) was compared for the same coal sample under different particle size conditions (median diameters of 0.2 mm and 1 mm). The coal sample surface was leveled multiple times, and five repeated measurements were conducted under each particle size condition.

The results show that changes in surface particle distribution significantly affected spectral stability, with larger-particle samples exhibiting greater spectral fluctuations compared to smaller-particle samples. Spectral stability refers to the consistency of spectral data over time and under varying conditions, characterized by minimal spectral fluctuations. In our experiment, smaller-particle samples maintained more consistent spectral characteristics after each leveling, indicating better spectral stability.

For NIRS spectra, 1 mm particle samples displayed higher absorbance. Larger particles caused stronger light scattering and longer optical path lengths, enhancing light–sample interaction and increasing absorbance. Poor surface uniformity in large-particle samples further increased light capture and absorption efficiency due to variations in porosity. Additionally, the uneven distribution of chemical components accentuated absorption peaks at specific wavelengths.

For XRF energy spectra, characteristic emission lines of various elements were labeled. Small-particle samples exhibited significantly higher fluorescence intensity for elements such as S, Ti, Fe, and Co. This is because fine-particle samples had a more uniform surface, enhancing fluorescence signal output, while larger particles with rough surfaces and larger particle spacing caused signal attenuation.

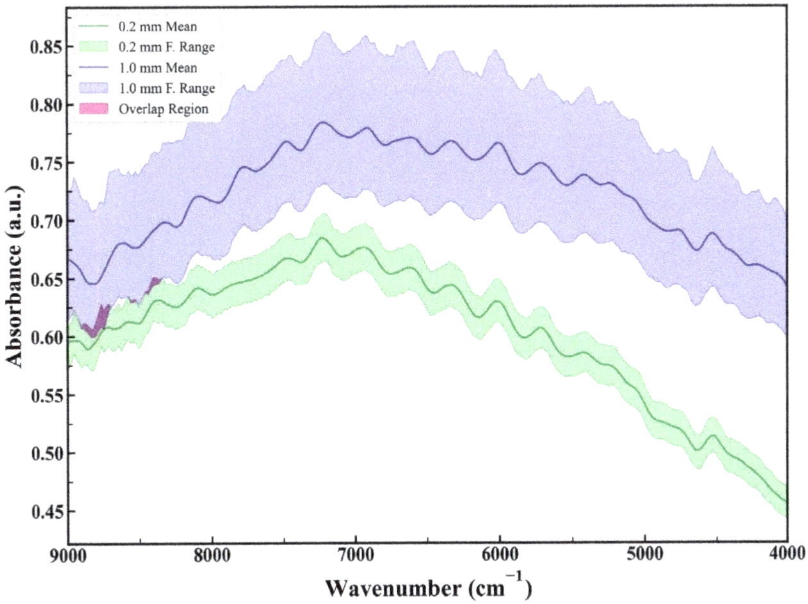


Figure 7. NIRS spectra of the same coal sample leveled repeatedly with different particle sizes.

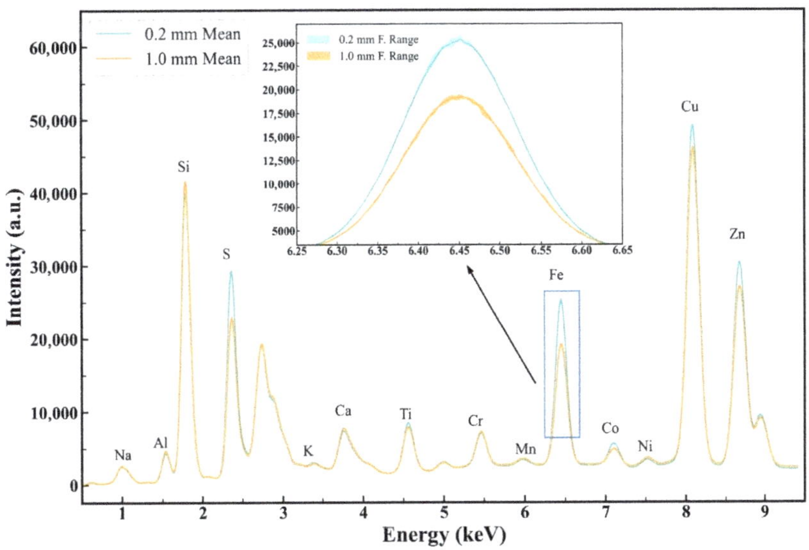


Figure 8. XRF energy spectra of the same coal sample leveled repeatedly with different particle sizes.

## 3.2. Training and Evaluation of the Correction Model

During the training and evaluation phase of the ash correction model, we used the SAM model to extract particle size features in the task of precise coal particle segmentation in microscopic images, ensuring the accuracy of the particle size effect correction model training.

To adapt to this specific task, we adjusted the SamAutomaticMaskGenerator parameters in the SAM model to minimize the impact of large coal particles on the segmentation results. The optimized parameters are detailed in Table 1. These adjustments significantly reduced the interference caused by large coal particles, making the segmentation results more aligned with the true morphology of the coal particles.

**Table 1.** Parameter settings for the SamAutomaticMaskGenerator.

| Parameter | Value | Type |
|---|---|---|
| points_per_side [1] | 32 | int |
| points_per_batch [2] | 128 | Int |
| pred_iou_thresh [3] | 0.87 | float |
| stability_score_thresh [4] | 0.8 | float |
| box_nms_thresh [5] | 0.8 | float |
| min_mask_region_area [6] | 200 | int |

[1] The number of points to be sampled along one side of the image. [2] Sets the number of points run simultaneously by the model. [3] A filtering threshold in [0,1], using the model's predicted mask quality. [4] A filtering threshold in [0,1], based on the mask's stability when changing the cutoff for binarizing the mask. [5] The box IoU cutoff used by non-maximal suppression to filter duplicate masks. [6] Remove disconnected regions and holes in masks with area smaller than min_mask_region_area.

Figure 9 illustrates the complete workflow from capturing the raw images to generating the final segmented coal particle images. Initially, the raw images are acquired at a resolution of 1920 × 1080, containing mixed information of coal particles and background. To improve the effectiveness of subsequent segmentation, the images undergo preprocessing, including cropping and denoising, resulting in images resized to 1000 × 1000 pixels.

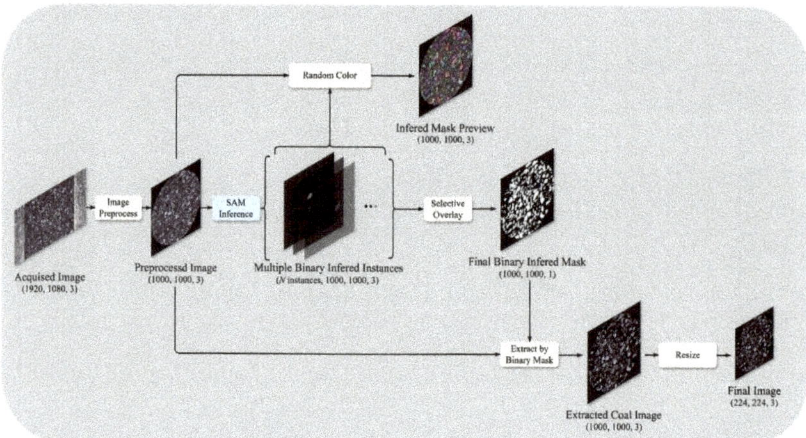


**Figure 9.** Image processing workflow.

The preprocessed images are then input into the SAM model for segmentation, which generates multiple binary segmentation instances, each representing an independent coal particle region. During segmentation, the instances output by the SAM model are visualized using randomly assigned colors with a transparency of 0.6 to facilitate evaluation and verification of the segmentation results. This produces an integrated mask preview.

Next, the segmentation results are optimized through filtering and overlay operations, retaining only regions that meet the particle size requirements. This step generates the final binary segmentation mask (a single-channel image) that clearly delineates coal particle regions while masking irrelevant background information.

The binary mask is then used to extract coal particle regions from the original images. The extracted images are standardized by resizing them to 224 × 224 × 3 pixels, making them suitable as input for deep learning models. This comprehensive workflow, combining image preprocessing, segmentation, filtering, and standardization, ensures the generated images are of high quality and consistency, providing reliable input data for subsequent analysis and modeling.

This processing pipeline demonstrates the efficiency of the SAM model, not only achieving precise coal particle segmentation but also eliminating over-segmentation and regions with abnormal sizes through post-processing. This significantly improves the consistency between the segmentation mask and the actual geometry of coal particles, providing high-quality input data that enhance the accuracy and stability of the ash prediction model.

Figure 10 shows five coal particle images from the dataset. The top row represents the original color images with circular masks applied, while the bottom row displays the color images generated after segmentation and post-processing by the SAM model. The results demonstrate the SAM model's robust ability to extract and segment individual coal particles from images, producing outputs closely aligned with the actual geometric features of coal particles.

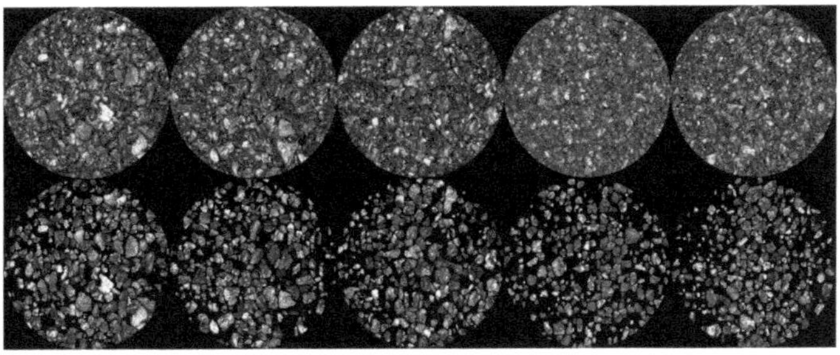


**Figure 10.** Comparison of coal particle images in the dataset.

During the training phase, a custom regression model based on the DeiT architecture was implemented using the PyTorch [44] framework and executed on a GPU to accelerate computation. The MSELoss function was selected as the loss criterion, and the Adam optimizer was used with an initial learning rate of 0.0001, ensuring stable training and convergence.

To further enhance the model's training effectiveness and adaptability, a Cosine Annealing Learning Rate Scheduler was introduced. This scheduler dynamically adjusts the learning rate over the total number of training epochs (num_epochs), gradually decaying it from the initial value to a minimum value of 0.00001. This learning rate strategy allows the model to explore a broader learning space in the early stages of training and refine its parameters during later stages through the gradual reduction in the learning rate.

## 4. Discussion

### 4.1. Significance of Particle Size Effects on Spectral Stability

The results highlight the critical impact of particle size on the stability of NIRS and XRF spectra. Large-particle samples exhibited greater spectral fluctuations due to factors such as stronger light scattering, uneven porosity, and inconsistent chemical composition. For NIRS, higher absorbance in larger particles was attributed to enhanced light-sample interaction. For XRF, the fluorescence intensity was significantly higher in fine-particle samples due to their uniform surface. These findings underscore the necessity of correcting for particle size effects to improve measurement accuracy and stability.

### 4.2. Impact of Correction on Ash Prediction Accuracy

The validation set experiments showed significant improvements in the SD of ash predictions after correction (Figure 11). For example, the SD of sample #1 decreased from

0.37% to 0.30%, and sample #2 from 0.35% to 0.28%. Similarly, the SD of samples #3 and #4 dropped from 0.33% and 0.32% to 0.26% and 0.24%, respectively. Other samples, such as #5, #6, #7, and #8, also exhibited varying degrees of reduction, with sample #6 showing the most notable improvement, decreasing from 0.34% to 0.27%. Overall, the average SD of ash predictions decreased from 0.34% to 0.27% after correction, representing a reduction of approximately 20.59%. These results indicate that particle size effect correction not only improves the accuracy of ash predictions but also enhances their repeatability, providing more reliable support for coal quality analysis.

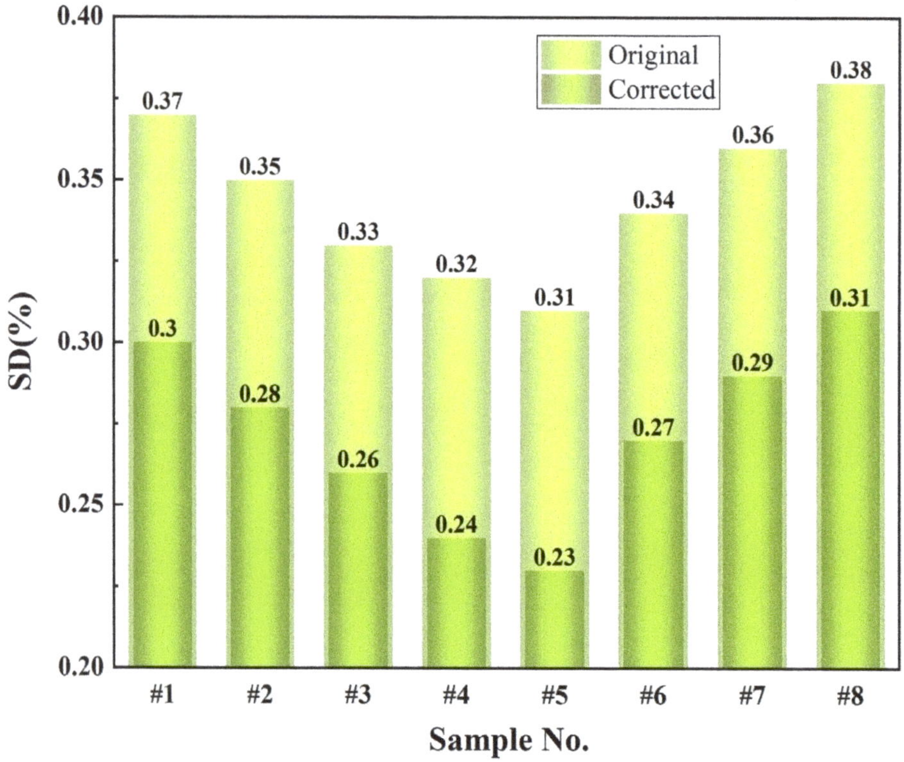


**Figure 11.** Comparison of standard deviation (SD) before and after correction.

Figure 12 presents the changes in RMSE of ash predictions before and after correction. After correction, RMSE showed a significant reduction. For instance, the RMSE of sample #1 decreased from 0.40% to 0.34%, sample #3 from 0.37% to 0.30%, sample #4 from 0.36% to 0.26%, and sample #8 from 0.39% to 0.27%. Overall, the average RMSE of the samples decreased from 0.36% to 0.28% after correction, representing a reduction of approximately 22.22%. These results clearly demonstrate that particle size effect correction significantly improves the model's predictive accuracy and adaptability to samples with different particle sizes.

In summary, the model correction significantly improved the performance of ash prediction in terms of both SD and RMSE: the reduction in SD indicates enhanced stability and repeatability of the model's predictions, while the decrease in RMSE reflects reduced prediction errors, improved accuracy, and more consistent predictive performance across different samples.

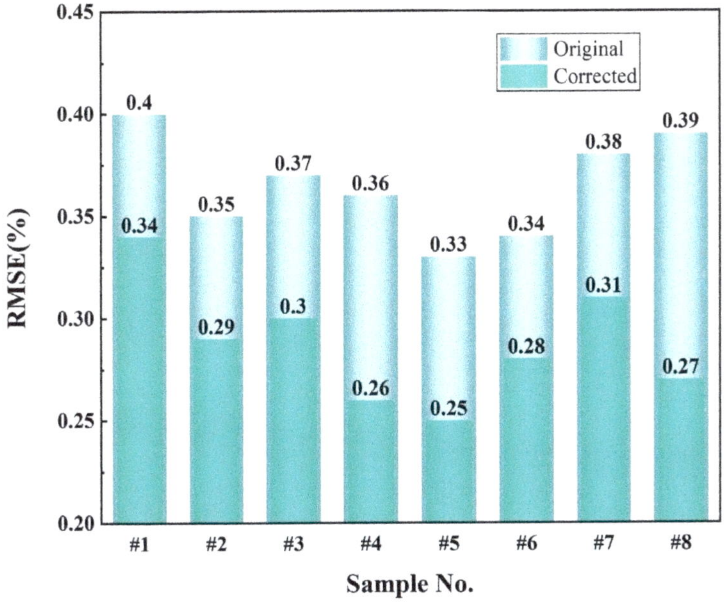


**Figure 12.** Comparison of root mean square error (RMSE) before and after correction.

## 5. Conclusions

To address the impact of particle size effects on the accuracy of spectral analysis for coal samples, this study proposed a correction method based on the SAM and DeiT models. This method successfully established a more comprehensive and efficient particle size effect correction mechanism, offering a novel technical solution to tackle complex interference factors in coal quality analysis.

During the experiments, the DeiT model was utilized to extract deep features from microscopic images of coal samples. Leveraging DeiT's transformer architecture, the model captured comprehensive global information on particle size distribution and morphological characteristics. Subsequently, DeiT's regression capability modeled the extracted high-dimensional features, learning the complex nonlinear relationships between particle size features and target parameters, such as ash content.

Compared to traditional spectral correction methods, this approach eliminates the reliance on spectral data alone by integrating spatial distribution characteristics and geometric structures of coal samples into the correction model. This significantly enhances adaptability and correction accuracy for particle size effects.

The experimental results demonstrate that the DeiT-based correction method substantially improved ash prediction accuracy, reducing SD from 0.34% to 0.27% and RMSE from 0.36% to 0.28%. These outcomes highlight the method's significant advantages in mitigating particle size effect interference and enhancing the precision of spectral analysis.

The innovation of this study lies not only in the application of the DeiT model but also in the in-depth exploration and utilization of complex spatial characteristics of samples. By incorporating the global modeling capabilities of transformer models, this method constructs a precise and generalizable particle size effect correction mechanism, providing a novel solution for handling complex interferences in coal quality analysis. Moreover, the method has broad application potential, extending to other tasks requiring particle size effect correction in complex sample analyses, and laying a foundation for the innovative development of spectral analysis technology.

The particle size effect correction method proposed in this study has potential applications not only in coal quality analysis but also in various other industries. For instance, in environmental monitoring, this method may improve the accuracy of pollutant concentration predictions in soil and water samples. In the mining sector, it could enhance ore composition testing and potentially improve assessment precision. Furthermore, in the field of food science, this method might aid in better particle analysis of powdered food products, contributing to a deeper understanding of their compositional characteristics. In medical diagnostics, particularly in cancer detection, this approach may help analyze the particle characteristics of biological samples, potentially improving disease prediction. Additionally, drug development may benefit from this method by optimizing the analysis of drug release characteristics and possibly increasing the accuracy of drug efficacy assessments. In summary, this research offers a novel perspective on addressing particle size effects in the analysis of various complex samples, and we will continue to explore its broader application prospects in the future.

**Author Contributions:** Conceptualization, J.Y. and L.Z.; methodology, J.Y.; software, J.Y.; validation, J.Y. and R.L.; formal analysis, J.Y.; investigation, J.Y. and R.L.; resources, J.Y.; data curation, R.L.; writing—original draft preparation, J.Y. and R.L.; writing—review and editing, J.Y.; visualization, R.L.; supervision, W.Y. and S.J.; project administration, L.Z. All authors have read and agreed to the published version of the manuscript.

**Funding:** This research was funded by Fund for Shanxi "1331KSC".

**Institutional Review Board Statement:** Not applicable.

**Informed Consent Statement:** Not applicable.

**Data Availability Statement:** The raw data supporting the conclusions of this article will be made available by the authors on request.

**Acknowledgments:** We would like to extend our thanks to Institute of Laser Spectroscopy of the Shanxi University for the resources to allow us to complete the study.

**Conflicts of Interest:** The authors declare no conflicts of interest.

## References

1. Cheng, F.; Zhang, Y.; Zhang, G.; Zhang, K.; Wu, J.; Zhang, D. Eliminating Environmental Impact of Coal Mining Wastes and Coal Processing By-Products by High Temperature Oxy-Fuel CFB Combustion for Clean Power Generation: A Review. *Fuel* **2024**, *373*, 132341. [CrossRef]
2. Liu, K.; He, C.; Zhu, C.; Chen, J.; Zhan, K.; Li, X. A Review of Laser-Induced Breakdown Spectroscopy for Coal Analysis. *TrAC Trends Anal. Chem.* **2021**, *143*, 116357. [CrossRef]
3. Sheta, S.; Afgan, M.S.; Hou, Z.; Yao, S.-C.; Zhang, L.; Li, Z.; Wang, Z. Coal Analysis by Laser-Induced Breakdown Spectroscopy: A Tutorial Review. *J. Anal. At. Spectrom.* **2019**, *34*, 1047–1082. [CrossRef]
4. Hower, J.C.; Finkelman, R.B.; Eble, C.F.; Arnold, B.J. Understanding Coal Quality and the Critical Importance of Comprehensive Coal Analyses. *Int. J. Coal Geol.* **2022**, *263*, 104120. [CrossRef]
5. Yao, S.; Mo, J.; Zhao, J.; Li, Y.; Zhang, X.; Lu, W.; Lu, Z. Development of a Rapid Coal Analyzer Using Laser-Induced Breakdown Spectroscopy (LIBS). *Appl. Spectrosc.* **2018**, *72*, 1225–1233. [CrossRef] [PubMed]
6. Tian, Z.; Li, J.; Wang, S.; Bai, Y.; Zhao, Y.; Zhang, L.; Zhang, P.; Ye, Z.; Zhu, Z.; Yin, W.; et al. Development and Industrial Application of LIBS-XRF Coal Quality Analyzer by Combining PCA and PLS Regression Methods. *J. Anal. At. Spectrom.* **2023**, *38*, 1421–1430. [CrossRef]
7. Kelloway, S.J.; Ward, C.R.; Marjo, C.E.; Wainwright, I.E.; Cohen, D.R. Quantitative Chemical Profiling of Coal Using Core-Scanning X-Ray Fluorescence Techniques. *Int. J. Coal Geol.* **2014**, *128*, 55–67. [CrossRef]
8. Andrés, J.; Bona, M. Analysis of Coal by Diffuse Reflectance Near-Infrared Spectroscopy. *Anal. Chim. Acta* **2005**, *535*, 123–132. [CrossRef]
9. Wang, H.; Guo, X.; Zhang, Y.; Zhang, J. Research Progress and Application of Online Coal Quality and Coal Quantity Analyses. *Coal Sci. Technol.* **2024**, *52*, 219–237.

10. Von Ketelhodt, L.; Bergmann, C. Dual Energy X-Ray Transmission Sorting of Coal. *J. South. Afr. Inst. Min. Metall.* **2010**, *110*, 371–378.
11. Li, J.; Gao, R.; Zhang, Y.; Wang, S.; Zhang, L.; Yin, W.; Jia, S. Coal Calorific Value Detection Technology Based on Nirs-Xrf Fusion Spectroscopy. *Chemosensors* **2023**, *11*, 363. [CrossRef]
12. Gao, R.; Wang, S.; Li, J.; Tian, Z.; Zhang, Y.; Zhang, L.; Ye, Z.; Zhu, Z.; Yin, W.; Jia, S. Development and Application of a Rapid Coal Calorific Value Analyzer Based on NIRS-XRF. *J. Anal. At. Spectrom.* **2023**, *38*, 2046–2058. [CrossRef]
13. Wang, S.; Feng, X.L.; Zhou, J.; Wang, X.M. Fourier Transform near Infrared Spectroscopy Analysis of Power Plant Coal Quality. *Adv. Mater. Res.* **2011**, *236*, 799–803. [CrossRef]
14. Acquafredda, P. XRF Technique. *Phys. Sci. Rev.* **2019**, *4*, 20180171. [CrossRef]
15. Gao, R.; Li, J.; Dong, L.; Wang, S.; Zhang, Y.; Zhang, L.; Ye, Z.; Zhu, Z.; Yin, W.; Jia, S. Accurate Analysis of Coal Calorific Value Using NIRS-XRF: Utilizing RF Classification and PLSR Subtype Modeling. *Microchem. J.* **2024**, *201*, 110716. [CrossRef]
16. Li, J.; Gao, R.; Zhang, Y.; Zhang, L.; Dong, L.; Ma, W.; Yin, W.; Jia, S. Research on Accurate Analysis of Coal Quality Using NIRS-XRF Fusion Spectroscopy in Complex Coal Type Scenarios. *Opt. Laser Technol.* **2025**, *181*, 111734. [CrossRef]
17. Blanco, M.; Coello, J.; Iturriaga, H.; Maspoch, S.; De La Pezuela, C. Near-Infrared Spectroscopy in the Pharmaceutical Industry. *Anal.-Lond.-Soc. Public Anal. Then R. Soc. Chem.* **1998**, *123*, 135R–150R. [CrossRef] [PubMed]
18. Sitko, R.; Zawisza, B. Quantification in X-Ray Fluorescence Spectrometry. In *X-Ray Spectroscopy*; IntechOpen: London, UK, 2012; pp. 137–162.
19. Myers, T.L.; Brauer, C.S.; Su, Y.-F.; Blake, T.A.; Johnson, T.J.; Richardson, R.L. The Influence of Particle Size on Infrared Reflectance Spectra. In *Algorithms and Technologies for Multispectral, Hyperspectral, and Ultraspectral Imagery XX*; SPIE: Bellingham, WA, USA, 2014; Volume 9088, pp. 61–68.
20. Martens, H.; Jensen, S.A.; Geladi, P. Multivariate Linearity Transformation for Near-Infrared Reflectance Spectrometry. In *Proceedings of the Nordic Symposium on Applied Statistics*; Stokkand Forlag Publishers: Stavanger, Norway, 1983; pp. 205–234.
21. Isaksson, T.; Kowalski, B. Piece-Wise Multiplicative Scatter Correction Applied to near-Infrared Diffuse Transmittance Data from Meat Products. *Appl. Spectrosc.* **1993**, *47*, 702–709. [CrossRef]
22. Geladi, P.; MacDougall, D.; Martens, H. Linearization and Scatter-Correction for Near-Infrared Reflectance Spectra of Meat. *Appl. Spectrosc.* **1985**, *39*, 491–500. [CrossRef]
23. Martens, H.; Nielsen, J.P.; Engelsen, S.B. Light Scattering and Light Absorbance Separated by Extended Multiplicative Signal Correction. Application to Near-Infrared Transmission Analysis of Powder Mixtures. *Anal. Chem.* **2003**, *75*, 394–404. [CrossRef]
24. García-Sánchez, F.; Galvez-Sola, L.; Martínez-Nicolás, J.J.; Muelas-Domingo, R.; Nieves, M. Using Near-Infrared Spectroscopy in Agricultural Systems. In *Developments in Near-Infrared Spectroscopy*; Kyprianidis, K.G., Skvaril, J., Eds.; IntechOpen: London, UK, 2017; pp. 97–127.
25. Krämer, K.; Ebel, S. Application of NIR Reflectance Spectroscopy for the Identification of Pharmaceutical Excipients. *Anal. Chim. Acta* **2000**, *420*, 155–161. [CrossRef]
26. Kirillov, A.; Mintun, E.; Ravi, N.; Mao, H.; Rolland, C.; Gustafson, L.; Xiao, T.; Whitehead, S.; Berg, A.C.; Lo, W.-Y. Segment Anything. In Proceedings of the IEEE/CVF International Conference on Computer Vision, Paris, France, 2–6 October 2023; pp. 4015–4026.
27. Touvron, H.; Cord, M.; Douze, M.; Massa, F.; Sablayrolles, A.; Jégou, H. Training Data-Efficient Image Transformers & Distillation through Attention. In Proceedings of the International Conference on Machine Learning, Shenzhen, China, 26 February 2021; pp. 10347–10357.
28. Minaee, S.; Boykov, Y.; Porikli, F.; Plaza, A.; Kehtarnavaz, N.; Terzopoulos, D. Image Segmentation Using Deep Learning: A Survey. *IEEE Trans. Pattern Anal. Mach. Intell.* **2021**, *44*, 3523–3542. [CrossRef] [PubMed]
29. Pavlidis, T.; Liow, Y.-T. Integrating Region Growing and Edge Detection. *IEEE Trans. Pattern Anal. Mach. Intell.* **1990**, *12*, 225–233. [CrossRef]
30. Kornilov, A.S.; Safonov, I.V. An Overview of Watershed Algorithm Implementations in Open Source Libraries. *J. Imaging* **2018**, *4*, 123. [CrossRef]
31. Shi, J.; Malik, J. Normalized Cuts and Image Segmentation. *IEEE Trans. Pattern Anal. Mach. Intell.* **2000**, *22*, 888–905.
32. Ronneberger, O.; Fischer, P.; Brox, T. U-Net: Convolutional Networks for Biomedical Image Segmentation. In *Medical Image Computing and Computer-Assisted Intervention—MICCAI 2015*; Navab, N., Hornegger, J., Wells, W.M., Frangi, A.F., Eds.; Lecture Notes in Computer Science; Springer International Publishing: Cham, Switzerland, 2015; Volume 9351, pp. 234–241, ISBN 978-3-319-24573-7.
33. He, K.; Gkioxari, G.; Dollár, P.; Girshick, R. Mask R-Cnn. In Proceedings of the IEEE International Conference on Computer Vision, Venice, Italy, 22–29 October 2017; pp. 2961–2969.
34. Mazurowski, M.A.; Dong, H.; Gu, H.; Yang, J.; Konz, N.; Zhang, Y. Segment Anything Model for Medical Image Analysis: An Experimental Study. *Med. Image Anal.* **2023**, *89*, 102918. [CrossRef] [PubMed]

35. Ren, S.; Luzi, F.; Lahrichi, S.; Kassaw, K.; Collins, L.M.; Bradbury, K.; Malof, J.M. Segment Anything, from Space? In Proceedings of the IEEE/CVF Winter Conference on Applications of Computer Vision, Waikoloa, HI, USA, 4–8 January 2024; pp. 8355–8365.
36. Kwakye, K.; Seong, Y.; Yi, S.; Aboah, A. DriveSAM: Cognitive Perspective on Driving Maneuvers Based on Drivers' Attention Using Eye Gaze Data. In Proceedings of the IEOM International Conference on Smart Mobility and Vehicle Electrification, Detroit, MI, USA, 10–12 October 2023. [CrossRef]
37. Yang, W.; Chen, X.-D.; Wu, W.; Qin, H.; Yan, K.; Mao, X.; Song, H. Boosting Deep Unsupervised Edge Detection via Segment Anything Model. *IEEE Trans. Ind. Inform.* **2024**, *20*, 8961–8971. [CrossRef]
38. Olsson, M. Early Detection of Bark Beetle Attacks: Integrating Segment Anything Model (SAM) Zero-Shot Segmentation and Spectral Indices for Tree Health Assessment. Master's Thesis, Lund University, Lund, Sweden, 2024.
39. Qing, J.; Deng, X.; Lan, Y.; Xian, J. Intelligently Counting Agricultural Pests by Integrating SAM with FamNet. *Appl. Sci.* **2024**, *14*, 5520. [CrossRef]
40. LeCun, Y.; Bengio, Y.; Hinton, G. Deep Learning. *Nature* **2015**, *521*, 436–444. [CrossRef] [PubMed]
41. Vaswani, A. Attention Is All You Need. In *Advances in Neural Information Processing Systems*; Curran Associates, Inc.: Red Hook, NY, USA, 2017.
42. LeCun, Y.; Kavukcuoglu, K.; Farabet, C. Convolutional Networks and Applications in Vision. In Proceedings of the 2010 IEEE International Symposium on Circuits and Systems, Paris, France, 30 May 2010–2 June 2010; IEEE: Piscataway, NJ, USA, 2010; pp. 253–256.
43. Hinton, G. Distilling the Knowledge in a Neural Network. *arXiv* **2015**, arXiv:1503.02531.
44. Paszke, A.; Gross, S.; Massa, F.; Lerer, A.; Bradbury, J.; Chanan, G.; Killeen, T.; Lin, Z.; Gimelshein, N.; Antiga, L. Pytorch: An Imperative Style, High-Performance Deep Learning Library. In *Advances in Neural Information Processing Systems 32*; Curran Associates, Inc.: Red Hook, NY, USA, 2019.

sensors

Article

# A Framework of State Estimation on Laminar Grinding Based on the CT Image–Force Model

Jihao Liu [1,*], Guoyan Zheng [2,*] and Weixin Yan [3]

1 State Key Laboratory of Ocean Engineering, School of Ocean and Civil Engineering, Shanghai Jiao Tong University, Shanghai 200240, China
2 Institute of Medical Robotics, School of Medical Engineering, Shanghai Jiao Tong University, Shanghai 200240, China
3 Institute of Robotics, School of Mechanical Engineering, Shanghai Jiao Tong University, Shanghai 200240, China; xiaogu4524@sjtu.edu.cn
* Correspondence: jihao.liu@sjtu.edu.cn (J.L.); guoyan.zheng@sjtu.edu.cn (G.Z.)

**Abstract:** It is a great challenge for a safe surgery to localize the cutting tip during laminar grinding. To address this problem, we develop a framework of state estimation based on the CT image–force model. For the proposed framework, the pre-operative CT image and intra-operative milling force signal work as source inputs. In the framework, a bone milling force prediction model is built, and the surgical planned paths can be transformed into the prediction sequences of milling force. The intra-operative milling force signal is segmented by the tumbling window algorithm. Then, the similarity between the prediction sequences and the segmented milling signal is derived by the dynamic time warping (DTW) algorithm. The derived similarity indicates the position of the cutting tip. Finally, to overcome influences of some factors, we used the random sample consensus (RANSAC). The code of the functional simulations has be opened.

**Keywords:** state estimation; CT image; milling force prediction

## 1. Introduction

In spinal surgeries, it is significantly risky to undertake mechanical operations, including bone drilling and milling [1]. In general, bone milling is used for bone removal to relieve compression on the spinal cord [2,3]. The surgeons have to perform complex operations in a narrow surgical field, and prevent a cutting tip from damaging soft tissues, such as nerves, blood vessels, and ligaments. It is extremely high dependent on the surgeons' experience [4,5].

The image-based navigation system has been developed for surgeons to conduct surgical planning through patient-to-image registration [6,7]. It integrates with a stereotaxy device, which can track the surgical tools with markers [8]. It is critical for a safe surgery to determine the position of the cutting tip. However, it is impossible to not only sense the deflection of a cutting bit but also to obtain the position of the cutting tip [9].

To address this problem, many researchers have been developing state recognition methods [10]. Some methods employ the intra-operative signal to identify the bone state during cutting. These signals consist of the cutting force/torque [11], sound pressure [12], vibration [13], and motor power of a cutting tool [14]. The bone state is recognized by detecting the signal feature of the stepwise breakthrough in the time domain. Qu et al. [15] developed a backpropagation neural network for state recognition on vertebral laminar grinding. Four intra-operative signals, including the characteristic milling

 https://doi.org/10.3390/s25010238

force, milling speed, milling depth, and ultrasonic scalped power, were loaded to detect the state of bone breakthrough. Jiang et al. [16] proposed an analytical force model to estimate the cutting depth. Its accuracy was up to 0.2 mm, and this performance was dependent upon identification of the force coefficients inside the milling force model. Most of the intra-operative signals are affected by the heat released by the bone cutting, except for the vibration signal. Xia et al. [17] developed a vibration signal fusion method to predict the remaining thickness of the lamina in real time, from which, the lamina cutoff had a success rate of 98.4%. There can be variations in the bone cutting states and signal features for different specimens because those are functions of bone tissue properties [18–20]. Therefore, there existed a potential risk for the above methods from the perspectives of robustness and adaption.

The bone cutting force can be predictable. The mechanical model of the cutting force has been introduced from the field of metal manufacturing into the field of medical engineering [21–23]. In the mechanical model of the bone cutting, some force coefficients are different due to a change in the yield strength of bones. It is only through complex experiments that the force coefficients for the precious prediction on the drilling force can be calibrated [24].

Researchers have been focusing on the challenge of how to obtain some prior information and estimate the surgical states before an operation. The pre-operative CT image has been used to predict the cutting state [25]. CT images can digitize the bone shape and material properties well. Grayscale CT images can quantify the strength of the bone [26,27]. Williamson et al. [28] found that the drilling force sequence was similar to the grayscale array of the planning path extracted from the CT image. Therefore, Wang et al. [6] combined the pre-operative CT image and the intra-operative drilling force signal to estimate the drilling position. However, the accuracy was affected by the sampling synchronization of the drilling signal. Thus, the CT image is combined with the mechanical model of the drilling force to derive the CT image–force mapping model. Based on this model, Li et al. [25] developed the virtual sensing framework to predict the trend of the thrust change during the drilling process. The discrimination capacity of identification can achieve the voxel level of the CT images. According to the gray value array in the CT image subject to the surgical planning, Li et al. [29] proposed a strategy to adjust the cutting speed. Despite the existing models considering the mechanism between a cutting tool and bone tissue, and from the results of these published works, the prior force information derived from the CT images does not seem to be consistent with actual measurements [6,29].

The focus of this work is on estimating the position of the cutting tip, rather than directly avoiding injury to tissues. The relative code can be found at https://github.com/GHow-sjtu/LaminarStateEstimator-CT. Based on the existing knowledge of the CT image–force mapping model, we propose a method to estimate the real-time position of the cutting tip. The main contributions lie in three aspects:

- We develop an intra-operative state estimation for laminar grinding. The pre-operative CT image and the intra-operative milling force signal are combined to estimate the tip position. Simulation results show that the proposed estimation method is robust for different bones from various specimens, and it can adopt CT images from different centers.
- We establish a CT image–force model to generate prior knowledge of the bone milling state before an operation. The proposed method may not provide an accurate quantitative estimation of the milling force due to various bone properties. However, the prior knowledge contains the time-domain signal characteristics that are used to estimate the milling state.

- Experiments showed that the milling force sequence is relative to the density distribution along one milling path. The bone density distribution of one milling path in a lamina is independent. It can work as one of the identification features for positioning during cutting. It means that the proposed framework may no longer be effective when the object bone becomes brittle due to osteoporosis or degeneration.

Despite the strengths of our study, we acknowledge that there are certain limitations. We ignore the impact of the sampling frequency of the cutting force sensor in this work. We believe that addressing this limitation in future studies will provide a more robust method for clinical application. Moreover, the effectiveness of the proposed method depends on the characteristics of bone density distribution. Although we have conducted many tests, we cannot determine the specific conditions under which the proposed method becomes ineffective.

The paper is organized as follows. Section 2 presents the proposed method. Section 3 describes the experiments and results. Finally, we present discussions in Section 4, followed by our conclusion in Section 5.

## 2. Methods

### *2.1. Method Overview*

In this work, a framework is developed to estimate the tip position during the operation process, as shown in Figure 1. The proposed framework adopts the pre-operative CT images and real-time milling signal as the inputs, and it consists of five functional modules. Module 1 extracts the CT voxels according to the surgical planning. Module 2 utilizes the CT image–force model to predict milling sequences in view of the thrust force, torque, and lateral forces. Module 3 segments the milling force signal into four-channel sequences by a tumbling window. The above data flows are combined into Module 4 to estimate the instantaneous tip position. The fitting algorithms in Module 5 are used to eliminate the nonlinear disturbances, as well as to estimate the position of the milled part. Finally, we can obtain the estimations on the position of the cutting tip, as well as the deviation of the actual milled paths.

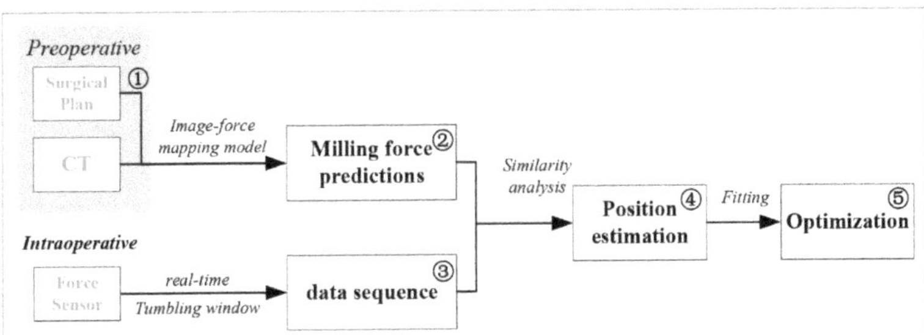


**Figure 1.** Framework of state estimation on laminar grinding.

The CT image–force model in Module 2 will be introduced in Section 2.2. This model is derived based on the mechanical model of ball-end milling. The tip position's estimation in Module 4 will be detailed in Section 2.3, and the fitting algorithms in Module 2 will be proposed in Section 2.4.

In this work, because the cutter–workpiece engagement (CWE) is considered in the milling force model, we can ignore the impact of the milling strategy. As shown in Figure 2, a common layer-by-layer policy is used as the milling strategy [17]. The planning paths are filled in a rectangular space. By using this policy, the milling cutter will remove the bone tissue through multi-layer horizontal movements. A Cartesian coordinate system is established to model actions of the milling cutter. The $x$-axis is defined by the direction of the feed rate of the cutter. The $z$-axis is defined by the direction of the milling depth. The $y$-axis is defined according to the right-hand rule. And the origin is defined by the starting position of the surgical task.

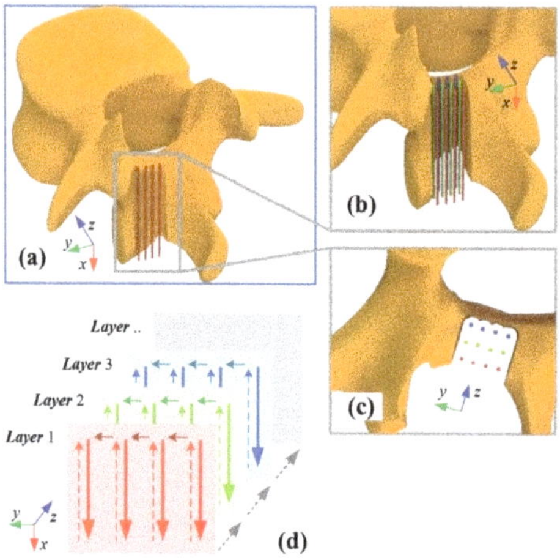


**Figure 2.** Schematic view of the layer-by-layer policy. (**a**) Schematic view of the thinned lamina, where four red lines represent the paths on the first milling layer. (**b**) Three groups of color lines represent the different layers, respectively. (**c**) Top view of the milling paths. (**d**) Spatial motions of the cutting tip during laminar grinding.

### 2.2. Ct Image–Force Mapping

The CT image–force model allows translation of the high-dimensional 3D images into several-dimensional virtual force sequences. The instantaneous milling force results from the contact force at the cutting edges engaging with the bone. The contact force at the micro-edge varies with the bone strength at the contacting location. Because the bone strength is quantified by the gray value in the CT image, the bone milling process can be regarded as the interaction process of the cutting edges with the corresponding image voxels of the object bone. Thus, the contact force of a micro-edge can be modeled by **Equation** (1).

$$f^i(t) = func(\mathbf{I}(\mathbf{P}_i(t))) \tag{1}$$

where $f^i(t)$ indicates the prediction of the instantaneous force at the $i$-th micro-edge at time $t$, $\mathbf{P}_i(t)$ indicates the position of the $i$-th micro-edge at time $t$, $\mathbf{I}(\cdot)$ indicates the extracted image gray value at the corresponding position, and $func(\cdot)$ indicates the milling force in a function of the gray value.

It is noteworthy that the proposed CT image–force model is inaccurate when predicting the milling force due to many factors that are mentioned above. However, the predicted sequences encompass the same time-domain signal features.

#### 2.2.1. Geometric Model of the Ball-End Cutter

For modeling of the milling process of a ball-end cutter, we establish four coordinate systems, including the milling cutter coordinate system (MCCS), the instantaneous milling cutter coordinate system ($i$-MCCS), the local working coordinate system ($l$-WCS), and the workpiece coordinate system (WCS). As shown in Figure 3, these four coordinate systems are used to define the geometric model of cutting edges, instantaneous cutting force, and milling motions.

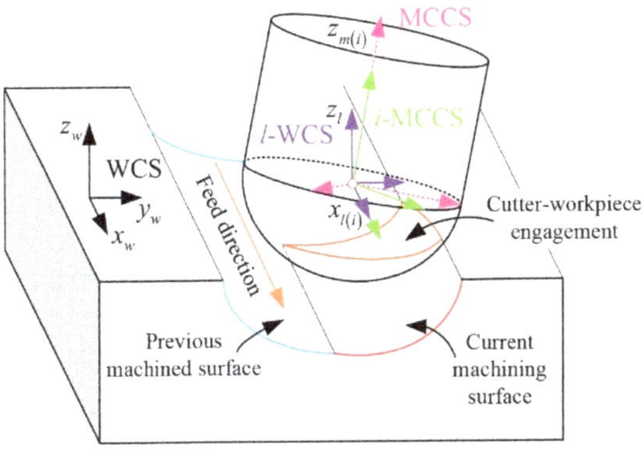


**Figure 3.** Schematic view of the bone milling process.

The MCCS, *i*-MCCS, and *l*-WCS are all defined at the ball-end cutter, and their origins are located at the centroid of the ball end, while the workpiece coordinate system (WCS) is defined at the object bone. The *x*-axis of the *i*-MCCS, *l*-WCS, and WCS is parallel to the feed direction of the milling cutter. The *z*-axis of the MCCS and *i*-MCCS is defined by the rod axis of the cutter. The *z*-axis of the *l*-WCS and WCS is normal to the milling layer. The *y*-axes of theses four coordinate systems are produced by the right-hand rule. During the milling process, there is an incline angle between the rob axis of the cutter and the bone surface.

In **Equation** (1), the coordinate position $\mathbf{P}_i(t)$ of a micro-edge is one of the indispensable parameters for the milling prediction function. In order to obtain the position $\mathbf{P}_i(t)$, the morphological and kinematic models of the ball-end cutter are built.

The morphological model of a ball-end cutter defines the position of cutting edges. In this work, a widely used orthopedic cutter with four flutes is chosen as the surgical tool. As shown in Figure 4, the position of the micro-edges on a ball-end cutter is modeled in the MCCS [21], as:

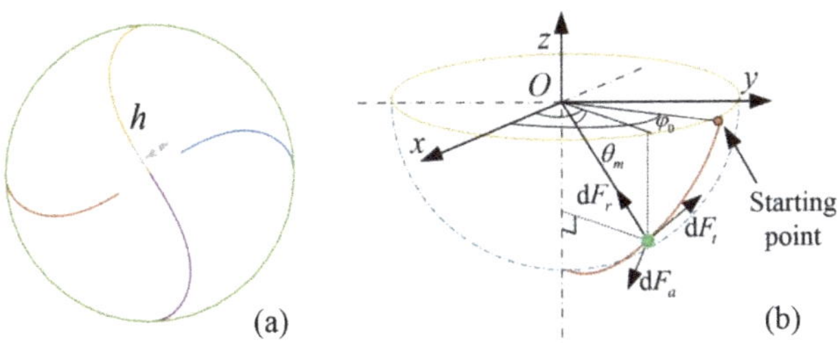


**Figure 4.** Geometric model of a four-flute ball-end cutter. (**a**) The bottom view of a four-flute cutter. (**b**) Isometric view of one cutting edge on a ball-end cutter.

$$\begin{cases} x_m = R\cos\theta_m\cos(\varphi_0 - \sin\theta_m\tan\beta_G) \\ y_m = R\cos\theta_m\sin(\varphi_0 - \sin\theta_m\tan\beta_G) \\ z_m = -R\sin\theta_m \end{cases} \tag{2}$$

where $R$ is the radius of the ball end; $\varphi_0$ is the circumferential starting angle that defines the starting point of the cutting edge; $\beta_G$ is the helical angle of the cutting edge, $\beta_G = 30°$; and $\theta_m$ is the axial position angle of one micro-edge. Some cutting edges do not pass the tool center at the apex. As shown in Figure 4a, $h$ is the distance from the edge to the center in the bottom view. Thus, the corresponding range of the axial position angle is within $[0, \arccos(h/R)]$.

2.2.2. Kinematic Model of the Ball-End Cutter

As the milling cutter grinds, the interactions of cutting edges with the bone occur on a complex helix trajectory. The real-time position of the micro-edges in the *l*-WCS can be obtained through a spatial transformation, which is written as:

$$ {}^{W}\mathbf{P} = {}^{W}_{t}\mathbf{T} \cdot {}^{t}\mathbf{P} \tag{3} $$

where ${}^{W}_{t}\mathbf{T}$ is the transformation matrix from the milling cutter coordinate system (MCCS) to the workpiece coordinate system (WCS), which indicates the grinding motion of the milling cutter, as follows:

$$ {}^{W}_{t}\mathbf{T} = \begin{pmatrix} {}^{w}_{l}\mathbf{T} \cdot \mathbf{\Omega}(t) & \mathbf{v}(t) \\ \mathbf{0} & 1 \end{pmatrix} \tag{4} $$

where $\mathbf{\Omega}(t)$ denotes the self-spinning motion of the cutter, $\mathbf{v}(t)$ denotes the feed motion, and ${}^{w}_{l}\mathbf{T}$ is the transformation matrix from the instantaneous milling coordinate system (*i*-MCS) to the local working coordinate system (*l*-WCS). It is defined by the incline angles $\delta_{mt}$ of the spindle axis in the workpiece coordinate system (WCS).

$$ {}^{w}_{l}\mathbf{T} = \begin{pmatrix} 1 & 0 & 0 & 0 \\ 0 & \cos\delta_{mt} & -\sin\delta_{mt} & 0 \\ 0 & \sin\delta_{mt} & \cos\delta_{mt} & 0 \\ 0 & 0 & 0 & 1 \end{pmatrix} \tag{5} $$

The spinning matrix $\mathbf{\Omega}(t)$ and the motion vector $\mathbf{v}(t)$ are modeled in the coordinate system *i*-MCCS, as follows:

$$ \mathbf{\Omega}(t) = \begin{pmatrix} \cos(\omega t + \phi_0) & -\sin(\omega t + \phi_0) & 0 \\ \sin(\omega t + \phi_0) & \cos(\omega t + \phi_0) & 0 \\ 0 & 0 & 1 \end{pmatrix} \tag{6} $$

$$ \mathbf{v}(t) = \begin{pmatrix} v_d \cdot t & 0 & 0 \end{pmatrix}^T \tag{7} $$

where $\omega$ is the self-spinning speed [rad/s], and $v_d$ is the feed rate [mm/s].

2.2.3. Cutter–Workpiece Engagement (CWE)

Cutter–workpiece engagement (CWE) relates to the section of the cutter interacting with the bone. During the bone milling process, the salient feature of the ball-end milling is that the geometry and material properties of the surgical object vary along the milling path. It leads to the continuous change in the section of cutting edges participating in milling, as shown in Figure 5. When the micro-edges are inside the area of CWE, they are valid for the milling interaction. Thus, the calculation of CWE is the precondition to obtaining the milling prediction [21,23].

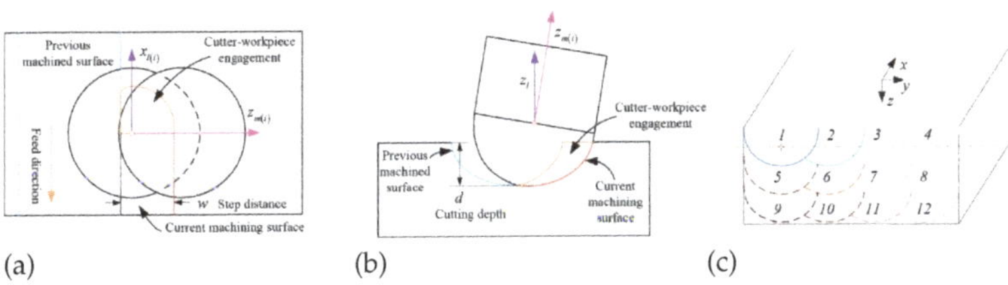


**Figure 5.** Schematic view of the cutter–workpiece engagement (CWE). (**a**) Top view. (**b**) Side View. (**c**) View of the CWE of several paths in the layer-by-layer policy.

The CWE area can be modeled by the boundary curves. The boundary of the CWE area is an intersection between the envelope surface formed by the previous machined path and the semi-spherical surface of the ball-end cutter. Due to the usage of a ball-end cutter, the previous machined surface is regarded as a nonstandard cylindrical surface. As shown in Figure 5c, the CWE area is relative to the milling depth $d$ and the step distance $w$ among the milling paths. As shown in Figure 6, there exist five types of CWE areas during the layer-by-layer milling process. These figures are created by Function *mesh* and *surf* in the software *MATLAB 2021b*. The detailed equations that model the boundary curves of CWE areas are listed in Appendix A.

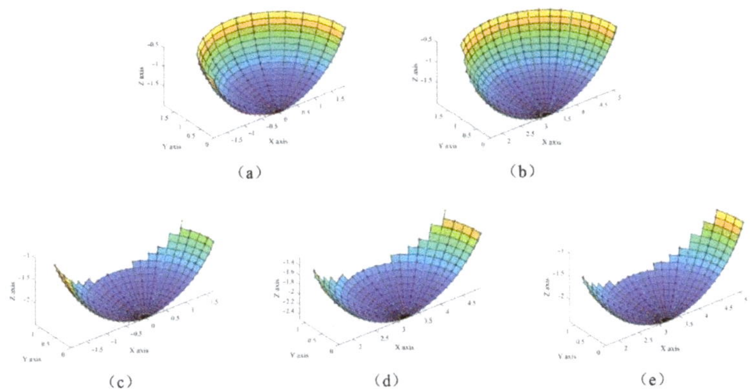


**Figure 6.** Schematic view of the CWE areas of different milling paths. (**a**) Valid CWE area of the first path on the top layer. (**b**) Valid CWE area of the others on the top layer. (**c**) Valid CWE area of the first path on the other layers. (**d**) Valid CWE area of the middle paths on the other layers. (**e**) Valid CWE area of the last path on the other layers.

### 2.2.4. Mechanical Model of Ball-End Milling

Lee and Altintas [22] propose the micro-element milling force model for orthogonal cutting, where the shearing mechanism and the plowing mechanism are considered separately. The formula that expresses the cutting forces at a micro-edge is shown in **Equation** (8).

$$\begin{cases} dF_r = K_{rc}t_n\mathrm{d}b + K_{re}\mathrm{d}s \\ dF_a = K_{ac}t_n\mathrm{d}b + K_{ae}\mathrm{d}s \\ dF_t = K_{tc}t_n\mathrm{d}b + K_{te}\mathrm{d}s \end{cases} \tag{8}$$

where $\mathrm{d}F_r$, $\mathrm{d}F_a$, and $\mathrm{d}F_t$ are the radial, axial, and tangential forces at the micro cutting edge [N]; $K_{rc}$, $K_{ac}$, and $K_{tc}$ are the shear coefficients [N/mm]; $K_{re}$, $K_{ae}$, and $K_{te}$ are the blade force coefficients, and also, namely, edge specific coefficients [N/mm]; $t_n$ is the thickness of the undeformed chip [mm]; and $\mathrm{d}b$ is the projection width of the micro-edge on the generatrix (the infinitesimal length of cutting edge) [mm], and is the projection length of the micro-edge on the generatrix (the crossing sectional area of cut) [$\mathrm{mm}^2$]. The shear coefficients and the blade force coefficients can be obtained by calibration methods [30–32]. However, it is impossible to calibrate the coefficients of the mechanical model for each patient.

The micro-edge chip width $\mathrm{d}b$ could be expressed in a function of the micro-axial position angle $\mathrm{d}\theta_m$ and the radius of cutter $R$, as follows:

$$\mathrm{d}b = R\mathrm{d}\theta_m \tag{9}$$

The micro-edge length $\mathrm{d}s$ is written as

$$\mathrm{d}s = R\sqrt{1+\cos^4\theta_m \tan^2\beta_G} \cdot \mathrm{d}\theta_m \tag{10}$$

The thickness of the undeformed chip $t_n$ is the projection of feed per tooth in the normal direction of the sphere. According to the theory of Merdol and Altintas [33], the thickness of the undeformed chip $t_n$ is shown as the equation:

$$t_n = \frac{\mathbf{v}_t \cdot \mathbf{n}_t}{|\mathbf{n}_t|} \tag{11}$$

where $\mathbf{v}_t$ denotes the projection of the feed rate per teeth of the cutter on the rotating milling cutter coordinate system (MCCS). $\mathbf{n}_t$ denotes a vector from the centroid of the ball end to the micro-edge, and $|\mathbf{n}_t| = R$. The feed rate per tooth is written as:

$$\mathbf{v}_t = \frac{60 \cdot {}^{i}\mathbf{v}_d}{n \cdot N} \tag{12}$$

where $N$ is the self-spinning speed of the cutter $[RPM]$, $n$ is the number of flutes on the cutter, and ${}^{i}\mathbf{v}_d$ is the tool feed data in the $i$-MCS [mm/s].

The cutting forces at the micro-edge are not parallel to the coordinate axes of the MCCS, which is modeled by the following equation:

$$\begin{pmatrix} \mathrm{d}F_{xT} \\ \mathrm{d}F_{yT} \\ \mathrm{d}F_{zT} \end{pmatrix} = \begin{pmatrix} -c\theta_m c\varphi_m & -s\theta_m c\varphi_m & s\varphi_m \\ -c\theta_m s\varphi_m & -s\theta_m s\varphi_m & -c\varphi_m \\ -s\theta_m & c\theta_m & 0 \end{pmatrix} \begin{pmatrix} \mathrm{d}F_r \\ \mathrm{d}F_a \\ \mathrm{d}F_t \end{pmatrix} \tag{13}$$

where $s$ and $c$ denote the trigonometric functions of $\sin()$ and $\cos()$, respectively. $\mathrm{d}F_{xT}$, $\mathrm{d}F_{yT}$, and $\mathrm{d}F_{zT}$ are the components of the cutting force on the coordinate axes. $\varphi_m$ is the circumferential angle of the micro-edge, which is expressed as:

$$\varphi_m = \varphi_0 - \sin\theta_m \tan\beta_G \tag{14}$$

Based on the finite element method, the instantaneous milling forces of the cutter in the MCCS could be obtained as follows:

$$\begin{cases} F_{xT} = \sum \mathrm{d}F_{xT}(P_i) \\ F_{yT} = \sum \mathrm{d}F_{yT}(P_i) \\ F_{zT} = \sum \mathrm{d}F_{zT}(P_i) \end{cases} \tag{15}$$

where $F_{xT}$, $F_{yT}$, and $F_{zT}$ are the components of the cutting force.

#### 2.2.5. CT Image–Force Mapping Model

During the bone cutting process, the cutter faces variations in bone shapes and bone material properties. The above mechanical model considers many factors but still lacks consideration of the time-varying material property. Some works have shown that bone materials' strength and modulus have a power relationship with density [27], and the bone density is proportional to the value in a CT image [26]. Thus, the CT image information is introduced into the bone milling model herein.

The cutting forces are weighted by the power of the grayscale value of the CT images. This is also consistent with the viewpoint of the literature [25]. **Equation** (16) reveals the weighted personalized bone milling forces.

$$\begin{cases} \mathrm{d}F_r = \lambda^{\mu} \cdot (K_{rc} \cdot t_n \cdot \mathrm{d}b + K_{re} \cdot \mathrm{d}s) \\ \mathrm{d}F_a = \lambda^{\mu} \cdot (K_{ac} \cdot t_n \cdot \mathrm{d}b + K_{ae} \cdot \mathrm{d}s) \\ \mathrm{d}F_t = \lambda^{\mu} \cdot (K_{tc} \cdot t_n \cdot \mathrm{d}b + K_{te} \cdot \mathrm{d}s) \end{cases} \tag{16}$$

where $\lambda$ is the image grayscale value at the infinitesimal element's position and $\mu$ is the power relationship coefficient.

In order to eliminate the gray shift due to changes in CT devices' performance, the image grayscale value extracted is normalized herein. In **Equation** (17), a piecewise linear function is used as the normalization rule.

$$\lambda = \begin{cases} 0, & x \le m_{\min}, \\ \frac{1}{m_{\max} - m_{\min}}(x - m_{\min}), & m_{\min} < x < m_{\max}, \\ 1, & x \ge m_{\max}. \end{cases} \tag{17}$$

where $x$ represents the grayscale value of a CT image voxel. $m_{\min}$ and $m_{\max}$ represent normalized parameters, which can be determined according to the gray distribution of the specified CT images. Typically, a bone contains both cortical bone and cancellous bone, $m_{\min}$ can be taken as the mean CT value of the cancellous bone area minus two times the standard deviation, and $m_{\max}$ is the mean CT value of the cortical bone area plus two times the standard deviation [25].

### 2.3. *Tip Position Estimation*

The local density distribution of the vertebrae can be used as the identifiable localization feature [28,34]. However, it is difficult to directly obtain real-time bone density during surgery. According to **Equation** (16), the fluctuation of the milling signals consists of information including the object density. In the clinical environment, many factors can introduce noise into the intra-operative signals, which affects the estimation of the milling states.

In the proposed method, the estimation principle of the tip position is to search the index of the maximum similarity between the milling prediction sequences and the real-time force signal. To improve the accuracy, the fitting methods are used for estimation of the tip position. As shown in Figure 7, the planned workspace is digitized into paralleled components subject to the planned paths. Each component is further divided into continuous grids. Each grid consists of several CT image voxels in series. The image voxel works as the basic metric unit in this work. According to the CT image–force model, each grid can be transformed into one data sequence with the same length.

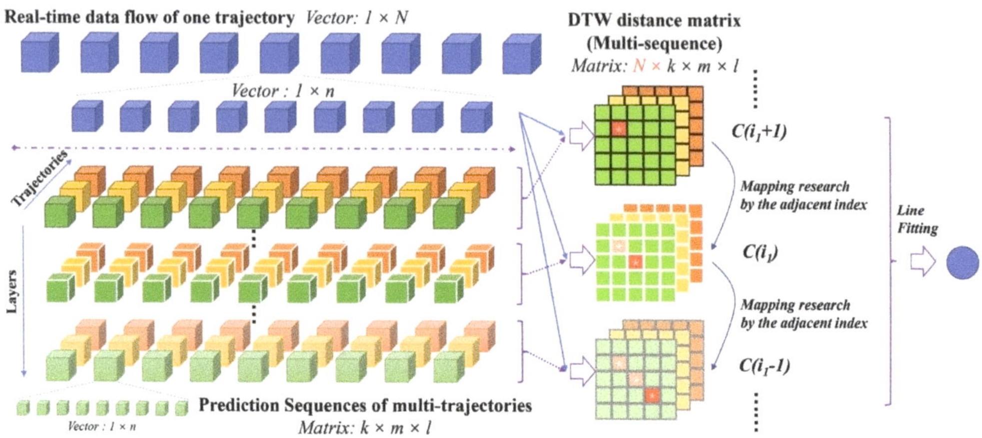


**Figure 7.** Tip position estimation by the method of similarity matching.

Every prediction sequence $g(i, j, k)$ can be regarded as the unique landmark indicating the position $P_p(i, j, k)$ of the $k$-th segment in the $j$-th path of the $i$-th layer inside the workspace of the surgical task, as shown in **Equation** (18).

$$g(i, j, k) \Rightarrow P_p(i, j, k) \tag{18}$$

The intra-operative real-time force signal is segmented into continuous sequences with the length of $n_s$ by a tumbling window. When the sampling frequency of the sensor is $f_s$ [Hz], the physical length $l$ [mm] of a signal sequence can be expressed as:

$$l = v_d n_s / f_s \tag{19}$$

The initial phase of the milling cutter has an influence on the milling signal. It can be ignored when the milling parameters agree with the following relationship:

$$\frac{60}{n \cdot N} v_d \ll \Delta x_{pix} \tag{20}$$

where $\Delta x_{pix}$ represents the physical size of one voxel of the CT images. It means that the ratio of the self-spinning speed of the cutter to the feed rate should be high enough.

Similarity mapping between the prediction sequences and the force signal segment enables estimation of the tip position. Due to the influence of bone motions, sensor noise, and signal synchronization, it is a great challenge to find precious paired sequences. To address this problem, the dynamic time warping (DTW) algorithm is employed to improve robustness.

Dynamic time warping (DTW) is a well-known machine learning method to measure the similarity of two temporal sequences, allowing similar shapes to match even if they are out of phase in the time axis [35–37]. It means that the sequences are warped in a nonlinear fashion to match each other. The steps of the position estimation method are as follows:

1. Calculate the similarity metric $M(S_{rm})$. $M(S_{rm})$ is a three-dimension matrix that is the optical DTW distance of the signal segment $S_{rm}$ and the predicted sequences. Its component $d_{i,j,k}$ in the metric $M(S_{rm})$ represents the similarity with the predicted sequence of the index $I[i, j, k]$, which can be expressed as:

$$d_{i,j,k}(S_{rm}) = DTW\left(S_{rm}, S_{i,j,k}\right) \tag{21}$$

where $1 \leq i \leq N_l, 1 \leq j \leq N_{traj}$, and $1 \leq k \leq N_s$. $N_r$, $N_{traj}$, and $N_l$ are the number of grids on one path, the number of paths on every layer, and the number of layers in the planning task, respectively.

2. The optical DTW distance is used to represent the similarity between two sequences, as follows:

$$d_{i,j,k} = C(N_s, N_s) \tag{22}$$

where $C(N_s, N_s)$ denotes the component value of the index $(N_s, N_s)$ in the DTW distance matrix $C$.
The optical DTW distance between two sequences is derived based on the principle of the shortest distance, as follows:

$$C(i,j) = D(i,j) + \min \begin{cases} C(i-1,j) \\ C(i,j-1) \\ C(i-1,j-1) \end{cases} \tag{23}$$

where $1 \leq i \leq N_s, 1 \leq j \leq N_s$, and $D$ is the distance matrix. In this work, we use the Euclidean metric to obtain the distance matrix $D$, as follows:

$$D(i,j) = \left| s_{rm}(i) - s_{i,j,k}(j) \right| \tag{24}$$

where $s_{rm}(i)$ indicates the $i$-th data point in the real-time sequence $S_{rm}$, and $s_{i,j,k}(j)$ indicates the $j$-th data point in the prediction sequences.

3. Find the index of the sequence with the highest similarity as the paired coordinate position:

$$I* = \arg\min_{I_{i,j,k}} (M) \tag{25}$$

The tip position is obtained according to **Equation** (18) as

$$\hat{P} = P(I*) \tag{26}$$

### 2.4. Optimization on the Position Estimation

By a fitting method, points of the real-time position of the cutting tip can be used to derive the location of the milling path. The schematic view of estimating on the real-time milling path is as shown in Figure 8. We adopt the random sample consensus (RANSAC) algorithm as the fitting method to estimate the milling path. This algorithm was proposed by Fishler and Bolles in 1981, and it is a widely used robust estimator [38].

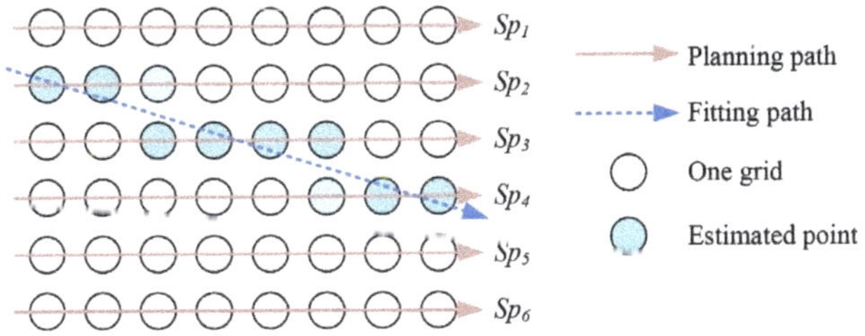


**Figure 8.** Schematic view of estimating the location of the milling path by a fitting algorithm. The blue circle indicates the estimated positions. The blue dashed line indicates the estimation on the current path. The red line indicates the planned paths.

The RANSAC algorithm for fitting the milling path is shown in Algorithm 1. In this step, $n_1$ is 2, $k_1$ is 2000, and $t_1$ is 1.0.

It is assumed that the deviation of every milled path from those planned is identical. During the milling operation, the space formed by the continued milled paths agrees with some geometric conditions. These are used as the geometric constraints to estimate the location of the milled space, as well as to evaluate the deviation from the planned paths. We also use the RANSAC algorithm to obtain the milling depth, and deviation of the milled part, as shown in Algorithm 2. In this step, $n_2$ is 30, $k_2$ is 2000, and $t_2$ is 1.0.

---

**Algorithm 1** RANSAC for fitting the milling path.

---

INPUT:

data—The matched coordinate point $\mathbf{P}_t$ on the current milling path, as well as the milled path.

fitting model—The model for fitting a 3D line:

$$\frac{x - x_0}{l} = \frac{x - y_0}{m} = \frac{x - z_0}{n} \tag{27}$$

where the vector $(l, m, n)$ indicates the direction of the fitted line in the 3D space, $\sqrt{l^2 + m^2 + n^2} = 1$.

evaluation model—the deviation distance from the data point to the fitting line:

$$\varepsilon = \frac{(\mathbf{P}_i - \mathbf{P}_0) \cdot (\mathbf{v}_0 \times (\mathbf{P}_i - \mathbf{P}_0) \times \mathbf{v}_0)}{\|\mathbf{P}_i - \mathbf{P}_0\|} \tag{28}$$

where $\mathbf{P}_0 = (x_0, y_0, z_0)$ and $\mathbf{v}_0$ indicate one point on the fitted line, and the line direction, respectively.

$n_1$—BestNum: Minimum number of data points to estimate model parameters.

$k_1$—Maximum number of iterations allowed in the algorithm.

$t_1$—The threshold value to determine data points that fit well by the above models.

OUTPUT:

bestFit—The parameters for the fitting line: $l, m, n$

---

**Algorithm 2** RANSAC for estimating the milling depth.

---

INPUT

data—The fitting lines of milled paths.

Fitting model—The model for fitting a displace deviation between the planned space and the current milled space:

$$\begin{cases} \Delta n_r = E(R_{i,j} - r_{i,j}) \\ \Delta n_l = E(L_{i,j} - l_{i,j}) \end{cases} \tag{29}$$

where $\Delta n_r$, and $\Delta n_l$ represent the deviations on the $y$-axis and the $z$-axis of the WCS, respectively. $E(\cdot)$ represent the mean function. $R_{i,j}$, and $r_{i,j}$ indicate the $y$-axis components of the estimation and planning value of a path. $L_{i,j}$, and $l_{i,j}$ indicate the $z$-axis component of the estimation and planning value of a path.

Evaluation model—The geometric constrain, as:

$$\varepsilon_s = \sqrt{(R_{i,j} - r_{i,j} - \Delta n_r)^2 + (L_{i,j} - l_{i,j} - \Delta n_l)^2} \tag{30}$$

$n_2$—BestNum: Minimum number of data points to estimate model parameters.

$k_2$—Maximum number of iterations allowed in the algorithm.

$t_2$—The threshold value to determine data points that fit well by the model.

OUTPUT:

bestFit—The deviation between the planning workspace and the actual milled workspace.

---

# 3. Experiments and Results

## 3.1. Simulations of the CT Image–Force Model

In order to depict the milling force to various densities, we built a virtual CT image with the stepped pixel gray level as the milling object. The size was 12.0 mm × 12.0 mm × 6.0 mm. The physical dimension of each voxel was defined as 0.25 mm × 0.25 mm × 0.25 mm. As shown in Figure 9, the grayscale in the image was divided into 10 step intervals from 0 to 1400. This range of grayscale conformed to that of the common CT images. Following the above definition of the $WCS$, a coordinate system was built, where the x-axis was defined by the gradient direction in this CT image.

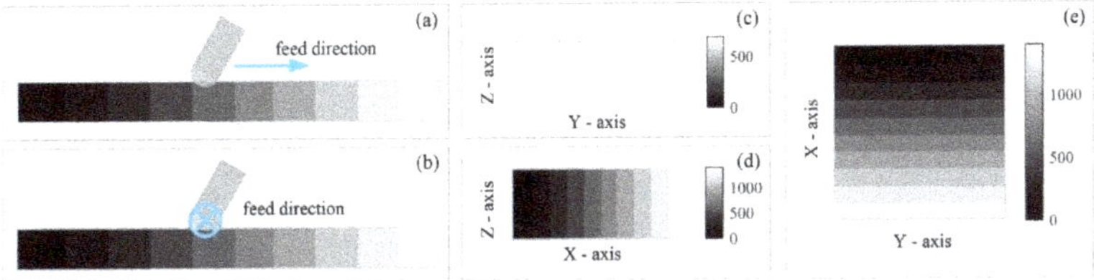


**Figure 9.** Schematic view of milling on one virtual object filled with gray gradient. (**a**) Simulation where milling paths paralleled the direction of the gray gradient, in which the color indicates its grayscale. (**b**) Simulation where milling paths ran vertical to the direction of the gray gradient, in which the color indicates its grayscale. (**c**) Front view of the virtual object. (**d**) Side view of the virtual object. (**e**) Top view of the virtual object.

It was assumed that the milling feed rate was 0.5 mm/s, the grinding speed was 800 $RPM$, the inclined angle of the cutter was 30°, the helix angle of the chisel edge was 30°, the one-layer milling depth was 0.8 mm, the number of the flutter was 4, the distance from the edge $h$ was 0.25 mm, and the step angle of the axial angel of cutting edges was 4°. The sampling frequency of the cutting force sensor was 20 Hz. In this simulation, the milling parameters and model parameters are listed in Table 1.

**Table 1.** Milling parameters in the CT image–force model simulations.

| Parameters | Symbol | Value |
|---|---|---|
| Feed rate | $v_d$ | 0.5 mm/s |
| Spinning speed | $N$ | 800 RPM |
| Milling depth | $d$ | 0.8 mm |
| Step distance | $w$ | 2.8 mm |
| Number of the flutter | $n_t$ | 4 |
| Radius of the cutter | $r_t$ | 2 mm |
| Helix angle of the cutter | | 30° |
| Inclined angle of the cutter | | 30° |
| Step angle of the axial angle | $d\theta_m$ | 4° |
| Distance between cutting edges | $h$ | 0.25 mm |
| Sampling frequency | | 20 Hz |
| Number of milling layers | | 3 |
| Number of paths on every layer | | 4 |
| Upper normalized parameter | $m_{\max}$ | 1400 |
| Lower normalized parameter | $m_{\min}$ | 80 |

We adopt the parameters in Table 2 for the force coefficients of **Equation** (16). In addition, it was assumed that the initial phase of the cutter on each milling path was random. Then, we obtained the milling forces $F_x$, $F_y$, $F_z$, and $M_z$ in the $i$-MCCS, as shown in Figure 10. The instantaneous gray was quantified by the average of the gray value of image voxels contacting with the valid micro-edges on the CWE area.

**Table 2.** Coefficients of the milling model.

| Symbol | Value |
|---|---|
| $K_{re}$ | $-1203.1\ \mathrm{N/mm^2}$ |
| $K_{ac}$ | $-105.2\ \mathrm{N/mm^2}$ |
| $K_{tc}$ | $2142.1\ \mathrm{N/mm^2}$ |
| $K_{te}$ | $-75\ \mathrm{N/mm^2}$ |
| $K_{ae}$ | $22.4\ \mathrm{N/mm^2}$ |
| $K_{te}$ | $-199.1\ \mathrm{N/mm^2}$ |
| $\mu$ | 1.815 |

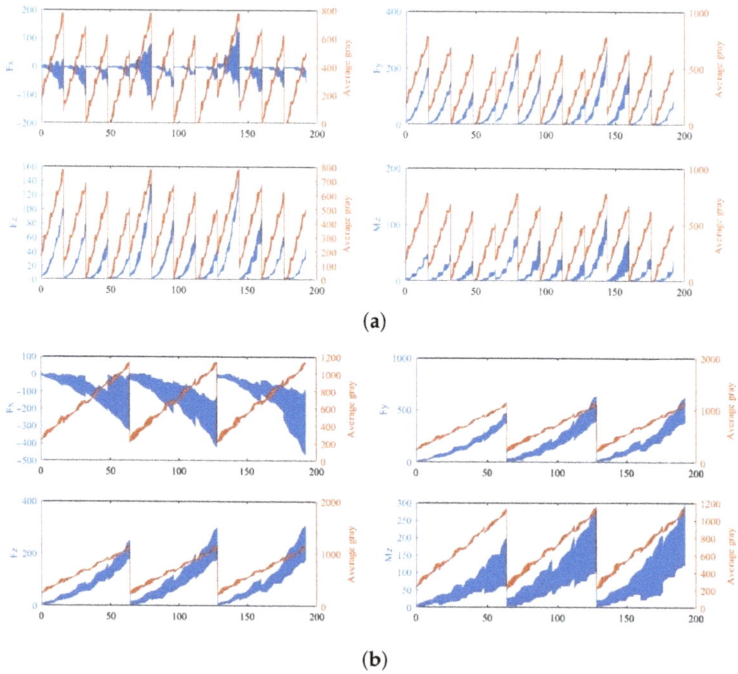

**Figure 10.** (**a**) Milling forces subject to the paths along the gray-gradient direction. (**b**) Milling force responding to the trajectories vertical to the gray gradient. The blue line depicts the prediction, while the red line depicts the gray average of the milling path in the CT image. The horizontal axis indicates the sequential order of the sampled predictions.

### 3.2. *Signal Analysis on the Laminar Milling*

According to studies [39,40], although the bone strength of humans is different from that of animals, the structural and functional properties of bone tissue are conserved. Animal experiments serve as the foundations for human trials in the field of bone tissue injury and repair [41]. Therefore, three groups of robot-assisted laminar milling experiments were conducted to verify the relationship between the bone density distribution and the milling force signal. Of these, two groups were conducted on porcine thoracic and lumbar laminas, respectively. The third group of experiments was on the plastic lumbar made by 3D printing technology (Material: R4600, Manufacturer: Wenext Technology Co., Ltd., Shenzhen, China). Different from porcine laminas, the plastic is profiled with uniform density. Every group of experiments was repeated three times. The milling force signal was collected during the operations. Through the spatial transformation as shown in **Equation** (31), we can obtain the milling force in the *i*-MCCS through the force/torque sensor.

$$^{m}\mathbf{F} = {}^{m}_{f}Ad \cdot {}^{f}\mathbf{F} \tag{31}$$

where ${}^{m}_{f}Ad$ is the adjoint transformation matrix from the robotic flange coordinate system to the *i*-MCCS, and ${}^{f}\mathbf{F}$ represents the force/torque data in the format of the vector $(f_x, f_y, f_z; m_x, m_y, m_z)^T$.

Following the proposed milling strategy, a UR 5e robot arm with a six-axis force/torque sensor was used to assist the milling operation, as shown in Figure 11a. During the milling operations, the milling tool was constrained by the guide as the end effector of the robot arm. The spinning speed of the cutter was manually controlled. In these experiments, we adopt the bi-direction milling during the bone milling. The path planning is listed in Table 3, where $n_{pos}$ indicates the number of paths in the positive direction, $n_{neg}$ indicates the number of paths in the negative direction, and $n_{data}$ indicates the length of every data sequence. Moreover, the milling depth was 0.6 mm, and the feed rate was about 1 mm/s. It was noticed that the cutter did not contact the object during the first-layer milling procedure.

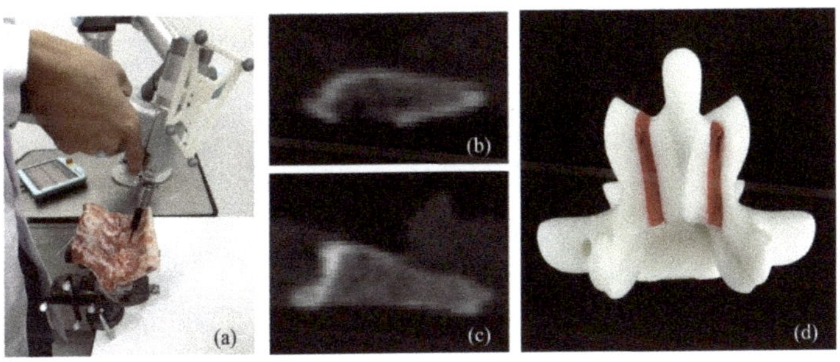


**Figure 11.** Experimental platform of the robot-assisted laminar milling and the experimental objects. (**a**) Robot-assisted milling operation. (**b**) CT image of porcine laminas. (**c**) CT image of porcine laminas. (**d**) The plastic model is made by 3D printing technology.

**Table 3.** Plan for the milling experiments.

| Objects | $n_{pos}$ | $n_{neg}$ | $n_{data}$ | Penetration? |
|---|---|---|---|---|
| Thoracic | 9 | 9 | 67 | Yes |
| Lumbar | 10 | 9 | 42 | Yes |
| Plastic | 16 | 16 | 51 | No |

Correlation analysis was used to determine the relation between the milling force signal and bone density. As shown in **Equation** (32), we used the Pearson correlation coefficient to quantify the similarity among the milling sequences subject to different paths on the same object. The result can be written by a matrix. The correlation matrix was shown in the format of a figure, as shown in Figure 12. The diagonal elements in the correlation matrix represented the autocorrelation coefficient, and all of them were scaled to 1.0. If the correlation coefficient of two sequences was below 0.4, their relationship was regarded to be independent.

$$\mathbf{R}(i,j) = corr(\mathbf{s}_i, \mathbf{s}_j) \tag{32}$$

where $1 \le i \le n_{seq}$, and $1 \le j \le n_{seq}$. $n_{seq}$ was the sum of the positive direction paths and the negative direction paths. $\mathbf{s}_i$ and $\mathbf{s}_j$ were the *i*-th and *j*-th sequences.

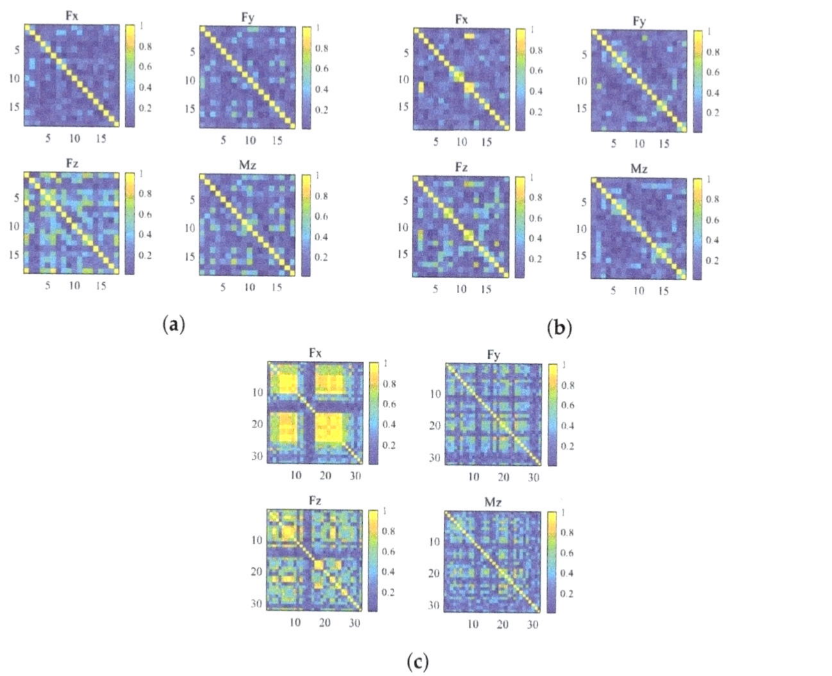


**Figure 12.** (**a**) Correlation relationship among the milling force sequences subject to the thoracic lamina. (**b**) Correlation relationship among the milling force sequence subject to the lumbar lamina. (**c**) Correlation relationship among the milling force sequence subject to the plastic model.

### 3.3. Functional Simulations of the Position Estimation

The commercial software MATLAB R2021b was used to conduct the functional simulation of the proposed tip position estimation on a computer (CPU: Intel i5-1135G7, RAM: 16.0 GB). Following the anatomical model in the commercial software Complete Anatomy [42], we created the segmentation annotation on the lamina in CT images using the open-source software ITK-SNAP [43]. An open-source library MNI2FS (MNI2FS: high-resolution surface rendering of MNI registered volumes) in MATLAB was used to extract the bone structure information, segmentation, and image information from the medical image files. In MATLAB, the point cloud method was used to demonstrate the segmented lamina and vertebra. The segmented lamina was marked by a frame. Further, we manually made the plan of the milling paths, as shown in Figure 13.

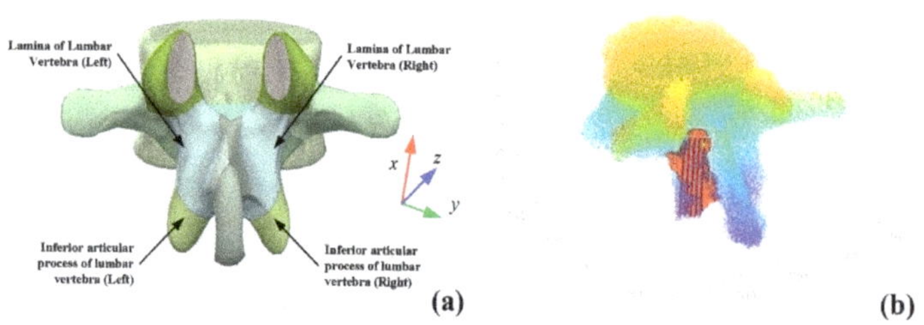


**Figure 13.** (**a**) Schematic view of the lumbar vertebra [42]. (**b**) The point cloud of a lumbar vertebra, where blue lines represent the planned paths, the red point represents the annotated lamina, and the yellow star represents the starting point of vertebra grinding. The color of the point cloud of the spinal bone indicates high information.

Milling efficiency is affected by the direction of feed motion. Thus, we employed the milling strategy to ensure that valid milling interactions occur during the motion along the positive direction. The milling parameters in Table 1 and the force coefficients in Table 2 were also utilized to generate the milling prediction sequences. Several factors, like bone motions, sensor noises, and unstable motions of a cutting tool, can introduce disturbance. Referring to the literature [7,44–46], it was assumed that the deviations in the simulated milling paths were limited and random. Moreover, the unstable feed rate of the milling cutter was modeled in a sine function.

In this simulation, nine sets of CT images with lumbar vertebra were randomly chosen from the VerSe dataset [47], including verse 503, 507, 620, 704, 714, 718, 756, 762, and 835. These cases and the CT images were from different centers. Every vertebra was profiled with different shapes, as well as the size of the voxel in the CT images being different. We chose randomly from lumbar vertebras in every case. Correspondingly, the surgical paths were different, as shown in Table 4.

**Table 4.** Path planning and initial deviations for the simulation cases.

| No. | Layers | Paths | Deviations (rad, rad, rad; mm, mm, mm) | Incline Angle (°) |
|---|---|---|---|---|
| 503 | 16 | 4 | 0.014, 0.011, 0.011; −0.65, −1.23,−0.27 | 1.19 |
| 507 | 11 | 5 | 0.021, 0.001, 0.010; 0.003, 0.24, −0.24 | 1.34 |
| 620 | 12 | 4 | 0.007, 0.004, 0.003; −0.12, −0.02, −0.16 | 0.48 |
| 704 | 11 | 3 | 0.005, 0.021, 0.024; 1.80, 0.69, −0.40 | 1.87 |
| 714 | 9 | 4 | 0.004, 0.013, 0.029; −0.67, −1.47, 1.17 | 1.86 |
| 718 | 10 | 5 | 0.060, 0.018, 0.007; −1.64, −1.87, 0.37 | 3.58 |
| 756 | 11 | 4 | 0.005, 0.013, 0.025; 0.65, −0.84, 1.26 | 1.65 |
| 835 | 15 | 7 | 0.026, 0.020, 0.015; 0.71, 0.09, 0.25 | 1.88 |

The estimation deviation can be divided into two parts, including the distance deviation and the milling depth deviation. Through a comparison of the similarity calculations, we verified the validity of the proposed estimation. The Pearson correlation was used to take the place of the DTW algorithm. The length of the data sequence was 15 herein. The errors of the tip position estimations are shown in Figure 14. The estimation error based on the correction coefficient was larger than that based on the optical DTW distance.

In the case of VerSe 762, the left lamina inside the second lumbar vertebra was narrow, so we only planned two paths on every layer, and 11 layers. In this group of simulations, the number of data for the fitting model was re-defined by eight in Algorithm 2. The initial deviations are listed in Table 5. Correspondingly, the estimation errors are shown in Figure 15. The means of the estimation error were all less than 1 mm.

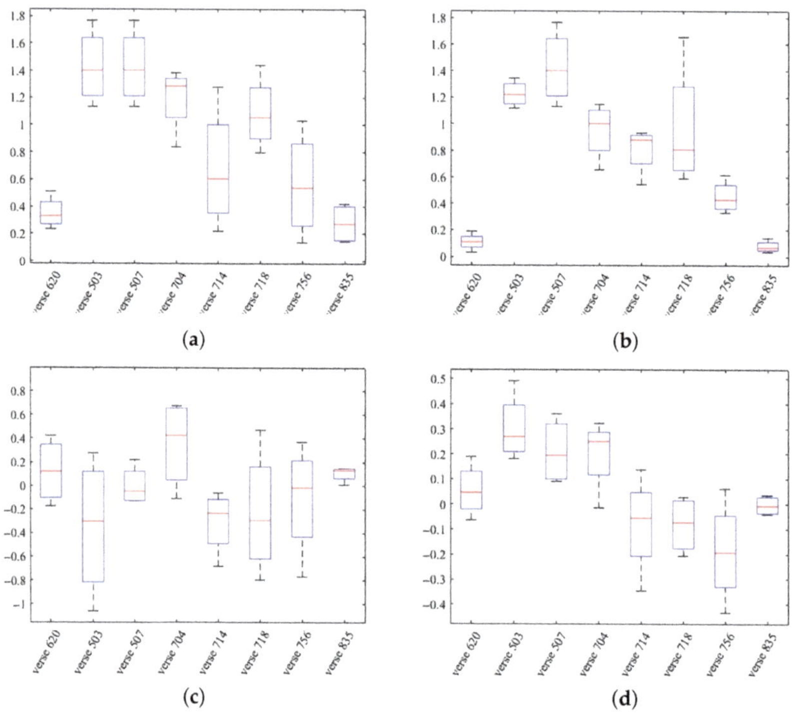

**Figure 14.** Estimation errors of the tip position. (**a**) Error of the distance deviation based on the correlation coefficient. (**b**) Error of the distance deviation based on the DTW distance. (**c**) Errors of milling depth estimation based on the correlation coefficient. (**d**) Errors of milling depth estimation based on the DTW distance. The unit of errors is millimeters.

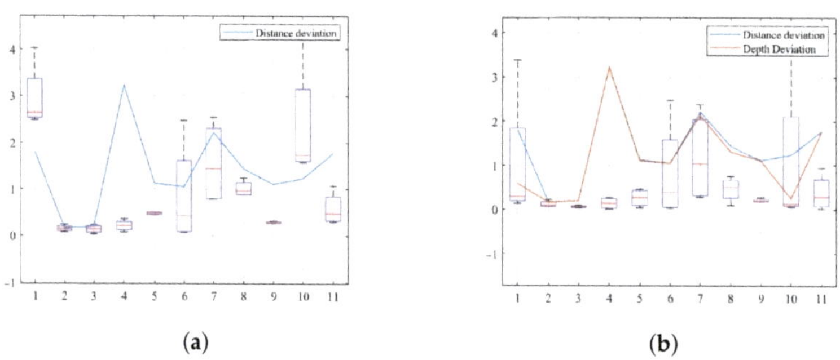

**Figure 15.** Estimation errors of simulations for Verse 762. (**a**) Absolute distance deviation. (**b**) Absolute milling depth deviation. The unit of the deviation is millimeters.

**Table 5.** Random deviation in the case of VerSe 762.

| No. | Deviations | Incline Angle (°) |
|---|---|---|
| 1 | 0.065, 0.024, 0.030; 0.43, 2.48, −0.24 | 4.35 |
| 2 | 0.054, 0.033, 0.024; −0.32, −0.01, 0.20 | 3.86 |
| 3 | 0.069, −0.000, 0.019; −0.35, 0.04, −0.21 | 4.11 |
| 4 | 0.053, 0.021, 0.022; 0.07, −0.18, −2.39 | 3.53 |
| 5 | 0.064, 0.010, 0.009; −1.43, 0.48, 0.97 | 3.78 |
| 6 | 0.055, 0.019, 0.022; 0.53, −0.02, 1.02 | 3.56 |
| 7 | 0.053, 0.029, 0.034; −1.24, −1.07, −1.43 | 3.97 |
| 8 | 0.009, 0.004, 0.004; 1.37, −0.89, −1.02 | 0.59 |
| 9 | 0.056, 0.031, 0.017; −0.77, 0.22, 1.19 | 3.77 |
| 10 | 0.064, 0.028, 0.029; 1.61, 1.74, 0.47 | 4.33 |
| 11 | 0.030, 0.003, 0.013; 1.36, −0.37, 1.43 | 1.89 |

In the case of VerSe 620, we chose the left lamina of the second lumbar vertebra as the target. In this case, we planned 12 milling layers, and four paths on every layer. The path planning and the pre-defined deviations are listed in Table 4. The corresponding milling predictions are shown in Appendix B. When the BestNum in Algorithm 2 was 30, the estimation errors based on the correlation coefficient and the DTW distance are shown in Appendix C.

We can estimate the tip position when the number of milled paths was more than the BestNum in Algorithm 2. Furthermore, when the BestNum values were 20, 25, 30, and 32, the estimation errors corresponding to various conditions are shown in Figure 16.

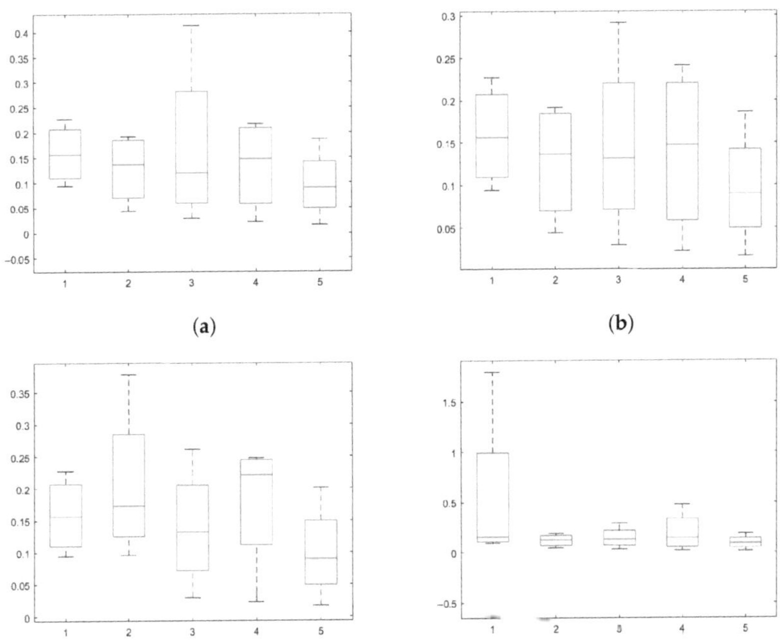

(a) (b) (c) (d)

**Figure 16.** Estimation error in the case of Verse 620. (**a**) BestNum20. (**b**) BestNum25. (**c**) BestNum30. (**d**) BestNum32. The unit of the errors is millimeters.

Due to bone motion and the deformation of the cutter, the feed rate was unstable during the operation. We used a sine function to model the unstable feed rate. With the amplitudes of 0.05 mm/s, 0.10 mm/s, 0.15 mm/s, 0.20 mm/s, and 0.30 mm/s, five groups of 0.5 mm/s feed rates were used. The initial phase of the milling cutter, as well as the deviation, was also random. Subject to different amplitudes, the estimation errors are shown in Figure 17. The results showed that the estimation error was less than 1.0 mm, and the error based on the DTW algorithm was less than 0.5 mm.

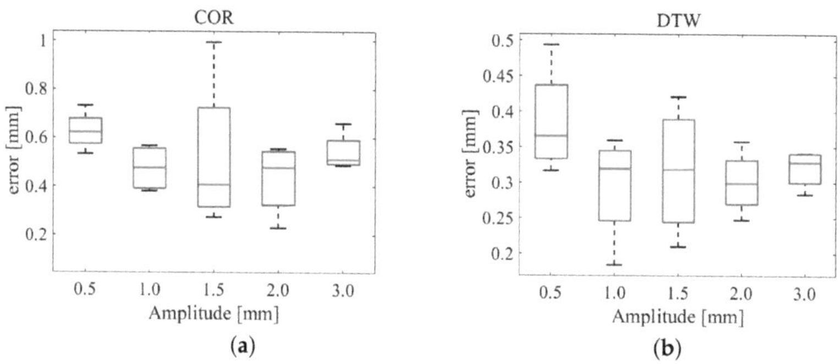


**Figure 17.** Estimation errors subject to various feed rates. (**a**) Estimation error based on Pierre's relevant analysis. (**b**) Estimation error based on the DTW algorithm.

## 4. Discussion

In other works, the principle of state recognition for spinal surgery is to detect the signal relieved when the cutter breaks through the second bone layer. As mentioned earlier, due to the difference in the bone properties of various specimens, the threshold for identified bone states is different. The focus of this paper is to address this problem. We take advantage of intra-operative CT images to predict the milling states. Then, we perform position estimation based on the similarity mapping between the predicted and real-time force signals by using the machine learning algorithm and the iterative algorithm. Therefore, we do not employ neural networks or deep learning algorithms in this work. Thus, the proposed method is not dependent on data samples, and does not require extensive training.

In the proposed CT image–force model, the force coefficients in **Equation** (16) should be obtained by a complex calibration process [23,30], whereas it is impossible to predict the milling force without loss of accuracy. In this work, through the prior knowledge gained from the CT image, we prefer to obtain the time-domain characteristics of milling forces rather than precious results. Moreover, the principle of position estimation is based on the similarity mapping of time-domain signal features. Various groups of CT images from the VerSe dataset were utilized to verify the validation of the proposed estimation method. The resolutions of CT images from different centers and CT devices are different. The results showed that the estimation method can adapt to CT images from different sources and CT devices.

To eliminate the influences of uncertain factors, such as bone motion, signal noise, signal synchronization, and so on, we make use of the DTW algorithm in the proposed framework. Compared with the linear algorithm, the usage of the DTW algorithm can improve estimation accuracy. The results showed that estimation accuracy can be up to the sub-millimeter level. However, the estimation is also affected by the step distances between the planning paths.

Time efficiency will degenerate with the increase in the milling volume of the surgical task, owing to the workload of the mapping calculation. In addition, time efficiency is affected by the length of the segmented data sequences. When the length is too long, the noise can affect the accuracy of the similarity matching. When the length is too short, the amount of location information is too little to generate the effective feature. Currently, application of the proposed framework is limited by the time-efficient performance.

## 5. Conclusions

This work has established a framework for state estimation of the intra-operative tip position during laminar grinding. Based on our proposed CT image–force model, we have demonstrated that prior knowledge of milling states, subject to specific surgical planning, can be extracted from pre-operative CT images. By integrating real-time milling force signals with this model, we have successfully estimated the tip position with improved robustness and accuracy, as evidenced by our simulation results. The DTW algorithm and the RANSCA algorithm have been effectively integrated to enhance performance; the estimation error is less than 1 mm, achieving an accuracy level up to the sub-millimeter. We employ many cases with different image resolutions from the VerSe dataset to verify that the proposed method is robust.

In future, our focus will shift towards optimizing the time efficiency of our framework from aspects of estimation algorithms. We plan to conduct laminar grinding experiments to empirically validate the proposed framework, aiming to assess and refine its performance under clinical conditions.

**Author Contributions:** Conceptualization, J.L. and G.Z.; formal analysis, J.L.; funding acquisition, J.L. and G.Z.; investigation, J.L.; methodology, J.L. and G.Z.; project administration, J.L. and G.Z.; resources, J.L. and G.Z.; supervision, J.L. and G.Z.; validation, J.L.; writing—original draft, J.L. and W.Y.; writing—review and editing, J.L. All authors have read and agreed to the published version of the manuscript.

**Funding:** This research was supported partially by the National Science Foundation of China (62203295 and U20A20199).

**Institutional Review Board Statement:** The study was conducted in accordance with the Declaration of Helsinki, and approved by the Institutional Review Board of the School of Biomedical Engineering, Shanghai Jiao Tong University, China (Approval No E20230356C, approved on 19 December 2023).

**Informed Consent Statement:** Not applicable.

**Data Availability Statement:** Data are contained within the article.

**Conflicts of Interest:** The authors declare no conflicts of interest.

## Abbreviations

The following abbreviations are used in this manuscript:

| | |
|---|---|
| CWE | Cutter–workpiece engagement |
| DTW | Dynamic time wrapping |
| $i$-MCCS | Instantaneous milling cutter coordinate system |
| $l$-WCS | Local working coordinate system |
| MCCS | Milling cutter coordinate system |
| RANSAC | Random sample consensus |
| WCS | Workpiece coordinate system |

## Appendix A. Equations for Boundary Curves of CWE

${}^{M}\mathbf{P}_{i,j}$ indicates a point on the surface of CWE in the case of the $j$-th path on the $i$-th layer in the workpiece coordinate system (WCS), and it is written as:

$$ {}^{W}\mathbf{P}_{i,j} \in \{ (x_{i,j}, y_{i,j}, z_{i,j}) | s.t. \} \tag{A1} $$

where $s.t.$ denotes the constrain condition subject to different paths.

(a) The constrain equations that model the boundary curves of the CWE area in the case of the first path on the top layer are as follows:

$$ \begin{cases} x_{1,1} \geq 0 \\ z_{1,1} \leq 0 \end{cases} \tag{A2} $$

(b) The constrain equations that model the boundary curves of the CWE area in the case of the other paths on the top layer are as follows:

$$ \begin{cases} x_{1,j} \geq 0 \\ z_{1,j} \leq 0 \\ \sqrt{\left(y_{1,j} - \widehat{y}_{1,j-1}\right)^2 + \left(z_{1,j} - \widehat{z}_{1,j-1}\right)^2} \geq R \end{cases} \tag{A3} $$

where $\widehat{z}_{i,j}$ denotes the projection decomposition of the centroid of the ball-end cutter along the $j$-th path of the $i$-th layer in the WCS.

(c) The constrain equations that model the boundary curves of the CWE area in the case of the first path on the other layers are as follows:

$$ \begin{cases} x_{i,1} \geq 0 \\ \sqrt{\left(y_{i,1} - \widehat{y}_{i-1,1}\right)^2 + \left(z_{i,1} - \widehat{z}_{i-1,j}\right)^2} \geq R \\ \sqrt{\left(y_{i,1} - \widehat{y}_{i-1,2}\right)^2 + \left(z_{i,1} - \widehat{z}_{i-1,2}\right)^2} \geq R \end{cases} \tag{A4} $$

(d) The constrain equations that model the boundary curves of the CWE area in the case of the middle paths on the other layers are as follows:

$$ \begin{cases} x_{i,j} \geq 0 \\ \sqrt{\left(y_{i,j} - \widehat{y}_{i,j-1}\right)^2 + \left(z_{i,j} - \widehat{z}_{i,j-1}\right)^2} \geq R \\ \sqrt{\left(y_{i,j} - \widehat{y}_{i-1,j}\right)^2 + \left(z_{i,j} - \widehat{z}_{i-1,j}\right)^2} \geq R \\ \sqrt{\left(y_{i,j} - \widehat{y}_{i-1,j+1}\right)^2 + \left(z_{i,j} - \widehat{z}_{i-1,j+1}\right)^2} \geq R \end{cases} \tag{A5} $$

(e) The constrain equations that model the boundary curves of the CWE area in the case of the last path on the other layers are as follows:

$$ \begin{cases} x_{i,j} \geq 0 \\ \sqrt{\left(y_{i,j} - \widehat{y}_{i,j-1}\right)^2 + \left(z_{i,j} - \widehat{z}_{i,j-1}\right)^2} \geq R \\ \sqrt{\left(y_{i,j} - \widehat{y}_{i-1,j}\right)^2 + \left(z_{i,j} - \widehat{z}_{i-1,j-1}\right)^2} \geq R \end{cases} \tag{A6} $$

## Appendix B. Relationships Between Cutting Forces and Bone Density

In the simulation case of VerSe 620, the milling force sequences and grayscale sequences subject to the planning path and the simulation path are shown in Figures A1–A5. The horizontal axis indicates the sequential order of the sample points. In this section, every groups of figures consists of 48 subplots subject to the order number of the milling layer and the order number of the path on one layer. For instance, the subject in the $i$-th row of the $j$-th column depicts sequences of the $i$-th path on the $j$-th layer.

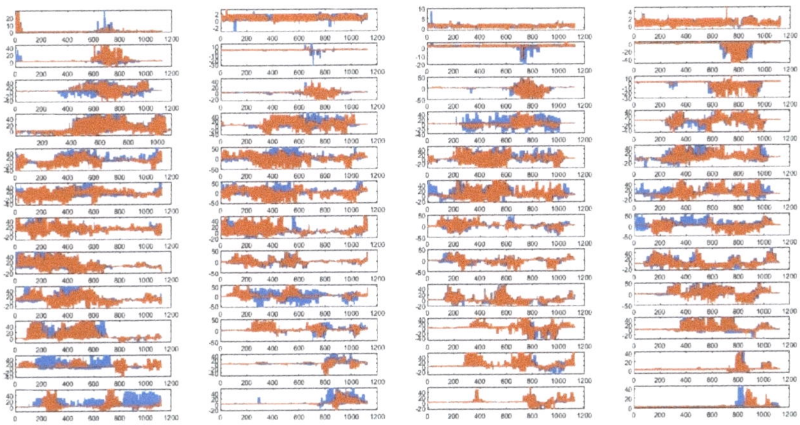

**Figure A1.** Sequences of milling force $F_x$. Red line indicates predictions on the planned paths, and blue line indicates intra-operative sequence in the simulation.

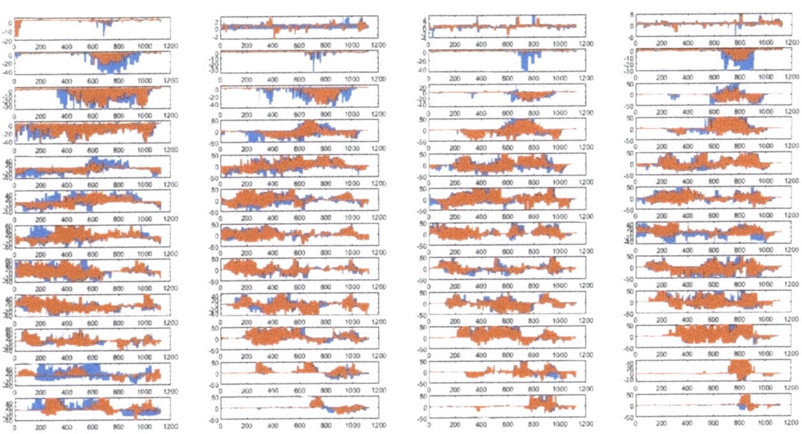

**Figure A2.** Sequences of milling force $F_y$. Red line indicates predictions on the planned paths, and blue line indicates intra-operative sequence in the simulation.

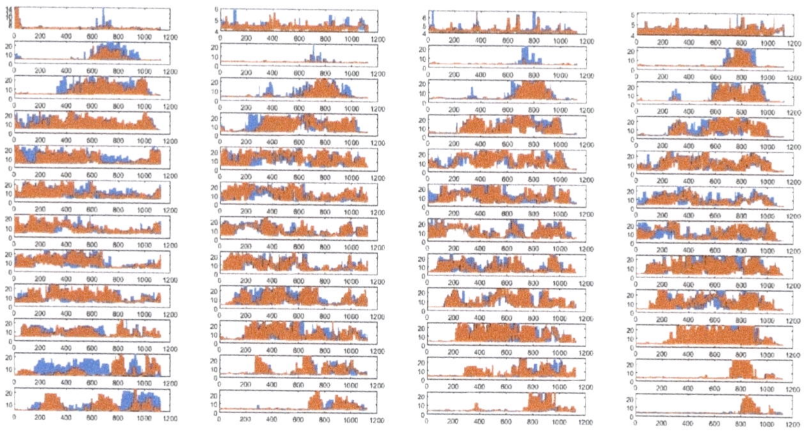

**Figure A3.** Sequences of milling force $F_z$. Red line indicates predictions on the planned paths, and blue line indicates intra-operative sequence in the simulation.

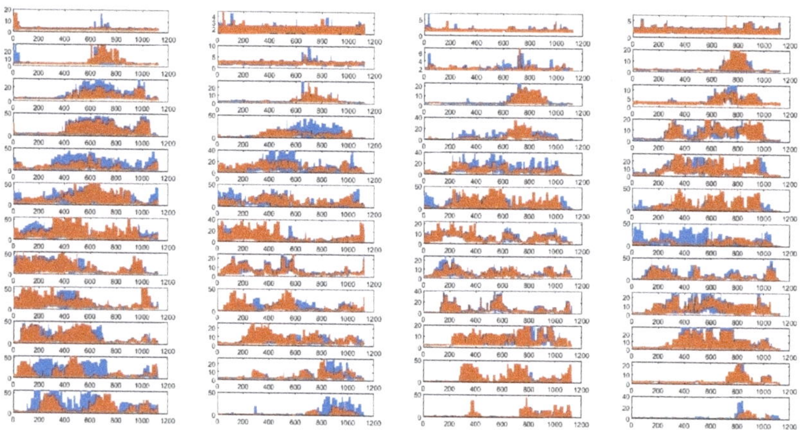

**Figure A4.** Sequences of milling force $M_z$. Red line indicates predictions on the planned paths, and blue line indicates intra-operative sequence in the simulation.

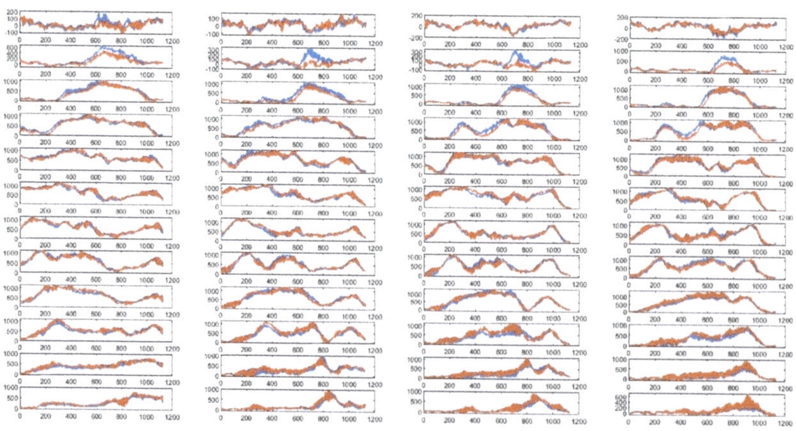

**Figure A5.** Sequences of grayscale values of real-time contact. Red line indicates gray value on plan paths, and blue line indicates intra-operative sequence in the simulation.

## Appendix C. State Estimation on the Milled Path

In the simulation case of VerSe 620, the distance deviation of every path was estimated from four channels of the milling forces. The errors of every path are shown in Figures A6–A9.

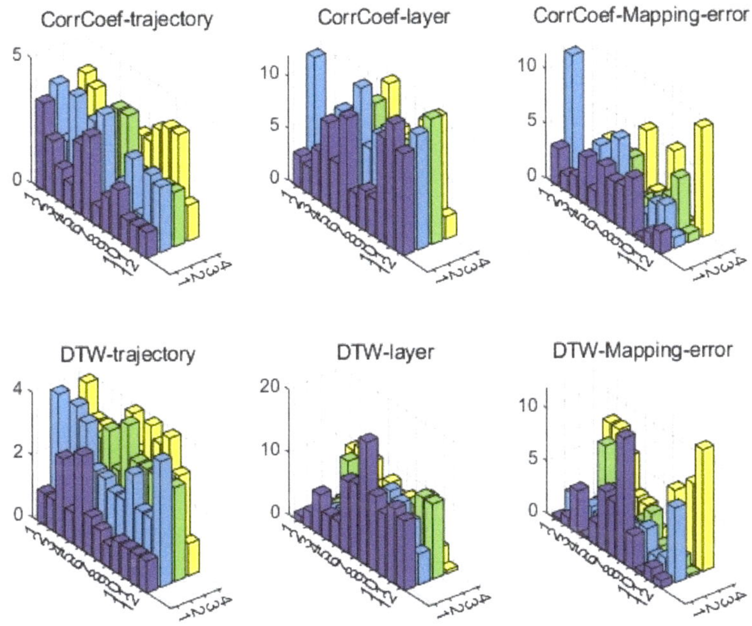


**Figure A6.** Errors of estimations based on $F_x$ sequences.

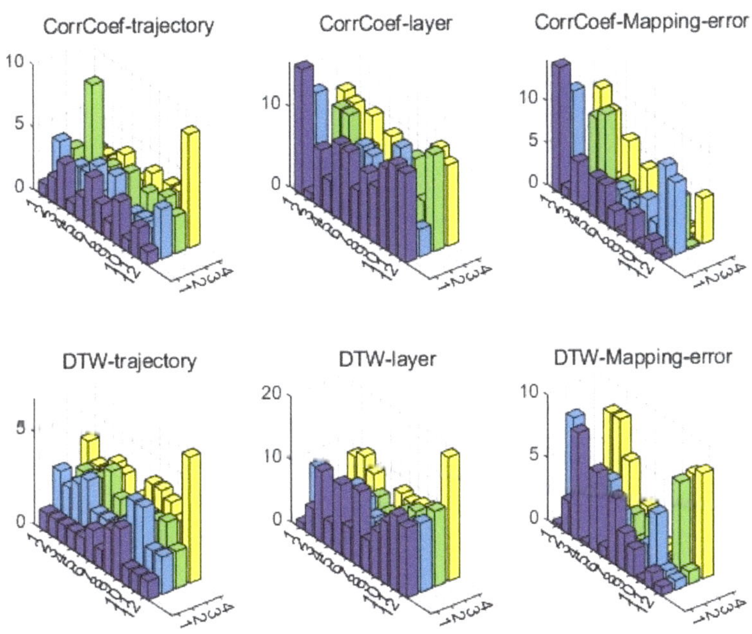


**Figure A7.** Errors of estimations based on $F_y$ sequences.

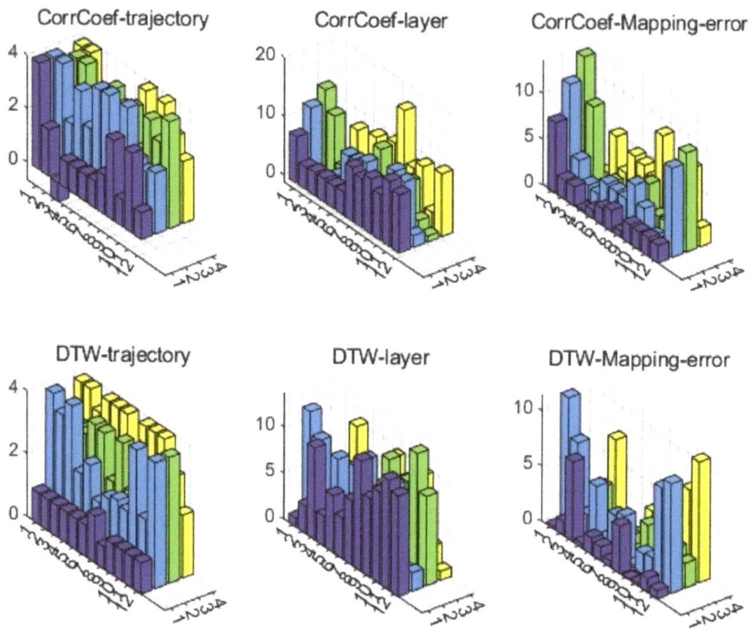


**Figure A8.** Errors of estimations based on $F_z$ sequences.

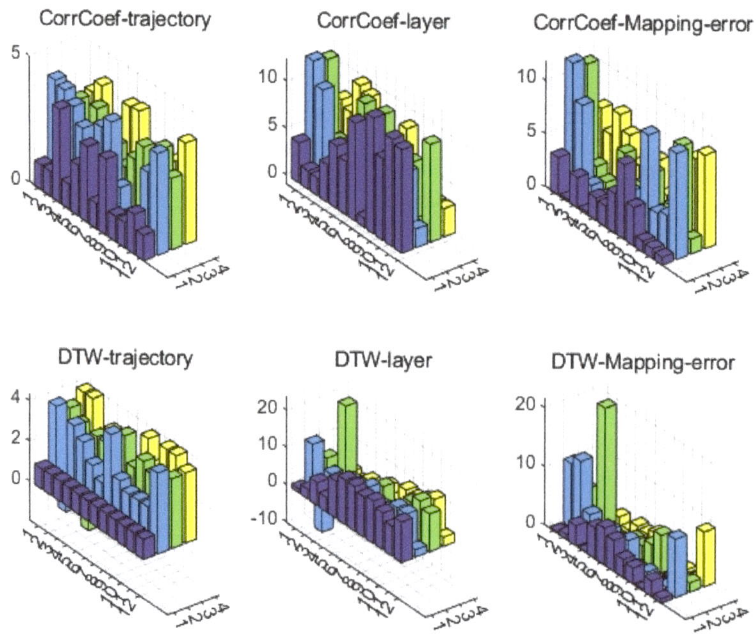


**Figure A9.** Errors of estimations based on $M_z$ sequences.

## References


1. Ratliff, J.K.; Cooper, P.R. Cervical Laminoplasty: A Critical Review. *J. Neurosurg.-Spine* **2003**, *98*, 230–238. [CrossRef] [PubMed]
2. Katz, J.N.; Harris, M.B. Lumbar Spinal Stenosis. *N. Engl. J. Med.* **2008**, *358*, 818–825. [CrossRef]

3. Weinstein, J.N.; Tosteson, T.D.; Lurie, J.D.; Tosteson, A.N.A.; Blood, E.; Hanscom, B.; Herkowitz, H.; Cammisa, F.; Albert, T.; Boden, S.D.; et al. Surgical versus Nonsurgical Therapy for Lumbar Spinal Stenosis. *N. Engl. J. Med.* **2008**, *358*, 794–810. [CrossRef] [PubMed]
4. Jin, H.; Hu, Y.; Tian, W.; Zhang, P.; Zhang, J.; Li, B. Safety Analysis and Control of a Robotic Spinal Surgical System. *Mechatronics* **2014**, *24*, 55–65. [CrossRef]
5. Fan, L.; Gao, P.; Zhao, B.; Sun, Y.; Xin, X.; Hu, Y.; Liu, S.; Zhang, J. Safety Control Strategy for Vertebral Lamina Milling Task. *CAAI Trans. Intell. Technol.* **2016**, *1*, 249–258. [CrossRef]
6. Wang, J.; Liu, H.; Ke, J.; Hu, L.; Zhang, S.; Yang, B.; Sun, S.; Guo, N.; Ma, F. Image-Guided Cochlear Access by Non-Invasive Registration: A Cadaveric Feasibility Study. *Sci. Rep.* **2020**, *10*, 18318. [CrossRef]
7. O'Connor, T.E.; O'Hehir, M.M.; Khan, A.; Mao, J.Z.; Levy, L.C.; Mullin, J.P.; Pollina, J. Mazor X Stealth Robotic Technology: A Technical Note. *World Neurosurg.* **2021**, *145*, 435–442. [CrossRef]
8. Mao, J.Z.; Soliman, M.A.R.; Karamian, B.A.; Khan, A.; Fritz, A.G.; Avasthi, N.; DiMaria, S.; Levy, B.R.; O'Connor, T.E.; Schroeder, G.; et al. Anatomical and Technical Considerations of Robot-Assisted Cervical Pedicle Screw Placement: A Cadaveric Study. *Glob. Spine J.* **2022**, 219256822110684. [CrossRef] [PubMed]
9. Puangmali, P.; Jetdumronglerd, S.; Wongratanaphisan, T.; Cole, M.O.T. Sensorless Stepwise Breakthrough Detection Technique for Safe Surgical Drilling of Bone. *Mechatronics* **2020**, *65*, 102306. [CrossRef]
10. Li, Z.; Yu, G.; Jiang, S.; Hu, L.; Li, W. Robot-Assisted Laminectomy in Spinal Surgery: A Systematic Review. *Ann. Transl. Med.* **2021**, *9*, 715. [CrossRef]
11. Al-Abdullah, K.I.; Lim, C.P.; Najdovski, Z.; Yassin, W. A Model-Based Bone Milling State Identification Method via Force Sensing for a Robotic Surgical System. *Int. J. Med. Robot.* **2019**, *15*, e1989. [CrossRef] [PubMed]
12. Zakeri, V.; Hodgson, A.J. Automatic Identification of Hard and Soft Bone Tissues by Analyzing Drilling Sounds. *IEEE/ACM Trans. Audio Speech Lang. Process.* **2019**, *27*, 404–414. [CrossRef]
13. Dai, Y.; Xue, Y.; Zhang, J. Milling State Identification Based on Vibration Sense of a Robotic Surgical System. *IEEE Trans. Ind. Electron.* **2016**, *63*, 6184–6193. [CrossRef]
14. Torun, Y.; Öztürk, A. A New Breakthrough Detection Method for Bone Drilling in Robotic Orthopedic Surgery with Closed-Loop Control Approach. *Ann. Biomed. Eng.* **2020**, *48*, 1218–1229. [CrossRef] [PubMed]
15. Qu, H.; Geng, B.; Chen, B.; Zhang, J.; Yang, Y.; Hu, L.; Zhao, Y. Force Perception and Bone Recognition of Vertebral Lamina Milling by Robot-Assisted Ultrasonic Bone Scalpel Based on Backpropagation Neural Network. *IEEE Access* **2021**, *9*, 52101–52112. [CrossRef]
16. Jiang, Z.; Qi, X.; Sun, Y.; Hu, Y.; Zahnd, G.; Zhang, J. Cutting Depth Monitoring Based on Milling Force for Robot-Assisted Laminectomy. *IEEE Trans. Automat. Sci. Eng.* **2020**, *17*, 2–14. [CrossRef]
17. Xia, G.; Zhang, L.; Dai, Y.; Xue, Y.; Zhang, J. Vertebral Lamina State Estimation in Robotic Bone Milling Process via Vibration Signals Fusion. *IEEE Trans. Instrum. Meas.* **2022**, *71*, 1–11. [CrossRef]
18. Lee, J.; Gozen, B.A.; Ozdoganlar, O.B. Modeling and Experimentation of Bone Drilling Forces. *J. Biomech.* **2012**, *45*, 1076–1083. [CrossRef]
19. Pandey, R.K.; Panda, S.S. Modelling and Optimization of Temperature in Orthopaedic Drilling: An in Vitro Study. *Acta. Bioeng. Biomech.* **2014**, *16*, 107–116. [PubMed]
20. Pandey, R.K.; Panda, S.S. Optimization of Bone Drilling Using Taguchi Methodology Coupled with Fuzzy Based Desirability Function Approach. *J. Intell. Manuf.* **2015**, *26*, 1121–1129. [CrossRef]
21. Mou, W.; Zhu, S.; Zhu, M.; Han, L.; Jiang, L. A Prediction Model of Cutting Force about Ball End Milling for Sculptured Surface. *Math. Probl. Eng.* **2020**, *2020*, 1–15. [CrossRef]
22. Lee, P.; Altintaş, Y. Prediction of Ball-End Milling Forces from Orthogonal Cutting Data. *Int. J. Mach. Tools Manuf.* **1996**, *36*, 1059–1072. [CrossRef]
23. Wei, Z.C.; Guo, M.L.; Wang, M.J.; Li, S.Q.; Wang, J. Prediction of Cutting Force for Ball End Mill in Sculptured Surface Based on Analytic Model of CWE and ICCE. *Mach. Sci. Technol.* **2019**, *23*, 688–711. [CrossRef]
24. Sui, J.; Sugita, N.; Ishii, K.; Harada, K.; Mitsuishi, M. Mechanistic Modeling of Bone-Drilling Process with Experimental Validation. *J. Mater. Process. Technol.* **2014**, *214*, 1018–1026. [CrossRef]
25. Li, L.; Yang, S.; Peng, W.; Ding, H.; Wang, G. A CT Image-Based Virtual Sensing Method to Estimate Bone Drilling Force for Surgical Robots. *IEEE Trans. Biomed. Eng.* **2022**, *69*, 871–881. [CrossRef] [PubMed]
26. Schreiber, J.J.; Anderson, P.A.; Rosas, H.G.; Buchholz, A.L.; Au, A.G. Hounsfield Units for Assessing Bone Mineral Density and Strength: A Tool for Osteoporosis Management. *J. Bone Joint Surg. Am.* **2011**, *93*, 1057–1063. [CrossRef] [PubMed]
27. Carter, D.R.; Hayes, W.C. The Compressive Behavior of Bone as a Two-Phase Porous Structure. *J. Bone Joint Surg. Am.* **1977**, *59*, 954–962. [CrossRef]
28. Williamson, T.M.; Bell, B.J.; Gerber, N.; Salas, L.; Zysset, P.; Caversaccio, M.; Weber, S. Estimation of Tool Pose Based on Force–Density Correlation During Robotic Drilling. *IEEE Trans. Biomed. Eng.* **2013**, *60*, 8. [CrossRef]

29. Li, Q.; Du, Z.; Yu, H. Grinding Trajectory Generator in Robot-Assisted Laminectomy Surgery. *Int. J. Comput. Assist. Radiol. Surg.* **2021**, *16*, 485–494. [CrossRef] [PubMed]
30. Cao, Q.; Zhao, J.; Han, S.; Chen, X. Force Coefficients Identification Considering Inclination Angle for Ball-End Finish Milling. *Precis. Eng.* **2012**, *36*, 252–260. [CrossRef]
31. Wang, H.; Wang, J.; Zhang, J.; Tao, K.; Wu, D. Identification and Analysis of Cutting Force Coefficients in the Helical Milling Process. *J. Adv. Mech. Des. Syst.* **2020**, *14*, JAMDSM0020. [CrossRef]
32. Wojciechowski, S. The Estimation of Cutting Forces and Specific Force Coefficients during Finishing Ball End Milling of Inclined Surfaces. *Int. J. Mach. Tools Manuf.* **2015**, *89*, 110–123. [CrossRef]
33. Merdol, S.D.; Altintas, Y. Virtual Cutting and Optimization of Three-Axis Milling Processes. *Int. J. Mach. Tools Manuf.* **2008**, *48*, 1063–1071. [CrossRef]
34. Weber, S.; Gavaghan, K.; Wimmer, W.; Williamson, T.; Gerber, N.; Anso, J.; Bell, B.; Feldmann, A.; Rathgeb, C.; Matulic, M.; et al. Instrument Flight to the Inner Ear. *Sci. Robot.* **2017**, *2*, eaal4916. [CrossRef] [PubMed]
35. Dynamic Time Warping. In *Information Retrieval for Music and Motion*; Müller, M., Ed.; Springer: Berlin/Heidelberg, Germany, 2007; pp. 69–84.
36. Keogh, E.J.; Pazzani, M.J. Derivative Dynamic Time Warping. In Proceedings of the 2001 SIAM International Conference on Data Mining, Online, 5–7 April 2001; Society for Industrial and Applied Mathematics: Philadelphia, PA, USA, 2001; pp. 1–11.
37. Keogh, E.; Ratanamahatana, C.A. Exact Indexing of Dynamic Time Warping. *Knowl. Inf. Syst.* **2005**, *7*, 358–386. [CrossRef]
38. Fischler, M.A.; Bolles, R.C. Random Sample Consensus: A Paradigm for Model Fitting with Applications to Image Analysis and Automated Cartography. *Commun. ACM* **1981**, *24*, 381–395. [CrossRef]
39. Stein, M.; Elefteriou, F.; Busse, B.; Fiedler, I.A.; Kwon, R.Y.; Farrell, E.; Ahmad, M.; Ignatius, A.; Grover, L.; Geris, L.; et al. Why Animal Experiments Are Still Indispensable in Bone Research: A Statement by the European Calcified Tissue Society. *J. Bone Miner. Res.* **2023**, *38*, 1045–1061 [CrossRef]
40. Peric, M.; Dumic-Cule, I.; Grcevic, D.; Matijasic, M.; Verbanac, D.; Paul, R.; Grgurevic, L.; Trkulja, V.; Bagi, C.M.; Vukicevic, S. The Rational Use of Animal Models in the Evaluation of Novel Bone Regenerative Therapies. *Bone* **2015**, *70*, 73–86. [CrossRef] [PubMed]
41. Li, Z.; Jiang, S.; Song, X.; Liu, S.; Wang, C.; Hu, L.; Li, W. Collaborative Spinal Robot System for Laminectomy: A Preliminary Study. *Neurosurg. Focus* **2022**, *52*, E11. [CrossRef] [PubMed]
42. Motsinger, S.K. Complete Anatomy. *J. Med. Libr. Assoc.* **2020**, *108*, 155–157. [CrossRef]
43. Yushkevich, P.A.; Piven, J.; Hazlett, H.C.; Smith, R.G.; Ho, S.; Gee, J.C.; Gerig, G. User-Guided 3D Active Contour Segmentation of Anatomical Structures: Significantly Improved Efficiency and Reliability. *NeuroImage* **2006**, *31*, 1116–1128. [CrossRef]
44. Chang, C.-J.; Lin, G.-L.; Tse, A.; Chu, H.-Y.; Tseng, C.-S. Registration of 2D C-Arm and 3D CT Images for a C-Arm Image-Assisted Navigation System for Spinal Surgery. *Appl. Bionics Biomech.* **2015**, *2015*, e478062. [CrossRef] [PubMed]
45. Soliman, M.A.; Khan, A.; O'Connor, T.E.; Foley, K.; Pollina, J. Accuracy and Efficiency of Fusion RoboticsTM Versus Mazor-XTM in Single-Level Lumbar Pedicle Screw Placement. *Cureus* **2021**, *13*, e15939. [PubMed]
46. Vardiman, A.B.; Wallace, D.J.; Crawford, N.R.; Riggleman, J.R.; Ahrendtsen, L.A.; Ledonio, C.G. Pedicle Screw Accuracy in Clinical Utilization of Minimally Invasive Navigated Robot-Assisted Spine Surgery. *J. Robot. Surg.* **2020**, *14*, 409–413. [CrossRef]
47. Sekuboyina, A.; Husseini, M.E.; Bayat, A.; Löffler, M.; Liebl, H.; Li, H.; Tetteh, G.; Kukačka, J.; Payer, C.; Štern, D.; et al. VerSe: A Vertebrae Labelling and Segmentation Benchmark for Multi-Detector CT Images. *Med. Image Anal.* **2021**, *73*, 102166. [CrossRef] [PubMed]

sensors

MDPI

*Article*

# 3D-BCLAM: A Lightweight Neurodynamic Model for Assessing Student Learning Effectiveness

**Wei Zhuang** [1,*], **Yunhong Zhang** [1], **Yuan Wang** [2] **and Kaiyang He** [3]

[1] School of Computer Science, Nanjing University of Information Science and Technology, Nanjing 210044, China; zhangyh@nuist.edu.cn
[2] School of Teacher and Education, Nanjing University of Information Science and Technology, Nanjing 210044, China; momo@nuist.edu.cn
[3] School of Mathematics and Physics, Xi'an Jiaotong-Liverpool University, Suzhou 215123, China; Kaiyang.He22@student.xjtlu.edu.cn
* Correspondence: zw@nuist.edu.cn

**Abstract:** Evaluating students' learning effectiveness is of great importance for gaining a deeper understanding of the learning process, accurately diagnosing learning barriers, and developing effective teaching strategies. Emotion, as a key factor influencing learning outcomes, provides a novel perspective for identifying cognitive states and emotional experiences. However, traditional evaluation methods suffer from one sidedness in feature extraction and high complexity in model construction, often making it difficult to fully explore the deep value of emotional data. To address this challenge, we have innovatively proposed a lightweight neurodynamic model: 3D-BCLAM. This model cleverly integrates Bidirectional Convolutional Long Short-Term Memory (BCL) and dynamic attention mechanism, in order to efficiently capture emotional dynamic changes in time series with extremely low computational cost. 3D-BCLAM can achieve a comprehensive evaluation of students' learning outcomes, covering not only the cognitive level but also delving into the emotional dimension for detailed analysis. Under testing on public datasets, 3D-BCLAM has demonstrated outstanding performance, significantly outperforming traditional machine learning and deep learning models based on Convolutional Neural Networks (CNN) and Recurrent Neural Networks (RNN). This achievement not only validates the effectiveness of the 3D-BCLAM model, but also provides strong support for promoting the innovation of student learning effectiveness assessment.

**Keywords:** emotion recognition; brain-computer interface; student learning effectiveness

## 1. Introduction

Emotions are the psychological reactions that humans experience when faced with external events, such as happiness or sadness. It has a significant impact on our perception, memory, and expression. Nowadays, emotion recognition technology is becoming increasingly important in fields such as human-computer interaction and emotion computing. Whether it's smart speakers, mobile phones, or our commonly used social media, they are all using this technology to analyze users' emotions. Based on the results of emotion recognition, these systems can better understand our needs and provide us with more thoughtful and personalized services.

During the learning process, students' emotions play a crucial role. Research has found that when students are in a good mood, such as feeling interested or enjoying learning, they are more proactive, engaged, and learn better. On the contrary, if students feel anxious or depressed, their learning will be hindered and their grades may also decline. Therefore, if we can take into account students' emotions when evaluating their learning effectiveness, we can have a more comprehensive understanding of their learning status. At the same time, teachers can develop more suitable teaching methods based on each student's emotional and cognitive needs. This assessment method that combines emotions and learning can assist teachers in teaching.

Currently, facial expressions are a relatively common method for human emotion recognition. This approach is based on computer vision and uses methods such as machine learning for classification and prediction. Avula et al. [1] suggested a methodology where facial emotions are initially learned through a CNN. Subsequently, an emotion-to-speech model is trained. Ultimately, this approach integrates hand gestures with the recognized facial emotions to comprehend and produce emotion alongside speech. Gupta et al. [2] focused on facial emotion recognition using thermal imaging. The primary goal of this work is to enhance the efficiency, robustness, and accuracy of emotion recognition systems to improve human-computer interaction, mental health monitoring, personalized education, marketing effectiveness, and security. The proposed CNN architecture is designed to recognize human emotions by classifying facial images into six distinct categories (happiness, sadness, anger, fear, disgust, and surprise). Foo et al. [3] devised a system for recognizing facial emotions aimed at detecting mental stress. Salma et al. [4] presented a machine learning model based on CNN to predict the face expressions. However, this method of recognizing human emotions through facial expressions has certain disadvantages. This is because facial expressions are not necessarily the most intuitive expression of human emotions. Some people may express emotions that are different from their inner thoughts under special circumstances. Therefore, physiological signals, as one of the characteristics of the human body, can intuitively display the inner activities of the human body and are an important basis for emotion detection.

The various life activities of humans rely on the core central control system: the brain. The human brain is composed of tens of thousands of neurons, and the activity between neurons generates electrical signals. In 1924, Berger measured the first human electroencephalogram (EEG) through the activity of electric eels. This discovery greatly promoted human interest in the study of the connection between the human body and the outside world, giving rise to brain computer interface technology.

In recent years, emotion detection research using EEG signals has gained significant attention. Analyzing EEG signals allows for the direct observation and quantification of attention levels, offering the advantages of objectivity and accuracy. Some early proposed methods took advantage of the huge advantages of EEG signals in feature band matching, such as Alpha, Beta, Theta, Gamma, etc. They all improved traditional frequency band power feature extraction algorithms by introducing machine learning methods, optimizing the algorithm's processing and results through classic frameworks such as K-Nearest-Neighbor (KNN), K-means, Support Vector Machines (SVM), and auto regressive models. Using artificial neural networks to automatically capture the time-domain and frequency-domain features of EEG signals, and effectively extract and analyze these features, thereby directly learning the complex nonlinear relationship between the original EEG signal and physiological features; Meanwhile, these technologies can be trained through a large amount of data, thus having high prediction accuracy. Li et al. [5] used Fast Fourier Transform (FFT) and Continuous Wavelet Transform (CWT) to extract the features of EEG signals. Liu et al. [6] introduced a novel approach employing a three-dimensional convolutional attention neural network (3DCANN) specifically designed for the emotion recognition based on EEG signals. Zhao et al. [7] proposed Differential Entropy-Recurrent Neural Network-Convolutional Neural Network (DE-CNN-RNN) model to explore emotion recognition.

Graph Neural Network (GNN) is a kind of deep learning models designed to process graph-structured data, which have garnered increasing attention in EEG-based emotion recognition. GNNs excel at capturing the spatial relationships among electrodes in EEG signals, thereby extracting more discriminative features. Guo et al. [8] proposed a novel model that integrates graph neural network-based prototype representation across multiple source domains with clustering similarity loss. Zhong et al. [9] proposed a regularized graph neural network (RGNN) for EEG-based emotion recognition, which considerd the biological topology among different brain regions to capture both local and global relations among different EEG channels. On the other hand, the Transformer architecture, renowned for its powerful sequence modeling capabilities, initially achieved remarkable success in the field of natural language processing. More recently, research has begun to utilize a unique self-attention mechanism to efficiently process long-range dependencies and temporal features in EEG signals. These studies typically serialize EEG signals into a sequence of time steps or feature vectors, subsequently leveraging Transformers for feature extraction and classification. Liu et al. [10] designed a hybrid architecture combining CNN and transformer for analyzing human psychological states. However, these methods have certain shortcomings in feature selection and model construction, and one-dimensional features have accuracy defects in time, frequency band and spatial feature analysis.

Traditional convolutional neural networks cannot capture precise features in time. At the same time, in order to cope with major emotional changes in the human body, it is necessary to preprocess the EEG signals. Therefore, we propose a lightweight neurodynamic emotion recognition model: 3D-BCLAM. For the raw dataset, we propose a new pre-processing process and selects differential-entropy as the input feature. The model is based on the CNN and Bi-LSTM module, and combines the dynamic Attention mechanism to classify the features of the emotional dataset. This model has certain advantages in parameter quantity and running time. The model is stable and robust and has good applicability. The primary contributions of this study are outlined below:

1. This paper proposes a novel preprocessing process for EEG emotional raw data, which involves designing a bandpass filter to optimize signal quality and stacking the processed data into a three-dimensional form to enhance the model's ability to represent features.
2. This paper introduces the Bi-LSTM model, which can simultaneously consider the forward and backward information of time series data, thereby capturing emotional features in EEG signals more comprehensively.
3. This paper integrates dynamic Attention Mechanism that enables the model to focus more on EEG signal features that are more important for emotion recognition tasks, ignoring irrelevant or redundant information, thereby improving the model's discriminative power and robustness.
4. Experiment on open-source datasets and real-time monitor: In this study, the robustness of emotion recognition is ensured through rigorous experimental validation using extensive public datasets. Additionally, real-time monitoring is implemented to assess performance across a wide range of samples and scenarios.
5. This paper proposes an evaluation model for student learning effectiveness that integrates emotion classification. The model categorizes students' various learning states based on calculated scores, and its efficacy has been validated in real-world scenarios.

## 2. Related Work

EEG signals are potential changes recorded from the scalp of humans or other animals, mainly reflecting the electrical activity characteristics of the brain. It is the overall reflection of the electrophysiological activity of brain nerve cells in the cerebral cortex or scalp surface [11]. In the human brain, the cerebral cortex is related to the cognitive level and emotions of the human body, and the analysis of EEG signals is mainly based on the cerebral cortex. When the human brain is active, a large number of neurons in the brain synchronize, and their postsynaptic potentials can be obtained by high-precision EEG sensors, which are local EEG signals. EEG signals are weak bioelectrical signals, with amplitudes mainly ranging from 0 to 60 μV, the frequency distribution is between 0 and 100 Hz. This type of signal has the characteristics of non-stationary and strong randomness. EEG signals from different frequency bands have different characteristics. Table 1 introduces some common bands that can be used for research on emotion recognition.

Regarding the task of recognizing emotions through EEG, current methods can generally be divided into conventional machine learning techniques and deep learning strategies. The traditional EEG-based emotion recognition methods using machine learning typically follow a sequence of steps: data acquisition, preprocessing, feature extraction, feature selection (optional), classifier design and training, and testing and evaluation. Among these steps, feature extraction and classifier design are the core components. Feature extraction aims to distill crucial information related to emotional states from raw EEG signals, while the classifier identifies different emotional states based on these extracted features. Li et al. [12] segmented EEG signals into four frequency ranges utilizing the discrete wavelet transform method, and computed entropy and energy as characteristics for the K-nearest neighbor classifier. Chen et al. [13] introduced an EEG-based emotion identification approach that relies on the Library for Support Vector Machines (LIBSVM) as the classification tool, and the average sentiment recognition rates on DEAP were 74.88% and 82.63%. Zheng et al. [14] transformed the initial one-dimensional EEG vector signal into a two-dimensional matrix signal that incorporated channel position data. Subsequently, they introduced a recognition technique grounded on an Adaptive Neural Decision Tree (ANT). Xiao et al. [15] introduced the Attention-based Temporal Learner with Dynamic Graph Neural Network (AT-DGNN), the results achieved accuracy of 83.74% in arousal recognition and 86.01% in valence recognition.

**Table 1.** Various Bands and Characteristics of EEG Signals.

| Type | | Frequency | Characteristics |
|---|---|---|---|
| Theta | | 4–8 Hz | Generated in a latent state of consciousness |
| Alpha | Low Alpha | 8–9 Hz | Blurred and confused before going to bed |
| | Mid Alpha | 9–12 Hz | Relaxed body and mind, focused attention |
| | Fast Alpha | 12–14 Hz | Highly alert |
| Beta | Low Beta | 14–16 Hz | Relax but concentrate |
| | Mid Beta | 16.5–20 Hz | Think and process receiving external information |
| | Fast Beta | 20.5–31 Hz | Exciting or anxiety |
| Gamma | | 31–45 Hz | Stress relief and meditation |

As mentioned before, traditional machine learning methods rely on manually designed features, which may not fully capture the complex emotional information. The feature extraction process often depends on the researchers' experience, which may potentially lead to information loss or redundancy. In contrast, 3D-BCLAM eliminates the need for tedious manual feature engineering through integrating Bi-LSTM and dynamic attention mechanisms. The model is capable of automatically learning features from raw EEG signals. Furthermore, traditional machine learning models may exhibit limited generalization capabilities when dealing with complex emotional states and cross-dataset tasks. This is primarily due to overfitting to specific datasets or sensitivity to variations in data distribution. 3D-BCLAM may possess better generalization abilities to adapt to different datasets and task requirements.

## 3. Methods

### *3.1. Baseline Drift Elimination*

EEG baseline drift refers to a slow and sustained change in the baseline of a signal (i.e., the potential level when there is no electrical activity) [16]. This change may manifest as an increase or decrease in baseline level, causing the background potential of EEG signals to deviate from the normal zero potential level. When collecting emotional data from subjects, baseline drift can occur due to changes in their physiological state, including breathing, heartbeat, and muscle activity. Baseline drift presents a challenge to the analysis and interpretation of EEG signals, as it may mask real brain electrical activity and diminish the accuracy and reliability of the signals.

Wavelet transform [17,18], as a time-frequency analysis method, is capable of analyzing local characteristics of signals at different scales. To deal with baseline drift in EEG signals, this method can effectively decompose the signal into components at multiple scales, identify and remove the low-frequency components associated with baseline drift, and subsequently reconstruct the signal. This process ensures that useful information in the signal is well-preserved while effectively eliminating baseline drift. The formula of using wavelet transform to remove baseline drift is shown in (1):

$$WT(a,\tau) = \frac{1}{\sqrt{a}} \int_{-\infty}^{\infty} f(t) * \varphi\left(\frac{t-\tau}{a}\right) dt \quad (1)$$

The variables in wavelet transform contain displacement $\tau$ and scale $a$, and the scale control signal waveform shrinks while the displacement control signal waveform shifts. Wavelet basis functions constitute a specific set of functions that efficiently decompose signals into their constituent components across various frequencies and time scales. Owing to their unique localization properties, these functions exhibit finite characteristics in both the time and frequency domains, enabling them to precisely capture the local features of signals. When multiplying the wavelet basis function with the signal function, the relationship between the current scale contained in the signal and the corresponding frequency components can be obtained.

When selecting wavelet basis functions, it is imperative to consider factors such as signal characteristics, orthogonality, compact support, and vanishing moments. Therefore, in this paper, the biore wavelet is used as the wavelet basis function, which is commonly represented as *biore x.y* (where $x$ is the reconstruction coefficient and $y$ is the decomposition coefficient). Symmetric wavelets can be used for signal decomposition and reconstruction, respectively. The individual wavelets have tight support, and the support length for reconstruction and decomposition is $2N + 1$ (where $N$ is the coefficient $x$, $y$). Here, the reconstruction coefficient is selected as 4 and the decomposition coefficient is selected as 3. The wavelet coefficients after thresholding are used for signal reconstruction. The reconstruction process is the inverse of wavelet decomposition, which combines the processed wavelet coefficients into an EEG signal with baseline drift removed through layer-by-layer upsampling and filtering operations. The reconstructed signal retains as much useful information from the original signal as possible, while eliminating baseline drift and noise. Figure 1 shows the comparison after baseline drift elimination.

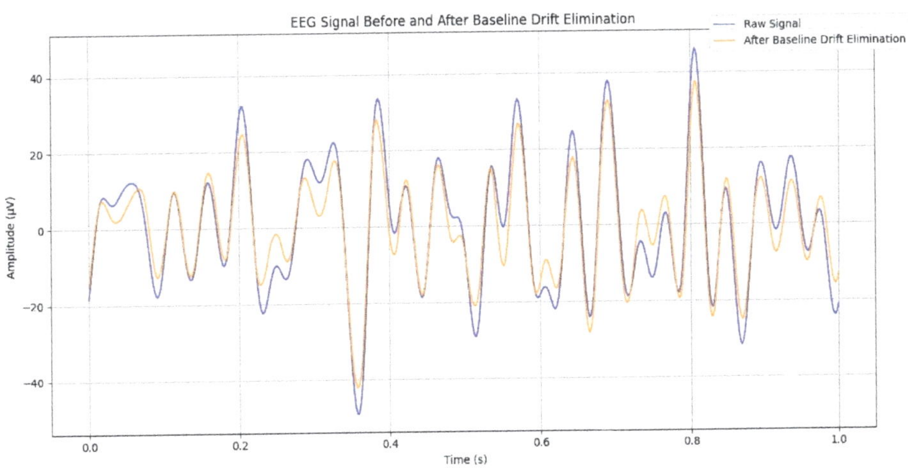


**Figure 1.** Baseline drift elimination based on wavelet transform.

As is shown in Figure 1, zero drift caused by both the device itself and external factors interferes with the true EEG signals, making it challenging to accurately capture and analyze brain electrical activity. However, the reconstructed signal, obtained through wavelet transform, eliminates these negative effects, thereby facilitating further processing.

### 3.2. Pre-Processing

The raw signal collected through a portable headset contains a large amount of noise and artifacts, and certain pre-processing is required for the original signal to facilitate subsequent feature extraction and model classification.

The main frequency of EEG is from 0 to 100 Hz [19], and in practical research, different rhythmic bands represent different physiological meanings. In order to obtain the band we want to study, it is necessary to filter the original signal. According to the characteristic table of EEG signals, band-pass filters are mainly used in this paper. A zero-phase band-pass filter based on Bessel filter has been designed to filter out signals of 0.5 to 40 Hz. The filter has an almost constant group delay throughout the entire pass-band, thereby maintaining the waveform of the filtered signal in the pass-band. The Bessel transfer function [20] in the filter aims to obtain a linear phase (i.e., the smoothest delay), and the impulse response has no oscillation characteristics. The Bessel transfer function is implemented by (2):

$$T_n(s) = \frac{B_n(0)}{B_n(s)} \tag{2}$$

Among them, $B_n$ is the Bessel polynomial, as (3) shows:

$$B_n(s) = \sum_{k=0}^{n} a_k s^k,\ a_n = 1 \tag{3}$$

The expression of the coefficient is shown in (4):

$$a_k = \frac{(2n-k)!}{k!(n-k)!2^{n-k}} \tag{4}$$

$n$ is the order of the Bessel filter, which is used to observe the signal characteristics of EEG signals with non-stationary digital signal processing type using a 4th order Bessel filter.

Due to the possibility of the same frequency domain components of the signal in different time domains, windowing analysis based on Hamming window [21] is required for the signal, which can be achieved through the (5):

$$\omega(n) = \begin{cases} 0.5[1-\cos\left(\frac{2\pi n}{M-1}\right)], 0 \le n \le M-1 \\ 0, others \end{cases} \tag{5}$$

In this paper, the application of the Hamming window plays a significant role. The Hamming window effectively smooths the EEG signals, significantly reducing spectral leakage and edge effects, thereby enhancing the accuracy of spectral analysis. Furthermore, by applying windowing processing, critical features in the signals are accentuated [22,23], effectively suppressing noise and unnecessary frequency components, which establishes a strong groundwork for the ensuing feature extraction and classification endeavors.

### 3.3. Feature Extraction

To analyze EEG signals in the time domain is the most direct and effective method, which facilitates the extraction of intuitive features. Time domain analysis is mainly based on the time series analysis of EEG signals.

The differential entropy [24] of sub frequency bands is shown in (6), which describes the temporal variation patterns of different frequency components in EEG signals, which can effectively transform high-dimensional and low signal-to-noise ratio temporal signals (one-dimensional temporal vectors) into descriptive values of several sub frequency bands (scalar values), and has strong discriminative power for emotional and other brain activities.

$$DE = \frac{1}{2}\log\left(2\pi e\sigma^2\right) \tag{6}$$

In Table 1, it is noted that EEG signals within distinct frequency bands reflect varying characteristics of brain activity. Consequently, we performed a bandpass filtering process on the raw EEG signals, utilizing the bandpass filters designed previously, to isolate the signals into their constituent frequency components. The purpose of this breakdown was to reveal the unique brain activity patterns present within various frequency ranges. In particular, we divided the EEG signals into four main categories: theta (4–8 Hz), alpha (8–14 Hz), beta (14–31 Hz), and gamma (31–45 Hz). The frequency specific analysis allows us to gain a deeper understanding of the neural activity behind various cognitive and emotional states [25].

### 3.4. 3D-BCLAM Framework

As is shown in Figure 2, 3D-BCLAM framework includes two primary components: the neurodynamic data generation module and the BCLAM framework. The neurodynamic data generation module is designed for transforming EEG signals into a three-dimensional neurodynamic data format, which is then sequentially sent into the nodes of the BCLAM framework. This facilitates temporal interactions among nodes and enables the learning of temporal features in the data.

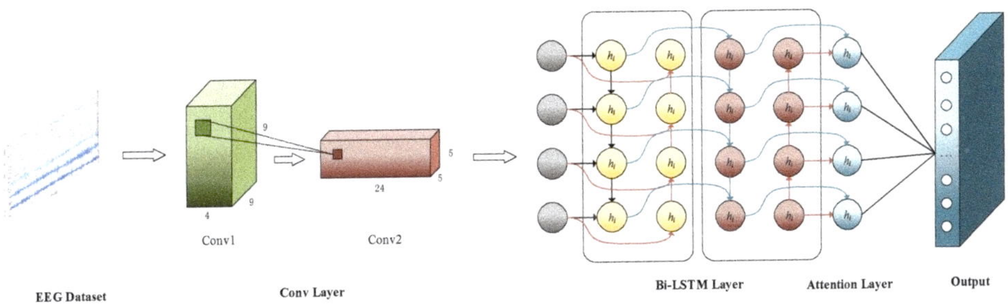


**Figure 2.** 3D-BCLAM Framework.

The BCLAM framework consists of three layers: two-dimensional convolutional (2D-Conv) layer, Bi-LSTM layer, and dynamic Attention Mechanism layer. This design enables the framework to efficiently capture complex features in both space and time from converted EEG data. The 2D-Conv layer is used for extracting local features from the original 3D data at beginning; Subsequently, the Bi-LSTM layer further processes these features to capture their long-term dependencies over time; After that, the dynamic attention mechanism layer analyzes the correlation between emotional data by focusing on key features.

The output of BCLAM framework is passed through fully-connected layer, which performs the classification of EEG emotional data. The approach introduces a novel and effective solution for emotion recognition from EEG signals by integrating neuromorphic data generation and deep learning methods.

#### 3.4.1. 3D Data Generation

In this paper, we design a specific data transformation way that efficiently converts one-dimensional EEG data into a three-dimensional format. We employ a custom data reshaping algorithm to transform each processed one-dimensional data segment, corresponding to features extracted from distinct frequency bands, into a two-dimensional matrix, denoted as data_2D. This step relies on a particular mapping rule that allocates consecutive elements from the one-dimensional data to specific locations within the two-dimensional matrix, resulting in a spatially structured feature representation.

To construct a three-dimensional dataset, we stack all these two-dimensional matrices along the feature dimension. In our case, this entails assembling the two-dimensional matrices, each representing a different frequency band, into a four-dimensional array with dimensions $(s, f, h, w)$, where $s$ is the number of samples, $f$ is the number of frequency bands, $h$ is the height, and $w$ is the width. However, to maintain compatibility with common deep learning frameworks, we can alternatively consider the last dimension $f$ as the number of channels $c$ in the feature maps, yielding a three-dimensional array of shape $(s, c, h, w)$, where $c$ corresponds to the number of channels. This process not only preserves the temporal and spectral information inherent in the original one-dimensional EEG signals but also enhances their representational power by introducing a spatial dimension. Consequently, it provides a richer set of features as input to subsequent deep learning models, facilitating improved performance in emotion recognition and other related tasks.

### 3.4.2. Long-Short Time Memory Node

EEG is a kind of time series data, and its characteristics have dynamic changes in time. Through LSTM, we can model the dynamic characteristics of EEG signals at different time points [26,27]. There may be long-term dependencies in EEG signals, that is, past emotional states may affect future emotional expressions. Traditional recurrent neural networks have the problem of gradient disappearance or gradient explosion, and LSTM effectively solves this problem by introducing gating mechanisms, especially forget gates and input gates. This enables LSTM to better capture long-term dependencies in sequence data, thereby improving the emotion recognition model's ability to understand sequence data.

The structure of the LSTM node is shown in Figure 3, which reveals its internal working mechanism. In this design, $c_t$ and $h_t$ represent the memory state and hidden layer state of the unit respectively, which are key components of the model when processing sequence data. At the same time, $x_t$ and $y_t$ serve as the input and output of the model respectively, interacting with the external world. The $\sigma$ symbol represents the sigma activation function, which plays an important role in LSTM. In addition, LSTM is equipped with three gating mechanisms to finely manage the flow of information:

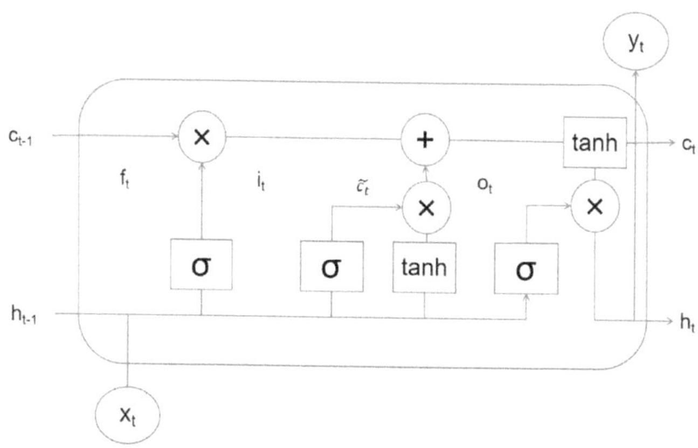


**Figure 3.** LSTM node.

The forget threshold, controlled by $f_t$, determines which memory states should be discarded, thereby helping the model "forget" unimportant information.

The input threshold, controlled by $i_t$, is responsible for screening which parts of $\widetilde{c_t}$ should be included in the current memory state to achieve the effective integration of new information.

The output threshold, controlled by $o_t$, determines which memory states should be read and used as output in the current time step, affecting the update of the hidden state $h_t$.

As the memory state $c_{t-1}$ is passed through the network, it first filters and discards information through the forget threshold, and then selectively absorbs new memory content through the input threshold. This mechanism ensures that the memory state of the model can be dynamically updated and optimized at each time step. Finally, after a series of operations, the content of the memory state is copied and passed to the function for processing, and then filtered by the output threshold, and finally a new hidden state $h_t$ is generated to prepare for the processing of the next time step.

#### 3.4.3. Bi-Convolutional-LSTM Layer

We introduce a lightweight neurodynamic model to recognize complex emotional data from human. The convolution kernel of two-dimensional Convolutional layer operates in the temporal or spatial dimension, while the three-dimensional convolution kernel performs convolution in two dimensions and extracts useful classification information. CNN extracts local features of the input data by using convolutional layers and pooling layers [28,29]. The same convolution kernel is slid across the entire input data to detect similar features at different locations.

In one-way LSTM, the hidden state at the current moment can only rely on the past input sequence, while bidirectional LSTM can use both past and future information to update the hidden state at the current moment. This helps reduce the risk of information loss, especially when processing longer sequences, and better preserves important information in the sequence. Bi-Convolutional-LSTM (BCL) maps the LSTM output to the space of attention weights through a fully connected layer. This fully-connected layer maps the hidden state of each time step output by the LSTM to a scalar value representing the importance of that time step.

#### 3.4.4. Dynamic Attention Mechanism

In tasks such as EEG emotion recognition, sequence data usually have a long-time span, in which some time steps may contain more critical information, while other time steps may contain relatively less or less important information. By introducing an attention mechanism [30], the model can dynamically adjust the degree of attention paid to different time steps, thereby more effectively capturing important features in sequence data, and giving different importance to information at different time steps.

Then, these scalar values are converted into attention weights via the softmax function such that the sum of all weights equals 1. These weights represent the relative importance of each time step, which means the degree to which the model should focus at that time step. The LSTM outputs are weighted and summed using the calculated attention weights to obtain a weighted representation. Specifically, for each time step, the LSTM output is multiplied with the corresponding attention weight, and then all weighted results are summed. This results in a weighted representation, where the contribution of each time step is determined by the attention weight. (7) is the formula of the attention mechanism:

$$Attention(Q,K,V) = Softmax\left(\frac{QK^T}{\sqrt{d_k}}\right) \tag{7}$$

$Q, K, V$ refer to Query, Key and Value respectively [31]. Query is obtained by linear transformation of the LSTM output and represents the hidden state of the current time step. Key represents the hidden state of the input sequence. They are used to measure the correlation between the hidden state of the current time step and the hidden states of other time steps. Value is the original representation of the LSTM output, that is, the hidden state without any linear transformation. It is used to represent the hidden state of each time step in the input sequence, and will be weighted and summed according to the calculated attention weight to obtain the final output. The weighted depiction is propagated through a fully connected layer to acquire the ultimate output forecast.

## 4. Discussion

### 4.1. Dataset Introduction

DEAP [32,33] is a physiological signal database used for emotion analysis. It contains physiological data and emotional ratings of multiple participants while watching multiple music video clips. Participants rated their emotional experience based on a discrete 9-point rating after watching each music video clip. These emotions include joy, excitement, anger, pressure, sadness, fear, surprise, calmness, and boredom. There are four values in each label: arousal, valence, dominance, and like. Valence represents the positive or negative nature of emotions. Arousal stands for the intensity or level of emotional activity. Dominance can reflect whether an individual is capable to control their emotional response, which is often expressed as confidence or a sense of authority. By dividing emotions into these three dimensions, they can help people better identify and classify emotions, and provide more accurate methods for emotion recognition.

To comprehensively evaluate students' learning effectiveness, we propose an assessment framework based on the VAD (Valence-Arousal-Dominance) model, with a scoring range of 0–9 for each dimension. Specifically, Valence measures students' interest and engagement in the learning content. Arousal reflects their mental activation and capacity for innovation. Dominance assesses their self-regulatory skills. Arousal, which directly relates to students' attention and emotional activation, is assigned the highest weight (0.4) due to its importance in efficient learning. Valence and Dominance, reflecting students' emotional disposition towards the lesson and their sense of control over the task, respectively, are each given equal weight (0.3) to balance their contributions to the learning effectiveness assessment. By assigning appropriate weights to each dimension and calculating score, we obtain a quantitative indicator that validly represents students' learning effectiveness. This comprehensive approach not only facilitates a thorough understanding of students' learning effectiveness, but also is helpful to develop personalized teaching plans and interventional strategies. The formula for calculating learning effectiveness score is shown in (8):

$$Score = 0.3 * V + 0.4 * A + 0.3 * D \tag{8}$$

To illustrate the purpose of the formula, we have designed a classification standard based on scores derived from the VAD dimensions. The standard is shown in Table 2. This standard describes different learning states corresponding to different score ranges, each with specific characteristics, aimed at providing teachers with targeted teaching strategies.

**Table 2.** Learning State Evaluation Standard.

| Aggregated Score Range | Learning State | Characteristics |
|---|---|---|
| 0–3 | Ineffective | Lack of interest, distracted attention, weak self-management |
| 3–4 | Moderate | Moderate interest, but attention and self-control lacking |
| 4–6 | Good | Equitable learning state |
| 6–9 | Excellent | High engagement, focused attention, strong self-control |

To assess the practical applicability of the model, a graduate student (aged 23, female) and an undergraduate student (aged 19, female) were recruited as the experimental subjects in this study. Both subjects have signed the experimental consent form. As is shown in Figure 4, they wore non-invasive dry electrode caps and used OpenBCI Cyton to accurately capture raw EEG signals. In order to simulate real classroom settings and situations, the student was prompted to simulate a series of classroom states during the lessons. The EEG data acquisition was conducted at a high sampling rate of 256 Hz across eight channels, ensuring comprehensive and accurate data collection for subsequent analysis.

The SEED-IV [34] (SJTU Emotion EEG Dataset for Emotion Recognition with Four Emotions) dataset, developed by the Brain and Computational Intelligence Lab (BCMI) at Shanghai Jiao Tong University, is a comprehensive dataset for emotion recognition encompassing four emotion categories: happiness, sadness, fear, and neutrality. This dataset meticulously selected 72 movie clips as stimuli to induce these four emotions and recorded EEG and eye movement data from 15 healthy Chinese subjects. Each subject participated in three experiments, with at least a three-day interval between each session to mitigate any lingering emotional effects. The signals were acquired using a 62-channel ESI NeuroScan system with a sampling rate of 1000 Hz, which was subsequently downsampled to 200 Hz. These emotion categories are pre-defined and mutually exclusive, conforming to the characteristics of discrete data. In the dataset, each movie clip was designed to elicit one of these four discrete emotions, and participants were asked to self-evaluate based on these discrete emotion categories after watching.

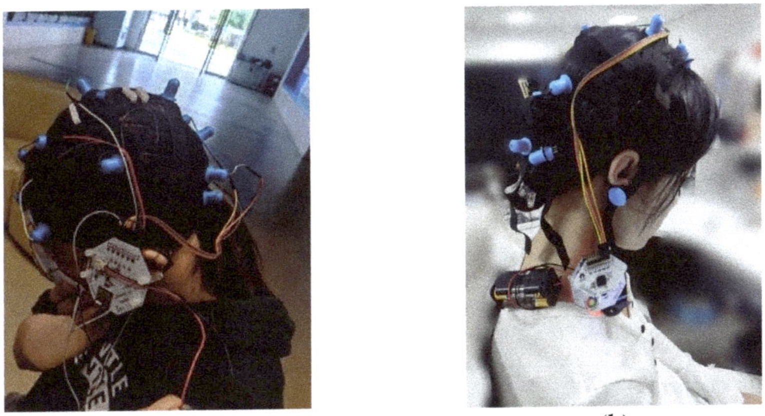

(a) (b)

**Figure 4.** Practical application subjects. (**a**) a graduate student (aged 23, female); (**b**) an undergraduate student (aged 19, female).

### 4.2. Experimental Setup

#### 4.2.1. Labels Generation

In this paper, we employ the MATLAB interface to retrieve DEAP datasets that encompass emotional labels. Subsequently, we implement a binarization process for these labels, setting a threshold value of 5. Labels exceeding this threshold are designated as representing positive emotions, whereas those falling below are classified as negative emotions. This binarization step aims to simplify subsequent analyses. To align with the multiple temporal windows obtained from the differential entropy decomposition of EEG signals, each original emotional label is replicated and extended to match the corresponding number of windows. This ensures that each window is associated with its respective emotional label, facilitating the investigation of the relationship between EEG signal features and emotional states through deep learning.

The SEED-IV dataset has been down sampled to 200 Hz. We employ a specially designed bandpass filter to process the data, aiming to minimize artifacts to the greatest extent possible. Following this, we take into account the temporal dynamics of emotional states and employ the moving average method to smooth out the filtered data, thereby further eliminating irrelevant components. To ensure experimental balance, we still select differential entropy as the feature. The EEG signals from each experiment are segmented into individual samples, with a 1-s time window between each sample and no overlap. In the SEED-IV dataset, emotions are categorized into four distinct classes, hence the labels are mapped in a one-hot encoding format.

#### 4.2.2. Framework Settings

In this study, all experimental procedures were conducted within the Windows 11 environment. The construction and training of deep learning models were facilitated by PyTorch 2.1.0. All computational tasks were executed on NVIDIA GeForce 4070Ti GPU (NVIDIA Corporation, Santa Clara, CA, USA). BrainFlow library utilizes dual threading and dual process programming methods to achieve real-time raw data reading, which is used to obtain raw EEG signals on OpenBCI Cyton and analyze learning effectiveness.

A comprehensive overview of the crucial hyperparameters for each component is shown in Table 3.

**Table 3.** Function Block and Hyperparameters of 3D-BCLAM.

| Function Block | | Hyperparameter |
|---|---|---|
| 2D-Convolutional-layer | 2D_Conv1 | In_channels: 4<br>Out_channels: 24<br>Kernel size = 5 * 5 |
| | 2D_Conv2 | In_channels: 24<br>Out_channels: 128<br>Kernel size = 2 * 2 |
| Bi-LSTM layer | | Batch_size = 32<br>Embedding_size: 16<br>bidirectional = True |
| Full-Connected layers | FC1 layer | Input_features = 128 * 2 * 2<br>Output_features = 96 |
| | FC2 layer | Input_features = 96<br>Output_features = 16 |
| Attention Mechanism layer | | Input_features = 16<br>Output_features = Softmax |

The DEAP dataset employed in this experimental study originates from pre-processed dataset. We divided this dataset into three different subsets using a ratio of 6:2:2. The first 60% of the data is designated as the training set for training the model and adjusting its parameters. The remaining 20% is used as a validation set, allowing us to evaluate the performance of the model and make any necessary adjustments during the training process. The remaining 20% constitutes the test set for evaluating the final performance.

For the SEED-IV dataset, our experimental design adopted widely accepted standards proposed by Zhong et al. [9], utilizing the first 16 trials as the training set and the latter 8 trials as the test set. For each test sample, the model outputs a predicted category and then compares it with the true category to calculate accuracy. After completing the prediction of all test samples, we calculated the average accuracy of all these samples, in order to calculate the overall average accuracy.

For the optimization of our model during the training process, we have chosen the Adam optimizer. Adam [35] is a widely-used optimization algorithm that stands out due to its adaptive learning rates. In our experiment, we initiated the model with a learning rate of 0.0001, a batch size of 32, and conducted training for a total of 500 iterations to ensure thorough convergence and optimization of the model.

#### 4.2.3. Experimental Metrics

When evaluating the performance of emotion recognition models, it is common practice to adopt a multifaceted approach by selecting multiple evaluation metrics. This ensures a thorough assessment of the model's capabilities. In the context of our experiment, we carefully chose three evaluation metrics: the F1 Score, Standard Deviation (STD), and Area Under the Curve (AUC). By combining these evaluation metrics, we aim to gain a holistic understanding of our emotion recognition model's performance, ensuring that it not only achieves high accuracy but also demonstrates consistency and reliability in its predictions.

1. F1 Score

In classification tasks, F1 score [36] plays a key role as a comprehensive measure for evaluating model performance. By integrating two crucial indicators, precision and recall, the F1 score is designed to provide a more comprehensive and balanced perspective on assessment, particularly in situations involving imbalanced datasets. Precision predicts the ratio of positive instances to true positive instances, while the recall represents the proportion of true positive instances accurately predicted by the model as positive. The formula for calculating F1 score is shown in (9):

$$F1 = \frac{2 * Precision * Recall}{Precision + Recall} \tag{9}$$

As is shown in the (9), the F1 score spans from 0 to 1, where a larger number represents improved model effectiveness.

2. STD

In emotion recognition models, the role of standard deviation [37] is mainly reflected in the degree of data dispersion or variation, which is helpful to evaluate the performance stability of the model in different samples or batches of data. The formula is shown in (10):

$$S = \sqrt{\frac{\sum(x_i - \overline{x})^2}{N - 1}} \tag{10}$$

3. AUC

The AUC [38] serves as an indicator measuring a model's capacity to prioritize positive instances over negative ones. Specifically, there are two approaches to determining the AUC: the first involves graphing the Receiver Operating Characteristic (ROC) curve and computing the enclosed area; the second entails arranging the anticipated scores of both positive and negative instances and determining the likelihood that a positive instance will be placed above a negative one. In the empirical studies presented here, we opt for the latter technique to ascertain the AUC figure, thereby assessing the efficacy of various classification models.

### 4.3. Experimental Results

According to Table 4, 3D-BCLAM achieved good results on the DEAP dataset. On the DEAP dataset, 3D-BCLAM s' valence classification accuracy, arousal classification accuracy and dominance classification accuracy were 95.47%, 95.83% and 96.88% respectively. It can be observed that different stimuli in different subjects tend to trigger different emotional dimensions.

**Table 4.** 3D-BCLAM Performance on DEAP.

| Subjects | VA [1] | AA [2] | DA [3] |
|---|---|---|---|
| S1 | 92.52 | 96.62 | 95.15 |
| S2 | 97.98 | 97.22 | 93.84 |
| S3 | 94.06 | 100 | 100 |
| S4 | 94.14 | 93.80 | 96.76 |
| S5 | 94.38 | 95.21 | 100 |
| S6 | 94.66 | 98.71 | 93.73 |
| S7 | 95.26 | 94.37 | 92.67 |
| S8 | 88.87 | 99.15 | 95.54 |
| S9 | 95.78 | 94.90 | 97.66 |
| S10 | 98.51 | 90.53 | 97.88 |
| S11 | 93.30 | 97.01 | 98.44 |
| S12 | 92.71 | 99.56 | 95.52 |
| S13 | 98.26 | 95.66 | 100 |
| S14 | 95.69 | 95.01 | 100 |
| S15 | 96.18 | 95.99 | 94.03 |
| S16 | 90.61 | 92.59 | 100 |
| S17 | 100 | 94.41 | 96.84 |
| S18 | 96.34 | 96.55 | 95.79 |
| S19 | 92.92 | 97.35 | 100 |

**Table 4.** *Cont.*

| Subjects | VA [1] | AA [2] | DA [3] |
|---|---|---|---|
| S20 | 95.74 | 94.27 | 98.59 |
| S21 | 95.81 | 98.11 | 96.72 |
| S22 | 98.68 | 98.62 | 90.03 |
| S23 | 94.52 | 96.89 | 98.61 |
| S24 | 94.45 | 95.24 | 93.14 |
| S25 | 97.86 | 95.75 | 97.96 |
| S26 | 95.54 | 93.01 | 95.61 |
| S27 | 90.37 | 92.02 | 97.72 |
| S28 | 100 | 95.37 | 97.77 |
| S29 | 88.8 | 97.81 | 96.31 |
| S30 | 96.4 | 91.41 | 96.77 |
| S31 | 98.03 | 100 | 96.73 |
| S32 | 100 | 99.8 | 97.11 |

[1] Valence accuracy. [2] Arousal accuracy. [3] Dominance accuracy.

Table 5 shows the typical experimental metrics of 3D-BCLAM in three states, which has good performance. To further confirm the impact of time series length in emotion recognition. 3D-BCLAM was tested on different time series lengths. Figure 5 shows that the classification accuracy of 3D-BCLAM differs in different time series, and the best performance was achieved when the sequence length is 8. Therefore, personalized models based on important features such as representative channels and appropriate time periods are of great value to achieve human emotion recognition.

**Table 5.** Evaluation Metrics of 3D-BCLAM on DEAP.

| Metrics | Valence | Arousal | Dominance |
|---|---|---|---|
| Average Accuracy | 95.47 | 95.83 | 96.88 |
| Average STD | 3.64 | 2.83 | 2.31 |
| F1 Score | 0.9555 | 0.9639 | 0.9718 |
| AUC | 0.9566 | 0.9642 | 0.9825 |

As is shown in Tables 6 and 7, 3D-BCLAM also achieved good results on the SEED-IV dataset. Among the 15 subjects, there were sessions where the accuracy rate surpassed 95%, indicating that our proposed model can be applied across different sessions with good generalization performance. However, there were also sessions where the accuracy rate fell below 65%, which might be caused by factors such as the quality of the collected EEG signals or similar brain activities among the subjects.

**Table 6.** 3D-BCLAM Performance on SEED-IV.

| Subjects | Session 1 | Session 2 | Session 3 |
|---|---|---|---|
| S1 | 93.96 | 96.34 | 82.39 |
| S2 | 91.68 | 85.86 | 69.92 |
| S3 | 63.01 | 78.04 | 71.39 |
| S4 | 75.19 | 66.34 | 99.95 |
| S5 | 97.69 | 75.25 | 93.08 |
| S6 | 66.49 | 88.74 | 75.41 |
| S7 | 69.40 | 91.16 | 61.43 |
| S8 | 95.91 | 69.85 | 87.99 |
| S9 | 85.82 | 85.24 | 62.48 |
| S10 | 84.78 | 97.67 | 70.65 |
| S11 | 65.20 | 90.26 | 74.34 |
| S12 | 80.42 | 98.84 | 67.79 |
| S13 | 80.59 | 68.13 | 90.84 |
| S14 | 83.29 | 86.75 | 81.39 |
| S15 | 65.79 | 88.86 | 67.87 |

**Table 7.** Evaluation Metrics of 3D-BCLAM on SEED-IV.

| Metrics | SEED-IV |
|---|---|
| Average accuracy | 80.52 |
| Average STD | 5.39 |
| F1 Score | 0.8148 |

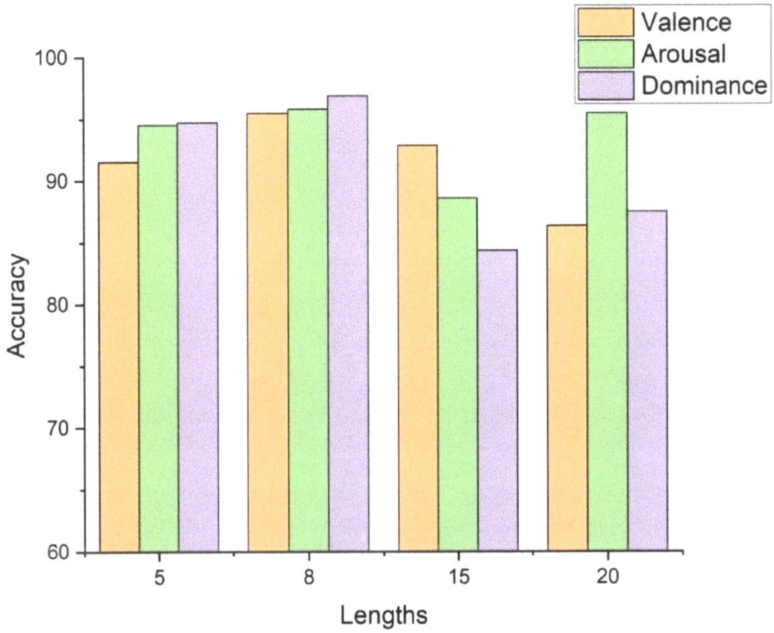


**Figure 5.** Applied time lengths of sequence and accuracy on DEAP.

As shown in the Figure 6, the student's learning effectiveness exhibited variation over a single testing cycle. During the initial time, the student's learning scores remained above 5, indicating a favorable learning outcome. This can be attributed to the initial novelty of the course, which likely enhanced the student's attention and engagement. However, in the subsequent test points, the student's learning scores declined, gradually falling below 5, reflecting a moderate learning performance. This decline may be attributed to a gradual waning of the student's patience and the emergence of a weariness towards learning as the course progressed.

Besides, the disparity in learning outcome assessments between graduate and undergraduate students can be largely attributed to the distinctiveness in their respective educational orientations and cognitive paradigms. Graduate subject education emphasizes the cultivation of academic abilities, thereby fostering highly autonomous learning methods. This self-regulated learning mode not only deepens their subject knowledge, but also effectively improves their attention management skills through continuous exploration and practice. On the contrary, undergraduate education often emphasizes broad-based general education, and students typically receive more structured knowledge transfer. Although equally valuable, this model may lead to relatively inadequate self-regulation and attention control among undergraduate students compared to graduate students. In our research, we invited three experts in the field of education to conduct manual evaluations. The evaluations provided by these experts are consistent with the results generated by our proposed evaluation model, thus validating our research findings.

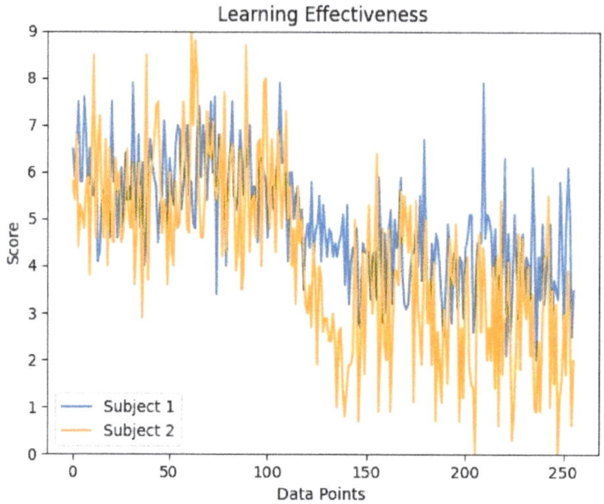


**Figure 6.** Learning Effectiveness.

### 4.4. Baseline Comparison

A comparative evaluation of 3D-BCLAM was conducted alongside several other methodologies, including the Linear Support Vector Machine (Linear-SVM) [39], the Spiking Neural Network enhanced with Transfer Learning (SNN + TL) [40], the Attention-based CNN-RNN (ACRNN) [41], the Synchronous Brain Network (SBN-STM) [42], the SNN integrated with Infinite Impulse Response Filters (SNN + IIR) [43], the Fractal SNN (Fra-SNN) [44], the Functional Connectivity Network (FCN) [45], and the NeuCube SNN [46]. Given the similarities between 3D-BCLAM and these methods in terms of model architecture and feature extraction, they were selected as benchmarks for comparison.

In addition, recently popular models based on graph neural networks and transformers were used for comparison, including Regularized Graph Neural Network (RGNN) [9], Attention-based Temporal Learner with Dynamic Graph Neural Network (AT-DGNN) [15], Dynamic graph convolutional neural networks (DGCNN) [47] and Emotion Recognition Transformer Net (ERTNet) [10]. The outcomes are presented in Table 8.

**Table 8.** Comparison Methods.

| Methods | VA [1] | AA [2] | DA [3] | SA [4] |
|---|---|---|---|---|
| Linear-SVM [39] | 66.47 | 60.33 | - | - |
| SNN + TL [40] | 82.75 | 84.22 | - | - |
| ACRNN [41] | 93.72 | 93.38 | - | - |
| SBN-STM [42] | 78.00 | 78.30 | - | - |
| ERTNet [10] | 73.31 | 80.99 | - | - |
| AT-DGNN [15] | 83.74 | 86.01 | - | - |
| SNN + IIR [43] | 61.15 | 53.86 | 67.50 | - |
| Fra-SNN [44] | 69.84 | 69.61 | 73.20 | - |
| FCN [45] | 45.55 | 62.73 | 59.60 | - |
| NeuCube SNN [46] | 78.00 | 74.00 | 80.00 | - |
| RGNN [9] | - | - | - | 79.37 |
| DGCNN [47] | - | - | - | 69.88 |
| 3D-BCLAM | 95.47 ± 3.64 | 95.83 ± 2.83 | 96.88 ± 2.31 | 80.52 ± 5.39 |

[1] Valence accuracy. [2] Arousal accuracy. [3] Dominance accuracy. [4] SEED-IV accuracy.

In comparison to these methodologies on DEAP, the accuracy variance ranged from 1.75% to 41.97%. Notably, when compared to approaches utilizing the frequency domain feature, Power Spectrum Density (PSD) (such as Linear-SVM and SNN + TL), 3D-BCLAM demonstrated enhancements of at least 12.72% and 11.61% in valence and arousal, respectively. Furthermore, when juxtaposed against methods employing DE (Fra-SNN), 3D-BCLAM exhibited improvements of 25.63%, 26.22%, and 23.68% in valence, arousal, and dominance, respectively. In comparison to these methodologies on SEED-IV, the accuracy variance ranged from 1.15% to 10.64%.

### 4.5. Ablation Study

To validate the efficacy of our proposed framework, we undertook a series of ablation studies [48]. Specifically, we systematically excluded certain components from the 3D-BCLAM model—namely, those modules instrumental in extracting EEG temporal features and those focusing on emotional attributes—and performed experiments. Ensuring consistency, the parameter inputs for each modified submodel were maintained akin to the original 3D-BCLAM configuration, thereby allowing us to rigorously assess the contributions of these components to the overall model performance. The results are shown in the Table 9.

**Table 9.** Ablation Study Results.

| Methods | VA [1] | AA [2] | DA [3] | SA [4] |
|---|---|---|---|---|
| 3D-BCLAM without AM | 90.88 ± 2.97 | 90.71 ± 4.66 | 88.41 ± 3.85 | 76.45 ± 8.31 |
| 3D-BCLAM without Bi-LSTM | 66.25 ± 5.31 | 62.93 ± 5.18 | 64.16 ± 4.95 | 49.67 ± 5.87 |
| 3D-BCLAM without Bi-LSTM and AM | 64.47 ± 7.13 | 60.31 ± 6.48 | 62.13 ± 5.22 | 48.35 ± 6.53 |
| 3D-BCLAM | 95.47 ± 3.64 | 95.83 ± 2.83 | 96.88 ± 2.31 | 80.52 ± 5.39 |

[1] Valence accuracy. [2] Arousal accuracy. [3] Dominance accuracy. [4] SEED-IV accuracy.

## 5. Conclusions

In this study, we present 3D-BCLAM, for student learning effectiveness assessment through emotion recognition. The model integrates a Bi-Convolutional-LSTM architecture with a dynamic Attention Mechanism, utilizing differential entropy as the key emotional feature. A Bessel filter, combined with a Hamming window, is employed to preprocess data, transforming one-dimensional signals into three-dimensional representations to capture spatiotemporal relationships. This design enables more effective learning of data characteristics, improving the model's performance in emotion recognition. Evaluated on the public dataset, 3D-BCLAM outperforms CNN, SVM, GNN, Transformer and hybrid SNN structures in recognizing emotions from EEG signals. By monitoring students' emotional states, educators can gain valuable insights into their engagement, cognitive load, and overall learning experience. Despite its strengths, the model's feature extraction capabilities could be further enhanced, particularly when handling complex EEG signals. Future work will involve applying the model in real-time EEG monitoring systems in educational environments, refining its performance on noisy or irregular data, and expanding its applicability across diverse student populations. These improvements would enhance the model's robustness and provide deeper insights into the role of emotions in learning, potentially transforming educational practices.

**Author Contributions:** Conceptualization, W.Z.; methodology, W.Z.; software, Y.Z.; validation, W.Z., Y.Z. and Y.W.; formal analysis, Y.Z.; investigation, Y.Z.; resources, K.H.; data curation, Y.Z.; writing—original draft preparation, W.Z.; writing—review and editing, Y.Z.; visualization, Y.W.; supervision, K.H.; project administration, W.Z.; funding acquisition, W.Z. All authors have read and agreed to the published version of the manuscript.

**Funding:** This research was funded by National Natural Science Foundation of China grant number 61802196.

**Institutional Review Board Statement:** Not applicable.

**Informed Consent Statement:** Informed consent was obtained from all subjects involved in the study.

**Data Availability Statement:** Data are contained within the article.

**Acknowledgments:** The authors would like to thank the Assistant Editor of this article and the anonymous reviewers for their valuable suggestions and comments.

**Conflicts of Interest:** No potential conflicts of interest were reported by the author.

## References

1. Avula, H.; Ranjith, R.; Pillai, A.S. CNN based recognition of emotion and speech from gestures and facial expressions. In Proceedings of the 2022 6th International Conference on Electronics, Communication and Aerospace Technology, Coimbatore, India, 1–3 December 2022; IEEE: Piscataway, NJ, USA, 2022; pp. 1360–1365.
2. Gupta, S.; Sengupta, A. Unlocking Emotions Through Heat: Facial Emotion Recognition via Thermal Imaging. In Proceedings of the 2023 3rd International Conference on Emerging Frontiers in Electrical and Electronic Technologies (ICEFEET), Patna, India, 21–22 December 2023; IEEE: Piscataway, NJ, USA, 2023; pp. 1–5.
3. Ming, F.J.; Anhum, S.S.; Islam, S.; Keoy, K.H. Facial Emotion Recognition System for Mental Stress Detection among University Students. In Proceedings of the 2023 3rd International Conference on Electrical, Computer, Communications and Mechatronics Engineering (ICECCME), Canary Islands, Spain, 19–21 July 2023; IEEE: Piscataway, NJ, USA, 2023; pp. 1–6.
4. AlWardany, S.; Hossam, S.; Moussa, K.; Darweesh, M.S. Emotion to Detect: Facial Expression Recognition by CNN. In Proceedings of the 2023 Intelligent Methods, Systems, and Applications (IMSA), Giza, Egypt, 15–16 July 2023; IEEE: Piscataway, NJ, USA, 2023; pp. 38–42.
5. Li, Q.; Liu, Y.; Liu, C.; Yan, F.; Zhang, Q.; Liu, Q.; Gao, W. EEG signal processing and emotion recognition using Convolutional Neural Network. In Proceedings of the 2021 International Conference on Electronic Information Engineering and Computer Science (EIECS), Changchun, China, 23–26 September 2021; IEEE: Piscataway, NJ, USA, 2021; pp. 81–84.
6. Liu, S.; Wang, X.; Zhao, L.; Li, B.; Hu, W.; Yu, J.; Zhang, Y.D. 3DCANN: A spatio-temporal convolution attention neural network for EEG emotion recognition. *IEEE J. Biomed. Health Inform.* **2021**, *26*, 5321–5331. [CrossRef] [PubMed]
7. Zhao, Q.; Dong, Y.; Yin, W. Emotion Recognition Based on EEG and DE-CNN-RNN. In Proceedings of the 2023 China Automation Congress (CAC), Chongqing, China, 17–19 November 2023; IEEE: Piscataway, NJ, USA, 2023; pp. 3376–3380.
8. Guo, Y.; Tang, C.; Wu, H.; Chen, B. GNN-based multi-source domain prototype representation for cross-subject EEG emotion recognition. *Neurocomputing* **2024**, *609*, 128445. [CrossRef]
9. Zhong, P.; Wang, D.; Miao, C. EEG-based emotion recognition using regularized graph neural networks. *IEEE Trans. Affect. Comput.* **2020**, *13*, 1290–1301. [CrossRef]
10. Liu, R.; Chao, Y.; Ma, X.; Sha, X.; Sun, L.; Li, S.; Chang, S. ERTNet: An interpretable transformer-based framework for EEG emotion recognition. *Front. Neurosci.* **2024**, *18*, 1320645. [CrossRef] [PubMed]
11. Kirschstein, T.; Köhling, R. What is the source of the EEG? *Clin. EEG Neurosci.* **2009**, *40*, 146–149. [CrossRef]
12. Li, M.; Xu, H.; Liu, X.; Lu, S. Emotion recognition from multichannel EEG signals using K-nearest neighbor classification. *Technol. Health Care* **2018**, *26*, 509–519. [CrossRef]
13. Chen, T.; Ju, S.; Ren, F.; Fan, M.; Gu, Y. EEG emotion recognition model based on the LIBSVM classifier. *Measurement* **2020**, *164*, 108047. [CrossRef]
14. Zheng, Y.; Ding, J.; Liu, F.; Wang, D. Adaptive neural decision tree for EEG based emotion recognition. *Inf. Sci.* **2023**, *643*, 119160. [CrossRef]
15. Xiao, M.; Zhu, Z.; Jiang, B.; Qu, M.; Wang, W. MEEG and AT-DGNN: Improving EEG Emotion Recognition with Music Introducing and Graph-based Learning. *arXiv* **2024**, arXiv:2407.05550.
16. Gupta, S.; Singh, H. Preprocessing EEG signals for direct human-system interface. In Proceedings of the IEEE International Joint Symposia on Intelligence and Systems, Rockville, MD, USA, 4–5 November 1996; IEEE: Piscataway, NJ, USA, 1996; pp. 32–37.
17. Zhang, D.; Zhang, D. Wavelet transform. In *Fundamentals of Image Data Mining: Analysis, Features, Classification and Retrieval*; Springer: Cham, Switzerland, 2019; pp. 35–44.
18. Osipov, A.; Pleshakova, E.; Liu, Y.; Gataullin, S. Machine learning methods for speech emotion recognition on telecommunication systems. *J. Comput. Virol. Hacking Tech.* **2024**, *20*, 415–428. [CrossRef]
19. Newson, J.J.; Thiagarajan, T.C. EEG frequency bands in psychiatric disorders: A review of resting state studies. *Front. Hum. Neurosci.* **2019**, *12*, 521. [CrossRef] [PubMed]
20. Beşkirli, M.; Kiran, M.S. Optimization of Butterworth and Bessel Filter Parameters with Improved Tree-Seed Algorithm. *Biomimetics* **2023**, *8*, 540. [CrossRef] [PubMed]
21. Ibrahim, D.G.A. Calibration of a step height standard for dimensional metrology using phase-shift interferometry and Hamming window: Band-pass filter. *J. Opt.* **2024**, *53*, 1420–1428. [CrossRef]
22. Ruan, C.; Zhang, Z.; Jiang, H.; Dang, J.; Wu, L.; Zhang, H. Wideband Near-Field Channel Covariance Estimation for XL-MIMO Systems in the Face of Beam Split. *IEEE Trans. Veh. Technol.* **2024**, 1–15. [CrossRef]
23. Shi, W.; Jiang, H.; Xiong, B.; Chen, X.; Zhang, H.; Chen, Z.; Wu, Q. RIS-empowered V2V communications: Three-dimensional beam domain channel modeling and analysis. *IEEE Trans. Wirel. Commun.* **2024**, *23*, 15844–15857. [CrossRef]
24. Liu, G.; Wen, Y.; Hsiao, J.H.; Zhang, D.; Tian, L.; Zhou, W. EEG-Based Familiar and Unfamiliar Face Classification Using Filter-Bank Differential Entropy Features. *IEEE Trans. Hum.-Mach. Syst.* **2023**, *54*, 44–55. [CrossRef]

25. Wang, T.; Huang, X.; Xiao, Z.; Cai, W.; Tai, Y. EEG emotion recognition based on differential entropy feature matrix through 2D-CNN-LSTM network. *EURASIP J. Adv. Signal Process.* **2024**, *2024*, 49. [CrossRef]
26. Zaheer, S.; Anjum, N.; Hussain, S.; Algarni, A.D.; Iqbal, J.; Bourouis, S.; Ullah, S.S. A multi parameter forecasting for stock time series data using LSTM and deep learning model. *Mathematics* **2023**, *11*, 590. [CrossRef]
27. Yedukondalu, J.; Sharma, D.; Sharma, L.D. Subject-Wise Cognitive Load Detection Using Time–Frequency EEG and Bi-LSTM. *Arab. J. Sci. Eng.* **2024**, *49*, 4445–4457. [CrossRef]
28. Rajwal, S.; Aggarwal, S. Convolutional neural network-based EEG signal analysis: A systematic review. *Arch. Comput. Methods Eng.* **2023**, *30*, 3585–3615. [CrossRef]
29. Wang, X.; Ma, Y.; Cammon, J.; Fang, F.; Gao, Y.; Zhang, Y. Self-supervised EEG emotion recognition models based on CNN. *IEEE Trans. Neural Syst. Rehabil. Eng.* **2023**, *31*, 1952–1962. [CrossRef] [PubMed]
30. Lu, S.; Liu, M.; Yin, L.; Yin, Z.; Liu, X.; Zheng, W. The multi-modal fusion in visual question answering: A review of attention mechanisms. *PeerJ Comput. Sci.* **2023**, *9*, e1400. [CrossRef] [PubMed]
31. Liu, T.; Xu, C.; Qiao, Y.; Jiang, C.; Chen, W. News recommendation with attention mechanism. *arXiv* **2024**, arXiv:2402.07422.
32. Koelstra, S.; Muhl, C.; Soleymani, M.; Lee, J.-S.; Yazdani, A.; Ebrahimi, T.; Pun, T.; Nijholt, A.; Patras, I. Deap: A database for emotion analysis; using physiological signals. *IEEE Trans. Affect. Comput.* **2011**, *3*, 18–31. [CrossRef]
33. Scherer, K.R. What are emotions? And how can they be measured? *Soc. Sci. Inf.* **2005**, *44*, 695–729. [CrossRef]
34. Zheng, W.L.; Liu, W.; Lu, Y.; Lu, B.L.; Cichocki, A. Emotionmeter: A multimodal framework for recognizing human emotions. *IEEE Trans. Cybern.* **2018**, *49*, 1110–1122. [CrossRef]
35. Kingma, D.P. Adam: A method for stochastic optimization. *arXiv* **2014**, arXiv:1412.6980.
36. Yacouby, R.; Axman, D. Probabilistic extension of precision, recall, and f1 score for more thorough evaluation of classification models. In Proceedings of the First Workshop on Evaluation and Comparison of NLP Systems, Online, 20 November 2022; pp. 79–91.
37. Lee, D.K.; In, J.; Lee, S. Standard deviation and standard error of the mean. *Korean J. Anesthesiol.* **2015**, *68*, 220–223. [CrossRef]
38. Lobo, J.M.; Jiménez-Valverde, A.; Real, R. AUC: A misleading measure of the performance of predictive distribution models. *Glob. Ecol. Biogeogr.* **2008**, *17*, 145–151. [CrossRef]
39. Jahromy, F.Z.; Bajoulvand, A.; Daliri, M.R. Statistical algorithms for emotion classification via functional connectivity. *J. Integr. Neurosci.* **2019**, *18*, 293–297. [CrossRef]
40. Yan, Z.; Zhou, J.; Wong, W.-F. EEG classification with spiking neural network: Smaller, better, more energy efficient. *Smart Health* **2022**, *24*, 100261. [CrossRef]
41. Li, D.; Xie, L.; Wang, Z.; Yang, H. Brain emotion perception inspired EEG emotion recognition with deep reinforcement learning. *IEEE Trans. Neural Netw. Learn. Syst.* **2023**, *35*, 12979–12992. [CrossRef] [PubMed]
42. Huang, L.; Su, Y.; Ma, J.; Ding, W.; Song, C. Research on Support Tensor Machine Based on Synchronous Brain Network for Emotion Classification. *J. Electron. Inf. Technol.* **2020**, *42*, 2462–2470.
43. Fang, H.; Shrestha, A.; Zhao, Z.; Qiu, Q. Exploiting neuron and synapse filter dynamics in spatial temporal learning of deep spiking neural network. *arXiv* **2020**, arXiv:2003.02944.
44. Li, W.; Fang, C.; Zhu, Z.; Chen, C.; Song, A. Fractal spiking neural network scheme for EEG-based emotion recognition. *IEEE J. Transl. Eng. Health Med.* **2023**, *12*, 106–118. [CrossRef]
45. Li, P.; Liu, H.; Si, Y.; Li, C.; Li, F.; Zhu, X.; Huang, X.; Zeng, Y.; Yao, D.; Zhang, Y.; et al. EEG based emotion recognition by combining functional connectivity network and local activations. *IEEE Trans. Biomed. Eng.* **2019**, *66*, 2869–2881. [CrossRef]
46. Luo, Y.; Fu, Q.; Xie, J.; Qin, Y.; Wu, G.; Liu, J.; Jiang, F.; Cao, Y.; Ding, X. EEG-based emotion classification using spiking neural networks. *IEEE Access* **2020**, *8*, 46007–46016. [CrossRef]
47. Song, T.; Zheng, W.; Song, P.; Cui, Z. EEG emotion recognition using dynamical graph convolutional neural networks. *IEEE Trans. Affect. Comput.* **2018**, *11*, 532–541. [CrossRef]
48. Long, X.; Zhuang, W.; Xia, M.; Hu, K.; Lin, H. SASiamNet: Self-adaptive Siamese Network for change detection of remote sensing image. *IEEE J. Sel. Top. Appl. Earth Obs. Remote Sens.* **2023**, *17*, 1021–1034. [CrossRef]

*sensors*

MDPI

*Article*

# Node Classification Method Based on Hierarchical Hypergraph Neural Network

**Feng Xu [1,2], Wanyue Xiong [1], Zizhu Fan [3,*] and Licheng Sun [4]**

1 School of Electrical and Automation Engineering, East China Jiaotong University, Nanchang 330013, China; 2022029081100008@ecjtu.edu.cn (F.X.); 2021088085400002@ecjtu.edu.cn (W.X.)
2 School of Mechanical and Electrical Engineering, Quzhou College of Technology, Quzhou 324000, China
3 College of Computer Science and Technology, Shanghai University of Electric Power, Shanghai 200090, China
4 Mechanical and Electrical Room, Quzhou Special Equipment Inspection & Testing Research Institute, Quzhou 324000, China; amenslc@163.com
* Correspondence: zzfan3@163.com

**Abstract:** Hypergraph neural networks have gained widespread attention due to their effectiveness in handling graph-structured data with complex relationships and multi-dimensional interactions. However, existing hypergraph neural network models mainly rely on planar message-passing mechanisms, which have limitations: (i) low efficiency in encoding long-distance information; (ii) underutilization of high-order neighborhood features, aggregating information only on the edges of the original graph. This paper proposes an innovative hierarchical hypergraph neural network (HCHG) to address these issues. The HCHG combines the high-order relationship-capturing capability of hypergraphs, uses the Louvain community detection algorithm to identify community structures within the network, and constructs hypergraphs layer by layer. In the bottom-level hypergraph, the model establishes high-order relationships through direct neighbor nodes, while in the top-level hypergraph, it captures global relationships between aggregated communities. Through three hierarchical message-passing mechanisms, the HCHG effectively integrates local and global information, enhancing the multi-resolution representation ability of node representations and significantly improving performance in node classification tasks. In addition, the model performs excellently in handling 3D multi-view datasets. Such datasets can be created by capturing 3D shapes and geometric features through sensors or by manual modeling, providing extensive application scenarios for analyzing three-dimensional shapes and complex geometric structures. Theoretical analysis and experimental results show that the HCHG outperforms traditional hypergraph neural networks in complex networks.

**Keywords:** hypergraph neural networks; hierarchical representations; Node classification

## 1. Introduction

Graph neural networks (GNNs) have garnered significant attention recently, emerging as powerful tools for processing graph-structured data. They are widely applied in various domains such as social networks [1,2], Photogrammetry [3,4], 3D object classification [5,6], the Internet of Things [7], and bioinformatics [8,9]. GNNs can effectively capture local relationships between nodes within a graph by aggregating information from neighboring nodes, enabling tasks such as node classification and link prediction [10,11]. For instance, in 3D object classification, GNNs utilize point cloud and depth data from sensors like LiDAR and RGB-D cameras, leveraging spatial relationships among nodes to enhance classification accuracy by capturing geometric features, especially in complex scenes. Classic GNN models, including GCN [12], GAT [13], and GraphSAGE [8], have achieved substantial advances in representation learning for graph data. However, these models exhibit limitations when handling complex graph structures and long-range dependencies among nodes.

Specifically, the flat message-passing mechanism of traditional GNNs makes it difficult to capture relationships between distant nodes effectively [14,15]. Furthermore, existing graph structures are often overly simplistic, primarily designed for binary relationships, which limits their ability to express multi-relational interactions fully. This directly results in traditional graph neural networks performing poorly in capturing global and local graph information, affecting classification effectiveness. Lastly, GNNs face memory and GPU memory constraints when handling complex graphs, making it challenging to scale to practical applications such as community detection [8].

The introduction of hypergraph structures presents a new approach to addressing these issues. Hypergraphs can capture high-order relationships among multiple nodes, transcending superficial binary relationships, thus better representing multilateral interactions in complex networks [16]. For example, hypergraphs are embedded into a low-dimensional space for clustering analysis, revealing the underlying group structures within the data. However, traditional hypergraph structures may have limitations when handling dynamically changing datasets, as they cannot adapt to rapidly evolving relationships, leading to delayed classification results [17]. At the same time, although hyperedge convolution layers can learn higher-order relationships in complex data, their high computational complexity affects the practicality of the model [18].

The hierarchical mechanism offers a new approach to addressing long-range dependencies and expressing hierarchical information. The hierarchical message-passing mechanism, which progressively aggregates local and global information, can effectively enhance the robustness and expressiveness of node representations [19]. For instance, hierarchical graph pooling methods, such as G-U-Net and DiffPool, have significantly improved in graph classification tasks [20,21]. Although some studies have combined hierarchical structures with graph learning models, there remains a lack of research on integrating hierarchical mechanisms with hypergraph neural networks for node classification.

To address key challenges in traditional GNNs and hypergraph neural networks, we introduce the Hierarchical Hypergraph Neural Network (HCHG). While GNNs struggle with long-range dependencies and global context, hypergraph neural networks excel at capturing higher-order relationships but are computationally expensive. HCHG constructs hypergraphs layer by layer, with the first layer capturing local relationships and subsequent layers aggregating community nodes to model global relationships, enhancing the model's ability to represent local and global interactions. Additionally, HCHG uses a multi-layer message-passing mechanism, including bottom-up, lateral, and top-down flows, which strengthens node representations and reduces the computational burden, efficiently handling complex networks.

The main contributions of this paper are as follows:

1. We propose the HCHG model. This novel approach combines hierarchical structures with hypergraph neural networks to effectively capture local and global relationships in node classification and link prediction tasks, improving performance on complex graphs.
2. The HCHG model introduces a hierarchical construction method, using the Louvain community detection algorithm to build higher-order relationship networks, enhancing the model's ability to represent complex network structures.
3. Our method performs excellently on six classification datasets and three link prediction datasets, achieving significant performance improvements across multiple tasks.

## 2. Related Work

Node classification is a core task in graph representation learning, aiming to predict a node's category based on its structure and attributes. Although Graph Neural Networks (GNNs), such as GCNs [12] and GraphSAGE [8], have achieved significant progress in node classification tasks, they still face challenges in capturing long-range dependencies and handling sparse graph structures, which are critical for node classification in complex networks.

In recent years, hypergraph representation learning has provided new solutions by modeling higher-order relationships between nodes. For example, end-to-end hypergraph convolution [22] and Dynamic Hypergraph Neural Networks (DHGNN) [23] effectively capture complex node interactions. While simplifying computation, HyperGCN [24] may lose some high-order structural information. Furthermore, HyperSAGE [25] enhances generalization capabilities through an inductive message-passing mechanism. However, these methods still face limitations in integrating global and local information, particularly in dynamic and complex network scenarios. Researchers have introduced hierarchical structures into node classification tasks to enhance the capacity for multi-granularity semantic modeling. Methods such as DiffPool [21] and ASAP [19] significantly improve representation through node aggregation, but their applications in node-level tasks remain limited by the shortcomings of single-layer models.

We propose the HCHG, which leverages a multi-layer structure and diverse message-passing mechanisms to effectively integrate local and global information while enhancing adaptability and generalization. Experiments demonstrate that HCHG achieves outstanding performance across multiple node classification datasets, particularly excelling in modeling higher-order relationships and complex node interactions.

## 3. Motivation and Background

Given a hypergraph structure $HG = (V, E, H)$, the objective is to construct a mapping function $F : HG \to Z \in \mathbb{R}^{|V| \times d}$ that captures the features of node $v_i$ and its relationships within the hypergraph. The effectiveness of $F$ will be evaluated through tasks such as node classification and link prediction.

In hypergraph neural networks, the node update mechanism differs from traditional Graph Neural Networks. A hypergraph consists of nodes and edges (hyperedges); each can connect multiple nodes. Below, we will detail the fundamental mechanism of node updates in hypergraph neural networks. Consider the hypergraph $HG = (V, E, H)$, where $V$ is the set of nodes, $E$ is the set of edges, and $H$ is the set of hyperedges. Each hyperedge $h_i \in H$ connects multiple nodes. The node update process in hypergraph neural networks typically involves the following two steps:

1. Message Aggregation

At layer $l$, the message aggregation for node $v$ is completed through all hyperedges connected to $v$. The aggregation can be represented as follows:

$$m_{agg}^{(l)} = \text{Aggregate}_N\left(\{W_{kv}^{(l)}, h_k^{(l)} \mid k \in N(v)\}\right) \tag{1}$$

where $\text{Aggregate}_N(\cdot)$ is a differentiable aggregation function, $W_{kv}^{(l)}$ is the association matrix between node $k$ and node $v$, $h_k^{(l)}$ represents the features of node $k$ at layer $l$, and $N(v)$ is the set of neighbor nodes directly connected to node $v$.

2. Node Feature Update

Using the aggregated message $m_{agg}^{(l)}$, the feature of node $v$ is updated as follows:

$$\begin{cases} h_v^{(l)} = \text{Combine}(m_{agg}^{(l)}, m_{vgg}^{(l)}) \\ m_{vgg}^{(l)} = \text{Aggregate}_I\left(\{W_{kv}^{(l)} \mid k \in N(v)\}\right) h_v^{(l-1)} \end{cases} \tag{2}$$

where $\text{Combine}(\cdot)$ is a nonlinear fusion function, $\text{Aggregate}_I(\cdot)$ is another aggregation function, and $h_v^{(l-1)}$ refers to the features of node $v$ from the previous layer.

## 4. Hierarchical Hypergraph Neural Networks

We propose the HCHG framework to enable node representations to receive long-range messages and multi-granularity semantics through a hierarchical hypergraph structure. As illustrated in Figure 1, this framework first creates a progressively refined hierarchical structure, processing the input hypergraph in layers. Next, hypergraphs are constructed to facilitate message-passing between supernodes based on the connectivity among hierarchical nodes. To ensure adequate information flow, we design three message propagation mechanisms: bottom-up, intra-layer, and top-down. These mechanisms ensure information exchange both within the same level and across different levels. Finally, we train the model using task-specific loss functions and gradient descent algorithms, optimizing node representations and overall performance.

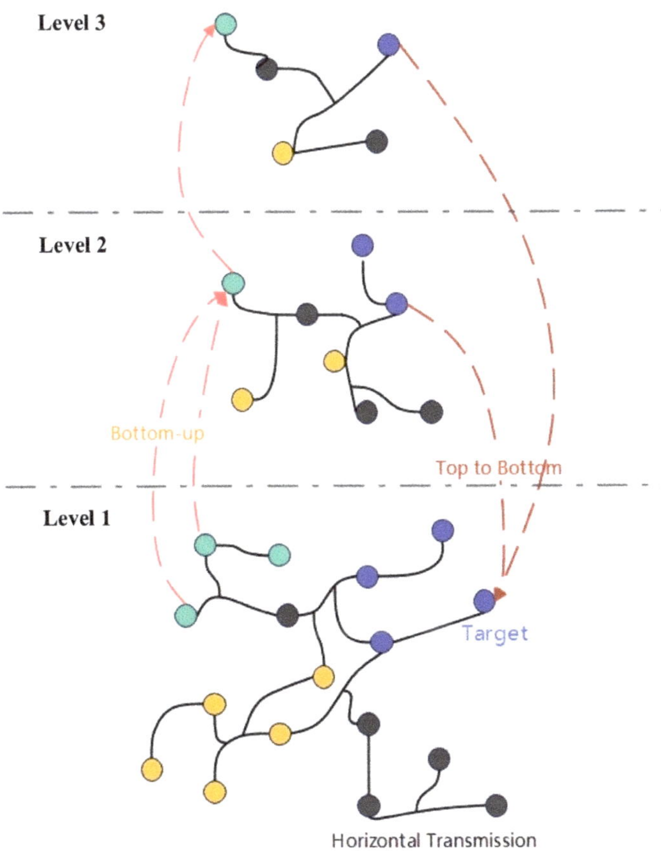


**Figure 1.** Hierarchical Hypergraph Neural Network Framework (Different colors represent different types of nodes).

### 4.1. Hierarchical Structure Partitioning

For complex multi-node relational systems, we first represent the raw data as a graph $G = (V, E)$, where $V$ is the set of nodes representing different entities, and $E$ is the set of edges depicting relationships between these entities. To capture the higher-order relationships among nodes more effectively, we introduce hyperedges $H$, defined as $h = \{v_1, v_2, \ldots, v_n\}$, where $v_i \in V$. This constructs a hypergraph $HG = (V, E, H)$.

On this basis, our study employs a hierarchical mechanism that simplifies the graph's structure through layer-wise abstraction and aggregation. In each layer, we convert the node-set $V$ into a higher-level set of supernodes by partitioning the nodes into communities. For instance, the supernodes in the first layer arise from the community partitioning of the original nodes. In contrast, subsequent layers' supernodes are formed by combining the supernodes from the preceding layer. This approach allows the hierarchical structure to evolve progressively from the lower to the upper layers, facilitating higher-level analysis and modeling.

### 4.2. Hierarchical Hypergraph Construction

In constructing the hypergraph, the first layer hypergraph starts from the original. We utilize the Louvain community detection algorithm to identify communities within the node set $V$ through modularity optimization. Each identified community $C_i \subseteq V$ forms a supernode, resulting in a supernode set $S_1 = \{SC_1^1, SC_2^1, \ldots, SC_p^1\}$, considered the first layer. Once the supernodes are established, we create edges between them. Suppose an edge exists between two communities, $C_i$ and $C_j$ (for example, through common original nodes or connecting hyperedges). In that case, we create an edge $e_{ij}$ between their corresponding supernodes $SC_i$ and $SC_j$.

We view the original nodes within each community as components of the hyperedges for hyperedge construction. Specifically, for the set of original nodes $V_{C_i} = \{v_k \mid v_k \in C_i\}$ within each community $C_i$, we define a hyperedge $h_i$ that includes all original nodes within community $C_i$, i.e., $h_i = V_{C_i}$. Thus, the set of hyperedges $H_1$ of the first layer hypergraph $HG_1$ consists of all hyperedges corresponding to the communities: $H_1 = \{h_i \mid i = 1, 2, \ldots, p\}$. Ultimately, the first layer hypergraph can be represented as $HG_1 = (S_1, E_1, H_1)$, where $E_1$ is the set of edges between supernodes, and $H_1$ is the collection of hyperedges within $S_1$.

When generating the second layer hypergraph, we again apply the Louvain community detection algorithm to aggregate the first layer supernodes, forming the second layer supernode set $S_2 = \{SC_1^2, SC_2^2, \ldots, SC_m^2\}$. During this process, if there exists an edge between the second layer supernodes $SC_k^2$ and $SC_l^2$, we establish an edge $e_{kl}$ between them. Additionally, we construct hyperedges for the second layer supernodes, defining each hyperedge $h_k$ formed by the supernodes in community $C_k$. Specifically, each hyperedge $h_k$ in the second layer consists of all first layer supernodes $SC_i^1$ that belong to community $C_k$, i.e., $h_k = \{SC_i^1 \mid SC_i^1 \in C_k\}$. Ultimately, the second layer hypergraph is represented as $HG_2 = (S_2, E_2, H_2)$, where $H_2$ is the collection of hyperedges within $S_2$.

### 4.3. Hierarchical Information Propagation

The hierarchical message-passing mechanism enhances node representations through long-range interaction and neighborhood aggregation. This mechanism does not interfere with the process of learning planar node representations, thereby effectively preserving the original information of the nodes. The hierarchical message-passing mechanism consists of the following three methods.

After obtaining the node representations of the $(t-1)$-th layer hypergraph $h_{s_j^{t-1}}^{(l)}$ using the node update mechanism, these representations are aggregated to update the supernode representations in the $t$-th layer. A schematic illustration is shown in Figure 2, with the mathematical expression for aggregation given by:

$$a_{SC_i^t}^{(l)} = \frac{1}{|SC_i^t| + 1} \left( \sum_{s_j^{t-1} \in SC_i^t} h_{s_j^{t-1}}^{(l)} + h_{SC_i^t}^{(l-1)} \right) \tag{3}$$

where $SC_i^t$ is the supernode in the $t$-th layer, $s_j^{t-1}$ represents the nodes belonging to $SC_i^t$ in the $(t-1)$-th layer, $|SC_i^t|$ is the number of nodes belonging to $SC_i^t$ in the $(t-1)$-th layer, and $h_{SC_i^t}^{(l-1)}$ represents the node representations of the supernode $SC_i^t$ in the $t$-th layer of the $(l-1)$-th layer.

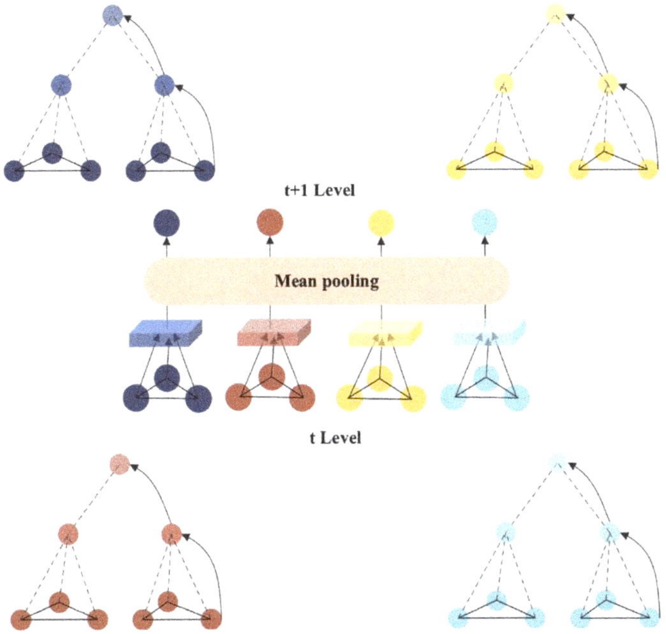


**Figure 2.** Schematic Diagram of Bottom-Up Propagation.

## 4.4. Inter-Layer Propagation

Inter-layer propagation primarily relies on hypergraph neural networks' planar message-passing mechanism to aggregate neighboring information and update node representations within the same layer. A schematic illustration is shown in Figure 3. Based on the bottom-up propagation, the aggregation process of information from higher-layer supernodes is represented as follows:

$$\begin{cases} m_{agg}^{(l)} = \text{Aggregate}_N\left(\{W_{kv}^{(l)}, a_u^{(l)} \mid k \in N(v)\}\right) \\ m_{vgg}^{(l)} = \text{Aggregate}_I\left(\{W_{kv}^{(l)} \mid k \in N(v)\}\right)h_v^{(l-1)} \\ b_v^{(l)} = \text{Combine}(m_{agg}^{(l)}, m_{vgg}^{(l)}) \end{cases} \quad (4)$$

where $a_u^{(l)}$ is the representation of supernode $u$ after bottom-up propagation, and $b_v^{(l)}$ is the updated feature representation of node $v$ in layer $l$. The meanings of the remaining parameters are consistent with those in Section 3.

The node representations from the hypergraphs $\{G_2, \ldots, G_T\}$ are used to update the node representations in the original graph $G$. The importance of information from different layers varies depending on the specific task. Therefore, an attention mechanism proposed by Veličković et al. is employed to adaptively learn the weights of the information during the top-down integration process [26]. A schematic illustration is shown in Figure 4, represented as follows:

$$h_v^l = \text{ReLU}\left(\sum_{u \in N^l(v)} \alpha_{uv}^l W^l \cdot \text{MEAN}(b_u^l)\right) \quad (5)$$

where $\alpha_{uv}^l$ is a trainable attention coefficient that represents the connection weight between nodes $v$ and $u$ across different layers. Here, $b_u$ is the bias term, MEAN denotes the element-wise average operation, and ReLU is the activation function. Ultimately, the node information representation from the last layer $L$ is output using the following formula [27]:

$$z_v = \sigma\left(\sum_{u \in N^L(v)} \alpha_{uv}^L W^L \cdot \text{MEAN}(b_u^L)\right) \tag{6}$$

where $\sigma$ is the Euclidean normalization function that adjusts values to the range of $[0, 1]$. The final generated node representations $Z \in \mathbb{R}^{n \times d}$ are used for classification, with each row $z_v \in Z$ representing the representation of a node $v$.

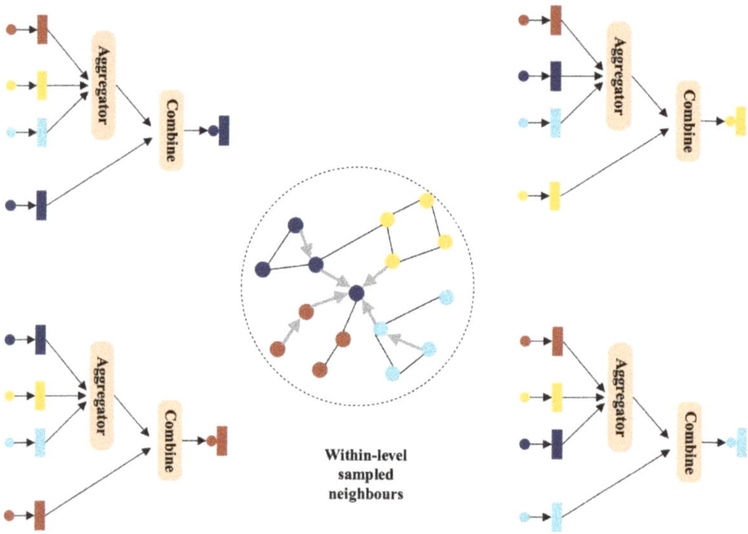


**Figure 3.** Schematic Diagram of Inter-Layer Propagation.

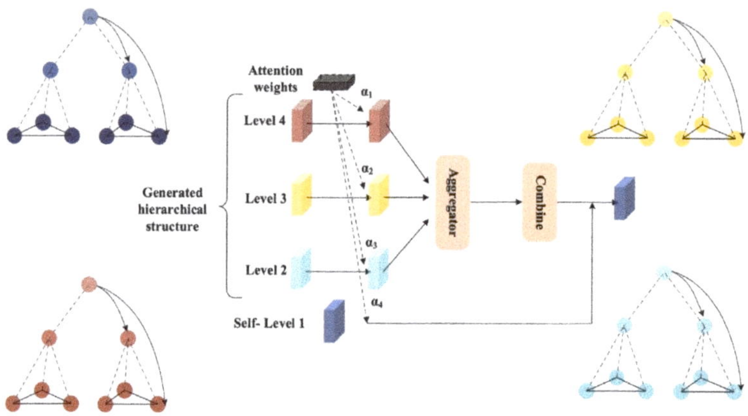


**Figure 4.** Schematic Diagram of Top-Down Propagation.

### 4.5. Model Training

In the experimental section, HCHG is applied to the training and prediction of semi-supervised node classification. The designed cross-entropy loss function is defined as follows:

$$L = -\sum_{v \in V} y_v^T \log(\mathrm{Softmax}(z_v)) \tag{7}$$

where $y_v^T$ is the one-hot encoded label vector representing node $v$. The loss function $L$ can be specifically modified based on different tasks.

The computational complexity analysis presented in this paper consists of three main components: the hierarchical construction of graphs, the construction of hypergraphs, and the information propagation mechanism. The time complexity of the Louvain algorithm during the hierarchical construction process at each layer is $O(m_t \log n_t)$. The complexity of hypergraph construction is $O(n_t + e_t)$. The complexity of the information propagation mechanism is $O(n_t d_t + e_t)$. Ultimately, the overall computational complexity can be expressed as:

$$O\left(\sum_{t=1}^{T} (m_t \log n_t + n_t + e_t + n_t d_t)\right) \tag{8}$$

where $T$ is the number of layers in the graph, and $m_t$, $n_t$, $e_t$, and $d_t$ represent the number of edges, nodes, hyperedges, and the average degree of nodes in layer $t$, respectively.

The following Algorithm 1 provides a brief summary of the construction process of the HCHG model.

**Algorithm 1:** Hierarchical Hypergraph Neural Network

**Input** : Graph $HG = (V, E, H)$
**Output:** Node representation $Z \in \mathbb{R}^{n \times d}$

$h_v^{(0)} \leftarrow x_v$;
$H = \{G_t \mid t = 1, 2, \ldots, T\}$;
**for** $l \leftarrow 1$ **to** $L$ **do**
    $h_v^{(l)} = \mathrm{ReLU}\left(\sum_{u \in N(v)} \frac{W^{(l)} h_u^{(l-1)}}{\sqrt{|N(u)||N(v)|}} + \frac{W^{(l)} h_v^{(l-1)}}{\sqrt{|N(v)||N(v)|}}\right)$;
    **for** $t \leftarrow 2$ **to** $T$ **do**
        $a_{SC_i^t}^{(l)} = \frac{1}{|SC_i^t|+1}\left(\sum_{s_j^{t-1} \in SC_i^t} h_{s_j^{t-1}}^{(l)} + h_{SC_i^t}^{(l-1)}\right)$
        $b_v^{(l)} = \mathrm{ReLU}\left(\sum_{u \in N(v)} \frac{W^{(l)} a_u^{(l)}}{\sqrt{|N(u)||N(u)|}} + \frac{W^{(l)} a_v^{(l)}}{\sqrt{|N(v)||N(v)|}}\right), \forall v \in HG$;
    **end**
    **for** $v \in G$ **do**
        **if** $l < L$ **then**
            $h_v^l = \mathrm{ReLU}\left(\sum_{u \in N^l(v)} \alpha_{uv}^l W^l \cdot \mathrm{MEAN}(b_u^l)\right)$
        **end**
        **else**
            $z_v = \sigma\left(\sum_{u \in N^L(v)} \alpha_{uv}^L W^L \cdot \mathrm{MEAN}(b_u^L)\right)$
        **end**
    **end**
**end**

## 5. Experimental Analysis

### 5.1. Datasets

To verify the model's overall performance, several commonly used datasets were used in the experiments, including graph-structured and multiview datasets. The graph-structured datasets contain rich node and edge relationships. In contrast, multi-view datasets can be generated by creating images from 3D models or using sensors to capture data from different angles, providing a comprehensive representation of the objects. Table 1 summarizes all the datasets used in the experiments.

**Table 1.** Categorical Dataset.

| Dataset | Nodes/Feature | Train/(val)/Test | Class |
|---|---|---|---|
| Cora | 2708/1433 | 140/500/1000 | 7 |
| Citeseer | 3312/3703 | 140/500/1000 | 6 |
| Pubmed | 19,717/500 | 60/500/1000 | 3 |
| Zoo | 101/16 | 66/35 | 7 |
| Grid | 400 | - | - |
| ModelNet40 | 12,311/(2048/4096) | 9843/2468 | 44 |
| NTU2012 | 2012/(2048/4096) | 1640/372 | 67 |

1. Graph-structured Datasets

Cora and Citeseer are citation network datasets introduced by Sen et al. [28]. Cora consists of 2708 scientific publications and 5429 links. Each publication is represented as a node with a 1433-dimensional word vector as its feature. Citeseer consists of 3312 scientific publications and 4660 links, with each node having a 3703-dimensional word vector.

Pubmed, introduced by Namata et al. [29], includes 19,717 scientific publications about diabetes from the Pubmed database, divided into three classes. Each node is represented by a TF/IDF weighted word vector consisting of 500 words.

The Zoo dataset is downloaded from the UCI website. Each sample contains 17 Boolean attributes. Hyperedges are created for nodes with the same classification feature value.

Grid is a synthetic 2D grid graph representing a $20 \times 20$ grid with 400 nodes and no node features. This dataset is only for link prediction.

2. Multiview Datasets

The ModelNet40 dataset consists of 12,311 objects from 40 popular categories, split into training and test sets, with 9843 objects for training and 2468 objects for testing. NTU2012 (National Taiwan University (NTU) 3D Dataset) is a dataset from the computer vision/graphics field. It comprises 2012 3D shapes from 67 categories, including cars, chairs, chessboards, chips, clocks, cups, doors, frames, pens, plant leaves, etc. In the NTU2012 dataset, 80% of the data is used for training, and the remaining 20% is used for testing.

In the experiments, each 3D object is represented by extracted features. Two state-of-the-art shape representation methods, Multi-View Convolutional Neural Network (MVCNN) and Group-View Convolutional Neural Network (GVCNN), are adopted here. These two methods have shown satisfactory performance in representing 3D objects. Following the experimental settings of MVCNN and GVCNN, multiple views of each 3D object are generated.

### 5.2. Experimental Setup and Results

Applying the HCHG model to the node classification task on the dataset, multiple averaged results are preserved in the experiments. For HGNN convolutional layers $\{256, 128, 64, 32\}$, experiments are conducted with 2 or 3 convolutional layers and a $1 \times 10^{-5}$ learning rate. The correlation between different views is modeled for the multiview data by generating a hypergraph $G$. For each view's data, an adjacency matrix $H_i$ of the hypergraph is constructed based on the HGNN proposed by Feng et al. [22]. As shown in Figure 5, the adjacency matrices $H_i$ of different views are concatenated to construct the adjacency matrix $H$ of the multiview hypergraph, thus creating a hypergraph structure with multiview features. Since the macro-level graph, $G_T$ of the macro-level layer is relatively small, during the experiment, we averaged the input label information by pooling $G_T$ and added the loss function separately to calculate the edge information in the $T$ layer. The experimental results showed no impact on the data. The possible reason is that the macro-level layer contains very little information and has minimal influence on the target nodes after top-down propagation. Therefore, the small changes in the node connection mode in $G_T$ have a negligible effect on the results.

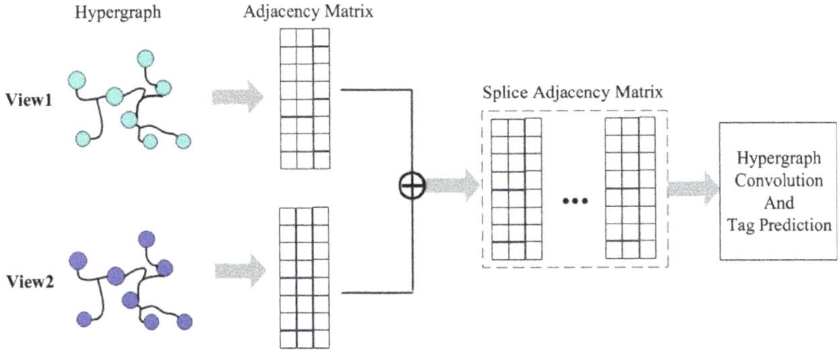


**Figure 5.** Multimodal Data Fusion.

A comparison of the HCHG model with other graph neural network models for node classification was conducted. Experimental results were collected for eight models, including Hyper-Conv, HC-GNN [27], GCN [12], GAT [13], FastGCN [30], LADIES [31], and DNGNN [32], HJRL [33] on standard datasets, as shown in Table 2. For the link prediction, six models—GCN, GraphSAGE [8], GIN [14], G-U-Net [20], GXN [34], and HC-GNN—were compared, as shown in Table 3. The results with node and without node features were evaluated in the experiments with the Cora dataset. The results show that HCHG performs well in terms of node classification and link prediction accuracy.

**Table 2.** Average Test Accuracy (%) ± Standard Deviation for Node Classification Tasks.

| Model (Author, Year) | Zoo | Cora | Pubmed | Citeseer |
|---|---|---|---|---|
| GCN [12] | 60.0 ± 1.5 | 80.2 ± 0.9 | 77.9 ± 1.1 | 64.8 ± 1.4 |
| GAT [13] | 48.5 ± 1.2 | 77.2 ± 1.0 | 77.5 ± 0.8 | 62.0 ± 1.3 |
| FastGCN [30] | 37.8 ± 1.6 | 78.0 ± 0.8 | 74.4 ± 1.3 | 63.5 ± 1.5 |
| LADIES [31] | 37.8 ± 1.7 | 78.3 ± 0.7 | 76.8 ± 1.2 | 65.0 ± 1.1 |
| Hyper-Conv [27] | 93.1 ± 0.4 | 82.7 ± 0.5 | 78.4 ± 0.6 | 71.2 ± 0.7 |
| LE [27] | 97.0 ± 0.2 | 82.3 ± 0.4 | 78.7 ± 0.5 | 70.4 ± 0.6 |
| HC-GNN [27] | 85.7 ± 0.5 | 79.0 ± 0.6 | 78.7 ± 0.4 | 65.9 ± 1.0 |
| HJRL [29] | 96.3 ± 0.3 | 77.6 ± 0.5 | 77.3 ± 0.6 | 65.1 ± 1.2 |
| HCHG (Ours) | 97.1 ± 0.2 | 79.8 ± 0.6 | 79.4 ± 0.5 | 66.2 ± 1.0 |

**Table 3.** Average Test Accuracy (%) ± Standard Deviation for Link Prediction Tasks.

| Model (Author, Year) | Grid | Cora-Feat | Cora-noFeat |
|---|---|---|---|
| GCN [12] | 76.3 ± 1.2 | 86.9 ± 0.9 | 78.5 ± 1.1 |
| GraphSAGE [8] | 77.5 ± 1.1 | 87.0 ± 0.7 | 74.1 ± 1.3 |
| GIN [14] | 75.6 ± 1.0 | 86.2 ± 0.8 | 78.2 ± 1.2 |
| G-U-Net [20] | 70.1 ± 1.5 | 90.9 ± 0.6 | 77.2 ± 1.0 |
| GXN [34] | 64.2 ± 1.4 | 88.9 ± 0.8 | 78.1 ± 1.1 |
| HC-GNN [27] | 80.1 ± 1.3 | 89.4 ± 0.7 | 77.6 ± 1.0 |
| HCHG (Ours) | 87.8 ± 0.9 | 82.1 ± 1.2 | 78.5 ± 1.1 |

For the multiview dataset (Table 4), a comparison was made between Hyper-Conv, LADIES, HGNN, HJRL, HGNN+ [35], and HC-HGNN. HCHG showed an improvement of approximately 6% on the NTU2012 dataset compared to other models, while HCHG and HC-GNN showed improvements on the ModelNet40 dataset. The superior performance of HCHG may be attributed to its hierarchical structure, which allows the model to capture the topological information of the graph, i.e., the message propagated from distant nodes in the graph. Moreover, the intermediate and macro-level semantics reflected in the hierarchical structure are encoded through bottom-up, intra-layer, and top-down propagation. On the ModelNet40 dataset, the HCHG model achieved an accuracy of 97%, surpassing other models such as Hyper-Conv, which attained 92%, demonstrating its adaptability to diverse data structures.

**Table 4.** Average Test Accuracy (%) ± Standard Deviation for Node Classification Tasks.

| Model (Author, Year) | NTU2012 | ModelNet40 |
|---|---|---|
| Hyper-Conv [27] | 79.4 ± 0.8 | 91.1 ± 1.2 |
| LE [27] | 83.2 ± 1.6 | 94.1 ± 1.3 |
| HGNN [35] | 84.2 ± 1.4 | 96.7 ± 1.2 |
| HGNN+ [35] | 84.2 ± 1.5 | 96.9 ± 1.1 |
| HC-GNN [27] | 83.3 ± 1.0 | 98.1 ± 0.8 |
| HJRL [29] | 86.1 ± 1.3 | 95.8 ± 1.4 |
| HCHG (ours) | 90.0 ± 1.1 | 97.4 ± 1.3 |

Additionally, with its ability to simultaneously aggregate information from multiple nodes, the hypergraph structure enables better capture of community structure information during the learning process. For example, on the NTU dataset, the HCHG model achieved an accuracy of 90%, a significant improvement compared to other models like HC-GNN, which achieved 85%.

The HCHG model demonstrates strong generalization capabilities when handling multimodal data, effectively adapting to various datasets. Its performance across diverse datasets, including Cora, Pubmed, Citeseer, Zoo, NTU, and ModelNet40, surpasses other models.

By integrating hypergraph structures and hierarchical information, the HCHG model can more effectively capture complex relationships surrounding nodes. In ablation experiments, the HCHG model consistently yielded favorable results across different numbers of node neighbors, confirming its adaptability to graphs of varying scales.

In summary, by combining hypergraph structures and hierarchical information, the HCHG model efficiently captures the intricate associations among multimodal data and achieves outstanding performance in node classification across various datasets.

Finally, in the experiments, HC-GNN, which is constructed using GCN, was compared to HCHG to investigate the impact of the hypergraph structure on the experimental results. It was found that the effect varies for different datasets. Not all graph community structures are suitable for the hypergraph structure, and this needs to be considered in different problem scenarios. Table 5 presents the ablation experiments on the multiview data, comparing the classification results for the same nodes under various scenarios of single-view and multiview. The results from the three models in the experiment demonstrated that multiview data carries more information, which is beneficial for classification. Finally, a comparison was made on the number of neighboring nodes using the ModelNet40 and NTU2012 datasets. As shown in Figure 6, the different performances of the HC-GNN and the proposed HCHG model with varying numbers of neighboring nodes are displayed. It can be observed that the HCHG model achieves the best results even with fewer neighboring nodes, indicating that the hypergraph structure can aggregate neighbor information more quickly and accurately.

**Table 5.** Average Test Accuracy (%) ± Standard Deviation for Multi-view Data vs. Single-view Data Comparison.

| View | HC-GNN [27] | HGNN [35] | HJRL [29] | HCHG (Ours) |
|---|---|---|---|---|
| NTU (mvcnn) | 73.7 ± 1.1 | 69.8 ± 0.9 | 69.6 ± 1.2 | 70.7 ± 1.0 |
| NTU (gvcnn) | 69.7 ± 0.8 | 79.5 ± 0.7 | 80.3 ± 1.6 | 85.7 ± 1.2 |
| NTU (mvc. and gvc.) | 83.3 ± 1.0 | 84.2 ± 1.4 | 86.1 ± 1.3 | 90.0 ± 0.8 |
| ModelNet40 (mvcnn) | 98.1 ± 1.3 | 90.8 ± 1.0 | 92.3 ± 1.7 | 93.9 ± 1.1 |
| ModelNet40 (gvcnn) | 97.3 ± 1.1 | 92.8 ± 0.9 | 90.5 ± 1.4 | 81.5 ± 1.5 |
| ModelNet40 (mvc. and gvc.) | 98.1 ± 0.8 | 96.7 ± 1.2 | 95.8 ± 1.4 | 97.4 ± 1.3 |

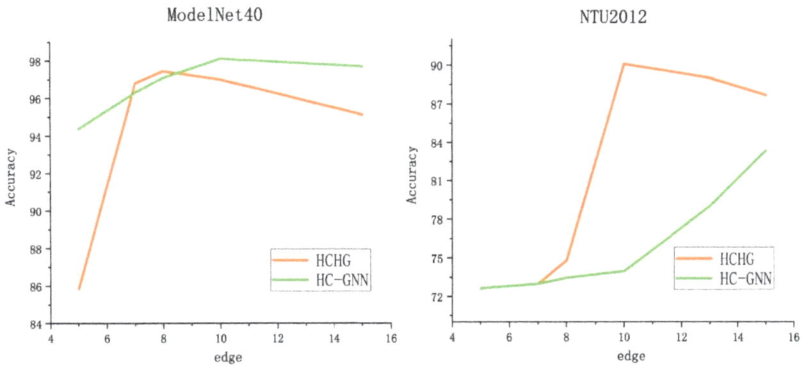


**Figure 6.** The number of neighboring node points affects the classification.

### 5.3. Visualization

The core dataset was visualized to compare the learning abilities of graph-based and hypergraph-based methods intuitively. The t-SNE method was used to visualize the output of the last layer convolution. The results are shown in Figure 7. It can be seen from the results that compared to the graph-based method; the hypergraph-based HCHG method produces recognizable clusters, which qualitatively validates the effectiveness of the proposed method.

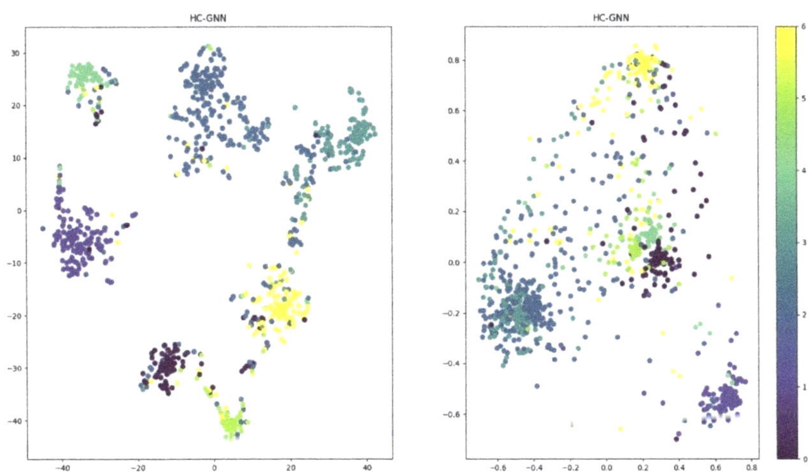


**Figure 7.** *Cont.*

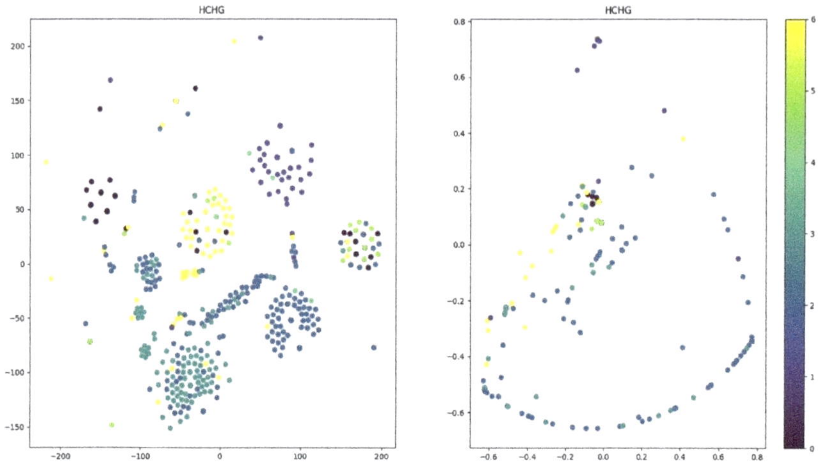


**Figure 7.** Visualization of the clustering results.

## 6. Conclusions

This paper proposes a novel Hierarchical message-passing Hypergraph Convolutional (HCHG) model that combines hypergraphs and hierarchical message-passing using a layered community detection algorithm. The HCHG model constructs a hierarchical structure of hypergraph neural networks and performs layered message-passing to handle multi-view data. The model structure of HCHG enables nodes to capture information-rich interactions from distant nodes effectively. Extensive experiments are conducted on five datasets, and the results are analyzed. The experiments demonstrate that HCHG performs excellently in graph-structured dataset classification and 3D model classification tasks. HCHG allows for different choices and customized designs of hierarchical structures, making it easily applicable to various task-specific data. In the future, our goal is to optimize the learning of hypergraph hierarchical structures further and extend the framework to handle complex multimodal data in real-life scenarios.

## 7. Limitations and Future Work

Despite the impressive performance of the HCHG model on multiple datasets, there are still some limitations. Future work will focus on improving the model's computational efficiency, particularly its scalability in complex networks, and developing more efficient algorithms to reduce computational complexity. Additionally, we plan to optimize the model's ability to handle complex social hierarchies and nested structural networks. Finally, we will conduct an in-depth analysis of how different community detection methods impact the generation of hierarchical structures, exploring their applicability and limitations in real-world scenarios. Overall, future research will further enhance the performance and broad applicability of the HCHG model.

**Author Contributions:** Conceptualization, W.X. and F.X.; methodology, F.X. and W.X.; software, F.X. and W.X.; validation, F.X. and L.S.; formal analysis, Z.F.; resources, F.X.; writing—original draft preparation, F.X. and Z.F.; supervision, Z.F.; funding acquisition, F.X., L.S. and Z.F. All authors have read and agreed to the published version of the manuscript.

**Funding:** This research was funded by the Quzhou City Science and Technology Plan Project (2023K263, 2023K265, 2023K045), the General Research Project of the Zhejiang Provincial Department of Education (2023) (Y202353440, Y202353289), and Quzhou Vocational and Technical College university-level scientific research project (QZYZ2305-2023).

**Institutional Review Board Statement:** Not applicable.

**Informed Consent Statement:** Not applicable.

**Data Availability Statement:** The data presented in this study are available in the article.

**Conflicts of Interest:** The authors declare no conflict of interest.

## References


1. Min, S.; Gao, Z.; Peng, J.; Wang, L.; Qin, K.; Fang, B. STGSN—A spatial–temporal graph neural network framework for time-evolving social networks. *Knowl.-Based Syst.* **2021**, *214*, 106746. [CrossRef]
2. Dhelim, S.; Aung, N.; Ning, H. Mining user interest based on personality-aware hybrid filtering in social networks. *Knowl.-Based Syst.* **2020**, *206*, 106227. [CrossRef]
3. Leahy, J.; Jabari, S. Enhancing Aerial Camera-LiDAR Registration through Combined LiDAR Feature Layers and Graph Neural Networks. *Int. Arch. Photogramm. Remote Sens. Spat. Inf. Sci.* **2024**, *48*, 25–31. [CrossRef]
4. Yuan, W.; Yuan, X.; Fan, Z.; Guo, Z.; Shi, X.; Gong, J.; Shibasaki, R. Graph neural network based multi-feature fusion for building change detection. *Int. Arch. Photogramm. Remote Sens. Spat. Inf. Sci.* **2021**, *43*, 377–382. [CrossRef]
5. Shi, W.; Rajkumar, R. Point-gnn: Graph neural network for 3d object detection in a point cloud. In Proceedings of the IEEE/CVF Conference on Computer Vision and Pattern Recognition, Seattle, WA, USA, 13–19 June 2020; pp. 1711–1719.
6. Meraz, M.; Ansari, M.A.; Javed, M.; Chakraborty, P. DC-GNN: Drop channel graph neural network for object classification and part segmentation in the point cloud. *Int. J. Multimed. Inf. Retr.* **2022**, *11*, 123–133. [CrossRef]
7. Wu, Y.; Dai, H.N.; Tang, H. Graph neural networks for anomaly detection in industrial Internet of Things. *IEEE Internet Things J.* **2022**, *9*, 9214–9231. [CrossRef]
8. Hamilton, W.; Ying, Z.; Leskovec, J. Inductive representation learning on large graphs. In Proceedings of the International Conference on Advances in Neural Information Processing Systems (NeurIPS), Long Beach, CA, USA, 4–9 December 2017; Volume 30, pp. 1025–1035.
9. Huang, K.; Xiao, C.; Glass, L.M.; Zitnik, M.; Sun, J. SkipGNN: Predicting molecular interactions with skip-graph networks. *Sci. Rep.* **2020**, *10*, 21092. [CrossRef] [PubMed]
10. Zitnik, M.; Agrawal, M.; Leskovec, J. Modeling polypharmacy side effects with graph convolutional networks. *Bioinformatics* **2018**, *34*, 457–466. [CrossRef]
11. Zhang, M.; Chen, Y. Link prediction based on graph neural networks. In Proceedings of the 2018 Annual Conference on Neural Information Processing Systems (NeurIPS), Montréal, QC, Canada, 3–8 December 2018; pp. 5171–5181.
12. Kipf, T.N.; Welling, M. Semi-supervised classification with graph convolutional networks. In Proceedings of the International Conference on Learning Representations (ICLR), Toulon, France, 24–26 April 2017.
13. Veličković, P.; Cucurull, G.; Casanova, A.; Romero, A.; Liò, P.; Bengio, Y. Graph attention networks. In Proceedings of the International Conference on Learning Representations (ICLR), Vancouver, BC, Canada, 30 April–3 May 2018.
14. Xu, K.; Hu, W.; Leskovec, J.; Jegelka, S. How powerful are graph neural networks? In Proceedings of the 2019 International Conference on Machine Learning (ICML), Long Beach, CA, USA, 9–15 June 2019.
15. Min, Y.; Wenkel, F.; Wolf, G. Scattering GCN: Overcoming oversmoothness in graph convolutional networks. In Proceedings of the 2020 Annual Conference on Neural Information Processing Systems (NeurIPS), New Orleans, LA, USA, 10–16 December 2020.
16. Perozzi, B.; Al-Rfou, R.; Skiena, S. Deepwalk: Online learning of social representations. In Proceedings of the 20th ACM SIGKDD International Conference on Knowledge Discovery and Data Mining, New York, NY, USA, 24–27 August 2014; pp. 701–710.
17. Zhou, D.; Huang, J.; Schölkopf, B. Learning with hypergraphs: Clustering, classification, and embedding. In Proceedings of the Advances in Neural Information Processing Systems, Kelowna, BC Canada, 4–7 December 2006; Volume 19, pp. 1601–1608.
18. Feng, Y.; You, H.; Zhang, Z.; Ji, R.; Gao, Y. Hypergraph neural networks. In Proceedings of the AAAI Conference on Artificial Intelligence, Honolulu, HI, USA, 27 January–1 February 2019; Volume 33, pp. 3558–3565.
19. Ranjan, E.; Sanyal, S.; Talukdar, P.P. ASAP: Adaptive structure aware pooling for learning hierarchical graph representations. In Proceedings of the 2020 AAAI Conference on Artificial Intelligence (AAAI), New York, NY, USA, 7–12 February 2020; pp. 5470–5477.
20. Gao, H.; Ji, S. Graph U-Nets. In Proceedings of the 2019 International Conference on Machine Learning (ICML), Long Beach, CA, USA, 9–15 June 2019.
21. Ying, R.; You, J.; Morris, C.; Ren, X.; Hamilton, W.L.; Leskovec, J. Hierarchical graph representation learning with differentiable pooling. In Proceedings of the 2018 Annual Conference on Neural Information Processing Systems (NeurIPS), Montréal, QC, Canada, 3–8 December 2018; pp. 4805–4815.
22. Bai, S.; Zhang, F.; Torr, P.H. Hypergraph convolution and hypergraph attention. *Pattern Recognit.* **2021**, *110*, 107637. [CrossRef]
23. Jiang, J.; Wei, Y.; Feng, Y.; Cao, J.; Gao, Y. Dynamic hypergraph neural networks. In Proceedings of the IJCAI, Macao, China, 10–16 August 2019; pp. 2635–2641.
24. Yadati, N.; Nimishakavi, M.; Yadav, P.; Nitin, V.; Louis, A.; Talukdar, P. Hypergcn: A new method for training graph convolutional networks on hypergraphs. In Proceedings of the Advances in Neural Information Processing Systems, Vancouver, BC, Canada, 8–14 December 2019; Volume 32.

25. Arya, D.; Gupta, D.K.; Rudinac, S.; Worring, M. Hypersage: Generalizing inductive representation learning on hypergraphs. *arXiv* **2020**, arXiv:2010.04558.
26. Ye, Z.; Zhao, H.; Zhang, K.; Zhu, Y.; Xiao, Y. Tri-party deep network representation learning using inductive matrix completion. *J. Cent. South Univ.* **2019**, *26*, 2746–2758. [CrossRef]
27. Zhong, Z.; Li, C.T.; Pang, J. Hierarchical message-passing graph neural networks. *Data Min. Knowl. Discov.* **2023**, *37*, 381–408. [CrossRef]
28. Sen, P.; Namata, G.; Bilgic, M.; Getoor, L.; Galligher, B.; Eliassi-Rad, T. Collective classification in network data. *AI Mag.* **2008**, *29*, 93–93. [CrossRef]
29. Namata, G.; London, B.; Getoor, L.; Huang, B. Query-driven active surveying for collective classification. In Proceedings of the 2012 International Workshop on Mining and Learning with Graphs, Edinburgh, UK, 1 July 2012; p. 8.
30. Chen, J.; Ma, T.; Xiao, C. FastGCN: Fast learning with graph convolutional networks via importance sampling. *arXiv* **2018**, arXiv:1801.10247.
31. Yang, C.; Wang, R.; Yao, S.; Abdelzaher, T. Hypergraph learning with line expansion. *arXiv* **2020**, arXiv:2005.04843.
32. Sunil, K.M. Feature Selection: Key to Enhance Node Classification with Graph Neural Networks). *CAAI Trans. Intell. Technol.* **2023**, *8*, 14–28. Available online: https://ietresearch.onlinelibrary.wiley.com/doi/full/10.1049/cit2.12166 (accessed on 29 October 2024).
33. Yan, Y.; Chen, Y.; Wang, S.; Wu, H.; Cai, R. Hypergraph Joint Representation Learning for Hypervertices and Hyperedges via Cross Expansion. In Proceedings of the AAAI Conference on Artificial Intelligence, Vancouver, BC, Canada, 26–27 February 2024; Volume 38, pp. 9232–9240.
34. Li, M.; Chen, S.; Zhang, Y.; Tsang, I.W. Graph cross networks with vertex infomax pooling. In Proceedings of the 2020 Annual Conference on Neural Information Processing Systems (NeurIPS), Virtual, 6–12 December 2020.
35. Gao, Y.; Feng, Y.; Ji, S.; Ji, R. HGNN+: General Hypergraph Neural Networks. *IEEE Trans. Pattern Anal. Mach. Intell.* **2023**, *45*, 3181–3199. [CrossRef] [PubMed]

sensors

MDPI

*Article*

# Facial Anti-Spoofing Using "Clue Maps"

**Liang Yu Gong *,†, Xue Jun Li †,‡ and Peter Han Joo Chong †,‡**

Department of Electrical and Electronic Engineering, Auckland University of Technology, Auckland 1010, New Zealand; xuejun.li@aut.ac.nz (X.J.L.); peter.chong@aut.ac.nz (P.H.J.C.)
* Correspondence: liangyu.gong@autuni.ac.nz
† Current address: Auckland University of Technology, 6 Saint Paul Street, Auckland 1010, New Zealand.
‡ These authors contributed equally to this work.

**Abstract:** Spoofing attacks (or Presentation Attacks) are easily accessible to facial recognition systems, making the online financial system vulnerable. Thus, it is urgent to develop an anti-spoofing solution with superior generalization ability due to the high demand for spoofing attack detection. Although multi-modality methods such as combining depth images with RGB images and feature fusion methods could currently perform well with certain datasets, the cost of obtaining the depth information and physiological signals, especially that of the biological signal is relatively high. This paper proposes a representation learning method of an Auto-Encoder structure based on Swin Transformer and ResNet, then applies cross-entropy loss, semi-hard triplet loss, and Smooth L1 pixel-wise loss to supervise the model training. The architecture contains three parts, namely an Encoder, a Decoder, and an auxiliary classifier. The Encoder part could effectively extract the features with patches' correlations and the Decoder aims to generate universal "Clue Maps" for further contrastive learning. Finally, the auxiliary classifier is adopted to assist the model in making the decision, which regards this result as one preliminary result. In addition, extensive experiments evaluated Attack Presentation Classification Error Rate (APCER), Bonafide Presentation Classification Error Rate (BPCER) and Average Classification Error Rate (ACER) performances on the popular spoofing databases (CelebA, OULU, and CASIA-MFSD) to compare with several existing anti-spoofing models, and our approach could outperform existing models which reach 1.2% and 1.6% ACER on intra-dataset experiment. In addition, the inter-dataset on CASIA-MFSD (training set) and Replay-attack (Testing set) reaches a new state-of-the-art performance with 23.8% Half Total Error Rate (HTER).

**Keywords:** anti-spoofing detection; Swin Transformer; ResNet; auto-encoder

## 1. Introduction

Since facial recognition is widely applied in many fields of daily life (e.g., accessing personal accounts via facial identification), face spoofing is becoming a big threat to users and making some online systems vulnerable. The presentation attacks (PAs), such as paper print attacks, replay attacks, and 3D facial masks are widely used and easily controlled by hackers. Thus, developing a reliable facial anti-spoofing (FAS) method [1–4] is important to avoid security risks and financial losses.

Among the proposed FAS methods, handcrafted feature-based [5] and deep learning-based methods [6] are common, and these methods are popular in processing single-modal data (RGB images). However, those models that only utilize hand-crafted features are not reliable, with low representation capacity due to different novel types, and some physiological signals [7] and handcrafted clues cannot be effectively learned by only spoofing images with a single model. Therefore, one major method is to combine multiple modalities of data such as depth and infrared (IR) images or design an ensembled system to distinguish spoofing attacks, which is the mainstream to reach the state of the art. On the other hand, another approach is to create a more advanced model architecture and combine different learning methods to extract as rich and effective spoofing features as possible.

As some datasets cannot provide corresponding depth or physiological information, it is undeniable that this type of method is rather promising and challenging in future work.

Enlightened by the approach to combining different learning methods, this paper proposes a novel Encoder–Decoder face anti-spoofing structure which utilizes Transformer as the Encoder and ResNet as the Decoder. The total loss is determined by three loss functions instead of using cross-entropy loss only. In the Encoder part, we only utilize the Swin Transformer as an extractor with an auxiliary classifier to achieve preliminary classification work. In addition, we assume the Transformer-based feature extractor could extract more useful features with correlations of patches, the combination of softmax and cross-entropy loss is used directly after applying L2 Normalization on extracted features. In the Decoder part, we regard this part as a "Clue Map" generator, the proposed method applies a semi-hard triplet loss [8] to minimize intra-class sample distances and maximize the inter-class sample distances first. This is useful to find out the minor differences between spoof images and live images. The main purpose of the Decoder is to revert the extracted features in the latent space to the "Clue Map" for live and spoof images and we apply pixel-wise loss to supervise them. Because live images should not have any "spoof clues", thus, the generated Clue Maps for live images should tend to be all-zero maps. In contrast, the generated Clue Maps for spoofing images should tend to be all-one maps. Even though the proposed work is based on the existing works, this method is a new attempt that combines Swin Transformer and ResNet to design a new model architecture. Based on the experimental results, it is proven to be robust and could enhance performance compared with previous methods. In addition, few papers apply the Swin Transformer as a feature extractor in the FAS field, and our preliminary work compares Swin Transformer with other Convolutional Networks and proves that Swin Transformer also has excellent spoofing feature extraction capabilities on Face Anti-spoofing. In addition, the generated "Clue Maps" by our proposed methods could directly be applied in other unsupervised learning such as consistency calculation or contrastive learning methods. In conclusion, the main contribution of this work is threefold:

(1) Design an Auto-Encoder structure based on Swin Transformer and ResNet. The Swin Transformer aimed to extract features with patch correlation and ResNet aimed to generate the corresponding "Clue Maps".
(2) Combine cross-entropy loss, and semi-hard triplet loss with Smooth L1 pixel-wise loss to supervise the spoof detector, which has proven to increase the model's generalization ability.
(3) Compared with some feature fusion methods, it could reach a new state-of-the-art performance, and the generated Clue Maps could be utilized in future contrastive learning methods.

## 2. Related Work

In this section, we revisit several representative anti-spoofing methods, which are divided into two main categories: convolutional neural network (CNN) anti-spoofing and hybrid learning methods. The CNN anti-spoofing methods usually include a direct supervised learning framework, pixel-wise supervision, and generative models. However, hybrid learning methods always combine hand-crafted features with CNN-extracted features. The main research directions and trends are more inclined to develop different feature fusion methods. Finally, we make a summary of the proposed backbone: the Swin Transformer as well.

### *2.1. CNN Anti-Spoofing Detection*

Advanced end-to-end CNN models could effectively map input images to spoofing detection, and most previous work used binary cross-entropy loss for direct supervised learning. These methods are efficient to use because cross-entropy loss could supervise Face Anti-Spoofing work to converge faster. But it easily causes the model to overfit and the reals and Presentation Attacks always hold asymmetric distribution [9], which makes models struggle to learn a latent space with smaller intra-class distance and larger inter-class distance between samples. For example, Xu et al. [10] designed a fine-grained classification network that contains different spoofing attack methods. This multi-class supervision work could represent some detailed properties (paper attack and replay). On the other hand, applying different losses, such as adopting focal loss or angular margin softmax loss, is also useful in solving hard sample challenges and is widely used in some anti-spoofing research. The second method is pixel-wise supervision with an auxiliary classifier, some PAs do not have facial depth information, so generating pixel-wise pseudo labels [11] could be regarded as discriminative supervision signals. Then, the pseudo-labels enforce the models to predict the depth maps for live images while the zero-maps for spoof ones. Overall, pixel-wise supervision is beneficial for explaining feature learning and reaching a higher evaluation performance. However, the main limitation is the high demand for training data resolution.

### 2.2. Hybrid Learning Methods

The hybrid learning method is described as a technique combining hand-crafted features with deep learning features, because hand-crafted features such as HOG [12] descriptors have proven to be strongly discriminative in some commercial RGB cameras in real life. There are three main hybrid learning approaches (see Figure 1) in the previous studies. Firstly, they extract hand-crafted features from the original input faces, and then send them to a deep-learning network. For example, Khamari [13] extracted LBP and Weber descriptors and then encoded them with CNN features which aims to obtain local intensity and edge information with semantic features. However, using hand-crafted methods at the initial stage will lose pixel-wise information, which causes low performances of these models. Secondly, some approaches choose hand-crafted methods to filter out irrelevant deep features. Li et al. [14] used Principle Components Analysis (PCA) to reduce unrelated redundancy of deep features extracted from the VGG face model. Although traditional hand-crafted methods increase the discriminative ability, the semantic representation of the overall model degrades to some extent. The last method is to fuse hand-crafted features with deep features together and send to binary classification which is the commonly used method in recent studies.

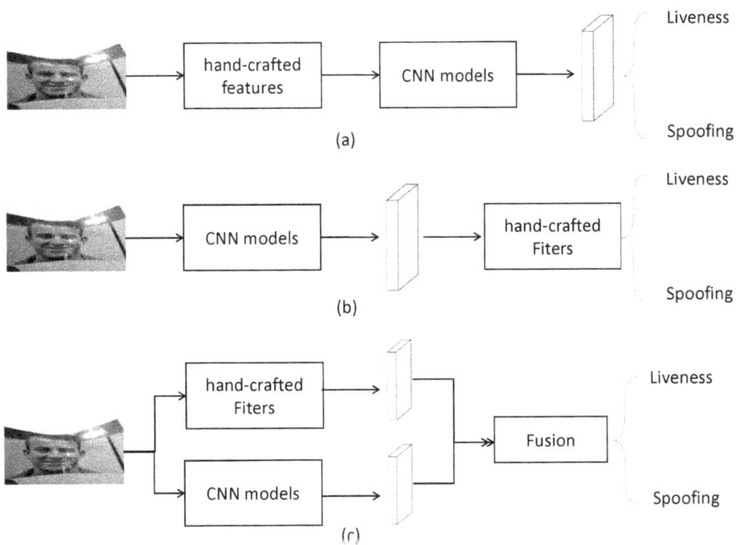


**Figure 1.** Three common hybrid learning methods for FAS. (**a**) represents CNN features from hand-crafted features. (**b**) represents CNN features filtered by hand-crafted methods. (**c**) represents feature fusion of hand-crafted features and deep learning features.

### 2.3. Swin Transformer

Convolutional Neural Networks such as ResNet [15] and Xception [16] are widely applied in image classification work; however, Vision Transformers [17], inspired by the self-attention mechanism [18], reached a new domain on distinguishing images in the computer vision field, which split images into several patches and combined their correlations. Swin Transformer [19] is a hierarchical architecture with shifted windows and has become increasingly powerful among different Vision Transformer (ViT) models. The main contribution of the Swin Transformer is to design a shifted window and apply a cyclic shift to obtain the interaction information between separated patches, which is unlike computing global self-attention by other ViTs. This could largely solve the shortcomings of some traditional vision transformers that do not have overlapping image patches. On the other hand, patch merging performs an important role in building hierarchical feature maps by adjusting each stage feature's resolution and channels. Swin Transformer reduces computation complexity and proves that it could be a general backbone for dense recognition tasks. In ImageNet classification, this approach currently has state-of-the-art accuracy with appropriate FLOPs and parameters.

To prove that the Swin Transformer could effectively extract the spoofing features, we only utilize the Swin Transformer as a feature extractor and directly make a binary classification on RGB images of CASIA-MFSD. Then, we chose an Equal Error Rate (EER), which is the point on the ROC curve that corresponds to having an equal probability of miss-classifying a positive or negative sample, then we compared with some CNN-based methods and handcrafted methods, the results are shown in Table 1.

**Table 1.** The comparison of different EER methods. The Swin Transformer only utilizes cross-entropy loss to make binary classification.

| Methods | EER (%) |
|---|---|
| Fine-tuned VGG-Face [14] | 5.20 |
| CNN [20] | 6.20 |
| Colour Texture [21] | 6.20 |
| Patch-based CNN [11] | 4.44 |
| Depth-based CNN [11] | 2.85 |
| Swin Transformer | 4.77 |

By the preliminary experiments, we can conclude that the Swin Transformer could work more effectively than some traditional backbones and handcrafted methods. However, depth maps could examine whether the inputs have face-like depth information, which largely enhances models' performances in the current stage.

## 3. Proposed Methods

In this section, we will explain our work from three aspects: data pre-processing, network design, and loss function design. Among them, the data pre-processing part only localizes, aligns, and crops human faces, and finally, the random geometric data augmentation methods are applied to the images obtained. The purpose of network design is to extract more variety of features and restore them to the corresponding Clue Maps. The last stage is to more effectively regulate the difference between the predicted value and the Ground Truth labels.

### 3.1. Data Pre-Processing

This method is designed based on extracting spatial information features of images; thus, we need to extract video frames and locate face position information for specific datasets such as CASIA-MFSD [4]. Since there is no obvious change in the expression and postures of the human faces in most video frames, we choose to calculate the total number of video frames in each video and obtain three video frames from each video to prevent the duplication of facial content information. At the same time, we reprocess the provided bounding box information of the OULU dataset [22] and use the facial detector to obtain facial areas of original data in CASIA-MFSD. Then, we expand the width and height of the face area by 20% to ensure that the edge information of the face is not lost. After we applied facial alignment and cropped facial areas, the samples (see Figure 2) were sent to random data augmentations to enrich input varieties, which is the first stage to avoid overfitting in our design. Specifically, we set a confidence threshold of 0.5 and a Non-Maximum Suppression (NMS) as 0.5 for facial detector "scrfd". There are several parameters we set for the data augmentations. Firstly, we selected the random data augmentation methods, which combine base transformation, horizontal flipping, vertical flipping, random rotation, and random resize crop. Then, there is a probability of 0.8 that vertical and horizontal flipping will flip the original input images. Additionally, we set the rotation angle from 60 degrees to 90 degrees for random rotation augmentation to increase the input varieties. Finally, the Random resize Crop scale is from 0.77 to 1 and the ratio is from 0.9 to 1.1.

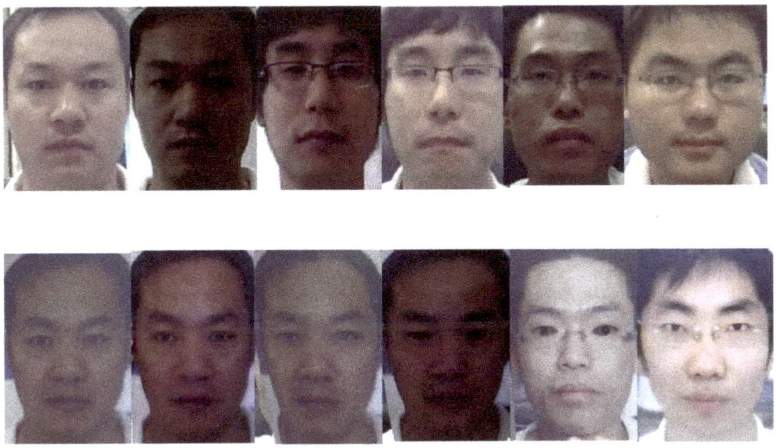

**Figure 2.** The cropped samples of CASIA-MFSD detected by facial area detector, the first row pictures are all liveness faces shot by different cameras, the second-row images include paper attack, paper mask and replay attack.

### *3.2. Network Architecture*

The proposed network architecture which consists of a shared parameter Transformer-based Encoder (Stage 1) and two ResNet-based Decoders (Stage 2) is illustrated in Figure 3. The main purpose of the Encoder (Stage 1) is to extract features and then save them into latent space; Stage 2 can be divided into three main branches: two Clue Map generators (Decoders) and one binary auxiliary classifier. The main purpose of designing the entire model framework as an Auto-Encoder with an auxiliary classifier is avoiding fully supervised learning for the training model. Auto-Encoder is an unsupervised learning model in nature which could largely reduce the dependence of data on annotations. In addition, the input data for the entire model has already been compressed into low-dimensional representations and stored in the latent space before passing through the Decoder part. This could allow the most important feature information to be extracted and minimize the impact of noise on the recognition model. Another benefit of Auto-Encoder is that its architecture is flexible and is not limited to the number of layers of the network model. Additionally, the latent representations can be used for classification work or clustering.

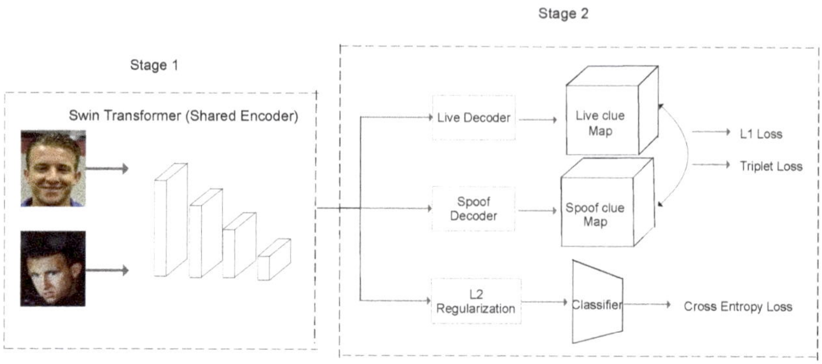


**Figure 3.** The proposed network architecture. The Transformer-based Encoders have shared parameters, but Decoders are trained separately and designed based on the ResNet structure with 27 convolutional layers without linear layers.

In Stage 1, the input images are firstly split into several non-overlapping patches, and regarded the patches as "tokens", which is the same as the operation of other Vision Transformers. Then, the corresponding patch size is set as $7 \times 7$, and patch embeddings are processed by 12 Swin Transformer blocks with self-attention computation to obtain features $f$ with the size of $[7, 7, 768]$. Specifically, the query ($Q$), key ($K$) and value ($V$) are input vectors after applying linear projection on the embeddings, the query and key are with the same vector dimension of $d$. By computing the dot product of the query and key and adding bias, we utilize the Softmax function to squeeze the output range from 0 to 1. The corresponding self-attention computation is written as in Equation (1). All features $f$ are saved in the latent space, and Stage 2 is to further process these saved features. In addition, we set the dropout rate as 0.8 in Multiple Layer Perceptron (MLP) to avoid over-fitting in this stage. After obtaining the original output features extracted by the Encoder, we reshape the tensor size to two-dimensional, which is $[49, 768]$.

$$Attention(Q, K, V) = Softmax(QK^T / \sqrt{d} + B)V \tag{1}$$

where query ($Q$), key ($K$), and value ($V$) are obtained from linear projection; $1/\sqrt{d}$ is the scale factor of query and key; and $B$ is the bias of query, key, and value.

In Stage 2, the features are first reshaped to $[12, 56, 56]$, which is for Decoders to generate corresponding Clue Maps. The Decoders are all ResNet-based structures, but with separate parameters to generate spoof or live Clue Maps. Specifically, the Decoders include one CBL module and 13 basic residual blocks, which are shown in Table 2. To illustrate the details of the Decoder structure, the designed ResNet-based decoder is shown in Figure 4 After obtaining the Clue Maps, we utilize Smooth L1 pixel-wise loss, because we assume that the live Clue Map should tend to be an all-zero map, and the spoof Clue Map tends to be an all-one map after model training. Additionally, considering strongly distinguishing the intra-class and inter-class samples, the second branch applies semi-hard triplet loss, which allows the distances between anchor and negative samples to be longer than the distances between anchor and positive samples. The bottom branch is a supervised learning branch only connected with Multi-layer Perceptron (MLP) for classification work. In addition, L2 regularization is applied to extracted features to avoid overfitting before the MLP. Thus, the final output of Stage 2 is to compute Smooth L1 pixel-wise loss, triplet loss and cross-entropy loss separately.

**Table 2.** The Decoder's components. Each Basic block contains two convolutional layers with kernel size 3, and strides are all set as 2.

| Layer Name | Output Size | Layer Components |
|---|---|---|
| Decoder Conv1 | $64 \times 28 \times 28$ | $2 \times 2$, stride = 2 |
| Decoder Basic Block1 | $128 \times 28 \times 28$ | $[3 \times 3, 3 \times 3] \times 3$ |
| Decoder Basic Block2 | $256 \times 14 \times 14$ | $[3 \times 3, 3 \times 3] \times 4$ |
| Decoder Basic Block3 | $1024 \times 7 \times 7$ | $[3 \times 3, 3 \times 3] \times 6$ |
| Reshape | $224 \times 224$ | None |

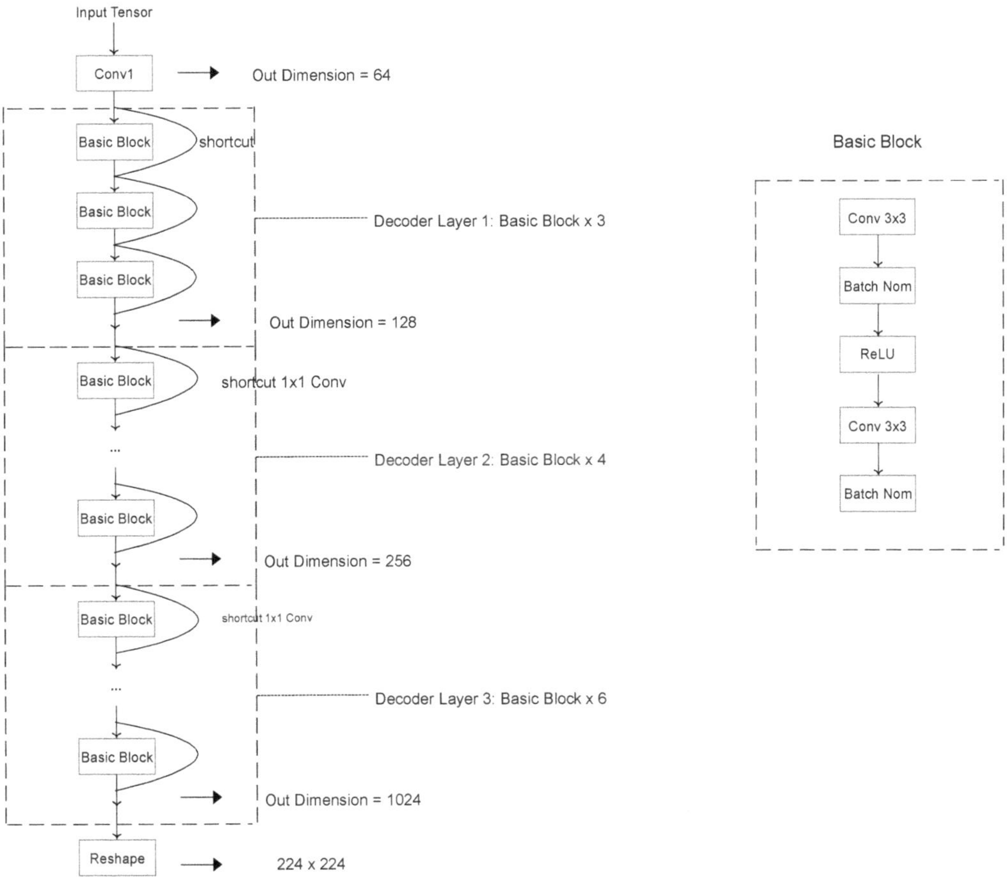


**Figure 4.** The proposed Decoder architecture. The liveness and spoofing Clue Maps generators are with the same architecture but with separate training parameters.

### 3.3. Loss Functions

For cross-entropy loss, as a traditional categorical loss function, its gradient calculation is much simpler, which leads to the faster convergence speed of the model in the training process and updates training parameters quicker in the limited training epochs. In contrast, using Mean Square Error (MSE) loss in logistic regression tasks could slow down convergence in classification due to its smoother gradient change, especially when it may produce a smaller gradient update in the early stage of training, and result in a slower training speed. Semi-hard triplet loss is a loss function commonly used in metric learning methods. It pushes the model to embed samples of the same class into the closer position of the feature space while separating samples of different classes from a theoretical perspective. In addition, this loss function largely prevents over-fitting, and its negative samples are slightly larger from the anchor than the positive ones. In this way, the model can avoid extremely difficult triples and excessive gradient changes. In conclusion, semi-hard triplet loss is effective in learning minor differences between samples by using "semi-hard" negative samples, and it could not only distinguish obviously different samples but also better capture the differences between samples that are visually similar but belong to different categories.

The embeddings obtained from the Transformer-based Encoder are represented by $f_p$ and $f_n$, where we regard them as live (positive) embeddings and spoof (negative) embeddings separately. Additionally, we want to ensure the anchor embeddings $f_a$ belong to the same class with positive embeddings and avoid manually grouping anchor, positive, and negative embeddings. We choose to generate positives and semi-hard negatives within a mini-batch, which is an online method. To distinguish intra-class and inter-class samples more effectively, we enforce that the Euclidean distance between the anchor and positive is shorter than the distance of the anchor with negative samples, but the positive exemplars with margin are further away from anchors than the negative samples. In other words, we let negative embeddings lie in the margin area to separate the minor differences between live and spoofs. The relationship between the embedding distances can be illustrated in Equation (2), and the triplet loss could be rewritten in Equation (3).

$$d(a,p) < d(a,n) < d(a,p) + margin \tag{2}$$

$$L_{tri} = \frac{1}{n}\sum_{i=0}^{n}[\| f_a - f_n \|_2^2 - \| f_a - f_p \|_2^2 - margin] \tag{3}$$

where $a$ represents the anchor sample and $f_a$ is the anchor feature correspondingly; $p$ represents the positive sample which belongs to the same class as the anchor and $f_p$ is the positive embedding; $n$ represents the negative samples and $f_n$ is the negative embedding; margin is an enforced distance between positives and negatives.

In this work, we did not take an anomaly detection approach to design a one-class classification task for FAS or regard the live samples as a closed set. We would like to apply pixel-wise supervision of samples on the spoof set as well, so we assume that the "Clue Maps" should be an all-one or all-zero map ideally; for example, the generated Spoof Clue Maps $M_S$ should approximately tend to be an all-one map, and Live Clue Maps $M_L$ are all-zero maps after training. To measure the difference between generated "Clue Maps" and ideal "Clue Maps" (all-one or all-zero matrix) better, we choose the Smooth L1 loss to supervise the generated clues. This is because L1 loss is not smooth at the zero point, which means that the gradient derivative cannot be well performed. In addition, using L2 loss alone is more sensitive to outliers to cause the gradient explosion. Thus, we select Smooth L1 loss which combines the advantages of both losses, modifies the non-smoothing at zero-point, and is more robust to outliers. Specifically, the Smooth L1 loss for Spoof Clue Maps can be illustrated in Equation (4).

$$L_{pixel} = \frac{1}{n}\sum_{i=0}^{n}\begin{cases} 0.5(M_1 - M_S)^2 & if\ |M_1 - M_S| < 1 \\ |M_1 - M_S| & otherwise \end{cases} \tag{4}$$

where $M_1$ represents all-one map; $M_S$ represents generated Spoof Clue Maps.

Similarly, the Smooth L1 loss for Live Clue Maps can be illustrated in Equation (5).

$$L_{pixel} = \frac{1}{n}\sum_{i=0}^{n}\begin{cases} 0.5(M_L - M_0)^2 & if\ |M_L - M_0| < 1 \\ |M_L - M_0| & otherwise \end{cases} \tag{5}$$

where $M_0$ represents all-zero map; $M_L$ represents generated liveness Clue Maps.

Finally, we design an auxiliary classifier to assist the model in making decisions, and cross-entropy loss is applied as a supervised learning method for model training. We only utilize the extracted features from Encoder with MLP to calculate the predicted matrix for spoofing and live images. Cross-entropy loss is used as one of the basic logistic regression factors for the final decision. The cross-entropy loss can be determined by Equation (6).

$$L_{CE} = -\frac{1}{n}\sum_{i=0}^{n}[ylogp + (1-y)log(1-p)] \tag{6}$$

where $y$ is the Ground Truth; $P$ is the predicted probability of the class; $n$ is the sample number.

In the final loss function design, we only want the CE loss to be used as an auxiliary loss function, while the triplet loss function and the pixel-wise loss function are used as the main loss measures to supervise the model to update the parameters. So, we combine these three loss functions linearly to obtain the final function in the end. Since the total loss is determined by three loss functions, we initially set the learnable weight balance for these three losses as 0.333. Then, the total loss function can be expressed as Equation (7).

$$L_{tot} = \alpha L_{CE} + \beta L_{tri} + \gamma Lpixel \tag{7}$$

where $\alpha$, $\beta$ and $\gamma$ are the initial learnable hyper-parameters.

## 4. Experiments

### *4.1. Datasets and Metrics*

In this experiment, we used three datasets: CelebA-Spoof [23], OULU [22], and CASIA-MFSD [4]. CelebA-Spoof is one of the largest scale anti-spoofing datasets, containing 625,537 images of 10,117 subjects. The total number of live images is more than 202,599, which originated from the Celeb-A dataset; some subjects are filtered to guarantee the balance of spoof instruments. In addition, it is famous for its various diversity and four illumination conditions, and two environments are considered. Unlike other spoofing datasets, CelebA-Spoof provides 43 attributes with rich annotations, 40 of them are for live images and three attributes (spoof types, environments, and illumination) are well-labelled for spoofing images. Specifically, spoof types consist of paper print, paper cut, 3D mask, and replay attack, which are the most common attack methods in recent years.

The OULU dataset consists of 4950 real and attack videos, collected from different sensors, illuminations, and background scenes. Additionally, there are four protocols for evaluating the generalization ability, including unseen environment conditions of a PAD attack, the effects of different printers and displays, and the sensor's interoperability. The dataset files define the category of data with the last string of the file names, including real faces (class 1), two paper attacks (classes 2 and 3), and two replay attacks (classes 4 and 5) separately.

Compared with CelebA-Spoofing, CASIA-MFSD is a small spoofing dataset that contains 600 video clips and 50 subjects for the training and testing phases. In each subject, there are 12 video clips, and only 1.avi, 2.avi, and HR1.avi belong to genuine classes shot by different cameras. In addition, we checked all the publicly available face anti-spoofing datasets, and found that they were all published on an older date. For example, the earliest dataset is Replay-attack published in 2012, and the CelebA-spoofing dataset was published in 2020. The main reason why we selected OULU-NPU, CASIA-MFSD, and Replay-attack is that most current works also utilize these datasets to prove their models' generalization ability. Lastly, images and videos from these datasets are of good quality. Except for the Replay-attack dataset, other datasets contain various spoofing attack methods and different shooting cameras, which are adequate to cover and deal with face spoofing attacks in the real world. Thus, our research work also tests these datasets to compare with the previous benchmark results.

For evaluating metrics, we calculate the confusion matrix to obtain True Positive (TP), False Positive (FP), False Negative (FN), and True Negative (TN) separately first.

Then, we utilize the Error Rate metrics including Attack Presentation Classification Error Rate (APCER), Bona fide Presentation Classification Error Rate (BPCER), and Average Classification Error Rate (ACER) to evaluate our approach performance and compare it with previous work. In addition, we also use Half Total Error Rate (HTER) as the cross-testing evaluating metric. The calculation is the same as ACER. The equations of APCER, BPCER, and ACER (HTER) are shown below:

$$APCER = \frac{FP}{TN + FP} \tag{8}$$

$$BPCER = \frac{FN}{TP + FN} \tag{9}$$

$$ACER(HTER) = \frac{APCER + BPCER}{2} \tag{10}$$

where $FP$ represents False Positives, $TP$ represents True Positives, $FN$ represents False Negatives, and $TN$ represents True Negatives.

### 4.2. Implementation Details

For data augmentation, we choose the random data augmentation method, which contains four geometric data augmentations (Horizontal Flipping, Vertical Flipping, Random Resized Crop, and Random Rotation). These four methods [24] could generally perform better results than others in small-scale datasets. Since the fine-grained categories of spoofing (such as phone attack, paper attack, pad attack, etc.) have different sensitivities to colour, we do not apply colour transformations to prevent confusion among different fine-grained categories. For image processing work, all images are resampled and located in facial areas by SCRFD [25] with 0.5 NMS and enlarged by 1.2 of the bounding box. Then, we resize them to $3 \times 224 \times 224$. For the training phase, we utilize the AdamW optimizer with a 0.0001 learning rate and $5 \times 10^{-4}$ weight decay. There is a 0.2 dropout rate applied on the Linear layer to prevent overfitting. The triplet loss margin is set as 0.5, and learnable weight parameters of three loss functions are initialized as 0.333 in the first epoch. In addition, we select "swin tiny patch4 window7 224.pth" as pre-trained model parameters for Encoder, the batch size is 32 and the total training epoch is set to 30.

### 4.3. Ablation Test

Before we compared our model's performance with other benchmark models, we performed a preliminary test to prove that the generation of "Clue Maps" with triplet loss and Smooth L1 loss is useful in live/spoofing classification work. There are three testing methods, which are the Swin Transformer with cross-entropy loss, the Swin Transformer with triplet loss and cross-entropy loss, and our proposed method. Specifically, the Swin Transformer architectures (as the Encoder part) are totally the same in this preliminary experiment. The triplet loss is applied to the extracted features of the Encoder part in the second testing method, but our method applied the triplet loss and Smooth L1 loss on the "Clue Maps" (Decoder part). In addition, we utilized CelebA-Spoofing as the intra-training set, and we randomly selected 20,000 images for training and 5000 images for validating. Then, we compute accuracy, APCER, BPCER, and ACER separately within 30 epochs, and the results are shown in Table 3. The updated hyper-parameters of loss functions' weights are 0.27 for cross-entropy loss, 0.45 for semi-hard triplet loss and 0.28 for Smooth L1 loss, respectively. This preliminary experiment illustrates that the supervised learning method for anti-spoofing is not the most effective, adding triplet loss on Encoder will slightly increase the APCER, which means the model will wrongly predict more spoof samples, but the BPCER drop by 6% approximately, thus the combination of cross-entropy and triplet loss on Encoder could enhance the validating accuracy and classification ability, especially on the live sample set. Finally, our approach only utilizes cross-entropy loss as an assisted supervision loss function, which is applied on the auxiliary classifier, and the pixel-wise loss and triplet loss are all applied on the generated "Clue Maps", then all Error Rates decrease largely, and the validating accuracy is significantly increasing as well. Thus, it is feasible to restore the features extracted from the Encoder to the "Clue Maps" of the original input size, and the unsupervised loss which applies to the Decoder part could both increase the classification ability on spoof and live sample sets.

**Table 3.** Preliminary validating results for three methods. The training and validating data are from CelebA-Spoofing.

| Methods | Epoch | Accuracy (%) | APCER (%) | BPCER (%) | ACER (%) |
|---|---|---|---|---|---|
| Method 1 | 18 | 86.35 | 4.444 | 17.672 | 11.507 |
| Method 2 | 22 | 89.75 | 7.401 | 11.494 | 9.448 |
| This work | 17 | 93.52 | 2.184 | 8.773 | 5.479 |

Method 1: Swin Transformer with cross-entropy loss; Method 2: Swin Transformer with cross-entropy and triplet loss.

### 4.4. Intra-Dataset Experiment

We carry out intra-dataset experiments on the first two protocols of OULU-NPU. For Protocol 1, the methods we compare the performances include the CNN baseline, CNN + MIL [26], GRADIENT [27], STASN [28], and FaceDS [29]. The results of APCER, BPCER, and ACER of OULU-NPU Protocol 1 are shown in Table 4. Our method outperforms all compared anti-spoofing methods on the first protocol to a large extent. Additionally, we also investigate one hand-crafted feature extraction method LBP's performances; it could reach 5.0% APCER, 20.8% BPCER, and 12.9% ACER, respectively. Thus, we can conclude that the traditional CNN classification algorithm and manual feature extraction are gradually losing their competitiveness in this task.

**Table 4.** The intra-dataset validating results for five compared methods. This table only presents the relative performances of the Protocol 1 scenario of OULU-NPU.

| Methods | APCER (%) | BPCER (%) | ACER (%) |
|---|---|---|---|
| CNN (baseline) | 7.8 | 22.3 | 10.1 |
| CNN + MIL | 3.3 | 9.2 | 6.3 |
| GRADIENT | 1.3 | 12.5 | 6.9 |
| STASN | 1.2 | 2.5 | 1.9 |
| FaceDS | 1.2 | 1.7 | 1.5 |
| This work | 0.9 | 1.5 | 1.2 |

For Protocol 2, it focuses on different spoofing attack methods. Thus, we select CNN baseline, GRADIENT, STASN, FaceDS, and Auxiliary [30] as the state-of-the-art models, and compare their relative Error Rate with ours. The validating results are reported in Table 5. Our model has slightly worse BPCER on this protocol, but could reach the lowest APCER and ACER, which are 1.5% and 1.6%. The STASN method has the lowest BPCER among the comparing methods.

**Table 5.** The intra-dataset validating results for five compared methods. This table only presents the relative performances of the Protocol 2 scenario of OULU-NPU.

| Methods | APCER (%) | BPCER (%) | ACER (%) |
|---|---|---|---|
| CNN (baseline) | 7.6 | 2.6 | 8.1 |
| GRADIENT | 3.1 | 1.9 | 2.5 |
| STASN | 4.2 | 0.3 | 2.2 |
| FaceDS | 4.2 | 4.4 | 4.3 |
| Auxiliary | 2.7 | 2.7 | 2.7 |
| This work | 1.5 | 1.7 | 1.6 |

### 4.5. Cross-Dataset Experiment

To demonstrate our model's generalization ability, we set up several cross-dataset experiments. Firstly, we use the largest spoofing dataset CelebA-Spoofing as the training set and then test on Protocol 1 and 2 on OULU-NPU. The ACER results are 13.7% and 19.0%, respectively. We have found that our algorithm is slightly less effective at a wide range of forgery attacks (Protocol 2). However, the versatility of our model is relatively good, and the stability of recognition is high in the case of multiple scenarios (Protocol 1). Furthermore, we utilize CASIA-MFSD and Replay-attack [31] to perform cross-dataset experiments, because it is the current benchmark result which is widely used in the academic research field. Table 6 presents the cross-testing HTER of the previous methods. Our proposed method reduces the Error Rate by 3.6% in the first cross-testing experiment but increases by 9.4% on the second cross-testing HTER.

**Table 6.** The inter-dataset testing results for six compared methods. The second column uses the CASIA-MFSD database as the training set, and the Replay-attack as the testing set. The third column is training on Replay-attack and testing on CASIA-MFSD.

| Method | CASIA-MFSD Replay-Attack | Replay-Attack CASIA-MFSD |
|---|---|---|
| Motion | 50.2% | 47.9% |
| CNN | 48.5% | 45.5% |
| LBP | 47.0% | 39.6% |
| Auxiliary | 27.6% | 28.4% |
| FaceDS | 28.5% | 41.1% |
| Spoof Cues [32] | 27.4% | **23.7%** |
| This work | **23.8%** | 33.1% |

We reviewed the recently published papers, and found out they utilize different protocols to prove their models' abilities to process unseen data. To ensure that our experimental data, protocols, and comparison methods are consistent, we used works that are relatively consistent and published in 2020. In addition, these selected works all used the same training and test datasets and protocols, which helped us to achieve a fair comparison. Furthermore, some of the recently published works did not publish their code. We aim to reproduce their code and compare our work with them as part of our future work.

## 5. Conclusions and Future Work

We reformulated the Face Anti-Spoofing task in an Auto-Encoder architecture with three supervised losses. The main innovation is to design a "Clue Maps" generator that is also the Decoder part of the whole network. Since there is less work to solve the FAS problem by using the Swin Transformer as a feature extractor, our work first shows that it could extract more useful information to a certain extent. Furthermore, Smooth L1 pixel-wise loss and triplet loss applied to the generated "Clue Maps" could help the model update parameters more efficiently and complete the liveness and spoofing classification task. This paper also identifies the importance of Decoder and the combination of Smooth L1 loss and semi-hard triplet loss in the ablation test. Meanwhile, we conduct extensive experiments on popular anti-spoofing datasets such as CelebA-Spoofing and prove our model's generalization ability. Finally, we hope our generated Clue Map method could be useful for further investigators to complete more comprehensive contrastive learning and achieve better FAS performances.

Future works have two main aspects. The first aspect is to investigate whether fine-grained classification could outperform binary classification work. Due to the gradual diversification of the counterfeiting methods of spoofing and the categories of sensors, the fine-grained attribute classification task may help the model learn more spoofing information to a certain extent. With the differences in the shooting environment and shooting equipment of the samples, we also believe that the fine-grained attribute classification task of FAS will be a research trend in the future.

The second aspect is to develop an efficient and lightweight network for extracting the depth information for the training samples, which we hope to apply to the pre-processing work of the entire architecture. For the task of biological detection of living human faces, the extraction of depth map information can be achieved by computer vision technology. From previous experiments, it can be confirmed that the multi-modal detection task containing depth map information often greatly improves the testing metrics. A commonly used hybrid learning architecture is shown in Section 2.2, and the obtaining of depth maps with proper feature fusion methods is required to analyse in future works.

Face anti-spoofing is mainly used to unlock an individual's financial system, but most liveness detection applications are still applying interactive FAS detection. For example, the testers follow the random instructions on the screen (such as closing eyes or shaking heads) to perform specific actions to determine whether the interacting individual is live or spoofing. Thus, our proposed silent FAS method can be used as an auxiliary tool in practical scenarios. Compared with other silent FAS methods, our method needs to be trained and tested in more scenarios and protocols. Since ViTs often require a large amount of data for training to ensure the excellent recognition ability of the model, we hope to fuse some datasets in future work and study the effect of cross-dataset data. In addition, our work does not include situations where multiple face images are used as input in data pre-processing. This issue may cause the recognition system to misjudge the face in the background, resulting in a degraded FAS performance.

**Author Contributions:** Conceptualization, L.Y.G. and X.J.L.; methodology, L.Y.G. and X.J.L.; software, L.Y.G.; validation, L.Y.G.; formal analysis, L.Y.G.; investigation, L.Y.G.; resources, L.Y.G. and X.J.L.; data curation, L.Y.G. and X.J.L.; writing—original draft preparation, L.Y.G., X.J.L. and P.H.J.C.; writing—review and editing, L.Y.G., X.J.L. and P.H.J.C.; visualization, L.Y.G. and X.J.L.; supervision, X.J.L. and P.H.J.C.; project administration, X.J.L. and P.H.J.C. All authors have read and agreed to the published version of the manuscript.

**Funding:** This research received no external funding.

**Institutional Review Board Statement:** Not applicable.

**Informed Consent Statement:** Not applicable.

**Data Availability Statement:** Data are contained within the article.

**Conflicts of Interest:** The authors declare no conflicts of interest.

## References

1. Liu, A.; Tan, Z.; Wan, J.; Liang, Y.; Lei, Z.; Guo, G.; Li, S.Z. Face Anti-Spoofing via Adversarial Cross-Modality Translation. *IEEE Trans. Inf. Forensics Secur.* **2021**, *16*, 2759–2772. [CrossRef]
2. Liu, A.; Wan, J.; Escalera, S.; Escalante, H.J.; Tan, Z.; Qi, Y. Multi-Modal Face Anti-Spoofing Attack Detection Challenge at CVPR2019. In Proceedings of the 2019 IEEE/CVF Conference on Computer Vision and Pattern Recognition Workshops (CVPRW), Long Beach, CA, USA, 16–17 June 2019; pp. 1601–1610. [CrossRef]
3. Yu, Z.; Qin, Y.; Zhao, H.; Li, X.; Zhao, G. Dual-Cross Central Difference Network for Face Anti-Spoofing. In Proceedings of the Thirtieth International Joint Conference on Artificial Intelligence, IJCAI-21, Montreal, QC, Canada, 19–27 August 2021; pp. 1281–1287.
4. Zhang, Z.; Yan, J.; Liu, S.; Lei, Z.; Yi, D.; Li, S.Z. A face antispoofing database with diverse attacks. In Proceedings of the 2012 5th IAPR International Conference on Biometrics (ICB), New Delhi, India, 29 March–1 April 2012; pp. 26–31. [CrossRef]
5. Zhou, J.; Shu, K.; Liu, P.; Xiang, J.; Xiong, S. Face Anti-Spoofing Based on Dynamic Color Texture Analysis Using Local Directional Number Pattern. In Proceedings of the 2020 25th International Conference on Pattern Recognition (ICPR), Milan, Italy, 10–15 January 2021; pp. 4221–4228. [CrossRef]
6. Cai, R.; Li, Z.; Wan, R.; Li, H.; Hu, Y.; Kot, A.C. Learning Meta Pattern for Face Anti-Spoofing. *IEEE Trans. Inf. Forensics Secur.* **2022**, *17*, 1201–1213. [CrossRef]

7. Liu, S.Q.; Lan, X.; Yuen, P.C. Multi-Channel Remote Photoplethysmography Correspondence Feature for 3D Mask Face Presentation Attack Detection. *IEEE Trans. Inf. Forensics Secur.* **2021**, *16*, 2683–2696. [CrossRef]
8. Schroff, F.; Kalenichenko, D.; Philbin, J. FaceNet: A unified embedding for face recognition and clustering. In Proceedings of the 2015 IEEE Conference on Computer Vision and Pattern Recognition (CVPR), Boston, MA, USA, 7–12 June 2015; pp. 815–823. [CrossRef]
9. Yu, Z.; Qin, Y.; Li, X.; Zhao, C.; Lei, Z.; Zhao, G. Deep Learning for Face Anti-Spoofing: A Survey. *IEEE Trans. Pattern Anal. Mach. Intell.* **2023**, *45*, 5609–5631. [CrossRef] [PubMed]
10. Xu, X.; Xiong, Y.; Xia, W. On Improving Temporal Consistency for Online Face Liveness Detection System. In Proceedings of the 2021 IEEE/CVF International Conference on Computer Vision Workshops (ICCVW), Montreal, BC, Canada, 11–17 October 2021; pp. 824–833.
11. Atoum, Y.; Liu, Y.; Jourabloo, A.; Liu, X. Face anti-spoofing using patch and depth-based CNNs. In Proceedings of the 2017 IEEE International Joint Conference on Biometrics (IJCB), Denver, CO, USA, 1–4 October 2017; pp. 319–328. [CrossRef]
12. Dalal, N.; Triggs, B. Histograms of oriented gradients for human detection. In Proceedings of the 2005 IEEE Computer Society Conference on Computer Vision and Pattern Recognition (CVPR'05), San Diego, CA, USA, 20–25 June 2005; Volume 1, pp. 886–893. [CrossRef]
13. Khammari, M. Robust face anti-spoofing using CNN with LBP and WLD. *IET Image Process.* **2019**, *13*, 1880–1884. [CrossRef]
14. Li, L.; Feng, X.; Boulkenafet, Z.; Xia, Z.; Li, M.; Hadid, A. An original face anti-spoofing approach using partial convolutional neural network. In Proceedings of the 2016 Sixth International Conference on Image Processing Theory, Tools and Applications (IPTA), Oulu, Finland, 12–15 December 2016; pp. 1–6. [CrossRef]
15. He, K.; Zhang, X.; Ren, S.; Sun, J. Deep Residual Learning for Image Recognition. In Proceedings of the 2016 IEEE Conference on Computer Vision and Pattern Recognition (CVPR), Las Vegas, NV, USA, 27–30 June 2016; pp. 770–778.
16. Chollet, F. Xception: Deep Learning with Depthwise Separable Convolutions. In Proceedings of the 2017 IEEE Conference on Computer Vision and Pattern Recognition (CVPR), Honolulu, HI, USA, 21–26 July 2017; pp. 1800–1807.
17. Dosovitskiy, A. An image is worth 16x16 words: Transformers for image recognition at scale. *arXiv* **2020**, arXiv:2010.11929.
18. Vaswani, A.; Shazeer, N.; Parmar, N.; Uszkoreit, J.; Jones, L.; Gomez, A.N.; Kaiser, L.; Polosukhin, I. Attention is all you need. In Proceedings of the 31st International Conference on Neural Information Processing Systems, Red Hook, NY, USA, 4–9 December 2017; NIPS'17; Curran Associates Inc.: Red Hook, NY, USA, 2017; pp. 6000–6010.
19. Liu, Z.; Lin, Y.; Cao, Y.; Hu, H.; Wei, Y.; Zhang, Z.; Lin, S.; Guo, B. Swin Transformer: Hierarchical Vision Transformer using Shifted Windows. In Proceedings of the 2021 IEEE/CVF International Conference on Computer Vision (ICCV), Montreal, QC, Canada, 10–17 October 2021; pp. 9992–10002.
20. Xu, Z.; Li, S.; Deng, W. Learning temporal features using LSTM-CNN architecture for face anti-spoofing. In Proceedings of the 2015 3rd IAPR Asian Conference on Pattern Recognition (ACPR), Kuala Lumpur, Malaysia, 3–6 November 2015; pp. 141–145. [CrossRef]
21. Boulkenafet, Z.; Komulainen, J.; Hadid, A. Face Spoofing Detection Using Colour Texture Analysis. *IEEE Trans. Inf. Forensics Secur.* **2016**, *11*, 1818–1830. [CrossRef]
22. Boulkenafet, Z.; Komulainen, J.; Li, L.; Feng, X.; Hadid, A. OULU-NPU: A Mobile Face Presentation Attack Database with Real-World Variations. In Proceedings of the 2017 12th IEEE International Conference on Automatic Face and Gesture Recognition (FG 2017), Washington, DC, USA, 30 May–3 June 2017; pp. 612–618. [CrossRef]
23. Zhang, Y.; Yin, Z.F.; Li, Y.; Yin, G.; Yan, J.; Shao, J.; Liu, Z. CelebA-Spoof: Large-Scale Face Anti-Spoofing Dataset with Rich Annotations. In Proceedings of the European Conference on Computer Vision, Glasgow, UK, 23–28 August 2020.
24. Shijie, J.; Ping, W.; Peiyi, J.; Siping, H. Research on data augmentation for image classification based on convolution neural networks. In Proceedings of the 2017 Chinese Automation Congress (CAC), Jinan, China, 20–22 October 2017; pp. 4165–4170. [CrossRef]
25. Guo, J.; Deng, J.; Lattas, A.; Zafeiriou, S. Sample and Computation Redistribution for Efficient Face Detection. *arXiv* **2021**, arXiv:2105.04714.
26. Lin, C.; Liao, Z.; Zhou, P.; Hu, J.; Ni, B. Live face verification with multiple instantialized local homographic parameterization. In Proceedings of the 27th International Joint Conference on Artificial Intelligence, Stockholm, Sweden, 13–19 July 2018.
27. Boulkenafet, Z.; Komulainen, J.; Akhtar, Z.; Benlamoudi, A.; Samai, D.; Bekhouche, S.E.; Ouafi, A.; Dornaika, F.; Taleb-Ahmed, A.; Qin, L.; et al. A competition on generalized software-based face presentation attack detection in mobile scenarios. In Proceedings of the 2017 IEEE International Joint Conference on Biometrics (IJCB), Denver, CO, USA, 1–4 October 2017; pp. 688–696.. [CrossRef]
28. Pan, G.; Sun, L.; Wu, Z.; Lao, S. Eyeblink-based Anti-Spoofing in Face Recognition from a Generic Webcamera. In Proceedings of the 2007 IEEE 11th International Conference on Computer Vision, Rio De Janeiro, Brazil, 14–21 October 2007; pp. 1–8. [CrossRef]
29. Jourabloo, A.; Liu, Y.; Liu, X. Face De-spoofing: Anti-spoofing via Noise Modeling. In Proceedings of the Computer Vision—ECCV 2018: 15th European Conference, Munich, Germany, 8–14 September 2018; Proceedings, Part XIII.
30. Liu, Y.; Jourabloo, A.; Liu, X. Learning Deep Models for Face Anti-Spoofing: Binary or Auxiliary Supervision. In Proceedings of the 2018 IEEE/CVF Conference on Computer Vision and Pattern Recognition, Salt Lake City, UT, USA, 18–23 June 2018; pp. 389–398. [CrossRef]

31. Chingovska, I.; Anjos, A.; Marcel, S. On the effectiveness of local binary patterns in face anti-spoofing. In Proceedings of the 2012 BIOSIG—Proceedings of the International Conference of Biometrics Special Interest Group (BIOSIG), Darmstadt, Germany, 6–7 September 2012; pp. 1–7.
32. Learning Generalized Spoof Cues for Face Anti-Spoofing. Available online: https://github.com/VIS-VAR/LGSC-for-FAS (accessed on 10 October 2024).

sensors

MDPI

*Article*

# Coal and Gangue Detection Networks with Compact and High-Performance Design

**Xiangyu Cao [1], Huajie Liu [1], Yang Liu [1,2], Junheng Li [1] and Ke Xu [1,*]**

[1] Collaborative Innovation Center of Steel Technology, University of Science and Technology Beijing, Beijing 100083, China; clovey_cxy@163.com (X.C.); lhjk2s@163.com (H.L.); leosea88@gmail.com (Y.L.); lijunheng0906@163.com (J.L.)

[2] Hebei Puyang Iron & Steel Co., Ltd., East of Yangyi Town, Wu'an City 056305, China

* Correspondence: xuke@ustb.edu.cn

**Abstract:** The efficient separation of coal and gangue remains a critical challenge in modern coal mining, directly impacting energy efficiency, environmental protection, and sustainable development. Current machine vision-based sorting methods face significant challenges in dense scenes, where label rewriting problems severely affect model performance, particularly when coal and gangue are closely distributed in conveyor belt images. This paper introduces CGDet (Coal and Gangue Detection), a novel compact convolutional neural network that addresses these challenges through two key innovations. First, we proposed an Object Distribution Density Measurement (ODDM) method to quantitatively analyze the distribution density of coal and gangue, enabling optimal selection of input and feature map resolutions to mitigate label rewriting issues. Second, we developed a Relative Resolution Object Scale Measurement (RROSM) method to assess object scales, guiding the design of a streamlined feature fusion structure that eliminates redundant components while maintaining detection accuracy. Experimental results demonstrate the effectiveness of our approach; CGDet achieved superior performance with AP50 and AR50 scores of 96.7% and 99.2% respectively, while reducing model parameters by 46.76%, computational cost by 47.94%, and inference time by 31.50% compared to traditional models. These improvements make CGDet particularly suitable for real-time coal and gangue sorting in underground mining environments, where computational resources are limited but high accuracy is essential. Our work provides a new perspective on designing compact yet high-performance object detection networks for dense scene applications.

**Keywords:** coal–gangue detection; object distribution density measurement (ODDM); relative resolution object scale measurement (RROSM); label rewriting problem; compact neural network

## 1. Introduction

Coal, as a cornerstone of global economic development, serves dual roles as an essential energy source and critical chemical raw material [1]. The imperative to address environmental concerns while maintaining coal's economic utility has led to the emergence of green and intelligent mining technologies [2]. These technologies represent a significant advancement in sustainable mining practices, integrating underground gangue separation with sophisticated backfilling techniques to minimize environmental impact and prevent mining-induced geological hazards [3]. Such integration not only reduces surface pollution from coal preparation facilities but also effectively mitigates the risk of ground subsidence, marking a substantial advancement in sustainable mining practices. A critical challenge in implementing green mining technologies lies in the spatial constraints of underground operations, which preclude the use of conventional surface processing equipment [4,5]. The dimensional limitations and operational complexities of traditional surface equipment pose significant barriers to underground deployment, necessitating innovative solutions for in situ coal processing. While intelligent sorting robots offer a promising solution due to their compact design [6], their effectiveness fundamentally depends on accurate machine vision systems for real-time coal and gangue discrimination [7]. The development of efficient and accurate machine vision methods is crucial for enabling these robots to perform swift and precise gangue removal during raw coal transportation, thereby facilitating the transition toward environmentally sustainable coal production practices.

Recent developments in convolutional neural networks have demonstrated remarkable potential in object detection tasks [8–10], particularly in coal–gangue discrimination applications [11]. Bounding boxes are used by object detection algorithms based on convolutional neural networks to identify the category and location of objects in images [12–14]. The evolution of deep learning architectures has revolutionized machine vision capabilities, enabling unprecedented accuracy in object detection and classification tasks. However, the application of these technologies in underground mining environments presents unique challenges that current solutions have yet to adequately address. Existing approaches primarily fall into two categories: two-stage detectors and single-stage detectors. Two-stage detectors, exemplified by Faster R-CNN [15], CG-RPN [16], and FCCN [17], achieve impressive accuracy through sophisticated proposal generation mechanisms but suffer from substantial computational overhead that impedes real-time processing capabilities [7]. These algorithms, while effective in controlled environments, face significant challenges in meeting the speed requirements of online sorting applications. Conversely, single-stage detectors like YOLO [18] offer enhanced processing efficiency but frequently compromise on detection accuracy [19]. Various optimization attempts, including cascaded architectures combining YOLOV3 with support vector machines [20] and implementations of deformable convolutions [21], have been proposed to address these limitations. However, these approaches have not fully resolved the fundamental speed-accuracy trade-off, particularly in dense scene detection scenarios.

The subsequent evolution of YOLOv3 variants, incorporating more sophisticated feature extraction networks and optimized training methodologies, has yielded significant improvements in coal and gangue perception accuracy [22–25]. These advanced models demonstrate enhanced detection capabilities but are characterized by large parameter spaces and substantial computational requirements, presenting significant challenges for deployment on edge devices with limited resources. This limitation has catalyzed research interest in lightweight object detection models [26,27]. Current model lightweighting approaches can be broadly categorized into two types [28]. The first is network architecture design, which includes manual design [29–32] and AutoML design [33]. The second is model compression, achieved through techniques such as network pruning [34], low-rank decomposition [35,36], low-bit quantization [37], and knowledge distillation [38]. Contemporary approaches to model compaction have primarily focused on network substitution strategies, such as replacing heavyweight networks with lighter alternatives. Common approaches include substituting DarkNet53 with ResNet18 [39] or MobileNetV3 [20] in YOLOv3 implementations, or replacing VGG16 with GhostNet [40] or MobileNetV1 [41] in SSD (Single Shot MultiBox Detector) architectures [42]. SSD is a single-stage object detection algorithm optimized based on the VGG16 architecture. It leverages feature maps at multiple levels for multi-scale detection, employing convolutional operations and predefined anchor boxes. While these modifications effectively reduce model parameters and computational demands, they often result in compromised detection performance, particularly in challenging dense-scene scenarios. To improve the performance of lightweight models, attention mechanisms are usually added, but adding attention mechanisms does not help to solve the label rewriting problem. Using a larger input image or feature map resolution for detection can alleviate the label rewriting problem, but blindly increasing the resolution of the input image and feature map will increase the computational complexity and seriously weaken the inference speed of the lightweight model [40,43]. In compact convolutional neural networks designed for recognizing coal and gangue, many high-performing models have emerged [44–48]. However, these models often overlook the dense distribution of coal and gangue, as well as the relatively small proportion of pixels occupied by coal and gangue in the images. Therefore, when compacting convolutional neural networks, how to continuously subtract so that they can maintain high performance and speed in dense scenarios while avoiding label rewriting is an important research question.

Recent advances in multi-scale feature learning and multi-view analysis have provided valuable insights for dense object detection. Wang et al. proposed a progressive learning strategy with multi-scale attention network, demonstrating the importance of scale-adaptive feature extraction [49]. Similarly, Wang et al. introduced a bi-consistency guided approach for incomplete multi-view clustering, highlighting the significance of consistent feature representation [50]. Furthermore, Wang et al. developed a graph-collaborated auto-encoder framework for multi-view clustering, offering novel perspectives on feature fusion [51]. Building upon these works, our CGDet advances the field by introducing ODDM and RROSM methods specifically designed for dense coal–gangue detection, while maintaining computational efficiency through optimized feature fusion strategies.

The current state of research faces three critical challenges that previous studies have failed to adequately address: (1) Performance Degradation in Dense Scenes: existing lightweight models struggle to maintain detection accuracy when confronted with densely distributed objects, a common scenario in coal–gangue sorting applications. (2) Computational Overhead: the integration of attention mechanisms and other performance-enhancing features often introduces significant computational burden, contradicting the primary goal of achieving a lightweight model. (3) Label Rewriting Issues: the problem of label rewriting becomes particularly acute in high-density scenes, where multiple objects compete for detection resources within limited spatial regions.

To address these fundamental challenges, this paper introduces CGDet, a novel lightweight convolutional neural network specifically designed for dense coal–gangue detection. Our approach introduces two innovative methodologies: (1) Object Distribution Density Measurement (ODDM): A systematic approach for analyzing and optimizing object detection in dense distributions. This methodology enables precise calibration of input image and feature map resolutions while maintaining high performance and computational efficiency. (2) Relative Resolution Object Scale Measurement (RROSM): A novel technique for characterizing object scale variations and optimizing feature fusion structures. This approach facilitates the development of efficient multi-scale detection strategies while minimizing computational requirements.

The primary objective of this research was to develop a high-performance, computationally efficient object detection system capable of accurate coal–gangue discrimination in dense underground mining environments. Specifically, we aimed to: (1) design a lightweight model architecture that maintains high detection accuracy in dense scenes while minimizing computational requirements. (2) Develop novel methodologies for optimizing input resolution and feature fusion based on object distribution characteristics. (3) Demonstrate the effectiveness of our approach through comprehensive experimental validation.

The primary innovations and contributions of this research are synthesized into three interconnected aspects: (1) The Object Distribution Density Measurement (ODDM) methodology is proposed, enabling optimal resolution selection, circumventing label rewriting issues, and providing a systematic analytical framework for object distribution patterns, with both theoretical foundations and practical guidance established for parameter optimization in dense detection scenarios. (2) The Relative Resolution Object Scale Measurement (RROSM) technique is introduced, facilitating the optimization of feature fusion design through precise quantification of object scale variations, with model complexity significantly reduced and detection accuracy maintained. (3) Based on these innovations, the CGDet architecture is constructed, integrating the advantages of ODDM and RROSM within a unified framework.

Optimal performance is achieved in dense coal–gangue detection tasks, while computational efficiency is preserved for edge device deployment, offering a viable solution for practical engineering applications. Together, these innovations form a cohesive technical system, establishing a new paradigm for lightweight object detection in dense environments.

## 2. Materials and Methods

### *2.1. YOLOX Object Detector*

YOLOX [52] is one of the state-of-the-art single-stage object detectors known for its fast detection speed and high accuracy. It has been widely utilized in object detection tasks and it is advantageous for real-time and high-precision perception of coal and gangue in dense scenes. The YOLOX detector still follows the YOLO detection paradigm, which involves gridding the image, and if an object's center is within a grid cell, that grid cell is responsible for detecting the object. The structure of the YOLOX-s model is shown in Figure 1. As shown in Figure 1, the YOLOX-s model encompasses three main parts: the backbone is used to extract features from the image, the neck is used to fuse feature maps at different scales, and the heads use the feature maps generated by the neck for detection. The backbone of the YOLOX-s model primarily consists of the Focus, CBS, CSP1_X, and SPP (Spatial Pyramid Pooling) modules. Through the Focus layer, the image is sliced, resulting in a reduction of its resolution. The CBS module amalgamates 2D convolution, batch normalization, and SiLU activation functions, encompassing an effective combination. The bottleneck layer incorporates CBS modules and assumes the responsibility of extracting features. The CSP1_X module serves as a feature extraction unit, where X denotes the count of bottleneck layers. For instance, CSP1_3 comprises three bottleneck layers, while CSP2_1 contains one CBS module. The PAN [53] (Path Aggregation Network) structure is an extension of the FPN [54] (Feature Pyramid Network) and is integrated into the neck of the YOLOX-s model. Feature fusion is achieved through CSP2_X, with X implying the number of CBS modules utilized. The heads of the YOLOX-s model encompass three decoupled heads, namely head 1, head 2, and head 3. These heads are responsible for generating the detection outputs.

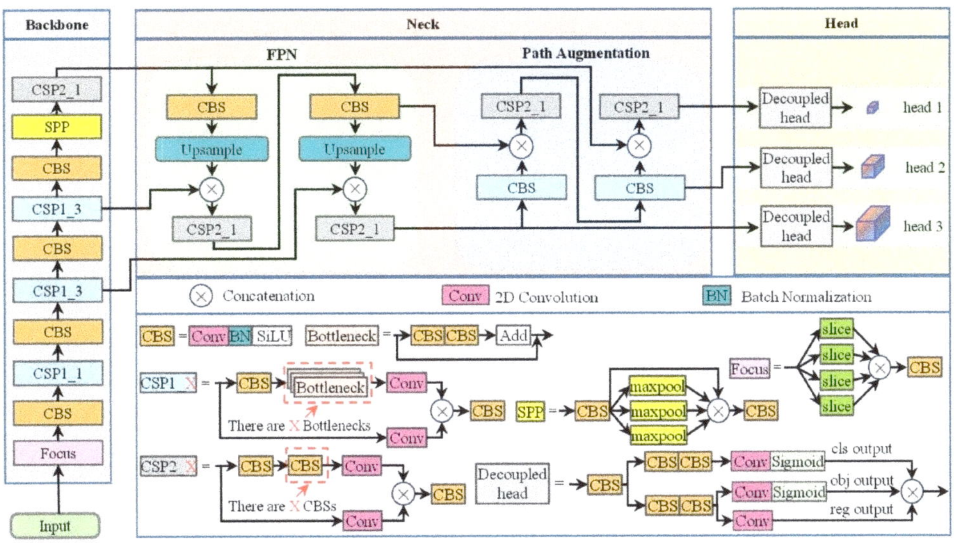


**Figure 1.** Structure of the YOLOX-s model.

### *2.2. Definition of the Label Rewriting Problem*

When a large number of objects are densely distributed in an image, the label rewriting problem occurs if the centers of two actual ground truth bounding boxes are located within the same image grid cell. As shown in Figure 2, the yellow color represents labels that have the label rewriting problem, while the blue color represents normal labels. The label rewriting problem can lead to a decrease in the detection performance of the CGDet model. Consider a set B = {b1, . . ., bt} consisting of the center coordinates of the ground truth bounding boxes in the image, where t represents the total number of ground truth bounding boxes within the image. The label will undergo rewriting when the following condition is fulfilled:

$$\exists(b_i, b_j \in C) : b_i^x\%w - b_j^x\%w = 0,\ b_i^y\%h - b_j^y\%h = 0 \tag{1}$$

where $b_i$ represents the center coordinate of the $i$-th ground truth bounding box, $b_j$ represents the center coordinate of the $j$-th actual ground truth bounding box. $b_i^x$ and $b_i^y$ denote the $x$ and $y$ coordinates of the center of the $i$-th ground truth bounding box. $b_i^x$ and $b_i^y$ represent the $x$ and $y$ coordinates of the center of the $j$-th ground truth bounding box. $w$ is the number of columns in the grid, and $h$ is the number of rows in the grid.

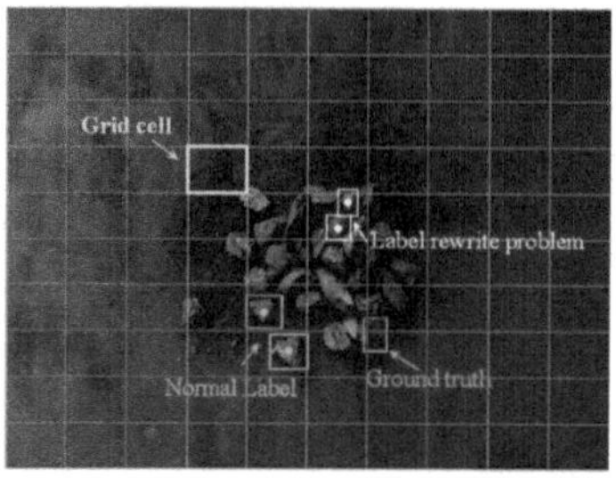


**Figure 2.** Illustration of CGDet model meshing and label rewriting.

Label rewriting introduces several negative impacts: (1) detection performance degradation, as some objects may be missed; (2) reduced localization accuracy due to competition among multiple objects within the same grid cell; (3) lower classification accuracy caused by feature interference between adjacent objects; and (4) unstable training performance, as label reassignment affects loss function computation. Therefore, it is essential to mitigate these impacts.

### *2.3. Measure the Distribution Density of Objects in Images*

To mitigate the adverse effects of label rewriting on CGDet's performance, the problem of label rewriting is transformed into a problem of measuring object distribution density. By selecting images with low object distribution density and low resolution for detection, label rewriting can be prevented. Using the ODDM method [55] to calculate the object distribution density in images allows the detector to determine high-performance, low-computation input image resolution, and feature map resolution, thereby improving detector performance while reducing computational load. The calculation formula for ODDM is shown in Equation (2).

$$\beta = \frac{1}{n}\sum_{i=1}^{n}\frac{img_i^g - img_i^d}{img_i^g} \tag{2}$$

where $n$ denotes the number of images, $img_i^g$ denotes the number of objects in the $i$-th image, On the feature map of the $i$-th image, $img_i^d$ represents the amount of grids which contain objects, $\beta$ represents the density level. A larger $\beta$ value leads to poorer detection performance of the model.

### *2.4. Measure the Scale of an Object in an Image*

To optimize the neck structure based on the object scale within the image, the scale of the objects has to be measured. The COCO dataset [56] employs an absolute image resolution to measure object scale, which, unfortunately, leads to inaccurate measurements when dealing with images of varying resolutions. Therefore, RROSM [55] was introduced in this study to accurately capture object scales, which aligns with the scale classification criteria utilized in the COCO dataset. RROSM is calculated as follows.

$$\begin{cases} S = [s_1, s_2, \cdots, s_n] \\ X = \left[\frac{1}{x_1}, \frac{1}{x_2}, \cdots, \frac{1}{x_n}\right] \\ G = \{g_{ij}\} n \times m \end{cases} \quad (3)$$

$$\alpha = X \cdot S \cdot G \quad (4)$$

For $n$ images, the multiplication of the width and height of the input resolution of each image is computed to obtain the vector $S$. At the original resolution of each image, the reciprocal of the multiplication of width and height produces the vector $X$. The matrix $G$ is composed of the areas of the actual bounding boxes for objects in all images, where $i \in \{1, 2, \ldots, n\}$ and $j \in \{1, 2, \ldots, m\}$. The maximum value of object quantity in the images is represented by $m$. Each element $g_{ij}$ symbolizes the multiplication of the width and height of the actual bounding box of a specific object. If $0 < a_{ij} <= 32^2$, it is classified as a small object. If $32^2 < a_{ij} <= 96^2$, it is classified as a medium object, and if $a_{ij} > 96^2$, it is classified as a large object. When the majority of objects are small, using only the P3 feature map for detection can yield good results.

### 2.5. The Structure of the CGDet Model

Through theoretical analysis, although YOLOX-s exhibits relatively small parameters and computational costs, its structure still presents optimization potential. Based on feature representation theory in deep learning, model performance demonstrates significant correlation with feature map resolution and object distribution density. Consequently, we propose the density theory-based ODDM method to calculate β values, quantitatively evaluating the impact of object distribution on feature extraction. When β values decrease significantly, indicating optimal object distribution density, the corresponding resolution is selected for training and detection, effectively mitigating label rewriting issues and enhancing feature learning quality.

Guided by multi-scale feature representation theory, we employ the RROSM method to analyze object scale distribution characteristics. Experimental evidence indicates that in the absence of large-scale objects, high-level feature maps (such as P5) contribute minimally to feature representation, justifying the removal of corresponding detection heads. When datasets predominantly contain medium and small-scale objects, according to feature pyramid theory, utilizing only the high-resolution P3 feature map suffices for comprehensive feature representation capability. Based on these theoretical analyses, we propose the CGDet model through objective-oriented reconstruction of YOLOX-s.

CGDet maintains the original backbone network structure due to its demonstrated efficacy in feature extraction. Quantitative analysis through RROSM reveals relatively concentrated object scale distribution in our application scenario, negating the necessity for complex feature fusion mechanisms. Therefore, based on information entropy theory, we eliminate the computationally redundant PAN structure, adopting a more concise FPN for feature fusion. ODDM density analysis demonstrates optimal feature representation achievable on the P3 feature map, justifying the retention of only head3 for object detection—a design that ensures detection performance while significantly reducing computational complexity. The backbone network's CSP1_1, CSP1_3, and CSP2_1 layers constitute a multi-level feature extraction structure, with outputs {C2, C3, C4, C5} and downsampling strides {4, 8, 16, 32} forming progressive feature abstraction levels.

As illustrated in Figure 3, regarding feature fusion, the neck network employs an enhanced FPN structure. Following feature pyramid theory, high-level features (C5) processed through the CBS layer generate semantically rich P5 feature maps. Through upsampling and feature concatenation operations, P5 merges with C4 through CSP2_1 processing to generate P4, achieving effective integration of high and low-level features. Similarly, P4 fuses with C3 to generate P3, establishing a progressive multi-scale feature fusion mechanism. The final feature maps {P3, P4, P5} maintain spatial consistency with {C3, C4, C5}. To further optimize computational efficiency, based on depthwise separable convolution theory, we replace the second CBS in the CSP2_X bottleneck layer with depthwise separable convolution, constructing the FPND structure [32]. This enhancement significantly reduces parameter count and computational complexity while maintaining feature representation capability. The notation X = 1 or X = 3 indicates different levels of feature extraction depth, enabling flexible feature optimization at various levels.

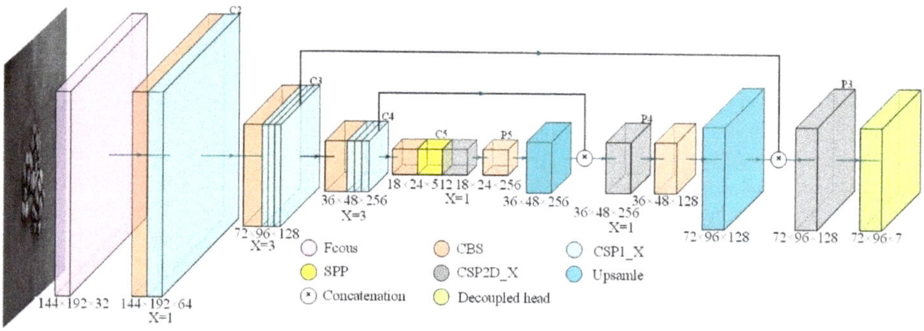


**Figure 3.** Structure of the CGDet model.

This architectural design, underpinned by solid theoretical foundations, demonstrates the following advantages: (1) optimal resolution selection based on density distribution theory; (2) scale-adaptive feature extraction guided by multi-scale representation theory; (3) efficient feature fusion mechanism supported by information entropy theory; and (4) computational optimization through advanced convolution theories. The integration of these theoretical foundations with practical architectural innovations results in a model that achieves both computational efficiency and detection accuracy in dense object detection scenarios.

## 3. Experiment

*Experimental Environment Settings and Dataset*

The experimental hardware resources include an AMD Ryzen 5 3600 CPU and NVIDIA RTX 2060 graphics card. The experiments were conducted on a system running Ubuntu 22.04 LTS with PyTorch 1.9.1, CUDA 10.2, and Python 3.8. In the experiments, the input resolution of the images was set to $512 \times 704$. The batch size was set to eight, and the initial learning rate was set to 0.003125. The YOLOXWarmCos method was used to update the learning rate during training. The default training duration was set to 300 epochs.

In the experiment, anthracite and claystone gangue were utilized as the experiment materials. The dataset employed in the experiment is displayed in Figure 4. Image acquisition was carried out using KinectV2 under various lighting conditions, resulting in significant variations in brightness between different images. The contrast between the coal and gangue in the images is relatively low, accompanied by minor differences in surface textures. Moreover, there is a substantial disparity in the distribution of coal and gangue within the images. Whether the objects in an image are densely distributed is determined by calculating the distribution density $\beta$ using Equation (2) in Section 2.3. A dense distribution is defined as $\beta > 1.5 \times 10^{-4}$, and a sparse distribution as $\beta < 1.5 \times 10^{-4}$. It was observed that 55% of the images in the dataset exhibited dense distributions of coal and gangue, while 45% exhibited sparse distributions. Via random sampling, 400 images from 608 images were taken as the training set, 100 images were taken as the validation set and finally, the remaining 108 images were taken as the test set. All these images were of $1470 \times 1080$ pixels resolution.

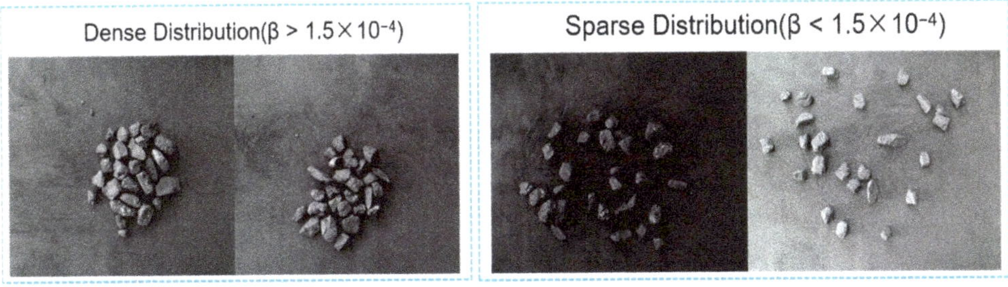


**Figure 4.** Images of coal and gangue in the dataset.

The evaluation of the proposed model encompasses several metrics, including the parameter count, GFLOPs (Giga Floating-point Operations), AP (Average Precision), and AR (Average Recall). AP and AR are computed using the COCO API [52]. Specifically, AP50 and AR50 denote the AP and AR values, respectively, corresponding to an Intersection over Union (IOU) threshold of 0.5. Higher values of AP and AR signify superior model performance.

## 4. Results, Discussion, and Analysis

### *4.1. Ablation Experiments with Different Components*

The AP50 and AR50 in this chapter are the results obtained by the model on the test set. The performance comparison of the model on the test set is shown in Table 1.

**Table 1.** Ablation experiments with different components.

| Model | Improvement Method | | | Performance | | | | | |
|---|---|---|---|---|---|---|---|---|---|
| | FPN | FPND | Head | AP50 (%) | AR50 (%) | $mAP_{50}$ (%) | Parameters (M) | GFLOPs | Inference Time (ms) |
| YOLOX-s | | | 3 | 93.8 | 99.5 | 69.6 | 8.94 | 23.55 | 19.87 |
| A | √ | | 3 | 96.5 | 99.0 | 98.0 | 6.72 | 21.04 | 16.11 |
| B | | √ | 3 | 96.7 | 99.3 | 97.9 | 5.00 | 12.66 | 15.57 |
| CGDet | | √ | 1 | 96.7 | 99.2 | 98.3 | 4.76 | 12.26 | 13.61 |

(In Table 1, the "√" symbol indicates that the corresponding module is used or integrated within the model).

As shown in Table 1, YOLOX-s had the lowest AP50 in training, with more parameters, computational workload, and inference time. Model A was derived by substituting the original PAN (Path Aggregation Network) structure in YOLOX-s with FPN (Feature Pyramid Network), while Model B was developed through the integration of depthwise separable convolution into the network architecture. Quantitative analysis demonstrates that Model A achieved significant performance improvements over the baseline YOLOX-s architecture: a 28.4% enhancement in $mAP_{50}$ (mean Average Precision at IoU threshold 0.5), while concurrently reducing parameter count by 24.83%, computational complexity by 10.66%, and inference latency by 3.76 ms. Model B achieved a 44.07% reduction in parameters and computation, along with a 4.3 ms faster inference time. Compared to the YOLOX-s baseline, the proposed CGDet demonstrated substantial improvements across multiple performance metrics by achieving a 28.7% increase in $mAP_{50}$, while significantly reducing model parameters and computational complexity by 46.76% and 47.94%, respectively. Furthermore, the model exhibited a 2.9% enhancement in AP50 while decreasing inference latency to 13.61 ms. Using a single detection head on the P3 feature map further reduced parameter, computation, and inference time while maintaining the model's high-precision detection capability.

### 4.2. Using ODDM to Measure the Distribution Density of Objects in Images

To investigate the distribution density of coal and gangue in different resolution feature maps, while maintaining the aspect ratio of the images, the object distribution density in different resolution feature maps was calculated based on Equation (2). The results are shown in Figure 5. The feature maps, denoted as P3, P4, and P5, were obtained by downsampling the input image by 8, 16, and 32 times, respectively. In Figure 5, the height of the image is represented by the vertical axis, which varies from 32 × 224 to 896 × 1088 in resolution. Comparing the feature maps at the same input resolution, the object distribution density was highest in P5 due to its lower resolution, while P3 had the lowest distribution density because of its higher resolution. The object distribution density in P4 fell between that of P3 and P5 since its resolution lay between the two.

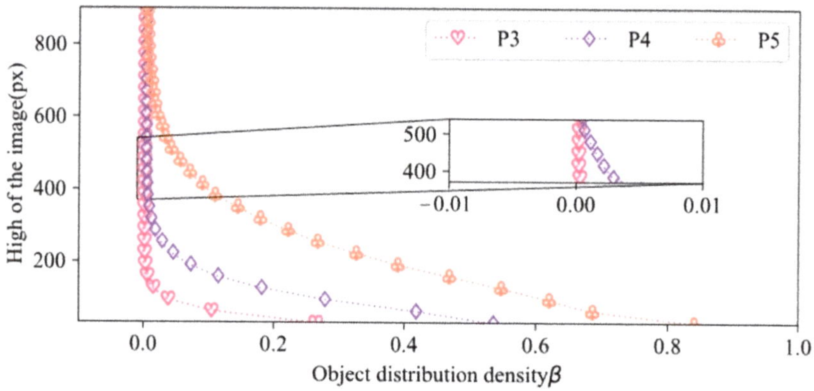


**Figure 5.** Distribution density of objects in different input resolution images in different resolution feature maps.

As shown in Figure 5, the input image's resolution rose, and the density of object distribution steadily decreased in the P3, P4, and P5 feature maps. For the P3 feature map, the density gradually decreased beyond an input resolution of 256 × 448. Once the input resolution surpassed 416 × 608, the distribution density of objects decreased at a stable rate. In the zoomed-in section of Figure 5, the object distribution density in P3 had an input resolution of 384 × 576 is $1.64 \times 10^{-4}$, which was an order of magnitude higher than the distribution density of $7.81 \times 10^{-5}$ for an image resolution of 416 × 608. For input resolutions of 416 × 608, 448 × 640, 480 × 672, and 512 × 704, the object distribution density in P3 remained constant. Within the range of 416 × 608 to 512 × 704, the object distribution density was lower in the P3 feature map than in the P4 feature map. The distribution density in the P4 feature map decreased slowly for input image resolutions higher than 640 × 832. P5 consistently had a decreasing density as the input resolution increased from 32 × 224 to 896 × 1088. To counter the impact of densely distributed objects, the CGDet model selects the P3 feature map for detection based on the density results in Figure 5. CGDet uses an image resolution of 512 × 704 for training and detection because the object distribution density is low at this resolution.

### 4.3. Using RROSM to Measure the Scale of Objects in Images

To enhance the accuracy of measuring the scale of coal and gangue in images, RROSM was employed specifically for the training set. The outcomes obtained from this measurement approach are illustrated in Figure 6, which presents the results derived from the utilization of RROSM. The vertical axis represents the quantities of small, medium, and large objects in the dataset, while the horizontal axis represents the input image resolutions. The image resolution ranges from 32 × 224 to 896 × 1088, and the aspect ratio of the images was maintained during the measurement. Figure 6 depicts the relationship between image resolution and object sizes in the dataset. As resolution increases, small objects decrease while medium objects increase. Small objects transform into medium objects as their resolution on the image grows. Before 416 × 608 resolution, small objects dominate (over 50%), but afterward, medium objects become more prominent. When resolution exceeds 800 × 992, medium objects start transforming into large objects, resulting in a decrease in the number of medium objects and an increase in large objects.

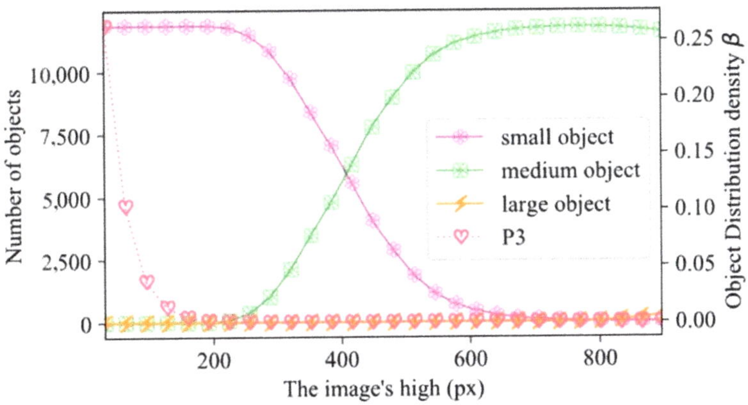


**Figure 6.** The Scale of objects in the training set.

As shown in Figure 6, the y-axis represents the distribution density of objects. Figure 6 depicts the correlation between the input image resolution and the density of object distribution in the P3 feature map. As resolution increases, the distribution density decreases, along with the number of small objects. When the resolution is below 256 × 448, the density is higher, and the dataset is mostly composed of small objects. Model performance is limited by both object distribution density and the presence of small objects at resolutions below 256 × 448.

The distribution density of objects in the P3 feature map decreases as image resolution goes from 256 × 448 to 416 × 608, but small objects still dominate the dataset. From the 416 × 608 to 736 × 928 resolution range, the lowest density of object distribution is in the P3 feature map. At this resolution, the model's performance is less affected by object distribution density, reducing the impact of small objects on perception. Resolutions above 736 × 928 have almost no small objects and neglectable object distribution density. While higher resolutions improve model performance, training and inference at such resolutions are costly. CGDet uses a 512 × 704 feature map for detection. At this resolution, coal and gangue, which are relatively measured in terms of object scale, are mainly composed of medium and small objects. As deep features are helpful for large object recognition, they are not very helpful for small and medium objects [53]. Therefore, CGDet chooses to use FPN for feature fusion, discarding the path enhancement part in PAN.

To provide additional evidence of the benefits associated with the relative object scale measurement method, Table 2 provides pertinent data regarding the model's performance and allows for a comparison of the performance between the PAN, FPN, and FPND models.

**Table 2.** Performance comparison of different neck structures.

| Neck | AP50 (%) | AR50 (%) | mAP$_{50}$ (%) | mAR$_{50}$ (%) | Parameters (M) | GFLOPs | Inference Time (ms) |
|---|---|---|---|---|---|---|---|
| PAN | 96.2 | 98.9 | 98.0 | 99.6 | 8.94 | 23.55 | 19.87 |
| FPN | 96.5 | 99.0 | 98.0 | 99.6 | 6.72 | 21.04 | 16.11 |
| FPND | 96.7 | 99.3 | 97.9 | 99.6 | 5.00 | 12.66 | 15.57 |

When the input image resolution is 512 × 704, removing the path enhancement module in PAN, which propagates shallow features to deeper layers, results in no change in the model's $mAP_{50}$. This suggests that the path enhancement component in PAN is redundant. Eliminating this redundant module improves AP50 and AR50 by 25%, reduces the number of parameters by 25%, decreases computational cost by 8%, and shortens inference time by 19%. FPND employs depthwise separable convolutions within the FPN, achieving reductions in parameter count, computational cost, and inference time at the expense of a slight 0.1% decrease in $mAP_{50}$. Compared to PAN, FPND reduces the number of parameters by 44%, decreases computational cost by 46%, and improves inference speed by 22%. These results further demonstrate that accurately measuring object scale in an image based on relative resolution provides valuable guidance for model architecture design.

### 4.4. Elimination of Redundant Detection Heads via ODDM

To illustrate the negative impact of object distribution density on model perception performance, detection experiments were conducted using feature maps with varying object distribution densities, as shown in the experimental results in Table 3. The P5 feature map, which had the highest object distribution density, impeded the model's perceptual capability, resulting in AP50, AR50, $mAP_{50}$, and $mAR_{50}$ values all below 90%. In contrast, the P4 feature map, with higher resolution and lower object distribution density, enhanced the model's perception, increasing AP50 and AR50 by 10.7% and 8.2%, respectively, compared to P5. Furthermore, the model's $mAP_{50}$ and $mAR_{50}$ improved by 10.7% and 20%, respectively, when using the P4 feature map compared to P5. Increasing the resolution further, the P3 feature map, which had the lowest object distribution density, provided an additional boost to the model's AP50 and AR50 by 2.9% and 3.3%, respectively, compared to P4. The model's $mAP_{50}$ and $mAR_{50}$ also increased by 3.5% and 2.8%, respectively, relative to using the P4 feature map. However, using the P3 feature map for detection required additional convolutional layers to fuse the feature maps, leading to increased model parameters and computational complexity. As the resolution of the P5, P4, and P3 feature maps gradually increased, the object distribution density within the feature maps progressively decreased, and the model's AP50, AR50, $mAP_{50}$, and $mAR_{50}$ steadily improved. Nevertheless, there was a diminishing marginal effect between the improvement in model perception performance and the increase in feature map resolution.

**Table 3.** The impact of feature maps with different levels of density on model performance.

| Feature Map | AP50 (%) | AR50 (%) | $mAP_{50}$ (%) | $mAR_{50}$ (%) | Parameters (M) | GFLOPs |
|---|---|---|---|---|---|---|
| P5 | 83.1 | 87.7 | 85.1 | 77.0 | 4.35 | 9.80 |
| P4 | 93.8 | 95.9 | 95.8 | 97.0 | 4.68 | 10.76 |
| P3 (CGDet) | 96.7 | 99.2 | 98.3 | 99.8 | 4.76 | 12.26 |

While increasing the input resolution of images or enhancing the resolution of feature maps used for detection can reduce the density of object distribution, the impact of increasing input image resolution and feature map resolution on improving model perceptual performance gradually diminishes. Since CGDet uses the P3 feature map for detection, which has a resolution eight times lower than that of the input image, we conducted experiments to investigate the relationship between input image resolution and model performance. During model training and testing, experiments were conducted with images of different resolutions ranging from 32 × 224 to 896 × 1088, and the results are shown in Figure 7. In Figure 7, as the image resolution increased, the model's $mAP_{50}$, $mAR_{50}$, and computational load gradually increased. When the image resolution was below 224 × 416, increasing the image resolution significantly improved the model's $mAP_{50}$ and $mAR_{50}$. When the image resolution ranged from 256 × 448 to 512 × 704, the contribution of increasing image resolution to improving the model's $mAP_{50}$ and $mAR_{50}$ gradually decreased.

Once the image resolution exceeds 512 × 704, the model's perceptual performance stabilized; further increasing the image resolution hardly improved the model's performance. Figure 7 reveals a noticeable diminishing return on model performance with increasing image resolution. While higher resolution input images are advantageous in reducing object density and enhancing the resolution of small objects, excessively increasing the input image resolution is counterproductive, leading to a significant increase in redundant computational load. Estimating the density of object distribution in images through methods like object density estimation allows for the determination of high-performance, low-computation image resolutions, thereby reducing the computational burden while maintaining high model performance.

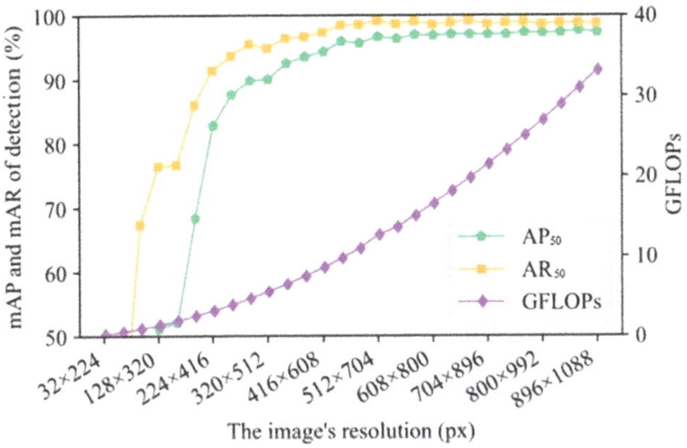


**Figure 7.** $mAP_{50}$, $mAR_{50}$, and GFLOPs were obtained for images with different input resolutions.

### 4.5. Visualization and Analysis of Results

The AP50 and AR50 of CGDet quantitatively represent the performance of the detector. However, they are difficult to observe. Therefore, CGDet was used to detect images in the test set, and the results are visualized in Figure 8.

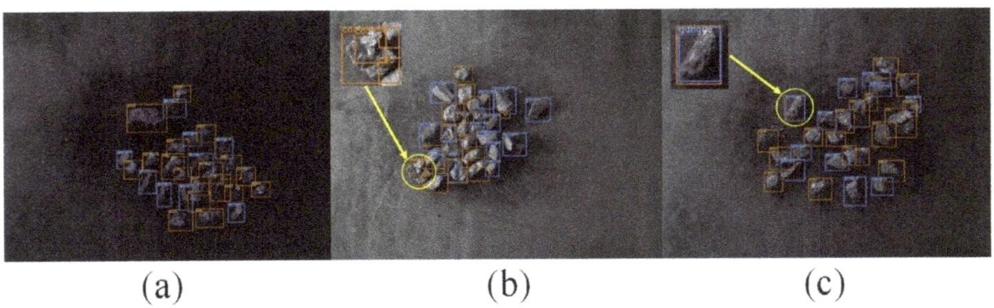


**Figure 8.** Visualization of CGDet's detection results on the test set. (**a**) Predicted Bounding Boxes for Gangue (Blue) and Coal (Yellow); (**b**) Redundant Predictions with the Same Class Label (Coal); (**c**) Redundant Predictions with Different Class Labels (Coal and Gangue).

In Figure 8a, the blue predicted bounding boxes represent gangue, while the yellow predicted bounding boxes represent coal. Most of the predicted boxes cover the corresponding objects in the image, but there are also a few instances where the object is redundantly predicted by two bounding boxes. There are two cases of redundant predictions. In one case, the two boxes with redundant predictions have the same class. As shown in Figure 8b, a piece of coal in the image is simultaneously predicted by two bounding boxes with the class label 'coal'. In the other case, the two boxes with redundant predictions have different classes. As shown in Figure 8c, the same piece of gangue in the image is predicted as both 'coal' and 'gangue' by two different bounding boxes. Due to the small area occupied by coal and gangue in the images, this results in a lower amount of discernible surface information for the coal and gangue in images. This makes it more difficult to distinguish them and leads to redundant predictions.

### 4.6. Comparison of the Performance of Different Detectors for Detecting Coal and Gangue

To demonstrate the advantage of CGDet in perceiving coal and gangue in low-resolution dense scenes, comparative experiments were conducted using MMDetection3. The Faster R-CNN, YOLOF, and AutoAssign detectors were utilized for the experiments, all of which employed ResNet50 as the backbone and FPN structure. The batch size in the experiment was eight and the input resolution of the images was set to 512 × 704, using the same dataset and evaluation metrics as CGDet. The results of the comparison experiment are shown in Table 4. Faster R-CNN is an excellent two-stage object detector, and its performance dominance in detecting coal and gangue is not obvious. Although YOLOF also performs detection using a single feature map, its AP50, and AR50 were 0.3% and 2.1% lower than CGDet, respectively. Despite CGDet utilizing only a single feature map for detection, it outperformed YOLOF. AutoAssign employs a dynamic label assignment strategy, but in this experiment, its AP50 and AR50 were 5.7% and 2.4% lower than CGDet, respectively. While YOLOV8n has fewer parameters and computational requirements than CGDet, its performance significantly lagged behind CGDet. YOLOV8s, despite having substantially more parameters and computational demands than CGDet, did not exhibit superior performance either. In this experiment, CGDet demonstrated a clear advantage, achieving AP50 and AR50 values of 96.7% and 99.2%, respectively, in comparison to Faster R-CNN, YOLOF, AutoAssign, and YOLOV8 detectors. Furthermore, CGDet achieved these results with an order of magnitude fewer parameters and significantly reduced computational requirements.

**Table 4.** Performance comparison of different detectors.

| Model | AP50 (%) | AR50 (%) | Parameters (M) | GFLOPs |
|---|---|---|---|---|
| Faster R-CNN | 96.4 | 97.1 | 41.35 | 81.66 |
| YOLOF | 96.2 | 98.4 | 42.36 | 34.49 |
| AutoAssign | 91.0 | 96.8 | 36.25 | 69.54 |
| YOLOV8n | 95.6 | 99.7 | 3.2 | 8.7 |
| YOLOV8s | 95.6 | 99.4 | 11.2 | 28.6 |
| CGDet | 96.7 | 99.2 | 4.76 | 12.26 |

### 4.7. Comparison of Different Coal and Gangue Perception Methods

Many excellent convolutional neural network models have been developed for the classification and localization of coal and gangue in images, but their performances vary. To provide a rough comparison of the performance of these outstanding models, this study selected convolutional neural network models that perceive coal and gangue using color images for comparison. Since these models use different datasets and the source code is not publicly available, the comparative results in Table 5 can only reflect the overall progress in the field.

As shown in Table 5, the proposed CGDet achieved the highest AP50, indicating that CGDet is highly competitive in the perception of coal and gangue. At the same time, CGDet had minimal inference time, indicating its ability to quickly perceive coal and gangue in images. Furthermore, CGDet has fewer parameters and computations, demonstrating its lightweight nature. By comparing with different models listed in the table, it can be seen that many models either suffer from lightweight but poor performance, or good performance but insufficient compacting and longer inference times. CGDet strikes a balance between model compaction and performance, exhibiting outstanding performance and efficiency in perceiving densely distributed coal and gangue in images.

Table 5. Comparison of different coal and gangue perception methods.

| Reference | AP50 (%) | Parameters (M) | GFLOPs | Inference Time (ms) |
|---|---|---|---|---|
| Q. Liu [23] | 96.45 | - | - | 30.67 |
| D. Yang [25] | 91.90 | 6.64 | 14.30 | - |
| P. Yan [24] | 96.00 | - | - | 19.00 |
| G. Xue [39] | 96.27 | - | - | 21.97 |
| J. Liu [40] | 78.50 | - | - | 28.41 |
| Y. Liu [43] | 80.24 | 5.97 | 6.83 | 11.12 |
| B. Zhang [41] | 91.33 | - | - | 40.00 |
| Z. Lv [20] | 88.54 | - | - | 30.20 |
| CGDet | 96.70 | 4.76 | 12.26 | 11.96 |

## 5. Conclusions

This paper presents CGDet, a compact convolutional neural network model specifically designed for the perception of coal and gangue in dense scenes. Through extensive experimental validation, the following key scientific and practical findings were established:

Model Performance and Efficiency: CGDet operates with only 4.76 million parameters and 12.26 GFLOPs of computational load, achieving an AP50 of 96.7% and an AR50 of 99.2%. This demonstrates that incorporating object distribution density and scale considerations allows for significant model lightweighting without sacrificing performance, thereby informing the design of efficient deep learning models.

Input Image and Feature Map Selection: The Object Distribution Density Measurement (ODDM) method determined an optimal input image resolution of $512 \times 704$, utilizing P3 as the feature map for detection. These configurations yielded excellent performance in dense scenarios, underscoring the importance of tailored input and feature map resolutions for object detection to mitigate issues associated with label rewriting.

Structural Optimization and Cost Reduction: By employing the Relative Resolution Object Scale Measurement (RROSM) method to assess object scale and optimizing the model's neck structure, CGDet achieved a 46.76% reduction in parameters and a 47.94% decrease in computational costs, while slightly enhancing both AP50 and AR50. This indicates that the RROSM method is effective at evaluating object scale, playing a crucial role in structural design and the elimination of redundant parameters.

Practical Recommendations: For the specific task of detecting densely distributed coal and gangue, it is advisable for designers and mechanical engineers to develop customized object detection models, as these may outperform general-purpose detectors. Despite CGDet's superior performance, it remains susceptible to duplicate detections. Future work should focus on addressing this issue, potentially through the integration of fine-grained classification methods to enhance detection accuracy.

**Author Contributions:** Conceptualization, H.L. and X.C.; methodology, H.L. and Y.L.; software, X.C., Y.L. and J.L.; validation, H.L. and X.C.; investigation, X.C. and K.X.; resources, K.X.; data curation, J.L., Y.L. and X.C.; writing—original draft preparation, H.L. and X.C.; writing—review and editing, K.X. and J.L.; funding acquisition, K.X. All authors have read and agreed to the published version of the manuscript.

**Funding:** This work was sponsored by the Fundamental Research Funds for the Central Universities (No. FRF-BD-23-02), and the Beijing Science and Technology Planning Project (No. Z221100005822012).

**Institutional Review Board Statement:** Not applicable.

**Informed Consent Statement:** Not applicable.

**Data Availability Statement:** The data presented in this study are available on request from the corresponding author.

**Conflicts of Interest:** The authors declare no conflicts of interest.

## References


1. Wang, X.-P.; Zhang, Z.-M.; Guo, Z.-H.; Su, C.; Sun, L.-H. Energy Structure Transformation in the Context of Carbon Neutralization: Evolutionary Game Analysis Based on Inclusive Development of Coal and Clean Energy. *J. Clean. Prod.* **2023**, *398*, 136626. [CrossRef]
2. Zhang, J.X.; Zhang, Q.; Spearing AJ, S.; Miao, X.X.; Guo, S.; Sun, Q. Green Coal Mining Technique Integrating Mining-Dressing-Gas Draining-Backfilling-Mining. *Int. J. Min. Sci. Technol.* **2017**, *27*, 17–27. [CrossRef]
3. Wei, Y.; Zhang, W.X.; Lin, B.Q.; Si, G.Y.; Zhang, J.G.; Wang, J.L. Integration of Protective Mining and Underground Backfilling for Coal and Gas Outburst Control: A Case Study. *Process Saf. Environ. Prot.* **2022**, *157*, 273–283.
4. Sotoudeh, F.; Nehring, M.; Kizil, M.; Knights, P. Integrated Underground Mining and Pre-Concentration Systems; a Critical Review of Technical Concepts and Developments. *Int. J. Mining Reclam. Environ.* **2021**, *35*, 153–182. [CrossRef]
5. Liu, H.; Xu, K. Recognition of Gangues from Color Images Using Convolutional Neural Networks with Attention Mechanism. *Measurement* **2023**, *206*, 112273. [CrossRef]
6. Luo, X.; He, K.; Zhang, Y.; He, P.; Zhang, Y. A Review of Intelligent Ore Sorting Technology and Equipment Development. *Int. J. Miner. Met. Mater.* **2022**, *29*, 1647–1655. [CrossRef]
7. Yang, J.; Peng, J.; Li, Y.; Xie, Q.; Wu, Q.; Wang, J. Gangue Localization and Volume Measurement Based on Adaptive Deep Feature Fusion and Surface Curvature Filter. *IEEE Trans. Instrum. Meas.* **2021**, *70*, 1–13. [CrossRef]
8. Wang, J.; Zhao, M.; Xia, C. An improved classification diagnosis approach for cervical images based on deep neural networks. *Pattern Anal. Appl.* **2024**, *27*, 79. [CrossRef]
9. Campos, S.; Zamora, J.; Allende, H. Block-Wise Imputation EM Algorithm in Multi-Source Scenario: ADNI Case. *Pattern Anal. Appl.* **2024**, *27*, 44. [CrossRef]
10. Akbaba, E.E.; Gurkan, F.; Gunsel, B. Boosting Person ReID Feature Extraction via Dynamic Convolution. *Pattern Anal. Appl.* **2024**, *27*, 80. [CrossRef]
11. Zou, L.; Yu, X.; Li, M.; Lei, M.; Yu, H. Nondestructive Identification of Coal and Gangue via Near-infrared Spectroscopy Based on Improved Broad Learning. *IEEE Trans. Instrum. Meas.* **2020**, *69*, 8043–8052. [CrossRef]
12. Li, C.; Wang, J. Remote Sensing Image Location Based on Improved Yolov7 Target Detection. *Pattern Anal. Appl.* **2024**, *27*, 50. [CrossRef]
13. Bao, W.; Zhang, H.; Ding, Y.; Shen, F.; Li, L. EdgeNet: A Low-Power Image Recognition Model Based on Small Sample Information. *Pattern Anal. Appl.* **2024**, *27*, 82. [CrossRef]
14. Kim, S.; Jang, I.-S.; Ko, B.C. Domain-Free Fire Detection Using the Spatial–Temporal Attention Transform of the Yolo Backbone. *Pattern Anal. Appl.* **2024**, *27*, 45. [CrossRef]
15. Ren, S.; He, K.; Girshick, R.; Sun, J. Faster R-CNN: Towards Real-Time Object Detection with Region Proposal Networks. *IEEE Trans. Pattern Anal. Mach. Intell.* **2017**, *39*, 1137–1149. [CrossRef]
16. Li, D.; Zhang, Z.; Xu, Z.; Xu, L.; Meng, G.; Li, Z.; Chen, S. An Image-Based Hierarchical Deep Learning Framework for Coal and Gangue Detection. *IEEE Access* **2019**, *7*, 184686–184699. [CrossRef]
17. Lei, S.; Xiao, X.; Zhang, M.; Dai, J. Visual classification method based on CNN for coal-gangue sorting robots. In Proceedings of the 2020 5th International Conference on Automation, Control and Robotics Engineering (CACRE), Dalian, China, 19–20 September 2020; pp. 543–547.
18. Redmon, J.; Divvala, S.; Girshick, R.; Farhadi, A. You Only Look Once: Unified, Real-Time Object Detection. In Proceedings of the 2016 IEEE Conference on Computer Vision and Pattern Recognition (CVPR), Las Vegas, NV, USA, 27–30 June 2016; pp. 779–788.
19. Li, D.; Ren, H.; Wang, G.; Wang, S.; Wang, W.; Du, M. Coal Gangue Detection and Recognition Method Based on Multiscale Fusion Lightweight Network SMS-YOLOv3. *Energy Sci. Eng.* **2023**, *11*, 1783–1797. [CrossRef]
20. Lv, Z.; Wang, W.; Xu, Z.; Zhang, K.; Lv, H. Cascade Network for Detection of Coal and Gangue in the Production Context. *Powder Technol.* **2021**, *377*, 361–371. [CrossRef]
21. Li, D.; Wang, G.; Zhang, Y.; Wang, S. Coal Gangue Detection and Recognition Algorithm Based on Deformable Convolution Yolov3. *IET Image Process.* **2022**, *16*, 134–144. [CrossRef]
22. Yan, P.; Sun, Q.; Yin, N.; Hua, L.; Shang, S.; Zhang, C. Detection of Coal and Gangue Based on Improved Yolov5.1 Which Embedded Scse Module. *Measurement* **2022**, *188*, 110530. [CrossRef]
23. Liu, Q.; Li, J.G.; Li, Y.S.; Gao, M.W. Recognition Methods for Coal and Coal Gangue Based on Deep Learning. *IEEE Access* **2021**, *9*, 77599–77610. [CrossRef]
24. Yan, P.; Kan, X.; Zhang, H.; Zhang, X.; Chen, F.; Li, X. Target Recognition of Coal and Gangue Based on Improved Yolov5s and Spectral Technology. *Sensors* **2023**, *23*, 4911. [CrossRef] [PubMed]
25. Yang, D.; Miao, C.; Li, X.; Liu, Y.; Wang, Y.; Zheng, Y. Improved Yolov7 Network Model for Gangue Selection Robot for Gangue and Foreign Matter Detection in Coal. *Sensors* **2023**, *23*, 5140. [CrossRef] [PubMed]
26. Xu, S.; Zhou, Y.; Huang, Y.; Han, T. Yolov4-Tiny-Based Coal Gangue Image Recognition and FPGA Implementation. *Micromachines* **2022**, *13*, 1983. [CrossRef] [PubMed]

27. Zhou, Y.; Chen, S.; Wang, Y.; Huan, W. Review of Research on Lightweight Convolutional Neural Networks. In Proceedings of the 2020 IEEE 5th Information Technology and Mechatronics Engineering Conference (ITOEC 2020), Chongqing, China, 12–14 June 2020; pp. 1713–1720.
28. Chen, F.; Li, S.; Han, J.; Ren, F.; Yang, Z. Review of Lightweight Deep Convolutional Neural Networks. *Arch. Comput. Methods Eng.* **2024**, *31*, 1915–1937. [CrossRef]
29. Szegedy, C.; Liu, W.; Jia, Y.; Sermanet, P.; Reed, S.; Anguelov, D.; Erhan, D.; Vanhoucke, V.; Rabinovich, A. Going Deeper with Convolutions. In Proceedings of the IEEE Conference on Computer Vision and Pattern Recognition, Boston, MA, USA, 7–12 June 2015.
30. Christian, S.; Vanhoucke, V.; Ioffe, S.; Shlens, J.; Wojna, Z. Rethinking the Inception Architecture for Computer Vision. In Proceedings of the IEEE Conference on Computer Vision and Pattern Recognition, Las Vegas, NV, USA, 27–30 June 2016.
31. Christian, S.; Ioffe, S.; Vanhoucke, V.; Alemi, A. Inception-V4, Inception-Resnet and the Impact of Residual Connections on Learning. In Proceedings of the AAAI Conference on Artificial Intelligence, San Francisco, CA, USA, 4–9 February 2017.
32. Chollet, F. Xception: Deep Learning with Depthwise Separable Convolutions. In Proceedings of the 30th IEEE Conference on Computer Vision and Pattern Recognition, Honolulu, HI, USA, 21–26 July 2017; pp. 1800–1807.
33. Real, E.; Aggarwal, A.; Huang, Y.; Le, Q.V. Regularized Evolution for Image Classifier Architecture Search. In Proceedings of the AAAI Conference on Artificial Intelligence, Honolulu, HI, USA, 27 January–1 February 2019.
34. Vysogorets, A.; Kempe, J. Connectivity Matters: Neural Network Pruning through the Lens of Effective Sparsity. *J. Mach. Learn. Res.* **2021**, *24*, 1–23. [CrossRef]
35. Jaderberg, M.; Vedaldi, A.; Zisserman, A. Speeding up Convolutional Neural Networks with Low Rank Expansions. *arXiv* **2014**, arXiv:1405.3866.
36. Zhang, X.; Zou, J.; He, K.; Sun, J. Accelerating Very Deep Convolutional Networks for Classification and Detection. *IEEE Trans. Pattern Anal. Mach. Intell.* **2015**, *38*, 1943–1955. [CrossRef]
37. Guo, Y.; Yao, A.; Zhao, H.; Chen, Y. Network Sketching: Exploiting Binary Structure in Deep Cnns. In Proceedings of the IEEE Conference on Computer Vision and Pattern Recognition, Honolulu, HI, USA, 21–26 July 2017.
38. Hinton, G. Distilling the Knowledge in a Neural Network. *arXiv* **2015**, arXiv:1503.02531.
39. Xue, G.; Li, S.; Hou, P.; Gao, S.; Tan, R. Research on Lightweight Yolo Coal Gangue Detection Algorithm Based on Resnet18 Backbone Feature Network. *Internet Things* **2023**, *22*, 100762. [CrossRef]
40. Liu, J.; Qiao, H.; Yang, L.; Guo, J. Improved Lightweight Yolov4 Foreign Object Detection Method for Conveyor Belts Combined with Cbam. *Appl. Sci.* **2023**, *13*, 8465. [CrossRef]
41. Zhang, B.; Zhang, H.-B. Coal Gangue Detection Method Based on Improved SSD Algorithm. In Proceedings of the 2021 International Conference on Intelligent Transportation, Big Data Smart City, Xi'an, China, 27–28 March 2021; pp. 634–637.
42. Liu, W.; Anguelov, D.; Erhan, D.; Szegedy, C.; Reed, S.; Fu, C.-Y.; Berg, A.C. SSD: Single Shot MultiBox Detector. In Proceedings of the European Conference on Computer Vision 2016, Amsterdam, The Netherlands, 11–14 October 2016; Springer: Cham, Switzerland, 2016; pp. 21–37.
43. Liu, Y.; Wang, X.; Zhang, Z.; Deng, F. LOSN: Lightweight Ore Sorting Networks for Edge Device Environment. *Eng. Appl. Artif. Intell* **2023**, *123*, 106191. [CrossRef]
44. Cao, Z.; Li, Z.; Fang, L.; Li, J. Lightweight Coal and Gangue Detection Algorithm Based on Improved Yolov7-Tiny. *Int. J. Coal Prep. Util.* **2024**, *44*, 1773–1792. [CrossRef]
45. Yan, P.; Zhang, H.; Kan, X.; Chen, F.; Wang, C.; Liu, Z. Lightweight Detection Method of Coal Gangue Based on Multispectral and Improved Yolov5s. *Int. J. Coal Prep. Util.* **2024**, *44*, 399–414. [CrossRef]
46. Wang, S.; Zhu, J.; Li, Z.; Sun, X.; Wang, G. Gdps-Yolo: An Improved Yolov8s for Coal Gangue Detection. *Int. J. Coal Prep. Util.* **2024**. [CrossRef]
47. Xin, F.; Jia, Q.; Yang, Y.; Pan, H.; Wang, Z. A High Accuracy Detection Method for Coal and Gangue with S3DD-Yolov8. *Int. J. Coal Prep. Util.* **2024**, 1–19. [CrossRef]
48. Yan, P.; Wang, W.; Li, G.; Zhao, Y.; Wang, J.; Wen, Z. Detection of Coal Gangue Based on Spectral Technology and Enhanced Lightweight Yolov7-tiny. *Int. J. Coal Prep. Util.* **2024**, *44*, 1843–1863. [CrossRef]
49. Wang, Y.; Peng, J.; Wang, H.; Wang, M. Progressive Learning with Multi-Scale Attention Network for Cross-Domain Vehicle re-Identification. *Sci. China Inf. Sci.* **2022**, *65*, 160103. [CrossRef]
50. Wang, H.; Yao, M.; Chen, Y.; Xu, Y.; Liu, H.; Jia, W.; Fu, X.; Wang, Y. Manifold-Based Incomplete Multi-View Clustering via Bi-Consistency Guidance. *IEEE Trans. Multimed.* **2024**, *26*, 10001–10014. [CrossRef]
51. Wang, H.; Yao, M.; Jiang, G.; Mi, Z.; Fu, X. Graph-Collaborated Auto-Encoder Hashing for Multiview Binary Clustering. *IEEE Trans. Neural Netw. Learn. Syst.* **2023**, *35*, 10121–10133. [CrossRef]
52. Zheng, G.; Songtao, L.; Feng, W.; Zeming, L.; Jian, S. YOLOX: Exceeding YOLO Series in 2021. *arXiv* **2021**, arXiv:2107.08430.
53. Liu, S.; Qi, L.; Qin, H.; Shi, J.; Jia, J. Path Aggregation Network for Instance Segmentation. In Proceedings of the 2018 IEEE/CVF Conference on Computer Vision and Pattern Recognition (CVPR), Salt Lake City, UT, USA, 18–23 June 2018; pp. 8759–8768.
54. Lin, T.Y.; Dollar, P.; Girshick, R.; He, K.; Hariharan, B.; Belongie, S. Feature Pyramid Networks for Object Detection. In Proceedings of the 2017 IEEE Conference on Computer Vision and Pattern Recognition (CVPR), Honolulu, HI, USA, 21–26 July 2017; pp. 936–944.

55. Liu, H.; Wang, D.; Xu, K.; Zhou, P.; Zhou, D. Lightweight Convolutional Neural Network for Counting Densely Piled Steel Bars. *Autom. Constr.* **2023**, *146*, 104692. [CrossRef]
56. Lin, T.Y.; Michael, M.; Serge, B.; James, H.; Pietro, P.; Deva, R.; Piotr, D.; Zitnick, C.L. Lawrence Zitnick. Microsoft Coco: Common Objects in Context. In *Computer Vision—ECCV 2014*; Springer: Berlin/Heidelberg, Germany, 2014; pp. 740–755.

sensors

MDPI

*Article*

# Steering-Angle Prediction and Controller Design Based on Improved YOLOv5 for Steering-by-Wire System

**Cunliang Ye [1,2], Yunlong Wang [1], Yongfu Wang [1,*] and Yan Liu [3]**

[1] School of Mechanical Engineering and Automation, Northeastern University, Shenyang 110819, China; yecunliang123@126.com (C.Y.); wangyl@mail.neu.edu.cn (Y.W.)
[2] School of Mechanical Engineering, Ningxia Institute of Science and Technology, Shizuishan 753000, China
[3] School of Automobile and Traffic Engineering, Liaoning University of Technology, Jinzhou 121001, China; dannieliuy@outlook.com
* Correspondence: yfwang@mail.neu.edu.cn

**Abstract:** A crucial role is played by steering-angle prediction in the control of autonomous vehicles (AVs). It mainly includes the prediction and control of the steering angle. However, the prediction accuracy and calculation efficiency of traditional YOLOv5 are limited. For the control of the steering angle, angular velocity is difficult to measure, and the angle control effect is affected by external disturbances and unknown friction. This paper proposes a lightweight steering angle prediction network model called YOLOv5Ms, based on YOLOv5, aiming to achieve accurate prediction while enhancing computational efficiency. Additionally, an adaptive output feedback control scheme with output constraints based on neural networks is proposed to regulate the predicted steering angle using the YOLOv5Ms algorithm effectively. Firstly, given that most lane-line data sets consist of simulated images and lack diversity, a novel lane data set derived from real roads is manually created to train the proposed network model. To improve real-time accuracy in steering-angle prediction and enhance effectiveness in steering control, we update the bounding box regression loss function with the generalized intersection over union (GIoU) to Shape-IoU_Loss as a better-converging regression loss function for bounding-box improvement. The YOLOv5Ms model achieves a 30.34% reduction in weight storage space while simultaneously improving accuracy by 7.38% compared to the YOLOv5s model. Furthermore, an adaptive output feedback control scheme with output constraints based on neural networks is introduced to regulate the predicted steering angle via YOLOv5Ms effectively. Moreover, utilizing the backstepping control method and introducing the Lyapunov barrier function enables us to design an adaptive neural network output feedback controller with output constraints. Finally, a strict stability analysis based on Lyapunov stability theory ensures the boundedness of all signals within the closed-loop system. Numerical simulations and experiments have shown that the proposed method provides a 39.16% better root mean squared error (RMSE) score than traditional backstepping control, and it achieves good estimation performance for angles, angular velocity, and unknown disturbances.

**Keywords:** steer-by-wire (SbW) systems; steering-angle prediction; autonomous vehicles (AVs); convolutional neural network (CNN); barrier Lyapunov function

## 1. Introduction

### *1.1. Background*

According to the latest World Health Organization (WHO) reports, approximately 1.3 million individuals lose their lives annually due to road accidents, with human errors accounting for an estimated 90% of all car crashes [1]. The statistics above have prompted the proposition of autonomous vehicles (AVs) as a means to mitigate human errors. AVs exemplify a burgeoning application of automotive technology, attracting significant attention from both academia and industry due to their advanced functionalities, such as scene recognition, path planning, and motion control, which offer substantial driving convenience. AVs are now emerging as an innocuous alternative to human drivers, thereby significantly reducing the annual loss of thousands of lives [2]. Noteworthy ongoing research efforts in managing the diverse challenges faced by AVs include advancements in human recognition, traffic analysis, road and lane detection, steering controls, and path planning. Simultaneously, the prediction and control of the steering angle play a pivotal role in the realm of autonomous vehicles, garnering significant attention from researchers, manufacturers, and insurance companies alike [3].

### 1.2. Related Research

In the last few years, significant advancements have been made in the field of AVs. The current research methodologies on AVs can be classified into two primary approaches: mediated perception and end-to-end driving. The mediated perception approach focuses on breaking the driving task down (e.g., perception, localization, planning, and control to ensure safe driving) into standardized modules. Subsequently, it employs rule-based methods to establish connections between these distinct modules. The mediated perception method, however, exhibits inherent limitations. The primary disadvantage lies in the intricate task of developing and maintaining interconnections between all modules within the system. The modularity paradigm may be compromised in different scenarios that require varying connections between modules [4]. Additionally, constructing and sustaining such a pipeline incurs significant costs despite extensive efforts over many years; thus, it is far from achieving complete autonomy [5]. Consequently, these approaches necessitate a substantial endeavor in designing architectures that integrate all system components and are frequently susceptible to error propagation throughout the entire pipeline [6,7].

Deep learning (DL) techniques are gaining increasing popularity and have emerged as a valuable tool across various industries, including the automotive sector, owing to their exceptional capability to extract image features. DL has significantly impacted AVs' control, particularly in terms of steering-angle prediction, due to its efficient processing of unlabeled raw data and robust extraction of image features. These techniques have facilitated the emergence of the end-to-end driving approach, also called the behavior reflex approach, simplifying traditional subsystems considerably and alleviating the burden associated with vehicle modeling and control [8]. DL-based steering-angle prediction in the end-to-end driving approach offers several advantages, including error tolerance, rapid error identification, and an enhanced capability to manage unpredictable situations [9]. The work of [10] presents an intelligent driving assist system for the real-time prediction of the steering angle using DL and a raw data set collected from a real environment.

To date, many studies have employed deep learning techniques to predict steering angles and control lateral motion in autonomous vehicles. The earliest attempt at end-to-end driving can be traced back to ALVINN, where a three-layer, fully connected network was trained to predict the steering wheel angle based on camera and radar images [11]. Consequently, the researchers subsequently developed an end-to-end driving system specifically designed for off-road conditions. They extensively trained a six-layer convolutional network using a substantial amount of data to accurately simulate the obstacle avoidance behavior exhibited by human drivers [12], the small vehicle, known as DAVE. Ref. [13], expanded upon the DAVE system, training a three-camera model to perform steering control for a vehicle in a range of real-world driving scenarios. This work arguably brought end-to-end systems to the forefront of AV research. A convolutional neural network (CNN)-based end-to-end controller was proposed for steering autonomous vehicles [14]. The network was trained using road screenshots generated via the car simulator CARSIM and human driver steering angles. However, it is worth noting that the network architecture consists of only seven layers, which may limit its capacity, and the training data lack real-world derivation, leading to potential limitations in their generalization ability. The proposed framework in [15] introduces a multi-task demonstration learning (MT-LfD) approach, incorporating an end-to-end trainable network for emulating the driving commands of an expert demonstrator. Supervised auxiliary task prediction is employed to guide the primary task of predicting driving commands. A neural motion planner is proposed in [16] for autonomous driving in complex urban scenarios, encompassing traffic light processing, concessions, and interaction with multiple road users. To accomplish this, the authors developed a comprehensive model that utilizes raw liDAR data and high-definition maps as inputs to generate interpretable intermediate representations in the form of 3D detections and their future trajectories.

The ease of amassing extensive human driving data renders the end-to-end approach highly effective for straightforward tasks. However, intricate and infrequent traffic scenarios continue to pose challenges for this methodology [17]. From the relevant research above, the primary challenge in DL-based steering-angle prediction for AVs lies in the scarcity of real-world data sets, necessitating a heavy reliance on data generated from simulated environments. The limited depth of existing CNN-based networks has also constrained their training performance. Increasing the network depth can enhance performance. However, it also introduces challenges such as vanishing or exploding gradients and accuracy saturation, followed by rapid degradation [18].

Despite the numerous shortcomings and challenges that persist, end-to-end driving remains the most promising approach for AVs based on previous research findings. This approach offers significant advantages in terms of reducing hardware costs and research complexity compared to alternative methods. Furthermore, its incorporation of diverse data sets enables versatility across various scenarios [6]. The work of [19] presents an innovative approach to end-to-end steering-angle prediction and its control in electric power-steering (EPS) systems. The methodology integrates transfer learning-based computer vision techniques for prediction and control with fuzzy signature-enhanced fuzzy systems. Successfully applied transfer learning-based computer vision technology to extract corresponding visual data without the need for large data sets reduces data collection and the computer load. The experiment shows that the proposed model achieves good performance. Recently, with the rapid advancement of deep learning techniques, computer vision-based object detection, combined with deep learning, has gradually emerged as the predominant method in this field of AVs. This methodology eliminates the need for manual feature extraction and can be categorized into two main groups: two-stage object detection methods represented by Region with CNN (RCNN), Fast RCNN, Faster RCNN, and Mask RCNN [20], and one-stage object detection methods, represented by Single Shot MultiBox Detector (SSD) detection methods series, You Only Look Once (YOLO) detection methods series, and RetinaNet [21–23]. Among these approaches, YOLOv5 stands out as a cutting-edge representation due to its superior speed, enhanced detection accuracy, and reduced file size. Consequently, it finds extensive applications requiring precise object detection tasks in various domains. In this study, drawing inspiration from object detection methodologies, we transform the task of predicting steering angles into an object-detection problem and propose a novel steering controller.

A lot of research has been conducted on steering control in AVs. In order to obtain accurate tracking performance for SbW systems, for example, model-based linear quadratic feedback control [24], trajectory tracking control [25], and model predictive control [26] are widely used. Ref. [27] proposed an adaptive sliding-mode control method to improve control accuracy using self-aligning torque and friction as an external disturbance. Ref. [27] proposed a robust sliding-mode learning control scheme and designed a sliding-mode learning controller to drive the sliding-mode variable in order to converge the tracking error to zero. They ignore system-parameter uncertainty and external disturbances. Ref. [28] proposed a robust, adaptive, integral terminal sliding-mode control strategy based on extreme learning machines, which ensures the finite time convergence of errors and effectively estimates the total uncertainty in a system using a single hidden layer feed-forward network. The work of [29] presents a new, vertical noncontact angle sensor based on the electromagnetic induction principle and conducted nonlinear optimization. A sensor prototype was made and tested in a laboratory. The experimental results show that the nonlinearity of the sensor was significantly improved, making angle measurement more accurate. This provides accurate angle values in angle-control experiments, which helps improve control accuracy. However, although the above methods have achieved many results, there are still limitations in many areas. For example, it is necessary to accurately know the angular velocity signal, and in practice, additional sensors need to be installed, while using differential methods can amplify measurement noise. It cannot be guaranteed that the tracking error will always be within a specific range, and there may be sudden changes in the tracking error.

### 1.3. Motivation and Contributions

The remarkable advancements in automotive technology in recent years have been driven by a convergence of several interconnected trends, including the resurgence of deep learning, the rapid evolution of sensing devices and in-vehicle computing systems, the accumulation of annotated data, and significant breakthroughs in related research fields (particularly computer vision) [30]. The rapid progress of deep learning can be attributed to the emergence and extensive application of convolutional neural networks (CNNs) in computer vision and object detection, which has paved the way for autonomous vehicle development. However, numerous challenges still hinder the widespread adoption of AVs in practical applications. For instance, one such challenge pertains to vision-based steering-angle prediction for AV control and designing an effective lateral controller for dynamic path tracking in order to solve the existing problems in the corner prediction and tracking control of autonomous vehicles. For example, the traditional YOLOv5 applied to angle prediction entails high requirements for storage capacity and hardware. Unknown parameters are difficult to measure in steering-angle tracking control, the influence of external disturbance, and model uncertainty on the control effect.

In this paper, we address the challenges above by transforming the task of predicting steering angles into an object-detection problem, and we propose a steering controller. It imitates the driver's perception of road conditions, decision-making, and steering implementation during vehicle operation. It utilizes a camera positioned behind the windshield to translate the observed lane image into a steering control signal. The selection of a DL-based object detection algorithm plays a crucial role in addressing the challenge of steering-angle prediction. Undoubtedly, YOLOv5 has garnered significant attention and demonstrated remarkable accomplishments. However, the constraints on storage capacity and hardware limitations present substantial challenges for deploying the full-scale YOLOv5 network model in vehicular equipment [31]. Therefore, due to its performance merits, YOLOv5s is selected as the network model for predicting steering angles. To achieve accurate steering-angle prediction while enhancing computational efficiency, a lightweight steering-angle prediction network model called YOLOv5Ms is proposed, based on YOLOv5s.

To mimic the driver's behavior during autonomous driving, we categorized lane-line curves into 15 classes, based on their curvature, and we created a corresponding data set for training You Only Look Once version 5 with MobileNet version 3 (YOLOv5Ms) as a network model. During AVs' operation, a camera mounted on the vehicle captures information about lane lines on the road. The trained YOLOv5Ms model is utilized to predict steering angles using these camera images. The processed steering angle is then transmitted to the steering controller via a serial port. Subsequently, our proposed controller receives this data through the serial port to enable appropriate steering control.

In order to ensure that the steering system of AVs can accurately and in a timely manner track the reference angle signal, the steering system's modeling and the controller's design are crucial. In practical engineering, there are many unknown parameters in the SbW system, such as friction torque, self-aligning torque, external disturbance, and angular velocity, that are difficult to measure. With the development of adaptive control technology, neural networks can approximate nonlinear functions with high accuracy. Meanwhile, the state observer and disturbance observer exert a good estimation effect for the variables that are difficult to measure and the external disturbance. Therefore, neural networks, state observers, and perturbation observers can be used to model SbW systems in order to improve model accuracy for better control accuracy. However, during the angle tracking of AVs, the tracking error should be guaranteed to be within a specific range, which may lead to accidents if sudden changes occur instantaneously. Therefore, we are motivated to explore a control method in an SbW system with model uncertainty, an external disturbance, and difficult-to-measure variables to improve the tracking accuracy while ensuring that the tracking error is always within a specific range.

The contributions of this paper can be summarized as follows:

1. The present paper proposes a lightweight steering-angle prediction network model, namely YOLOv5Ms, based on YOLOv5s to achieve model compression while maintaining detection accuracy and speed. To address the issues of low localization accuracy and slow regression speed in object detection boxes during training, we employ Shape-IoU_Loss as the regression loss function for bounding box improvement.
2. To ensure that the steering system of the autonomous vehicle responds quickly and accurately to the predicted steering-angle signal, an adaptive output feedback control scheme with output constraints based on a neural network is proposed in this paper. The advantage of this control method is that it can constrain the tracking error within a given range, improving the tracking accuracy. Meanwhile, the effect of model uncertainty, external disturbance, and unmeasurable variables on the system are compensated for.
3. To enhance the generalization capability of the proposed detection model in this study, we conducted an extended data collection experiment at Western Xia Park in Yinchuan City, building upon our previously created lane-line data set. To ensure consistency with the previously collected steering-angle information, we once again experimented using a Borgward SUV (BX5) vehicle. This time, we recorded 40 h of real-world driving videos and increased the number of images from 8000 to 20,000 in order to augment the data set's diversity while maintaining an image size of $640 \times 640 \times 3$ pixels. To our knowledge, this manually labeled data set utilizing ImageLabel is currently the most prominent one encompassing lane lines.

The rest of the paper is organized as follows. Section 2 presents the lane-line detection algorithm based on YOLOv5, while Section 3 details the data set's organization and network training. The steering controller design and stability proof are discussed in Section 4, followed by an experimental evaluation in Section 5. Finally, conclusions are drawn in Section 6.

## 2. Methods

### 2.1. Lane-Line Detection Algorithm Description

The YOLOv5 algorithm, as the current representative deep learning algorithm in the YOLO series (Appendix A), exhibits exceptional performance in object detection with an accelerated training speed, enhanced accuracy, and broader applicability. Consequently, it holds significant potential for practical applications. Four models are derived based on network depth and feature map width, YOLOv5s, m, l, and x. Specifically, the four models share a consistent network structure comprising input, backbone, neck, and prediction-head components. The YOLOv5 network is categorized as a single-stage, end-to-end detection framework that treats object detection as a regression problem by predicting bounding boxes and class probabilities across the entire image. This model encompasses three crucial processes: boundary-box prediction, class prediction, and feature extraction. The well-designed network architecture enables flexibility and selectivity in diverse scenarios. Therefore, we adopt YOLOv5's one-staged detection framework as the foundational architecture for steering-angle prediction.

The YOLOv5 network model has achieved quite good results, but one of the problems with the steering-angle prediction model-based YOLOv5 is that the model is huge, with many parameters and large calculation amounts, and it is difficult to apply in embedded devices; moreover, steering-angle prediction scenarios require low latency or response speed. Imagine what terrible things could happen if the detection model for steering-angle prediction were slow. So, working on a small but efficient detection model is crucial in these scenarios, at least for now, although the hardware will also become faster in the future. Therefore, in the steering-angle prediction model based on YOLOv5, there is still room for improvement and enhancement. Optimizing the model architecture by employing smaller convolutional cores and reducing the number of pooling layers can effectively mitigate the parameters and computational load. Different improvement methods can be adopted, based on specific application scenarios with varying detection difficulties. Hence, this paper proposes a lightweight steering-angle prediction network model based on YOLOv5s to achieve a streamlined design while minimizing FLOPs, parameter counts, and the overall model size without compromising detection accuracy.

The MobileNet network exhibits superior advantages in lightweight neural networks due to its reduced size, decreased computational requirements, and enhanced accuracy. Furthermore, mobile models have been constructed using progressively more efficient building blocks. MobileNetV3 is an amalgamation of three models: MobileNetV1's depth-wise separable convolutions, MobileNetV2's inverted residual with a linear bottleneck, and MnasNet's lightweight attention model based on squeeze and excitation (SE) structures [32–34]. To optimize its performance on mobile phone CPUs, MobileNetV3 underwent a hardware-aware network architecture search (NAS) complemented by the NetAdapt algorithm, followed by further enhancements through novel architectural advancements. Two versions of MobileNetV3 are available: Large, for high-performance platforms, and Small, for low-performance platforms. Instead of using partial $3 \times 3$ deep convolutions, MobileNetV3 introduces a deep convolution of size $5 \times 5$. The SE module and h-swish (HS) activation function are incorporated to enhance model accuracy. These techniques can be effectively combined to discover optimized models tailored to specific hardware platforms.

YOLOv5 is a widely adopted object-detection algorithm, while MobileNetV3 represents a lightweight architecture for convolutional neural networks. Leveraging the strengths of these two models, we propose YOLOv5Ms, a lightweight steering prediction network model based on YOLOv5s. This model efficiently and accurately performs target-detection tasks, achieving a balance between accuracy and latency, making it suitable for deployment on mobile devices.

The schematic of steering-angle prediction and control based on the YOLOv5Ms network is illustrated in Figure 1. During autonomous driving, the vehicle-mounted camera captures road information in the form of images, which are then processed via a pre-trained YOLOv5 network. Subsequently, the predicted steering is transmitted to the steering controller. By mapping the steering-angle signal according to a predefined mapping relation, the input signal for the steering controller is obtained, resulting in corresponding steering outcomes through the actuation of the steering motor.

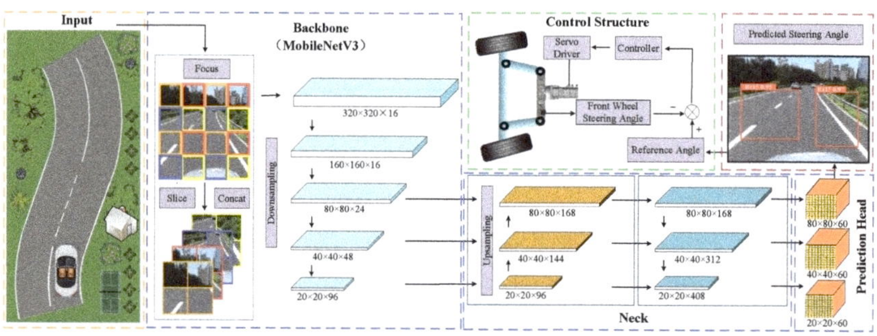


**Figure 1.** The lightweight steering-angle prediction network model, namely YOLOv5Ms, based on YOLOv5s and a control schematic network.

### 2.2. Improvement of YOLOv5Ms Network Architecture

In this section, we present a lightweight steering-angle prediction network model based on YOLOv5s. To enhance the performance of YOLOv5s, we have made two key improvements: replacing the original network backbone with MobileNetV3 and substituting the CIoU border regression function with Shape-IoU for better results. To reduce dimensionality without sacrificing features and computational efficiency, we have retained the focus structure at the input end of the network, as designed in YOLOv5. The resulting lightweight steering-angle prediction network model, named YOLOv5Ms, is built upon YOLOv5s, and its control schematic network is illustrated in Figure 1.

Focus: YOLOv5 incorporates a focused structure at the network input to reduce dimensionality without compromising features and computational efficiency. The focus structure divides the preprocessed image into four parts using slicing operations, and it concatenates them. A 20% overlap area is introduced between the two image parts to ensure that lane lines are not disrupted. The specific principles of slicing and concatenation are illustrated in Figure 2. This focus module achieves downsampling while increasing channel dimensions, reducing FLOPs, and improving speed.

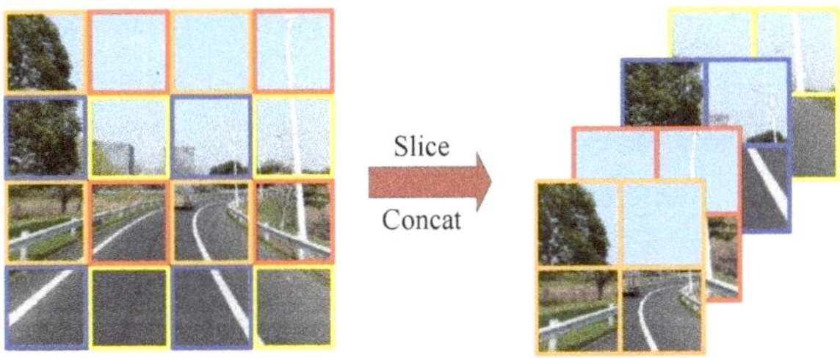


**Figure 2.** The specific slicing and concat principles.

Backbone: To achieve a lightweight network architecture, we modified the backbone of yolov5s by incorporating the large and small modules of MobileNetV3 as alternative backbones. We named them YOLOv5Ms and YOLOv5Ml, respectively. The specifications for YOLOv5Ms and YOLOv5Ml of the backbone can be seen in Tables 1 and 2. In the table, the input represents the shape transformation of each feature layer, while the operator signifies the block structure to be executed at each feature layer. The variables 'size' and '♯out' respectively denote the number of channels after the inverse residual structure is applied to the bottleneck and the number of channels in the feature layer when it is input into the bottleneck ('bk'). The term 'SE' indicates whether or not an attention mechanism, SE, is introduced in this module. In column six, 'NL' represents the type of activation function, where 'HS' denotes the h-swish, 'RE' represents ReLU, and 's' indicates the stride.

**Table 1.** Specifications for YOLOv5Ms of the backbone.

| Input | Operator | Size | ♯ Out | SE | NL | s |
|---|---|---|---|---|---|---|
| $640^2 \times 3$ | 2d, $3 \times 3$ | – | 16 | – | *HS* | 2 |
| $320^2 \times 16$ | bk, $3 \times 3$ | 16 | 16 | ✓ | *RE* | 2 |
| $160^2 \times 16$ | bk, $3 \times 3$ | 72 | 24 | – | *RE* | 2 |
| $80^2 \times 24$ | bk, $3 \times 3$ | 88 | 24 | – | *RE* | 1 |
| $80^2 \times 24$ | bk, $5 \times 5$ | 96 | 40 | ✓ | *HS* | 2 |
| $40^2 \times 40$ | bk, $5 \times 5$ | 240 | 40 | ✓ | *HS* | 1 |
| $40^2 \times 40$ | bk, $5 \times 5$ | 240 | 40 | ✓ | *HS* | 1 |
| $40^2 \times 40$ | bk, $5 \times 5$ | 120 | 48 | ✓ | *HS* | 1 |
| $40^2 \times 48$ | bk, $5 \times 5$ | 144 | 48 | ✓ | *HS* | 1 |
| $40^2 \times 48$ | bk, $5 \times 5$ | 288 | 96 | ✓ | *HS* | 2 |
| $20^2 \times 96$ | bk, $5 \times 5$ | 576 | 96 | ✓ | *HS* | 1 |
| $20^2 \times 96$ | bk, $5 \times 5$ | 576 | 96 | ✓ | *HS* | 1 |

**Table 2.** Specifications for YOLOv5Ml of the backbone.

| Input | Operator | Size | ♯ Out | SE | NL | s |
|---|---|---|---|---|---|---|
| $640^2 \times 3$ | 2d, $3 \times 3$ | – | 16 | – | *HS* | 2 |
| $320^2 \times 16$ | bk, $3 \times 3$ | 16 | 16 | – | *RE* | 1 |
| $320^2 \times 16$ | bk, $3 \times 3$ | 64 | 24 | – | *RE* | 2 |
| $160^2 \times 24$ | bk, $3 \times 3$ | 72 | 24 | – | *RE* | 1 |
| $160^2 \times 24$ | bk, $5 \times 5$ | 72 | 40 | ✓ | *RE* | 2 |
| $80^2 \times 40$ | bk, $5 \times 5$ | 120 | 40 | ✓ | *RE* | 1 |
| $80^2 \times 40$ | bk, $5 \times 5$ | 120 | 40 | ✓ | *RE* | 1 |
| $80^2 \times 40$ | bk, $3 \times 3$ | 240 | 80 | – | *HS* | 2 |
| $40^2 \times 80$ | bk, $3 \times 3$ | 200 | 80 | – | *HS* | 1 |
| $40^2 \times 80$ | bk, $3 \times 3$ | 184 | 80 | – | *HS* | 1 |
| $40^2 \times 80$ | bk, $3 \times 3$ | 184 | 80 | – | *HS* | 1 |
| $40^2 \times 80$ | bk, $3 \times 3$ | 480 | 112 | ✓ | *HS* | 1 |
| $40^2 \times 112$ | bk, $3 \times 3$ | 672 | 112 | ✓ | *HS* | 1 |
| $40^2 \times 112$ | bk, $5 \times 5$ | 672 | 160 | ✓ | *HS* | 2 |
| $20^2 \times 112$ | bk, $5 \times 5$ | 960 | 160 | ✓ | *HS* | 1 |
| $20^2 \times 160$ | bk, $5 \times 5$ | 960 | 160 | ✓ | *HS* | 1 |

The bottleneck structure is depicted in Figure 3, encompassing an inverse residual architecture that incorporates a linear bottleneck, depthwise separable convolution, and an SE attention mechanism. In the case of a stride value of 1 and input channels equal to output channels for the module, a shortcut connection is established between the input and output. Otherwise, subsequent operations follow the depthwise separable convolution operation, the SE attention mechanism, and the $1 \times 1$ point convolution operation. The depth separable convolution and squeeze-and-excitation block attention mechanism, SE, of the linear bottleneck are further described below.

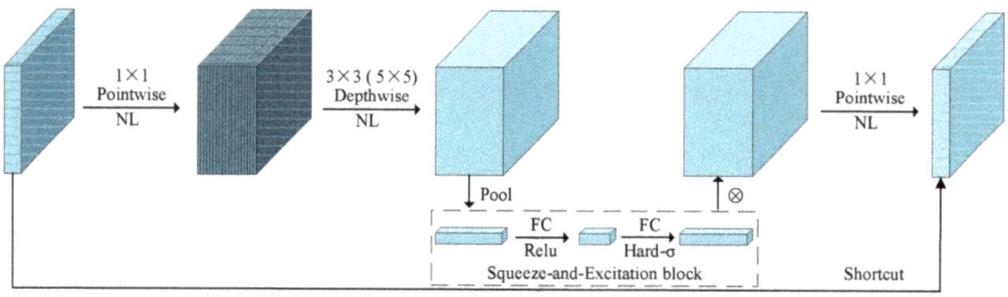


**Figure 3.** Bottleneck block structure.

(1) Depthwise separable convolution

The standard convolution operation takes an input tensor, $F$, of size $D_F \times D_F \times M$ and applies a convolutional kernel, $K \in R^{k \times k \times M \times N}$, to generate an output tensor, $G$, of size $D_G \times D_G \times N$. Here, $D_F$ represents the spatial width and height of a square input feature map, $M$ denotes the number of input channels (input depth), and $D_G$ corresponds to the spatial width and height of a square output feature map. Finally, $N$ signifies the number of output channels (output depth) [35].

The standard convolutional layer is parameterized by a square convolution kernel, $K$, with spatial dimensions of $D_K \times D_K \times M \times N$, where $M$ represents the number of input channels, and $N$ represents the number of output channels, as defined previously. Assuming stride one and padding, the computation for the output feature map in standard convolution can be expressed as follows:

$$G_{k,l,n} = \sum_{i,j,m} K_{i,j,m,n} \cdot F_{k+i-1,l+j-1,m} \quad (1)$$

Standard convolutions have the computational cost of

$$C_{s-cost} = D_F \times D_F \times D_K \times D_K \times M \times N \tag{2}$$

It is evident that the computational cost is multiplicatively dependent on various factors, including the number of input channels ($M$) and output channels ($N$), the kernel size ($D_K \times D_K$), and the feature map size ($D_F \times D_F$).

Depthwise separable convolutions serve as a fundamental component in numerous efficient neural network architectures, and we employed them in our current study as well. This form of factorized convolutions breaks a standard convolution down into two parts: depthwise convolution, which applies a single filter per input channel for lightweight filtering, and pointwise convolution (a $1 \times 1$ convolution), responsible for generating new features by computing linear combinations of the input channels [32]. This factorization significantly reduces the computation and model size. The standard and depthwise separable convolution principles are illustrated in Figures 4 and 5.

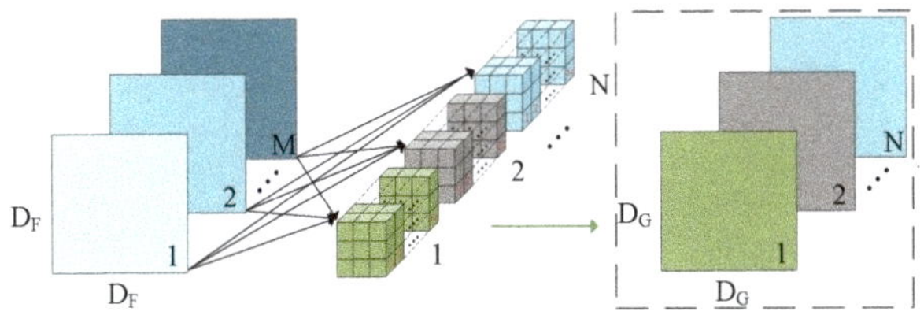


**Figure 4.** Standard convolution architecture.

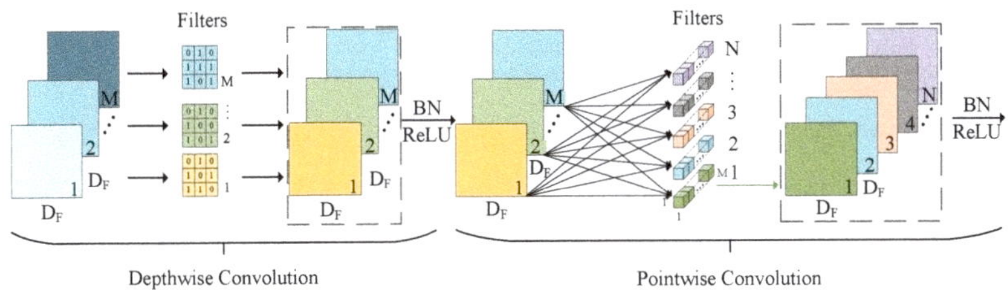


**Figure 5.** Depthwise separable convolution architecture.

Depthwise convolutions are employed to apply a singular filter for each input channel, while pointwise convolution, represented as a simple $1 \times 1$ convolution, is subsequently utilized to generate a linear combination of the output from the depthwise layer. The bottleneck block incorporates both batch normalization and rectified linear unit (ReLU) nonlinearities in both layers.

The depthwise convolution operation establishes a one-to-one correspondence between the convolution kernel and channel. Each channel is convolved with only one specific convolution kernel, generating feature map channels that exactly match the number of input channels. Mathematically, depthwise convolution can be represented as employing a single filter per input channel (input depth):

$$\widetilde{G}_{k,l,m} = \sum_{i,j} \widetilde{K}_{i,j,m} \cdot F_{k+i-1,l+j-1,m} \tag{3}$$

where $\widetilde{K}$ is the depthwise convolutional kernel of size $D_K \times D_K \times M$, and the $m_{th}$ filter in $\widetilde{K}$ is applied to the $m_{th}$ channel in $F$ in order to produce the $m_{th}$ channel of the filtered output feature map $\widetilde{G}$. Hence, depthwise convolution has a computational cost of

$$C_{Dw-cost} = D_F \times D_F \times D_K \times D_K \times M \tag{4}$$

The pointwise convolution operations resemble standard convolution operations, as they employ a $1 \times 1 \times M$ convolution kernel, where $M$ represents the number of channels in the preceding layer. Consequently, this convolution operation amalgamates the previous step's map in a depth-wise manner with appropriate weights to generate a novel feature map. Multiple output feature maps are produced for each convolution kernel. Pointwise convolution and depthwise separable convolutions have the computational cost of

$$\begin{aligned} C_{Pw-cost} &= D_F \times D_F \times 1 \times 1 \times M \times N \\ &= D_F \times D_F \times M \times N \end{aligned} \tag{5}$$

$$C_{dp-cost} = {D_F}^2 \times {D_K}^2 \times M + {D_F}^2 \times M \times N \tag{6}$$

By expressing convolution as a two-step process of filtering and combining, we achieve a reduction in the computation of

$$\frac{{D_F}^2 \times {D_K}^2 \times M + {D_F}^2 \times M \times N}{{D_F}^2 \times {D_K}^2 \times M \times N} = \frac{1}{N} + \frac{1}{{D_K}^2} \tag{7}$$

The depthwise separable convolution effectively reduces the computation compared to traditional layers by a factor of approximately $k^2$. When a $3 \times 3$ convolution kernel is assumed to be utilized in the depthwise separable convolution, it requires only 8 to 9 times less computation than the standard convolution without considering bias while maintaining a negligible decrease in accuracy. Figure 6 illustrates the comparison between standard convolution and depthwise, separable convolution with the batch norm and ReLU.

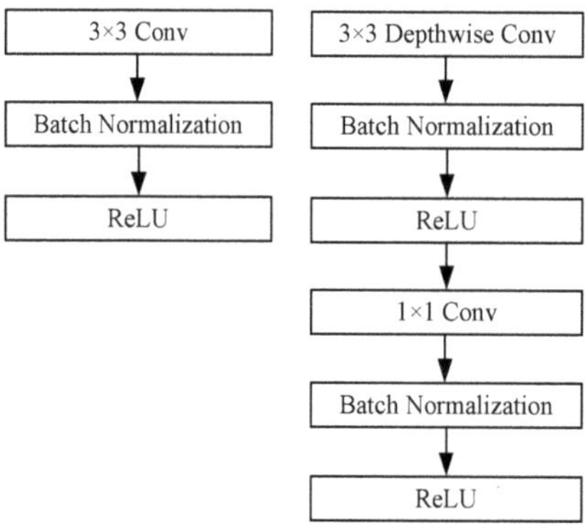


**Figure 6.** (**Left**): standard convolutional layer with batchnorm and ReLU. (**Right**): depthwise, separable convolution with depthwise and pointwise layers, followed by batchnorm and ReLU.

(2) Squeeze-and-excitation blocks

CNNs have emerged as valuable models for processing diverse visual tasks, making them the fundamental network structure employed in our study [36]. Recent research has demonstrated that incorporating attention mechanisms into CNN can enhance feature representations by effectively capturing spatial correlations. The attention mechanism is inspired by humans' ability to process external information, where individuals selectively attend to relevant information while filtering out irrelevant stimuli due to the limited processing capacity of the human brain [37,38].

In order to obtain a more robust representation, only the most significant attributes for predicting the steering angle in images captured via the front-mounted camera during driving are retained, thereby enhancing performance. We introduce a novel architectural unit called the squeeze-and-excitation (SE) block that explicitly models interdependencies between convolutional feature channels to improve network representations [39].

The structure of the SE building block is depicted in Figure 7. Assume that input feature maps of the SE block $\mathbf{X}$ have shape $W' \times H' \times C'$, where $W'$ is the width, $H'$ is height, and $C'$ is the channels of feature maps. $\mathbf{F}_{tr}$ can be thought of as a standard convolution operator. $\mathbf{F}_{tr}$ maps an input $\mathbf{X} \in \mathbb{R}^{W' \times H' \times C'}$ to feature maps $\mathbf{U} \in \mathbb{R}^{W \times H \times C}$. In the notation that follows, we use $\mathbf{K} = [\mathbf{k}_1, \mathbf{k}_2, \ldots, \mathbf{k}_C]$ to denote the learned set of filter kernels, where $\mathbf{k}_c$ refers to the parameters of the $c$th filter. We can then write the outputs as $\mathbf{U} = [\mathbf{u}_1, \mathbf{u}_2, \ldots, \mathbf{u}_C]$, where $\mathbf{u}_c$ can be expressed mathematically as follows:

$$\mathbf{u}_c = \mathbf{k}_c * \mathbf{X} = \sum_{m=1}^{C'} \mathbf{k}_c^m * \mathbf{x}^m \tag{8}$$

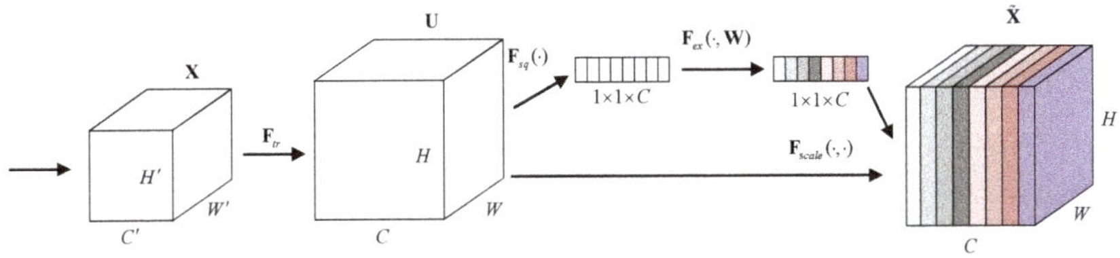


**Figure 7.** The structure of the SE building block.

Here, $\mathbf{k}_c = [\mathbf{k}_c^1, \mathbf{k}_c^2, \cdots, \mathbf{k}_c^{C'}]$, $*$ denotes a convolution operation, $\mathbf{X} = [\mathbf{x}^1, \mathbf{x}^2, \cdots, \mathbf{x}^{C'}]$, and $\mathbf{u}_c \in \mathbb{R}^{H \times W}$. $\mathbf{k}_c^m$ is a 2D spatial kernel representing a single channel of $\mathbf{k}_c$ that acts on the corresponding channel of $\mathbf{X}$. To enhance the clarity of notation, the inclusion of bias terms has been omitted.

In addition to high-level channel relationships, convolutional models inherently involve implicit and localized channel dependencies. We anticipate that explicitly modeling interdependencies between channels will enhance the learning of convolutional features, thereby improving the network's sensitivity to informative features that subsequent transformations can effectively utilize. Consequently, we aim to provide it with access to global information and recalibrate filter responses in two steps, namely squeezing and excitation, before they are fed into the next transformation. The SE attention mechanism enables the feature map to access global information and recalibrate the filter response through squeezing and excitation steps before proceeding with subsequent transformations [39].

After $\mathbf{F}_{tr}$ mapping an input, $\mathbf{X} \in \mathbb{R}^{W' \times H' \times C'}$, to feature maps, $\mathbf{U} \in \mathbb{R}^{W \times H \times C}$, to solve the problem of utilizing channel dependencies, we squeeze global spatial information into a channel description by using global average pooling operations to generate channel-wise statistics. The function of this descriptor is to generate an embedment of the corresponding global distribution of channel features, allowing all layers to use information from the global receptive domain (receptive field) of the network. Formally, the statistic $\mathbf{z} \in \mathbb{R}^C$ is generated via a shrinking of $\mathbf{U}$ through its spatial dimension $H \times W$, and the $c$-th element of $\mathbf{z}$ is calculated as follows:

$$z_c = \mathbf{F}_{sq}(\mathbf{u}_c) = \frac{1}{H \times W} \sum_{i=1}^{H} \sum_{j=1}^{M} u_c(i,j) \tag{9}$$

Here, $\mathbf{F}_{sq}$ represents the global average pooling of channels.

To take advantage of the information aggregated in the squeeze operation, the second operation (excitation operation) is performed to capture the channel-wise dependency fully. To limit the complexity of the model and facilitate generalization, parameterized gating mechanisms are parameterized by forming a bottleneck containing two fully connected layers (FCs) around the nonlinearity. The first fully connected layer compresses C channels into $\frac{C}{r}$ channels to reduce the computational load, and a ReLU nonlinear activation, $\delta$, is then used. The second fully connected layer returns to the number of the channel dimension to the original $C$ channels and then obtains the weight $\mathbf{s}$ through sigmoid activation, $\sigma$. Therefore, the weight, $\mathbf{W}$, of $C$ feature maps in $\mathbf{U}$ can be expressed as follows:

$$\mathbf{s} = \mathbf{F}_{ex}(\mathbf{z}, \mathbf{W}) = \sigma(g(\mathbf{z}, \mathbf{W})) = \sigma(\mathbf{W}_2\delta(\mathbf{W}_1\mathbf{z})) \tag{10}$$

where $r$ refers to the proportion of compression, and we take $r = 4$. $\mathbf{s} \in \mathbb{R}^{1\times1\times C}$, $\mathbf{W}_1 \in \mathbb{R}^{\frac{C}{r}\times C}$, $\mathbf{W}_2 \in \mathbb{R}^{C\times\frac{C}{r}}$. The final output of the squeeze-and-excitation block is obtained by rescaling $\mathbf{U}$ using the activation $\mathbf{s}$:

$$\widetilde{\mathbf{x}}_c = \mathbf{F}_{scale}(\mathbf{u}_c, s_c) = s_c\mathbf{u}_c \tag{11}$$

where $\widetilde{\mathbf{X}} = [\widetilde{\mathbf{x}}_1, \widetilde{\mathbf{x}}_2, \ldots, \widetilde{\mathbf{x}}_C]$, and $\mathbf{F}_{scale}(\mathbf{u}_c, s_c)$ refer to channel-wise multiplication between the scalar $s_c$ and the feature map $\mathbf{u}_c \in \mathbb{R}^{H\times W}$. SE blocks intrinsically introduce dynamics conditioned on the input, which can be regarded as a self-attention function on channels whose relationships are not confined to the local receptive field that the convolutional filters are responsive to. The SE blocks are also a flexible plug-and-play module. When a bottleneck module in the network backbone does not use SE, the bottleneck module can carry out the normal convolution process.

### 2.3. Loss Function

Object detection is a fundamental challenge in computer vision tasks, and bounding-box regression plays a pivotal role in accurately predicting the location of target objects. In our proposed YOLOv5Ms network, we make predictions for boxes at three different scales [40]. The final scale generates a 3D tensor that encodes information about bounding boxes, objectness scores, and class predictions. At each scale, we predict three boxes, resulting in a tensor of size $D \times D \times [3 \times (4 + 1 + 15)]$ to account for the four bounding box offsets, one objectness prediction, and fifteen class predictions. Herein, $D$ represents the grid size of the detection head.

Regarding the evaluation metric for bounding-box regression, conventional object detectors typically employ the mean square error (MSE) to directly regress the center-point coordinates, height, and width of the bounding box (BBox). However, treating each point of the BBox as independent variables when estimating their coordinate values fails to consider the holistic nature of the object itself. To address this issue and overcome the neglect of object integrity, a novel intersection over union (IoU) loss function was proposed for bounding boxes [41]. This loss function takes into consideration the coverage of both predicted and ground-truth bounding-box areas. It jointly regresses all bound variables as a unified unit by directly enforcing the maximal overlap between the predicted bounding box and the ground truth, as illustrated in Figure 8. The schematic diagram in Figure 8 demonstrates the process of bounding-box regression for this loss function. The X-axis represents the horizontal direction, while the Y-axis represents the vertical direction. The computation of the IoU loss involves calculating four coordinate points of the BBox by comparing them with the ground truth and then connecting these generated results to form a complete code. The most popular metric of IoU is as follows:

$$IoU = \frac{|G_T \cap P_b|}{|G_T \cup P_b|} \tag{12}$$

$$G_T = (x_2 - x_1) \times (y_2 - y_1) \tag{13}$$

$$P_b = (x_4 - x_3) \times (y_4 - y_3) \tag{14}$$

where $G_T$ is the ground truth area with lane lines, as labeled by our own bounding box, and $P_b$ is the predicted area of the object bounding box. $M(x_1, y_1)$, $N(x_2, y_2)$, $P(x_3, y_3)$, and $Q(x_4, y_4)$ are the left top and bottom right corners of the two bounding boxes, respectively. The intersection of $G_T$ and $P_b$ is calculated via Equation (15):

$$|G_T \bigcap P_b| = |(min(x_2, x_4) - max(x_1, x_3) \\ \times (min(y_2, y_4) - max(y_1, y_3)| \tag{15}$$

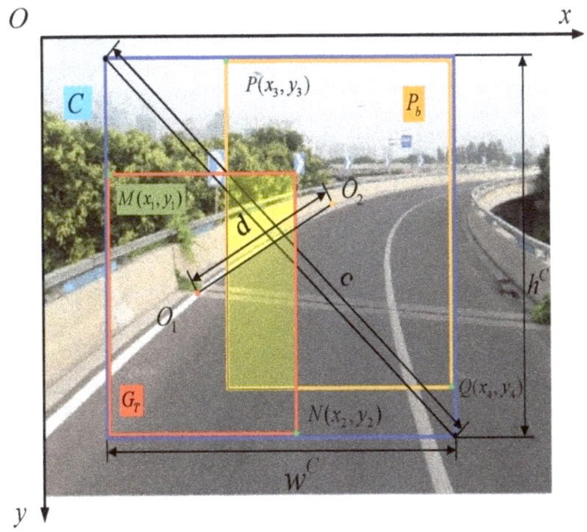


**Figure 8.** Schematic diagram of the bounding-box regression loss function.

Therefore, the IoU loss function can be expressed as follows:

$$L_{IoU} = 1 - \frac{|G_T \cap P_b|}{|G_T \cup P_b|} \tag{16}$$

However, the IoU loss only works when the bounding boxes have overlap and would not provide any moving gradient for non-overlapping cases, and then the generalized IoU loss (GIoU) was proposed in [42], adding a penalty term C expressed as follows:

$$|C| = |[\max(x_2, x_4) - \min(x_1, x_3)] \times \\ [\max(y_2, y_4) - \min(y_1, y_3)]| \tag{17}$$

The GIoU loss function can be expressed as follows:

$$L_{GIoU} = 1 - IoU + \frac{|C - G_T \cup P_b|}{|C|} \tag{18}$$

where C is the smallest box covering $G_T$ and $P_b$, as is shown in Figure 8. The GIoU loss includes the shape and orientation of the object, in addition to the coverage area. They proposed finding the smallest-area BBox that can simultaneously cover the predicted BBox and ground-truth BBox and using this BBox as the denominator to replace the denominator originally used in the IoU loss.

Introducing the penalty term facilitates the movement of the predicted box towards the target box in non-overlapping scenarios. Despite its ability to alleviate the gradient vanishing issue for such cases, GIoU still exhibits certain limitations. When bounding boxes enclose objects, the GIoU loss degrades to the IoU loss. A new approach called the distance-IoU (DIoU) loss is proposed for bounding-box regression to address this limitation. The DIoU loss incorporates a penalty term into the IoU loss to directly minimize the normalized distance between the central points of two bounding boxes, resulting in significantly faster convergence compared to the GIoU loss [43]. The objective of the DIoU loss is to simultaneously consider both the overlap area and the central-point distance when evaluating bounding boxes. Generally, the DIoU loss can be defined as follows:

$$L_{DIoU} = 1 - IoU + \frac{\rho^2(O_1, O_2)}{c^2} \tag{19}$$

As shown in Figure 8, $O_1$ and $O_2$ denote the central points of $G_T$ and $P_b$, respectively. $\rho(\cdot) = \|O_2 - O_1\|_2$ is the Euclidean central distance of the predicted BBox and ground-truth BBox, and $c$ is the diagonal length of $C$, which is the smallest enclosing box covering the two boxes.

The loss function for bounding-box regression should incorporate three crucial geometric measures, namely the overlap area, central-point distance, and aspect ratio. Consequently, building upon the DIoU loss, ref. [43] proposed a comprehensive IoU (CIoU) loss that integrates these aforementioned geometric measures. This novel approach facilitates faster convergence and yields superior performance compared to both IoU and GIoU losses. Then, the loss function can be defined as follows:

$$L_{CIoU} = 1 - IoU + \frac{\rho^2(O_1, O_2)}{c^2} + \alpha v \tag{20}$$

$$v = \frac{4}{\pi^2}(\arctan\frac{w^{G_T}}{h^{G_T}} - \arctan\frac{w^{P_b}}{h^{P_b}})^2 \tag{21}$$

$$\alpha = \frac{v}{(1 - IoU) + v} \tag{22}$$

where $\alpha$ is a positive trade-off parameter, and $v$ measures the consistency of the aspect ratio. $w^{G_T}$ and $h^{G_T}$ are the width and height of the ground-truth bounding box, while $w^{P_b}$ and $h^{P_b}$ represent the width and height of the predicted bounding box. The gradient of $v$ with reference to $w^{P_b}$ and $h^{P_b}$ should be specified as follows:

$$\begin{aligned}\frac{\partial v}{\partial w^{P_b}} &= \frac{8}{\pi^2}(\arctan\frac{w^{G_T}}{h^{G_T}} - \arctan\frac{w^{P_b}}{h^{P_b}}) \\ &\times \frac{h^{P_b}}{{w^{P_b}}^2 + {h^{P_b}}^2}\end{aligned} \tag{23}$$

$$\begin{aligned}\frac{\partial v}{\partial h^{P_b}} &= -\frac{8}{\pi^2}(\arctan\frac{w^{G_T}}{h^{G_T}} - \arctan\frac{w^{P_b}}{h^{P_b}}) \\ &\times \frac{w^{P_b}}{{w^{P_b}}^2 + {h^{P_b}}^2}\end{aligned} \tag{24}$$

The dominator ${w^{P_b}}^2 + {h^{P_b}}^2$ is usually a small value for the cases $w^{P_b}$ and $h^{P_b}$, with a range of [0, 1], which is likely to yield gradient explosion, and thus, in our implementation, the dominator ${w^{P_b}}^2 + {h^{P_b}}^2$ is simply removed for stable convergence, through which the step size $\frac{1}{{w^{P_b}}^2 + {h^{P_b}}^2}$ is replaced with 1, and the gradient direction is still consistent with Equations (23) and (24).

Since the $v$ only reflects the discrepancy of the aspect ratio, the CIoU loss may optimize the similarity unreasonably. To address the above problems, the work of [44] revised the CIoU loss and proposed a more efficient version of IoU (EIoU), the EIoU loss, which is defined as follows:

$$\begin{aligned}L_{EIoU} &= 1 - IoU + \frac{\rho^2(O_1, O_2)}{c^2} + \frac{\rho^2(w^{G_T}, w^{P_b})}{(w^C)^2} \\ &+ \frac{\rho^2(h^{G_T}, h^{P_b})}{(h^C)^2}\end{aligned} \tag{25}$$

where $h^C$ and $w^C$ are the width and height of the smallest enclosing box, C, covering the two boxes.

Based on previous research, SIoU further considers the influence of the angle between the bounding boxes on the bounding box regression, which aims to accelerate the convergence process by decreasing the angle between the anchor box and the $G_T$ box, which is the horizontal or vertical direction [45]. Its definition is as follows:

$$L_{SIoU} = 1 - IoU + \frac{\Delta + \Omega}{2} \tag{26}$$

$$\Delta = \sum_{t=w^{P_b},h^{P_b}} (1 - e^{-\gamma \rho_t}), \gamma = 2 - \Lambda \tag{27}$$

$$\Lambda = \sin(2\sin^{-1}\frac{min(|x_c^{G_T} - x_c^{P_b}|, |y_c^{G_T} - y_c^{P_b}|)}{\sqrt{(x_c^{G_T} - x_c^{P_b})^2 + (y_c^{G_T} - y_c^{P_b})^2 + \epsilon}}) \tag{28}$$

$$\begin{cases} \rho_{w^{P_b}} = (\frac{x_c^{G_T} - x_c^{P_b}}{w^C})^2 \\ \rho_{h^{P_b}} = (\frac{y_c^{G_T} - y_c^{P_b}}{h^C})^2 \end{cases} \tag{29}$$

$$\Omega = \sum_{t=w^{P_b},h^{P_b}} (1 - e^{-\varpi_t})^{\theta}, \theta = 4 \tag{30}$$

where the value of $\theta$ defines how much the shape costs and its unique value for each data set. The value of $\theta$ is a significant term in this equation; it controls how much attention should be paid to the cost of the shape. If a value of $\theta$ is set to be 1, it will immediately optimize the shape, thus harming the free movement of a shape. To calculate the value of $\theta$, the genetic algorithm is used for each data set; experimentally, the value of $\theta$ near to 4, and the range that the author defined for this parameter is from 2 to 6.

$$\begin{aligned} \varpi_{w^{P_b}} &= \frac{|w^{G_T} - w^{P_b}|}{max(w^{G_T}, w^{P_b})} \\ \varpi_{h^{P_b}} &= \frac{|h^{G_T} - h^{P_b}|}{max(h^{G_T}, h^{P_b})} \end{aligned} \tag{31}$$

In conclusion, the previous bounding box regression methods mainly achieve more accurate regression by adding new geometric constraints on top of IoU. The above methods considered the influence of the distance, shape, and angle of the $G_T$ box and the anchor box on the bounding-box regression but neglected the fact that the shape and scale of the bounding box itself will also exert influences on the bounding-box regression. In order to further improve the accuracy of the regression, the authors proposed a new generation of the bounding regression loss: Shape-IoU in [46].

$$w_{wt} = \frac{2 \times (w^{G_T})^{scale}}{(w^{G_T})^{scale} + (h^{G_T})^{scale}} \tag{32}$$

$$h_{wt} = \frac{2 \times (h^{G_T})^{scale}}{(w^{G_T})^{scale} + (h^{G_T})^{scale}} \tag{33}$$

$$D_{shape} = h_{wt} \times \frac{(x_c^{P_b} - x_c^{G_T})^2}{c^2} + w_{wt} \times \frac{(y_c^{P_b} - y_c^{G_T})^2}{c^2} \tag{34}$$

$$\Omega_{shape} = \sum_{t=w^{P_b},h^{P_b}} (1 - e^{-\varpi_t})^{\theta}, \theta = 4 \tag{35}$$

$$\begin{cases} \omega_{w^{P_b}} = h_{wt} \times \frac{|w^{GT} - w^{P_b}|}{max(w^{GT}, w^{P_b})} \\ \omega_{h^{P_b}} = w_{wt} \times \frac{|h^{GT} - h^{P_b}|}{max(h^{GT}, h^{P_b})} \end{cases} \tag{36}$$

where scale is the scale factor, which is related to the scale of the target in the data set, and $w_{wt}$ and $h_{wt}$ are the weight coefficients in the horizontal and vertical directions, respectively, whose values are related to the shape of the GT box. $D_{shape}$ is the distance shape. Its corresponding bounding box regression loss is as follows:

$$L_{Shape-IoU} = 1 - IoU + D_{shape} + 0.5 \times \Omega_{shape} \tag{37}$$

YOLOv5 previously used GIoU; for the above reasons, in this paper, we use $L_{Shape-IoU}$ as the bounding-box regression-loss function. Moreover, the excellent performance of Shape-IoU as a bounding-box regression-loss function has been verified in [46].

The loss function used in the training of the YOLOv5Ms in the prediction of the steering angle mainly included the bounding-box location loss($L_{Shape-IoU}$), confidence loss ($L_{confidence}$), and classification loss ($L_{class}$), as follows:

$$Loss = L_{Shape-IoU} + L_{confidence} + L_{class} \tag{38}$$

$$\begin{aligned} &Loss = 1 - IoU + D_{shape} + 0.5 \times \Omega_{shape} - \\ &\sum_{i=0}^{S^2} \sum_{j=0}^{B} I_{ij}^{obj} [\tilde{C}_i^j \log(\acute{C}_i^j) + (1 - \tilde{C}_i^j) \log(1 - \acute{C}_i^j)] - \\ &\lambda_{noobj} \sum_{i=0}^{S^2} \sum_{j=0}^{B} I_{ij}^{noobj} [\tilde{C}_i^j \log(\acute{C}_i^j) + (1 - \tilde{C}_i^j) \log(1 - \acute{C}_i^j)] \\ &- \sum_{i=0}^{S^2} I_i^{obj} \sum_{\tilde{c} \in class} [\tilde{p}_i(\tilde{c}) \log(\acute{p}_i(\tilde{c})) + \\ &(1 - \tilde{p}_i(\tilde{c})) \log(1 - \acute{p}_i(\tilde{c}))] \end{aligned} \tag{39}$$

where S is the number of grids (the image is divided into S×S grids to find the position containing lane lines one by one), and B is the number of anchors for each grid to predict the lane line. $I_{ij}^{obj}$ denotes that the *jth* bounding box predictor in cell *i* is responsible for that prediction; its value is 1 if there is an object in the jth anchor of the ith grid, and otherwise, it is 0. $I_i^{obj}$ denotes whether the object (lane line) appears in cell *i*. $\tilde{C}_i^j$ and $\acute{C}_i^j$ stand for confidences. $I_{ij}^{noobj}$ denotes that the *jth* bounding-box predictor in cell *i* is responsible for that prediction. $\lambda_{noobj}$ is a parameter to decrease the loss from confidence predictions for boxes that do not contain lane lines. $\tilde{p}_i(\tilde{c})$ and $\acute{p}_i(\tilde{c})$ represent the probability that the lane line in cell *i* belongs to class $\tilde{c}$, while $\tilde{c}$ is the number of classes (lane-camber category).

## 3. Data Sets' Descriptions and Detector Model Training

In this section, we present our own data set, elaborate on the training process, and report the evaluation results of the proposed network model.

### 3.1. Data Sets' Descriptions

The task of creating custom data sets has been previously addressed in our prior research. To collect lane lines and steering angles, a Borgward SUV (BX5) was utilized at 20 km per hour within the Shenyang Qipanshan Scenic Area. Building upon our previous work, we conducted an expansion acquisition experiment at Western Xia Park in Yinchuan. To ensure consistency with the collected steering-angle information from before, we employed the BX5 vehicle once again for experimentation purposes. This time, we recorded 40 h of real-time driving video and augmented the data set by increasing the number of images from its original count of 8000 to 20,000, maintaining the image size of 640 × 640 × 3 pixels. Following statistical analysis on the distribution of collected steering angles, which ranged between −50 and 60 degrees, we divided these angles into 15 categories, ranging from −60 to +60 degrees, as illustrated in Table 3. The label denotes the sequential number of the data sets' labels. The classification of images in a data set is exemplified in Figure 9. Subsequently, we partitioned our data set into three subsets: a training set (70%), a validation set (20%), and a test set (10%), based on a predetermined ratio.

**Table 3.** Lane-turning categories and steering angles.

| Classes | L60 | L45 | L35 | L25 | L15 | L10 | L05 | G | R05 | R10 | R15 | R25 | R35 | R45 | R60 |
|---|---|---|---|---|---|---|---|---|---|---|---|---|---|---|---|
| Angle | −60 | −45 | −35 | −25 | −15 | −10 | −5 | 0 | 5 | 10 | 15 | 25 | 35 | 45 | 60 |
| Label | 14 | 13 | 12 | 11 | 10 | 9 | 8 | 0 | 1 | 2 | 3 | 4 | 5 | 6 | 7 |

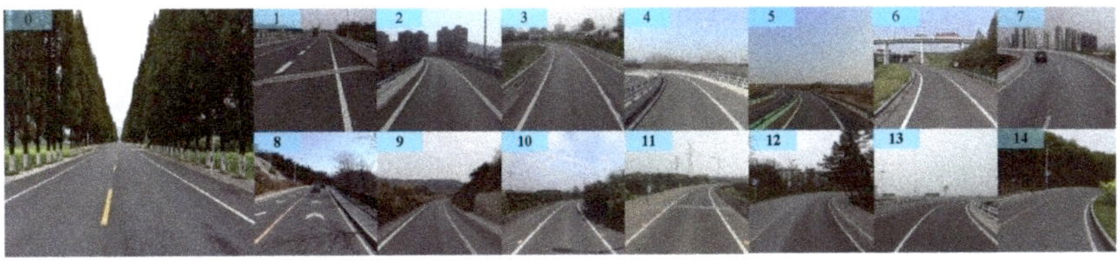

**Figure 9.** Illustrative images extracted from the acquired unprocessed training data.

### 3.2. Measurement Metrics

The performance evaluation of the proposed YOLOv5Ms, based on YOLOv5s, was conducted using precision, recall, mean average precision (mAP@0.5; mAP@0.5:0.95), average detection processing time, parameter count, FLOPs, and model size as measurement metrics [47].

Precision is calculated as the proportion of the number of positive samples correctly predicted to those predicted as positive. It is defined as follows:

$$Precision = \frac{TP}{TP + FP} \tag{40}$$

Recall is calculated as the proportion of all targets that are correctly predicted. It is defined as follows:

$$Recall = \frac{TP}{TP + FN} \tag{41}$$

The average precision (AP) represents the mean precision rate, which should be maximized while ensuring accuracy as the recall rate gradually increases from 0 to 1. The calculation formulas of mAP@0.5 and mAP@0.5:0.95 are as follows:

$$mAP = \frac{\sum_{\hat{c}=1}^{\hat{C}} AP(\hat{c})}{\hat{C}} \tag{42}$$

where TP, FP, and FN represent the counts of true positive (TP) cases (indicating correctly predicted lane lines in the model), false positive (FP) cases (denoting situations where no lane line exists but a lane is falsely predicted in the model), and false negative (FN) cases (referring to scenarios where lane lines exist but are incorrectly predicted as absent in the model), respectively. Additionally, $\hat{C}$ denotes the number of curvature categories for lane lines. In this study, we categorized lane-line curves into 15 classes, resulting in $\hat{C}$ being equal to 15. The term mAP@0.5 refers to the mean average precision across all categories when the intersection over union (IoU) is set to 0.5, while mAP@0.5:0.95 represents the average mAP at various IoU thresholds, ranging from 0.5 to 0.95, with a step size of 0.05.

### 3.3. Training and Test Results

Training object detection is a computationally intensive task, particularly following the completion of data-set collection and tagging. In supervised training, the network's weights or independent parameters are iteratively adjusted to optimize performance for a specific training data set. The proposed model's training process is executed using the PyTorch framework on the Windows operating system. The software environment includes CUDA 11.0 and Python 3.8. For data-set training, an Advanced Micro Devices (AMD) Ryzen 2700X processor was employed, alongside an NVIDIA GeForce RTX 2080Ti with 11 GB of memory.

Details of the training process and results are shown in Table 4 and Figures 10 and 11. The number of training epochs was set to 500 during network training; hence, 'Epoch' in Figures 10 and 11 corresponds to a total of 500 iterations. After the training, the weights of the 6 models were 10.1 M, 36.2 M, 14.5 M, 40.3 M 88.7 M, and 173.3 M, respectively. The total number of parameters of the six models is $5.07 \times 10^6$, $17.85 \times 10^6$, $7.05 \times 10^6$, $20.93 \times 10^6$, $46.19 \times 10^6$, and $86.32 \times 10^6$, respectively. Comparing the training results of our proposed YOLOv5Ms models and the four YOLOv5 models can reveal that the total number of parameters in YOLOv5Ms is reduced by $1.98 \times 10^6$ compared to YOLOv5s, resulting in a 28.09% decrease and a weight reduction of 4.4 M, which represents a decline of 30.34%. In terms of the training time, under identical hardware conditions, YOLOv5Ms exhibits a training speed that is 5.19 h faster than that of YOLOv5s. Furthermore, regarding precision metrics such as mAP@0.5 and mAP@0.5:0.95, the performance improvement achieved using YOLOv5Ms surpasses that of YOLOv5s, with enhancements reaching 6.59%, 0.41%, and 5.01%, respectively. The experimental results demonstrate that incorporating an attention mechanism into YOLOv5s effectively enhances model precision in reducing both total parameters and weights.

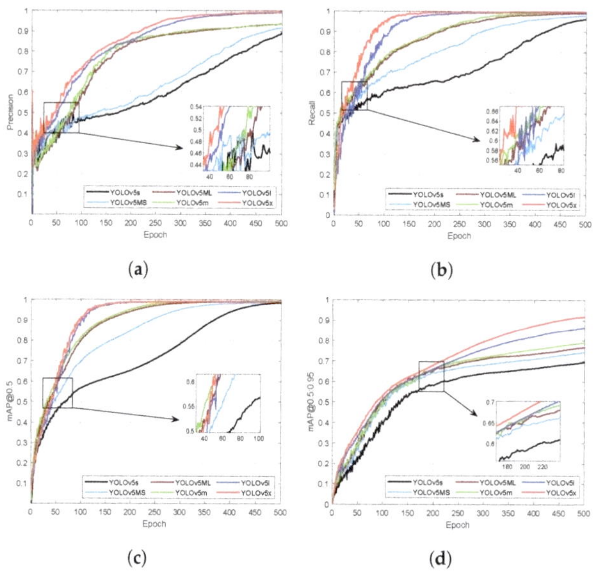


(a) (b)

(c) (d)

**Figure 10.** Comparison of the precision, recall rate, mAP@0.5, and mAP@0.5:0.95 of the six models of YOLOv5 in the training and verification stages: (**a**) precision, (**b**) recall, (**c**) mAP@0.5, and (**d**) mAP@0.5:0.95.

**Table 4.** Details of training process and results.

| Model | Params ($\times 10^6$) | Weight (M) | Loss ($\times 10^{-3}$) $T_C^1$ | $T_O^1$ | $T_{cl}^1$ | Pre (%)$^2$ | Rec (%)$^2$ | mAP (%) $m_{0.5}^2$ | $m_{.5:.95}^2$ | $T(h)^2$ |
|---|---|---|---|---|---|---|---|---|---|---|
| YOLOv5Ms | 5.07 | 10.1 | 19.80 | 11.57 | 5.71 | 95.83 | 96.28 | 99.10 | 74.60 | 16.67 |
| YOLOv5Ml | 17.85 | 36.2 | 18.82 | 10.51 | 3.54 | 97.32 | 97.93 | 99.42 | 76.89 | 25.95 |
| YOLOv5s | 7.05 | 14.5 | 19.59 | 12.61 | 7.55 | 89.24 | 90.09 | 98.69 | 69.57 | 21.86 |
| YOLOv5m | 20.93 | 40.3 | 15.52 | 9.18 | 3.32 | 99.05 | 99.09 | 99.49 | 79.16 | 41.67 |
| YOLOv5l | 46.19 | 88.7 | 14.49 | 7.85 | 2.71 | 99.22 | 99.40 | 99.41 | 86.59 | 58.09 |
| YOLOv5x | 86.32 | 173.3 | 13.38 | 6.59 | 2.14 | 99.50 | 99.64 | 99.42 | 91.85 | 76.27 |

[1] $T_C$, $T_O$, and $T_{cl}$: represent each error of training, respectively. [2] Pre: precision; Rec: recall; $\mathbf{m}_{0.5}$: mAP@0.5; $\mathbf{m}_{.5:.95}$: mAP@0.5:0.95; T(h): training time (hours).

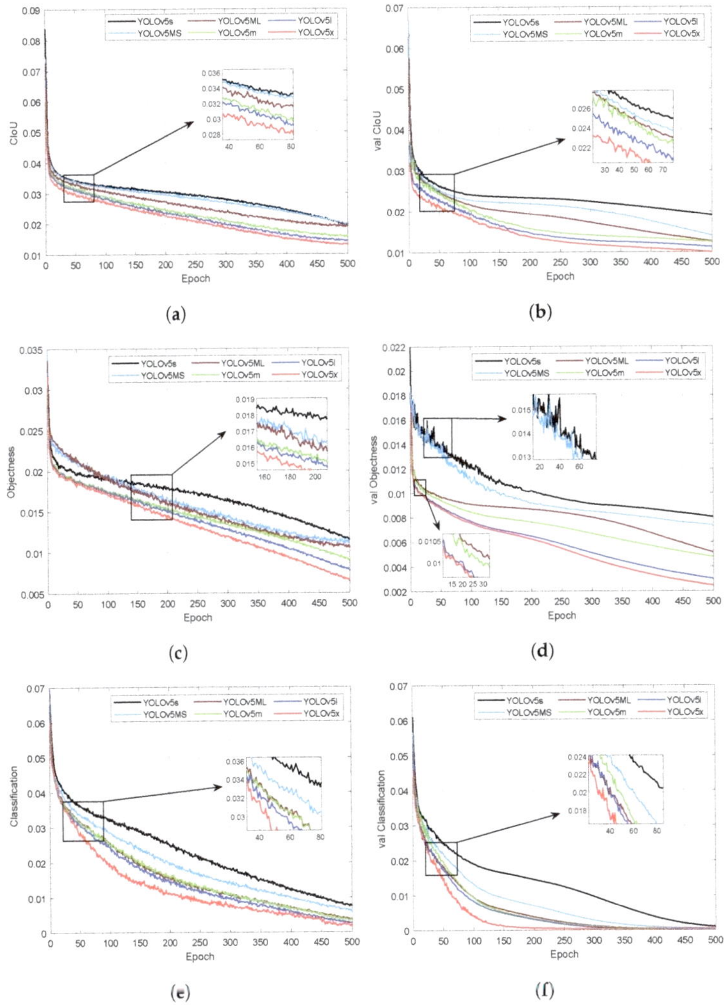


**Figure 11.** Comparison of the bounding-box regression, confidence, and classification of the six models of YOLOv5 in the training and validation stages: (**a**) CIoU, (**b**) val CIoU, (**c**) objectness, (**d**) val objectness, (**e**) classification, and (**f**) val classification.

Through a comparison between our proposed YOLOv5Ml model and YOLOv5s and YOLOv5m models, we observed that the various indicators of YOLOv5Ml outperform those of YOLOv5s but are similar to those of YOLOv5m. However, its overall performance is slightly inferior to that of YOLOv5m due to dominant factors such as model size, weight size, and training time. Compared with YOLOv5m, the total number of parameters in our model was reduced by $3.08 \times 10^6$, the weight size decreased by 4.1 M, and the training time was shortened by 15.72 h.

YOLOv5x and YOLOv5l exhibit superior performance, irrespective of the associated time and hardware costs. However, in practical applications, a common approach is to balance the model cost and overall performance. Therefore, it is generally preferred to consider lower-cost factors such as hardware utilization and execution time while ensuring that the model's performance meets real-world requirements.

The test results of the trained model are shown in Figure 12. In Figure 12, the "tags" represent the YOLOv5Ms network subsequent to 500 epochs of training. Following the evaluation of images containing lane lines, the letters denote their respective categories, while the numbers indicate their corresponding probabilities. It can be seen from the test results that the training of the network achieved the expected performance. We discuss the real-time predictive performance of the trained YOLOv5Ms detector by verifying experiments in Section 5.

This paper proposes a composite controller that integrates a novel adaptive updating law and disturbance observer to ensure that AVs' steering system promptly and accurately responds to the predicted steering-angle signal. Subsequently, we elaborate on the proposed controller in the following section of this paper and conduct a comparative experiment to validate its control performance.

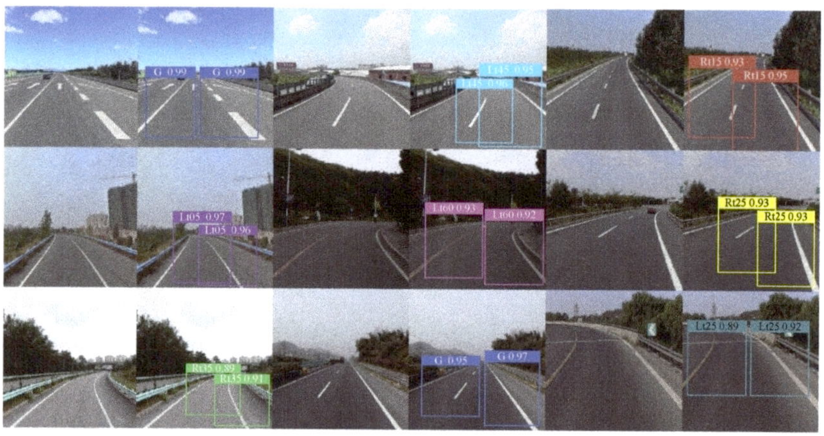

**Figure 12.** Images labeled with tags and the outcomes of tests.

## 4. Mathematical Model of SbW System and Controller Design

### *4.1. Dynamics Model*

Figure 13 shows the schematic diagram of the SbW system. The SbW system consists mainly of mechanical and electrical structures. It mainly includes a handwheel, a steering column, a steering motor, a motor controller, a gear reducer, an angle sensor, and a feedback motor. On the handwheel side, the angle sensor is mounted on the steering column, and it measures the angle of the handwheel. The motor controller receives the angle signal through CAN to control the motor rotation, and the motor rotation drives the front-wheel rotation through the gear reducer. The sensors mounted on the steering-tie rods measure the steering angle of the front wheels and feedback to the motor controller. The motor controller receives the feedback signal for closed-loop control to track the reference angle.

For simplicity, the modeling of the steering system consists of the steering motor and the front wheel, and the dynamic equations of the steering motor are as follows:

$$J_{sm}\ddot{\delta}_s + B_{sm}\dot{\delta}_s + \tau_1 + \tau_d = \tau_m \tag{43}$$

where $\delta_s$ is the angle of the steering motor shaft. $J_{sm}$ is the inertia of the steering motor. $B_{sm}$ is the viscous friction of the steering motor. $\tau_1$ represents the torque applied via the front wheels to the steering motor shaft. $\tau_d$ is the disturbance torque. $\tau_m$ is the torque output via the steering motor.

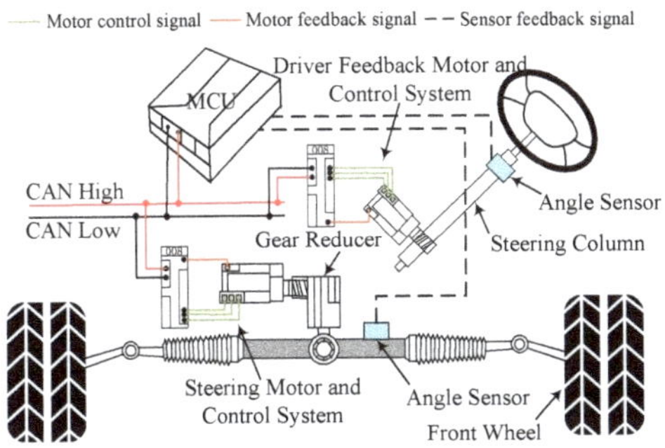


**Figure 13.** Overall structure diagram of SbW system.

The dynamic equation for the front wheels is as follows:

$$J_{fw}\ddot{\delta}_f + B_{fw}\dot{\delta}_f + \tau_f + \tau_e = \tau_2 \tag{44}$$

where $\delta_f$ is the angle of the steering motor shaft. $J_{fw}$ is the inertia of the front wheels. $B_{fw}$ is the viscous friction of the steering motor. $\tau_f$ is the friction torque on the front wheels. $\tau_e$ is the self-aligning torque on the front wheels. $\tau_2$ represents the torque transmitted via the steering motor to the front-wheel steering arms. The self-aligning moment is expressed as a hyperbolic tangent function:

$$\tau_e = \varrho \tanh(\delta_f) \tag{45}$$

where $\varrho$ is the positive constant related to the road adhesion.

The friction model friction torque is defined as follows [48]:

$$\tau_f = \alpha_1[\tanh(\beta_1\dot{\delta}_f) - \tanh(\beta_2\dot{\delta}_f)] + \alpha_2 \tanh(\beta_3\dot{\delta}_f) + \alpha_3\dot{\delta}_f \tag{46}$$

where $\alpha_i$ and $\beta_i$ are positive constants. According to (46), the friction model contains many features of other friction models. Therefore, the friction model (46) provides a more comprehensive description of friction and provides a more accurate model for controller design.

Regardless of the backlash exiting the rack and pinion gear teeth, we have the following relationship:

$$\frac{\delta_f}{\delta_s} = \frac{\dot{\delta}_f}{\dot{\delta}_s} = \frac{\ddot{\delta}_f}{\ddot{\delta}_s} = \frac{1}{i_{mc}} = \frac{\tau_1}{\tau_2} \tag{47}$$

where $i_{mc}$ is the steering ratio.

Using (47) and eliminating $\delta_s$, we obtain the following:

$$J_e\ddot{\delta}_f + B_e\dot{\delta}_f + i_{mc}\tau_d + \tau_f + \tau_e = i_{mc}\tau_m \tag{48}$$

where $J_e = J_{fw} + i_{mc}^2 J_{sm}$ is the moment of inertia. $B_e = B_{fw} + i_{mc}^2 B_{sm}$ is the the system damping.

We rewrite (48) as follows:

$$\ddot{\delta}_f = \frac{i_{mc}}{J_e}\tau_m - \frac{B_e\dot{\delta}_f + \tau_e + \tau_f}{J_e} - \frac{i_{mc}\tau_d}{J_e} \tag{49}$$

We define $x_1 = \delta_f, x_2 = \dot{\delta}_f$ and rewrite (49) as the state space equation as follows:

$$\begin{cases} \dot{x}_1 = x_2 \\ \dot{x}_2 = i_e\tau_m - \tau_{ef} - \tau_D \end{cases} \tag{50}$$

where $i_e = \frac{i_{mc}}{J_e}$. $\tau_{ef} = \frac{B_e\dot{\delta}_f+\tau_e+\tau_f}{J_e}$ is the lumped uncertainty. $\tau_D = \frac{i_{mc}\tau_d}{J_e}$ is the external disturbance. The design of the controller requires accurate model parameters such as $J_{fw}$, $J_{sm}$ and $i_{mc}$. In engineering practice, these parameters can be obtained through offline parameter identification methods such as the half-period integration method [49] and the zero-mean sinusoidal perturbation method [50]. The transmission ratio $i_{mc}$ can be calculated from the number of gear teeth. However, the accurate friction model $\tau_f$ and self-aligning torque $\tau_e$ present difficulty in obtaining accurate values. The coefficients $\alpha_i$ and $\beta_i$ of the friction model are related to road adhesion, and it is difficult to obtain accurate values. The self-aligning torque, $\tau_e$, is an estimated model, and the coefficient $\rho$ is related to road adhesion. Therefore, the friction model and the self-aligning torque need to be approximated using other methods in the controller design.

**Lemma 1** ([51]). *For any $(x, y) \in \mathcal{R}^2$, the following Young's inequality is satisfied:*

$$xy \le \frac{\varpi^p}{p}|x|^p + \frac{1}{q\varpi^q}|y|^q \tag{51}$$

*where $\varpi > 0$, $p > 1$, and $q > 1$ are constants satifying that $(q-1)(p-1)$=1.*

**Lemma 2** ([52]). *A function, $F(\mathbf{X})$: $\Omega_\mathbf{X} \to \mathcal{R}$, with a compact set, $\Omega_\mathbf{X} \in \mathcal{R}^m$, can be approximated using a radial basis function neural network (RBFNN):*

$$F(\mathbf{X}) = \mathbf{W}^{*T}\mathbf{G}(\mathbf{X}) + \varepsilon^* \tag{52}$$

*where $\mathbf{W}^* = [W_1^*, W_2^*, ..., W_l^*]^T \in \mathcal{R}^l$ is the ideal weight vector. $\mathbf{X} = [X_1, X_2, ..., X_m]^T \in \mathcal{R}^m$ is the input vector. $\varepsilon^*$ is an optimal approximation. There exists a positive constant, $\bar{\varepsilon}_1$, that satisfies $\varepsilon^* < \bar{\varepsilon}_1$. $\mathbf{G}(\mathbf{X}) = [G_1(\mathbf{X}), G_2(\mathbf{X}), ..., G_l(\mathbf{X})] \in \mathcal{R}^l$ is the basis function vector. The Gaussian function is chosen as the basis function as follows.*

$$G_j(\mathbf{X}) = \exp(-\frac{||\mathbf{X} - \mathbf{c}_j||^2}{2b_j^2}) \tag{53}$$

*where $\mathbf{c}_j = [c_{1j}, c_{1j}, ..., c_{mj}]^T$ is the center, and $b_j$ is the width of the Gaussian function.*

**Remark 1.** *The disturbance $\tau_D$ satisfies the following conditions: $\tau_D \le \tau_{D\max}$ and $\dot{\tau}_D \le \varepsilon_D$ ($\tau_{D\max}$; $\varepsilon_D \in R^+$). In much of the previous literature [53], it has been assumed that the perturbations and the derivatives of the perturbations are bounded. In this paper, the external disturbances $\tau_D = \frac{i_{mc}\tau_d}{J_e}$, $i_{mc}$ and $J_e$ are intrinsic parameters of the system, which are related only to the system itself and not to the external world. In engineering practice, $\tau_d$ is mainly an external disturbance including the following: internal disturbances in the steering motor, sensor measurement noise, external forces acting on the SbW system, and so on. These disturbances and their derivatives exist in practice with unknown maximum values. Therefore, the unknown $\tau_{D\max}$ and $\varepsilon_D$ exist such that $\tau_D \le \tau_{D\max}$ and $\dot{\tau}_D \le \varepsilon_D$.*

### 4.2. Observer Design

Given that the angular position can be measured directly by the sensor in practice, the angular velocity needs to be measured with an additional sensor, and it is difficult to find a suitable location for the sensor. In observer design, the parameters in the state space equations need to be known. However, model uncertainty and external disturbance make it difficult to obtain accurate values. According to Lemma 2, $\tau_{ef}$ can be approximated via RBFNN as follows:

$$\tau_{ef}(x_1, \hat{x}_2) = \mathbf{W}_0^{*T}\mathbf{G}_0(x_1, \hat{x}_2) + \varepsilon_0^* \tag{54}$$

where $\mathbf{W}_0^*$ is the ideal weight. $\hat{x}_2$ is the angular velocity obtained by the state observer designed later.

Define the estimate of $\tau_{ef}$ as follows:

$$\hat{\tau}_{ef} = \hat{\mathbf{W}}_0\mathbf{G}_0(x_1, \hat{x}_2) \tag{55}$$

Define $\Delta\tau_{ef} = \tau_{ef}(x_1, x_2) - \tau_{ef}(x_1, \hat{x}_2)$, and satisfy $|\Delta\tau_{ef}| \leq h_f|x_2 - \hat{x}_2|$; $h_f$ is a designed positive constant. Therefore, the dynamic of $x_2$ can be represented as follows:

$$\dot{x}_2 = i_e\tau_m - \Delta\tau_{ef} - \mathbf{W}_0^{*T}\mathbf{G}_0(x_1, \hat{x}_2) + \varepsilon_0^* - \tau_D \tag{56}$$

Define $\hat{x}_1$ as the estimate of the angular position, $\hat{x}_2$ as the estimate of angular velocity, $\tilde{x}_1 = x_1 - \hat{x}_1$ as the angular position estimation error, and $\tilde{x}_2 = x_2 - \hat{x}_2$ as the angular velocity estimation error. Inspired by [54], the state observer design is as follows:

$$\begin{cases} \dot{\hat{x}}_1 = \hat{x}_2 + k_1\tilde{x}_1 \\ \hat{x}_2 = S_1 + k_3\tilde{x}_1 \\ \dot{S}_1 = i_e\tau_m - \hat{\mathbf{W}}_0\mathbf{G}_0(x_1, \hat{x}_2) - \hat{\tau}_D + k_2\tilde{x}_1 \end{cases} \tag{57}$$

where $k_i(i = 1, 2, 3)$ is the designed positive constants. $\hat{\tau}_D$ is the estimate of $\tau_D$. According to (50), (56), and (57), the following error dynamics equation is obtained:

$$\begin{cases} \dot{\tilde{x}}_1 = -k_1\tilde{x}_1 + \tilde{x}_2 \\ \dot{\tilde{x}}_2 = -\Delta\tau_{ef} - \tilde{\mathbf{W}}_0\mathbf{G}_0(x_1, \hat{x}_2) - \tilde{\tau}_D + \tilde{x}_1(k_1k_3 - k_2) \\ \qquad - k_3\tilde{x}_2 \end{cases} \tag{58}$$

where $\tilde{\tau}_D = \tau_D - \hat{\tau}_D$ is the disturbance estimation error.

To estimate the disturbance, the auxiliary variable $\lambda$ is introduced as follows:

$$\lambda = \tau_D + \alpha x_2 \tag{59}$$

where $\alpha$ is a designed constant. The disturbance is estimated as follows:

$$\hat{\tau}_D = \hat{\lambda} - \alpha\hat{x}_2 \tag{60}$$

Deriving $\lambda$ with respect to time gives the following:

$$\dot{\lambda} = \dot{\tau}_D + \alpha(i_e\tau_m - \tau_{ef} - \lambda + \alpha x_2) \tag{61}$$

The design of $\dot{\hat{\lambda}}$ is as follows:

$$\dot{\hat{\lambda}} = \alpha(i_e\tau_m - \hat{\lambda} + \alpha\hat{x}_2) \tag{62}$$

Define $\tilde{\lambda} = \lambda - \hat{\lambda}$ and combine it with (61) and (62) with the derivation for time to obtain the following:

$$\begin{aligned} \dot{\tilde{\lambda}} =& \dot{\lambda} - \dot{\hat{\lambda}} \\ =& \dot{\tau}_D + \alpha(-\mathbf{W}_0^*\mathbf{G}_0(x_1, \hat{x}_2) + \varepsilon_0^* + \Delta\tau_{ef} - \tilde{\lambda} + \alpha\tilde{x}_2) \end{aligned} \tag{63}$$

The Lyapunov function is selected as follows:

$$V_0 = \frac{1}{2}\tilde{x}_1^2 + \frac{1}{2}\tilde{x}_2^2 + \frac{1}{2}\tilde{\lambda} \tag{64}$$

Taking the derivative of (64) yields the following:

$$\begin{aligned}\dot{V}_0 =& \tilde{x}_1\dot{\tilde{x}}_1 + \tilde{x}_2\dot{\tilde{x}}_2 + \tilde{\lambda}\dot{\tilde{\lambda}} \\ =& \tilde{x}_1\tilde{x}_2 - k_1 x_1^2 + \tilde{x}_2\Delta\tau_{ef} - \tilde{x}_2\tilde{\mathbf{W}}_0^T\mathbf{G}_0(x_1,\hat{x}_2) + \tilde{x}_2\varepsilon_0^* \\ & - \tilde{x}_2\tilde{\tau}_D + \tilde{x}_1\tilde{x}_2(k_1k_3 - k_2) - k_3\tilde{x}_2^2 + \tilde{\lambda}\dot{\tau}_D + \alpha\tilde{\lambda}\varepsilon_0^* \\ & + \alpha\tilde{\lambda}\Delta\tau_{ef} - \alpha\tilde{\lambda}^2 + \alpha^2\tilde{\lambda}\tilde{x}_2 - \alpha\tilde{\lambda}\mathbf{W}_0^{*T}\mathbf{G}_0(x_1,\hat{x}_2)\end{aligned} \tag{65}$$

Using Lemma 1 yields the following:

$$\begin{cases} \tilde{x}_1\tilde{x}_2 \le \frac{\mu_0}{2}\tilde{x}_1^2 + \frac{1}{2\mu_0}\tilde{x}_2^2 \\ \tilde{x}_2\Delta\tau_{ef} \le |h_f|\tilde{x}_2^2 \\ \tilde{x}_2\tilde{\mathbf{W}}_0^T\mathbf{G}_0(x_1,\hat{x}_2) \le \frac{\mu_2}{2}\tilde{x}_2^2 + \frac{1}{2\mu_1}\tilde{\mathbf{W}}_0^T\tilde{\mathbf{W}}_0 \\ \tilde{x}_2\tilde{\tau}_D \le (\frac{\mu_2}{2} + \frac{\alpha^2}{\mu_2})x_2^2 + \frac{1}{\mu_2}\tilde{\lambda}^2 \\ \tilde{\lambda}\dot{\tau}_D \le \frac{\mu_3}{2}\tilde{\lambda}^2 + \frac{1}{2\mu_3}\varepsilon_D^2 \\ \alpha\tilde{\lambda}\mathbf{W}_0^{*T}\mathbf{G}_0(x_1,\hat{x}_2) \le \frac{\mu_4}{2}\tilde{\lambda}^2 + \frac{1}{2\mu_4}\alpha^2\mathbf{W}_0^{*T}\mathbf{W}_0^* \\ \alpha^2\tilde{\lambda}\tilde{x}_2 \le \frac{\mu_5}{2}\tilde{\lambda}^2 + \frac{1}{2\mu_5}\alpha^4\tilde{x}_2^2 \\ \alpha\tilde{\lambda}\Delta\tau_{ef} \le \frac{\mu_6}{2}\tilde{\lambda}^2 + \frac{1}{2\mu_6}\alpha^2 h_f^2\tilde{x}_2^2 \\ \alpha\tilde{\lambda}\varepsilon_0^* \le \frac{\mu_7}{2}\tilde{\lambda}^2 + \frac{\alpha^2}{2\mu_7}\varepsilon_0^{*2} \\ \tilde{x}_2\varepsilon_0^* \le \frac{\mu_8}{2}\tilde{x}_2^2 + \frac{1}{2\mu_8}\varepsilon_0^{*2} \end{cases} \tag{66}$$

According to the above inequalities, we can get the following:

$$\begin{aligned}\dot{V}_0 \le& -(k_1 - \frac{\mu_0(k_1k_3 - k_2 + 1)}{2})\tilde{x}_1^2 - [k_3 - \frac{k_1k_3 - k_2 + 1}{2\mu_0} \\ & + \frac{\mu_8}{2} - \frac{\mu_1}{2} - (\frac{\mu_2}{2} + \frac{\alpha^2}{\mu_2}) - \frac{1}{2\mu_5}\alpha^4 - \frac{1}{2\mu_6}\alpha^2 h_f^2]\tilde{x}_2^2 \\ & - (\alpha - \frac{1}{\mu_2} - \frac{\mu_3}{2} - \frac{\mu_4}{2} - \frac{\mu_5}{2} - \frac{\mu_6}{2} - \frac{\mu_7}{2})\tilde{\lambda}^2 + \frac{1}{2\mu_3}\varepsilon_D^2 \\ & + \frac{1}{2\mu_1}\tilde{\mathbf{W}}_0^T\tilde{\mathbf{W}}_0 + \frac{1}{2\mu_4}\alpha^2\mathbf{W}_0^{*T}\mathbf{W}_0^* + (\frac{\alpha^2}{2\mu_7} + \frac{1}{2\mu_8})\varepsilon_0^{*2}\end{aligned} \tag{67}$$

where $\kappa_1 = k_1 - \frac{\mu_0(k_1k_3-k_2+1)}{2}$, $\kappa_2 = k_3 - \frac{k_1k_3-k_2+1}{2\mu_0} + \frac{\mu_8}{2} - \frac{\mu_1}{2} - (\frac{\mu_2}{2} + \frac{\alpha^2}{\mu_2}) - \frac{1}{2\mu_5}\alpha^4 - \frac{1}{2\mu_6}\alpha^2 h_f^2$, $\kappa_3 = \alpha - \frac{1}{\mu_2} - \frac{\mu_3}{2} - \frac{\mu_4}{2} - \frac{\mu_5}{2} - \frac{\mu_6}{2} - \frac{\mu_7}{2}$, $\kappa_4 = \frac{1}{2\mu_3}\varepsilon_D^2 + \frac{1}{2\mu_1}\tilde{\mathbf{W}}_0^T\tilde{\mathbf{W}}_0 + \frac{1}{2\mu_4}\alpha^2\mathbf{W}_0^{*T}\mathbf{W}_0^* + (\frac{\alpha^2}{2\mu_7} + \frac{1}{2\mu_8})\varepsilon_0^{*2}$.

According to (67), if $\kappa_1 > 0$, $\kappa_2 > 0$, $\kappa_3 > 0$, and $\kappa_4$ is bounded, it follows from Lyapunov's stability theory that the estimation errors $\tilde{x}_1$, $\tilde{x}_2$, and $\tilde{\lambda}$ are ultimately and consistently bounded. Therefore, this paper aims to design a suitable adaptive control method to guarantee that all states of the closed-loop system, including the observer, are bounded.

### 4.3. Controller Design

In order to improve the tracking accuracy, a barrier Lyapunov function is used on the basis of the traditional backstepping control method. The proposed controller design is divided into two steps.

Step 1: Define the variables $z_1 = x_1 - x_d$ and $z_2 = \hat{x}_2 - \alpha_1$. Select the barrier Lyapunov function as follows:

$$V_1 = \frac{1}{2}\ln\frac{z_1^2}{b_1^2 - z_1^2} \tag{68}$$

where $b_1$ is a designed positive constant for the boundary.

The derivation of (68) yields the following:

$$\dot{V}_1 = \frac{z_1\dot{z}_1}{b_1^2 - z_1^2} = \frac{z_1}{b_1^2 - z_1^2}(z_2 + \alpha_1 + \tilde{x}_2 - \dot{x}_d) \tag{69}$$

The virtual control law $\alpha_1$ is designed as follows:

$$\alpha_1 = -k_{d1}z_1 + \dot{x}_d - \frac{z_1}{b_1^2 - z_1^2} - \frac{5}{2}(b_1^2 - z_1^2)z_1 \tag{70}$$

Substituting (70) into (69) yields the following:

$$\begin{aligned}\dot{V}_1 =& \frac{z_1}{b_1^2 - z_1^2}(z_2 - k_{d1}z_1 + \dot{x}_d - \frac{z_1}{b_1^2 - z_1^2} - \frac{5}{2}(b_1^2 - z_1^2) \\ & - \dot{x}_d + \tilde{x}_2) \\ =& \frac{z_1 z_2}{b_1^2 - z_1^2} - \frac{k_{d1}z_1^2}{b_1^2 - z_1^2} - \frac{z_1^2}{(b_1^2 - z_1^2)^2} - \frac{5}{2}z_1^2 + \frac{z_1\tilde{x}_2}{b_1^2 - z_1^2}\end{aligned} \tag{71}$$

Using Lemma 1 yields the following:

$$\begin{cases} \dfrac{z_1 z_2}{b_1^2 - z_1^2} \le \dfrac{1}{2}\dfrac{z_1^2}{(b_1^2 - z_1^2)^2} + \dfrac{1}{2}z_2^2 \\ \dfrac{z_1\tilde{x}_2}{b_1^2 - z_1^2} \le \dfrac{1}{2}\dfrac{z_1^2}{(b_1^2 - z_1^2)^2} + \dfrac{1}{2}\tilde{x}_2^2 \end{cases} \tag{72}$$

Substituting (72) into (71) yields the following:

$$\dot{V}_1 \le -\frac{k_{d1}z_1^2}{b_1^2 - z_1^2} + \frac{1}{2}z_2^2 - \frac{5}{2}z_1^2 + \frac{1}{2}\tilde{x}_2^2 \tag{73}$$

Step 2: Select the barrier Lyapunov function as follows:

$$V_2 = \frac{1}{2}\ln\frac{z_2^2}{b_2^2 - z_2^2} + \frac{1}{2r_0}\tilde{\mathbf{W}}_0^T\tilde{\mathbf{W}}_0 + \frac{1}{2r_1}\tilde{\mathbf{W}}_1^T\tilde{\mathbf{W}}_1 \tag{74}$$

where $b_2$ is a designed positive constant for the boundary. $r_0$ and $r_1$ are positive constants.

The derivation of (74) yields the following:

$$\begin{aligned}\dot{V}_2 =& \frac{z_2\dot{z}_2}{b_2^2 - z_2^2} - \frac{1}{r_0}\tilde{\mathbf{W}}_0^T\dot{\mathbf{W}}_0 - \frac{1}{r_0}\tilde{\mathbf{W}}_1^T\dot{\mathbf{W}}_1 \\ =& \frac{z_2}{b_2^2 - z_2^2}(i_e\tau_m - \hat{\tau}_{ef} - \hat{\tau}_D + k_3\tilde{x}_2 + (k_2 - k_1k_3)\tilde{x}_1 \\ & - \dot{\alpha}_1) - \frac{1}{r_0}\tilde{\mathbf{W}}_0^T\dot{\mathbf{W}}_0 - \frac{1}{r_1}\tilde{\mathbf{W}}_1^T\dot{\mathbf{W}}_1\end{aligned} \tag{75}$$

Define $F = \dot{\alpha}_1$; according to Lemma 2, $F$ can be approximated via RBFNN as follows:

$$F = \mathbf{W}_1^{*T}\mathbf{G}_1(x_1, \hat{x}_2) + \varepsilon_1^* \tag{76}$$

Define the estimate of $F$ as follows:

$$\hat{F} = \hat{\mathbf{W}}_1\mathbf{G}_1(x_1, \hat{x}_2) \tag{77}$$

The control input $u$ is designed as follows:

$$\begin{aligned}\tau_m =& \frac{1}{i_e}[\hat{\tau}_{ef} + \hat{\tau}_D - (k_2 - k_1k_3)\tilde{x}_1 - k_{d2}z_2 - \frac{k_3^2 z_2}{b_2^2 - z_2^2} \\ &- \frac{3z_2}{2(b_2^2 - z_2^2)} - z_1 - \frac{5}{2}(b_2^2 - z_2^2)z_2 + \hat{F}]\end{aligned} \tag{78}$$

The neural network adaptive law is designed as follows:

$$\begin{cases}\dot{\hat{\mathbf{W}}}_0 = r_0(z_1 + z_2)\mathbf{G}_0 - m_0\hat{\mathbf{W}}_0 \\ \dot{\hat{\mathbf{W}}}_1 = r_1(z_1 + z_2)\mathbf{G}_1 - m_1\hat{\mathbf{W}}_1\end{cases} \tag{79}$$

where $r_i, m_i (i = 1, 2)$ is the designed positive constants.

Substituting (77)–(79) into (75) yields the following:

$$\begin{aligned}\dot{V}_2 =& \frac{k_3z_2\tilde{x}_2}{b_2^2 - z_2^2} - \frac{z_2}{b_2^2 - z_2^2}\tilde{\mathbf{W}}_1^T\mathbf{G}_1 + \frac{z_2}{b_2^2 - z_2^2}\varepsilon_1^* - \frac{k_{d2}z_2^2}{b_2^2 - z_2^2} \\ &- \frac{3z_2^2}{2(b_2^2 - z_2^2)^2} - \frac{k_3^2z_2^2}{2(b_2^2 - z_2^2)^2} - \frac{z_1z_2}{b_2^2 - z_2^2} - \frac{5}{2}z_2^2 \\ &- \tilde{\mathbf{W}}_0^T(z_1 + z_2)\mathbf{G}_0 + \frac{m_0}{r_0}\hat{\mathbf{W}}_0 - \tilde{\mathbf{W}}_1^T(z_1 + z_2)\mathbf{G}_1 + \frac{m_1}{r_1}\hat{\mathbf{W}}_1\end{aligned} \tag{80}$$

Using Lemma 1 yields the following:

$$\begin{cases}\frac{k_3z_2\tilde{x}_2}{b_2^2 - z_2^2} \le \frac{k_3^2z_2^2}{2(b_2^2 - z_2^2)^2} + \frac{1}{2}\tilde{x}_2^2 \\ \frac{z_2}{b_2^2 - z_2^2}\tilde{\mathbf{W}}_1\mathbf{G}_1 \le \frac{z_2^2}{2(b_2^2 - z_2^2)^2} + \frac{1}{2}\tilde{\mathbf{W}}_1^T\tilde{\mathbf{W}}_1 \\ \frac{z_2\varepsilon_1^*}{b_2^2 - z_2^2} \le \frac{z_2^2}{2(b_2^2 - z_2^2)^2} + \frac{1}{2}\varepsilon_1^{*2} \\ \frac{z_1z_2}{b_2^2 - z_2^2} \le \frac{z_2^2}{2(b_2^2 - z_2^2)^2} + \frac{1}{2}z_1^2 \\ -\tilde{\mathbf{W}}_0^T(z_1 + z_2)\mathbf{G}_0 + \frac{m_0}{r_0}\hat{\mathbf{W}}_0 \le z_1^2 + z_2^2 + \frac{1}{2}\tilde{\mathbf{W}}_0^T\tilde{\mathbf{W}}_0 \\ -\frac{m_0}{2r_0}\tilde{\mathbf{W}}_0^T\tilde{\mathbf{W}}_0 + \frac{m_0}{2r_0}\mathbf{W}_0^{*T}\mathbf{W}_0^* \\ -\tilde{\mathbf{W}}_1^T(z_1 + z_2)\mathbf{G}_1 + \frac{m_1}{r_1}\hat{\mathbf{W}}_1 \le z_1^2 + z_2^2 + \frac{1}{2}\tilde{\mathbf{W}}_1^T\tilde{\mathbf{W}}_1 \\ -\frac{m_1}{2r_1}\tilde{\mathbf{W}}_1^T\tilde{\mathbf{W}}_1 + \frac{m_1}{2r_1}\mathbf{W}_1^{*T}\mathbf{W}_1^*\end{cases} \tag{81}$$

The control principles and procedures of the constraint-based adaptive neural network-output feedback controller proposed in this paper is shown in Figure 14.

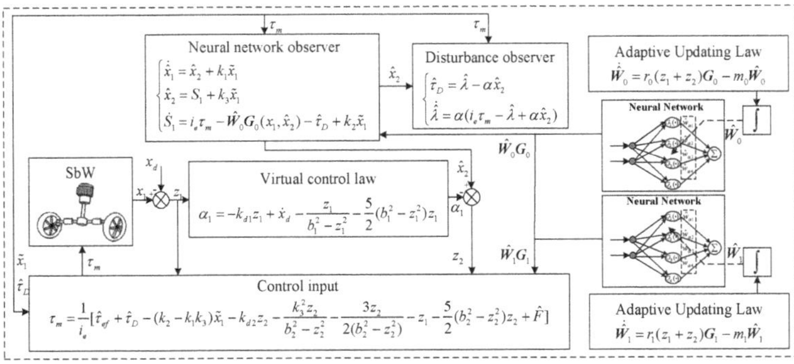


**Figure 14.** The control principles and procedures of the method proposed in this paper.

Substituting (81) into (80) yields the following:

$$\begin{aligned}\dot{V}_2 \leq &\frac{1}{2}\tilde{x}_2^2 - \frac{k_{d2}z_2^2}{b_2^2 - z_2^2} - (\frac{m_0}{2r_0} - \frac{1}{2})\tilde{\mathbf{W}}_0^T\tilde{\mathbf{W}}_0 - (\frac{m_1}{2r_1} - \frac{1}{2})\tilde{\mathbf{W}}_1^T\tilde{\mathbf{W}}_1 \\ &+ \frac{1}{2}\varepsilon_1^* - \frac{1}{2}z_2^2 + \frac{5}{2}z_1^2 + \frac{m_0}{2r_0}\mathbf{W}_0^{*T}\mathbf{W}_0^* + \frac{m_1}{2r_1}\mathbf{W}_1^{*T}\mathbf{W}_1^*\end{aligned} \tag{82}$$

### 4.4. Stability Analysis

**Theorem 1.** *For the SbW control system (50), the neural network state observer (57) and disturbance observer (60), the virtual controller (70), and the controller (78) are used. The adaptive law of the neural network is defined in (79); then, all signals of the closed-loop system converge to a compact set.*

**Proof.** Select the Lyapunov function as follows:

$$V = V_0 + V_1 + V_2 \tag{83}$$

Substituting (67), (73), and (82) into (83) yields the following:

$$\begin{aligned}\dot{V} \leq &-(k_1 - \frac{\mu_0(k_1k_3 - k_2 + 1)}{2})\tilde{x}_1^2 - (k_3 - \frac{k_1k_3 - k_2 + 1}{2\mu_0} \\ &+ \frac{\mu_8}{2} - \frac{\mu_1}{2} - \frac{\mu_2}{2} - \frac{\alpha^2}{\mu_2} - \frac{1}{2\mu_5}\alpha^4 - \frac{1}{2\mu_6}\alpha^2h_f^2 - 1)\tilde{x}_2^2 \\ &- (\alpha - \frac{1}{\mu_2} - \frac{\mu_3}{2} - \frac{\mu_4}{2} - \frac{\mu_5}{2} - \frac{\mu_6}{2} - \frac{\mu_7}{2})\tilde{\lambda}^2 \\ &- (\frac{m_0}{2r_0} - \frac{1}{2} - \frac{1}{2\mu_1})\tilde{\mathbf{W}}_0^T\tilde{\mathbf{W}}_0 - (\frac{m_1}{2r_1} - \frac{1}{2})\tilde{\mathbf{W}}_1^T\tilde{\mathbf{W}}_1 \\ &- k_{d1}\frac{z_1^2}{b_1^2 - z_1^2} - k_{d2}\frac{z_2^2}{b_2^2 - z_2^2} + \frac{1}{2\mu_3}\varepsilon_D^2 + \frac{1}{2\mu_4}\mathbf{W}_0^{*T}\mathbf{W}_0^* \\ &+ (\frac{\alpha^2}{2\mu_7} + \frac{1}{2\mu_4})\varepsilon_0^{*2} + \frac{1}{2}\varepsilon_1^* + \frac{m_0}{2r_0}\mathbf{W}_0^{*T}\mathbf{W}_0^* + \frac{m_1}{2r_1}\mathbf{W}_1^{*T}\mathbf{W}_1^*\end{aligned} \tag{84}$$

where $C_1 = 2(k_1 - \frac{\mu_0(k_1k_3-k_2+1)}{2})$, $C_2 = 2(k_3 - \frac{k_1k_3-k_2+1}{2\mu_0} + \frac{\mu_8}{2} - \frac{\mu_1}{2} - \frac{\mu_2}{2} - \frac{\alpha^2}{\mu_2} - \frac{1}{2\mu_5}\alpha^4 - \frac{1}{2\mu_6}\alpha^2h_f^2 - 1)$, $C_3 = 2(\alpha - \frac{1}{\mu_2} - \frac{\mu_3}{2} - \frac{\mu_4}{2} - \frac{\mu_5}{2} - \frac{\mu_6}{2} - \frac{\mu_7}{2})$, $C_4 = 2k_{d1}$, $C_5 = 2k_{d2}$, $C_6 = 2(\frac{m_0}{2r_0} - \frac{1}{2} - \frac{1}{2\mu_1})$, $C_7 = 2(\frac{m_1}{2r_1} - \frac{1}{2})$, $C_0 = +\frac{1}{2\mu_3}\varepsilon_D^2 + \frac{1}{2\mu_4}\mathbf{W}_0^{*T}\mathbf{W}_0^* + (\frac{\alpha^2}{2\mu_7} + \frac{1}{2\mu_4})\varepsilon_0^{*2} + \frac{1}{2}\varepsilon_1^* + \frac{m_0}{2r_0}\mathbf{W}_0^{*T}\mathbf{W}_0^* + \frac{m_1}{2r_1}\mathbf{W}_1^{*T}\mathbf{W}_1^*$.

Define the compact set $\Omega_z = \{z_i||z_i| \leq b_i, i = 1,2\}$; then, on $\Omega_z$, the following is obtained: $\ln \frac{z_i^2}{b_i^2 - z_i^2} \leq \frac{z_i^2}{b_i^2 - z_i^2}$. Therefore, (84) can be expressed as follows:

$$\dot{V} \leq -aV + C_0 \tag{85}$$

where $a = \min\{C_1, C_2, C_3, C_4, C_5, C_6, C_7\}$.

According to A, $\tilde{x}_1$, $\tilde{x}_2$, $\lambda$, $z_1$, $z_2$, $\tilde{\mathbf{W}}_0$, and $\tilde{\mathbf{W}}_1$are bounded. Since $\alpha$ is bounded, it follows that $\hat{x}_2 = z_2 + \alpha$ is bounded, and $x_2 = \hat{x}_2 + \tilde{x}_2$ is bounded. It can be inferred from (70) and (78) that the virtual control law and control input are also bounded. Theorem 1 has been proven. □

## 5. Simulation and Experimental Validation

In this section, to verify the effectiveness of the proposed controller in the online control SbW system, we conducted simulations and hardware loop experiments.

### 5.1. Simulation

The parameters of the SbW system are chosen to be the same with [22], which are listed in Table 5. In this numerical simulation, the parameters are set as follows: $\alpha_1 = 0.25$, $\alpha_2 = 20$, $\alpha_3 = 0.01$, $\beta_1 = 100$, $\beta_2 = 1$, and $\beta_3 = 100$. To verify the robustness under different loads, different external disturbance are added as follows:

$$\tau_D = \begin{cases} 2, 0 < t \leq 40 \\ 1 + 0.5tanh(0.1(t-40)), 40 < t \leq 80 \\ 2 + 0.3tanh(0.1(t-80)), 80 < t \leq 120 \\ 3 - 120tanh(0.1(t-120)), 120 < t \leq 160 \end{cases} \tag{86}$$

To verify the superiority of the proposed method, three methods are selected for comparison. In order to ensure a fair comparison of the three methods, the parameters of each method are adjusted to achieve the best control effect under the same conditions.

**Table 5.** Parameters for SbW system.

| Parameters | Value |
|---|---|
| $J_{fw}$ (kg· m$^2$) | 3.8 |
| $J_{sm}$ (kg· m$^2$) | 0.0045 |
| $B_{fw}$ (Nms/rad) | 10 |
| $B_{sm}$ (Nms/rad) | 0.05 |
| $i_{mc}$ | 18 |

(1) The controller proposed in Theorem 1 is expressed as follows:

$$\begin{aligned} \tau_m = & \frac{1}{i_e}[\hat{\tau}_{ef} + \hat{\tau}_D - (k_2 - k_1 k_3)\tilde{x}_1 - k_{d2} z_2 - \frac{k_3^2 z_2}{b_2^2 - z_2^2} \\ & - \frac{3z_2}{2(b_2^2 - z_2^2)} - z_1 - \frac{5}{2}(b_2^2 - z_2^2)z_2 + \hat{F}] \end{aligned} \tag{87}$$

The parameters of the proposed method are set as follows: $k_1 = 0.001$, $k_2 = 150$, $k_3 = 50$, $r_0 = 100$, $m_0 = 20$, $r_1 = 100$, $m_1 = 15$, $k_{d1} = k_{d2} = 10$, $b_1 = b_2 = 5$, $\alpha = 1$. The neural network parameters are set as follows: $b_j = 5$, $c_1 = [0,0]^T$, $c_2 = [0.05, 0.05]^T$, $c_3 = [0.1, 0.1]^T$, $c_4 = [0.15, 0.15]^T$, $c_5 = [0.2, 0.2]^T$, $c_6 = [0.25, 0.25]^T$, $c_7 = [0.3, 0.3]^T$, $c_8 = [0.35, 0.35]^T$, $c_9 = [0.4, 0.4]^T$, $c_{10} = [0.45, 0.45]^T$, $c_{11} = [0.5, 0.5]^T$, $c_{12} = [0.55, 0.55]^T$, $c_{13} = [0.6, 0.6]^T$, $c_{14} = [0.65, 0.65]^T$, $c_{15} = [0.7, 0.7]^T$, $c_{16} = [0.75, 0.75]^T$, $c_{17} = [0.8, 0.8]^T$, $c_{18} = [0.85, 0.85]^T$, $c_{19} = [0.9, 0.9]^T$, $c_{20} = [0.95, 0.95]^T$, $c_{21} = [1,1]^T$.

(2) To verify the effectiveness of the disturbance observer, this method removes the disturbance observer from the proposed method, and the controller parameters remain consistent with the proposed method.

(3) The traditional backstepping control method (BSC) differs from the proposed method by removing the state constraints and keeping the other parts the same. The controller is expressed as follows:

$$\begin{cases} \alpha_1 = -k_{d1} z_1 + \dot{x}_d \\ \tau_m = \dfrac{1}{i_e}(\hat{\tau}_{ef} + \hat{\tau}_D + \dot{\alpha}_1 - (k_2 - k_1 k_3)\tilde{x}_1 - k_{d2} z_2 - z_1) \end{cases} \tag{88}$$

The parameters of BSC are set as follows: $k_{d1} = k_{d2} = 70$. The parameters of the state observer and the disturbance observer are consistent with the proposed method. The simulation reference signal is set to $x_d = \sin(t)$. In order to evaluate the performance of the three controllers, a performance index is introduced: the root mean square error (RMSE), RMSE=$\sqrt{\frac{1}{n}\sum_{i=1}^{n} e_i^2}$. The simulation results are shown in Figure 15.

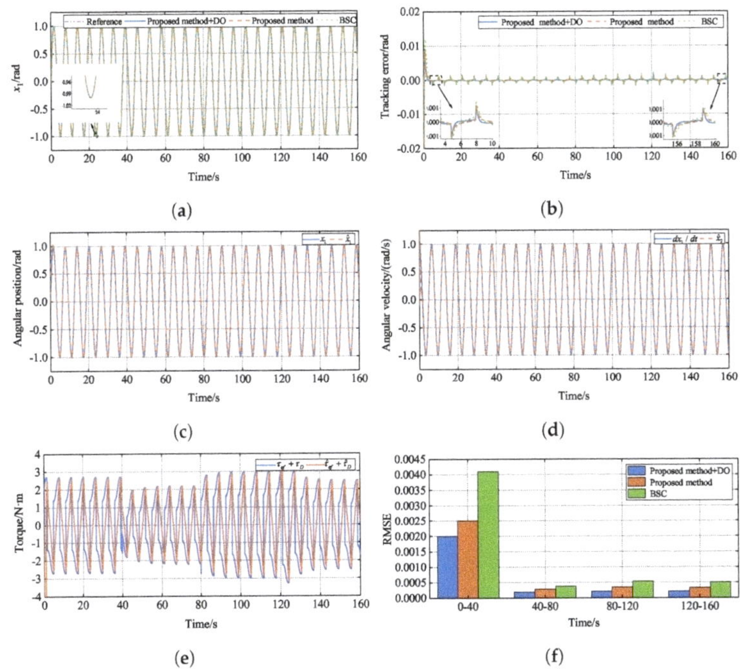


**Figure 15.** The simulation results. (**a**) Position-tracking performance; (**b**) tracking error; (**c**) angular position; (**d**) angular velocity; (**e**) friction and torque; (**f**) RMSE.

Figure 15 shows the curves of the numerical simulation. Figure 15a,b show the position-tracking performance and tracking error of the three methods, respectively. From Figure 15a, it can be seen that all three methods can track the reference signal well, the errors are very close to each other, and it is difficult to see the difference between the three methods intuitively. However, the tracking error curve shows that the tracking error of BSC is more than 0.01 rad in the starting tracking stage, while the other two methods are within 0.01 rad, which indicates that the proposed method achieves a faster response speed. During the tracking process, the tracking error of BSC is larger than that of the other two methods. The tracking error of the proposed method with a disturbance observer is smaller, and the tracking error converges near zero faster. Figure 15c,d show the curves of the estimation results of the state observer for $x_1$ and $x_2$, respectively. As can be seen from Figure 15c, at the beginning stage, the curves of $\hat{x}_1$ and $x_1$ have a slightly larger error and do not fit perfectly. But soon after that, the two curves almost coincide, and the state observer can estimate the angular position well. As can be seen from Figure 15d, since the simulation is an ideal environment to derive the angular velocity directly for the angular position without noise, a smooth curve is obtained. The curves of $\hat{x}_2$ and $dx_1/dt$ almost coincide, and the state observer can estimate the angular velocity well. Figure 15e shows the curve of the neural network approximation of friction and the disturbance observer estimation of external disturbance; from the simulation results, it can be seen that the neural network and the disturbance observer are quickly adjusted by updating the adaptive law to accurately estimate the friction and the external disturbance when the load changes. Figure 15f shows RSME histograms of the three methods, from which it can be seen that, in each period, the proposed method with the disturbance observer achieved lower values in RMSE, indicating better tracking results.

### 5.2. Experiment

In order to better validate the effectiveness of the proposed method, and for safety reasons, hardware-in-the-loop (HIL) experiments were conducted to verify the effectiveness of the proposed control method in practice. The schematic diagram of the steering control YOLOv5-based end-to-end for an autonomous vehicle is shown in Figure 16. The SbW system mainly consists of a steering test bench, dSPACE1401, a monocular camera, and a computer. The steering test bench mainly consists of a steering motor, a reducer, a servo controller, a tension controller, a magnetic powder brake, a steering gear, a cable sensor, and a table frame. In order to verify the proposed method's effectiveness and superiority in comparison with two other methods, firstly, the steering-angle signal received via the controller is artificially given, which causes the steering wheel to traverse the categorized steering angles sequentially, starting from the original position, which ranges between $-60°$ and $60°$.

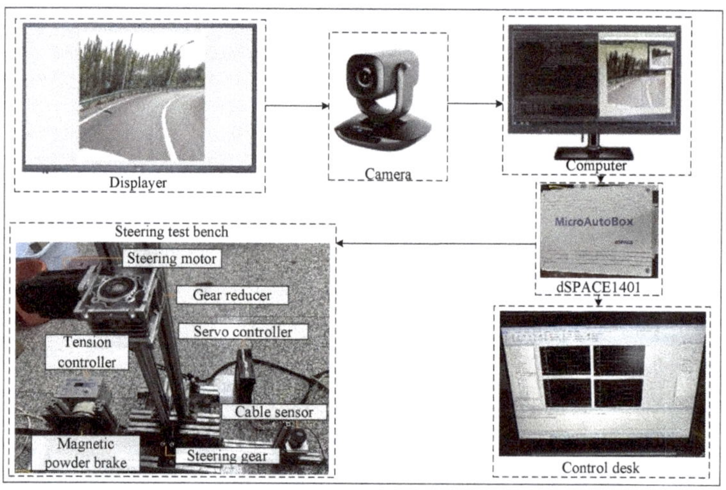


**Figure 16.** The schematic diagram of the YOLOv5-based end-to-end steering control for an autonomous vehicle.

The parameters of the methods in the hardware-in-the-loop experiments are different from those in the simulation, and the parameters of the three methods are set as follows:

(1) The parameters of the proposed method are set to $k_1 = 0.001$, $k_2 = 180$, $k_3 = 100$, $k_{d1} = 70$, $k_{d2} = 1$, $b_1 = 0.2$, $b_2 = 0.3$, and $\alpha = 0.7$. The parameters of the neural network are consistent with those in the simulation.

(2) The parameters of BSC are set to $k_{d1} = 85$, $k_{d2} = 2$. The other parameters are consistent with the proposed method.

The experimental results are shown in Figure 17. Figure 17a,b show the position-tracking performance and tracking error, respectively. From Figure 17a, it can be seen that the tracking performance curve is not as smooth as in the simulation due to the noise in the angular position of the sensor measurement in the experiment. Compared to the other two methods, the proposed method with the disturbance observer exhibits a faster response and a smaller steady-state error. This is more intuitive in the tracking error curve. As Figure 17b shows, the maximum tracking error of the BSC is 0.055 rad, and the maximum tracking errors of the other two methods are within 0.055 rad. Within 50 s to 120 s, it is clearly seen that the proposed method with perturbation observer has a smaller tracking error. In the final stage of tracking, the proposed method with the perturbed observer has a smaller steady-state error, and the tracking error is closer to zero. Figure 17c,d show the estimated curves for the angular position and angular velocity, respectively. From Figure 17c, it can be seen that the $\hat{x}_1$ curve derived from the state observer is very close to that of $x_1$. Between 0 and 50 s, due to the initial operation of the SbW system, there is significant resistance between various components, such as the gap between the gear and the rack, and the gap between the steering motor and the gear reducer. After running for a period of time, the system operates in normal working condition. This can also be seen in Figure 17e, where the estimation of friction and external disturbances from 0 to 50 s is larger than after 50 s. Therefore, the estimation of the angle position has a certain impact, and the error from 0 to 50 s is larger than that after 50 s. From Figure 17d, it can be seen that the derivation of $x_1$ leads to an amplification in the noise due to the presence of noise in the sensor measurements of the experiment. The $\hat{x}_2$ derived from the state observer, on the other hand, is much closer to the real value of $x_2$, has much less noise, and meets the requirements of the controller design. Figure 17e shows the neural network approximation friction and the external disturbance curve estimated via the disturbance observer. Figure 17f shows the RMSE curves of the three methods; at each stage, the proposed method has smaller values, indicating that the proposed method with the disturbance observer achieves better tracking performance.

From the above simulation and experiment, it can be seen that, although the experimental conditions added in the simulation are different from the environment in the actual experiment, it is difficult to achieve consistency with the simulation in the actual experimental environment; for instance, noise is present in the sensors, the actuator has a response delay, added friction occurs, and the external perturbation is inconsistent, etc. However, the trend in the results obtained from the numerical simulation and HIL experiment is consistent, indicating the superiority of the method proposed in this paper.

For safety reasons, we verified the real-time steering prediction and steering control of the trained YOLOv5 on the SbW experimental bench. The experimental results are shown in Figure 18. Figure 18a shows the randomly selected real-time validation images; the trained YOLOv5 outputs the predicted steering angle based on the image and sends it to follow the controller via a serial protocol. Figure 18b shows the output predicted steering angle. When the predicted angle changes, the reference signal is a step-signal change. While, in practice, there are delays in the communication between the steering motor and the controller, it is difficult to track the step signal, and the actual tracking performance is fully and smoothly shifted. Therefore, a filter is added after the predicted steering angle of the output to obtain a smoothed reference signal, as shown in Figure 18c. The adaptive neural network output feedback controller proposed in this paper is used to track the reference signal derived earlier, as shown in Figure 18d, from which it can be seen that, in real-time turn angle variation, the method proposed in this paper can still track the reference angle well and achieves good tracking performance. Figure 18e,f show the estimation curves of the state observer, from which it can be seen that $\hat{x}_1$ and $\hat{x}_2$ derived from the state observer achieve good accuracy when the reference turning angle varies randomly, which is consistent with the previous simulation and experiment. From the experimental results in Figure 18, it can be seen that the trained detector and the proposed controller achieve better prediction and control capabilities.

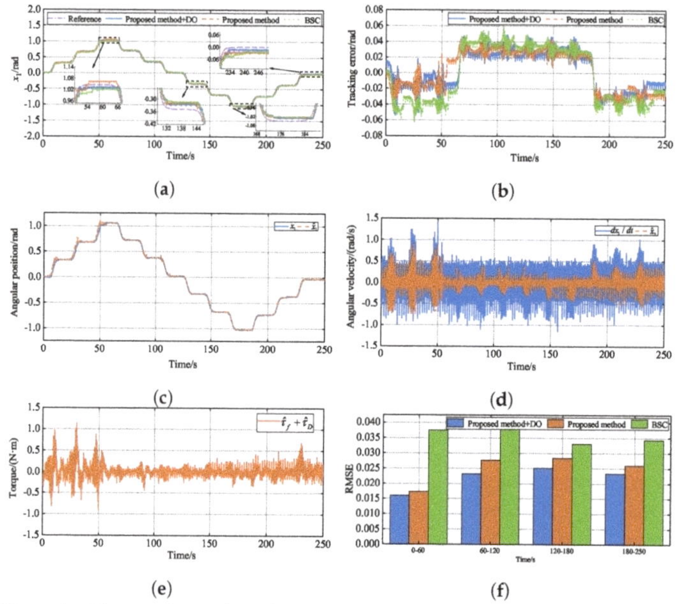

Figure 17. The experimental results. (a) Position-tracking performance; (b) tracking error; (c) angular position; (d) angular velocity; (e) friction and torque; (f) RMSE.

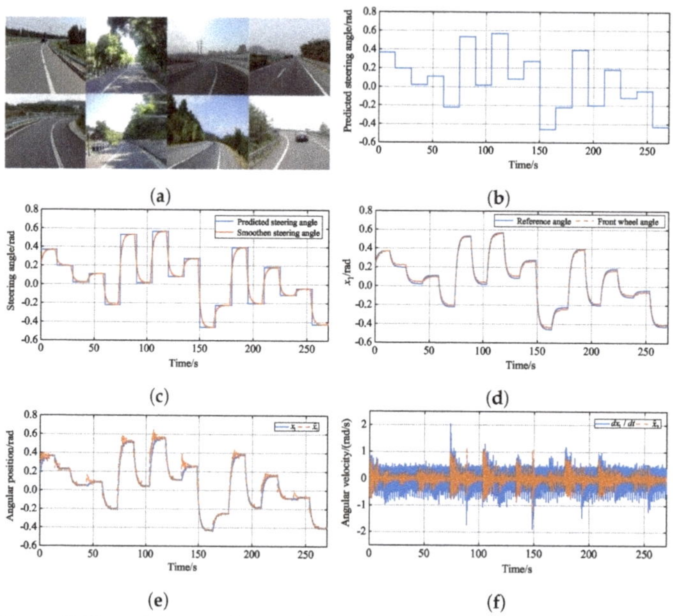

Figure 18. The real-time prediction and execution of the steering angle. (a) Randomly selected images; (b) predicted angle; (c) reference angle; (d) position tracking performance; (e) angular position; (f) angular velocity.

## 6. Conclusions

In this paper, a lightweight steering-angle prediction network model based on YOLOv5 and an adaptive output feedback control scheme with output constraints based on neural networks has been introduced to regulate the predicted steering angle of YOLOv5Ms effectively. We used YOLOv5Ms as a detector to solve the challenging task of steering-angle prediction in this paper. Meanwhile, an adaptive output feedback control scheme with output constraints based on neural networks has been proposed to ensure that the steering system responds quickly and accurately to the desired steering-angle signal. To train the YOLOv5Ms detector and enhance the generalization capability of the proposed detection model in this study, we conducted an extended data-collection experiment at Western Xia Park in Yinchuan City, building upon our previously created lane-line data set. The images of the data sets were labeled one by one by comparing the steering angle collected in the videos. The accuracy and response speed of the detector can meet the actual requirements after real-time testing. Furthermore, the proposed controller can improve the convergence of the tracking error and eliminate the influence of disturbance. Meanwhile, the proposed controller enhances the steering control accuracy of the steering angle predicted via YOLOv5Ms. The experimental results show that the trained network and the proposed controller perform well. The research in this paper can be further extended to other aspects. Firstly, due to the limited experimental conditions, the prediction and tracking of the angle are only experimented in the SbW experimental bench, and they will be experimentally verified in the actual car in the future. In the controller design, only angle tracking was considered, and the angle tracking of the SbW system will be combined with the trajectory tracking control of the AV in the future.

**Author Contributions:** Conceptualization, C.Y. and Y.L.; methodology, C.Y. and Y.W. (Yunlong Wang); software, C.Y. and Y.L.; validation, C.Y., Y.L., and Y.W. (Yunlong Wang); formal analysis, C.Y.; investigation, Y.W. (Yongfu Wang); resources, Y.L. and Y.W. (Yongfu Wang); data curation, C.Y. and Y.W. (Yongfu Wang); writing—original draft preparation, C.Y.; writing—review and editing, C.Y. and Y.L.; visualization, C.Y. and Y.L.; supervision, Y.L.; project administration, Y.L.; funding acquisition, C.Y. All authors have read and agreed to the published version of the manuscript.

**Funding:** This work was supported by the Natural Science Foundation of the Ningxia Hui Autonomous Region (2022AAC03338), supported by the National Natural Science Foundation of China under Grant 52405535, supported by the Postdoctoral Science Foundation of Northeastern University under Grant 20240103, supported by the Fundamental Research Funds for the Central Universities of China under Grant N2303026, supported by the Natural Science Foundation of Liaoning Province under Grant 2023-BSBA-101.

**Institutional Review Board Statement:** Not applicable.

**Informed Consent Statement:** Not applicable.

**Data Availability Statement:** Data are contained within the article.

**Conflicts of Interest:** The authors declare no conflicts of interest.

## Abbreviations

| | | | |
|---|---|---|---|
| AVs | Autonomous vehicles | GIoU | Generalized intersection |
| SbW | Steer by wire | CNN | Convolutional neural network |
| WHO | World Health Organization | DL | Deeping learning |
| MT-LfD | Multi-task demonstration learning | SE | Squeeze and excitation |
| HS | h-swish | ReLU | Rectified linear unit |
| FCs | Fully connected layers | MSE | Mean square error |
| BBOX | Bounding box | IoU | Intersection over union |
| DIoU | Distance-IoU | CIoU | Comprehensive IoU |

| | | | |
|---|---|---|---|
| EIoU | Efficient version of IoU | AP | Average precision |
| TP | True positive | FP | False positive |
| FN | False negative | AMD | Advanced Micro Devices |
| CAN | Controller area network | RBFNN | Radial basis function neural network |
| BSC | Backstepping control method | HIL | Hardware-in-the-loop |
| NAS | Network architecture | RCNN | Region with CNN |
| SSD | Single Shot MultiBOX Detector | YOLO | You Only Look Once |
| YOLOv5Ms | You Only Look Once version 5 with MobilNet version 3 | | |

## Appendix A

The algorithm followed in this study is presented in Algorithm A1.

**Algorithm A1** Steering Angle prediction and control

**Require:** Input image sequences
**Ensure:** Controlled motor position
1. nput_size = (640, 640, 3), nc= 15, anchors = [(10, 13), (16, 30), (33, 23), (30, 61), (62, 45), (59, 119), (116, 90),
(156, 198), (373, 326)], numanchors = len(anchors)
2. Input picture: Image = read_image(path)
3. Image preprocess: Processed_image = preprocess_image(Image)
4. Loading model: Model = load_model('YOLOv5Ms')
5. Image reasoning: Outputs = Model(Processed_image)
6. Analytical prediction result: Predictions = Parse_predictions(Outputs)
7. Filter prediction result: Filtered_predictions = Filter_predictions(Predictions)
8. Output the final prediction result to controller: Final prediction result=Ym
9. Estimate angular velocity, model uncertainty, and external disturbance: $\hat{x}_2$, $\hat{\tau}_{ef}$, $\hat{\tau}_D$.
10. Adaptive neural network output feedback controller provides output $\tau_m$, and controls motor position
based on this controller output.
11. Adjust motor position.
12. **return** Controlled motor position

## References

1. Elallid, B.B.; Benamar, N.; Hafid, A.S.; Rachidi, T.; Mrani, N. A Comprehensive Survey on the Application of Deep and Reinforcement Learning Approaches in Autonomous Driving. *J. King Saud Univ.-Comput. Inf. Sci.* **2022**, *34*, 7366–7390. [CrossRef]
2. Fagnant, D.J.; Kockelman, K. Preparing a nation for autonomous vehicles: Opportunities, barriers and policy recommendations. *Transp. Res. Part A Policy Pract.* **2015**, *77*, 167–181. [CrossRef]
3. Gidado, U.M.; Chiroma, H.; Aljojo, N.; Abubakar, S.; Popoola, S.; Mohammed, A. A survey on deep learning for steering angle prediction in autonomous vehicles. *IEEE Access* **2020**, *8*, 163797–163817. [CrossRef]
4. Peng, B.; Sun, Q.; Li, S.E.; Kum, D.; Yin, Y.; Wei, J.; Gu, T. End-to-end autonomous driving through dueling double deep Q-network. *Automot. Innov.* **2021**, *4*, 328–337. [CrossRef]
5. Ma, Y.; Wang, Z.; Yan, G.; Yang, L. Artificial intelligence applications in the development of autonomous vehicles: A survey. *IEEE/CAA J. Autom. Sin.* **2020**, *7*, 315–329. [CrossRef]
6. Tampuu, A.; Matiisen, T.; Semikin, M.; Fishman, D.; Muhammd, N. A Survey of End-to-End Driving: Architectures and Training Methods. *IEEE Trans. Neural Netw. Learn. Syst.* **2022**, *33*, 1364–1384. [CrossRef]
7. Yurtsever, E.; Lambert, J.; Carballo, A.; Takeda, K. A Survey of Autonomous Driving: Common Practices and Emerging Technologies. *IEEE Access* **2020**, *8*, 58443–58469. [CrossRef]
8. Russakovsky, O.; Deng, J.; Su, H.; Krause, J.; Satheesh, S.; Ma, S.; Huang, Z.; Karpathy, A.; Khosla, A. Imagenet large scale visual recognition challenge. *Int. J. Comput. Vision* **2015**, *115*, 211–252. [CrossRef]
9. Polack, P.; Altch, F.; Andr, B.; Fortelle, A. The kinematic bicycle model: A consistent model for planning feasible trajectories for autonomous vehicles? In Proceedings of the 2017 IEEE Intelligent Vehicles Symposium (IV), Los Angeles, CA, USA, 11–14 June 2017; pp. 812–818.
10. Mohammed, M.S.; Abduljabar, A.M.; Faisal, M.M.; Mahmmod, B.M.; Abdulhussain, S.H.; Khan, W.; Liatsis, P.; Hussain, A. Low-cost autonomous car level 2: Design and implementation for conventional vehicles. *Results Eng.* **2023**, *17*, 100969. [CrossRef]
11. Pomerleau, D.A. Alvinn: An autonomous land vehicle in a neural network. *Adv. Neural Inf. Process. Syst.* **1988**, *1*, 305–313

12. Muller, U.; Ben, J.; Cosatto, E.; Flepp, B.; Cun, Y. Off-road obstacle avoidance through end-to-end learning. In Proceedings of the Advances in Neural Information Processing Systems, Montreal, QC, Canada, 7–12 December 2005; Volume 18.
13. Bojarski, M.; Del, T.D.; Dworakowski, D.; Firner, B.; Flepp, B.; Goyal, P.; Jackel, L.D. End to end learning for self-driving cars. *arXiv* **2016**, arXiv:1604.07316.
14. Mohseni, F.; Voronov, S.; Frisk, E. Deep learning model predictive control for autonomous driving in unknown environments. *IFAC-PapersOnLine* **2018**, *51*, 447–452. [CrossRef]
15. Mehta, A.; Subramanian, A. Learning end-to-end autonomous driving using guided auxiliary supervision. In Proceedings of the 11th Indian Conference on Computer Vision, Graphics and Image Processing, Hyderabad, India, 18–22 December 2018; pp. 1–8.
16. Zeng, W.; Luo, W.; Suo, S.; Sadat, A.; Yang, B.; Casas, S.; Urtasun, R. End-to-end interpretable neural motion planner. In Proceedings of the IEEE/CVF Conference on Computer Vision and Pattern Recognition, Long Beach, CA, USA, 15–20 June 2019; pp. 8660–8669.
17. Le M.; Yi, D.; Dianati, M.; Mouzakitis, A. A survey on imitation learning techniques for end-to-end autonomous vehicles. *IEEE Trans. Intell. Transp. Syst.* **2022**, *23*, 14128–14147.
18. He, K.; Zhang, X.; Ren, S.; Sun, J. Deep residual learning for image recognition. In Proceedings of the IEEE Conference on Computer Vision and Pattern Recognition, Las Vegas, NV, USA, 27–30 June 2016; pp. 770–778.
19. Karadeniz, A.M.; Ballagi, Á.; Kóczy, L.T. Transfer Learning-Based Steering Angle Prediction and Control with Fuzzy Signatures-Enhanced Fuzzy Systems for Autonomous Vehicles. *Symmetry* **2024**, *16*, 1180. [CrossRef]
20. Ren, S.; He, K.; Girshick, R.; Sun, J. Faster r-cnn: Towards real-time object detection with region proposal networks. *Adv. Neural Inf. Process. Syst.* **2015**, *28*. [CrossRef]
21. Bochkovskiy, A.; Wang, C.; Liao, H.M. Yolov4: Optimal speed and accuracy of object detection. *arXiv* **2020**, arXiv:2004.10934.
22. Ye, C.; Wang, Y.; Wang, Y.; Tie, M. Steering angle prediction yolov5-based end-to-end adaptive neural network control for autonomous vehicles. *Proc. Inst. Mech. Eng. Part D J. Automob. Eng.* **2022**, *236*, 1991–2011. [CrossRef]
23. Dong, X.; Yan, S.; Duan, C. A lightweight vehicles detection network model based on yolov5. *Eng. Appl. Artif. Intell.* **2022**, *113*, 104914. [CrossRef]
24. Marumo, Y.; Nagai, M. Steering control of motorcycles using steerby-wire system. *Veh. Syst. Dyn.* **2007**, *45*, 445–458. [CrossRef]
25. Setlur, P.; Wagner, J.R.; Dawson, D.M.; Braganza, D. A trajectory tracking steer-by-wire control system for ground vehicles. *IEEE Trans. Veh. Technol.* **2006**, *55*, 76–85. [CrossRef]
26. Huang, C.; Naghdy, F.; Du, H. Delta operatorbased fault estimation and fault-tolerant model predictive control for steer-by-wire systems. *IEEE Trans. Control Syst. Technol.* **2018**, *26*, 1810–1817. [CrossRef]
27. Sun, Z.; Zheng, J.; Man, Z.; Wang, H. Robust control of a vehicle steer-by-wire system using adaptive sliding mode. *IEEE Trans. Control Syst. Technol.* **2016**, *63*, 2251–2262. [CrossRef]
28. Ye, M.; Wang, H. Robust adaptive integral terminal sliding mode control for steer-by-wire systems based on extreme learning machine. *Comput. Electr. Eng.* **2020**, *86*, 106756. [CrossRef]
29. Chen, J.; Guo, Y. Design and Non-Linearity Optimization of a Vertical Brushless Electric Power Steering Angle Sensor. *Sensors* **2024**, *24*, 2469. [CrossRef]
30. Garcia, G.; Molina, C.; Luque, B.; Rafael, M.; Juan, M. Road pollution estimation from vehicle tracking in surveillance videos by deep convolutional neural networks. *Appl. Soft Comput.* **2021**, *113*, 107950. [CrossRef]
31. Yao, J.; Qi, J.; Zhang, J.; Shao, H.; Yang, J.; Li, X. A real-time detection algorithm for kiwifruit defects based on yolov5. *Electronics* **2021**, *10*, 1711. [CrossRef]
32. Howard, A.G.; Zhu, M.; Chen, B.; Kalenichenko, D.; Wang, W.; Wey, T.; Andreetto, M.; Adam, H. Mobilenets: Efficient convolutional neural networks for mobile vision applications. *arXiv* **2017**, arXiv:1704.04861.
33. Sandler, M.; Howard, A.; Zhu, M.; Zhmoginov, A.; Chen, L.C. Mobilenetv2: Inverted residuals and linear bottlenecks. In Proceedings of the IEEE Conference on Computer Vision and Pattern Recognition, Salt Lake City, UT, USA, 18–23 June 2018; pp. 4510–4520.
34. Zhao, L.; Wang, L. A new lightweight network based on mobilenetv3. *KSII Trans. Internet Inf. Syst.* **2022**, *16*, 1–15.
35. Gu, J.; Wang, Z.; Kuen, J.; Ma, L.; Shahroudy, A.; Shuai, B.; Liu, T.; Wang, X.; Wang, G.; Cai, J. Recent advances in convolutional neural networks. *Pattern Recognit.* **2018**, *77*, 354–377. [CrossRef]
36. Krizhevsky, A.; Sutskever, I.; Hinton, G.E. Imagenet classification with deep convolutional neural networks. *Adv. Neural Inf. Process. Syst.* **2012**, *25*. [CrossRef]
37. Niu, Z.; Zhong, G.; Yu, H. A review on the attention mechanism of deep learning. *Neurocomputing* **2021**, *452*, 48–62. [CrossRef]
38. Guo, M.H.; Xu, T.X.; Liu, J.J.; Liu, Z.N.; Jiang, P.T.; Mu, T.J.; Zhang, S.H.; Martin, R.R.; Cheng, M.M.; Hu, S.M. Attention mechanisms in computer vision: A survey. *Comput. Vis. Media* **2022**, *8*, 331–368. [CrossRef]
39. Hu, J.; Shen, L.; Sun, G. Squeeze-and-excitation networks. In Proceedings of the IEEE Conference on Computer Vision and Pattern Recognition, Salt Lake City, UT, USA, 18–23 June 2018; pp. 7132–7141.
40. Redmon, J.; Farhadi, A. Yolov3: An incremental improvement. *arXiv* **2018**, arXiv:1804.02767.
41. Yu, J.; Jiang, Y.; Wang, Z.; Cao, Z.; Huang, T. Unitbox: An advanced object detection network. In Proceedings of the 24th ACM international conference on Multimedia, Amsterdam, The Netherlands, 15–19 October 2016; pp. 516–520.

42. Rezatofighi, H.; Tsoi, N.; Gwak, J.; Sadeghian, A.; Reid, I.; Savarese, S. Generalized intersection over union: A metric and a loss for bounding box regression. In Proceedings of the IEEE/CVF Conference on Computer Vision and Pattern Recognition, Long Beach, CA, USA, 15–20 June 2019; pp. 658–666.
43. Zheng, Z.; Wang, P.; Liu, W.; Li, J.; Ye, R.; Ren, D. Distance-iou loss: Faster and better learning for bounding box regression. *Proc. AAAI Conf. Artif. Intell.* **2020**, *34*, 12993–13000. [CrossRef]
44. Zhang, Y.F.; Ren, W.; Zhang, Z.; Jia, Z.; Wang, L.; Tan, T. Focal and efficient iou loss for accurate bounding box regression. *Neurocomputing* **2022**, *506*, 146–157. [CrossRef]
45. Gevorgyan, Z. Siou loss: More powerful learning for bounding box regression. *arXiv* **2022**, arXiv:2205.12740.
46. Zhang, H.; Zhang, S. Shape-iou: More accurate metric considering bounding box shape and scale. *arXiv* **2023**, arXiv:2312.17663.
47. Visa, S.; Ramsay, B.; Ralescu, A.L.; Van Der Knaap, E. Confusion matrix-based feature selection. *Maics* **2011**, *710*, 120–127.
48. Na, J.; Chen, Q.; Ren, X.; Guo, Y. Adaptive prescribed performance motion control of servo mechanisms with friction compensation. *IEEE Trans. Ind. Electron.* **2014**, *61*, 486–494. [CrossRef]
49. Kim, S. Moment of inertia and friction torque coefficient identification in a servo drive system. *IEEE Trans. Ind. Electron.* **2019**, *66*, 60–70. [CrossRef]
50. Liu, K.; Zhu, Z. Determination of moment of inertia of permanent magnet synchronous machine drives for design of speed loop regulator. *IEEE Trans. Ind. Electron.* **2017**, *25*, 1816–1824. [CrossRef]
51. Deng, H.; Krstic, M. Stochastic nonlinear stabilization-i: A backstepping design. *Syst. Control Lett.* **1997**, *32*, 143–150. [CrossRef]
52. Li, Y.; Qiang, S.; Zhuang, X.; Kaynak, O. Robust and adaptive backstepping control for nonlinear systems using rbf neural networks. *IEEE Trans. Neural Netw.* **2004**, *15*, 693–701. [CrossRef]
53. Chen, M.; Ge, S. Direct adaptive neural control for a class of uncertain non-affine nonlinear systems based on disturbance observer. *IEEE Trans. Cybern.* **2013**, *43*, 1213–1225. [CrossRef]
54. Peng, Z.; Wang, J.; Wang, D. Distributed containment maneuvering of multiple marine vessels via neurodynamics-based output feedback. *IEEE Trans. Ind. Electron.* **2017**, *64*, 3831–3839. [CrossRef]

sensors

MDPI

Article

# Adaptive FPGA-Based Accelerators for Human–Robot Interaction in Indoor Environments

**Mangali Sravanthi [1,2], Sravan Kumar Gunturi [1], Mangali Chinna Chinnaiah [3,4,*], Siew-Kei Lam [4], G. Divya Vani [3], Mudasar Basha [3], Narambhatla Janardhan [5], Dodde Hari Krishna [3] and Sanjay Dubey [3]**

1 Department of Electronics and Communication Engineering, Koneru Lakshmaiah Education Foundation, Aziznagar, Hyderabad 500075, Telangana, India; sravanthi.engg@gmail.com or sravanthi.engg@mriet.ac.in (M.S.); sravankumar.gunturi@gmail.com (S.K.G.)
2 Department of Electronics and Communication Engineering, Malla Reddy Institute of Engineering and Technology, Maisammaguda, Hyderabad 500014, Telangana, India
3 Department of Electronics and Communications Engineering, B. V. Raju Institute of Technology, Medak, Narsapur 502313, Telangana, India; divyavani.g@bvrit.ac.in (G.D.V.); mudasar.basha@bvrit.ac.in (M.B.); harikrishna.dodde@bvrit.ac.in (D.H.K.); sanjay.dubey@bvrit.ac.in (S.D.)
4 College of Computing and Data Science (CCDS), Nanyang Technological University, Singapore 639798, Singapore; siewkei_lam@pmail.ntu.edu.sg
5 Department of Mechanical Engineering, Chaitanya Bharati Institute of Technology, Gandipet, Hyderabad 500075, Telangana, India; njanardhan_mech@cbit.ac.in
* Correspondence: chinnaaiah.mc@bvrit.ac.in or chinnaiah.mangali@ntu.edu.sg

**Abstract:** This study addresses the challenges of human–robot interactions in real-time environments with adaptive field-programmable gate array (FPGA)-based accelerators. Predicting human posture in indoor environments in confined areas is a significant challenge for service robots. The proposed approach works on two levels: the estimation of human location and the robot's intention to serve based on the human's location at static and adaptive positions. This paper presents three methodologies to address these challenges: binary classification to analyze static and adaptive postures for human localization in indoor environments using the sensor fusion method, adaptive Simultaneous Localization and Mapping (SLAM) for the robot to deliver the task, and human–robot implicit communication. VLSI hardware schemes are developed for the proposed method. Initially, the control unit processes real-time sensor data through PIR sensors and multiple ultrasonic sensors to analyze the human posture. Subsequently, static and adaptive human posture data are communicated to the robot via Wi-Fi. Finally, the robot performs services for humans using an adaptive SLAM-based triangulation navigation method. The experimental validation was conducted in a hospital environment. The proposed algorithms were coded in Verilog HDL, simulated, and synthesized using VIVADO 2017.3. A Zed-board-based FPGA Xilinx board was used for experimental validation.

**Keywords:** posture recognition; localization; FPGA; service robot; sensor fusion

## 1. Introduction

Human–robotic interaction (HRI) systems have become increasingly integrated into healthcare environments [1] (Alzheimer elders assistance), playing a vital role in assisting with tasks such as patient monitoring, medication delivery, and physical support. These robots must not only interact with their surroundings but also adapt to dynamic changes in real time to provide effective assistance. One of the key challenges in developing such systems is the precise localization of a human subject at stationary and moving positions [2]. Reliable and accurate human localization is essential for enabling robots to provide timely and context-aware responses and enhance the patient care and safety. Over the past 30 years, significant research has been conducted on human posture, sleep analysis, and sleep monitoring. In HRI systems, the early stage is about sensing and analyzing human activity recognition to serve as a better way of interacting with autonomous attendants. In this regard, human activities are confined to the sleep and activity stages.

According to the authors of a review analysis [3], sleep apnea affects between 9% and 38% of the general population, and this number is expected to increase in the future. Services navigate towards the localization point of elders/people with Alzheimer's. Human localization has been classified into three categories: monitor-based localization (MBL), device-based localization (DBL), and proximity-based localization. The proposed HRI system is driven by ultrasound MBL algorithms [4]. In the HRI system, the next stage is service robot-based Simultaneous Localization and Mapping (SLAM) navigation. Recent market trends in statistical analysis shows that the global robotic healthcare AI market is expected to reach INR 188 billion by 2030, increasing CAGR by 37% from 2022 to 2030 [5].

In an HRI system, sensing has been performed in two ways by humans and autonomous robots. In this process, estimating the human pose in the environment plays a critical role in enabling the robot to assist humans in delivering necessary services. Human localization analysis using various sensing methods has been presented over the last two decades by researchers. The main challenge involved in pose estimation analysis relies on the quality of sensor data acquisition and pre-processing. Researchers have used pressure, non-contact, wearable, and non-wearable sensing devices to collect data [6–8]. The author focuses on in-bed human pose estimation, including sleep and sitting positions, using a multimodal conditional variational auto encoder (MC-VAE) and HRNet for single-modality inference [9,10]. A novel body posture recognition system on a bed, which accurately estimates sleep postures (supine, left lateral, prone, right lateral) using ballistocardiogram signals, enhancing comfort and reliability, was presented by the authors of [11]. The author of [12] focused on predicting sleep postures, including sitting using a Bayesian network algorithm with a heartbeat rate and image monitoring for accurate posture recognition in wireless body area networks. Similarly, a human sleep posture recognition method using millimeter-wave radar and interactive learning to overcome the sensitivity of radar signals to different individuals was presented by the authors of [13]. Wearable and non-wearable sensors, including three-axis accelerometers, multi-modal sensor fusion, electroencephalography (EEG), and thermometers, have been used to capture data on sleep posture [14,15]. The proposed system was developed using ultrasonic sensor fusion data and a contactless sensing approach to estimate human poses in the environment.

For autonomous robot navigation, SLAM approaches have been used. A robotic assistance system can provide care and support for humans, including those localized on a bed, thereby demonstrating the potential of robots to collaborate in various care scenarios [16]. Ultrasonic sensor fusion data are provided to the robot for effective navigation, allowing it to accurately detect human positions and assess distances, thus enabling smoother and more efficient movement through its environment. The authors have developed robotic delivery systems such as MEDROBO, which can enhance patient care by automating medicine delivery and monitoring vital signs for bedridden individuals using RFID tags attached to the bed [17]. A multifunctional intelligent bed (MIB) integrates autonomous movement, position adjustment, and interaction interfaces to assist mobility-impaired individuals, showing the potential for robotic assistance for bed-localized humans [18]. The challenges involved in the above approaches include maintaining accurate optimization and adaptability, particularly in adaptive healthcare environments. Issues such as RFID tag misplacement and the need for continuous real-time sensing can affect its efficiency in automating medicine delivery and assisting individuals with mobility impairment. Therefore, there is a need for IoT-based systems that enhance healthcare robotics by enabling real-time data collection and communication, thereby improving the task automation and accuracy. IoT-based robotic medicine delivery systems for bedridden individuals, improving outcomes, and overall healthcare efficiency in hospitals, have been addressed by the authors of [19]. Hu. Q. et al. proposed a system that employed a pressure sensor array integrated into a bed sheet with 1024 nodes for comprehensive data collection [20]. The author focused on a mobile robot using ZigBee for bed localization and drug identification based on a central processing unit (CPU) [21]. The key literature findings are that human localization and robot navigation progress independently in the best way. The major challenge is dynamic human localization [2] versus robot services [22], which has been addressed by a few researchers. SLAM methods have been addressed in the last four decades, and the navigation algorithm [23,24] is a subset of the data structure, as well as the shortest path algorithm, tree algorithm, and graph models such as Dijkstra, A* algorithms, and heuristic approaches. Bresson et al. [25] proposed an autonomous navigation method. A challenge mentioned is that navigation methods for person-following mobile robots are required in services. This challenge motivated the proposed research, and recent studies have developed a person-following approach using computer vision methods [26].

The HRI final stage has been accomplished with computational devices, and active research has been conducted using edge computation devices such as the Central Processing Unit (CPU), Graphical Processing Unit (GPU), and field programmable gate array (FPGA). Processing large amounts of data with a high computational speed is not sufficient with a CPU. An FPGA offers parallel data processing with lower latency and power consumption, making it ideal for real-time IoT features such as real-time sensor data collection, processing, and communication for efficient and adaptive systems. The authors of [27] discussed an FPGA-based smart delivery bot for goods, not medicine, utilizing sensors and the Dijkstra algorithm for efficient navigation. The authors developed an Internet-of-Things controlled robot using FPGA, enabling remote navigation via voice commands from a mobile app, with sensor data uploaded to the cloud for task completion [28]. The authors presented FPGA-based robotic accelerators as competitive alternatives to CPU and GPU platforms [29,30], focusing on their performance and energy efficiency, while analyzing optimization techniques and technical challenges within the robotic system pipeline, including commercial and space applications [31]. By leveraging FPGA architectures, the authors proposed an adaptive FPGA-based accelerator for human–robot interactions in indoor environments.

Utilizing an FPGA as a hardware accelerator represents a significant advancement, greatly enhancing computational speed and parallel processing capabilities. The emphasis of this algorithm on FPGA technology makes it particularly suitable for real-time application. The key contributions of the proposed approach are as follows:

- Novel Hardware Schemes are presented for static and adaptive human localization analyses in indoor environments.
- The proposed accelerator is a novel heuristic-triangulation-based navigation algorithm for achieving adaptive SLAM.
- FPGA-based accelerators are proposed for establishing interactions between human localization and robot systems.

The research presented in this paper includes the following components. Section 1 outlines the background and motivation behind human sleep posture analysis using the FPGA implementation. Sections 2 and 3 details the proposed methodology, including both theoretical and hardware aspects. In Section 4, the proposed method is validated using results related to the synthesis, power consumption, and experimental comparisons. The final section summarizes the research findings and discusses future research directions.

## 2. Hardware-Based Algorithms

Human–service robot interactions are embedded with the localization of the human and robot and the robot provides services based on the navigation algorithm under event-driven conditions. Hardware-based algorithms were developed to analyze human localization in both static and adaptive scenarios. Based on human localization, the proposed hardware-based triangulation-navigation algorithm was developed using a service robot. Table 1 represents the related symbols and abbreviations used through out this research work.

**Table 1.** Proposed research-related abbreviations.

| Symbol | Abbreviation |
|---|---|
| $S_{PR}$ | S: ultrasonic sensors, as {H_R, H_L, A_R, A_L, R_L & L_L}<br>P: Position of sensor at Head (H), Abdomen (A), Limb(L)<br>R: Position at sides as Right ®, left(L) |
| PP | Past Position |
| CP | Current Position |
| $S_R$ | Service Robot |
| Dest_ Node | Destination Node |

### 2.1. *Hardware-Based Algorithm for Human–Robot Interaction*

Figure 1 presents an overall flowchart of the proposed hardware-based human–robot interaction (HRI). The proposed HRI methods depend on the localization of the subject (human) and robot. Human localization was performed using contactless sensing. Localization is associated with both static and adaptive forms. The same information is transmitted to the service robot. Before planning to serve the human, the service robot self-localizes based on direction and triangulation methods. After receiving the coordinates of the human localization, it navigates towards the destination using a triangulation-based navigation algorithm. After the successful accomplishment of the task, it retrieves to its parking station using the same navigation algorithm.

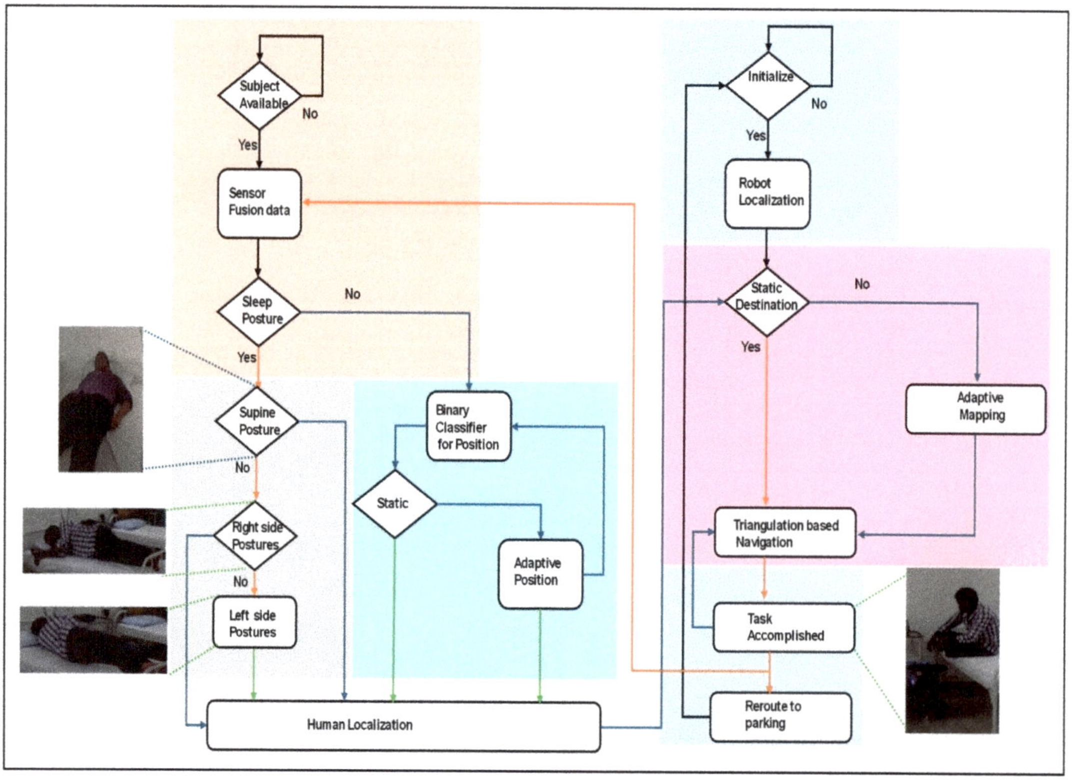


**Figure 1.** Flowchart of proposed hardware-based human–robot interaction.

#### 2.1.1. Hardware-Based Algorithm for Human Localization in an Indoor Environment

This portion focuses on determining human localization within an indoor environment.

The pseudocode for locating humans in various scenarios is outlined in Algorithm 1. The explanation of the pseudocode in Algorithm 1 is represented in the form of a flowchart, as shown in Figure 2.

Algorithm 1 describes the human localization process using a hardware-based algorithm. As shown in Figure 1, sensor data were acquired using distance and PIR sensors (line 1). All parameters were initialized with a reset and operated based on clk (lines 2 and 3). The proposed human-localization algorithm was executed when the PIR sensor was evaluated for human availability. Distance sensor fusion was arranged in the form of six-bit posture values. When the position values were more than two, the sleep posture was considered (line 8). Sleep postures were classified in simple forms, such as supine and left- and right-side sleep postures (lines 9 to 11). In addition to the sleeping posture, the sitting posture is considered by the proposed algorithm (lines 12 to 18).

**Algorithm 1:** Pseudo code for Hardware-Based human localization

```
1.  Initialize sensory fusion distance data
2.  always @ (posedge clk) begin
3.  {PIR, Human available, Position values, Two Positions, Sleep posture, sitting posture, one
    hot} = 0.
4.  state = INIT.
5.  Case (state)
6.  State_1: (PIR = 1)? Human available: state.
7.    Case (Human available)
8.    State_11: (Position values > Two Positions) Sleep posture: Sitting posture.
9.      Case (Sleep posture)
10.     State_1a: (Posture = 6′b111111)? Supine: State_1b.
11.     State_1b: (Posture = 6′bxx0101)? Right side posture: Left side posture.
12.     Case (Sitting posture)
13.      State_1as: (((Position && Time) = Static)? State static: Adaptive.
14.      Case (State static)
15.      State_a1: (Position = one hot)? State_a2: Aliasing_pose.
16.      State_a2: (Position = 6′dx)? Position Binary Classifier: state.
17.      Case (Aliasing_pose)
18.      State_b1: (Position = 6′dy)? Position Binary Classifier: state.
19.      Case (Adaptive)
20.      State_b11: if (count && CP == end position) begin
21.                   count && CP <= start position.
22.                     else {count <= count + 1, CP <= CP + 1}, {PP_n = CP}.
23.      State_b12: (count = 0)? State static: State_b14.
24.      State_b13: (CP = PP)? State static: State_b14.
25.      State_b14: (CP = PP_n)? Position Binary Classifier: State b15.
26. default: state = INIT.
27. end case, End.
```

The sitting pose was evaluated based on the sensor distance, and its position was vital to the service robot to analyze whether the subject is in a sitting posture at a static position; if the subject traverses from one position to another, it is considered as an adaptive sitting position, which has been evaluated based on the time and position parameters (line 13). Adaptive positions were evaluated using lines 19–25. The static pose positions depend on the coverage of the sensor fusion. The sensor coverage of sitting positions includes complete individual sensors and aliasing situations (sensing of more than one human sensor). Digital one-hot-based sensor fusion was evaluated for the subject position among the six positions on the bed. Positions were classified using a binary classifier (line 16).

In the aliasing situation, sensor fusion coverage with an encoded one-hot approach was embedded and classified using a position binary classifier (line 18).

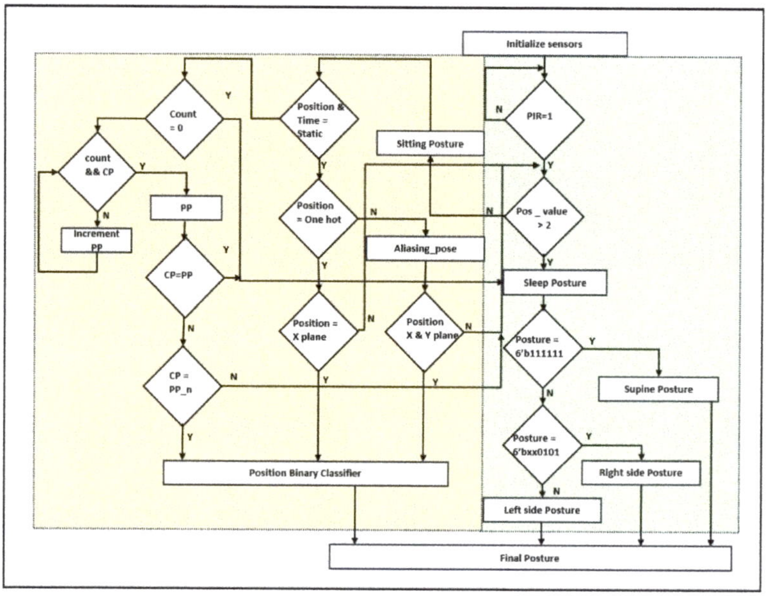


**Figure 2.** Flowchart for hardware-based human localization.

The hardware-based adaptive sitting position analysis is the first of its kind to provide better services using robots. Thus, the proposed method provides superior robotic services. Count, past position (PP), and current position (CP) are parameters for adaptive sitting position evaluation. The start position was initialized by sensors, and every step of the movement from one position to another position was recorded until the subject stopped moving (lines 20 to 22). Each stage's past position was memorized as PP_n, and the proportional adaptive time was registered as the count value. Adaptive current positioning was then classified and shared with the updated new position of the service robot (line 25). Table 2 presents the classification of the positions in the lines into a binary classifier using sensor fusion data.

**Table 2.** Sensor fusion data for human localization.

| Subject Seated at | Head_Right (HR) | Head_Left (HL) | Abdomen_Right (AR) | Abdomen_Left (AL) | Right Lower Limb_(RL) | Left Lower Limb_(LL) |
|---|---|---|---|---|---|---|
| Top position of right | 1 | 0 | 0 | 0 | 0 | 0 |
| Top position of left | 0 | 1 | 0 | 0 | 0 | 0 |
| Middle position of right | 0 | 0 | 1 | 0 | 0 | 0 |
| Middle position of left | 0 | 0 | 0 | 1 | 0 | 0 |
| Lower position of right | 0 | 0 | 0 | 0 | 1 | 0 |
| Lower position of left | 0 | 0 | 0 | 0 | 0 | 1 |
| Aliasing top of right | 1 | 0 | 1 | 0 | 0 | 0 |
| Aliasing top of head | 1 | 1 | 0 | 0 | 0 | 0 |
| Aliasing top of left | 0 | 1 | 0 | 1 | 0 | 0 |
| Aliasing middle of right | X | 0 | 1 | 0 | X | 0 |

Table 2. *Cont.*

| Subject Seated at | Head_Right (HR) | Head_Left (HL) | Abdomen_Right (AR) | Abdomen_Left (AL) | Right Lower Limb_(RL) | Left Lower Limb_(LL) |
|---|---|---|---|---|---|---|
| Aliasing middle of left | 0 | X | 0 | 1 | 0 | X |
| Aliasing lower of right | 0 | 0 | 1 | 0 | 1 | 0 |
| Aliasing lower of limbs | 0 | 0 | 0 | 0 | 1 | 1 |
| Aliasing lower of left | 0 | 0 | 0 | 1 | 0 | 1 |

### 2.1.2. Hardware-Based Adaptive SLAM

The proposed hardware-based adaptive Simultaneous Localization and Mapping (SLAM) was used to serve humans in an indoor environment. In robotics, localization and mapping are embedded in navigation systems. In the generic approach, the robot navigates to the destination early using robot navigation. In this process, SLAM plays a vital role in allowing the robot to continuously update its localization. Based on the obtained path, it plans to retain its route by mapping. When serving a human (subject), the subject changes from one portion of the bed to another. In this regard, the proposed adaptive SLAM approach was developed to serve adaptive situations according to human movement.

The proposed method was developed as a heuristic-type triangulation-based navigation algorithm to achieve an adaptive SLAM.

Figure 3 shows a service-based robot in an indoor environment, initially a robot at a parking station. As mentioned in Algorithm 2, the robot executes services based on task assignment. Standard services have been used during the COVID pandemic, such as service robots serving subjects (humans) in isolation/individual. Standard tasks include food and medical services along with standard timings. Simultaneously, the robot registers the tasks of either food or medical services. As presented in Algorithm 2, the robot is assigned to either a multitask or a single task in line 4. In the case of the multitask, the sorting of the path is performed using the bubble sort technique, and the robot traverses to the task point (line 7). SLAM retains its localization and is mapped in line with triangulation-based navigation. The task coordinates were registered and utilized until the task was completed. The path plan mapping was computed using the angles of the robot localization coordinates and task coordinates (lines 9–13).

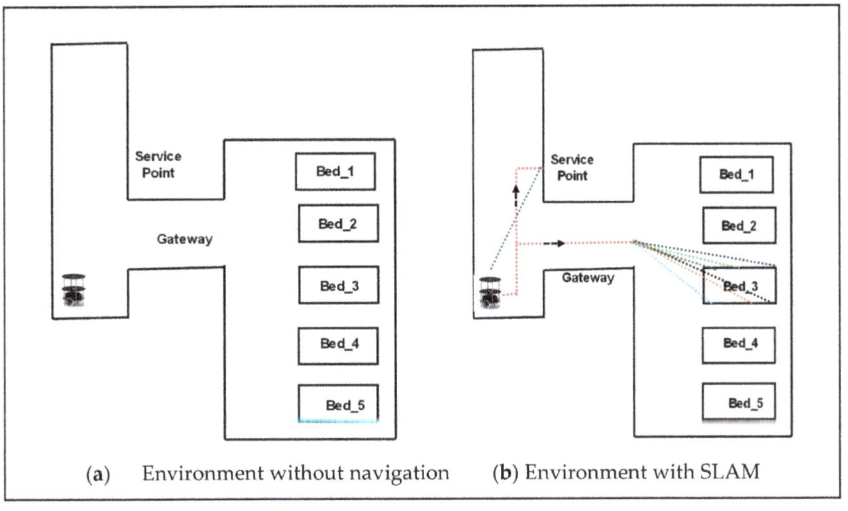


**Figure 3.** Triangulation-based navigation for service robots in an indoor environment. Different colored lines shows the representation of receiving signals from all sensors.

Adaptive SLAM was established once the robot received the delivery point (task destination) in the traversing mode. The robot adapts its path based on the adaptive movements of the subjects. If the subject moves to a new location, the robot can adapt the path and travel to deliver the item (lines 14 to 17). The explanation of Algorithm 2 is represented in the form of a flowchart, as shown in Figure 4. The use of triangulation navigation is shown in the lines presented in Figure 5. Triangulation navigation supports the performance of static and adaptive SLAM, as indicated by Algorithm 2. Figure 5 shows the subject in bed at various locations. Paths 3a and 3b are the shortest paths among the path distance weights when the robot navigates. Similarly, the longest distances for the robot navigating from the gateway to the destination of the task were paths 6a and 6b. The robot moves back using the same route that it has taken to accomplish the task until the endpoint of the gateway (i.e., the entrance gateway). It then transitions to the parking station if no other tasks are scheduled. If any task is assigned, Algorithm 2 follows.

**Algorithm 2:** Pseudo code of hardware based Adaptive SLAM for robotic services

```
1.   Service Robot (S_R) initialize services and ready at parking station.
2.   If (Task assigned)
3.   Case (Task type)
4.   State_1: (Task type = Multitask)? State_2: Static SLAM.
5.   State_2: (Task sort)? Task destination: Task sort.
6.   Case (Task_destination)
7.   State_11: (Task_destination = Static Task sort _n)? State_12: Accomplished.
8.   State_12: (Task_destination = Adaptive Task)? Adaptive SLAM: SLAM static.
9.   Case (Static SLAM)
10.     State_SS1: (Navigation sort_n = Task_destination_n)? Accomplished: State_SS2.
11.     State_SS2: if (Current Node == Dest_ Node) begin
12.                    Current Node <= start position.
13.                    else {Current Node <= Current Node + 1}.
14.  Case (Adaptive SLAM)
15.     State_AS1: (Adaptive task)? Task assigned <= Adaptive task: Task_destination.
16.     State_AS2: (Adaptive task sort)? State_AS3: State_AS2.
17.     State_AS3: (Task destination <= Task sort)? Static SLAM: State_AS3.
18.     end case, End.
```

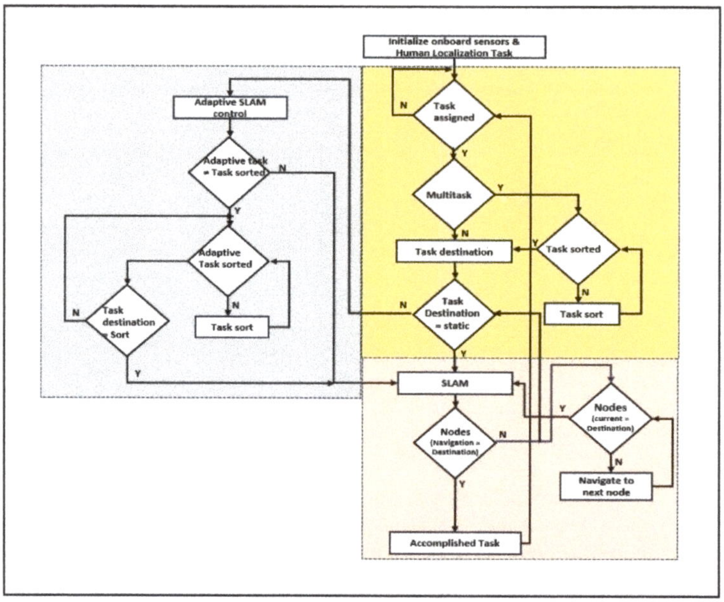


**Figure 4.** Flowchart for adaptive SLAM for robotic services.

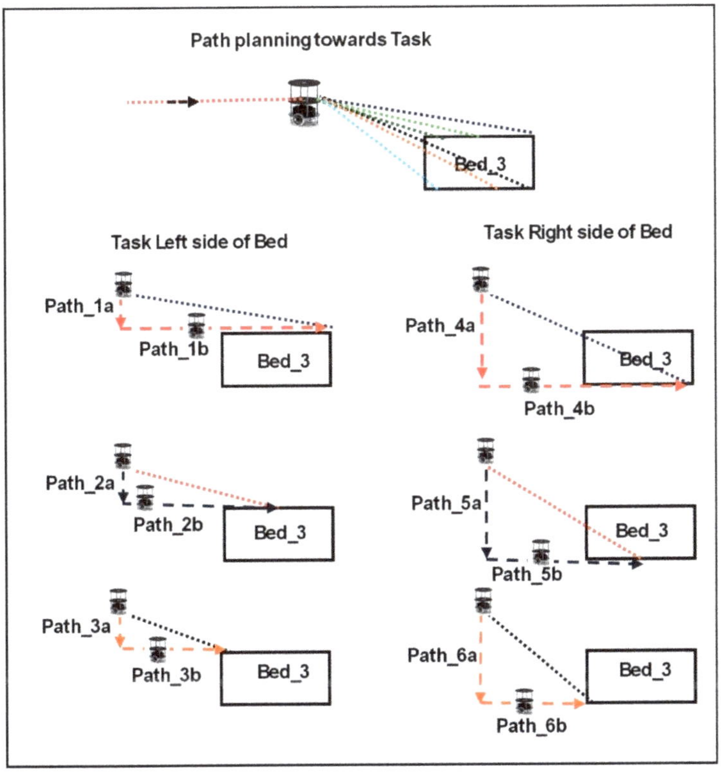


**Figure 5.** Path planning of service robots based on task in an indoor environment with different colors.

## 3. Hardware Schemes for Human–Robot Interaction in an Indoor Environment

Section 3 deals with FPGA-based accelerators that are equivalent to accomplishing the proposed hardware-based algorithms for human–robot interactions. Concurrently, human and robot localization has been confined to different reconfigurable devices. The robot continuously receives static or adaptive human localization because it navigates to the destination using the triangulation approach.

### *3.1. Hardware Accelerator for Human–Robot Interaction*

The proposed hardware accelerator is versatile for human–service robot interactions, as illustrated in Figure 6. It was integrated with human localization, robot localization, and navigation. In this research, two FPGA reconfigurable edge computing devices were incorporated; the first of these was for the human, and the other was for the robot. The pose control unit (PCU) is a part of the FPGA position for evaluating human localization. This is performed using the lines in Algorithm 1. Initially, the algorithm was triggered based on the PIR sensor information. Human availability was evaluated using PIR, which enables human localization computations. Six ultrasonic sensors {SH_R, SH_L, SA_R, SA_L, SR_L, and SL_L} were positioned on the roof to capture the human localization on the bed. These sensors were triggered by the PCU, and echo signals were captured and digitized at a distance from the sensor-distance fusion module. It is compiled with all the 20-bit sensor distances in the fusion with respect to the event conditions. Human localization was performed with five Processing Elements (PEs): sleep posture, static sitting position, adaptive sitting position, aliasing sitting position, and position binary classifier. The PCU verifies the classification of the subject during sleep or in the sitting position. Under these conditions, humans are versatile in the sitting position. If the subject is at one position until the robot begins its services, it is considered as a static position with six-bit information. Under certain conditions, the subject is positioned between two or three sensor coverage areas, and the subject is considered to be in an aliasing sitting position. This was addressed based on the maximum position zone. The adaptive sitting position evaluates the change in position by the participant with respect to time. All positions were evaluated using a position binary classifier and shared with the other end-edge computing device for human localization using ESP8266. It is operated at 9600 baud rates with the UART protocol to transmit the human localization details continuously.

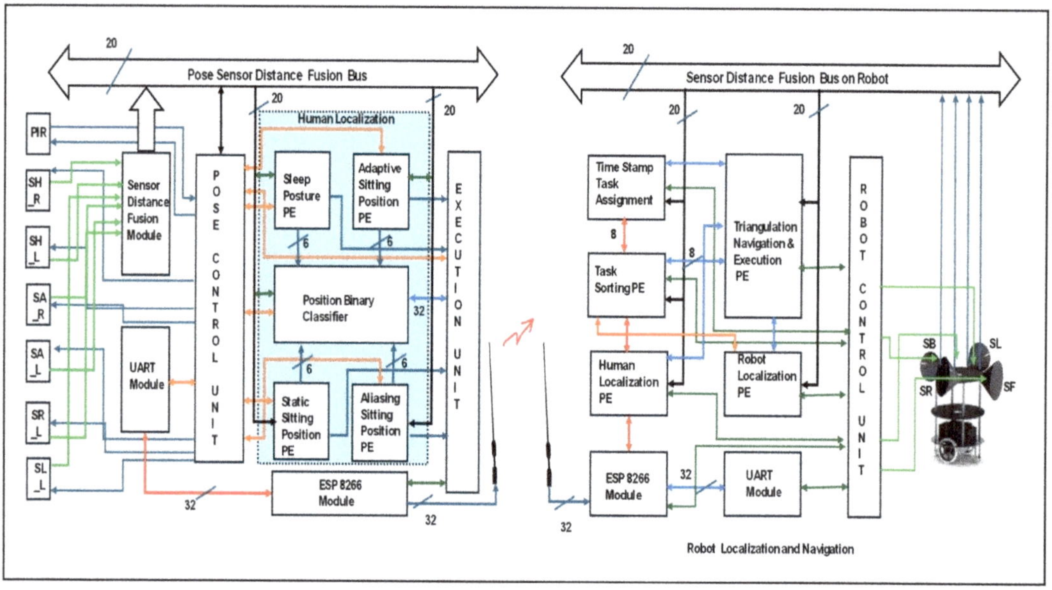


**Figure 6.** Overall hardware accelerator for human–robot interaction.

An FPGA reconfigurable edge computing device was placed on the robot. It operates according to Algorithm 2. Four ultrasonic sensors {SF, SL, SR, and SB} were used on board to sense the environment. A Robot Control Unit (RCU) plays a vital role under various conditions. It triggers all the sensors and the communication module ESP8266. The proposed service robot was assigned a task based on its timestamp. For example, a robot can serve diabetic tablets based on the time at which the human wakes up from sleep (evaluated based on human movements). All services are registered in DDR3 memory. The AXI lite protocol was used to drive the data from memory. The pickup nodes were registered as tasks. Task sorting is in the sleep module for a regular navigation path until the human is positioned at a new location on the bed, compared to the previous destination task. Task-sorting PE has been revamping route nodes with mapping as per the human localization PE. Rerouted mapping nodes were provided to the navigation module. Robot localization is another parallel task that self-evaluates an edge device by using sensory information. Navigation develops a route according to the task nodes and robot localization using triangulation-based navigation approaches. Simultaneous Localization and Mapping (SLAM) was performed with 20-bit sensor distances and their fusion along with continuous destination task estimation.

### 3.2. *Hardware Schemes for Human Localization*

Figure 7 presents the detailed human localization information with internal architectures. The ultrasonic sensors were operated at a 40 KHz frequency and captured at a rate of 1/8 s. Distance data fusion was captured and stored in FIFO {H_R to L_L}. Prior to normalizing the six sensors' distance as 6′bxxxxxx, it had been decoded as in the sleep position. For Sitting position at different levels, the sensory digital value is given as '1' when it is in the availability range. Otherwise, this value is '0'. The sampling data are presented in Table 2. These data were used to classify either sleep or sitting postures using a pose-selection encoder. Sleep postures have been presented. There are more than two positions and the sensor data logic value is '1'. Then, it enables the sleep posture PE. Sensor data have been compared with the reference FIFO data on sleep posture, including supine posture (SP), left-side posture (LP), and right-side posture (RP), and they are encoded and transferred to the position binary classifier.

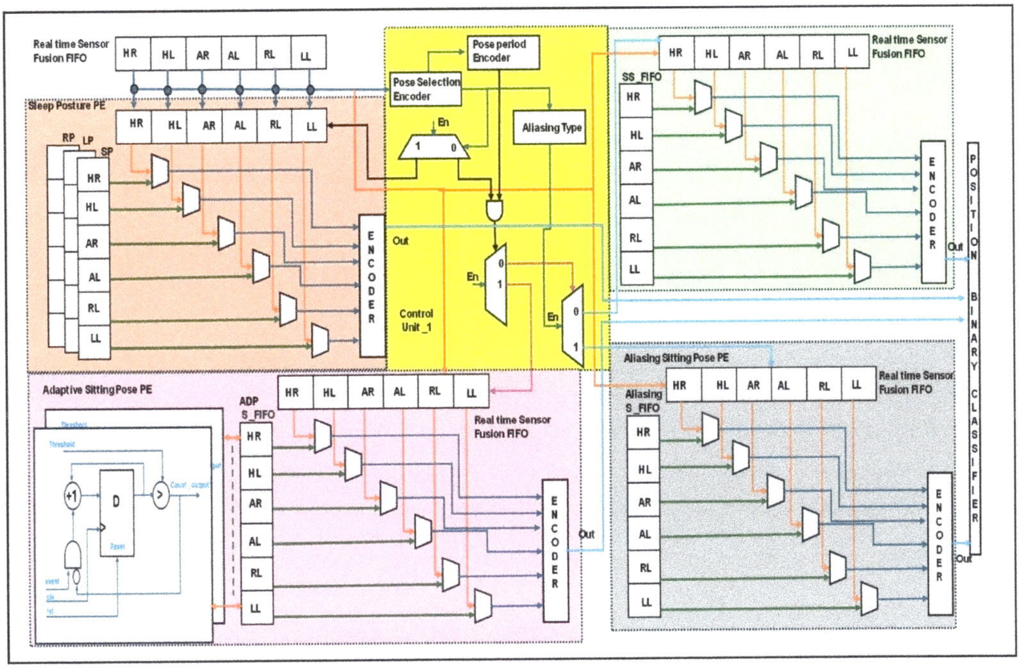


**Figure 7.** Internal architecture of the human localization process.

A pose-period encoder distinguishes between static and adaptive position modules. The static position has been presented in two ways: the static sitting pose PE and aliasing sitting pose PE. In the static sitting position PE, real-time sensor data were compared with the reference FIFO position. Similarly, aliasing and adaptive approaches have been used. To replace the sitting PE, an encoder was designed along the logic computation module. The logic computation module normalizes the aliasing coverage data with the adjacent higher grouping logic '1'. e.g., when HR = 1, HL = 1, and AR = 1 is 6′b111000, the subject is sitting in the cross mode between the left and right sides of the bed. Normalization confines the subject's position to the right side of the bed. The adaptive position was confined to the pose period and the array of sensor data were compared. For example, if the subject initially sat at the HR, the sensor data weere presented as 6′b100000 at time T. It compares the subject's movement from one position to another over time. The same is true for the PBC module. In this case, T + 1 with 6′b001000 and T + 2 with 6′b000010 indicate moving around the right side of the bed. Finally, the human was positioned at the right-limb coverage spot (RL). The relative information is shared with a binary classifier, and human localization is provided to the robot through IoT communication. The position binary classifier has been continuously evaluated in lines [32,33] of the binary search.

### 3.3. Hardware Schemes of Robot Localization and Triangulation-Based Navigation

Figure 8 shows the internal hardware schemes for robot localization and navigation.

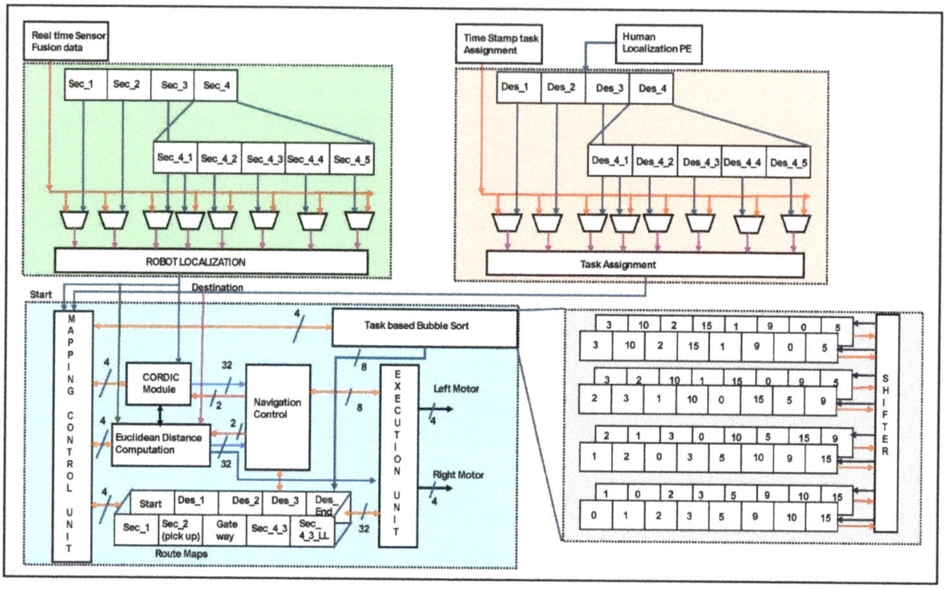


**Figure 8.** Hardware scheme robot localization and triangulation-based navigation.

The real time sensor data of robot localization is represented in red color lines where as human localization is represented in blue color. The processing of data inside the architecture is represented in different colors. The environments were sectioned into sectors (sec_1... sec_n). Each sector was divided into multilevel sectors, e.g., sec_4 into sec_4_1 to sec_4_n. Robot localization was performed by comparing the real-time sensor fusion data and the location of the reference sector (s _1 to s _4_5). Human localization PE provides the destination of the human position, which is used for the assigned task. Every node has been considered a destination, and all sub-destinations (Des_1... Des_4_5) are routed to the end destination (Des-end), which has been assigned as the task. Concurrently, the time-stamp task assignment is aligned with human localization PE as a task assignment. The assigned tasks were sorted according to bubble sorting techniques. A task-based bubble sorting technique was constructed using eight register arrays and shifters. Four clock cycles were used to obtain the task-based sorted information. The information was shared with the mapping control unit to develop the route maps. Route maps were established based on triangulation-based navigation using a CORDIC IP core. The robot localization output is driven into the CORDIC and Euclidean distance computation modules. Triangulation computation inherent modules are CORDIC, which have been computed with 32 bits for the angles and their square root of distance calculation. Based on the task sort, information route maps were registered as static routes and adapted for routing in SLAM lines. Euclidean distance computation is performed with the two-bit navigation control and it estimates the distance with 32 bits between two nodes. The same procedure was performed by mapping the control unit to update the route maps. As shown in Figure 5, CORDIC and Euclidean provide an accurate distance to travel by the robot. The longest route from the gateway to the destination in the service sector is on the right side of the bed at the HR sensor-coverage node. Concurrently, an on-board reconfigurable computing device provides distances as paths 4a and 4b. The travel distance was evaluated using an odometer-based soft code as part of the execution unit. The execution controls the left and right motors of the robot with four bits each (two-bit acceleration control and two-bit direction).

## 4. Results

The proposed human–robot interaction was developed with FPGA-based accelerators. Human localization was evaluated at one edge of the FPGA device, and the robot on the other side on board was directed to the right destination (human positions) under both static, adaptive, and even driven conditions. The validation of the proposed algorithms is discussed in Section 2 and the hardware schemes are discussed in Section 3. The results were obtained with resource utilization at both ends along with power consumption. An experimental setup was established as a platform for validating the proposed algorithm in the form of experimental studies.

### 4.1. Resource Utilization

The proposed HRI utilizes Xilinx products from the Xilinx University program. The hardware accelerator proposed in Section 3 was developed with equivalent code by using Verilog HDL and was tailored as per the proposed HRI. The functional verification of the system was performed using the Xilinx simulator; Xilinx tools were used for the synthesis and implementation steps.

The reconfigurable devices are part of the Xilinx Zynq family, and their design has been mentioned by Xilinx (San Jose, CA, USA) as an XC7Z020-1CSG484 Zed board. The proposed approach utilizes the processing system (PS) to capture time-stamped tasks while executing the services. Control logic and interfacing were performed using the programming logic (PL) of the zed-board device. PS and PL were interfaced at the system level using the AXI lite protocol for synchronization at the complete system level. The Block RAM (BRAM) (140 blocks, 36 kb equal to 4.9 Mb) and 220 Digital Signal Processing (DSP) slices were on the zed board, which has been utilized to a certain extent to pursue this method.

Resources are consumed in the execution of human localization, as mentioned in Table 3, and robot localization and navigation are listed in Table 4. Among the computing methods, edge computation provides the fastest and most accurate method; FPGA reconfigurable devices consume less power and perform concurrently [34–36]. FPGAs for HRI solutions are the first to provide solutions under adaptive position–event conditions. Consumption in an FPGA was evaluated using lookup table (LUT), Block RAM (BRAM), and Digital Signal Processing (DSP) slices. Human localization consumed LUT (48%), BRAM (42%), and DSP slices (38%). Similarly, robot localization and navigation were used for LUT (57%), BRAM (46%), and DSP slices (39%).

**Table 3.** FPGA resource utilization for human localization accelerator on Zed board.

| Module | LUT | BRAM | DSP Slice |
|---|---|---|---|
| External modules and pose control unit | 5246 | 14 | 22 |
| Sleep posture PE | 2714 | 06 | 08 |
| Position binary classifier PE | 1846 | 06 | 10 |
| Adaptive sitting position PE | 6330 | 18 | 18 |
| Static and aliasing sitting position PE | 4702 | 08 | 16 |
| Execution modules, UART, and display | 4342 | 6 | 08 |
| Total | 25180 | 58 | 82 |

**Table 4.** FPGA resource utilization for robot localization and navigation accelerator on Zed board.

| Module | LUT | BRAM | DSP Slice |
|---|---|---|---|
| External modules and robot control unit | 5246 | 14 | 22 |
| Human localization PE | 4404 | 10 | 12 |
| Task assignment and sort PE | 3916 | 12 | 10 |
| Robot localization PE | 5140 | 08 | 18 |
| Triangulation navigation PE | 7268 | 14 | 16 |
| Execution modules, UART, and display | 4342 | 6 | 08 |
| Total | 30,316 | 64 | 86 |

Figures 9 and 10 show the details of the consumption of each module as percentages. The adaptive sitting position PE for human localization and triangulation navigation PE for service robot implementation consumed the highest resource utilization. The architectures of service robot localization and navigation-based adaptive target positions were deployed in the FPGA and are presented in Figure 8. Table 3 and Figure 9 illustrate human localization resource utilization. Control units and interfacing implicit communication modules, such as UART, are consumed, as described above. The resource utilization of the other modules was as follows: sleep posture PE (11%, 10%, and 10%), position binary classifier PE (8%, 10%, and 12%), adaptive sitting position PE (25%, 31%, and 22%), and static and aliasing sitting positions PE (18%, 14%, and 20%). Similarly, Table 4 and Figure 10 show the device consumption as LUT, BRAM, and DSP slices of FPGA-based robots, such as the external modules and robot control unit (17%, 22%, and 25%), human localization PE (15%, 16%, and 14%), task assignment and sort PE (13%, 19%, and 12%), robot localization PE (17%, 12%, and 21%), triangulation navigation PE (24%, 22%, and 19%), and execution modules, UART, and display (14%, 10%, and 9%).

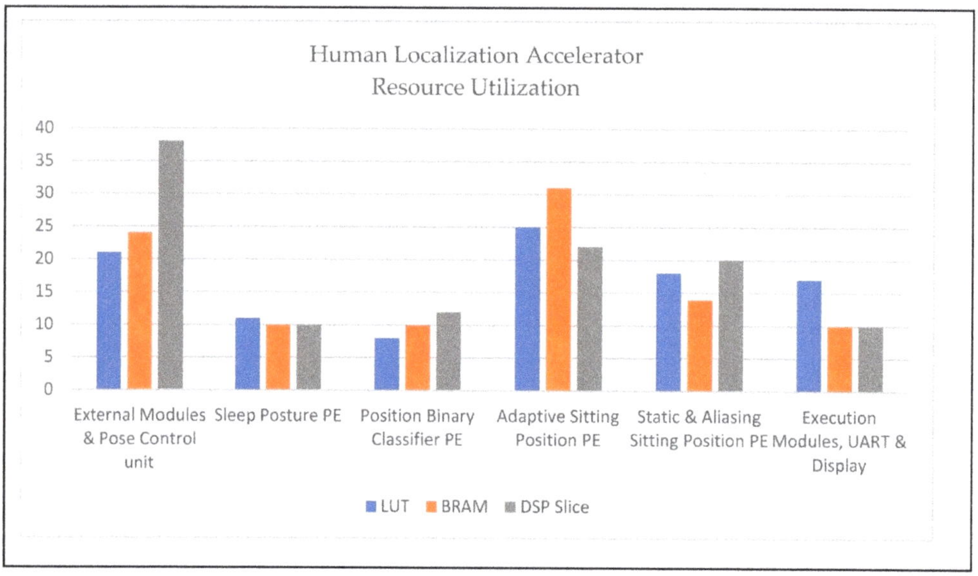


**Figure 9.** Resource utilization of human localization accelerator.

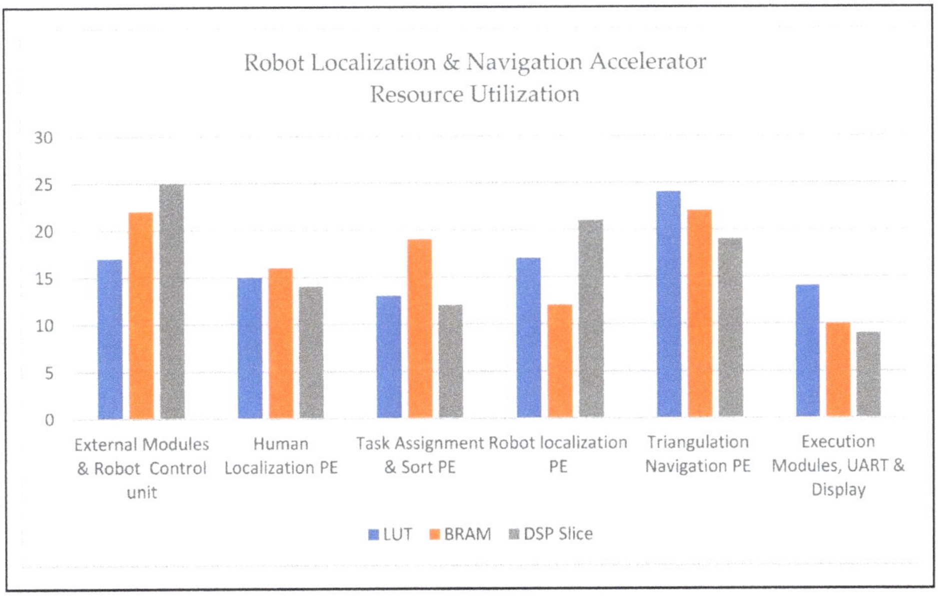


**Figure 10.** Resource utilization of robot localization and navigation accelerator.

Figure 11 illustrates the power consumption of a human localization accelerator of 1.2 watts. The power consumption was registered using the Xilinx power estimation tool. The power consumption details of each hardware module are provided in percentage form in the pie chart in Figure 11. The adaptive sitting PE consumed 27% power; compared to other modules in human localization tasks, this value is high. The power consumption details of the other modules were as follows: pose control (23%), PE (18%), position binary classifier PE (12%), static and aliasing sitting PE (14%), and execution (6%).

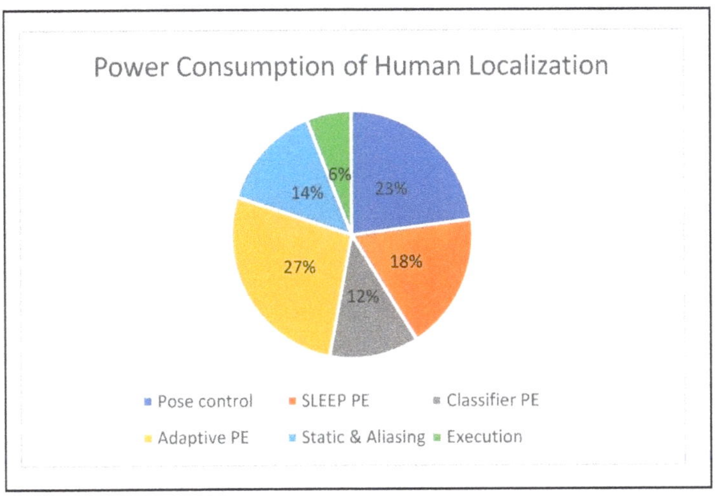


**Figure 11.** Device power consumption of human localization accelerator.

Figure 12 shows the power consumption of the service-based robot localization and navigation accelerator. The overall device consumes 1.8 watts of power and presents the consumption of each module in percentage form, whereas the control unit and execution consume the same amount of power. The preferred tool is XPE, and the power consumption of each module is as follows: human localization (12%), task assignment and sorting (16%), data driven from the PS through the AXI protocol, robot localization (18%), and triangulation-based navigation PE (25%). Triangulation PE consumes more power than the other modules on the FPGA-based robots. The interfacing and control unit modules had the second highest share of power consumption.

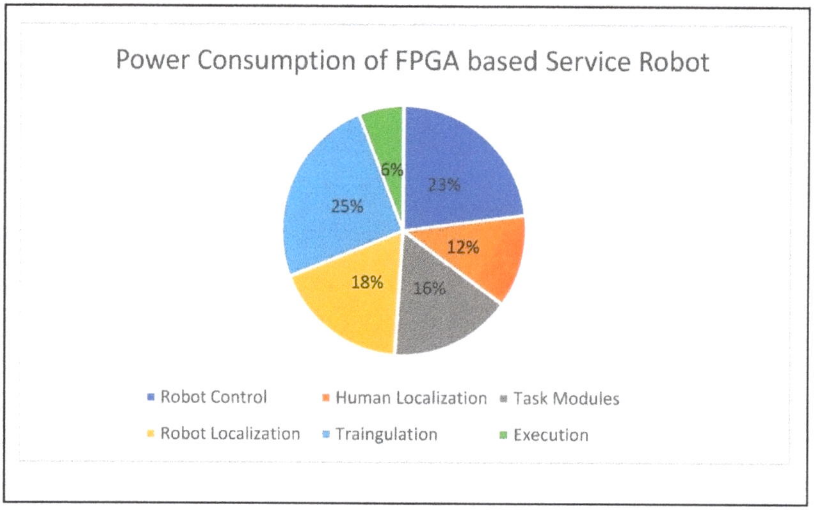


**Figure 12.** Device power consumption of service-based robot localization and navigation accelerator.

## 4.2. *Experimental Results*

This section describes the experimental setup for human and robot interactions based on their localization under static and adaptive conditions.

### 4.2.1. Experimental Setup

Figure 13 presents the experimental setup with two parts: one regarding the human posture and position analysis setup and another regarding the service-type FPGA-based robot. The human localization process is illustrated in Figure 13a,b. The service-based robot is shown in Figure 13c. A real-time experimental setup was used for the proposed hardware-based algorithms validated with the experimental setup in Figure 14a–d. Figure 14a shows the sensor coverage bed for capturing the human posture and positions. Figure 14b presents the human reverse supine sleep posture and the subject in the HL sensor coverage area in Figure 14c. The other subject was positioned in the RL sensor coverage area at the same time as the robot travelled to serve the subject.

Both experimental setups were embedded with ultrasonic sensors to capture human positions and explore the environment. The major experimental setups are sensing devices and other auxiliary devices such as a digital compass and PIR. The ultrasonic sensors were operated at 40 KHz and 5 volts, and the sensor array was operated using FPGA control units. A digital compass was deployed on the FPGA-based service robot to estimate the angles, which was also applied to CORDIC. Implicit communication was performed between the two devices using the ESP8266 Wi-Fi modules operated at a baud rate of 9600. The main unit in the proposed method is the FPGA. Xilinx-manufactured FPGAs are edge-computing devices, as mentioned in Section 4.1. The other parts of the robot experiment were embedded with two driven wheels and driving circuits, based on the control logic received from the triangulation-based navigation algorithm module. This is operated with driving circuits with LED acid batteries at 24 V/7 Amp. These batteries are charged every 6 h, and the operational time can be improved by replacing it with new battery technology. The FPGA and sensors are powered around 3.3–5 V from batteries through voltage regulators using 7805 IC modules. Figure 14c,d show the experimental details about the proposed hardware approaches. The robot frame was developed in in-house by local design experts. The robot frame has three layers: a bottom layer with batteries and voltage regulators, a middle layer with computational devices, and a layer on top of the service robot where service modules were positioned.

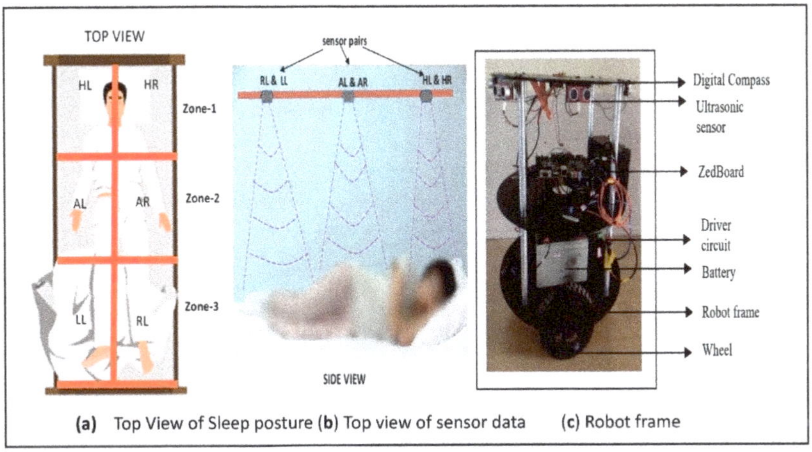


**Figure 13.** Human and robot interaction experimental setup.

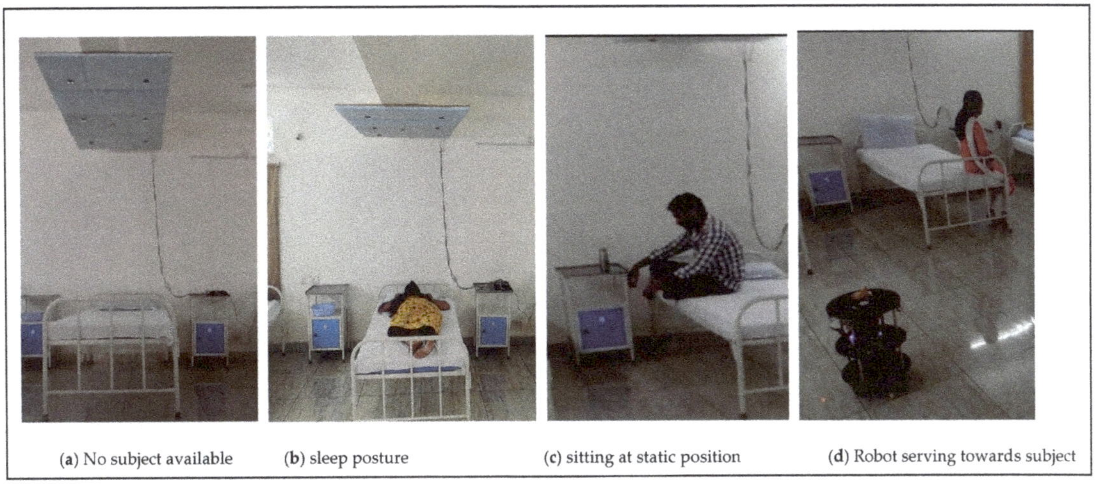


**Figure 14.** Real-time experimental setup of human and robot interaction.

4.2.2. Experimental Results of Human and Robot Interaction at Static Position

The FPGA-based robot services towards human localization at static positions are shown in Figure 15a–h. The versatile approach of the proposed method is that duo FPGAs are performed concurrently and communicate regularly through IoT modules. The FPGA-based robot initially triggered it to navigate from the parking point with respect to the timestamp task assignment, as illustrated in Figure 15a. Implicit communication has continued with the human localization analysis of FPGA accelerator devices.

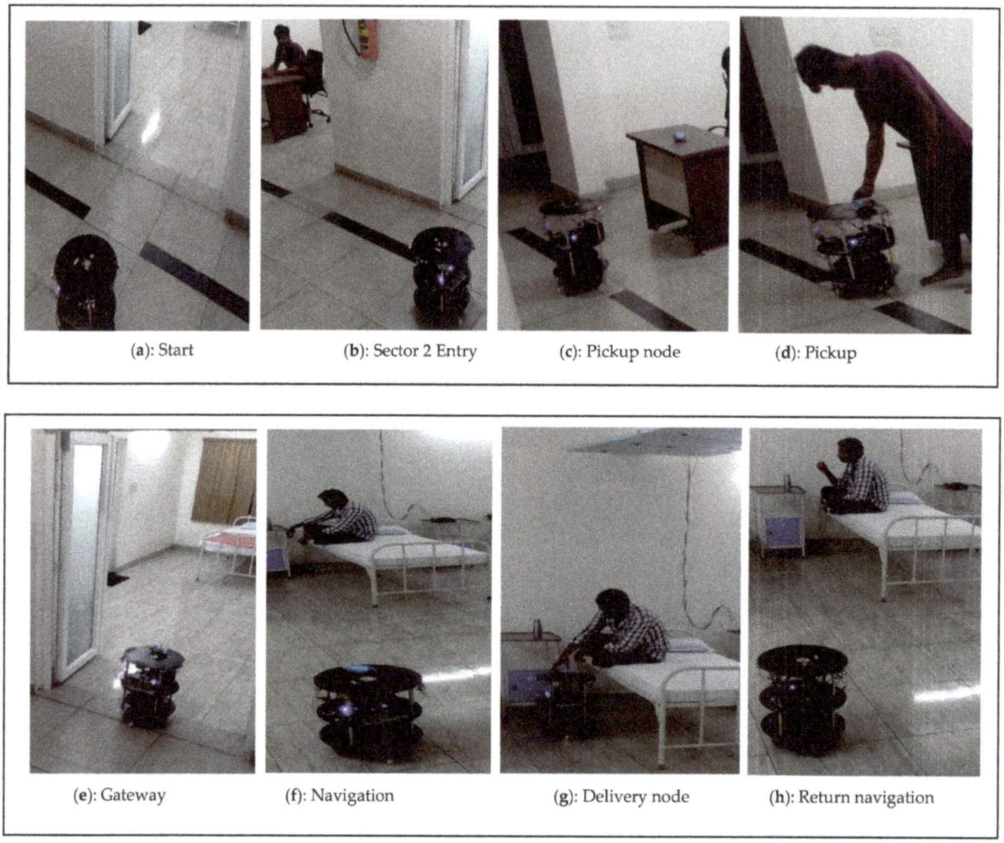


**Figure 15.** (**a–d**) Demonstration results of robot navigation from parking to pick up. (**e–h**) Demonstration results of human and robot interaction at static position.

The navigation was performed in lines of TNA to pick up the food/medicine drives towards sector 2, as presented in Figure 15b. The navigation in sector 2 continued until the pickup node was reached (Figure 15c) and the robot waits until the human positioned the food (PIR and ultrasonic sensor signal patterns were evaluated) on the robot (Figure 15d). The mapping module in Figure 8 provides a route map for navigating from sector 2 to sector 3 (gateway). Robotic turns are continuously evaluated by the CORDIC modules, and the distance to travel is provided by the Euclidean distance for successful navigation. Robot localization and self-positioning, along with kinematics and movements, are operated with robot control, and the positions are corrected based on the TNA with CORDIC modules.

The robot navigates from the gateway entry (Figure 15e) to sector 4 (Figure 15f) of the delivery bed and human localization. Based on human localization, a route map was mapped, and SLAM was performed using TNA to reach the destination point, as shown in Figure 15g. Similar to the pickup node, the human pattern identification of the subject indicated that food and medicine were collected. The proposed environment was considered ethical and not false or misleading in the collection of foods/medicines by the subjects. The FPGA-based robot returned from the delivery node to the parking station using a reroute with similar mapping techniques, as shown in Figure 15h. The return navigation by the FPGA adapts the mapping modules and TNA to reach the parking station. When the continuous task assignment continues to the robot, it is performed according to the assignments. In this approach, the delivery modes are inclined toward first-come, first-serve methods.

The static human-position-based services provided by the FPGA-based robot demonstration are as follows: https://www.youtube.com/watch?v=xIjKWfpmPIU (accessed on 25 September 2024).

#### 4.2.3. Experimental Results of Human and Robot Interaction at Adaptive Position

A demonstration of the adaptive-based position service by the FPGA-based robot is shown in Figure 16a–h. Similar to the previous experiment, it starts and collects the essential material from the pickup node (Figure 16a) and the navigates through gateway (Figure 16b). Adaptive human localization was initially observed at the HL sensor coverage area (Figure 16c). When the subject is in continuous motion, the human localization-side FPGA shares information with the FPGA-based robot. In this study, we considered coverage up to 50 cm from the bed. This coverage was provided to avoid false positives during the inference stage using the proposed method. The FPGA-based robot adapts to adaptive human localization, and proportional adaptive SLAM was performed (Figure 16e). In this demonstration, the subject reached the destination node as the RL coverage point (Figure 16f). The time duration was recorded to determine the rate of speed of the subject switching from one sensor to another, and the proportional total duration captured from the HL to RL nodes was 14.20 s. The robot moves from the delivery point to the parking station/next task point (Figure 16g,h). The experimental results are as follows: https://www.youtube.com/watch?v=cPasjy0F528&t=14s (accessed on 25 September 2024).

Table 5 presents a qualitative analysis comparing the contributions of various studies in this field of interest. Adaptive human localization-based services using autonomous robots have drawn attention owing to their effectiveness. In this regard, researchers are working on analyzing subject/human posture position groups [20,37–39]. Other robotics have been developed to serve subjects with different interaction methods, using face recognition and other methods. The integration of both ends has been attempted by very few researchers [40,41]. The proposed research contribution involves integrating both human localization and FPGA-based robot services; it is first of its kind to use adaptive-based robot services. FPGA edge computation provides better results than the other computation methods at the inference level [30].

The edge device clock frequency = 100 MHz, voltage applied for the device = 3.3 V, switching capacitance = 4.41 PF, dynamic power (P_dynamic) = 0.96 W, static power (P_static) = 0.24 W, and total power consumed for human localization is 1.2 W. The number of pipeline stages in hardware (S) is eight, clock time (Tclk) is 10 ns, and latency per iteration (S × Tclk) is 80 ns. The total number of iterations (N) was 30, and the total latency as (N + S − 1) × Tclk was 370 ns. The number of correct predictions was 29 and the total number of predictions was 30. The resulting accuracy was 98.4% and the error rate was 1.6%.

$$\text{Accuracy} = \frac{No\ of\ Correct\ Predictions}{Total\ Prediction} \times 100 = 98.4\% \tag{1}$$

$$\text{Error} = 1 - \frac{No\ of\ Correct\ Predictions}{Total\ Prediction} \times 100 = 1 - \frac{29}{30} = 1.6\% \tag{2}$$

The average response time for each path is represented as static in Figure 17 and adaptive in Figure 18. The time responses are the same up to the early delivery node, based on the Euclidean distance triangulation navigation towards various nodes around the bed. The return response time was the critical return time. The average response time of adaptive human–robot interaction (HRI) presents adaptive human localization and robot navigation. The adaptive response time changes when humans move from node1 to node4; its critical path and time response is 5 min 10 s.

**Table 5.** Comparison of human and robot interaction with relevant research methods.

| Reference Papers | Sensory Approach | | Algorithm | Hardware | Number of Postures/Position | Pros | Accuracy | Cons |
|---|---|---|---|---|---|---|---|---|
| | Method | Fusion | | | | | | |
| Q. Hu et al. 2021 [20] | 1024 sensors Pressure sensor | Yes | HOG, SVM, and CNN | Arduino Nano and CPU | 6 | <400 ms, sampling and processing | 86.94% to 91.24% | Contact approach |
| Matar et al. 2020 [37] | 1728 FSR sensors | Yes | HOG + LBP, FFANN | CPU | 4 | Health monitoring | 97% | More usage of sensors |
| R. Tapwal et al. 2023 [38] | Two flex force sensors | Yes | K-means | Arduino Uno and CPU | 4 | Health monitoring | ~99.3% | consumes 17.5 W, contact approach |
| Hu, D et al. 2024 [39] | 32 Piezoelectric sensor | Yes | $S^3$CNN | N/A | 4 | Effectively detects nuanced pressure disturbances | 93.0% | not applicable |
| Y. Tanaka et al. 2020 [40] | Camera | No | Amygdala | FPGA | – | Interaction with subject based face recognition | >90% | not applicable |
| T.Kim et al. 2024 [41] | Multi sensors and Camera | Yes | DFS, 3D routes, Vision algorithms | Intel NUC and Nvidia Jetson Xavier | | Multi floor service and mapping | N/A | Costlier in implementation |
| Proposed | 10 Ultrasonic sensors | Yes | Human Localization, Triangulation Navigation algorithm | FPGA | | Parallel computing, <200 ns, sampling, and computation. Adaptive localization-based robot services | 98.4% | PR flow will be preferred in future usage |

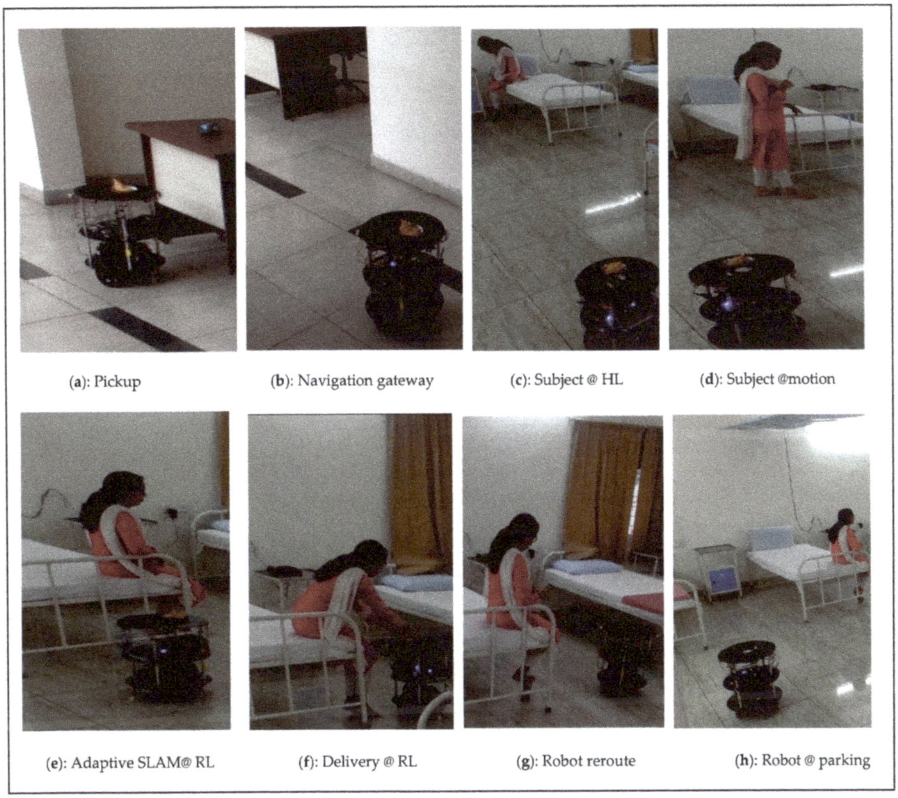


**Figure 16.** (**a**–**h**) Demonstration results of human and robot interaction at adaptive position.

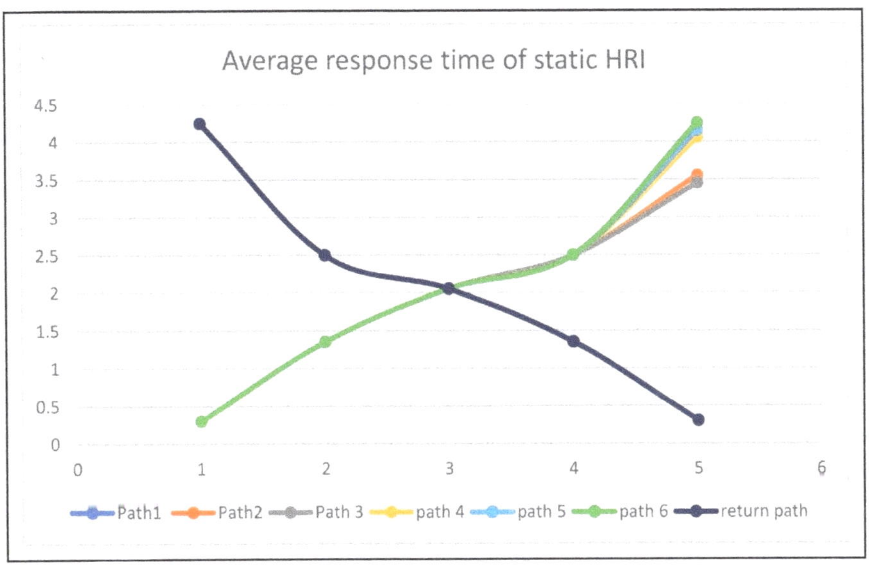


**Figure 17.** Average response time of human–robot interaction at static conditions.

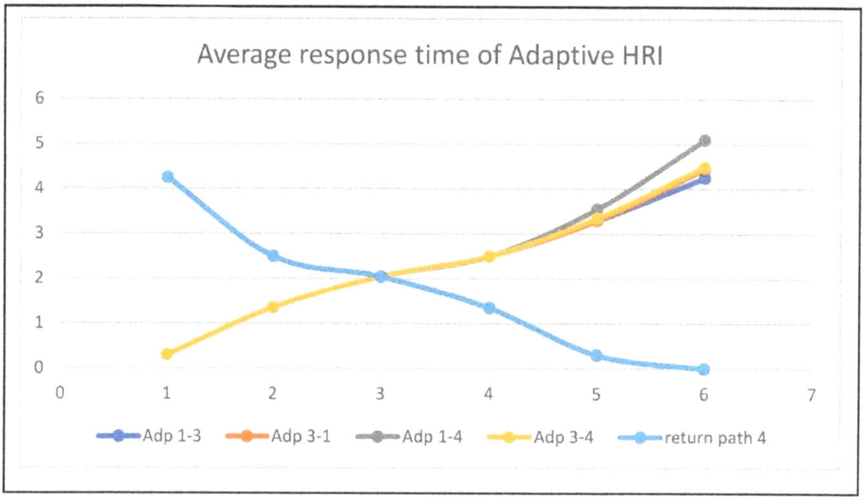


**Figure 18.** Average response time of human–robot interaction at adaptive conditions.

## 5. Conclusions

In this article, we presented a service-based human–robot interaction system in healthcare environments. The proposed methodology successfully addresses a solution for human–robot interactions in delivering a task by analyzing adaptive human positions in a static or dynamic manner. FPGA-based accelerators have been developed as key solutions to address the challenges in healthcare assistance. Equivalent hardware accelerators were developed and deployed on a Xilinx FPGA XC7Z020-1CSG484 Zed board. The resource utilization of the proposed HRI for a human localization accelerator on a Zed board consumes 48%, 42%, and 38% for the LUT, BRAM, and DSP slices, respectively. Similarly, the robot localization and navigation consumed 57%, 46%, and 39% of the LUT, BRAM, and DSP slices, respectively. The device power consumption of the human localization accelerator is 1.2 watts and that of the service-based robot localization and navigation accelerator is 1.8 watts. The proposed human localization and triangulation navigation algorithm with parallel computing provided 98.4% accuracy compared with previous methods. In the future, the proposed method could be integrated with partial reconfigurations for multi-tasking services.

**Author Contributions:** Conceptualization, S.K.G., M.C.C., S.-K.L., G.D.V., N.J. and S.D.; methodology, M.S., S.K.G., M.C.C., S.-K.L. and S.D.; validation, M.S., M.C.C., G.D.V., M.B., D.H.K. and N.J.; writing—original draft preparation, M.S., M.C.C., S.K.G., M.B., D.H.K. and S.-K.L.; writing—review and editing, M.C.C., S.-K.L., S.K.G., G.D.V., N.J. and S.D. All authors have read and agreed to the published version of the manuscript.

**Funding:** This research received no external funding.

**Institutional Review Board Statement:** Not applicable.

**Informed Consent Statement:** Not applicable.

**Data Availability Statement:** Data are contained within the article.

**Acknowledgments:** The EDA Tool and FPGA hardware were supported by the B V Raju Institute of Technology, Medak (Dist.), Narsapur.

**Conflicts of Interest:** The authors declare no conflicts of interest.

## References


1. Koumakis, L.; Chatzaki, C.; Kazantzaki, E.; Maniadi, E.; Tsiknakis, M. Dementia Care Frameworks and Assistive Technologies for Their Implementation: A Review. *IEEE Rev. Biomed. Eng.* **2019**, *12*, 4–18. [CrossRef] [PubMed]
2. Wu, C.; Yang, Z.; Zhou, Z.; Liu, X.; Liu, Y.; Cao, J. Non-Invasive Detection of Moving and Stationary Human with Wi-Fi. *IEEE J. Sel. Areas Commun.* **2015**, *33*, 2329–2342. [CrossRef]
3. Senaratna, C.V.; Perret, J.L.; Lodge, C.J.; Lowe, A.J.; Campbell, B.E.; Matheson, M.C.; Hamilton, G.S.; Dharmage, S.C. Prevalence of obstructive sleep apnea in the general population: A systematic review. *Sleep Med. Rev.* **2017**, *34*, 70–81. [CrossRef]
4. Zafari, F.; Gkelias, A.; Leung, K. A Survey of Indoor Localization Systems and Technologies. *IEEE Commun. Surv. Tutor.* **2019**, *21*, 2568–2599. [CrossRef]
5. Global AI in Health-Care Market Analysis Overview. Available online: https://radixweb.com/blog/ai-in-healthcare-statistics (accessed on 14 September 2024).
6. Liu, S.; Huang, X.; Marcenaro, L.; Ostadabbas, S. Privacy-Preserving in-Bed Human Pose Estimation: Highlights from the IEEE Video and Image Processing Cup 2021 Student Competition [SP Competitions]. *IEEE Signal Process. Mag.* **2022**, *39*, 121–129. [CrossRef]
7. Fallmann, S.; Chen, L. Computational Sleep Behavior Analysis: A Survey. *IEEE Access* **2019**, *7*, 142421–142440. [CrossRef]
8. Leelaarporn, P.; Wachiraphan, P.; Kaewlee, T.; Udsa, T.; Chaisaen, R.; Choksatchawathi, T.; Laosirirat, R.; Lakhan, P.; Natnithikarat, P.; Thanontip, K.; et al. Sensor-Driven Achieving of Smart Living: A Review. *IEEE Sens. J.* **2021**, *21*, 10369–10391. [CrossRef]
9. Lluvia, I.; Lazkano, E.; Ansuategi, A. Active Mapping and Robot Exploration: A Survey. *Sensors* **2021**, *21*, 2445. [CrossRef]
10. Cao, T.; Armin, M.A.; Denman, S.; Petersson, L. In-Bed Human Pose Estimation from Unseen and Privacy-Preserving Image Domains. In Proceedings of the 2022 IEEE 19th International Symposium on Biomedical Imaging (ISBI), Kolkata, India, 28–31 March 2022. [CrossRef]
11. Liu, M.; Ye, S. A Novel Body Posture Recognition System on Bed. In Proceedings of the 2018 IEEE 3rd International Conference on Signal and Image Processing (ICSIP), Shenzhen, China, 13–15 July 2018. [CrossRef]
12. Roshini, A.; Kiran, K.V.D. An Enhanced Posture Prediction-Bayesian Network Algorithm for Sleep Posture Recognition in Wireless Body Area Networks. *Int. J. Telemed. Appl.* **2022**, *2022*, 3102545. [CrossRef]
13. Luo, B.; Yang, Z.; Chu, P.; Zhou, J. Human Sleep Posture Recognition Method Based on Interactive Learning of Ultra-Long Short-Term Information. *IEEE Sens. J.* **2023**, *23*, 13399–13410. [CrossRef]
14. Fallmann, S.; van Veen, R.; Chen, L.; Walker, D.; Chen, F.; Pan, C. Wearable accelerometer based extended sleep position recognition. In Proceedings of the 2017 IEEE 19th International Conference on e-Health Networking, Applications and Services (Healthcom), Dalian, China, 12–15 October 2017; pp. 1–6.
15. Chung, K.; Song, K.; Shin, K.; Sohn, J.; Cho, S.H.; Chang, J.-H. Noncontact sleep study by multi-modal sensor fusion. *Sensors* **2017**, *17*, 1685. [CrossRef] [PubMed]
16. Collecchia, G.; De Gobbi, R. The robotic assistance system. In *AI in Clinical Practice: A Guide to Artificial Intelligence and Digital Medicine*; Academic Press: Cambridge, MA, USA, 2024. [CrossRef]
17. Kalpana, G.; Poojitha, S.R.; Varun, M.; Sriharsha, P. MEDROBO: Automated Medicine Delivery and Patient Monitoring System. *J. Electron Inform.* **2024**, *6*, 212–226. [CrossRef]
18. Zhao, D.; Wu, Y.; Yang, C.; Yang, J.; Liu, H.; Wang, S.; Jiang, Y.; Hiroshi, Y. A novel multifunctional intelligent bed integrated with multimodal human–robot interaction approach and safe nursing methods. *IET Cyber-Syst. Robot.* **2023**, *5*, e12097. [CrossRef]
19. Selvaraj, S.; Dhanalakshmi, B.; Prabha, P.S.; Verma, A.; Muniyandy, E.; Sridhar, S. An IoT Intelligent Approach for Safety and Efficiency of Robotic Medicine Delivery in Hospitals. *J. Electr. Syst.* **2024**, *20*, 820–827. [CrossRef]
20. Hu, Q.; Tang, X.; Tang, W. A Real-Time Patient-Specific Sleeping Posture Recognition System Using Pressure Sensitive Conductive Sheet and Transfer Learning. *IEEE Sens. J.* **2021**, *21*, 6869–6879. [CrossRef]
21. Naik, U.; Bhuatara, S.; Chougala, B. An Experimental Framework for Automated Bed Localization and Drug Identification Using ZigBee Signal Strength and Mobile Robot. In Proceedings of the 2019 IEEE International Conference on Distributed Computing, VLSI, Electrical Circuits and Robotics (DISCOVER), Manipal, India, 11–12 August 2019. [CrossRef]
22. Saunders, J.; Syrdal, D.S.; Koay, K.L.; Burke, N.; Dautenhahn, K. "Teach Me–Show Me"—End-User Personalization of a Smart Home and Companion Robot. *IEEE Trans. Hum.-Mach. Syst.* **2016**, *46*, 27–40. [CrossRef]
23. Cahn, D.F.; Phillips, S.R. ROBNAV: A Range-Based Robot Navigation and Obstacle Avoidance Algorithm. *IEEE Trans. Syst. Man Cybern.* **1975**, *5*, 544–551. [CrossRef]
24. Durrant-Whyte, H.; Bailey, T. Simultaneous localization and mapping: Part I. *IEEE Robot. Autom. Mag.* **2016**, *13*, 99–110. [CrossRef]
25. Bresson, G.; Alsayed, Z.; Yu, L.; Glaser, S. Simultaneous Localization and Mapping: A Survey of Current Trends in Autonomous Driving. *IEEE Trans. Intell. Veh.* **2017**, 2194–2220. [CrossRef]
26. Zhang, C.Z.; Li, Z.H.; Chen, M.S.; Lin, Y.C.; Wang, G.Q.; Wang, Q.; Zeng, W.D. Advanced Multi-Sensor Person-Following System on a Mobile Robot: Design, Construction and Measurements. *IEEE Instrum. Meas. Mag.* **2024**, *27*, 38–44. [CrossRef]
27. Sakthi Ram, T.; Yogesh, L.; Vetriashwath, S.; Nishanth, G.; Swathika, O.G. FPGA-Based Smart Delivery Bot. In *Smart Grids as Cyber Physical Systems: Artificial Intelligence, Cybersecurity, and Clean Energy for Next Generation Smart Grids*; Wiley: Hoboken, NJ, USA, 2014. [CrossRef]

28. Basha, M.; Vamshi, K.; Bhavana, K.; Bhavitha, M. Command Control Robot using Internet of Things on Field Programmable Gate Array. In Proceedings of the 2020 International Conference on Electronics and Sustainable Communication Systems (ICESC), Coimbatore, India, 2–4 July 2020; pp. 1068–1073. [CrossRef]
29. Qasaimeh, M.; Denolf, K.; Lo, J.; Vissers, K.; Zambreno, J.; Jones, P.H. Comparing energy efficiency of CPU, GPU and FPGA implementations for vision kernels. In Proceedings of the 2019 IEEE International Conference on Embedded Software and Systems (ICESS), Las Vegas, NV, USA, 2–3 June 2019; pp. 1–8.
30. Ulusel, O.; Picardo, C.; Harris, C.B.; Reda, S.; Bahar, R.I. Hardware acceleration of feature detection and description algorithms on lowpower embedded platforms. In Proceedings of the 2016 26th International Conference on Field Programmable Logic and Applications (FPL), Lausanne, Switzerland, 19 August–2 September 2016; pp. 1–9.
31. Wan, Z.; Yu, B.; Li, T.Y.; Tang, J.; Zhu, Y.; Wang, Y.; Raychowdhury, A.; Liu, S. A Survey of FPGA-Based Robotic Computing. *IEEE Circuits Syst. Mag.* **2021**, *21*, 48–74. [CrossRef]
32. Thathsara, M.; Lam, S.K.; Kawshan, D.; Piyasena, D. Hardware Accelerator for Feature Matching with Binary Search Tree. In Proceedings of the 2024 IEEE International Symposium on Circuits and Systems (ISCAS), Singapore, 19–22 May 2024; pp. 1–5.
33. Schlegel, D.; Grisetti, G. Hbst: A hamming distance embedding binary search tree for feature-based visual place recognition. *IEEE Robot. Autom. Lett.* **2018**, *3*, 3741–3748. [CrossRef]
34. Nurvitadhi, E.; Sheffield, D.; Sim, J.; Mishra, A.; Venkatesh, G.; Marr, D. Accelerating Binarized Neural Networks: Comparison of FPGA, CPU, GPU, and ASIC. In Proceedings of the 2016 International Conference on Field-Programmable Technology (FPT), Xi'an, China, 7–9 December 2016; pp. 77–84.
35. Basha, M.; Siva Kumar, M.; Chinnaiah, M.C.; Lam, S.-K.; Srikanthan, T.; Narambhatla, J.; Dodde, H.K.; Dubey, S. Hardware Schemes for Smarter Indoor Robotics to Prevent the Backing Crash Framework Using Field Programmable Gate Array-Based Multi-Robots. *Sensors* **2024**, *24*, 1724. [CrossRef] [PubMed]
36. Karumuri, S.R.; Lam, S.K.; Narambhatlu, J.; Dubey, S. Hardware-Efficient Scheme for Trailer Robot Parking by Truck Robot in an Indoor Environment with Rendezvous. *Sensors* **2023**, *23*, 5097. [CrossRef]
37. Matar, G.; Lina, J.-M.; Kaddoum, G. Artificial neural network for in-bed posture classification using bed-sheet pressure sensors. *IEEE J. Biomed. Health Informat.* **2020**, *24*, 101–110. [CrossRef]
38. Tapwal, R.; Misra, S.; Deb, P.K. i-Sheet: A Low-Cost Bedsheet Sensor for Remote Diagnosis of Isolated Individuals. *IEEE Sens. J.* **2023**, *23*, 906–913. [CrossRef]
39. Hu, D.; Gao, W.; Ang, K.K.; Hu, M.; Chuai, G.; Huang, R. Smart Sleep Monitoring: Sparse Sensor-Based Spatiotemporal CNN for Sleep Posture Detection. *Sensors* **2024**, *24*, 4833. [CrossRef]
40. Tanaka, Y.; Morie, T.; Tamukoh, H. An Amygdala-Inspired Classical Conditioning Model Implemented on an FPGA for Home Service Robots. *IEEE Access* **2020**, *8*, 212066–212078. [CrossRef]
41. Kim, T.; Kang, G.; Lee, D.; Shim, D.H. Development of an Indoor Delivery Mobile Robot for a Multi-Floor Environment. *IEEE Access* **2024**, *12*, 45202–45215. [CrossRef]

sensors

MDPI

*Article*

# PDeT: A Progressive Deformable Transformer for Photovoltaic Panel Defect Segmentation

**Peng Zhou [1,2], Hong Fang [3] and Gaochang Wu [1,*]**

[1] State Key Laboratory of Synthetical Automation for Process Industries, Northeastern University, Shenyang 110819, China
[2] School of Artificial Intelligence and Data Science, Hebei University of Technology, Tianjin 300130, China
[3] School of Information and Electronic Engineering, Zhejiang Gongshang University, Hangzhou 310018, China
* Correspondence: wugc@mail.neu.edu.cn

**Abstract:** Defects in photovoltaic (PV) panels can significantly reduce the power generation efficiency of the system and may cause localized overheating due to uneven current distribution. Therefore, adopting precise pixel-level defect detection, i.e., defect segmentation, technology is essential to ensuring stable operation. However, for effective defect segmentation, the feature extractor must adaptively determine the appropriate scale or receptive field for accurate defect localization, while the decoder must seamlessly fuse coarse-level semantics with fine-grained features to enhance high-level representations. In this paper, we propose a Progressive Deformable Transformer (PDeT) for defect segmentation in PV cells. This approach effectively learns spatial sampling offsets and refines features progressively through coarse-level semantic attention. Specifically, the network adaptively captures spatial offset positions and computes self-attention, expanding the model's receptive field and enabling feature extraction across objects of various shapes. Furthermore, we introduce a semantic aggregation module to refine semantic information, converting the fused feature map into a scale space and balancing contextual information. Extensive experiments demonstrate the effectiveness of our method, achieving an mIoU of 88.41% on our solar cell dataset, outperforming other methods. Additionally, to validate the PDeT's applicability across different domains, we trained and tested it on the MVTec-AD dataset. The experimental results demonstrate that the PDeT exhibits excellent recognition performance in various other scenarios as well.

**Keywords:** photovoltaic panel defects; defect segmentation; deformable attention; feature aggregation

## 1. Introduction

Defects in photovoltaic (PV) cell substrates can reduce photoelectric conversion efficiency, leading to a decrease in system power generation [1]. These defects may also cause uneven current distribution in localized areas, resulting in hotspot effects [2]. This abnormal temperature increase in defect regions not only further decreases power generation efficiency but can also damage PV panels and even pose safety hazards, such as fire risks. Therefore, incorporating defect detection technology in PV quality control processes is crucial for identifying and preventing such defects in advance, ensuring the efficient and safe operation of PV systems. Defect segmentation (pixel-level defect detection) [3] provides detailed information about defects, including their precise location, shape, and size. With accurate segmentation data, PV manufacturers can detect potential issues in the panels early, preventing further problems and losses during the system's operational phase [4]. This not only boosts the economic benefits for enterprises but also contributes to the sustainable development of clean energy.

Recent research has utilized deep learning-based segmentation models [5–15] to segment defects in solar panels. Compared to manual inspection, deep learning techniques offer significant advantages. First, deep learning can automatically process and analyze large amounts of data, greatly improving inspection efficiency, especially in large-scale production settings. Second, deep learning models exhibit high consistency and precision in identifying complex features, avoiding fatigue and subjective errors that are common in manual inspections. Additionally, deep learning can continuously optimize and improve through data training, adapting to new types of defects and changing environments, which manual inspection cannot match in terms of adaptability and continuous improvement.

However, current defect segmentation algorithms still struggle with detecting elongated cracks and tend to miss or falsely detect small flaws around grid lines. During the feature extraction stage (encoding phase), Convolutional Neural Networks (CNNs) are limited by their fixed position sampling of input features. This constraint makes it difficult for models to handle fine-grained recognition tasks like detecting elongated cracks, leading to confusion or the loss of important features [3]. Although Vision Transformers (ViTs) [16] have been proven to effectively capture long-range feature relationships, the dense attention mechanism in ViTs results in high memory and computational costs. In the feature fusion and upsampling stage (decoding phase), the transmission of high-level semantic information to shallow layers gets disrupted and diluted by a large number of local patterns in the shallow layers [17].

Therefore, learning-based methods for PV defect segmentation need to address the following challenges. First, in the feature extraction phase, the encoder needs to adaptively select feature sampling locations. Second, in the feature fusion and upsampling phase, the decoder must refine features based on coarse-level semantics and prevent the dilution of fine-grained information.

In this paper, we propose a novel Progressive Deformable Transformer, dubbed PDeT, to effectively learn the offset of spatial sampling positions and progressively refine features based on coarse-level semantics for enhancing defect segmentation in PV panels. Specifically, we employ a deformable self-attention module in the encoder, which generates reference points as a unified network and takes query features as input for learning offsets, generating corresponding offsets for all reference points. In this way, the candidate keys/values can focus on defect regions and other crucial areas, enabling precise localization of defect features in complex backgrounds. This module is more flexible and efficient, allowing the dynamic adjustment of attention regions, thereby capturing the edges and details of defects more effectively and improving the accuracy of segmentation. In the decoder, we introduce a semantic aggregation module that combines feature differences across four different scales, reassembling coarse-level features with fine-grained ones. This approach effectively distinguishes between background and defect features in PV panels, providing clear and detailed spatial boundaries without losing semantic information. Our PDeT is capable of flexibly adjusting spatial sampling positions and progressively refining feature extraction using coarse-level semantic information, thereby improving the accuracy and reliability of PV defect detection.

The main contributions of this paper are summarized as follows:

- A progressive deformable Transformer is proposed to achieve high-quality segmentation of PV panel defects, significantly enhancing the ability to detect complex defect features.
- A deformable self-attention module is introduced to adaptively learn spatial feature sampling locations. This module adjusts sampling positions based on the shape and structure of input features, flexibly capturing irregular or deformed features.
- A semantic aggregation module is designed to ensure the retention and integration of both coarse and fine-grained information, effectively balancing these features while incorporating contextual information for better segmentation accuracy.

We conducted extensive experiments to validate the effectiveness of the introduced modules. On the solar cell defect dataset, our model achieved 88.41% mIoU. Additionally, we also conducted training and evaluation on the MVTec-AD [18] dataset. The experimental results indicate that the PDeT demonstrates exceptional recognition capabilities across different scenarios.

## 2. Related Work

This paper focuses on photovoltaic defect segmentation using a Vision Transformer backbone. To provide context, we present a brief overview of relevant research in this area.

### 2.1. Photovoltaic Defect Segmentation

The photovoltaic industry has extensively adopted deep learning-based methods for defect detection, offering significant improvements in both detection efficiency and accuracy compared to traditional approaches. By analyzing features from large-scale datasets, deep learning enables the precise identification of defects in photovoltaic panels. Tang et al. [15], for instance, used limited samples to generate high-resolution electroluminescence images and employed CNNs to automatically classify defects. Jiang et al. [13] proposed an m-shaped architecture to extract and fuse shallow and deep features in segmentation networks, incorporating an attention module to suppress the photovoltaic background and improve segmentation accuracy. Xie et al. [12] embedded a domain discriminator into the CNN to distinguish between data domains, allowing the feature extractor to learn domain-invariant features. Pratt et al. [19] evaluated four deep learning models (U-Net, PSPNet, and DeepLabv3+) for detecting cracks, inactive areas, and grid line defects in photovoltaic panels. Jha et al. [11] introduced a semi-supervised semantic segmentation method for defect detection with limited labeled data, significantly reducing manual annotation costs. Kaligambe et al. [10] developed a lightweight CNN model and compared its performance against a fine-tuned VGG16 model. Fioresi et al. [8] used ResNet50 and DeepLabv3 as backbone networks and segmentation decoders to identify defects such as cracks, contact interruptions, cell interconnection failures, and contact corrosion in both polycrystalline and monocrystalline silicon cells. Chen et al. [7] fine-tuned a U-Net model with a pre-trained VGG16 encoder, achieving excellent segmentation results for cracks and busbars. Similarly, Zhang et al. [6] refined CNN-extracted features using a global pairwise similarity module and a connection saliency module, enhancing defect detection in photovoltaic images.

### 2.2. Vision Transformer

The Vision Transformer (ViT) [16] has revolutionized computer vision tasks by leveraging the self-attention mechanism originally designed for natural language processing. By treating images as sequences of patches, ViT captures global context more effectively than traditional convolutional neural networks (CNNs). However, the high computational complexity and large data requirements have led to the development of more efficient Transformer variants. One such model is the Data-Efficient Image Transformer (DeiT), introduced by Touvron et al. [20], which improves the training process of ViT through data augmentation and advanced techniques, making it more suitable for smaller datasets.

In addition to image classification, ViT has been successfully applied to tasks like object detection and segmentation [21,22]. To enhance Transformer-based architectures further, Liu et al. [23] developed the Swin Transformer, which utilizes a hierarchical structure and local window self-attention, significantly improving computational efficiency and achieving state-of-the-art performance across multiple benchmarks.

Beyond these advancements, the neighborhood attention Transformer [24] offers an alternative approach by refining local attention mechanisms. Unlike the standard self-attention mechanism that emphasizes global information, NAT focuses on attention within local neighborhoods, making it particularly effective for tasks requiring fine-grained feature extraction. In summary, while ViTs laid the foundation for Transformer-based models in computer vision, optimizations in models like the DeiT, Swin Transformer, and neighborhood attention Transformer have addressed challenges such as computational complexity and fine feature extraction, broadening their applicability to a wider range of visual tasks.

## 3. Methodology

In this section, we delve into the specific architecture of the proposed Progressive Deformable Transformer (PDeT) designed for photovoltaic panel defect segmentation. The ViT [16] was the first to demonstrate the viability of Transformer mechanisms in computer vision. Unlike CNNs, Transformer-based models, with their Multi-Head Self-Attention (MHSA) mechanism, excel at capturing long-range dependencies, making them particularly effective for target localization. Building on this foundation, we introduce a deformable sampling operation before the MHSA in each Transformer encoder. This operation enables the network to focus more effectively on relevant regions. In the decoder, we propose a semantic aggregation module, which enhances the fusion of multi-stage features, improving overall segmentation accuracy. The following subsections will provide a detailed explanation of the network framework, the Deformable Transformer Block, and the Semantic Aggregation Block.

### 3.1. PDeT Overall Architecture

Our PDeT follows the widely used encoder–decoder structure. The encoder extracts feature information from the input image, while the decoder progressively restores the spatial dimensions to generate pixel-level segmentation results. As illustrated in Figure 1, the input image of shape $H \times W \times 3$ is first processed through two convolutional and normalization embedding layers, producing patch embeddings of size $H/4 \times W/4 \times C$ (where $C = 128$). Each convolution employs a kernel size of $3 \times 3$, with a stride of 2 and padding of 1, expanding output channels from 3 to 64 and then to 128. To construct a multi-level feature pyramid, our backbone is organized into four stages, each with a progressively increasing stride. Each stage comprises $N$ stacked neighborhood attention Transformer blocks (NATs) [24] and Deformable Transformer Blocks (DTBs). In our implementation, $\{N_1, N_2, N_3, N_4\}$ are set to $\{1, 2, 9, 1\}$, respectively. The feature maps extracted at each stage are downsampled by a factor of 4, 8, 16, and 32 times the input size, denoted as $f = \{f_i \mid 1 \leq i \leq 4\}$.

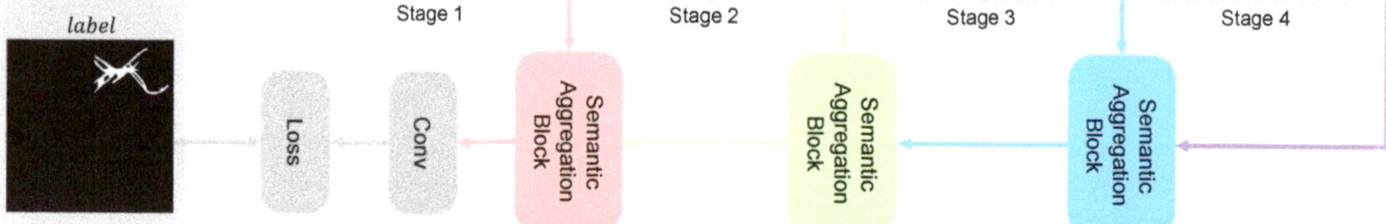


**Figure 1.** Overall architecture of the proposed PDeT for photovoltaic defect segmentation.

Next, we aim to seamlessly fuse and upsample the multi-level features in the decoder stage. We employ the Semantic Aggregation Block (SAB) to fuse adjacent features $\{f_i, f_{i+1}\}$, with the output serving as the input to the subsequent SAB. This process reduces inconsistencies between feature levels, allowing coarse-level semantic information to effectively refine finer features, thereby achieving a balance between global semantics and local details. The output from the encoder is processed through two rounds of bilinear interpolation and convolution operations to generate the predicted output.

### 3.2. Deformable Transformer Block

Before introducing deformable attention into the Transformer, we will first review the vanilla MHSA mechanism in the Transformer. Given an input feature map $x \in R^{H \times W \times C}$, the MHSA mechanism with $M$ attention heads is applied, where each attention head independently learns different relationships. The outputs from these attention heads are then concatenated. The vanilla MHSA mechanism can be formulated as follows:

$$\begin{aligned} q &= xW_q, k = xW_k, v = xW_v, \\ y^{(m)} &= \text{softmax}\left(\frac{q^{(m)}k^{(m)T}}{\sqrt{d}}\right)v^{(m)}, m \in \{1, \ldots, M\}, \\ y &= \text{concat}(y^{(1)}, \ldots, y^{(M)})W_o, \end{aligned} \tag{1}$$

where $d = \frac{C}{M}$ represents the dimension of each attention head, and $q^{(m)}, k^{(m)}, v^{(m)}$ denote the query, key, and value embeddings, respectively. The output of the $m$-th attention head is represented as $y^{(m)}$. The learnable parameters $W_q, W_k, W_v, W_o \in R^{C \times C}$ are the projection matrices for the feature embeddings. The formulation for the $i$-th Transformer block is given as follows:

$$\begin{aligned} y_i' &= \text{MHSA}(\text{LN}(y_{i-1})) + y_{i-1}, \\ y_i &= \text{MLP}(\text{LN}(y_i')) + y_i', \end{aligned} \tag{2}$$

where $LN(\cdot)$ represents Layer Normalization [25], MHSA$(\cdot)$ denotes the MHSA mechanism in Equation (1), and MLP$(\cdot)$ is the MLP with two linear layers.

Despite the vanilla MHSA mechanism's effectiveness in capturing global information, it has certain limitations when processing local features and irregular shapes. To address these issues, we incorporate deformable operations into our PDeT. Deformable operations allow flexible attention adjustments, enabling the model to better focus on critical information. This is especially effective for handling complex or irregular features in PV defect segmentation. Next, we will provide a detailed explanation of how deformable operations are integrated into MHSA to enhance the performance of Transformer models.

As shown in Figure 2, our goal is to enable the key–value pairs to adaptively sample feature information based on offsets provided by the offset network. First, given the input feature $x \in R^{H \times W \times C}$, a uniform grid of reference points $r \in R^{H_r \times W_r \times 2}$ is generated. This grid is downsampled by a factor of relative to the size of the input feature, where $H_r \in \frac{H}{r}$ and $W_r \in \frac{W}{r}$. The values of the reference points correspond to 2D coordinates $(0,0), \ldots (H_r - 1, W_r - 1)$. The ranges of the two dimensions, $[0, (H_r - 1)]$ and $[0, (W_r - 1)]$, are then normalized to $[-1, +1]$, where $(-1, -1)$ represents the reference point at the top-left corner and $(+1, +1)$ represents the reference point at the bottom-right corner.

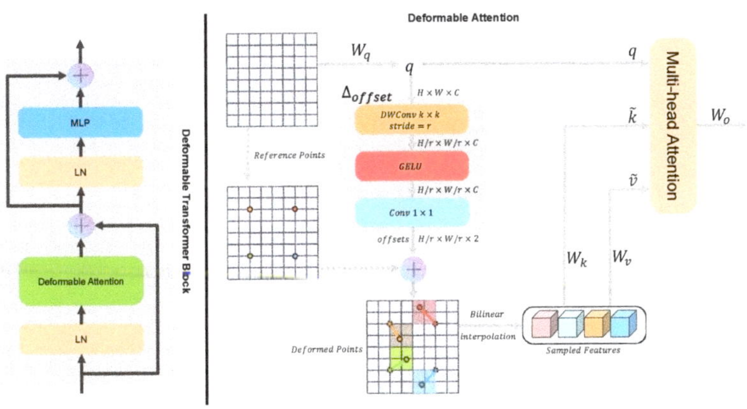


**Figure 2.** Detailed structure of the Deformable Transformer Block (DTB).

Next, we need to obtain the offsets for each reference point. We start by using $W_q$ to generate the query tokens $q$, which are then input into the $\Delta_{offset}$ module to learn the offsets for the reference points. This module consists of a depth-wise convolution, a GELU activation function, and $1 \times 1$ convolution, resulting in an output with the same shape as the reference points. The calculated offsets are then added to the reference points to derive the positions of the deformable points. Sampling is performed at these deformable points, and the keys and values are computed using the projection matrices. At this stage, we obtain the deformable keys $\tilde{k}$ and values $\tilde{v}$, which are combined with $q$ to compute the MHSA. Consequently, Equation (1) is updated to:

$$\begin{aligned} q &= xW_q, \tilde{k} = \tilde{x}W_k, \tilde{v} = \tilde{x}W_v \\ \Delta_{\mathbf{p}} &= \Delta_{offset}(q), \\ \tilde{x} &= \varphi(x; \mathbf{p} + \Delta_{\mathbf{p}}), \end{aligned} \tag{3}$$

where $\Delta_{\mathbf{p}}$ represents the offset of the reference point, $\mathbf{p}$ represents the position of the reference point, and $\varphi(a; \mathbf{b})$ denotes the sampling result at location $\mathbf{b}$ in the feature map $a$.

This deformable operation enables the Transformer structure to adaptively sample based on the query features, allowing the model to flexibly adjust the shape and position of the self-attention, particularly when handling features that span large scales. Moreover, by integrating the deformable operation, the only component that introduces a small number of learnable parameters is the $\Delta_{offset}$ module. This is one reason why we employ lightweight depth-wise convolution, ensuring that the model remains efficient while maintaining performance.

### 3.3. Semantic Aggregation Block

The encoder of our PDeT incorporates multiple stages to generate feature maps at different hierarchical levels. To progressively fuse the feature maps extracted from each stage, we integrate the Semantic Aggregation Block (SAB), which extracts and merges features across these levels. This block effectively preserves coarse semantic information while retaining fine-grained details, ultimately leading to high-quality segmentation results. Figure 3 illustrates the detailed structure of the SAB.

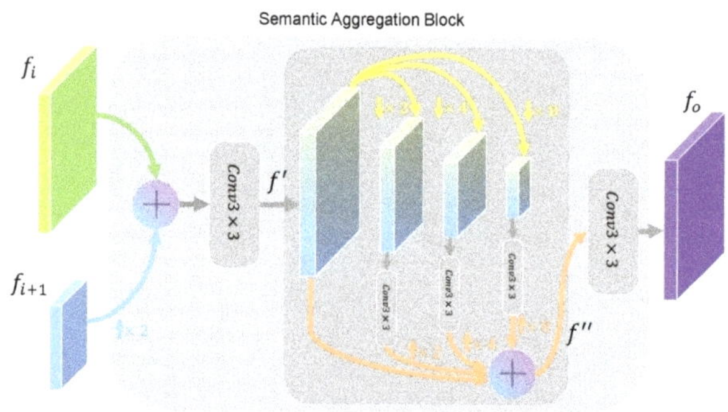


**Figure 3.** Detailed structure of the Semantic Aggregation Block (SAB).

The SAB processes feature maps from two different stages, $f_i$ and $f_{i+1}$, where $i \in \{1,2,3\}$. We first align the channel dimensions of the feature maps into $C = 256$ via a $1 \times 1$ convolution. Then, a bilinear interpolation is applied to upsample the higher-level semantic feature $f_{i+1}$, resizing it to match the dimensions of the lower-level feature $f_i$. These operations lay the groundwork for subsequent feature fusion. The interpolated feature is then added to the lower-level feature, followed by a $3 \times 3$ convolution layer for initial feature extraction. This step not only enhances the fused feature representation but also captures richer detail information. The process is formulated as:

$$f' = \mathrm{Conv}_{3\times3}(f_i + \phi_{bi}(f_{i+1};2)), \tag{4}$$

where $\phi_{bi}(\cdot;2)$ indicates the $2 \times 2$ bilinear upsampling operation, $\mathrm{Conv}_{3\times3}$ represents the $3 \times 3$ convolution layer, and $f'$ is the intermediate feature map within the SAB.

Next, the SAB applies an average pooling operation at multiple scales, transforming the feature map into various spatial resolutions. This multi-scale processing allows the model to capture features comprehensively, from local details to global context. It enhances the model's ability to perceive defect regions at different scales and improves its adaptability to diverse scenes and variations. After convolutional processing, the features from each sub-branch are upsampled to the original size and combined with the input feature map through residual connections. These connections ensure that original feature information is not lost during multi-scale transformations, preserving both fine-grained details and global semantic information, thereby enhancing the stability and expressiveness of the fusion. The process can be formulated as:

$$f'' = f' + \sum_{j\in\{2,4,8\}} \phi_{bi}(\mathrm{Conv}_{3\times3}(\mathrm{Pool}(f';j));j), \tag{5}$$

where $\mathrm{Pool}(\cdot;j)$ indicates the average pooling operation at scale $j \in \{2,4,8\}$.

Finally, a $3 \times 3$ convolution layer is applied to the fused features for further refinement and smoothing, generating the output of the SAB as $f_o = \mathrm{Conv}_{3\times3}(f'')$. This step enhances the features after multi-scale processing, improving the model's contextual awareness and leading to more robust feature representations.

Overall, the proposed SAB achieves a balance between coarse and fine-grained information through multi-scale processing, enabling the model to generalize effectively when dealing with targets of varying scales, shapes, and distributions, thereby improving its adaptability and expressive power in complex photovoltaic environments.

## 4. Experiments

We conducted ablation and comparison experiments on the photovoltaic dataset to validate the performance of the PDeT network. Additionally, to assess the applicability of the PDeT network in other industrial scenarios, we selected four industrial scenes from the public MVTec-AD [18] dataset for further evaluation.

### *4.1. Implementation*

All experiments were conducted using an NVIDIA GeForce RTX 3060 (12GB) and an Intel Core i5-12490F processor, both sourced from Santa Clara, CA, USA. The model was built and trained using the PyTorch 1.12.0 framework. During training, the AdamW [26] optimizer was employed with an initial learning rate of 0.0001 and a weight decay coefficient of 0.0001. The exponential decay rates for computing the first- and second-moment estimates of gradients were set to 0.9 and 0.999, respectively. A polynomial learning rate schedule (with a power of 0.9) was adopted, allowing dynamic adjustment of the learning rate throughout training. The maximum number of iterations was set to 160,000, with model evaluations performed every 8000 iterations using the mIoU as the evaluation metric. Cross-entropy loss was used to calculate the loss, ensuring efficient model convergence and accurate classification.

The photovoltaic dataset used in our experiments contains a total of 1024 images, which were split into training and validation sets at a 2:1 ratio. Each image has a resolution of $640 \times 640$, and the segmentation results are classified into two categories: defect and background. During training, we applied random cropping as a data augmentation technique to both the input images and their corresponding labels.

### 4.2. Ablation Study

We conducted ablation experiments using the photovoltaic panel dataset. To validate the effectiveness of the deformable convolution, we sequentially replaced the NAT Block in the feature extraction stage with the DTB. In the overall network structure described in Section 3, we stack $N_i$ Transformer blocks in each stage. Each Transformer block originally consisted of two NATs in series as the baseline, and then, we replaced the second NAT in each Transformer with the DTB. The results, as shown in Table 1, indicate that while adding the DTB only in the fourth stage slightly decreases model performance, incorporating the DTB in the third stage yields an improvement of about one percentage point. When all stages utilize the DTB, the model performance increases by approximately three percentage points compared to the baseline.

**Table 1.** Ablation study on the application of deformable attention at different stages. ✗ and ✓ indicate whether DTB is used in the stage.

| Stage #/Deformable Attention | | | | mIoU |
|---|---|---|---|---|
| **Stage 1** | **Stage 2** | **Stage 3** | **Stage 4** | |
| ✗ | ✗ | ✗ | ✗ | 85.27 |
| ✗ | ✗ | ✗ | ✓ | 85.05 |
| ✗ | ✗ | ✓ | ✓ | 88.22 |
| ✗ | ✓ | ✓ | ✓ | 86.17 |
| ✓ | ✓ | ✓ | ✓ | 88.41 |

As shown in Figure 1, we replaced the SAB with standard convolution and bilinear interpolation to establish a comparison baseline, effectively omitting the transition from $f'$ to $f''$ . We then sequentially integrated multi-scale methods into the different stages of the decoder. As shown in Table 2, using SAB in stages 1 and 2 resulted in a performance improvement of 0.62%, while adding SAB from stages 2 to 3 further increased performance by 1.12%.

**Table 2.** The results of the ablation experiment for the SAB module in the encoding structure. The check mark (✓) signifies the utilization of the SAB, whereas the cross (✗) indicates its exclusion.

| Stage #/SAB | | | mIoU |
|---|---|---|---|
| **Stage 1–Stage 2** | **Stage 2–Stage 3** | **Stage 3–Stage 4** | |
| ✗ | ✗ | ✗ | 87.25 |
| ✓ | ✗ | ✗ | 87.87 |
| ✓ | ✓ | ✗ | 88.37 |
| ✓ | ✓ | ✓ | 88.41 |

To evaluate the impact of different Decoder heads on model performance while keeping the encoder architecture unchanged, we conducted comparative experiments. This experiment utilized the encoder proposed in this paper as the baseline architecture and introduced various Decoder heads to observe their performance in specific tasks. The experimental results, as shown in Table 3, indicate that the IoU for the background class remained consistent across all Decoder heads. However, significant differences were observed in the IoU for the defect class among the various Decoder heads.

Specifically, the IoU for the defect class with the FPN [27] head is 74.52%, resulting in an overall mIoU of 87.25%. The UPer [28] head shows a slight improvement, with a defect class IoU of 75.36% and an overall mIoU of 87.67%. The most significant enhancement is observed with the proposed PDeT model I, achieving a defect class IoU of 76.85% and an overall mIoU of 88.41%. This indicates that the PDeT demonstrates advantages in fine-grained feature aggregation when processing defect features, significantly improving the model's performance in defect detection tasks.

**Table 3.** A comparison of the experimental results with other Decoder heads.

| Decoder Head | IoU | | mIoU |
|---|---|---|---|
| | Background | Defect | |
| FPN head [27] | 99.98 | 74.52 | 87.25 |
| UPer head [28] | 99.98 | 75.36 | 87.67 |
| PDeT head (ours) | 99.98 | 76.85 | 88.41 |

Figure 4 illustrates the training process of the PDeT model. During the initial phase of training, the loss fluctuates significantly, indicating that the model is still learning and adjusting its parameters. However, as training progresses, the model gradually learns to capture the characteristics of the data, leading to a steady improvement in both the overall mIoU and mAcc metrics. Notably, the best mIoU is achieved at the 300th epoch, reaching 88.41%, which reflects the model's superior performance at this stage. Meanwhile, the loss value gradually converges and stabilizes at a lower level, indicating that the model effectively reduced its error rate during training.

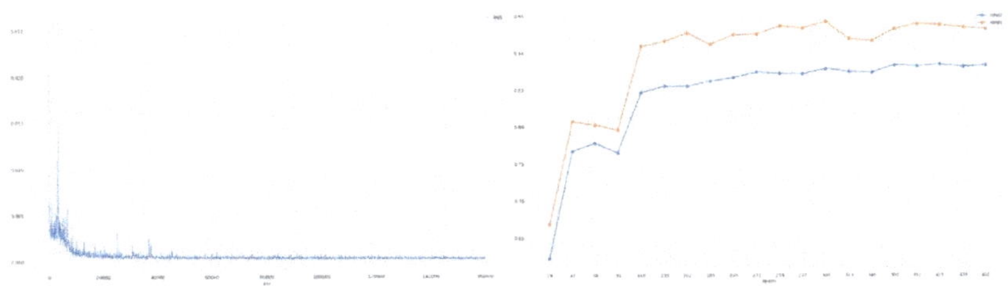

**Figure 4.** The training process of the PDeT is assessed using three metrics: loss, mIoU, and mAcc. These metrics offer valuable insights into the model's performance and effectiveness during training. The left panel displays the loss at each iteration, while the right panel presents the validation results throughout the training process.

## 4.3. *Comparison with Other Segmentation Networks*

In this section, we compare our method with existing semantic segmentation networks, including EMANet [29], STDC [30], DDRNet [31], K-Net [32], DNLNet [33], CCNet [34], ANN [35], DMNet [36], PIDNet [37], ISANet [38], GCNet [39], and SIIF [3].

Table 4 provides a detailed comparison of various models in the task of defect detection on photovoltaic panels, including metrics such as model parameters (Params), floating-point operations per second (FLOPs), frames per second (FPS), precision, recall, F1 score, and mIoU. Precision represents the proportion of true positive samples among those predicted as positive by the model. High precision indicates that most of the detected defects are genuine. Recall, on the other hand, measures the proportion of correctly identified positive samples out of all actual positive cases. High recall signifies that the majority of actual defects have been successfully detected. Additionally, mIoU reflects the model's ability to distinguish between defect areas and the background. A higher mIoU ensures greater detection accuracy and fewer missed defects.

Analysis reveals that the PDeT model outperforms others by at least four percentage points in mIoU, demonstrating its exceptional performance in photovoltaic defect segmentation. This advantage is primarily due to PDeT's feature extraction network, which employs a Transformer architecture. However, this comes at the cost of a relatively large number of parameters, leading to increased computational overhead. Thus, there is still room for optimization in the inference efficiency of the PDeT. In contrast, models like DDRNet-S and STDC, while having fewer parameters and higher computational efficiency, generally perform worse in the actual segmentation results, showing a significant gap compared to the PDeT. Despite their successes in lightweight design, these models exhibit relatively limited feature extraction capabilities when dealing with complex defect backgrounds, making it challenging to accurately capture the details of defect regions.

**Table 4.** Comparison of experimental results of various indicators with other segmentation networks.

| Method | Params | FLOPs | FPS | Precision | Recall | F1 | mIoU |
|---|---|---|---|---|---|---|---|
| EMANet [29] | 42.08M | 263.17G | 15.37 | 34.03 | 40.53 | 37.00 | 61.78 |
| STDC [30] | 8.57M | 13.24G | 78.05 | 64.88 | 51.99 | 57.72 | 70.02 |
| DDRNet-S [31] | 7.72M | 9.267G | 143.24 | 68.20 | 58.62 | 63.50 | 73.00 |
| K-Net [32] | 62.29M | 285.92G | 5.99 | 33.69 | 82.87 | 47.91 | 74.65 |
| DNLNet [33] | 50.1M | 312.25G | 5.75 | 58.91 | 79.89 | 67.82 | 75.82 |
| CCNet [34] | 49.81M | 313.09G | 12.97 | 65.29 | 79.81 | 71.83 | 78.15 |
| ANN [35] | 46.22M | 289.28G | 14.00 | 72.78 | 78.24 | 75.41 | 80.20 |
| DMNet [36] | 53.16M | 305.64G | 13.15 | 73.95 | 78.65 | 76.23 | 80.61 |
| PIDNet-L [37] | 36.93M | 53.83G | 26.23 | 71.70 | 81.40 | 76.25 | 80.79 |
| ISANet [38] | 37.69M | 233.42G | 15.37 | 81.46 | 75.67 | 78.46 | 81.84 |
| GCNet [39] | 49.62M | 308.89G | 13.85 | 76.93 | 80.35 | 78.60 | 82.51 |
| SIIF [3] | 58.72M | 75.74G | 25.09 | 79.80 | 83.03 | 81.38 | 84.30 |
| PDeT (our) | 104.15M | 200.22G | 10.49 | 90.12 | 89.37 | 89.66 | 88.41 |

Figure 5 presents a detailed comparison of different networks in the segmentation of defects on photovoltaic panels. By examining the results, we can clearly observe the differences among models when addressing specific types of defects, particularly in the segmentation of elongated cracks, where the discrepancies are especially pronounced. From the segmentation results in the first and third rows, it is evident that many models struggle with elongated cracks, often producing coarse results. These defects typically exhibit fine, elongated features, and conventional segmentation networks tend to overlook edge information when dealing with such detail-rich defects, leading to imprecise segmentation outcomes. For instance, while K-Net, a model with a larger number of parameters, has strong global perception capabilities during feature extraction, allowing it to capture the general outline of defects, the edges of the cracks in its output still appear blurred, failing to accurately segment the detailed parts of elongated defects.

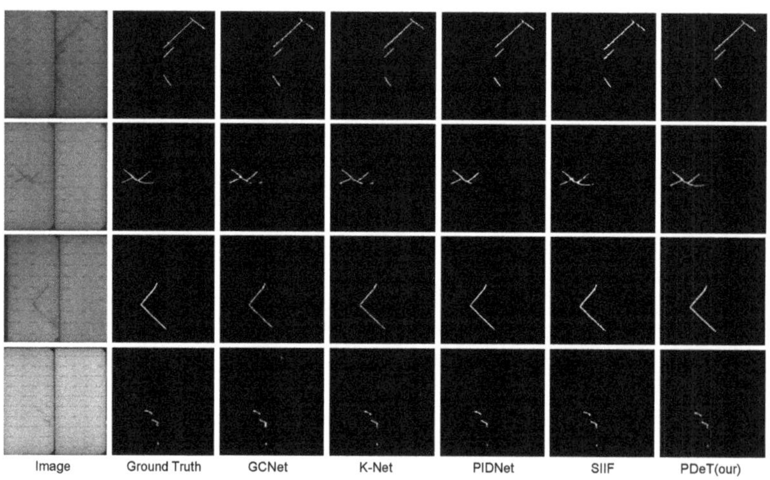


**Figure 5.** Quantitative comparison with other segmentation networks.

In contrast, the PDeT demonstrates superior capability in handling such defects. The model employs deformable self-attention, which allows for dynamic adjustment of sampling point positions, enabling a more flexible focus on the edges of cracks and, thus, accurately capturing these details. Moreover, during the decoding process, the SAB module plays a crucial role in refining segmentation. This module progressively aggregates coarse and fine feature information by fusing multi-scale features, allowing for precise segmentation of defect edges without losing semantic information. Due to the need for further optimization of the model's parameter count and computational load, we will consider employing pruning and quantization methods suitable for Transformer architectures in the future. These approaches aim to reduce the model's computational cost and memory usage. Figure 5 clearly illustrates that the PDeT's segmentation results outperform other models in detailing and edge treatment of cracks. This refined segmentation ability enables the PDeT to maintain global perception while flexibly adjusting its focus areas and enhancing the feature aggregation process, ultimately improving defect detection accuracy.

### 4.4. Applicability in Other Industrial Fields

To validate the application potential of the PDeT photovoltaic defect detection model in other industrial scenarios, we selected four typical scenes from the MVTec-AD [18] anomaly detection dataset for experimentation. These scenes include Wood, Metal Nut, Tile, and Hazelnut, representing common complex backgrounds and diverse defect types in industrial manufacturing, thus providing high representativeness. The selection of these scenes aims to ensure that the PDeT model demonstrates good adaptability across different materials and defect patterns, further validating its broad potential for practical industrial applications.

The MVTec-AD dataset is primarily used for anomaly detection and contains both normal and abnormal data. In our experimental design, we performed stratified sampling for each scene, dividing the normal and abnormal data into training and testing sets at a 2:1 ratio. This approach simulates real industrial defect detection tasks and aligns more closely with actual application requirements. The evaluation metric for the model is mIoU, which is widely used in semantic segmentation tasks and provides a comprehensive assessment of the model's recognition performance across various categories.

In this experiment, we compared the performance of K-Net, UPerNet, GCNet, and SIIF models across four scenes in the MVTec-AD dataset. The experimental results are presented in Table 5, with each column representing the mIoU for the respective scenes.

**Table 5.** Comparative experimental results of the model across the four scenes: Hazelnut, Metal Nut, Tile, and Wood. All values shown in the table represent the mIoU for assessing the model's recognition performance in each scene.

| Method | Hazelnut | Metal Nut | Tile | Wood |
|---|---|---|---|---|
| K-Net [32] | 76.06 | 95.29 | 92.81 | 74.17 |
| UPerNet [28] | 93.57 | 96.6 | 95.44 | 88.35 |
| GCNet [39] | 93.27 | 95.32 | 95.07 | 87.93 |
| SIIF [3] | 94.13 | 95.22 | 92.95 | 87.86 |
| PDeT (our) | 94.34 | 95.32 | 92.46 | 88.54 |

The performance of K-Net [32] across the four scenes is relatively low, with an mIoU of 76.06% for Hazelnut and 74.17% for Wood, indicating its limited recognition capability in complex backgrounds. In contrast, UPerNet [28] performed exceptionally well in all scenes, achieving mIoU of 93.57% and 96.6% for Hazelnut and Metal Nut, respectively, demonstrating its superior feature extraction ability. The performances of GCNet [39] and SIIF [3] are comparable to UPerNet, maintaining high mIoU values across the scenes. Notably, in the Metal Nut scene, GCNet [39] achieved an mIoU of 95.32%, indicating a certain advantage in detecting defects in metal nuts. It is noteworthy that the proposed PDeT model performed well across all four scenes: Hazelnut, Metal Nut, Tile, and Wood. The mIoU for the Hazelnut scene was 94.34%, while for the Metal Nut scene, it was 95.32%. This indicates that the PDeT model demonstrates strong adaptability and stability across different materials and defect patterns.

Figure 6 presents a quantitative display of the segmentation results of the comparative models across four different scenes. In the first row, under the wood scene, the model effectively segments the liquid and combined areas, while the K-Net model shows relatively poor segmentation results. In the tile scene (third row), the model struggles with segmenting fine cracks, resulting in discontinuities; in contrast, our PDeT model performs significantly better. In the hazelnut scene (fifth and sixth rows), the results indicate that K-Net's segmentation is subpar, while other models demonstrate notably superior performance. In the Metal Nut scene, all models are capable of effectively identifying anomalous defects, showcasing their robust segmentation capabilities.

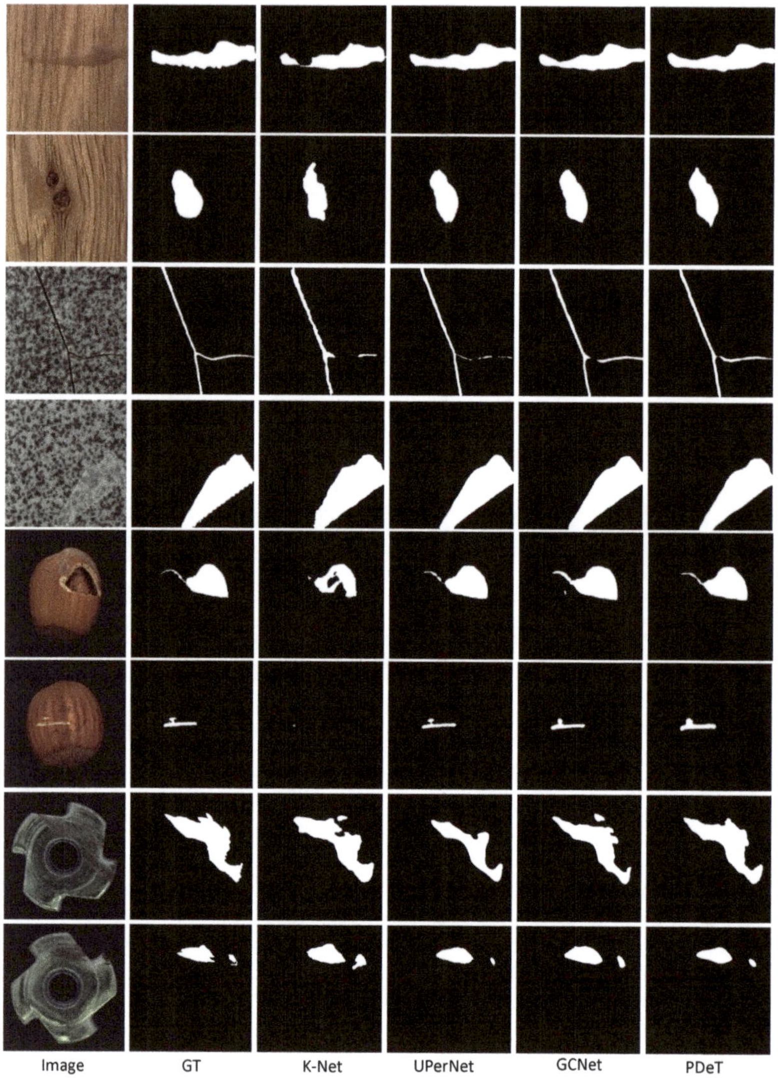


**Figure 6.** Quantitative display of segmentation results from multiple models across four distinct scenes, with each scene presenting two quantitative outcomes. The columns represent the segmentation results of the model.

These results underscore the practical applicability of our model, especially in diverse industrial contexts. By incorporating deformable self-attention and semantic aggregation modules, we not only enhance the geometric distinction capabilities but also refine the representation of semantic features. The introduction of these modules facilitates efficient collaboration between the encoder and decoder, ensuring precise feature transmission and gradual reconstruction, thereby allowing the PDeT to exhibit greater adaptability and stability in real-world applications.

## 5. Conclusions

Our research leverages image sensors for defect detection in photovoltaic panels. Compared to traditional electrical sensor-based methods, such as open-circuit voltage and short-circuit current measurements, we employ electroluminescence (EL) imaging to capture high-resolution, two-dimensional signals, significantly enhancing defect detection accuracy. Additionally, the deep learning techniques incorporated in our study not only improve the perception of defects in photovoltaic panels but also pave the way for advancements in intelligent recognition systems. To further advance this field, we have successfully proposed a Progressive Deformable Transformer for photovoltaic panel defect segmentation, which enhances the segmentation of defects in solar panels. By incorporating deformable self-attention and a semantic aggregation module, we not only improved the ability to differentiate geometric shapes but also refined the representation of semantic features. Furthermore, the introduction of these modules facilitates efficient collaboration between the encoder and decoder, ensuring precise feature transfer and progressive reconstruction. Researchers can flexibly adjust the model based on practical application needs to optimize its performance in specific scenarios. This achievement has significant implications not only for photovoltaic defect segmentation but also provides insights and exploration avenues for research in other industrial defect segmentation fields. The comprehensive experimental results indicate that our method achieved an mIoU of 88.41% on the photovoltaic dataset, outperforming existing segmentation algorithms. Additionally, the network demonstrated comprehensive and high-precision recognition capabilities across four scenarios in the MVTec-AD industrial dataset. By assisting companies in implementing rigorous quality inspections, our approach enhances product quality and economic benefits, promoting the development of sustainable energy systems. By leveraging defect information, photovoltaic manufacturers can optimize production processes, reduce resource waste, and transition to more sustainable manufacturing.

**Author Contributions:** Conceptualization, G.W.; methodology, G.W. and P.Z.; software, P.Z. and H.F.; validation, P.Z.; formal analysis, G.W. and P.Z.; investigation, P.Z.; resources, G.W.; data curation, P.Z.; writing—original draft preparation, P.Z.; writing—review and editing, G.W. and P.Z.; visualization, P.Z.; supervision, G.W.; project administration, G.W.; funding acquisition, G.W. All authors have read and agreed to the published version of the manuscript.

**Funding:** This research was funded in part by the National Natural Science Foundation of China (NSFC; grant numbers: 62103092 and U20A20189), in part by the Major Program of National NSFC (grant numbers: 61991404 and 61991401), and in part by the Research Program of the Liaoning Liaohe Laboratory (No.: LLL23ZZ-05-01).

**Institutional Review Board Statement:** Not applicable.

**Informed Consent Statement:** Not applicable.

**Data Availability Statement:** The original contributions presented in this study are included in the article; further inquiries can be directed to the corresponding author.

**Acknowledgments:** The authors appreciate the constructive criticism and suggestions from the editor(s) and all anonymous reviewers.

**Conflicts of Interest:** The authors declare no conflicts of interest.

## Abbreviations

The following abbreviations are used in this manuscript:

| | |
|---|---|
| mIoU | Mean Intersection over Union |
| IoU | Intersection over Union |
| mAcc | Mean Accuracy |

## References


1. Sun, C.; Zou, Y.; Qin, C.; Zhang, B.; Wu, X. Temperature effect of photovoltaic cells: A review. *Adv. Compos. Hybrid Mater.* **2022**, *5*, 2675–2699. [CrossRef]
2. Garcìa, M.C.; Herrmann, W.; Böhmer, W.; Proisy, B. Thermal and electrical effects caused by outdoor hot-spot testing in associations of photovoltaic cells. *Prog. Photovolt. Res. Appl.* **2003**, *11*, 293–307. [CrossRef]
3. Zhou, P.; Wang, R.; Wang, C.; Chen, H.; Liu, K. SIIF: Semantic information interactive fusion network for photovoltaic defect segmentation. *Appl. Energy* **2024**, *371*, 123643. [CrossRef]
4. Shaik, A.; Balasundaram, A.; Kakarla, L.S.; Murugan, N. Deep Learning-Based Detection and Segmentation of Damage in Solar Panels. *Automation* **2024**, *5*, 128–150. [CrossRef]
5. Hou, D.; Ma, J.; Huang, S.; Zhang, J.; Zhu, X.T. Classification of defective photovoltaic modules in ImageNet-trained networks using transfer learning. In Proceedings of the 2021 IEEE 12th Energy Conversion Congress & Exposition-Asia (ECCE-Asia), Singapore, 24–27 May 2021; pp. 2127–2132.
6. Zhang, J.; Shen, Y.; Jiang, J.; Fang, S.; Chen, L.; Yan, T.; Li, Z.; Zhang, K.; Wei, H.; Guo, W. Automatic detection of defective solar cells in electroluminescence images via global similarity and concatenated saliency guided network. *IEEE Trans. Ind. Inform.* **2022**, *19*, 7335–7345. [CrossRef]
7. Chen, X.; Karin, T.; Libby, C.; Deceglie, M.; Hacke, P.; Silverman, T.J.; Jain, A. Automatic crack segmentation and feature extraction in electroluminescence images of solar modules. *IEEE J. Photovolt.* **2023**, *13*, 334–342. [CrossRef]
8. Fioresi, J.; Colvin, D.J.; Frota, R.; Gupta, R.; Li, M.; Seigneur, H.P.; Vyas, S.; Oliveira, S.; Shah, M.; Davis, K.O. Automated defect detection and localization in photovoltaic cells using semantic segmentation of electroluminescence images. *IEEE J. Photovolt.* **2021**, *12*, 53–61. [CrossRef]
9. Wang, C.; Chen, H.; Zhao, S.; Wang, Y.; Cao, Z. A Low-Cost Defect Segmentation System Based On IoT for Large-Scale Photovoltaic Manufacturing. *IEEE Internet Things J.* **2024**, *11*, 16928–16940. [CrossRef]
10. Kaligambe, A.; Fujita, G. A Deep Learning-Based Framework for Automatic Detection of Defective Solar Photovoltaic Cells in Electroluminescence Images Using Transfer Learning. In Proceedings of the 2023 4th International Conference on High Voltage Engineering and Power Systems (ICHVEPS), Bali, Indonesia, 6–10 August 2023; pp. 81–85.
11. Jha, A.; Rawat, Y.; Vyas, S. PV-S3: Advancing Automatic Photovoltaic Defect Detection using Semi-Supervised Semantic Segmentation of Electroluminescence Images. *arXiv* **2024**, arXiv:2404.13693.
12. Xie, X.; Lai, G.; You, M.; Liang, J.; Leng, B. Effective transfer learning of defect detection for photovoltaic module cells in electroluminescence images. *Sol. Energy* **2023**, *250*, 312–323. [CrossRef]
13. Jiang, Y.; Zhao, C. Attention classification-and-segmentation network for micro-crack anomaly detection of photovoltaic module cells. *Sol. Energy* **2022**, *238*, 291–304. [CrossRef]
14. Otamendi, U.; Martinez, I.; Quartulli, M.; Olaizola, I.G.; Viles, E.; Cambarau, W. Segmentation of cell-level anomalies in electroluminescence images of photovoltaic modules. *Sol. Energy* **2021**, *220*, 914–926. [CrossRef]
15. Tang, W.; Yang, Q.; Xiong, K.; Yan, W. Deep learning based automatic defect identification of photovoltaic module using electroluminescence images. *Sol. Energy* **2020**, *201*, 453–460. [CrossRef]
16. Alexey D. An image is worth 16x16 words: Transformers for image recognition at scale. *arXiv* **2020**, arXiv: 2010.11929.
17. Liu, J.J.; Hou, Q.; Cheng, M.M.; Feng, J.; Jiang, J. A simple pooling-based design for real-time salient object detection. In Proceedings of the IEEE/CVF Conference on Computer Vision and Pattern Recognition, Long Beach, CA, USA, 15–20 June 2019; pp. 3917–3926.
18. Bergmann, P.; Fauser, M. A comprehensive real-world dataset for unsupervised anomaly detection. In Proceedings of the IEEE/CVF Conference on Computer Vision and Pattern Recognition, Long Beach, CA, USA, 15–20 June 2019; pp. 9592–9600.
19. Pratt, L.; Mattheus, J.; Klein, R. A benchmark dataset for defect detection and classification in electroluminescence images of PV modules using semantic segmentation. *Syst. Soft Comput.* **2023**, *5*, 200048. [CrossRef]
20. Touvron, H.; Cord, M.; Douze, M.; Massa, F.; Sablayrolles, A.; Jégou, H. Training data-efficient image transformers & distillation through attention. In Proceedings of the International Conference on Machine Learning, Virtual, 18–24 July 2021; pp. 10347–10357.
21. Carion, N.; Massa, F.; Synnaeve, G.; Usunier, N.; Kirillov, A.; Zagoruyko, S. End-to-End Object Detection with Transformers. In *European Conference on Computer Vision*; Springer International Publishing: Cham, Switzerland, 2020; pp. 213–229.
22. Chen, J.; Lu, Y.; Yu, Q.; Luo, X.; Adeli, E.; Wang, Y.; Lu, L.; Yuille, A.L.; Zhou, Y. Transunet: Transformers make strong encoders for medical image segmentation. *arXiv* **2021**, arXiv:2102.04306.
23. Liu, Z.; Lin, Y.; Cao, Y.; Hu, H.; Wei, Y.; Zhang, Z.; Lin, S.; Guo, B. Swin transformer: Hierarchical vision transformer using shifted windows. In Proceedings of the IEEE/CVF International Conference on Computer Vision, Montreal, BC, Canada, 10 –21 October 2021; pp. 10012–10022.

24. Hassani, A.; Walton, S.; Li, J.; Li, S.; Shi, H. Neighborhood attention transformer. In Proceedings of the IEEE/CVF Conference on Computer Vision and Pattern Recognition, Vancouver, BC, Canada, 17–24 June 2023; pp. 6185–6194.
25. Xu, J.; Sun, X.; Zhang, Z.; Zhao, G. Layer normalization. *arXiv* **2016**, arXiv: 1607.06450.
26. Loshchilov, I. Decoupled weight decay regularization. *arXiv* **2017**, arXiv:1711.05101.
27. Lin, T.Y.; Dollár, P.; Girshick, R.; He, K.; Hariharan, B.; Belongie, S. Feature pyramid networks for object detection. In Proceedings of the IEEE Conference on Computer Vision and Pattern Recognition, Honolulu, HI, USA, 21–26 July 2017; pp. 2117–2125.
28. Xiao, T.; Liu, Y.; Zhou, B.; Jiang, Y.; Sun, J. Unified perceptual parsing for scene understanding. In Proceedings of the European Conference on Computer Vision (ECCV), Munich, Germany, 8–14 September 2018; pp. 418–434.
29. Li, X.; Zhong, Z.; Wu, J.; Yang, Y.; Lin, Z.; Liu, H. Expectation-maximization attention networks for semantic segmentation. In Proceedings of the IEEE/CVF International Conference on Computer Vision, Seoul, Republic of Korea, 27 October–2 November 2019; pp. 9167–9176.
30. Fan, M.; Lai, S.; Huang, J.; Wei, X.; Chai, Z.; Luo, J.; Wei, X. Rethinking bisenet for real-time semantic segmentation. In Proceedings of the IEEE/CVF Conference on Computer Vision and Pattern Recognition, Nashville, TN, USA, 20–25 June 2021; pp. 9716–9725.
31. Hong, Y.; Pan, H.; Sun, W.; Jia, Y. Deep dual-resolution networks for real-time and accurate semantic segmentation of road scenes. *arXiv* **2021**, arXiv:2101.06085.
32. Zhang, W.; Pang, J.; Chen, K.; Loy, C.C. K-net: Towards unified image segmentation. *Adv. Neural Inf. Process. Syst.* **2021**, *34*, 10326–10338.
33. Yin, M.; Yao, Z.; Cao, Y.; Li, X.; Zhang, Z.; Lin, S.; Hu, H. Disentangled non-local neural networks. In Proceedings of the Computer Vision–ECCV 2020: 16th European Conference, Glasgow, UK, 23–28 August 2020; pp. 191–207.
34. Huang, Z.; Wang, X.; Huang, L.; Huang, C.; Wei, Y.; Liu, W. Ccnet: Criss-cross attention for semantic segmentation. In Proceedings of the IEEE/CVF International Conference on Computer Vision, Seoul, Republic of Korea, 27 October–2 November 2019; pp. 603–612.
35. Zhu, Z.; Xu, M.; Bai, S.; Huang, T.; Bai, X. Asymmetric non-local neural networks for semantic segmentation. In Proceedings of the IEEE/CVF International Conference on Computer Vision, Seoul, Republic of Korea, 27 October–2 November 2019; pp. 593–602.
36. He, J.; Deng, Z.; Qiao, Y. Dynamic multi-scale filters for semantic segmentation. In Proceedings of the IEEE/CVF International Conference on Computer Vision, Seoul, Republic of Korea, 27 October–2 November 2019; pp. 3562–3572.
37. Xu, J.; Xiong, Z.; Bhattacharyya, S.P. PIDNet: A real-time semantic segmentation network inspired by PID controllers. In Proceedings of the IEEE/CVF Conference on Computer Vision and Pattern Recognition, Vancouver, BC, Canada, 17–24 June 2023; pp. 19529–19539.
38. Huang, L.; Yuan, Y.; Guo, J.; Zhang, C.; Chen, X.; Wang, J. Interlaced sparse self-attention for semantic segmentation. *arXiv* **2021**, arXiv:1907.12273.
39. Cao, Y.; Xu, J.; Lin, S.; Wei, F.; Hu, H. Gcnet: Non-local networks meet squeeze-excitation networks and beyond. In Proceedings of the IEEE/CVF International Conference on Computer Vision Workshops, Seoul, Republic of Korea, 27–28 October 2019.

MDPI AG
Grosspeteranlage 5
4052 Basel
Switzerland
Tel.: +41 61 683 77 34

*Sensors* Editorial Office
E-mail: sensors@mdpi.com
www.mdpi.com/journal/sensors

www.ingramcontent.com/pod-product-compliance
Lightning Source LLC
Chambersburg PA
CBHW061551220926
51850CB00005B/310
*9783725862665*